Revolution and Change
in Central and Eastern Europe

Revised Edition

Roger East and Jolyon Pontin

First published in Great Britain in 1997 by
Pinter Publishers Ltd
Wellington House, 125 Strand, London WC2R 0BB

British Library Cataloguing in Publication Data

A catalogue record for this book is available from the British Library.

ISBN   1-85567-360-6 (hb)

            1-85567-361-4 (pb) ·.

Library of Congress Cataloging-in-Publication Data

East, Roger,
    Revolution and change in Central and Eastern Europe / Roger East and Jolyon Pontin
        p.   cm.
    Rev. and expanded ed. of: Revolutions in Eastern Europe / Roger East
    Includes bibliographical references and index.
    ISBN 1-85567-360-6 (hb) . — ISBN 1-85567-361-4 (pb)
    1. Europe, Eastern—Politics and government—1989-   2. Europe, Central—Politics and government—1989-   I. Pontin, Jolyon.
    II. East, Roger.   Revolutions in Eastern Europe.   III. Title.
DJK51.E24 1997
943—dc20   96-34614
                                                                        CIP

Computer Typeset by CIRCA Reference, Cambridge
Printed and Bound in Great Britain by
Creative Print and Design Wales, Ebbw Vale.

CONTENTS

NOTE: Each of the country chapters covers the period since 1918 in outline, and since 1945 in more detail, including the establishment of communist rule, the collapse of communism in the late 1980s and early 1990s, and the post-communist experience to 1995.

INTRODUCTION

This book has grown out of a first edition entitled *Revolutions in Eastern Europe*, published in 1992. Like that predecessor, it sets out to provide a clear record of the recent period of rapid change experienced by the region's former communist states. It seeks to set in context the main events of the collapse of communism, and the creation of post-communist political systems. The present volume takes the account through a further stage, describing the varying experience of political pluralism in the 1990s, against a background of profound economic transition.

The change in title reflects a shift in perception. Certainly 1989 was the most dramatic year, the end of an epoch and the "year of revolutions", but from the somewhat greater distance of 1996 we would now consider it more appropriate to characterise the whole recent period as one of "revolution and change". The label "Eastern Europe", too, while convenient enough as shorthand in the bipolar division of the Cold War era, is one which the present book abandons in favour of "Central and Eastern Europe". More complicated this may be, but it makes a distinction which reflects real differences both in historical tradition and in current position.

The list of countries covered in this book is markedly different from those of 1989. The region which westerners might mentally lump together as the "Eastern European bloc" then comprised eight states and the Soviet Union (within which the Baltic republics were incorporated). One of the eight, the GDR, no longer exists, while Czechoslovakia has become two countries and Yugoslavia, has disintegrated into five parts. There is no longer in any sense a bloc, although they may still be a residual Russian sphere of influence.. After the dramatic break-up of the Soviet Union in 1991, there are (in addition to the three now independent Baltic republics) a total of seven European states to the east of what was "Eastern Europe". Prague and Budapest at least, like Berlin and Vienna, clearly now rank with the principal cities of Central Europe once again.

The structure of the book - Comparisons between countries

The book begins with an introductory chapter, contrasting the historical antecedents of the states at the end of World War I, when the Versailles settlement marked in most cases the recognition of their modern independent existence. Thereafter, there are nine main chapters arranged essentially on a country-by-country basis - except that what begins as a Czechoslovakia chapter has a later subdivision into the Czech Republic and Slovakia, and the Yugoslavia chapter has separate treatments of Slovenia, Croatia, Bosnia-Hercegovina, Slovenia and Macedonia.

The country chapters have a consistent structure, to enable the reader to refer easily to the relevant experience of other countries at any point. Each section is identified within the country chapter by a heading in bold capitals. Thus, after the initial information on the geography and the population of the country concerned, there is a succinct **HISTORICAL NARRATIVE** for each country, with the emphasis on the events surrounding the fall of the communist regime and the experience of the post-communist years. In each case this is followed by an outline of changes in the **ECONOMY**, focusing in particular on privatisation and on property restitution. A section on **POST-COMMUNIST JUSTICE ISSUES** covers the process of administering justice over the worst transgressions of the communist era, and bringing to light and purging the perpetrators and collaborators of secret police surveillance and repression. Where appropriate, there are separate sections on the **MEDIA** and on **ETHNIC AND NATIONAL RELATIONS.** Thereafter the chapters deal in turn with **FOREIGN AFFAIRS, CONSTITUTIONAL ISSUES, PRINCIPAL PERSONALITIES, POLITICAL PARTIES,** and **ELECTIONS,** including full results for the period to the end of 1995. A comprehensive **CHRONOLOGY** completes the coverage for each country.

The final chapter considers the new shape of Europe: its alliances and defence framework, its institutions for political and functional co-operation and for economic integration. There is much debate on how the states of Central and Eastern Europe are being fitted into, and are crucially affecting, what were once mainly West European and Atlantic structures. In keeping with the factual emphasis throughout this book, however, the final chapter once again concerns itself primarily with recording what has actually taken place; it attempts to arrange this information in such a way as to help distinguish the wood from the trees.

A glossary of terms and acronyms is included to assist the reader who may wish to refer to any part of the text without necessarily following the full sequence of a particular chapter.

Acknowledgement for the maps in this volume is due to Carpress International Press Agency: the copyright in Carpress maps is the property of CARTO of Brussels.

Roger East and Jolyon Pontin

Cambridge/London, October 1996

OVERALL CHRONOLOGY

1914-18. The First World War. Defeat of Germany and destruction of the Austro-Hungarian and Ottoman empires, while the Russian Tsarist empire collapses and the Soviet Union comes into existence following the Bolshevik revolution of 1917.

1919. A short-lived communist regime is formed in Hungary but ousted after six months in favour of the right-wing authoritarian Adml. Horthy.

1918-20. The postwar settlement creates new democratic nation-states across central and eastern Europe. The 1919 Treaty of Versailles imposes a harsh settlement on Germany's new Weimar Republic; the 1919 Treaty of Neuilly defines borders in the Balkans, undoing Bulgaria's wartime expansion; and the 1920 Treaty of Trianon resolves the postwar settlement in former Austria-Hungary, with historic Hungary losing two-thirds of its territory whereas Romania has doubled in size.

1920. Albanian independence is restored; Ahmed Zogu (King Zog) takes over in 1924.

1921. A unitary constitution confirms the position of the Serb royal house in the south Slav state which came into existence in 1918 under the name of Kingdom of the Croats, Serbs and Slovenes (later renamed Yugoslavia).

1922. Foundation of the Soviet Union.

1926. The Pilsudski coup in Poland initiates a period of authoritarian government.

1929. King Alexander institutes a royal dictatorship in Yugoslavia.

1930. King Carol establishes an authoritarian regime in Romania.

March 1933. Hitler imposes Nazi rule after becoming German Chancellor.

March 1938. The *Anschluss*, the annexation of Austria by Nazi Germany.

September 1938. Czechoslovakia is abandoned by its Western allies, who acquiesce at Munich to Hitler's insistence on German annexation of the Sudetenland. When Czechoslovakia is dismembered in 1939, a Nazi puppet regime is set up in Slovakia.

23 August 1939. The Nazi-Soviet Pact.

August 1939. Croatia obtains substantial autonomy within Yugoslavia.

September 1939. The Second World War begins with the German invasion of Poland, which is partitioned between Germany and the Soviet Union.

June 1940. The Soviet Union annexes the Baltic States.

November 1940. Hungary formally aligns itself with the Axis powers, as do Bulgaria and Romania the following year.

April 1941. Axis forces invade Yugoslavia and the *Ustasa* fascist regime is set up in Croatia; Tito's communist Partisans provide the fiercest resistance.

June 1941. Collapse of the Nazi-Soviet Pact as Germany launches an invasion across Soviet-occupied territory and into Russia itself.

1939-44. German hegemony and the Nazi application of the genocidal "final solution", sending millions of Jews and others to death in the Holocaust.

July 1944-May 1945. German retreat in the east. The Red Army enters Romania, Bulgaria, Poland, Hungary and Czechoslovakia; Romania and Bulgaria change sides to ally with the Soviet Union, and a communist-led Fatherland Front takes power in Sofia, while Soviet troops liberate Bucharest in August 1944 (after Romania has changed sides), Warsaw in January 1945 (after allowing the Uprising to be crushed), Budapest in February, and Prague in May.

February 1945. The Yalta summit; Britain, the USA and the Soviet Union agree on the postwar division of Europe into spheres of influence.

May 1945. Nazi Germany surrenders to the Allies; eastern German areas liberated by the Red Army become the Soviet-occupied zone. Berlin is divided in July.

January 1946. Albania's communist government, formed from the wartime resistance, proclaims a republic under Enver Hoxha; the regime falls out with Yugoslavia in 1948, the Soviet Union in 1961 and China in 1978.

May 1946. The communists win most seats in elections in Czechoslovakia.

October 1946. Bulgarian communists predominate in the Fatherland Front's election victory; within a year they have eliminated their rivals.

November 1946. The communist-dominated front wins disputed Romanian elections.

January 1947. Elections in Poland, dominated by communists and allies.

June 1947. The USA launches its Marshall Plan to aid reconstruction in Europe; Stalin condemns it as imperialist and countries in the Soviet sphere do not participate.

August 1947. Hungary's communists overtake the Smallholders in elections, and use "salami tactics" to eliminate opponents; single-list elections follow in 1949.

December 1947. A people's republic is proclaimed in Romania.

February-March 1948. An effective coup by the communists in Czechoslovakia.

June 1948. The Soviet Union breaks relations with Tito's "deviationist" Yugoslavia.

July 1948-May 1949. The Berlin airlift withstands a Soviet attempt to blockade West Berlin and gain control over the whole city.

January 1949. Formation of Comecon, to bind a Soviet bloc together economically.

April 1949. Formation of the Western alliance, NATO, as Cold War tension rises.

7 October 1949. Proclamation of the German Democratic Republic (GDR).

June 1950. Workers' self-management is introduced in Yugoslavia.

1950-51. Political show trials reach their height while Stalinist economic policies are forced through across the Soviet bloc.

March 1953. Death of Stalin and beginning of a brief period of destalinisation.

June 1953. The Berlin riots, suppressed by Soviet forces, are followed by some efforts to improve living standards for hard-pressed East German workers.

May 1955. West Germany joins NATO; the Warsaw Pact is formed.

February 1956. Khrushchev's "secret speech" denounces Stalinism.

June-October 1956. Crisis in Poland, with riots and strikes demanding liberalisation; reinstatement of the popular Gomulka as party leader.

4 November 1956. The Soviet invasion crushes the reformist Hungarian revolution, after Hungary's decision to leave the Warsaw Pact, and cows reformists elsewhere.

13 August 1961. The Berlin Wall stops an outflow of East Germans to the West.

October 1964. Brezhnev takes over from Khrushchev as Soviet party leader.

March 1965. Ceausescu becomes Romanian party leader, instituting a regime with maverick foreign policies but repressing any internal dissent.

January 1968. Kadar's regime in Hungary introduces the "New Economic Mechanism" incorporating some elements of a market economy.

20-21 August 1968. The Warsaw Pact invasion of Czechoslovakia forcibly ends the eight-month Czechoslovak reform socialist experiment or "Prague spring" .

November 1968. The Brezhnev doctrine of "limited sovereignty" is enunciated, a clear warning that if there is a "threat to socialism" the Soviet Union and other socialist states will fulfil their "internationalist obligation" to intervene.

March-May 1970. West Germany recognises the GDR's existence and accepts postwar border arrangements.

December 1970. The Baltic crisis in Poland; troops kill hundreds to suppress strikes and riots in coastal cities, but the regime is shaken sufficiently to proclaim the following year that improving living standards is its supreme goal.

January 1977. Formation of Charter 77 in Czechoslovakia.

May 1980. Death of Tito.

August 1980. Formation of the Solidarity trade union in Poland; the government concedes the right to strike; Solidarity membership reaches ten million within a year.

13 December 1981. Martial law clampdown in Poland, including the arrest of Solidarity leaders, whose political demands include free elections.

March 1985. Gorbachev becomes CPSU general secretary.

October 1987. Slobodan Milosevic becomes leader of Serbia's League of Communists.

6 February 1989. Following the revival of Solidarity in Poland and demands for its relegalisation, the Jaruzelski regime opens "round table" talks which conclude on 5 April with fundamental government concessions.

11 February. Hungary's reformist-led communist party endorses a multi-party system.

2 May 1989. Hungary begins dismantling the "Iron Curtain" along the Austrian border.

May-July 1989. Declarations of sovereignty by the Lithuanian and Latvian legislatures reflect growing resistance to Soviet rule in the Baltic states.

June 1989. Solidarity triumphs and communists lose heavily in the Polish elections.

July 1989. Gorbachev renounces the Brezhnev doctrine at a Warsaw Pact summit.

August-September 1989. Tadeusz Mazowiecki becomes the first post-communist Prime Minister in Poland; his Solidarity-led government includes communist ministers.

11 September 1989. Hungary lifts restrictions on transit by East Germans, effectively breaking ranks with the rest of the communist bloc by allowing freedom of travel. This is denounced by East Germany but not by the Soviet Union.

18 September 1989. Hungarian round-table talks reach agreement on a framework for multi-party democracy, which are approved by parliament in October.

18 October 1989. Facing massive opposition demonstrations, veteran East German hardline leader Honecker steps down, making way for reformists.

9 November 1989. Fall of the Berlin Wall.

10 November 1989. Inflexible Bulgarian leader Zhivkov is ousted in a "palace coup".

17 November 1989. Major demonstrations mark the beginning of Czechoslovakia's "velvet revolution"; by 10 December there is a majority non-communist government.

7 December 1989. With the collapse of the short-lived East German reform communist regime, the Round Table convenes and agrees to hold democratic elections.

11 December 1989. Bulgaria's communist government proposes free elections.

21-25 December 1989. Ceausescu is shouted down by Romanian protesters following the suppression of riots in Timisoara; amid bloody fighting, the army changes sides and Ceausescu flees but is caught and killed.

30 December 1989. Former dissident Havel becomes interim Czechoslovak president.

January 1990. Poland begins "shock therapy" in pursuit of economic transformation.

January 1990. The Yugoslav League of Communists holds its last conference and surrenders its monopoly on power; Slovene and Croat elections in April reinforce the momentum towards secession.

11 March 1990. Lithuania's legislature declares independence.

18 March 1990. East German elections are won by the Christian Democrats and allies, encouraging West German Chancellor Kohl to press for rapid German unification.

25 March 1990. First round of Hungarian elections which result in a non-communist opposition victory and formation of the conservative Antall government.

20 May 1990. Romania's interim National Salvation Front confirms its hold on power through general elections.

8-9 June 1990. Elections in Czechoslovakia are won by Civic Forum and People against Violence; the communists finish second.

10-17 June 1990. Elections in Bulgaria leave the ex-communist BSP in a majority but it fails to form a government, this being eventually entrusted to technocrats.

3 October 1990. Unification of Germany by merger of GDR into the Federal Republic.

November-December 1990. Walesa is elected as president in Poland.

March-June 1991. Elections in Albania, reluctantly conceded by the ruling communists, leave the party in power, but ostensibly committed to a market economy. Strike protests force power-sharing, amid economic chaos and a refugee exodus.

25 June 1991. Croatia and Slovenia proclaim independence from Yugoslavia; after a 10-day war in Slovenia, and more protracted fighting in Croatia, both states win international recognition by January 1992.

28 June - 1 July 1991. Comecon and the Warsaw Pact are wound up.

19-21 August 1991. Failed coup attempt in Moscow by CPSU hardliners.

20-21 August 1991. Estonia and Latvia declare independence.

September 1991. Macedonia declares independence.

October 1991. Free elections produce a fragmented parliament in Poland, leading to the formation of a centre-right government in December.

October-November 1991. The United Democratic Front wins elections in Bulgaria, but its centre-right government falls within a year, replaced by a "government of experts".

25 December 1991. The Soviet Union is formally dissolved at midnight.

March 1992. Albania's former communist party is routed in fresh elections.

April 1992. Civil war begins in Bosnia, whose independence is recognised by the EC and USA, and by the UN in May.

5-6 June 1992. With leading Slovak politicians demanding sovereignty, elections in Czechoslovakia underline the polarisation between the two republics.

October-November 1992. Ex-communists win Lithuania's parliamentary elections.

1 January 1993. The Czech Republic and Slovakia become independent states in the so-called "velvet divorce".

19 September 1993. Former communist parties win elections in Poland.

May 1994. The former communist Hungarian Socialist Party wins elections, and its leader Gyula Horn forms a socialist-led coalition the following month.

30 September - 1 October 1994. A general election in Slovakia returns Meciar's centre-left nationalist HZDS to power.

December 1994. Bulgaria's former communist BSP wins a majority in elections and returns to power, forming a coalition the following month.

November 1995. Walesa is defeated by the former communist party leader Kwasniewski in Polish presidential elections.

December 1995. The Dayton accords formally end the war in former Yugoslavia.

HISTORICAL BACKGROUND

The countries of central and eastern Europe, as they emerged from the convulsion of the First World War, were shaped in broad terms as nation states and parliamentary democracies. However imperfectly applied (with some states incorporating substantial national minorities), the national principle and the democratic principle were the basis of the Versailles settlement, which radically redrew the map of the region in 1919-20.

The pre-1918 map of Europe consisted not of states but of empires built on dynastic principles - Tsarist Russia in the east, the Ottoman Turkish empire in the Balkan south and east, the Habsburg empire of Austria-Hungary, whose period as a great European power dated from the lifting of the Turkish siege of Vienna in 1683, and Germany, based on the power of Prussia in the north but only united in the Second Reich since 1871.

Nationalism in the Balkans, as has been so often said, provided the spark for the European war in 1914, the continental conflict which was then widened to become the first world war. Three of the four empires were wartime allies - Austria-Hungary and Germany, the so-called Central Powers, joined later in 1914 by Turkey. It was their defeat, and the revolutionary overthrow of the Tsarist empire in Russia, which opened the way for the Versailles settlement to implement the national principle so widely.

In territorial terms the dominance of the four empires had extended across the whole region since the late eighteenth century partitions of Poland. The experience of the French revolutionary wars and the Napoleonic empire in Europe, profoundly influential in the fostering of liberal nationalism, and disruptive of Habsburg rule, was nevertheless principally confined to the western half of the continent. The Confederation of the Rhine did briefly encompass Saxony, however, and Napoleonic Europe also involved the creation of the short-lived Grand Duchy of Warsaw (1807-13) and the Illyrian Provinces under French rule in what is now Croatia.

The states which gained sovereignty after 1918 (or up to several decades earlier in parts of the Balkans, with the Ottoman empire in a state of progressive collapse) had in common the lack of established traditions of running their central government. Hungary was a partial exception, the Austro-Hungarian Dual Monarchy created in 1867 having enhanced its already significant autonomy as a centre of power in the Habsburg empire. However, in terms of the experience of responsible government, central and eastern Europe as a whole might be differentiated from the more modernised societies and mature polities of western Europe. Germany was different, in that the German empire was inherently more national in character and the problems facing the German state post-1918 were more those of a defeated and humiliated nation than of an inchoate polity, although Germany's lack of firmly rooted democratic institutions helped encourage the recourse to authoritarianism which was such a common phenomenon further east in Europe in the inter-war period.

Beyond the one broadly common characteristic of having been imperial subjects, and the underlying shared feature that central and east European societies were economically and industrially less developed than those of western Europe (the Czech Lands of Bohemia and Moravia, and once again Germany, being exceptions here), it is however the differences between the states of the region which stand out as much as their similarities. In part these differences can be linked to contrasts in religious traditions, and in the degree of importance attached to mediaeval antecedents and historical symbols of statehood. In part of course it relates to geography (physical and human) and economic resource endowment. To a very significant extent, however, the particular characteristics of central and east European states at the beginning of the modern (i.e. post-1918) period can be ascribed to the varying nature of their experience of being governed (or ruled) under the four different empires.

The contrast in religious traditions

Christianity spread throughout central and eastern Europe in the ninth and tenth centuries. Albania, compulsorily Islamised after the defeat of Skanderbeg, is the only country in the region with a Muslim majority, although there are also important numbers of Muslims within Yugoslavia, mainly Albanians in Kosovo, as well as the Muslims of Bosnia-Hercegovina. In Bulgaria there was a sizeable Muslim population, mainly of ethnic Turks.

The main line of religious division is that between Orthodox Christianity, dominant throughout the southern part of the region, and Roman Catholics. Orthodox Churches dominate in Bulgaria, Romania, Serbia and Macedonia. Catholics are greatly in the majority among Croats, Slovenes and Slovaks, and overwhelmingly so among Poles; they also form a majority in Lithuania and in Hungary (and Transylvania), but alongside numerous protestants. The Czechs are mixed as between Catholics and the Hussite and other protestant denominations, while only in Estonia, Latvia and the former East Germany are the principal churches protestant (Lutheran and Evangelical).

Experiences under imperial rule

Estonia, Latvia and Lithuania were ruled from the late eighteenth century as provinces of Tsarist Russia. A policy of vigorous Russification was pursued there in the late nineteenth century. Much of Poland shared the Baltic states' relatively recent history of Russian domination and, latterly, Russification. Russian rule dated from 1772 in what is now Poland's eastern fringe, but was extended by annexation after 1815 through to Warsaw and Lodz. The war between Poland and Bolshevik Russia in 1920-21, essentially an opportunist venture on the Polish side, had deep roots in historical enmity. Polish-Russian relations had been one of the great European rivalries in the fourteenth, fifteenth and sixteenth centuries. Polish romantic nationalists look back on this as a heroic age, when the Polish and Lithuanian kingdom was the greatest power in Europe, its lands reaching down to the Black Sea. In 1683 Poland had led the anti-Ottoman coalition which relieved Vienna. Even by this time, however, the power of its elective monarchy was already in decline, a trend hastened when Russia eliminated, in the Great Northern War of 1700-21, the strong Swedish influence on the north-central European balance of power.

The territory formally annexed by Russia in the eighteenth century partitions of Poland was allowed some initial autonomy as the Congress Kingdom of Poland. The industries of Lodz and Warsaw became linked in with St Petersburg, however, in the earliest phase of Russian railway-building; the customs barrier was abolished in 1851, and anti-Russian revolts were crushed in 1830 and 1863, after which the separation was altogether eliminated and Polish culture in the Russian sphere was suppressed.

Elsewhere in Europe, Russia's influence, if not its rule, was felt most keenly (apart from in 1848-49 when Tsar Nicholas's armies took on the role of repressive "policeman") in the eastern Balkans, as the far from disinterested sponsor of nineteenth century nationalism.

The wider context of this was the slow disintegration of the Ottoman empire. For 500 years until the mid-nineteenth century Ottoman control extended over all of what became Albania, Macedonia, Montenegro, Serbia (apart from an area, now Vojvodina, which was under Hungarian rule in the Habsburg empire), Romania (apart from Transylvania) and Bulgaria.

Ottoman rule in the Balkans was that of a tyrannical colonial power, extracting revenue through high taxes and returning little or nothing of this in investment, and maintaining through a venal and arbitrary bureaucracy a regime which discouraged economic development or social change. For Albanians, as Muslim co-religionists, taxation was more lenient; elsewhere, Orthodox Christians were at least allowed a measure of toleration, whereas Catholics were more actively persecuted.

The first major Balkan nationalist revolt, that of Serbia in the Napoleonic era, was ultimately unsuccessful, but the Serbs won autonomy in 1830 and independence in 1878, the precursor to a struggle for Greater Serbia and the liberation of all the South Slavs from Habsburg and Turkish rule. Serbia had had an empire itself in the mediaeval period, which reached its height in the mid-fourteenth century, but had been overthrown by the Turks at the Battle of Kosovo in 1389 (a date whose commemoration by the Albanians of Kosovo is thus a highly potent symbol of national divisions).

Moldavia and Walachia (where in 1848 the liberal nationalists were put down by Russian intervention after they had succeeded in winning concessions from the Turkish governor of Bucharest) gained the status of autonomous principalities within the Ottoman empire at the end of the Crimean War, from 1856; they were unified in 1861, declared their independence in 1877 during the Russo-Turkish war, and were recognised, as independent Romania, in 1878 at the Treaty of Berlin.

Bulgaria had been a powerful empire in the tenth century before the rise of Ottoman power. Its experience of Ottoman rule was much more direct and culturally and economically intrusive than that of the Romanian provinces further north. There was a revival of cultural nationalism in the late eighteenth century, stemming from within the Orthodox Church rather than from the landed classes; Bulgaria lacked an indigenous aristocracy as a consequence of expropriations over the centuries by Turkish overlords. Its significant national revival continued through the nineteenth century to be based heavily around the identity of its Orthodox Church, which was eventually able in 1870 to constitute itself independently of the authority of the Greek patriarch. The church, with Russian encouragement, launched an agitation for national independence, and in 1876 an uprising was brutally crushed, but the Russian victory in the Russo-Turkish war gave them the ability temporarily to dictate the settlement terms, which they used to establish a "Big Bulgaria", from the Danube to the Aegean, under the Treaty of San

Stefano (1878). Russia was seen by the other main European powers, however, as having gained an unacceptable expansion of its Mediterranean influence under this settlement, and was forced to back down. Later in the year the Treaty of Berlin cut down Bulgaria both in size, so that it no longer reached south to the Aegean, and in status, leaving it as a principality nominally within the Ottoman empire.

Bulgaria's subsequent history, to 1918 (it achieved full independence in 1908) and indeed beyond, was dominated by the ambition of restoring the San Stefano frontiers. It was this objective which prompted its involvement in the Balkan Wars of 1912-1913 (which also made Albania, at least on paper, an independent state), and which led to its entering the first world war on the side of the Central Powers.

The boundary between the Habsburg and the Ottoman empires was pushed north and west in the early sixteenth century by Ottoman military power, whose invading forces crushed a peasant revolt in Hungary during this period. The last Ottoman onslaught, in the mid-seventeenth century in the reign of Sultan Mehmed IV, reached Vienna in 1683. Pushing back the Turkish armies thereafter, by 1699 the Habsburgs had reconquered Hungary (to whose throne the Habsburg dynasty had acceded in 1526), and they added to their empire at Ottoman expense in the subsequent decades notably in Transylvania and, temporarily, in northern Serbia.

Hungary, with its powerful and reactionary Magyar aristocracy dominating the countryside and a middle class nationalist element of growing significance in Budapest and other cities, swiftly acquired and jealously guarded a high degree of autonomy under the Habsburg empire. The events of 1848-49 in Hungary illustrated both the growth of liberal nationalist feeling in Budapest, and the extent to which distrust of the cosmopolitan attitudes of the city left it cut off from the conservative-nationalist power elites in the rest of the Hungarian part of the Habsburg empire. In March 1848 the Diet in Budapest, responding to news of revolution from Paris and the urgings of the poet Petofi and the lawyer and editor Kossuth, adopted the so-called March Laws, claiming that the government should be made responsible to the Diet. The Emperor Ferdinand initially accepted, but then exploited the divisive nationalisms within the Hungarian lands (including Transylvania, Croatia and Slovakia), encouraging the governor of Croatia to lead military moves against the Hungarian rebels, in return for the promise of Croat autonomy under Habsburg protection. Kossuth's citizen's defence forces held them off, but when Russian armies were brought into play in defence of the existing European order, they put down the Hungarian rebellion in August 1849.

From 1867 Hungary obtained equal status with Austria and a Dual Monarchy, under which only defence and foreign affairs were handled jointly. The bureaucracy which implemented imperial rule comprised both Germans and Magyars, but the imperial system was used to reinforce the power of the Magyar upper classes. It was markedly more conservative and authoritarian than the regime applied in the Austrian half of the Dual Monarchy, such as in Slovenia.

It was Hungary which exercised the Habsburg dominion not only over Transylvania but also over Slovakia (under Hungarian rule from the ninth century) and Croatia (which had a period of independent existence in the tenth century, but was thereafter joined to Hungary). In all these areas, Catholicism was the majority religion. Croatian nationalism, unsatisfied with limited autonomy from 1868, developed principally within an intellectual milieu. It was essentially pan-Slavist and anti-Hungarian in its initial conception and oriented towards Yugoslav aspirations. Its identification of Croatia as having a common destiny with neighbouring Serbia was partly pragmatic, in that a small independent Croatia on its own could be excessively vulnerable to Italian expansionism. The appeal to South Slav sentiment, however, was based on linguistic rather than religious or social affinities. Croatia, Catholic where Serbia was Orthodox, had also experienced an exposure to more mainstream European ideas as part of the Habsburg as opposed to the Ottoman empire. The administration had been less corrupt and had encouraged more economic development, while some resources had gone into infrastructure and education, although paradoxically it was this which produced a supply of Croatian graduates in excess of that still backward society's requirements, and thus a pool of disaffected intelligentsia which fed the ranks of Yugoslav nationalist movements.

Within the Austrian-administered portion of the Habsburg empire throughout this period were the Czech lands of Bohemia and Moravia. The Czechs had had their own cohesive state, formed in the tenth to twelfth centuries, and a Czech monarch, Charles IV, who in 1346 became Holy Roman Emperor. Czechs also looked back proudly to the religious reforms and associated national feelings stimulated by the Czech priest Jan Hus, who challenged the authority of Rome and was burned at the stake in 1415, provoking protracted resistance to the authority of the Emperor Sigismund. The Habsburgs acceded to the Czech throne in 1526 and crushed the rebellion by Czech nobles at the Battle of the White Mountain in 1620. The rise of a middle class Czech nationalism, in conflict with German national aspirations in an increasingly urban and industrialised environment, was held in check by Habsburg authority, bureaucracy, and, on occasion, armed force, as when Austrian armies bombarded Prague to crush a rebellion in 1848 sparked off by a pan-Slav congress and by Czech nationalist demonstrations.

Those Poles whose homelands came into Habsburg dominion at partition, in what is now southern Poland, kept some local autonomy and cultural freedoms, and even an independent republic of Krakow in 1815-46. This arrangement, initially due to Austrian and Russian differences over which side should annex it, allowed the old Polish capital and university centre to flourish as a haven for liberal and nationalist thinkers from all over the Habsburg empire, until Metternich in 1846 resolved to end their pernicious influence by annexation.

What Poles had undergone at Russian hands since partition, however, was more similar in some respects to the experience of Poles under Prussia/Germany. An emphasis on industrial development promoted the growth in particular of Breslau (Wroclaw) and Danzig (Gdansk), but in 1848 the incipient nationalist revolt was swiftly put down by German nationalists acting in the name of the Frankfurt Parliament.

Agrarian and urban societies

A major contrast in European history is to be seen between areas with a significant urban population and experience of the nineteenth century industrial revolution, and those which remained largely unaffected. In central and particularly eastern Europe, those in the former category were still very much the exception by 1918, and generally continued to be so until the all-consuming efforts of the postwar Stalin-influenced communist regimes to build a heavy industrial base.

Saxony in what became East Germany, as well as the Czech lands and parts of Poland and Hungary, were nevertheless substantially industrialised in the nineteenth century. Bohemia and Silesia in particular were in the forefront among the great industrial areas of Europe prior to 1914, while Warsaw and Lodz in the Russian part of Poland, Danzig/Gdansk and Breslau/Wroclaw in Posen (German Poland), and Brno in Moravia, were major industrial centres. Kosice in Slovakia had iron ore and a metals industry, and Budapest and other Hungarian cities were industrial producers, notably of textiles. Northern Bulgaria had a significant textile industry, Romania had petroleum and Serbia its coal mining, but large-scale industry especially in the southern part of eastern Europe was for the most part confined to the use of relatively unsophisticated technology in food processing or textiles, and to pockets of extractive industry. The urban population in Bulgaria was still only about one third of the total population as late as the 1930s, and the proportions in Romania, Yugoslavia and Albania were even smaller.

Few areas had any sizeable industrial proletariat in 1918, and when there was a substantial pocket of working class employment the recruitment was recently drawn from the peasantry, and the workers had yet to develop any strong political coherence. Exceptions to this were the Czech lands, with a strong nucleus of militant communism in heavy industry, and what later became East Germany, where the social democratic and trade unionist strand of left-wing politics was more in the ascendant.

Even such sizeable cities as did exist were often not integrated with their surrounding areas as centres of political and commercial exchange, with notable exceptions such as Vienna, Prague, Budapest and Lvov. Some were little more than garrison towns or administrative outposts of the imperial bureaucracy. Town and country in such circumstances may have existed side by side, but they formed not one but two mutually hostile and suspicious societies, each characterised by different systems of values. The relationship of the mainly agrarian local population with people from these towns was frequently non-existent, and was most acutely experienced when the peasantry suffered impositions at the hands of town dwellers, in the form of military conscription or the exaction of taxes.

These relationships served to reinforce the insular and anti-urban mentality of the mass of the peasantry, hostile to strangers and to change, and sustaining an existence outside the matrix of economic exchange. The church, Catholic or Orthodox, was often the main context in which the lives of such peasants were connected with others outside the family group, and there was a predisposition to consider political issues, if at all, in messianic terms.

The ranks of the better-off in agrarian societies were swelled by greater mobility and the increased economic mobilisation of economies for war in 1914-18. It was this class of *kulaks* (later to suffer most in Stalinist campaigns for collectivisation) who were most attracted to the peasant parties that gained much electoral support in the early years of the fledgling democratic states. They saw the advantage of this involvement in political organisation as a way of trying to use the state for generally conservative objectives, to protect their interests. In practice ruling government cadres were often able to use their greater experience of politics and powers of patronage to manipulate and co-opt the peasantist leaders, simply using the peasant parties' numerically large following to ensure themselves a compliant majority in ineffectual parliaments.

Such cities as Sofia, the only really significant city in Bulgaria, and to a large extent also Budapest and Bucharest and other urban centres, tended to be regarded by the non-urban elites and by the mass of the peasants alike as cosmopolitan implants, not as a coherent central element in an economic and social network with the surrounding area. This was particularly the case where, not only in Romania and Hungary but also notably in Poland, a significant element in the entrepreneurial middle class was ethnically distinct from the indigenous population. An indigenous entrepreneurial middle class was sizeable only in Saxony and the Czech lands by 1914; much of the expansion of economic activity in the previous century was due to the impetus from immigrant groups - in many cases Jews from Galicia and Russia, in some others (particularly in the Czech Lands) also containing a German element or, further south, Armenians. The perception that the value systems of these minorities were "alien" reinforced hostility to them among traditional ruling elites, and encouraged their belief that involvement in change, risk-taking and commercially-based networks of exchange were inimical to the real identity of the historic nation. Only in Bohemia and Moravia did a native entrepreneurial class achieve sufficient strength to make its necessary contribution to the building of the political structures of a modern and pluralist state. The ethnic divisions within a city like Prague or Budapest (even if Jews in Budapest were disposed to assimilate Hungarian culture rather than remain confined to the ghetto) were another factor in weakening the extent to which the bourgeoisie could develop as the nucleus of any relatively homogenous civil society.

The development of the intelligentsia, in the pre-1914 period, was to a large extent concentrated within the churches and the bureaucracies of empire, and recruits came mainly from among members of the gentry no longer able to make their living from landed estates. Where educational opportunities were expanded, particularly under Habsburg rule, this was generally not accompanied by a commensurate development of demand for graduates within a capitalist bourgeoisie. The educated elites accordingly for the most part found themselves promoting ideologies of nationalism in the service of political elites, or alternatively defending the values of loyalty to empire, apart from those who joined the growing ranks of the "pariah" intelligentsia in the nineteenth and early twentieth century revolutionary movements.

The turbulent events of 1848, across Europe's major capitals from Paris through Germany to Prague and Budapest, reflected the widespread frustration felt against the stifling conditions (both economic and political) of authoritarian regimes. This "year of revolutions" was a brief moment when nationalists, middle class pro-democracy groups and intellectuals, inspired by liberal ideologies and fired up to action by the news of what was happening in neighbouring capitals, proclaimed their right to independence and their faith in parliamentary structures. Their revolts were fuelled by economic recession, unrest and unemployment, the failure of harvests, and the consequent food shortages in the cities. However, the dramatic actions of 1848 were essentially the expression of an urban middle class opposition to the conservative imperial order, and in central and eastern Eurpe (certainly outside Germany) they lacked the deep roots and the cohesion with social forces in the surrounding countryside which might have made them a more durable threat to the traditional elites and governing bureaucracies.

The power elites of the four empires experienced no real obligation to demonstrate the legitimacy of their rule, nor to win allegiance to its civil institutions, since their rule was not founded on reciprocity, and since the power of civil society was too weak vis-a-vis the state to challenge it successfully when conflicts like those of 1848 did erupt. The weakness of liberal values was to be translated in the post-1918 period into a real problem of lack of attachment to the institutions which should have bound them together had they genuinely been more modern pluralist polities. This factor both militated against the effective functioning of democratic institutions, and contributed to the relative ease with which they could be usurped by an etatist governing elite, or challenged by authoritarian movements of a more radical right-wing character.

POLAND

The country was known officially as the Polish People's Republic (*Polska Rzeczpospolita Ludowa*) until Dec. 30, 1989, and thereafter simply as the Polish Republic (*Polska Rzeczpospolita*).

With the exception of Ukraine and Russia, Poland is the largest country in Central and Eastern Europe, in terms both of land area--312,680 sq. km--and population, which numbered 38,400,000 in 1990. It shares borders with Russia, Lithuania, Belarus, Ukraine, Slovakia, the Czech Republic and Germany. Along the Czech-Slovak border in the south are the only significant peaks which form part of the Carpathian and Sudety mountains. Most of Poland is low-lying, being part of the North European plain. The river Vistula (Wista in Polish) rises near Krakow, flows north through Warsaw (Warszawa) and enters the Baltic near Gdansk. The Oder (Odra), Poland's other major river, originates in Moravia and flows north to its confluence with the Neisse (Nysa), thenceforth delimiting much of the Polish-German border until it reaches the Baltic near Szczecin.

Although to this day Poland has a significant peasant population, the rapid industrialisation during the communist era urbanised many former peasants. Over 60 per cent of Poles are now urban-dwellers. The capital, Warsaw, is the largest city, with a population of 1,660,000. The second city is the old-established industrial centre of Lodz, which is about half the size of Warsaw. The upper Silesia mining region is highly industrialised and heavily polluted; its main centres are Katowice and the steel city of Krakow (which has a population of some 750,000). Other cities of comparable size are the two major regional centres of western Poland--namely Wroclaw (which was known under German rule as Breslau) and Poznan (Posnan)--and the two main Baltic ports, Gdansk (Danzig) and Szczecin (Stettin).

The Polish language (*jezyk polski*) is part of the West Slavic group, but differs significantly from others in the same group, notably Czech and Slovak.

Before the Second World War Poland's ethnic minorities had comprised some 30 per cent of the population of over 30 million. Apart from numbers of Ukrainians, White

Russians (Belorussians), Germans and Ruthenians, there were at least three million Jews. Following the Nazi Holocaust Poland has only about 12,000 Jews. The population exchanges of the postwar period led to even greater ethnic homogeneity and Poland is now 98.7% ethnically Polish. There are small minorities of Ukrainians, Belorussians and German-speakers.

About half a million Poles live in what is now Belarus and a substantial number also in the Baltic states, particularly Lithuania, whose capital Vilnius was once the Polish city of Wilna. There are significant emigré communities particularly in North America.

In religious terms Poland is more devoutly Catholic than any country in Europe, with the possible exception of Ireland. Catholicism claims the allegiance of 95 per cent of the population, three quarters of whom attend services on a regular basis. The Church is regarded by many Poles as the cornerstone of the Polish nation, although its political influence in post-communist Poland is limited. There is also a Polish Autocephalous Orthodox Church and other smaller Christian denominations (mainly Ukrainian Uniates, and Lutherans and other Protestants).

HISTORICAL NARRATIVE

Historic Poland was a considerable empire, which once stretched from the Baltic to the Black Sea. In 1795 it was partitioned between the stronger regional powers, Russia, Austria and Prussia. Austria and Germany overran Russia's Polish provinces in 1917-18. When they collapsed later in 1918 a unified Poland was recreated as part of the postwar peace settlement.

Marshal Jozef Pilsudski was proclaimed Chief-of-State of the Second Polish Republic on 14 November 1918. The republic's borders to the West and south were fixed at Versailles in 1919. Defeated Germany ceded Posen and West Prussia to the new state. East Prussia remained German, although separated by a corridor of Polish territory adjoining the Baltic. The Baltic port of Danzig became a "free city". In 1920-1 Poland took military action to expand its territory in the east, under the pretext of supporting the rebellious Russian White army against the Bolsheviks. The Red Army counter-attacked and reached Warsaw, but was decisively defeated there in August 1920. Under the Treaty of Riga in March 1921 Poland was awarded half of what is now Belarus and a great swathe of western Ukraine.

Poland had five years of parliamentary democracy under its March 1921 constitution, but Marshal Pilsudski, the dominant figure of the interwar period, lost patience with the fractious politicking of a series of weak coalition governments, and in May 1926 launched a military coup. Pilsudski's nine subsequent years of authoritarian rule are still regarded by many Poles as an enlightened dictatorship. The regime had democratic trappings; there were even multi-party elections in which the Communist Party was permitted to compete. Pilsudski's party, the Nonpartisan Bloc for Cooperation with the Government (BBWR), was a coalition of forces in favour of strong, technocratic government.

Although the Pilsudski regime enacted constitutional guarantees on racial and religious tolerance, his period as head of state was marked by a breakdown in inter-ethnic relations. Poland also faced the problem of the increasingly irredentist Germany, with which there was growing friction over Danzig and the Polish corridor. Pilsudski, who formally no longer held office but who nonetheless remained the effective dictator, died in May 1935, and power was thereafter exercised by a military council.

The Second World War

After the Western appeasement of Hitler at Munich in 1938, and the dismembering of Czechoslovakia, the Nazi threat was turned into devastating military action as soon as Hitler had reached a deal with Stalin. The Nazi-Soviet pact of August 1939 included secret protocols on the partition of Poland and Eastern Europe as a whole. British and French guarantees to Poland were now insufficient to deter Germany from invasion. The Second World War started in September 1939 when German troops, using blitzkrieg tactics, poured into Poland in spite of fierce Polish resistance. Much of western Poland was incorporated as *lebensraum* for the German Reich while the east was annexed to the Soviet Union. The remaining rump was the so-called *General Gouvernement* area, under a ferocious Nazi regime. By June 1941 the Nazi-Soviet pact had collapsed and German forces had swept east, occupying the whole of Poland and entering Soviet territory.

A Polish government-in-exile was established in London, headed by the pre-war leader Gen. Wladyslaw Sikorski until his death in 1943, and thereafter by Peasant Party leader Stanislaw Mikolajczyk.

In 1944 the Soviet army re-crossed Poland's eastern frontier, driving the retreating Germans before it, but German forces retained their grip on Warsaw. In August 1944 the government-in-exile launched the Warsaw uprising, an armed attempt to reclaim the capital before the Red Army could reach it, and thus to strengthen Poland's hand in postwar peace negotiations. Some 250,000 Polish rebels, including communists, died in a heroic but desperate struggle in which the city itself was virtually destroyed. Cynically, the Soviet advance was halted short of Warsaw, the Soviets having calculated that their best interests would be served by letting the Germans defeat the rebels. Warsaw was finally "liberated" by the Red Army in January 1945.

The strength of Polish resistance to the Germans, exemplified by the Warsaw uprising, demonstrated that Poles still nurtured a defiant nationalism, despite 200 years of domination by regional powers. But no country in Europe had a more terrible experience of World War II. Under the SS state, extermination camps were constructed in 1941 for the genocide of Jews, Roma (Gypsies) and others. Other Poles were conscripted to forced labour in Germany, or deported to the General Gouvernement area. From the eastern portion of Poland, which was under Soviet rule in the early stages of the war, over one million Poles were deported to the Soviet Union. In total Poland lost 20 per cent of its population -- six million people, half of whom were Jews. Poland's entrepreneurial class was virtually eradicated. The severe damage wrought to the country's infrastructure by the war was compounded by the Soviet seizure of industrial machinery, much of which was removed to the Soviet Union.

In the postwar world, Soviet hegemony in Eastern Europe was reflected in the fate of Poland, across which were the supply lines to the strategically crucial Soviet-controlled sector of Germany. The territorial settlement, formalised by the victorious powers at the Potsdam conference in August 1945, confirmed promises made by the Western allies to the Soviet Union at Teheran and Yalta in 1943 and 1945. Eastern Poland was thus incorporated into the Soviet Union, while Poland's frontier with Germany was moved some 250 km westward to the Oder-Neisse line. In the north-east, the formerly German enclave of East Prussia was divided between Poland and the Soviet Union, which took Königsberg/Kaliningrad. In major population exchanges 3.5 million Poles moved west, from the former Polish eastern territories; many were transferred to homes in western Poland vacated by 4.5 million Germans.

The communist takeover and the period of Stalinisation

In a series of barely concealed manoeuvres under Soviet direction, a communist single-party regime was established between 1944 and 1947.

The London-based Prime Minister Mikolajczyk resigned in the wake of the Warsaw uprising, pragmatically urging his supporters to co-operate with the communists, who had established a Committee of National Liberation, and who set up a provisional government at Lublin in December 1944. There were nonetheless bloody clashes between anti-communist militia and armed communists throughout the winter of 1944-5 and the spring of 1945. In June 1945, pending the holding of elections, a communist-dominated Polish Government of National Unity, led by the communist Boleslaw Bierut as acting President, was established in Warsaw and recognised by the Allied powers.

Legislative elections in January 1947 took place in an atmosphere of intimidation. Several associates of Mikolajczyk were murdered. Although the communist party's popularity had undoubtedly grown from its pre-war level (a peak of 7 per cent in 1927), the 1947 election results were rigged to ensure a large majority for the communists and their allies -- the Socialists, the Democratic Party and the United Peasant Party (ZSL). Bierut was confirmed as President. Opposition parties were then dissolved and their leaders, among them Mikolajczyk, were forced to flee the country. In 1949 the communists absorbed their partners, to form the Polish United Workers' Party (PZPR). (The Polish communist party, dissolved in 1938, had been revived in 1942 as the Polish Workers' Party, the PPR.)

Under a three-year plan completed in 1947-49, the economy began to recover, but was thenceforth distorted by the Stalinist preoccupation with investment in heavy industry and armaments, to the serious detriment of other sectors of the economy. This accelerated industrialisation was intended to bind Poland into Comecon as a centre of heavy industry and a cheap source of supplies to the Soviet Union.

While industry was nationalised, the agricultural sector escaped the full implementation of Soviet-style collectivisation. Although a collectivisation programme was formally adopted in July 1948, it was undermined by mainly passive peasant resistance. Among the programme's opponents within the PPR was the party general secretary Wladyslaw Gomulka, who for his pains was expelled from the party in September 1948 and imprisoned as a "right-wing nationalist deviationist".

The purge which brought down Gomulka was comparatively moderate, certainly by comparison with the more violent purges elsewhere in Central and Eastern Europe. This was the peak period of political Stalinisation, whose proponents outlasted for some years the death of the Soviet leader himself in 1953. Bierut died in March 1956, reputedly from shock over Soviet leader Nikita Khrushchev's repudiation of Stalin the previous month in his Secret Speech in Moscow.

Destalinisation

An amnesty in Poland in the spring of 1956 was accompanied by other destalinising measures, including legal limits on the powers of the security police. For a while events in Poland seemed to move in tandem with those in Hungary, apparently presaging a new liberal era in communist Eastern Europe.

On 28 June 1956, workers in Poznan demonstrating against conditions at their plant began a riot and attacked the local PZPR headquarters. Polish troops crushed the protest, killing 53 people and wounding some 300. The incident prompted a wave of strikes demanding liberalisation. The PZPR responded to this turmoil by bringing the popular Gomulka back from the wilderness and electing him as party general secretary, and by removing Soviet General Rokossovski as defence minister. At the PZPR central committee meeting in October, Gomulka conceded that the Poznan riots were the result of impoverishment. He reaffirmed Poland's determination to follow its own road.

The apparently successful Polish stand gave encouragement to radically-minded reformists in Hungary, where the return of Nagy paralleled the reinstatement of Gomulka. Conversely, the Soviet use of military force to crush the reforms in Hungary in November also served to cow Poland's Gomulka regime into political orthodoxy. Poland was required to maintain loyalty to the Soviet line. Twelve years later, in August 1968, Polish troops took part in the Warsaw Pact invasion of Czechoslovakia, to suppress that experiment in reform socialism.

Gomulka did, however, effectively abandon collectivisation, so that Poland became the only Soviet bloc state with a majority of the agricultural sector in private hands. This reversal represented a significant victory by Polish society over the communist state. In another significant concession, restrictions on religious and intellectual freedom were eased.

By the late 1960s Gomulka was vulnerable. He had become reliant on the support of a strongly anti-liberal element within the party. This element mobilised popular support with its anti-Zionist rhetoric, which struck a chord with the xenophobia and anti-Semitism of some Polish nationalists. In contrast to Hungary, where some innovation had been encouraged under Kadar, the Polish regime had continued to rely heavily on the stifling central planning system, and Gomulka failed to deliver the sustained improvement in living standards which he had pledged in 1956. Although massive food subsidies partially obscured the magnitude of Poland's economic problems, they merely stored up problems for the future.

In a belated attempt to cut these food subsidies, price increases of 30 per cent were announced on 12 December 1970 - just before Christmas. This insensitive measure provoked the "Baltic crisis" as protest strikes and rioting spread through several coastal cities, including Gdansk. Hundreds of people were killed when security forces opened fire on the crowds. Within a week of the price rises Edward Gierek, the Katowice communist leader and a respected manager, had replaced Gomulka. Strikes and protests continued in January and February 1971, and spread to Warsaw and Lodz. In mid-February Gierek announced a humiliating climbdown: prices would be frozen at their pre-December level for two years, the measure being funded by a Soviet loan.

The policy reversal prompted by the Baltic crisis marked a second major victory by Polish society over the communist state. The PZPR congress of December 1971 effectively conceded the major part of the protesters' demands by proclaiming the improvement of living standards as the party's "supreme goal". The Baltic crisis also marked the beginning of the opposition movement which developed into Solidarity.

The economy in the Gierek era

Gierek's economic objective was industrial development financed by borrowing. Continuing growth was to be driven by industry, rejuvenated and reoriented to the export market. This transformation was to be wrought through technology, principally by means of new imported machinery to boost industrial productivity. The imports were to be financed by foreign loans.

Under the Gierek strategy Poland rapidly accumulated a startlingly large foreign debt, but with little corresponding benefit to the economy. By the late 1970s economic growth had gone catastrophically into reverse. The allocation of investment had remained a highly centralised process, subject to bureaucratic interests and distortions, and with a pronounced bias towards heavy industry. The failures of the Polish bureaucracy had been compounded by developments in the world economy, as global recession from 1974 shrank the export market. There were serious balance-of-payments problems and shortages of consumer goods. The Polish regime faced increasing domestic pressure to divert foreign loans into subsidies designed to maintain living standards.

By 1976 food subsidies had reached 12 per cent of Polish GDP. Food price increases of 60 per cent were announced in June 1976, and inevitably prompted a new wave of strikes and demonstrations. Gierek at once dropped the price rises, but launched a crackdown on militant workers and students, thousands of whom were arrested. The harsh measures prompted the formation of the Committee for the Defence of Workers (KOR), the precursor of Solidarity, in September 1976.

Apart from economic stagnation, the most significant legacy of the Gierek era was the growth of the *nomenklatura*, the system for the appointment of a communist bureaucracy. The nomenklatura permeated every area of public life including government, local administration, the official unions, industrial management, the media, education and the arts. The party elite accrued wealth and privileges: Gierek himself had special facilities built in the Carpathians for party use. Venality and corruption spread into all aspects of life. Meritocratic or technocratic principles were often overlooked in favour of profit and nepotism.

The Polish Pope

The only major non-communist structure before the emergence of the Solidarity movement was the Roman Catholic Church, whose more radical elements gave important moral support to human rights activity and the emerging "workers' self-defence committees" of the late 1970s. Polish pride in nationality and Catholicism received a forceful boost with the October 1978 election of Cardinal Karol Wojtyla as the "Polish Pope" John Paul II. The following June he made his first triumphal papal visit to Poland.

Solidarity

The wave of strikes which was to bring Gierek down in 1980 began in mid-year, in the Baltic ports and Silesian coalfields, and was again sparked by price increases. Unofficial union organisations provided the focus for the workers' grievances, which were initially confined to demands for wage rises. Beyond the consensus that force should not be used, the government failed to agree a co-ordinated response to the strikes. Sensing the government's indecision, the workers' demands escalated. Workers at the Gdansk shipyard, led by electrician Lech Walesa, struck in mid-August to demand government acceptance of free trade unions, specifically the NPZZ Solidarnosc (Self-Governing Trade Union Solidarity). Negotiations began on 26 August with strike representatives including Walesa.

The talks led to the "Gdansk accords", the most significant concession yet by the communist state, and a critical turning point in the protracted demise of communism in Poland (and indeed in East-Central Europe as a whole). The accords, struck on 31 August 1980, conceded the right to strike and the right to form free trade unions. The striking workers had confronted the party, whose ideology was based upon its claim to represent the working class, and were seen to have won the right to operate outside the communist system.

The Solidarity free trade union, founded in September under Walesa's leadership, overcame legal obstacles to achieve registration by November, and membership grew rapidly from the ports, steelyards and mines to the countryside (Rural Solidarity was formally constituted in May 1981). Solidarity even attracted to its ranks as many as one third of the PZPR membership, and by mid-1981 claimed an astonishing 9,500,000 members.

Meanwhile the PZPR and government went through a succession of leadership changes. Gierek was replaced as PZPR leader in September 1980 by Stanislaw Kania, who pressed for reforms to restore party credibility, but was under constant counter-attack from entrenched hardline interests. Kania's appointment had been balanced by that of Gen. Wojciech Jaruzelski, a conservative, as prime minister in February 1981. Kania survived a PZPR extraordinary congress in July 1981, but was replaced by Jaruzelski in October.

For a year it was Solidarity which dominated the political agenda, with Walesa and other leaders urging restraint upon their militant membership, as the economic situation continued to deteriorate. Solidarity's national conference in September-October 1981 revealed the radicalisation of the movement. To achieve enduring economic changes, the delegates resolve, trade union demands and worker self-management were insufficient; political reforms were necessary, including free elections. Walesa had advocated restraint but as Solidarity became increasingly radical he now risked being outflanked by union militants.

Martial law

Whilst the Polish regime was under heavy pressure from the Solidarity movement, it also faced pressure from the Soviet Union, including the risk of military intervention. The Warsaw Pact's December 1980 summit had underscored its commitment to the Brezhnev doctrine by declaring that all socialist countries had an interest in Poland's problems. In 1981 hundreds of thousands of Soviet troops participated in a series of exercises near the border with Poland, while in the rest of Central and Eastern Europe the media campaign against Solidarity reached a new pitch.

In early November 1981 the Primate of Poland, Cardinal Glemp, brought Walesa and Jaruzelski together for talks, amid indications that the communist party would accept a division of responsibilities with the unions and the church in a broad national unity front. By the end of the month, however, talks had collapsed in failure, and the Jaruzelski government quickly announced a package of emergency laws, including a ban on strikes. Solidarity threw down the gauntlet by threatening a general strike.

In a bid to avert Soviet military intervention, which he now believed was otherwise inevitable, Jaruzelski declared martial law on 13 December 1981, arresting thousands of opposition activists including the Solidarity leaders, and revoking the Gdansk accords. Solidarity was abolished in autumn 1982. Forced underground, it nevertheless remained the most active dissident organisation in East-Central Europe, producing numerous *samizdat* publications, organising and mobilising demonstrations and strike action, and also urging boycotts of elections.

In October 1984 the pro-Solidarity priest Fr Jerzy Popieluszko was kidnapped and killed by state security agents. Although the agents responsible were convicted in 1985, claiming to have acted without orders, the murder tainted the regime and provided a focus for powerful moral criticism from the Church. As the regime sought to improve its image on human rights, successive amnesties led in 1986 to a decree on the release of all political prisoners.

During this period the economy faltered and declined. In 1982 prices were increased by 76 per cent, with a concomitant drop in living standards by 26 per cent. Economic growth rates of 6 per cent in 1983 and 1984 gave way to stagnation by 1986. And, most importantly, the level of foreign debt steadily increased as Poland failed to keep pace with repayments, partly due to US and other Western sanctions imposed in 1981-84 in response to martial law.

Disaffection among workers remained strong, and their grievances over pay and prices had deepened as the economy deteriorated further. In 1984 the officially-tolerated trade unions had formed a National Trade Union Accord (OPZZ), providing an alternative to Solidarity for limited demands on wages and price subsidies. The OPZZ's close links to the ruling PZPR were illustrated controversially when its leader, Alfred Miodowicz, joined the party politburo in mid-1986.

The round table talks

A fresh upsurge of strikes in August 1988 spread from the mining industry, effectively compelling Jaruzelski to abandon the attempt to rule against the people. Instead Jaruzelski began to explore the possibility of co-operation with workers and the political opposition to tackle the country's overwhelming problems. Jaruzelski's initiative resembled a 1986 offer by Solidarity leaders to end clandestine activity and open a dialogue with the government, which had been rebuffed.

Although Solidarity remained illegal, the government offered to negotiate with it, initially on trade union pluralism; the agenda was then widened to include the re-legalisation of Solidarity, and the extension of political reforms.

The round table talks, eventually convened in February 1989, were seen at the outset as a necessary search for consensus to deal with the current crisis. Only during the process itself did it become apparent that the round table talks were defining Poland's future political development.

In the historic Round Table agreement of April 1989, the PZPR became the first ruling communist party ever to give up its monopoly on power, agreeing to share power with an independent social organ. The revolutionary significance of this concession emerged after the partially-free June elections, in which Solidarity won a crushing victory in the openly-contested seats. The PZPR, having broken away from the two parties formerly allied to it (the Democratic Party and the United Peasant Party--ZSL), became the junior partner in a Solidarity-led government formed in August-September under Tadeusz Mazowiecki, while Jaruzelski was elected president, in conformity with the formula proposed by Solidarity intellectual Adam Michnik: "your president, our government". Poland thus became the only Warsaw Pact country with a non-communist government, but was pledged to remain within the existing security framework; the four government portfolios held by communist ministers included the ministries of defence and interior.

This marked the high point of Poland's revolution, a process which had begun in Gdansk nine years earlier, and whose second phase, after the long hiatus of 1982-88, had lasted just one year. By 1990 the PZPR had dissolved itself to form a successor party, the Social Democracy of the Polish Republic (SdRP), as part of a coalition of ex-communist groups, the Democratic Left Alliance (SLD). Under the leadership of a young former junior minister, Aleksander Kwasniewski, the SdRP and the SLD turned to mainstream European-style social democracy.

Solidarity, post-communism and economic "shock therapy"

Meanwhile, the new Solidarity-led government had introduced "shock treatment", in the form of an economic austerity programme masterminded by and named after Finance Minister Leszek Balcerowicz. The Balcerowicz Plan was the first attempt radically to reform a command economy on pro-market principles (*see also section on economy*). For two difficult years, successive governments held fast to this programme, effecting a relatively rapid conversion to a market economy with the aim of achieving prosperity in the medium term, but with divisive effects as standards of living dropped; Solidarity's working class constituency suffered particularly.

Shock treatment, and Walesa's leadership, were the main catalysts for the fragmentation of Solidarity. Always a demographically diverse movement, it comprised workers, peasants and intellectuals, and contained liberal, Christian democratic, nationalist, labourist and social democratic factions, many of which formed political parties in 1990-91.

Walesa's style of leadership had been causing consternation among Solidarity intellectuals by 1990. Many suspected him of irresponsible attempts to elevate himself as the candidate to replace Jaruzelski as president, at the expense of other Solidarity leaders. In particular Walesa's criticism of shock treatment provoked accusations of populism. In the presidential elections of autumn 1990 the prime minister and Solidarity intellectual Tadeusz Mazowiecki ran against Walesa. Hindered by rumours that he was Jewish, and by the unpopularity of radical reforms, Mazowiecki was beaten into third place, behind Walesa and the maverick candidate Stanislaw Tyminski, an emigré businessman with a demagogic programme promising prosperity for all. Once elected Walesa moderated his attacks on economic reform and appointed as Prime Minister Jan Krzysztof Bielecki of the Liberal Democratic Congress (KLD)--the party most associated with shock treatment.

The 1991 legislative elections completed the fragmentation of the Solidarity movement. Under the electoral system parties could win parliamentary seats with as little as 1 per cent of the vote, and 29 parties did so, while the low turnout of just over 43 per cent was a measure of the popular disenchantment with the now bewildering array of political parties.

The two most prominent pro-reform parties, the KLD and Mazowiecki's Democratic Union (UD), together secured under 20 per cent of the vote, reflecting widespread disillusion with the high social costs of economic reform. Meanwhile post-Solidarity Christian and Christian Democratic parties, who had received the implicit backing of the church, were a modest success. The two most prominent, the Centre Alliance (PC) and the Catholic Electoral Action grouping, of which the Christian National Union (ZChN) was the principal component, together won over 17 per cent of the *Sejm* vote. ZChN leader Wieslaw Chrzanowski was elected as speaker of the *Sejm* in November 1991.

The coalition which emerged from complex negotiations following the elections was dominated by these parties and led by Jan Olszewski of the Centre Alliance. Olszewski openly attempted to abandon radical economic reform; hiss failure taught all parties about the new post-communist political realities. In February 1992 the Olszewski cabinet published a new socio-economic programme designed to bring the economy out of recession by relaxing the austerity measures. Olszewski's plans rapidly unravelled: the finance minister immediately resigned, warning of hyperinflation; and in March the programme was rejected by the *Sejm*, having failed to satisfy either the left or the liberal right. Later that month Olszewski abandoned any further attempt radically to alter the course of economic policy, citing the need to win back essential IMF support suspended in October 1991.

Relations between Walesa and the Olszewski cabinet were poor throughout its term. A clash over control of the military forced the resignation of Defence Minister Jan Parys in May 1992, and later that month Walesa declared his loss of confidence in the government. Sensing its imminent dismissal by parliament, the Olszewski government provoked a major confrontation with Walesa. It chose to fight on the issue of de-communisation, its key political policy. Although it included in its ranks the ex-communist Polish Peasant Party (PSL, formerly ZSL), Olszewski's coalition had strongly advocated a campaign to break with the communist past. There was widespread resentment among voters that a former communist elite continued to occupy senior offices of state and had adapted itself to exploit the new economic conditions since 1989. Olszewski argued that those responsible for the injustices of the communist era should be punished, or at least removed from positions of authority.

In February 1992 a government-sponsored *Sejm* resolution pronounced the 1981 declaration of Martial Law illegal, paving the way for the prosecution of former communist leaders such as Gen. Jaruzelski. In a bid to expose an alleged "fifth column" of former secret police collaborators, the government then decided to distribute to party leaders a secret list of officials cited in communist-era secret police files as collaborators. Both liberal and left-wing parties denounced this as a politically-motivated smear directed at the regime's opponents, while Walesa, who was reputedly among those accused, also strongly opposed the move. The affair had the effect of tainting the de-communisation process with the suspicion of political manipulation.

The Olszewski government left a significant legacy considering how briefly it held office. Its abortive attempt to abandon radical economic reform revealed the narrow constraints restricting economic policy-making. Its other main policy, de-communisation, was all but discredited. Its shambolic fall from power further damaged prospects for co-operation among post-Solidarity groups, while its poor reputation badly damaged the performance of right-wing and Christian democratic parties in the 1993 legislative elections.

Olszewski was briefly succeeded by PSL leader Waldemar Pawlak, who thus became Poland's youngest ever prime minister; he failed to form a coalition and rapidly gave way to Poland's first woman prime minister, Hanna Suchocka of the UD. Suchocka's first achievement was to bring together a coalition at all. Her government included seven post-Solidarity parties from the liberal, Christian democratic and peasant wings of the movement, including both the UD and the ZChN, with most Solidarity union deputies lending tacit support.

Over the next ten months the Suchocka government piloted some highly significant legislation through parliament. This included the "Small Constitution", a much needed package designed to clarify the relationship between the *Sejm*, the cabinet and the presidency (which nevertheless failed to end constitutional disputes; *see below*); an electoral law designed to reduce the fragmentation of parliament; and measures imposing narrow criteria for legal abortions, which pleased the Christian parties within the coalition. In addition, a series of radical economic initiatives included new austerity measures, designed to reduce the budget deficit, and mass privatisation legislation, designed to broaden and accelerate the process of ownership transformation. Although radical plans to restructure the coal industry were rejected by the *Sejm*, Suchocka's economic policies pleased international investors, and in March 1993 the IMF approved its first loan since October 1991.

Important domestic backers of the coalition, however, were uncomfortable with the return to radical economics. In late April 1993 the Peasant Alliance withdrew from the government in protest at the lack of support for agriculture, and when the cabinet refused in May to sanction pay increases for striking health and education workers, Solidarity deputies backed a successful motion of no confidence. Suchocka's cabinet announced its resignation in late May. In a historic miscalculation, Walesa dissolved the legislature and called elections for September.

1993-5: the "velvet restoration"

The 1993 elections, held under Suchocka's new electoral law, represented a heavy blow for the divided post-Solidarity parties. The ex-communist SLD and PSL swept back to power, securing two thirds of the seats in the *Sejm*. The right, despite winning a similar proportion of the vote, suffered heavily for its fragmentation. Post-Solidarity parties--Walesa's Non-Party Bloc in Support of Reforms (BBWR), the UD, and the (socialist) Labour Union--won under 30 per cent of the seats, and the rest went to the extreme nationalist KPN.

The post-Solidarity parties performed poorly for a number of reasons. In the first place, the fragmentation of Solidarity in 1990-91 had led to a bewildering profusion of parties. Even on Solidarity's liberal wing, which had earned a reputation for pragmatism, the UD and the KLD failed to combine until 1994, while the right was even more fragmented. In consequence the non-left vote was so divided that over a third of the total vote went to parties which failed to clear the new electoral hurdles, and none of the parties on Solidarity's Christian democratic wing gained specific representation in the Polish parliament, a striking failure in a strongly Catholic country.

Secondly, in a country with a history of popular unrest related directly to sudden drops in standards of living, an economic policy which demanded material sacrifices for the sake of future prosperity had courted unpopularity. The authors of shock treatment, aware of the political risks of the strategy, had failed to deliver a substantial economic revival before the crucial 1993 election. Instead high unemployment and falling living standards understandably led many Poles to regard themselves as losers in the process.

Thirdly, in common with the generation of post-communist politicians across Eastern Europe, the political leaders who emerged from opposition in 1989 had no experience either of the execution of government or of the effective presentation of policies to voters. Many post-Solidarity leaders, although highly capable intellectuals, lacked the acute political skills necessary to rally voters behind controversial policies. On the other hand Walesa, probably Poland's most charismatic leader, deliberately distanced himself from shock treatment.

Fourthly, the success of Stanislaw Tyminski in capturing a quarter of the popular vote in 1990's presidential elections had already demonstrated the relative immaturity of the Polish electorate. Thus, although the opponents of shock treatment, including the parties of the left, frequently offered no practical alternative beyond vague promises to "moderate" reform, they attracted support through their continual criticism of aspects of the policy.

Finally, many Poles had come to regard the liberalism of the post-Solidarity governments as a new dogma imported from the West. Ideologies had for years been regarded with cynicism by workers and peasants as the artificial constructs of intellectuals. Walesa's BBWR, attempting to attract such voters with the offer of a government of technocrats above petty party bickering, failed to convince many voters, Walesa himself having been a highly political president.

1993: why the left won

To many post-Solidarity leaders the revival of the Polish left appeared to swim against the tide of history; however, it mirrored similar developments in other East European countries, not least in Russia itself.

The ex-communist parties had the advantage of inheriting extensive party organisations, and retained considerable support throughout the political transition from 1989. Some voters identified them as the most technically competent to govern, in view of their lengthy experience, while their new youthful leaders helped convince a relatively small but significant portion of the electorate that they had sincerely abandoned dogma in favour of a pragmatic programme embracing a mixed economy with adequate social protection. The PSL in particular also appealed successfully to the sectional interests of small-scale farmers. Moreover, Poland's communists had voluntarily relinquished power; by contrast with other East European states, where the communist regimes had departed with the greatest reluctance, they could thus more convincingly claim a place in the democratic process.

The ex-communist parties in government

In the wake of the elections PSL leader Pawlak formed a coalition cabinet including eight PSL and five SLD deputies. Among six independent ministers were those of foreign affairs, defence and internal affairs, who were effectively Walesa's nominees.

Pawlak stressed that the new government was committed to continuity in both foreign and economic policy, but that the economic reform would be slowed to an orderly pace, with a renewed emphasis on a more equal distribution of the benefits of transition. In practice, however, Pawlak controversially used a number of ruses to delay the privatisation process, exposing divisions within the coalition as SLD ministers objected that this appeared to undermine the party's claim to have embraced the mixed economy. Although Pawlak approved a third tranche of privatisation in October 1994, opinion polls showed that the Polish people were also becoming increasingly frustrated with the sluggish pace of economic reform.

Constitutional wrangling between Walesa and the ex-communist parties dominated Polish politics for two years. Exploiting the legal confusion surrounding policy prerogatives, Walesa repeatedly vetoed bills, sending legislation to the constitutional tribunal and threatening to dissolve parliament. Walesa's tactics encouraged the *Sejm* to pass a resolution in October 1994 requesting that the president cease activities which could threaten or destabilise democracy. A presidential spokesman revealed in October 1994 that Walesa was deliberately acting on the fringe of the law, in order to push his powers as far as possible. Seeking greater control over the appointment of government personnel, in November 1994 he effectively forced Pawlak to dismiss Defence Minister Adm. Piotr Kolodziejczik, his own nominee. It emerged that Walesa had encouraged the general staff to hold a vote of no confidence in Kolodziejczik, who accused Walesa of inciting insubordination by senior officers and of undermining civilian control over the military.

Economic policy was one of many areas of confrontation between President Walesa and the Pawlak government. In January 1995, at the height of a tax dispute which threatened the passage of a budget for 1995, Walesa urged citizens to ignore higher tax rates set by the government and instead to pay income tax at the previous, lower rate. Finance Minister Kolodko castigated Walesa for "activity aimed against the foundations of the state".

Walesa initially sought to portray the PSL and SLD as unreconstructed communists. Two *Sejm* decisions in July 1994, its deferment of consideration of the Concordat with the Vatican and its rejection of lustration legislation, were bitterly condemned as a resurgence of communism. This view was partially endorsed by other more moderate former Solidarity leaders; Adam Michnik argued that Poland was witnessing a "velvet restoration" of communist rule.

As the presidential elections neared, Walesa's criticism took a different tack. He conceded that the ex-communist parties were committed to economic reform, but argued that an ex-communist elite was unfairly positioned to exercise political and economic power in post-communist Poland. Walesa feared that the *nomenklatura* had effectively survived intact, with all its abuses of nepotism and corruption.

In February 1995 Walesa threatened to dissolve parliament if Pawlak remained prime minister. The *Sejm* countered with a threat to impeach Walesa. A constitutional crisis was narrowly averted when Pawlak agreed to resign. Walesa rapidly worked to undermine Pawlak's successor, the respected *Sejm* speaker Jozef Oleksy of the SLD, whom Walesa accused of "treasonable activities" when he strayed into Walesa's foreign policy responsibilities in May 1995.

The 1995 presidential elections

Walesa was narrowly defeated in the presidential elections of November 1995 by the SLD leader Aleksander Kwasniewski, marking the end of the Solidarity era and leaving Poland dominated by ex-communists in the parliament, cabinet and presidency.

Walesa's campaign had been defined by a negative: anti-communism. This revealed the narrow limits of his once-celebrated understanding for the mood of the people. Most Poles were weary of political confrontation. Kwasniewski, in contrast, had stressed one-nation social democracy, calling for reconciliation, compromise, political stability and social justice, and committing himself to continuity in economic policy and foreign affairs, reiterating his support for Poland joining NATO and the EC (EU) by 2000.

Walesa's record in office, moreover, was a highly controversial one. His repeated clashes with governments of varied political hues, and his obvious appetite for power, made him vulnerable to accusations of destabilising Polish politics and discrediting democratic institutions. His arrogant and belligerent style of leadership, including a tendency to make vulgar personal attacks on rivals, had led former ally Michnik tellingly to denounce him as a "master of destruction" guilty of "megalomania and coarseness". Pre-election opinion polls showed that Walesa was distrusted by more respondents, 45 per cent, than all other senior Polish politicians. In contrast Kwasniewski's distrust rating had been a modest 24 per cent.

Most importantly, Walesa's strategic vision of Poland seemed opaque, and much of his presidency seemed devoted to short-term political tactics, notably concerned with the acquisition of power, rather than with clear notions about policy. His willingness to change policy for the sake of political expediency, exemplified in his criticism of radical economic reform in 1990, betrayed a populist preoccupation with means before ends. Indicative of this was his failure to establish an effective political party with a clear programme; indeed his BBWR was handicapped from the beginning by its name, which had historical associations with the inter-war authoritarian regime.

The young and charismatic Kwasniewski succeeded notably in attracting the support of younger voters, as well as his natural constituency among the unemployed, farmers and office workers. Regarded as the technocratic candidate, he could benefit from the left's long experience of government whilst avoiding personal discredit for the abuses of the communist era.

Kwasniewski's victory was nonetheless a narrow one, and left the country divided. Walesa's response was to question the validity of the results. His supporters launched serious allegations against Kwasniewski, claiming that there had been electoral fraud, and that Kwasniewski had deliberately falsified his own educational qualifications. Walesa then turned on prime minister Oleksy, accusing him of having spied for the Soviet Union. The allegations could not prevent Kwasniewski's inauguration as president on 22 December, but they hinted that Walesa's future role in opposition could be potentially destabilising.

ECONOMY

Poland under its Solidarity-led coalition from 1989 was the first ex-communist state in East-Central Europe to adopt a radical economic reform programme, the so-called Balcerowicz Plan. Finance Minister Leszek Balcerowicz advocated "shock treatment", a rapid but painful transition to the market economy, expecting a sharp recession but calculating that the costs of the plan would be more than compensated by its medium- to long-term benefits. Balcerowicz argued that Poland had no option but radical market reforms, dismissed suggestions of a Polish "third way" between socialism and capitalism, and warned that gradual reform, far from escaping the costs of transition, would result in stagnation. Introduced in January 1990, shock treatment included an end to central planning, the abolition of state subsidies, the liberalisation of prices, and privatisation.

Seriously disrupted by the turmoil in its Comecon partners, Poland during this period was also establishing new trade links with Western Europe. As early as 1990 Germany had supplanted the Soviet Union as Poland's major trading partner.

GDP declined by 12 per cent in 1990, while living standards fell rapidly as inflation peaked at over 500 per cent. Public sector workers and social security recipients suffered particularly. The consequent political pressure on the post-Solidarity governments of 1990-3 was heavy, particularly after Walesa's criticism of shock treatment in 1990. Although Walesa swung behind the reforms once elected president, "shock treatment" was soon dropped as a slogan, and successive Polish cabinets demonstrated a reluctance to introduce further austerity measures, prompting the IMF to suspend its aid programme in 1991-3, citing Poland's failure to meet performance criteria.

Balcerowicz was dropped from government when the Olszewski cabinet took office in December 1991. Olszewski resolved to bring the economy out of recession by relaxing austerity measures, thus effectively abandoning shock treatment. Olszewski promised a new emphasis on social support. His proposals for a relaxation of monetary controls, however, were rejected by an unholy alliance of the left and economic liberals in the *Sejm* in March 1992. Olszewski dropped the proposals in mid-March, conceding that they would further jeopardise relations with the IMF and that this would in turn put in doubt a raft of loans, debt agreements and foreign investment.

The Suchocka cabinet placed a renewed emphasis on fiscal discipline, warning of the risk of hyperinflation. Tax increases and spending cuts in October 1992 were designed to reduce the budget deficit and quicken the privatisation process. The passage of a budget in February 1993 won back the support of the IMF. Suchocka was however limited by the fragility of her coalition, and radical plans to restructure the coal industry were rejected by the *Sejm* under pressure from striking Silesian miners. In late May 1993 the Suchocka cabinet fell after refusing to amend the budget to permit pay rises for striking health and education workers.

Although Poland officially came out of recession in 1992, recording real GDP growth of 2.4 per cent, the recovery was too limited to satisfy Polish voters. Pawlak's coalition of ex-communist parties in 1993 pledged to slow the reform process to an "orderly" pace and to distribute the benefits of reform more equally, maintaining an adequate level of social support. The SLD, however, became restless at the slow pace of reform, especially privatisation. By end-1995 the SLD was in a stronger position in the coalition, Pawlak having been replaced by SLD deputy Oleksy, and Kwasniewski having won the presidency.

The IMF continued to provide support and the economy made steady progress. By 1995 the Polish economy had become one of the strongest-performing in the region, recording GDP growth of some 6 per cent in 1995, with manufacturing industry staging a particularly strong recovery. Trade with new partners in the West had increased sharply and there was growing evidence of improving consumer confidence, while inflation was falling. Poland was therefore able to position itself with some confidence in its bid for membership of the EC (EU) by 2000.

Privatisation and restitution of property

The privatisation process in Poland advanced relatively slowly, despite a July 1990 privatisation bill opening the way for the sale of some 80 per cent of the state's holdings. Limited privatisation by direct sale got under way, with two tranches of privatisation in 1990-3, but a third was not approved until October 1994. In April 1993 the *Sejm* approved a mass privatisation programme under which 600 state firms were to be transferred to investment funds in preparation for flotation after ten years; shares in the funds were to be available for a nominal fee. Prime Minister Pawlak, however, used a variety of administrative and legal devices to delay the process, to the chagrin of his SLD coalition partners. Finance minister Kolodko insisted in 1995 that the government was not slowing privatisation but merely taking a strategic view, waiting for the "right moment" for particular sales. Although Pawlak was replaced in spring 1995, the PSL continued to influence privatisation policy.

Mass privatisation began in earnest only after the passage of further legislation in summer 1995. Opposition figures contended that a cumbersome approval process insisted on by the PSL, ostensibly to ensure "accountability" in the privatisation process, was in fact designed to cause delay. A second significant criticism of the legislation concerned measures permitting the officials controlling state enterprises to "commercialise" them (i.e. to convert them to a share ownership structure) without plans for subsequent sale of the state's shares, thus creating a self-perpetuating bureaucracy with no interest in full privatisation. The coalition passed the legislation with a two-thirds majority in July, overturning Walesa's veto.

The restitution of property, meanwhile, proceeded extremely slowly. Only the Church secured relatively prompt restitution. Other applications proceeded laboriously. In Warsaw, for example, where an October 1945 decree had "communalised" all real estate, only a handful of property certificates had been distributed by summer 1995. Thousands of applications for the restitution of city centre property were unresolved. Restitution legislation proposed by Walesa and the UW, which said that property should be returned or compensation offered, was rejected in June 1995, but parliament did decide in summer 1995 that restitution should be in the form of re-privatisation bonds and not in kind.

POST-COMMUNIST JUSTICE ISSUES

Accountability for Martial Law and past repression

The issue of postcommunist justice became highly politicised in Poland. The repression of the Martial Law period was vivid in the memory of former Solidarity activists and of Poles in general, but several ministers in the cabinets of Pawlak and Oleksy had served in the Martial Law-era government, and President Kwasniewski had been a junior minister in the mid-1980s.

The first postcommunist parliament passed a resolution on 1 February 1992 declaring that the imposition of Martial Law was illegal. The resolution also established a commission to explore the issue of compensation to the victims of Martial Law. Blame for the repression of the Martial Law period and its excesses was focused on key figures in the communist leadership. Gen. Jaruzelski, who insisted that only the declaration of Martial Law had prevented a Soviet military invasion, was charged along with 13 others in September 1992 with a variety of criminal offenses relating to its imposition. On 27 April 1993 Jaruzelski was also charged with having organised, as defence minister, the suppression of a workers' protest in December 1970, which had resulted in the death of at least 44 people.

One of the most notorious abuses of the communist era was the murder in November 1984 of pro-Solidarity priest Father Jerzy Popieluszko. Four low-ranking soldiers were convicted of the murder in February 1985. Former Interior Ministry Generals Wladyslaw Ciaston and Zenon Platek were acquitted in 1994 of aiding and abetting in the murder.

Lustration

Lustration (or "purification", a purge of state personnel "tainted" by their conduct in the communist era) proved highly controversial in Poland. Post-Solidarity politicians, particularly on the right, campaigned vigorously for the exposure of communist-era agents of the secret police and of their collaborators. The Committee for the Defence of Democracy, co-founded in February 1993 by Jan Olszewski, rallied the right under the lustration banner, claiming that a "fifth column" of communist sympathisers held positions of authority. In contrast the left opposed lustration, fearing that the move would generate a climate of anti-communist hysteria, while liberal and centre-left parties expressed doubts over the reliability of secret police files and fears over their use for political ends.

In the absence of a proper legal process, unsubstantiated accusations of collaboration with communist era secret police intermittently poisoned the political atmosphere. In the most recent case Walesa, in the wake of his defeat in the presidential elections of

November 1995, accused Prime Minister Josef Oleksy of having collaborated with Soviet and Russian intelligence agencies.

The crisis of the secret list

During Olszewski's tenure as prime minister a political storm blew up over the exposure of alleged collaborators. In a feverish political climate, Interior Minister Macierewicz in late May 1992 secured a mandate from the *Sejm* to expose former collaborators in positions of authority. Macierewicz duly delivered to the leaders of the main political parties an "informative" list of 64 ministers, deputies and civil servants allegedly cited in secret police files as collaborators. Among those named was rumoured to be President Walesa. The distribution of the list was widely regarded as an attempt by the weakened government to smear its political enemies and the episode itself tainted the lustration process.

After the Constitutional Tribunal had ruled as unconstitutional the *Sejm* resolution ordering the exposure of the officials, Macierewicz was charged in September 1993 with illegally revealing state secrets. Walesa, anxious to clear his own name, requested the publication of all secret police files on him, but this was refused on legal grounds. Olszewski's Committee for the Defence of Democracy subsequently repeatedly accused Walesa's closest aides, including his principal adviser Mieczyslaw Wachowski, of links with the communist-era secret police.

Rejection of lustration

On 7 July 1994 the *Sejm*, by then dominated by ex-communist parties, firmly rejected lustration legislation. A statement issued by the SLD faction asserted that the state "should not treat as criminals people who collaborated with the legal organs of power". Although the liberal UW concurred with the ex-communist parties on this point, *Gazeta Wyborcza* editor and prominent Solidarity intellectual Adam Michnik described the rejection as part of a "velvet restoration" of communism. Two further developments added to Michnik's case. In August 1994 a former secret policeman, Marian Zacharski (who was known as "superspy" having been jailed by the US authorities from 1981-6 for espionage), was appointed as head of the civilian State Security Office, but forced to resign within days following a storm of protest. Secondly, in December 1994 the ex-communist majority in the *Sejm* rejected a motion condemning the imposition of martial law.

MEDIA

Under the press freedom introduced by the round table agreement of spring 1989, newspapers and journals boomed. Many titles are foreign-owned. There has been some concern over the standard of journalism; material is often highly politicised and with weak factual content.

The fate of the broadcast media has been considerably more controversial. In January 1993 Walesa signed a law, after three years of debate, designed to end the state monopoly on broadcasting. The law also established a National Radio and Television Broadcasting Council (KRRT) with a brief to "protect the public interest". Walesa had insisted on a clause stipulating that private broadcasters should "respect the Christian system of values". In January 1994 Poland's first private television channel, Polsat, began to broadcast. Although Polish Television (TVP) and Polish Radio were transformed into private companies, the Treasury remained the sole shareholder.

Most controversy over the broadcast media since 1993 is concerned with apparent attempts by political leaders to control broadcasting officials. Whilst president, Walesa repeatedly protested at the alleged bias of the television news. In 1994-5 he made a series of changes in the board running both TVP and the KRRT, the most controversial being the appointment as KRRT chairman of the leader of the Christian National Union (ZChN), Marek Jurek, in May 1995. Many concluded that this appointment had been made in exchange for the ZChN's support in the presidential elections later in 1995. The appointment prompted the *Sejm* to introduce legislation removing Walesa's prerogative to nominate the KRRT Chair.

CHURCH-STATE RELATIONS

The exceptional significance of Church-state relations in Poland merits a separate section on the subject.

The role of the Catholic Church in Poland's post-communist order has caused considerable controversy. Polish national identity has historically been closely related to Polish Catholicism. Citing this centrality to traditional Polish values, the Church has sought to restore the formal privileges it lost under the communist system.

Nevertheless, many Poles resist the Church's campaign for an enlarged role in the political and social spheres. There is an anti-clerical strain in Polish opinion, and many on the left regard the Church as reactionary. Opinion polls show that even regular church-goers believe that the Church should remain aloof from politics. There is an emerging consensus in favour of a secular state in which political and religious spheres are clearly delineated. Church attendance, although still remarkably high by European standards, has fallen in the 1990s.

In the communist era the Church had been able gradually to win a relatively high degree of independence from the state. The election of the "Polish Pope" in 1978 and his series of papal visits commencing in June 1979 further boosted the Church. The Polish Papacy was a source of national pride, reassuring Poles that despite political bonds tying them into the Soviet orbit, they remained--at a cultural and spiritual level-- part of the family of European nations.

The Church was therefore in a strong position to play a role in the rise of Solidarity in the early 1980s. Church attendance boomed as the Church became the focus of much Solidarity activity, particularly after the declaration of Martial Law, when Solidarity was forced underground. The murder of the pro-Solidarity priest Fr. Jerzy Popieluszko by state security agents in October 1984 came to symbolise the brutality of the communist regime. The Church's role in the emergence of the political opposition strengthened its hand in the Round Table negotiations of 1989. The talks resulted in concessions unparalleled in the communist bloc, as a new legal framework for church-state relations guaranteed freedom of conscience and of religious belief, awarded the Church a role in education and social support and restored property confiscated in the 1950s.

With the fall of communism, the Church's attention moved quickly to abortion, freely available in Poland since 1956. In 1990 legislation restricted abortion, and a strict law was passed by parliament in January 1993, despite opinion polls showing its unpopularity, permitting abortion in only three cases: (i) when the mother's life was endangered by continued pregnancy; (ii) when pregnancy was the result of rape or incest; and (iii) when tests showed irreparable damage to the foetus. Most politicians, particularly those from post-Solidarity parties, regarded criticism of the Church as a political taboo.

An attempt to formalise Church-state relations was begun under the post-Solidarity governments of the early 1990s, leading to President Walesa's signature in July 1993 of a concordat with the Vatican in which Church and state were designated "independent and autonomous bodies".

The success of ex-communist parties in the elections of September 1993, and the decline in popularity of Christian and Christian Democratic parties, marked a watershed for the Church. When approval of the Concordat was blocked (as SLD deputies argued that it awarded the Church a privileged position) Cardinal Glemp, the Primate of Poland, complained that the Church was under attack, and Walesa condemned the "resurgence of communism".

The Church became involved in the 1995 presidential election campaign. In August 1995 the Polish episcopate urged Catholics to reject candidates who had "participated in the exercise of power at the highest levels under totalitarian rule". Kwasniewski countered that he had not held high office in the communist era, having been a junior minister, but the episcopate's letter was understood as a broadside against the ex-communist left. Kwasniewski campaigned in 1995 for a secular state, whereas Walesa advocated stronger links between church and state. As President, Kwasniewski has pledged to pursue a consensual approach in church-state relations, but it remained to be seen whether the Church and Christian politicians, Walesa included, would co-operate.

ETHNIC AND NATIONAL RELATIONS

In contrast to most of its neighbours in East-Central Europe, Poland's population is over 98 per cent Polish, an unusual ethnic homogeneity. Most of the members of Poland's interwar minorities had been dispersed or killed as a result of the Second World War. One of Poland's remaining minority groups is a tiny community of about 12,000 Jews. Despite its small size, there was evidence of anti-Semitism throughout the postwar period. Anti-Semitism has deep roots in the Polish peasantry, working class and clergy. This is exemplified in the controversial comments of a priest, Fr. Henryk Jankowski, who argued in June 1995 that Jews had played a role in the rise of Nazism and communism, and that Jews were responsible for injustices in the capitalist system through their activities in "banking and financial circles". Jankowski's comments might have been overlooked had he not been an adviser and close friend of President Walesa. Walesa duly issued a general condemnation of anti-Semitism, but observers noted the proximity of presidential elections and recalled that Walesa's main rival for the presidency in 1990, Tadeusz Mazowiecki, had probably been disadvantaged by rumours that he was Jewish. Soon after Jankowski's comments Walesa's rival for the presidency, Kwasniewski, was heckled by Solidarity supporters hurling anti-Semitic abuse at a meeting in Southern Poland. Kwasniewski responded robustly, denouncing Solidarity activists as "fascists and anti-Semites".

Although both right-wing party leaders and the nationalist press continued to make anti-Semitic comments, some observers noted a change in the climate in 1995, following the publicity surrounding the 50th anniversary of the liberation of the Auschwitz concentration camp. Many Poles had hitherto taken the view that the Jews' fate had been no worse than their own catastrophic experience of Nazi terror.

FOREIGN AFFAIRS

Constitutional problems with the making of foreign and defence policy

The making of Poland's foreign policy has been disrupted by constitutional problems. Once president, Lech Walesa pressed for foreign policy-making powers and, with the passage of the "Small Constitution" in 1992, he secured joint control with the prime minister over the "power ministries", including the foreign affairs and defence portfolios. Subsequently Walesa gradually gained more influence over foreign policy.

Perhaps the worst constitutional clash over foreign policy prerogatives came amid heightened political tension in the run-up to presidential elections in 1995. President Walesa announced that he would not attend forthcoming international ceremonies to mark the 50th anniversary of allied victory in the Second World War, having detected a German snub in the plans for protocol during the Berlin leg of those ceremonies. Prime Minister Oleksy defied Walesa by announcing that he would attend the ceremony, earning Walesa's bitter denunciation for "treasonable activities".

There was also persistent constitutional wrangling over political control of the military. Walesa, citing the constitutional designation of the president as head of the armed forces, was involved in a series of disputes with successive defence ministers from 1991 over control of the general staff. In practice the general staff has operated with near-autonomy and generals have showed a growing tendency to make political statements, notably demonstrating bias toward Walesa in the run-up to the 1995 presidential elections. In August 1995 Walesa vetoed legislation placing the military under the Cabinet's control.

Despite these constitutional problems Polish foreign policy since 1990 has been relatively consistent, in contrast to the instability of domestic policy-making. There was exceptional continuity at the ministry of foreign affairs, a portfolio held by Krzystof Skubiszewski from 1989 to 1993, by Andrzej Olechowski in 1993-5 and then by Wladyslaw Bartoszewski for nine months until Walesa's defeat in the 1995 presidential elections. Particularly since the re-unification of Germany and the collapse of the Soviet Union, Poland has been at the heart of the international debate over future European economic, political and security arrangements.

Relations with the Soviet Union and Russia

The renunciation of the Brezhnev doctrine by Soviet leader Mikhail Gorbachev in summer 1989 released Poland from the Soviet orbit and cleared the way for Poland's domestic revolution.

An official Soviet admission of responsibility for the 1940 massacre of Polish officers in Katyn was intended to draw a line under the sins of the Soviet imperial past, and to begin a process of reconciliation, marking the Soviet Union's transformation into a law-based state and a reliable international partner.

Poland was formally released from the Soviet-dominated security system with the dissolution of the Warsaw Treaty Organisation in February 1991. The Soviet Union collapsed later that year and in October Russian officials struck an agreement on the withdrawal of the estimated 40,000 troops hitherto based in Poland. Under the agreement combat troops had departed within 12 months, and the remaining 6,000 support troops quit the country in September 1994.

Polish officials aimed to rebuild ties with former communist allies, including Russia, on the basis of mutual interest. In November 1992 a new defence doctrine proclaimed that Poland had no natural enemies and no territorial claims on its neighbours. Accordingly, Poland has secured friendship treaties with all seven neighbours, including Russia and Lithuania (with which relations had been sensitive, due to the alleged mistreatment of the Polish minority there) and in May 1992 with Russia. Visiting Poland for the first time in August 1993 Russian President Boris Yeltsin welcomed a new phase in relations between the two states in which there was "no place for hegemony and diktat, the political psychology of big brother and little brother".

The debate over Polish NATO membership

Poland's post-Solidarity leaders, notably Walesa, consistently advocated Polish NATO membership. Skubiszewski pressed for NATO membership by 2000, a policy continued by Olechowski under the coalition of ex-communist parties from 1993. What domestic obstacles there were related to the establishment of demonstrable civilian control of the military (discussed above), a precondition of NATO membership.

Initially Russia raised few objections, Yeltsin declaring in his 1993 visit that a future Polish decision to join NATO "[would] not go against the interests of...Russia". Following the Russian elections of December 1993, however, Russian policy rapidly changed. Under pressure from nationalists and the military leadership, Yeltsin began to voice increasingly strident opposition to Polish NATO membership. The Russian position had enlisted vociferous support from neighbouring Belarus by summer 1994.

In February 1994 Poland acceded to NATO's Partnerships for Peace (PfP) scheme. Its NATO membership campaign continued to receive backing in principle from existing member states, and in July 1994 US President Bill Clinton, during a visit to Warsaw, warned Russia that "no one country should have the right to veto...any other democracy's integration into Western institutions, including those ensuring security". Nevertheless several Polish leaders expressed disappointment that Clinton had not suggested a timetable for full membership. By 1995 leading Polish figures, including Kwasniewski, continued to support NATO membership but demonstrated mounting concern at the implications of such a move for relations with Russia. Nevertheless in April 1995 Prime Minister Oleksy visited Brussels to impress on NATO ambassadors that Poland expected by 1996 a decision on Polish entry. US officials stressed that the election of Kwasniewski as Polish President did not detrimentally affect Poland's prospects of NATO membership.

In the absence of firm commitments from NATO, Poland pressed ahead with improving bilateral military co-operation with Western states, holding joint military exercises with French, German and combined NATO forces, and in February 1995 concluding an agreement with the USA to hold more extensive military manoeuvres and to share military information.

Economic integration with the West

As post-communist Poland rapidly reoriented its foreign trade, Germany had become Poland's principal trade partner by 1990. In June 1991 the communist-era economic co-operation agency Comecon was abolished. Instead Polish economic policy came under the heavy influence of Western-dominated international institutions, notably the IMF.

In December 1991 Poland secured an association agreement, effective as of February 1994, with the EC (EU). Poland's prompt adoption of economic reform, combined with its level of economic development relative to most other ex-communist states, put it in the fast track for EC membership, along with its Central European neighbours Hungary and Czechoslovakia. Again, Polish officials pressed for membership by 2000. Polish leaders, backed by a clear majority of Poles, saw considerable economic and security advantages to EC membership. Although Poland received strong backing from the UK, Germany and other EC states, there remained potentially major problems. Reconciling Polish and EC agricultural policy was perhaps the most significant. Polish officials pleaded for a transitional period in which Poland was granted EC membership but not required to fulfil the most stringent conditions of such status. In April 1995 Oleksy met European Commission president Jacques Santer to request the granting at least of observer status by end-1996.

Visegrad group

In the early stages of its campaign for membership of NATO and the EC, Poland and its central European allies Hungary and Czechoslovakia formed the Visegrad Triangle in February 1991 (known from January 1993, with the partition of Czechoslovakia, as the Visegrad group) in a campaign for co-ordinated European integration. This lost momentum in 1992-3 as members increasingly identified one another as rivals. Since the rise of Russian nationalism, however, there has been a renewed awareness of the common interests of the Visegrad states.

Relations with Germany

German officials have worked hard to establish good relations with Poland. Germany has been a staunch supporter of early EC and NATO membership for Poland, while German private investment in Poland has been considerable. Germany has offered Poland tangible evidence of its commitment to Polish integration with the West, including undertakings to improve road and rail links from Germany to Poland and a plan to site a gas pipeline from Siberia to Germany across Polish territory.

German diplomacy has demonstrated considerable skill in appealing for reconciliation between the two former enemies. German President Roman Herzog won praise in summer 1994 for his conciliatory comments at ceremonies to mark the 50th anniversary of the Warsaw uprising. (In contrast the Russian representative conspicuously failed to apologise for the Red Army's cynical decision to allow the defeat of the rebels.)

CONSTITUTIONAL ISSUES

Constitutional reform as of end-1995 consisted of piecemeal amendments to the communist-era constitution of 1952. Constitutional amendments passed by the *Sejm* on April 7, 1989, enacted the round table agreements on the creation of a national presidency and a new bicameral parliament. Laws passed at the same time guaranteed the right of free association. By the end of 1989 the Mazowiecki government had repealed Article 3 of the 1952 constitution confirming the leading role of the PZPR, and changed the country's formal title from the Polish People's Republic to the Polish Republic. Legislation passed in September 1990 established a system of direct presidential elections on a five-yearly basis. A new constitution was to be in place by the time fully free legislative elections were held in 1993. (Under a procedure agreed in

April 1992, a new constitution must be endorsed in a referendum, following approval by parliament.)

In the event, legislative and presidential elections were held ahead of schedule in 1990-91, before a new constitution was in place. The process of drafting the constitution was disrupted and delayed by political instability and disagreement, particularly after the victory of ex-communist parties in the legislative elections of 1993. The result has been a sequence of increasingly rancorous disputes between the parliament, the presidency and the cabinet over the division of powers.

Walesa strongly favoured a Gaullist presidential system, with considerable presidential powers, including the power to appoint and dismiss ministers. He openly admires Pilsudski, the authoritarian leader of Poland in the interwar period. During his term as head of state, Walesa operated on the "fringe of the law", in a bid to acquire more power for the presidency at the expense of the government and legislature, and repeatedly threatened to dissolve the *Sejm*, often on dubious legal grounds.

The "Small Constitution", approved during a brief respite from constitutional struggle under the premiership of Hanna Suchocka in August 1992, was an attempt to clarify the dispute over rival prerogatives pending the passage of a complete constitution. In particular the "Small Constitution" attempted to resolve the argument over appointments, with Walesa winning limited control over the "security ministries" of foreign affairs, defence and internal affairs. It failed, however, to end these disagreements, and the continued arguments, particularly over control of the defence ministry, blighted Polish politics in 1993-95, particularly after the success of postcommunist parties in the legislative elections of 1993. The election of the pragmatic ex-communist Kwasniewski, who served as Chair of the National Assembly constitutional commission in 1993-5, has synchronised the presidency and government, making a consensus on a new constitution more likely. From 1993 the ex-communists had a parliamentary majority close to the two-thirds of *Sejm* seats necessary to approve constitutional law.

PRINCIPAL PERSONALITIES

The communist era

Wladyslaw **Gomulka** (1905-1982). The man who briefly held out the hope of a reformist Polish road to socialism when he was reinstated as party leader in 1956. Gomulka had been imprisoned as a communist and union organiser in the 1930s; on escaping from captivity in 1939 he became the communists' foremost wartime resistance leader. When Boleslaw Bierut and others returned from Moscow they began to dominate the party. Gomulka retained the post of secretary-general but in 1948 he was dismissed and made to recant his "nationalist deviation". He was then expelled from the party and imprisoned for five years without charge. Gomulka was released amid the first signs of destalinisation in April 1956 and was party first secretary by the autumn. Although he persuaded Khrushchev not to order a Soviet clampdown in Poland, Hungary could not escape this fate, and few of the new liberal ideas survived in the harsher climate of the late 1950s. Gomulka himself became identified with the retention of tight party controls and with failure to tackle the endemic problems of the industry-oriented command economy. Worker unrest in 1970, and attempts to repress it by force, led to his downfall and replacement at the end of that year by Gierek.

Edward **Gierek** (b. 1913). Gierek made his name as party first secretary in Katowice in the 1960s, and was an increasingly influential member of the politburo, which he had joined in 1956. Gierek had worked as a miner in the French and Belgian coalfields before returning to Poland after the war. His appointment as Gomulka's successor in 1970 was based on his reputation as an effective economic manager and communicator with ordinary working people. His new policy of borrowing abroad to invest in industrial plant failed to achieve sustained export-led growth and saddled the country with a major international debt. Confronted by the growth of independent unions in 1980, Gomulka was indecisive. He was ousted in September 1980 after suffering a heart attack, and under martial law he was interned for a year from December 1981, but corruption charges against him were never pressed.

Gen. Wojciech **Jaruzelski** (b. 1923). A career soldier from a minor aristocratic family in the eastern part of Poland annexed by the Soviet Union in 1939, Jaruzelski had fought with the Polish Army in the Soviet Union in 1943-45. After 1945 his army career was combined with party posts and government service, leading to his appointment in 1968 as defence minister and a place on the PZPR politburo from 1970. Named Prime Minister in February 1981 as the regime faced the Solidarity crisis, he took over as PZPR first secretary in October and introduced martial law in December 1981. In November 1985 he took the post of President, while remaining party first secretary. Jaruzelski was never to be forgiven by the opposition as the man who imposed martial law and his cold and rigid military manner allowed him to be caricatured as a ruthless dictator. Perhaps surprisingly, however, he retained the respect of many Poles, who accepted his argument that were it not for the Polish crackdown Soviet military intervention would have been inevitable. Jaruzelski was the unlikely communist leader who took the party knowingly into the 1989 round-table negotiations to work out Eastern Europe's first pluralist system. The partially-free parliamentary elections in June showed the full extent of the rejection of the old PZPR, and Jaruzelski from this point took no part in shaping a future communist party. Instead he stood for the restyled post of President and was narrowly elected by the parliament, where key Solidarity votes were cast in his favour for the sake of stability. As president Jaruzelski briefly enjoyed high approval ratings, peaking at 74 per cent in September 1989, as measured by opinion polls. Accepting ultimately that he would always symbolise the old regime, and taking note of the revolutionary changes across Eastern Europe, Jaruzelski was persuaded within little over a year to step down and make way for the direct election of his successor, Lech Walesa. Jaruzelski now faces a lengthy legal process relating to the imposition of Martial Law, which was deemed a criminal act by the legislature in 1992, and over his role as defence minister in suppressing an earlier workers' protest in December 1970, which had resulted in the death of at least 44 people.

The post-communist era

Leszek **Balcerowicz** (b. 1947). The Deputy Prime Minister and Finance Minister in the governments of Mazowiecki and Bielecki from 1989-91 and leader of the principal post-Solidarity party, the Freedom Union, from 1995. Balcerowicz was an economist who had left the PZPR during the 1981 crisis to work as a consultant to Solidarity. He was the architect of the politically risky Balcerowicz Plan, the first and most radical pro-market reform programme in post-communist Central and Eastern Europe. As a leading advocate of "shock treatment", Balcerowicz planned a rapid transition to a free market economy; he believed the consequent short term social costs would be ameliorated by the revival of the economy in the medium term. He was sacrificed for political reasons with the appointment of the Olszewski government in 1991. Balcerowicz joined the Freedom Union (UW) on its formation in 1994 and in April 1995 he was elected UW leader.

Jacek **Kuron** (b. 1934). A historian and dissident liberal voice in the PZPR until his expulsion and detention in the mid-1960s, he was one of the intellectuals who co-founded (in 1976) the Workers' Defence Committee (KOR) and (in 1977) the Social Self-Defence Committee (KSS), a human rights pressure group with links with the Czechoslovak Charter 77. Involved from 1980 with Solidarity, he was imprisoned under martial law; although charged with conspiring to overthrow the state by force, he was released under amnesty. He was one of the Solidarity delegation members in the 1989 round table talks, and regarded as a possible prime minister; in the event, however, he took on the post of minister of labour and social policy. Kuron subsequently assumed the role of Poland's elder statesman, scoring highly in opinion polls for both visibility and trustworthiness. Despite his centre-left opinions, Kuron was nominated for the presidency by the liberal Freedom Union, but came third with a modest 9 per cent of the vote in the 1995 presidential election.

Aleksander **Kwasniewski** (b. 1954). President of Poland from December 1995 and leader from 1990 of the ex-communist Democratic Left Alliance bloc (SLD). Kwasniewski joined the PZPR in 1977 aged 23, and worked as an activist in the official communist youth movements in the late 1970s and early 1980s. He was editor-in-chief first of the state student weekly *Itd* (1981-4) and then of the daily newspaper *Sztandar Mlodych* (1984-5). In 1985-7 Kwasniewski was minister without portfolio responsible for youth affairs, and in 1987-90 he served as Chairman of the Committee for Youth and Physical Education. He participated in the Round Table negotiations of 1989. When the PZPR dissolved itself in 1990 Kwasniewski became leader of its successor, the Social Democracy of the Polish Republic (SdPR), and of the leftist bloc it dominates, the SLD. In 1991 he was elected to the *Sejm*. In 1993-5 Kwasniewski served as Chair of the National Assembly (joint *Sejm* and Senate) commission charged with drafting a new constitution. He won support by presenting himself as a moderate seeking political unity; for instance he initially backed the ratification of the Concordat between Poland and the Vatican, against the wishes of his party. Although critics suggested that the SLD remained considerably more radical than its pragmatic leader, Kwasniewski's personality impressed a crucial portion of the floating vote in the 1995 presidential election.

Tadeusz **Mazowiecki** (b. 1927). Leading Solidarity intellectual, the first prime minister of a Solidarity-led government, and leader of the liberal Democratic Union party until its dissolution. Mazowiecki was an editor with a long association with independent Catholic papers. In August 1980 he acted as an adviser to Solidarity during the negotiations which led to the Gdansk accords; Mazowiecki then became the first editor of the Solidarity newspaper *Tygodnik Solidarnosc*. He was interned under martial law. In 1989 Mazowiecki was on the Solidarity negotiating team at the round-table talks. As prime minister in 1989-90 he supported the use of the controversial "shock treatment" to overhaul Poland's economic system, encountering strong opposition from Walesa and the labour movement. Mazowiecki's supporters were disappointed by his unexpected humiliation in the first round of the presidential election in November 1990. He became leader of the Democratic Union from 1991 and led its successor party the Freedom Union from 1994-5. From 1992-5 Mazowiecki was UN Special Envoy on Human Rights in the Former Yugoslavia, responsible for investigating war crimes.

Jozef **Oleksy** (b. 1945). Member of the ex-communist Democratic Left Alliance (SLD), Speaker of the *Sejm* from 1993-95 and Prime Minister from March 1995. Oleksy, an economist, had been a cabinet minister in the communist era, responsible for relations with the trade unions, including Solidarity. He became a Deputy Chair of the SdRP, the successor party to the PZPR, and was elected to the *Sejm* as an SLD deputy in 1991. Following the victory of the ex-communist parties in the elections of 1993 Oleksy became speaker of the *Sejm*, and attracted praise for his pragmatic conduct. In March 1995 Oleksy replaced Pawlak as Prime Minister, thus becoming the first former PZPR member to lead a post-communist era government. In December 1995 Oleksy was accused by Walesa of having collaborated with Soviet intelligence, a claim dismissed by Oleksy's supporters as a crude smear.

Waldemar **Pawlak** (b. 1959). Leader of the leftist Polish Peasant Party (PSL) and Prime Minister in 1993-95. A former state farm manager and member of the communist-allied United Peasant Party (ZSL), he established a reputation as a reformist, and won a seat in the *Sejm* in 1989 on the ZSL list with the endorsement of Rural Solidarity. He played a key role in ousting the ZSL's discredited leadership, joined the ZSL's successor party the PSL in 1990, and was elected as its leader in June 1991. He was appointed as Poland's youngest-ever Prime Minister in June 1992, but failed to form a government and resigned in July. He was reappointed as Prime Minister in October 1993 following the success of the PSL in the 1993 elections, when it finished second. As Prime Minister Pawlak earned a reputation as a skilled tactician but was criticised for lacking political vision. He clashed with President Walesa on a number of issues, notably his tendency to delay economic reform, particularly privatisation. Pawlak resigned in February 1995 after Walesa lost patience with him.

Hanna **Suchocka** (b.1946). Poland's first woman prime minister, in 1992-93. A lecturer in constitutional law, Suchocka was elected to the *Sejm* as a Solidarity deputy in 1989. She joined the Democratic Union in 1990. Suchocka served on the *Sejm* legislation committee until from 1989-92. In July 1992 she was appointed as Prime Minister of a "government of national accord" bringing together seven post-Solidarity parties from the movement's liberal, Christian democratic and agrarian wings, a significant achievement in the poisoned political atmosphere following the demise of the Olszewski regime. Under Suchocka's tenure several key measures were steered through parliament, including an IMF-approved austerity programme, the "small constitution" and legislation on abortion, electoral reform and mass privatisation. The Suchocka cabinet submitted its resignation in May 1993 after its refusal to award pay rises to striking public sector workers led to defeat in a motion of no confidence. Suchocka remained in office until the appointment of the Pawlak cabinet in October 1993. She subsequently became a key figure in the Freedom Union.

Lech **Walesa** (b. 1943). Solidarity's leading figure in the communist era and President of Poland for five years from December 1990. A charismatic figure, latterly styling himself on the interwar dictator Pilsudski, he earned a reputation as a pugnacious and uncompromising leader. Walesa's political career began in 1970 when, as an electrician at the Lenin shipyard in Gdansk, he led a strike committee during the Baltic crisis. During the strikes of August 1980, Walesa headed the Gdansk inter-factory committee and then participated in negotiating the historic "Gdansk accords" which freed trade unions. When the Solidarity trade union formed the following month, Walesa became chairman of its national co-ordinating commission. Walesa was detained for 11 months in the Martial Law period, but then returned to work at the Lenin shipyard. In 1983 Walesa was awarded the Nobel Peace Prize in recognition of his iconic status internationally as an opponent of the authoritarian regime. When a fresh round of strikes began in 1988 Walesa was permitted a television appearance, during which he called for the re-legalisation of Solidarity. He participated in the round table talks which proved to be pivotal in the history of communism in Eastern Europe. Avoiding governmental responsibilities himself, he concentrated briefly on trade union activism, returning to the bread-and-butter issues on which he had built his career, and attacking the economic austerity measures introduced by a government staffed by his notional allies from Solidarity. Having successfully campaigned to have the presidential elections held early, he was overwhelmingly elected to the post himself in late 1990. He left Solidarity in order to appear to stand above party politics, but had already alienated many of his former Solidarity allies, particularly intellectuals such as Michnik and Mazowiecki who were suspicious of his abrasive style of leadership and ambitious drive to accumulate power. In 1992 Walesa was tainted by allegations of collaboration with the communist-era secret police. Many of his former allies in Solidarity were aghast, but Walesa worked hard to restore his credibility. He established a new party deliberately modelled on the party of government during Pilsudski's interwar authoritarian regime, called the Non-Party Bloc in Support of Reforms (BBWR), but it performed poorly in the legislative elections of 1993. The victory of the ex-communist parties in these elections gave Walesa the opportunity to re-establish his anti-communist credentials. He set on a strategy of stretching the law to its limits to secure his sometimes opaque political purposes. The result was a series of increasingly hostile confrontations with the leftist governments of Pawlak and Oleksy, which undermined public confidence in the political process. Walesa's bid for re-election as president in 1995 benefited from the absence of an obvious rival candidate from the post-Solidarity camp, and from a strong constituency of anti-communist opinion. For the second round of the election he won the endorsement of Mazowiecki and other leading liberals, but was nevertheless defeated, having alienated many voters with his confrontational style. His defeat was a heavy blow to the post-Solidarity parties. Walesa's bitter accusation of electoral fraud, coupled with his grave allegations of treason against Prime Minister Jozef Oleksy, hinted strongly at a future in zealous opposition.

POLITICAL PARTIES

The communist party and successors

The interwar Communist Party of Poland was dissolved in 1938 on Comintern orders. A successor, the Polish Workers' Party, was formed in Moscow in 1941-42. In 1948 it merged with the Socialist Party to become the **Polish United Workers' Party** (PZPR). The PZPR was wound up in January 1990. Its successor party, to which it ceded all its assets, adopted the name **Social Democracy of the Polish Republic** (SdPR) and elected former youth minister Aleksander Kwasniewski as its leader. The SdPR abandoned democratic centralism and the dictatorship of the proletariat and embraced parliamentary democracy and the mixed economy, although critics claimed that the grass roots of the bloc were still radical leftists. There were no serious moves to ban the activities of the former communist parties but in November 1990 the *Sejm* adopted a bill transferring most of the SdPR's considerable assets to the state on the grounds that they had been acquired illegally.

The SdPR became the principal force in an electoral bloc of ex-communist groups, the **Democratic Left Alliance** (SLD). Also led by Kwasniewski, the SLD has presented itself as a modern social democratic party in the Western European tradition. The SLD was the second largest group in a fragmented parliament in 1991-3; in the elections of 1993 the SLD was the main victor and formed a coalition with the Polish Peasant

Party. Kwasniewski was elected as President in 1995. The SLD increasingly convinced voters that it had abandoned ideology in favour of moderate, mainstream Polish values, and that it was the most technically competent political force in the country.

The **Polish Peasant Party** (PSL) was formed in May 1990, on the basis of the United Peasants' Party (which had been a junior partner of the PZPR in the communist era), a revived Polish Peasant Party (banned since 1947) and some defectors from Rural Solidarity. Its leader, the former Solidarity deputy Roman Bartoszcze, was ousted at an acrimonious congress in July 1991. Under the new leadership of Waldemar Pawlak, a former state farm manager, the party did relatively well in the 1991 elections, outpolling its rivals for the rural vote, the **Peasant Alliance** (PL). The PSL was then hailed as the only party successfully to target a social class (and one of considerable size, since some 3.7 million Poles were employed in the agricultural sector). The PSL was a junior coalition partner in the Olszewski government in December 1991, and Pawlak was briefly made Prime Minister in 1992 but failed to form a coalition. The PSL emerged from the 1993 elections as the second largest party in parliament and formed a coalition with the SLD. Pawlak served as Prime Minister in 1993-5, during which period the PSL more than punched its weight in the coalition. There were a number of policy disputes, particularly over the slow pace of privatisation favoured by Pawlak, and in 1995 he was replaced as Prime Minister by the SLD's Jozef Oleksy, although the coalition remained intact. Pawlak ran against SLD leader Kwasniewski in the presidential elections of 1995, but attracted only 4.3 per cent of the vote.

Labour Union (UP) was originally formed as Labour Solidarity and contested the 1991 elections under that name. The UP promoted a socialist programme and after its improved performance in 1993 it initially entered the coalition of ex-communist parties under Pawlak. Although it quickly withdrew it continued largely to support the coalition's policies.

Solidarity and its successors - Other parties

Solidarity was the mass anti-communist movement which swept the PZPR from power in 1989. The movement fragmented in 1990, leaving a rump trade union organisation with an affiliated political party. The fragmentation of the movement reflected its demographically broad membership, which had included workers, intellectuals and peasants. Many Solidarity deputies formed new parties to represent Christian Democrats, nationalists, liberals, socialists and agrarians. Some deputies continued to sit as the rump Solidarity Citizens' Committee, which championed the bread-and-butter issues on which the original movement had been built. Its campaign to reduce the social cost of reform earned it a place in parliament from 1991-3. In the general election of 1993 Solidarity lost all its *Sejm* seats, although it did win nine in the Senate.

The **Democratic Union** (UD) was a liberal party founded in 1990 by Solidarity intellectuals, and led by former prime minister Mazowiecki. The UD backed radical economic reform and a liberal political agenda. It participated in the post-Solidarity governments of 1990-91 and 1992-3. The UD emerged as the largest single party in a fragmented parliament in 1991, and co-operated with the Liberal Democratic Congress (KLD) and the small Polish Economic Programme in the parliamentary "Small Coalition". The UD was the only liberal party to retain seats in parliament after the 1993 elections. It merged with the KLD in 1994 to form the Freedom Union.

The **Liberal Democratic Congress** (KLD) was a post-Solidarity party in government from 1989-91 and 1982-3. The KLD was closely associated with the Balcerowicz plan, the economic austerity programme introduced by the early Solidarity-dominated coalitions. Formed in 1988, the KLD's prominent members included the radical economist Jan Bielecki, who was prime minister for most of 1991. The KLD failed to secure seats in the 1993 elections and in 1994 it merged with its ally the Democratic Union to form the Freedom Union.

The **Freedom Union** (UW) was formed in 1994 from a merger of the UD and the KLD. Mazowiecki led the UW for a year before giving way to the radical economist Leszek Balcerowicz. Although primarily a liberal party, the UW nominated the prominent centre-left politician Jacek Kuron for the 1995 presidential election. The UW has thus sought to appeal to a broad range of people beyond its intellectual leadership.

The **Conservative Liberal Movement** (RKL) was founded in April 1995 by the respected former foreign minister Andrzej Olechowski, an erstwhile ally of Walesa who strongly backed closer ties with Western institutions. The party aimed to counterbalance the UW, attracting the support of the centre-right by offering economic reforms combined with a relatively conservative social policy.

The **Centre Alliance** (PC) was formed within Solidarity in May 1990 by supporters of Lech Walesa, with Jaroslaw Kaczynski as its chairman, and was regarded as the Christian democratic right wing of the Solidarity movement. Relations with Walesa deteriorated after the latter reversed his opposition to radical economic reform. After the PC's modest success in the 1991 elections it became part of the centre-right parliamentary coalition and participated in the Olszewski government. Having failed to secure seats in 1993, it combined in May 1994 with several other right-wing parties, including the ZChN, in a loose confederation of right wing parties called Covenant for Poland (PdP).

The **Christian National Union** (ZChN) is a post-Solidarity party founded in October 1989 under the leadership of Wieslaw Chrzanowski. The ZChN attracted opponents of the Mazowiecki government and supported Walesa's campaign against shock treatment. Walesa's reversal on economic policy, however, made the ZChN one of Walesa's fiercest critics. The ZChN was a modest success in the 1991 elections and in November 1991 Chrzanowski was elected as speaker of the *Sejm*. The ZChN and the PC became the nucleus of the centre-right Olszewski coalition. After the party failed to win seats in the 1993 elections, the ZChN combined in May 1994 with several other right-wing parties, including the PC, in a loose confederation of right wing parties called Covenant for Poland (PdP).

The **Non-Party Bloc in Support of Reforms** (BBWR) was established by Lech Walesa in 1993. Designed to stand above the party fray, the BBWR took as its model the interwar entity which had supported the dictatorship of Jozef Pilsudski--the Non-Partisan Bloc for Cooperation with Government (also BBWR). It therefore advocated setting aside ideological differences in favour of a government of technocrats under a strong presidency, with policies based on consensus values such as Christianity and moderate economic reform with adequate social protection. Walesa failed to convince the rump Solidarity party to run joint candidates with the BBWR in the general elections of 1993. Voters viewed its claim to unify the nation with scepticism and the BBWR was instead regarded more narrowly as the presidential party; it only narrowly secured seats in the 1993 elections.

The **Confederation For An Independent Poland** (KPN), an anti-communist, nationalist right-wing party led by Leszek Moczulski, was originally founded in 1979.

Moczulski was imprisoned twice in the 1980s and the KPN was not permitted to compete in the 1989 elections, but won 46 seats in 1991. The KPN tapped into the intolerant strain in Polish nationalism (echoes of which had emerged in the anti-Semitic campaign within the communist party in the late 1960s). The party did not take part in government in 1991-3 and in the 1993 elections it secured only 22 seats.

ELECTIONS

Parliamentary and presidential elections since 1989 have followed a pattern familiar in several East European states. Initially the communist party was swept from power in a stunning defeat and the anti-communist opposition, in the Polish case Solidarity and its successors, took power. The social costs of reform, and divisions within the anti-communist movement, drove voters back to the ex-communist parties, who emerged victorious in legislative elections in 1993 and the presidential election of 1995.

Turnouts have been consistently low, reflecting the electorate's low (and declining) level of trust in both political institutions and politicians. Only with the second round of presidential elections in 1995 did turnout reach a respectable 68 per cent.

Legislative elections

Communist era: Under the 1952 constitution of the communist regime the legislature was a unicameral assembly, the *Sejm*, to which elections were held every four years; the 460 seats were divided in agreed proportions between the PZPR and two other approved parties, the United Peasants' Party and the Democratic Party. A turnout of nearly 79 per cent was claimed for the last of these elections in 1985.

Partially free elections in 1989: A new bicameral National Assembly was created under constitutional amendments in April 1989. The 460-seat *Sejm* became the key lower house, with a new 100-seat Senate as the upper house. Both chambers were to serve four-year terms. Direct elections to the National Assembly took place in June 1989. While all Senate seats were openly contested only 35 per cent of the *Sejm*, or 161 seats, were similarly contested. The remaining 299 *Sejm* seats were restricted, 35 being allocated to an unopposed "national list" of government and party leaders, 157 to candidates from the ruling PZPR, 65 to the United Peasants' Party, 24 to the Democratic Party, and 16 to lay Roman Catholic organisations.

In a major shock to the communist regime, the Solidarity Citizens' Committee won all but one of the seats in the Senate and all of the openly contested *Sejm* seats. To the regime's deep embarrassment 33 candidates for the 35 unopposed "national list" seats were rejected when more than half of the voters deleted their names from the ballot paper. Thus Solidarity finished with just 12 seats fewer than the PZPR. The first round election turnout on 4 June 1989 was only 62 per cent, and the second round turnout on 18 June, in which almost two thirds of the *Sejm* was elected, a mere 25 per cent.

	Sejm seats,	Senate seats
PZPR (communists)	173	0
United Peasant Party (ZSL)	76	0
Democratic Party (SD)	27	0
Approved Catholic groups	23	0
Solidarity Citizens' Committee	161	99
Independent	0	1
Total	460	100

First fully free legislative elections, October 1991. In the October 1991 general election all seats were freely contested. Although the elections featured a complex system of modified proportional representation designed to limit the number of independent deputies, there was no electoral hurdle for contesting parties and blocs. The 100 Senate seats were elected in 47 two-member counties and two three-member counties (Warsaw and Katowice). Of the *Sejm*'s 460 seats, 69 were elected on the basis of votes cast for party national lists, and 391 were allocated to 37 multi-member electoral counties. Voters cast ballots for individually named party representatives, but in each electoral county their vote was counted towards an aggregate total for the candidates' parties. Seats were then allotted to each party proportionately, but parties were required to award seats among their candidates in order of their popularity in the ballot. The 1991 elections resulted in a highly fragmented legislature comprising 29 parties (*see table for 11 main contending parties*). The turnout was only 43.2 per cent.

September 1993 legislative elections. A new electoral law designed to reduce the fragmentation of the legislature was signed by President Walesa in June in advance of elections on 19 September 1993. The law established hurdles of 5 per cent for parties and 8 per cent for alliances, in elections to 391 constituency seats. The 69 seats allocated from the national list ballot were to be awarded only to parties or alliances exceeding 7 per cent of the poll. Under these new rules, only six parties and alliances secured *Sejm* seats. Over 35 per cent of the vote went to groups which failed to clear the new hurdles, most of which were parties from Solidarity's fragmented right-wing. Although the postcommunist SLD and PSL achieved a striking success in taking 35.8 per cent of votes, the rules benefitted them still further, awarding them 65.9 per cent of seats in the *Sejm*. Turnout increased modestly compared with 1991, to 52.1 per cent.

	% 1991	seats 1991		%1993	seats 1993	
		Sejm	Senate		*Sejm*	Senate
SLD	11.9	60	4	20.4	171	37
PSL	8.7	48	8	15.4	132	36
UD	12.3	62	21	10.6	74	4
UP*	2.1	4	-	7.3	41	2
KPN	7.5	46	4	5.8	22	2
BBWR	-	-	-	5.4	16	2
GMO	n/a	7	1	0.7	4	1
KKW"O"+	8.7	49	12	6.4	0	1
Sol.	5.1	27	11	4.9	0	9
PC	8.7	44	9	4.4	0	1
KLD	7.5	37	6	4.0	0	1
PL	5.5	28	7	2.3	0	0
Others**	22.0	48	17	13.1	0	4
Total	100%	460	100	100%	460	100

*Labour Solidarity (SP) in 1991
+Catholic Electoral Action in 1991, and in 1993 the KKW"O" grouping, also called *Ojczyzna* or Homeland, which likewise included the Christian National Union (ZChN)
**Including independents and, in 1993, one Rural Solidarity senator.

SLD=Democratic Left Alliance; PSL=Polish Peasant Party; UD=Democratic Union; UP=Labour Union; KPN=Confederation for an Independent Poland; BBWR=Non-Party Bloc in Support of Reforms; GMO=German minority organisations; Sol.=Solidarity; PC=Centre Alliance; KLD=Liberal Democratic Congress; PL=Peasant Alliance.

Presidential elections

Prior to 1989 the head of state under the communist regime was chosen as the chairman of the Council of State, elected by the *Sejm*. Gen. Jaruzelski was the last holder of this ceremonial post, in 1985-89. The office of executive state President was created under the April 1989 constitutional amendments. The President was elected by a joint sitting of both houses of the National Assembly on 19 July 1989, notionally for a six-year term. As the only candidate Jaruzelski received 270 to 233 against with 34 abstentions, just one vote above the 50 per cent of valid votes required for election. Poland moved to a directly elected presidency in 1990 after a sustained campaign by Walesa's supporters. Jaruzelski agreed in September to step aside for an early poll.

Presidential election in November-December 1990: Voting was held in two rounds, the turnout being respectively 60 per cent and 55 per cent. Of six candidates, Walesa and prime minister Mazowiecki (backed by the centre-left ROAD faction) were regarded as the front runners, but a major surprise was sprung by the independent candidate, emigré Stanislaw Tyminski, whose populist programme promised prosperity with minimal social costs. In the first round on 25 November he attracted so many protest votes, especially in the countryside and small towns, that he finished second with 23.1 per cent, while Mazowiecki scored under 20 per cent. In the second round on 9 December Tyminski was comprehensively defeated by Walesa, who won 74.3 per cent with the lukewarm endorsement of the pro-Mazowiecki camp. Walesa was sworn in as President on 22 December 1990 for a five-year term.

	% of 1st round vote	% of second round vote
Lech Walesa	39.96	74.3
Stanislaw Tyminski (ind.)	23.10	25.7
Tadeusz Mazowiecki (ROAD)	18.08	
Wlodzimierz Cimoszewicz (SLD)	9.21	
Roman Bartoszcze (PSL)	7.15	
Leszek Moczulski (KPN)	2.50	

Presidential election in November 1995: Lech Walesa was defeated in presidential elections in 1995 by Aleksander Kwasniewski, the leader of the ex-communist SLD bloc. Walesa and Kwasniewski had emerged as the front-runners after the first round of the elections on 5 November, with other contenders in the field of 13 losing support as voters shifted to the two candidates deemed most likely to win a second round. Hanna Gronkiewicz-Waltz, the respected chair of the National Bank whom opinion polls had rated as a third major contender weeks before the elections, ended up with only 2.76 per cent of the vote, despite her endorsement by the centre-right National-Christian Alliance and other centre-right groups. The turnout was 64.7 per cent on the first round and 68.2 per cent on the second.

	% of 1st round vote	% of second round vote
Aleksander Kwasniewski (SLD)	35.11	51.72
Lech Walesa	33.11	48.28
Jacek Kuron (UW)	9.22	
Jan Olszewski	6.86	
Waldemar Pawlak (PSL)	4.31	
Tadeusz Zielinski	3.53	
Hanna Gronkiewicz-Waltz	2.76	
Janusz Korwin-Mikke (UPR)	2.40	
Others	2.70	

CHRONOLOGY

1795. The Polish Commonwealth, once a major European power, is divided between Austria, Prussia and Russia.

14 November 1918. Reunification of Poland in the postwar settlement. War hero Marshal Jozef Pilsudski becomes head of state.

1926. Coup d'etat by Pilsudski ends a period of fractious coalition government and weak presidency and ushers in an authoritarian regime with a government of technocrats.

1927. Legislative elections; the Communist Party of Poland achieves a pre-war peak of 7 per cent of the vote.

23 August 1939. Nazi-Soviet Pact.

September 1939. Germany invades Poland. Poland is partitioned between Germany and the Soviet Union.

1940. Katyn massacre: 15,000 Polish officers are deported from Soviet-occupied Poland to the forest of Katyn in the Soviet Union, and murdered by the Soviet security police. The Soviet Union subsequently claims that Nazi forces committed the massacres after occupying the Katyn area in 1941; the truth is admitted only in 1990.

1941. Collapse of Nazi-Soviet pact; German troops sweep across Poland. A government-in-exile is established in London.

1942. Establishment of Polish Workers' Party (PPR) as successor to communist party.

1939-44. Some six million Poles lose their lives under Nazi occupation, the greatest per capita loss borne by any warring party in the Second World War. Almost all of Poland's three million Polish Jews are murdered in Nazi concentration camps under the genocidal "Final Solution" policy.

July 1944. The Red Army re-enters Poland; establishment of Soviet-backed Polish Committee of National Liberation.

August-October 1944. Warsaw uprising: the city is razed and a quarter of a million Poles die in a failed attempt to wrest control of the capital from German forces. The Red Army advance pauses just short of Warsaw, allowing the Nazis to defeat the Polish rebels.

January 1945. The Red Army liberates Warsaw. Stalin recognises the communist-dominated provisional government.

February 1945. Britain, the USA and the Soviet Union agree at the summit meeting in Yalta on a division of postwar Europe into spheres of interest. Considerable Polish territory is awarded to the Soviet Union (and German territory to Poland), and the conference calls for the formation of Government of National Unity, which takes place in June 1945.

19 January 1947. The communists and their allies dominate rigged general elections and claim an overwhelming parliamentary majority. By the summer of 1947 membership of the communist Polish Workers' Party (PPR) numbers one million. Poland enters its Stalinist period.

July 1948. Poland adopts the Soviet model of central industrial planning and agricultural collectivisation.

September 1948. Gomulka is replaced as general secretary of the communist party and recants his "national deviationist" errors, including opposition to collectivisation; Boleslaw Bierut, the communist President, reassumes the party leadership.

December 1948. The PPR merges with the Socialist Party to form the Polish United Workers' Party (PZPR).

January 1949. Under the postwar peace settlement Poland officially incorporates German territory in the West but loses its eastern territories, including the cities of Wilno (Vilnius) and Lwow, to the Soviet Union. There follow mass population exchanges involving eight million people.

March 1954. The second PZPR congress brings in a collective leadership on the post-Stalin Soviet model.

February 1956. Political detainees are released and press censorship relaxed.

June-October 1956. Crisis in Poland and Hungary. On 28 June workers attack PZPR headquarters in Poznan; 53 are killed and 300 injured. A wave of strikes demanding liberalisation spreads. News of the turmoil in Hungary encourages protesting Poles. The popular Gomulka is reinstated as PZPR general secretary while Soviet Marshal Rokossovski is removed as defence minister. The Soviet invasion of Hungary in November then discourages reform. However, collectivisation in agriculture is reversed.

20-21 August 1968. The Warsaw Pact invasion of Czechoslovakia forcibly ends the Czechoslovak reform socialist experiment. In November Soviet party leader Leonid Brezhnev enunciates the "Brezhnev doctrine".

December 1970. Price increases provoke the "Baltic crisis", with strikes and rioting spreading through several coastal cities, including Gdansk. Hundreds of people are killed as security forces open fire on the crowds. Gomulka is replaced by Edward Gierek; the regime, shaken by the December riots, proclaims the improvement of living standards as the party's "supreme goal" at the party congress of December 1971.

June-July 1976. Proposed food price increases are abandoned after riots.

December 1976. Foundation of the Committee for the Defence of Workers (KOR), the first organisation to resist the communist authorities.

October 1978. Cardinal Karol Wojtyla is elected as Pope John Paul II, known as the "Polish pope".

August 1980. Foundation of Solidarity trade union after price rises again provoke strikes.

31 August 1980. In the historic Gdansk accords the government concedes the rights to strike and to form free trade unions.

September 1980. Gierek is replaced as PZPR leader by Stanyslaw Kania on health grounds.

10 November 1980. Solidarity is granted legal registration.

February 1981. The defence minister Gen. Jaruzelski becomes prime minister.

September 1981. Walesa is elected as Solidarity chairman at the first national delegate conference, but the meeting is dominated by radical demands for political action. Solidarity membership peaks at some ten million.

October 1981. Gen. Jaruzelski succeeds Kania as PZPR first secretary.

13 December 1981. Martial law is declared in response to Solidarity's increased political demands, which include free elections. Solidarity's leaders, including Walesa, are arrested, the Gdansk accords are revoked, a ban on strikes is introduced and trade unions are suspended. Walesa is eventually released in November 1982.

8 October 1982. Under a new trade union act Solidarity is effectively dissolved; for the next six years it maintains an underground existence.

30 December 1982. Martial law is suspended.

June 1983. The Pope, on a visit to Poland, calls for dialogue between the authorities and the people.

22 July 1983. Martial law is formally lifted.

October 1983. Walesa is awarded the Nobel Peace Prize.

October 1984. Pro-Solidarity priest Fr Jerzy Popieluszko is murdered; 250,000 people attend his funeral on 3 November, and four members of the state security forces are convicted of the murder on 7 February, 1985.

March 1985. Mikhail Gorbachev becomes general secretary of the Soviet communist party.

6 November 1985. Jaruzelski adds the office of head of state (succeeding Henryk Jablonski) to his position as PZPR first secretary, but gives up the post of prime minister to Zbigniew Messner.

June 1987. The Pope on his third official visit emphasises the importance of human rights, supports the right to form free trade unions and grants an audience to Walesa.

29 November 1987. A referendum is held on (i) an economic reform programme involving austerity measures and (ii) limited political liberalisation and decentralisation; the government gets less than the 50 per cent minimum support of the total electorate it has declared necessary.

August-October 1988. A bout of industrial unrest, as workers demand the re-legalisation of Solidarity, leads to talks between the government and Walesa.

September-October 1988. Messner is replaced as prime minister by Mieczyslaw Rakowski.

17-18 January 1989. An acrimonious PZPR plenum approves Jaruzelski's proposal to hold round table talks on relegalising Solidarity, resolving to "take into account pluralism of interests" within the trade union sphere and in politics.

6 February 1989. Round table talks begin in Warsaw, involving Solidarity, the Church, the government, the PZPR, official organs including the OPZZ trade union and the umbrella Patriotic Movement for National Rebirth.

7 March 1989. The Polish government for the first time openly blames the Soviet Union for the 1940 Katyn massacre.

5 April 1989. A historic deal marks the conclusion of the round table talks. There are to be partially free multi-party elections and free elections four years hence; constitutional changes, including the introduction of press freedom; and a package of economic reforms.

17 April 1989. Solidarity is legalised under the round table agreement.

8 May 1989. An independent daily newspaper *Gazeta Wyborcza* edited by leading Solidarity intellectual Adam Michnik is launched.

17 May 1989. The Roman Catholic Church is accorded a status unparalleled in the communist bloc under a new legal framework for church-state relations.

29 May 1989. Parliament pardons those convicted since the 1980 Gdansk accords for strikes, demonstrations and supporting banned organisations.

4 and 18 June 1989. Partially free elections to the new bicameral National Assembly are a triumph for Solidarity, whereas the ruling PZPR and its allies fail to win any openly contested seats.

6 June 1989. Gen. Jaruzelski offers to include Solidarity in a coalition government. The following day, Jaruzelski confirms that the PZPR would relinquish power if defeated in the fully free elections due in 1993.

July 1989. Gorbachev addresses an assembly of Warsaw Pact leaders in Bucharest to renounce the Brezhnev doctrine.

19 July 1989. Gen. Jaruzelski, the sole candidate, is elected as President by the National Assembly with the pragmatic support of senior Solidarity figures.

29 July 1989. Outgoing prime minister Mieczyslaw Rakowski succeeds Jaruzelski as PZPR first secretary; PZPR reformers benefit from a reshuffle in the politburo and secretariat.

1 August 1989. Food prices rise by up to 500 per cent after the abolition of state price controls.

2 August 1989. Kiszczak is elected by the *Sejm* as prime minister but is unable to muster a coalition because the PZPR's formerly allied parties, the ZSL and SD, are by now discussing possible coalition with Solidarity.

19 August 1989. The PZPR agrees to join a Solidarity-led coalition provided it secures key portfolios including the defence and interior ministries.

24 August 1989. Solidarity intellectual Tadeusz Mazowiecki becomes the first post-communist Prime Minister.

12 September 1989. The *Sejm* (the lower house of the National Assembly) swears in the first government in Eastern Europe since the 1940s which is not under communist control.

12 October 1989. The coalition government reveals its unprecedented, radical economic strategy defying Walesa's warnings of potential civil unrest. The so-called Balcerowicz Plan prescribes economic "shock treatment" and is implemented from early January 1990 with the imposition of dramatic price increases.

9 November 1989. The Berlin wall is breached, marking the symbolic end of Soviet domination of the "satellite states".

29-30 December 1989. The National Assembly formally renames the country as the Polish Republic rather than the People's Republic of Poland.

7-30 January 1990. The PZPR's last congress dissolves the party on 28 January and establishes a successor, the Social Democracy of the Polish Republic (SdRP), embracing parliamentary democracy and the market economy. Aleksander Kwasniewski becomes the SdRP chairman.

13 April 1990. The Soviet Union officially admits Soviet culpability in the massacre of Polish officers in Katyn in 1940.

24 June 1990. Senior figures including Adam Michnik resign from the Solidarity national committee on June 24 over Walesa's authoritarian leadership style.

6-7 July 1990. In a concession to Walesa, Mazowiecki replaces three former communist ministers, leaving only a fourth in office. Walesa and Mazowiecki jointly pledge to co-operate on economic reconstruction and "preserving social peace".

13 July 1990. The passage of a privatisation bill opens the way for the sale of state holdings amounting to 80 per cent of the economy. The bill includes provision for cheap share offers to workers.

1 October 1990. Jaruzelski, having agreed to step down, signs constitutional legislation ordering direct presidential elections.

25 November 1990. Walesa tops the poll in the first round of the presidential elections, winning 40 per cent of the vote in a 60 per cent turnout. The unpopular economic reform programme limits support for Mazowiecki to 18 per cent; he is beaten into third place by the flamboyant and erratic emigré businessman Stanislaw Tyminski. On 9 December 1990. Walesa wins three quarters of the vote to defeat Tyminski in the second round run-off. He resigns as chairman of Solidarity on 12 December, and is sworn in as President on 22 December.

12 January 1991. A government of Solidarity and post-Solidarity figures is sworn in under Jan Krzysztof Bielecki.

October 1991. IMF credit is suspended after Poland fails to meet performance criteria.

27 October 1991. Poland's first fully free multi-party elections since the beginning of the communist period result in a fragmented parliament of 29 parties. Communist and allied parties secure only about 20 per cent of the vote. The turnout of only 43 per cent reveals a degree of disaffection attributable to the unpopular austerity measures.

23 December 1991. A coalition of centre-right post-Solidarity parties, with Jan Olszewski as prime minister, is sworn in nearly two months after the elections.

1 January 1992. Steep energy price rises are introduced; they provoke a wave of strikes, peaking on 13 January, when some 2 million Solidarity union members stop work.

1 February 1992. A *Sejm* resolution pronounces Martial Law to have been illegal.

5 March 1992. The Olszewski government's economic programme, which aims to kick-start the Polish economy by relaxing monetary controls, is defeated in the *Sejm*.

26 May 1992. President Walesa declares his loss of confidence in the Olszewski government.

4 June 1992. Walesa is rumoured to be among those named in a list, distributed to political leaders by Interior Minister Macierewicz, of 64 senior officials allegedly cited in secret police files as collaborators. The following day Olszewski is defeated in a no confidence motion. A *Sejm* Extraordinary Commission subsequently accuses Macierewicz of actions which "could have led to the destabilisation of the state".

6 June - 10 July 1992. Waldemar Pawlak of the formerly communist-allied party PSL briefly holds the office of Prime Minister, having been proposed by Walesa. Pawlak fails to construct a coalition.

July 10 1992. Hanna Suchocka becomes Poland's first woman Prime Minister; her cabinet is a broad coalition of seven post-Solidarity parties, including liberal, Christian democratic and peasant parties.

1 August 1992. Passage through the *Sejm* of the "small constitution", designed to clarify the responsibilities of the legislature and the executive organs of the government and presidency. The small constitution takes effect on 8 December.

9 October 1992. Suchocka presents an IMF-approved austerity programme designed to reduce the budget deficit. The package is accepted by parliament on 6 November.

28 October 1992. Withdrawal of the last remaining Russian combat unit from Poland; some 6,000 Russian support troops remain to expedite the transit of Russian troops withdrawing from eastern Germany.

2 November 1992. The National Defence Committee adopts a new defence doctrine, proclaiming that Poland has no natural enemies and no territorial claims on its neighbours; and declaring that Poland's long-term security is best guaranteed by Polish membership of NATO.

December 1992. In the face of a wave of coal strikes the *Sejm* narrowly rejects government plans to restructure the coal industry.

7 January 1993. Strict legislation allowing abortion only under exceptional circumstances is passed by the *Sejm*; Walesa signs the bill into law on 15 February.

13 January 1993. Walesa signs legislation designed to end the state monopoly on broadcasting, the *Sejm* having accepted an amendment requiring broadcasters to respect Christian values.

12 February 1993. Walesa forces the *Sejm* to approve a budget for 1993, after threatening otherwise to dissolve the legislature.

8 March 1993. The IMF approves standby credit worth $655m, lifting the suspension of credit in place since 1991.

30 April 1993. The *Sejm* adopts a mass privatisation bill: 600 state firms are to be assigned to one of ten investment funds, shares in which are to be available to citizens for a nominal fee.

28 May 1993. The Suchocka cabinet submits its resignation after a motion of no confidence proposed by Solidarity deputies, following the cabinet's refusal to award pay rises to striking health and education workers. The cabinet stays in office pending the appointment of a successor.

31 May 1993. Walesa dissolves the parliament.

1 June 1993. Walesa signs an electoral law, passed by the *Sejm* in April, establishing hurdles for parties competing in the polls with the aim of ending the fragmentation of the legislature. Two days later he calls elections for September.

1 June 1993. The Suchocka Cabinet approves a concordat with the Vatican regulating relations between the Polish state and Roman Catholic Church. The Concordat awaits parliamentary approval.

24-26 August 1993. The first official visit to postcommunist Poland by a Russian head of state takes place; President Boris Yeltsin welcomes "a new phase in relations" between Russia and Poland and appears to countenance Polish membership of NATO.

19 September 1993. Legislative elections. Only six parties and alliances secure seats, compared with 29 in 1991. The postcommunist SLD (led by Kwasniewski) and PSL secure nearly two thirds of the seats, whereas the right fares poorly. The most successful post-Solidarity party, the UD, takes only 10.6 per cent of the vote.

26 October 1993. A left-wing SLD-PSL coalition takes office. PSL leader Pawlak becomes prime minister for the second time. The Government stresses its commitment to continued reform at a prudent pace. The cabinet includes several ministers who had held posts during communist rule.

10 May 1994. An economic plan for 1994-8, "Strategy for Poland", aims for macroeconomic stabilisation and pledges greater financial discipline.

1 July 1994. The *Sejm* postpones consideration of the Concordat with the Vatican until after the adoption of a new constitution. Walesa condemns the failure to ratify the concordat as a resurgence of communism.

6-7 July 1994. US President Bill Clinton visit Warsaw. Clinton warns Russia not to attempt to block an extension of NATO membership into central and eastern Europe.

8 September 1994. The last remaining Russian troops depart from Polish territory.

22 September 1994. Privatisation Minister Wieslaw Kaczmarek of the SLD accuses Prime Minister Pawlak of blocking the sale of state enterprises. He is supported by Walesa.

10 October 1994. Walesa requests the dismissal of Defence Minister Adm. Piotr Kolodziejczik; Pawlak eventually complies on 10 November. It emerges that Walesa, at a meeting of the general staff in late September, had organised a vote of no confidence in Kolodziejczik, who accuses Walesa of having incited insubordination by senior officers and of undermining civilian control over the military.

12 October 1994. A *Sejm* resolution requests that Walesa cease activities which could threaten or destabilise democracy.

19 October 1994. Pawlak approves a third tranche of privatisation after considerable delay.

3 January 1995. Walesa disputes the government's tax plans for 1995, urging citizens to pay only the lower rate of tax that he favours.

7 February 1995. Pawlak resigns as prime minister under heavy pressure from Walesa, averting a constitutional crisis.

1 March 1995. Jozef Oleksy of the SLD takes office as prime minister at the head of a new cabinet preserving the SLD-PSL alliance. Oleksy agrees on 3 March to appoint Walesa's nominees to the key portfolios of defence, foreign affairs and interior.

5 April 1995. Walesa announces that he will not attend international ceremonies in May to celebrate the 50th anniversary of the Allied victory in the Second World War, after an alleged snub by Germany over diplomatic protocol during the planned Berlin ceremony. Oleksy's decision to attend the ceremonies against Walesa's wishes is denounced by the president on 20 April as "treasonable".

26 May 1995. Walesa supports demonstrations by Solidarity supporters in Warsaw against unemployment and government economic policy.

16 August 1995. Walesa vetoes legislation placing the military under the Cabinet's control.

5 November 1995. Walesa and Kwasniewski emerge as the front runners in the first round of voting in presidential elections.

19 November 1995. Kwasniewski is narrowly elected president, winning 51.7 per cent of the vote compared to Walesa's 48.3 per cent.

9 December 1995. The Constitutional Tribunal rejects Walesa's bid to overturn the election results on the basis that Kwasniewski had misinformed voters about his educational qualifications. Allegations of electoral fraud await investigation.

December 1995. Walesa accuses Prime Minister Oleksy of having collaborated with Soviet intelligence.

22 December 1995. Inauguration of Kwasniewski as president.

HUNGARY

The country's official name was the Hungarian People's Republic (*Magyar Nepkoztarsasag*) until Oct. 23, 1989, and thereafter the Republic of Hungary (*Magyar Koztarsasag*).

Hungary is a landlocked country, with a total area of 93,030 sq. km and a population of 10,375,000 (less than half that of Romania, and a similar size to the Czech Republic). Over 50 per cent of Hungarians live in urban areas, and a quarter within metropolitan Budapest, the capital city. The Danube flows from the north-western corner of the republic, forming for some 150 km the country's northern border with Slovakia; it then flows south, past Budapest, with Lake Balaton to the west and the fertile Alfold plains to the east, until it reaches the southern border with former Yugoslavia, where it forms the boundary between Croatia and Serbia. A long border with Romania lies on Hungary's eastern flank. Apart from Budapest the principal towns are Debrecen and Miskolc in the north-east, Szeged and Pecs in the south, and the industrial centre of Gyor on the Danube in the north-west.

Hungary is in ethnic terms a relatively homogeneous country. 96.6 per cent of the population is classified as Magyar, a people whose ancestors arrived in the area from Asia before the 10th century AD. By religion Hungary is predominantly a Christian country, since the time of King Stephen (crowned in 1000 AD), and two-thirds of the population profess the Catholic faith, while one fifth are Lutherans. Magyar is the language of over 98 per cent of the population; there is a Romany population of some 320,000, many of whom are Romany-speakers, and

there are smaller German and Slovak minorities. Alone of the countries of Eastern Europe, Hungary still has a sizeable Jewish community, numbering some 88,000. [*See the Czechoslovakia, Romania, and Yugoslavia chapters for the ethnic Hungarian minorities in the region.*]

HISTORICAL NARRATIVE

Hungary's historic territories, conquered by the Magyars in the ninth century AD, were those lands encompassed by the Carpathian mountains, stretching from the northern border of present-day Slovakia, westward through much of what is now Romania, to reach Belgrade in the south.

For centuries the Hungarian monarchy formed an alliance with Austria under the Habsburgs. In 1867 the Dual Monarchy was created, extending Hungary's already significant autonomy. There were considerable distinctive features in the administration of the Hungarian portion of the empire (*see also Czechoslovakia*). In Hungary Magyars formed the landed upper class, and Magyars and Germans the bureaucratic elite; other ethnic groups were regarded as subject peoples. The imperial administration in Hungary was more authoritarian and more reactionary than in Austria and had a less efficient bureaucracy, with less investment in communications, education or economic development. The entrepreneurial classes were dominated by Jews. The economy was primarily an agrarian one and manufacturing industry was undeveloped and old-fashioned.

Hungary's case in the negotiations towards the epochal peace settlement following the First World War was damaged both by the country's wartime alliance with Germany, and by its brief experience of Bolshevik rule in 1919, which had brought communism to central Europe for the first time.

The communist Bela Kun had set up a Soviet Republic in March 1919 and rapidly implemented a radical Bolshevik-style programme. Large parts of the economy were nationalised, the church disestablished, revolutionary tribunals set up to administer justice and a radical land reform imposed. As Kun's popularity waned he announced the "dictatorship of the proletariat" in June 1919 and began a "red terror" in which hundreds of counter-revolutionaries died.

Instrumental in Kun's rise had been the support of demobbed soldiers restive over the anticipated loss of historic Hungarian territory, and in a desperate bid to win back nationalist support Kun launched military offensives to reclaim territory lost to Czechoslovakia and Romania. The failure of both (the first for diplomatic reasons, the second for military ones) fatally undermined the government and Kun fled from Hungary in August 1919 as Romanian troops marched on Budapest. Power was handed over to Adml. Miklos Horthy's regime, whose "white terror" eclipsed its red precursor in claiming many thousands of victims, including communists and Jews.

At the Treaty of Trianon historic Hungary was duly dismembered, losing more than two thirds of its territory, mostly to Czechoslovakia, Romania and Yugoslavia. The economic loss imposed by Trianon was also grave, with Hungary ceding territory containing vital raw materials and communications links. In addition, only a quarter of rump Hungary's new borders were natural frontiers. Historic Hungary also lost nearly 60 per cent of its population, and some 32 per cent of Magyars found themselves living outside Hungary's new borders.

The truncation of the country at Trianon was regarded by Hungarian patriots as a humiliation. It was compounded by a further Trianon clause binding Hungary to maintain only a token military capability, and prohibiting heavy weapons. The recovery of the lost land became for some Hungarian leaders the country's principal long-term priority, but most postponed the project, mindful of the failure to reclaim the territory by military force in 1919, choosing instead to consolidate Hungary's political and economic situation.

As regent (head of state) from 1920 to 1944, Horthy dominated interwar Hungary with his brand of conservatism, anti-communism, clericalism and increasing authoritarianism. Horthy represented Hungary's highly conservative ruling class.

Hungarian democracy in the interwar period was limited. The communist party was banned for most of this time and the outcome of Hungary's first notionally free elections in 1920, in which conservative, agrarian and Christian parties triumphed, was affected by the climate of fear created by the white terror. Subsequent elections were influenced by the abolition of the secret ballot in rural areas. Tight party discipline in the ruling Government Party also reduced debate.

Economically, Hungary staged a slow recovery during the 1920s, with state support for industry contributing to the expansion of that sector. However from 1929 the depression had severe consequences for the economy, driving unemployment up to some 35 per cent, and starvation struck the countryside. The economic downturn prompted a surge of opposition to Jewish-dominated capital and boosted the Hungarian fascists, the Right-Radicals. As Hungary's Prime Minister from 1932 until his death in 1936, Right-Radical leader Gyula Gombos established increasingly close ties with Nazi Germany, whose booming economy dragged Hungary out of recession.

Domestically, Horthy attempted to marshal a retreat from full Nazism after 1936. The ruling class of which he was the champion was highly suspicious of the Nazis as a mass, ideology-based party and was unsettled by German-Austrian *Anschluss* in March 1938, which made Nazi Germany a direct neighbour, and still more so by the German-Soviet pact and consequent partition of Poland in 1939. These fear were offset, however, by the opportunity that an alliance with Germany provided to reclaim historic Hungarian territory. Between 1938 and 1940 Hungary re-acquired considerable territory from southern Slovakia, Ruthenia and Romania. In November 1940 Hungary entered the Axis's tripartite pact and in 1941 Hungarian troops participated in the Axis invasion of Yugoslavia, reclaiming territory from Serbia.

From spring 1938 Hungary had passed a series anti-Semitic laws, and had participated in the deportation of some 100,000 Jews. Further mass deportations under Nazi supervision took place from 1944, claiming a further 500,000 victims. Hungarian leaders did not support the genocide, and some 260,000 Jews were spared. Uniquely in the region, Hungary thus retained a significant although much diminished Jewish community after the war.

As the tide of war turned against Germany, and the Red Army advanced towards Hungarian territory, Hungary sought to distance itself from the Germans and withdrew troops it had committed to the Axis invasion of the Soviet Union. Germany responded by occupying Hungary in March 1944. In October Red Army troops entered Hungary to take Szeged and Debrecen. Horthy attempted to end Hungarian participation in the war by signing an armistice with the USSR, whereupon he was deposed by the Germans and replaced by the leader of the pro-Nazi Arrow Cross movement, Ferenc Szalasi. By February 1945, however, the Red Army had reached Budapest, and by the spring the whole country had been liberated.

The fighting and looting of 1944-5 badly damaged Hungary and cost the country some 40 per cent of her national wealth. Nevertheless Hungary's close relationship with Germany during the Second World War had contributed to rapid economic development after 1938, bringing Hungary closer to European levels of development.

The victory of the Red Army placed Hungary under the administration of a broad-based anti-fascist provisional government. First formed in Debrecen in December 1944, the government was responsible for two major decisions; firstly, the signature of an armistice in January 1945 with the Allies, whereby Hungary formally renounced her annexations of Czechoslovak, Romanian and Yugoslav territory from 1938 onwards; and secondly the passage of a radical land reform act expropriating the feudal estates which had hitherto accounted for the greater part of the country's land. This land reform was the responsibility of agriculture minister Imre Nagy.

Municipal elections in Budapest in October 1945 indicated overwhelming backing for the mainly-agrarian Smallholders' Party. Soviet Marshal Voroshilov responded by directing that, to prevent "anarchy and civil war", the general elections due the following month should be based on a single government list. This was opposed by Britain and the USA, and a compromise formula allowed for separate lists, but with a commitment to form a broad coalition government, which was headed by Smallholder leader Ferenc Nagy.

The Soviet-backed communists then applied their notorious `salami tactics' to remove opponents one by one. In mid-1947 Ferenc Nagy was ousted from power and left the country and by mid-1948 the Socialists had been neutralised. In 1949 a single-list general election was held, returning to office a communist-dominated bloc whose single-party rule was enshrined in the 1949 Constitution of the People's Republic of Hungary.

There followed seven years of a brutal Stalinist dictatorship under Matyas Rakosi, who forced through an increasingly unpopular drive for industrialisation and agricultural collectivisation. The "Muscovite" communists in the central leadership eliminated their rivals in factional disputes, show trials and purges. The most prominent victim was foreign minister Laszlo Rajk, who was executed in October 1949 for "Titoism".

After Stalin's death in 1953 Imre Nagy's elevation to the post of prime minister raised hopes for a period of liberalisation, known officially as the New Course, but Nagy was then deposed in 1955 and dismissed from the party for right-wing deviationism. In political exile, Nagy developed his critique of the Stalinist elite and his coded proposals for a pluralist democracy in which the communist party effectively renounced its leading role.

The roots of the Hungarian revolution lay in Soviet leader Khrushchev's destalinisation programme. In February 1956 Khrushchev delivered his secret speech denouncing Stalinism; he then continued his liberal drive by holding a summit with Tito in the late summer. But whilst Khrushchev clearly favoured the displacement of the hardline elite in Hungary in favour of reform-communists, the Soviet leadership was unprepared for a mass uprising against Soviet domination.

Emboldened by the liberalisation in the Soviet Union, reform communist supporters of Nagy had begun to hold mass meetings in June to demand his reinstatement. A series of strikes, prompted by reports of the riots in Poznan in Poland, spread throughout Hungary. Rakosi had favoured a crackdown, but instead had been dismissed by the Soviets. In an officially-approved ceremony on 6 October the body of the newly-rehabilitated Rajk was re-buried. The ceremony was attended by some 200,000 people. From this moment the 1956 Hungarian uprising, or Hungarian revolution, developed with astonishing speed. Support for a new, responsive, democratic socialism burgeoned; many regarded the Yugoslav model, with workers' participation and apparent grass roots democracy, as the model.

On 23 October an illegal student demonstration swelled into a massive pro-democracy rally demanding Nagy's reappointment and the withdrawal of Soviet forces. Some protesters chanted pro-Yugoslav slogans. When Rakosi's successor Gero denounced the demonstration in a radio broadcast, protesters besieged the radio station in Budapest. Soviet tanks arrived to secure Budapest and clashed with hastily-armed

Hungarian rebels. There followed four days of fighting, which ended only when the Soviets agreed to withdraw their forces.

Imre Nagy, who had returned as prime minister on 25 October, had negotiated the withdrawal. He announced that multi-party "socialist democracy" would be restored. He duly formed a multi-party government on 30 October and disbanded the secret police. Having praised the rebels for defending Hungarian independence, Nagy next declared Hungary's intention to leave the Warsaw Pact. This step was unacceptable to the Soviets, who launched a brutal military invasion and a short war to suppress the revolution.

Soviet troops and tanks swept back into Hungary on 4 November 1956. They were fiercely resisted by thousands of armed Hungarians in Budapest and elsewhere. Unarmed civilian protesters in Budapest and the provinces were massacred by Hungarian militia. Total casualty figures are hotly disputed, and range from 2,500 to 60,000 people killed. In the wake of the revolution Nagy and four associates were executed for treason. The communist hegemony was reimposed and many centre-left and intellectual figures fled the country.

The Hungarian revolution is one of the defining moments for communism in East-Central Europe prior to 1989; subsequent events of comparable significance were the erection of the Berlin Wall in 1961, the Prague Spring of 1968 and the rise of Solidarity in 1981. The Soviet invasion shattered any pretence that Soviet power in eastern Europe had any democratic legitimacy, and forced a postponement of de-stalinisation across Eastern Europe.

The dominant figure in Hungary for the next 30 years following the revolution was Janos Kadar. In its first five years Kadar's regime consolidated its power with a ruthless crackdown in which thousands of opponents were executed, jailed or interned.

Kadar launched his crackdown from political necessity. He himself was no more a Stalinist than Khrushchev. Nevertheless, in its obedience to Soviet foreign policy, Hungary was orthodox to the point of slavishness.

By the early 1960s the Soviet leadership was ready to back a second wave of destalinisation in Central and Eastern Europe, the process which had been postponed after the turmoil of 1956 in Hungary. Kadar's tactics changed in the new climate. The party, he indicated, would not now demand the total allegiance of all, in the classic totalitarian model; there could be non-party contributions to national life, since "whoever is not against us is with us". Hungary, like Poland and others, laid a new emphasis on providing material benefits to its citizens, in order to mitigate political repression. The regime's New Economic Mechanism (NEM) earned Hungary an enduring reputation as the most innovative and economically liberal of the Soviet-bloc states, and Hungarians enjoyed a period of relative prosperity.

From the mid-1970s, however, the economic basis of this strategy of "depoliticised" communism began to fracture. The NEM had moved away from the classic command economy, using market mechanisms as a vehicle, but the regime was unwilling to allow for the harsher consequences of an unfettering of the market. It became dependent on heavy foreign borrowing to sustain the illusion of prosperity. By 1986 Hungary was the most heavily indebted communist state in Central or Eastern Europe, with its foreign convertible currency debt amounting to 62.2 per cent of GDP. Pro-reform communists called for more radical "reform of the reform", but instead the regime retreated into conservatism. Nevertheless Hungary retained an image of relative economic liberality in the West, and Western visitors to Budapest were often impressed by its thriving markets and shops.

Gorbachev's accession to power in the Soviet Union and his *perestroika* (restructuring) policy provided a changed international context. The hardline Hungarian leadership was isolated, and could no longer point to the Soviet threat as an excuse for failing to implement reforms. 1988-89 marked the success of the pro-reform communists in the peaceful takeover of the party leadership, ousting first the elderly Kadar and then his successor Karoly Grosz.

The party then introduced a series of increasingly audacious reforms, thus establishing itself as the driving force behind the Hungarian revolution of 1989-90. Changes included the legalisation of independent political parties and the announcement of partially free elections; the repudiation of the 1956 Soviet invasion and the full rehabilitation of Nagy, who was given a state funeral; and the first breach of the "Iron Curtain" as Foreign Minister Gyula Horn ceremonially cut the wire on the Austrian frontier, a vital moment in the mass exodus of East Germans to the West which ultimately caused the collapse of the GDR. In October the MSMP dissolved itself to establish a new, social democratic party, the Hungarian Socialist Party (MSzP).

The party's new leadership, although itself divided, had thus demonstrated considerable agility in positioning itself to play a key role in the coming democratic order. In contrast to the unbending leadership in neighbouring Czechoslovakia, the Hungarian reformists had calculated that the party's long-term interests were best served by being seen to embrace democracy. In this respect their approach had much in common with the strategy of the Polish party.

There had been mass public protests in Hungary during the last years of communism, putting public pressure on the regime from 1986 over two key issues - the controversial Gabcikovo-Nagymaros hydroelectric power scheme with Czechoslovakia, and the harsh mistreatment of the ethnic Hungarian minority in neighbouring Romania. "People Power", however, played a minimal role in the Hungarian revolution of 1989-90. Indeed, the first mass involvement in the transition came in the crucial general elections of 1990. Despite its careful manoeuvring, the MSzP secured only a disappointing 10.89 per cent of the vote, while anti-communist parties captured more than three quarters of the vote. Voters judged that with communism collapsing all over Eastern Europe, the ex-communist party was no longer relevant, and they saw little reason to reward the MSzP for having played a central role in setting the process rolling.

The broad conservative movement Hungarian Democratic Forum (MDF) emerged as the largest party, and formed a coalition with two minor right-wing parties, the Christian Democratic Party (KDNP) and the Smallholders (FKgP), all of them supporting Christian and national values. MDF leader and Prime Minister Jozsef Antall, a former historian and museum director, quickly imposed his dominance on the decision-making process. Meanwhile Arpad Goncz, a member of the liberal Alliance of Free Democrats (SzDSz), was elected by the new parliament to the mainly ceremonial presidency. Goncz proved an able and popular president, working hard to enhance the presidency's powers and prestige, although his pragmatic and non-partisan style sometimes marginalised him.

In June 1991 the last of over 50,000 Soviet soldiers left Hungary, and in July the Warsaw Treaty Organisation or Warsaw Pact was formally dissolved. Hungary set about staking its claim to membership of NATO, and in doing so sought common cause with Poland and Czechoslovakia, the Visegrad group. Meanwhile Comecon had been formally dissolved at a meeting in Budapest, and Hungary's trade rapidly reoriented itself so that by 1992 over half was with the European Communities (EC, subsequently EU), although Russia remained Hungary's second largest trading partner. In December 1991 Hungary, together with its Visegrad allies, signed association agreements with the EC providing for the introduction of free trade over a ten-year period. Hungary thus established itself with Poland and Czechoslovakia in the fast track towards European integration.

In the economic sphere, the Antall government eschewed both Polish-style "shock therapy" and the flagship mass privatisation schemes favoured by the Czechoslovaks, both of which were effectively vetoed by the populist wing of the MDF. Instead the Antall regime adopted a more pragmatic approach. Privatisation got under way in 1991 and proceeded in a rather piecemeal fashion as foreign investors and the former nomenklatura cherry-picked the most promising state enterprises.

In 1990-2 Hungary was widely regarded in the West as the incipient economic success story of the former communist bloc, and Hungary attracted by far the largest quantity of foreign investment of all countries in the region. In fact, however, the expected economic recovery failed to materialise. Output declined rapidly in 1990-91 and continued to fall in 1992-3, showing signs of recovery only in 1994. Unemployment doubled in 1992 alone, albeit from a low base, and the government found itself unable to maintain the previously generous social provision. Instead it was faced with making drastic and inevitably unpopular social spending cuts to stem the growing budget deficit, with general elections looming in 1994.

The government also struggled to counter the impression that economic gains under its term had not been equally distributed, and that the former communist elite had unfairly acquired a disproportionate share of the new wealth created in this period. Some populist figures in the MDF, such as its vice president Istvan Csurka, were claiming by 1992 that MDF liberals, the IMF and other supposedly malign "foreign" or Jewish interests had freed the market for their own self-interested reasons, and they called effectively for a return to state control. Csurka was expelled from the MDF in 1993.

The MDF's populist wing placed great emphasis on the establishment of a legal process to correct past injustices. There was also support for such measures across the more moderate right. Accordingly, the Antall government secured the passage of laws compensating those imprisoned or deported for political reasons between 1939 and 1989, and the families of those executed for political reasons in the same period. Another law facilitated the prosecution of the perpetrators of war crimes or crimes against humanity in 1956. Compensation was offered to those whose property had been nationalised under the communist regime.

Constitutional difficulties with several of these laws in some ways reflected the inexperience of legislators in drafting clear and unambiguous legislation. It added to the popular perception that the former dissidents who had taken power in 1990, whilst perhaps intellectually accomplished, were limited in their technical competence to govern (*see also Poland and Czechoslovakia*). Antall was among those accused of lacking the popular touch to communicate government policy to the electorate and to put its case in the face of allegations of incompetence. An early example of the government's failure in this respect was the strike and blockade of Budapest streets by taxi drivers in October 1990, prompted by a peremptory government reversal of previous assurances that fuel prices would be held down.

MDF leaders realised that their message was not convincing the electorate, but they blamed this failure on alleged bias in the broadcast media. The MDF-led government repeatedly attempted to dismiss the heads of state TV and radio in favour of its own nominees, and despite President Goncz's support for the broadcast chiefs, the MDF eventually got its way in 1993. As the general elections approached in 1994, there was increasing evidence of government interference in the broadcast media.

During this period, and particularly after the death of Antall in December 1993, the right-wing coalition increasingly gave itself up to visceral anti-communism. Divided amongst themselves and without an electoral "big idea" for 1994, the rightist parties united only in their mutual distrust of the ex-communist MSzP. The Hungarian right reached its nadir with the prominence given by the state media during the 1994 election campaign to allegations that during the 1956 revolution Gyula Horn had personally beaten rebel prisoners; the MDF denied any involvement in the story.

The MSzP campaign, in contrast to the MDF's, stressed national reconciliation, calling on voters to set aside the grievances of a past era and to unite in the national interest. Although the party thus invited voters to draw a line under the communist past, paradoxically it also appealed to history in claiming to be the most technically competent team, by invoking its long experience of government in the communist era. Perhaps the party's most successful tactic was to present a brand of one-nation social democracy, promising social justice to ensure a fair distribution of the proceeds of the economic transition. The party pledged to rule by consensus, and to pursue those goals around which the country could unite, such as EC (EU) and NATO membership.

The 1994 elections were a major failure for the right. Having won over 50 per cent of the vote in 1990, the leading right-wing and centre-right parties together attracted only a third of the vote in 1994. The MSzP campaign, in contrast, was highly successful. The MSzP alone won almost a third of the vote, more than tripling its share over 1990. Hungary's complex electoral system awarded the MSzP 209 seats, almost three times that of its nearest rival the SzDSz, while the MDF won just 37, and the right as a whole 105. The vote demonstrated the electorate's weariness with ideology, embodied in the highly political campaign of the MDF, and its desire for stable, consensual and competent government. Once again, events in Hungary had mirrored those in Poland (*see Polish legislative elections of 1993 and presidential election of 1995*).

Although the MSzP held an absolute majority in the new parliament, it opted to form a coalition with the SzDSz, lending credibility to its claim to be seeking a new brand of consensus politics. Under a favourable coalition deal, the SzDSz took three cabinet seats and an effective veto on government policy. Of the MSzP's 11 ministers, nine had at least 20 years' experience as MSMP members during the communist era. The new coalition controlled over two thirds of the seats in the parliament, sufficient to pass constitutional legislation.

The new coalition's foreign policy demonstrated remarkable continuity with its predecessor. The new prime minister, MSzP leader Gyula Horn, quickly stressed Hungary's continuing commitment to joining NATO and the EC (EU) at the earliest possible opportunity. In November 1994 Horn declared that the Central European states should persuade Russia that their prospective membership of NATO posed no threat, drawing opposition claims that Horn was advocating a Russian veto on NATO expansion. Horn rejected these claims, and at the end of 1995 Hungary remained a leading contender for early accession to NATO.

The economy dominated the new coalition's domestic agenda. Immediately after his party's election victory, Horn had warned Hungarians not to expect a rapid improvement in living standards. Measures were soon taken to reverse the alarming growth in the budget deficit, with a package of austerity measures in October 1994. Progress in other areas was initially halting, however, and the resignation in January 1995 of Ferenc Bartha, the senior privatisation official, and Finance Minster Laszlo Bekesi, coupled with the virtual halting of privatisation in the first six months of 1995, damaged Hungary's international reputation as a reforming country. The delays in the reform process reflected disquiet on the left wing of the MSzP.

However in spring 1995 the government introduced further austerity measures, and a new law put the privatisation process back on track. The first really large-scale privatisation came in December 1995 with the sale of the energy sector. Nevertheless, the resignation in December 1995 of Labour Minister Magda Kosa Kovacs, in protest at cuts in social benefits, was a further reminder of the divisions in the MSzP.

The government also secured the passage of crucial and long-delayed legislation on the state-owned broadcast media, establishing a system of independent supervision and formally distancing the radio and TV channels from state control.

ECONOMY

The Hungarian economy benefited post-1989 from Hungary's reputation as having been economically the most liberal and prosperous of the communist regimes. Trade during the communist era had made Hungary familiar to the Western market, convincing many Western investors that Hungarians had a natural affinity for the market. Hungary also benefited from a better existing legislative framework for investment. This, combined with the warm reception given to the reforms of the Antall government, made Hungary by far the most successful former communist country in the region in attracting foreign investment, more than $10bn in 1990-4. Even in the election year of 1994 Hungary took some 32 per cent of all foreign direct investment in Central and Eastern Europe, including the former Soviet Union. The result is that whilst average per capita investment in the region as of 1995 was some $41, the figure for Hungary was $528.

Several key economic reforms were introduced under Antall. In February 1992 the last remaining state-controls on prices were lifted, and in April 1992 bankruptcy legislation took effect, theoretically obliging all loss-making companies to close. Privatisation also got under way (*see below*). Nevertheless the expected economic recovery failed to materialise. In fact the economy continued to contract: in 1992 alone there was negative growth of 4.5 per cent, and unemployment doubled. Major budget deficit problems led to the suspension of IMF loans agreed in 1991.

The Horn government, when it took office in 1994, was keen to stress its commitment to continuing economic reform, although promising to place a renewed emphasis on social responsibility. Horn warned Hungarians not to expect rapid improvements in living standards. The government's economic priority was to reduce the budget deficit, but the consequent cuts in government expenditure caused political difficulties as those on the left of the MSzP protested. In January 1995 Finance Minister Bekesi resigned over the limited scale and slow pace of economic reform, warning that Hungary faced crisis over rapidly expanding foreign debt (which by the end of 1995 had reached some $33bn). Bekesi urged a resumption of privatisation to bring in much-needed revenues. In February, Finance Ministry officials conceded that the Hungarian economy was in worse shape than at any point over the preceding 10 to 15 years, mainly due to the "spiralling" public debt. Further austerity measures were introduced in March 1995 and the government has battled for a stabilisation programme designed to solve the budget deficit problem.

Privatisation

The privatisation process got slowly under way in 1991 with the sale of 20 flagship concerns, and continued in 1992. As at end-1992 some 80 per cent of the money invested in privatisation had come from foreign investors. By 1993 many of the most attractive enterprises had been sold, but strategic sectors of the economy and other more problematic companies remained in state ownership.

The privatisation process slowed still further after the MSzP election victory in 1994. In September 1994 the government announced an inquiry into allegedly corrupt privatisation, citing evidence that only two thirds of the revenue due from sales in 1993 had actually been collected by the state revenue service. Sales virtually halted in the first six months of 1995. The Horn government's commitment to privatisation was however in no serious doubt by the end of 1995, after the passage of a law in May designed to complete the privatisation process by 1997. The law streamlined the privatisation bureaucracy, facilitated quick cash sales, and permitted the sale of majority stakes in the strategic public utilities hitherto exempt from privatisation. The November 1995 sale of the energy sector was the first large-scale privatisation in the region.

Restitution

In June 1991 a compensation law awarded only partial compensation for nationalised property, in the form of vouchers. Only 500,000 people actually applied for compensation, well short of the 1.5 million originally projected by the government. A second law, passed in July 1991, restored some former church property, but not land.

The pusillanimity of the restitution legislation irritated leaders of the minor coalition party, the Smallholders, who campaigned on a virtual single-issue pro-restitution ticket. Smallholder leader Torgyan argued that without widespread restitution the former communist elite would continue to acquire property through "nomenklatura privatisation".

Further compensation laws passed in April-May 1992 covered the pre-communist period from 1939 to 1949, providing partial compensation for damaged caused to private property by the state and to those whose property was expropriated by the state for political reasons. Provision was also made for compensation payments to the victims (or their descendants) of politically motivated murder, deportation or imprisonment.

The Constitutional Court in February 1995 annulled the restitution legislation on the grounds that compensation claims from relatives of Jews killed or deported in 1939-44 had effectively been excluded. The Court ordered the passage of a new law by September 1995, but the legislation was delayed.

POST-COMMUNIST JUSTICE ISSUES

Issues of postcommunist justice bear a special significance in Hungary, which was the scene of the most violent and ruthless suppression of anti-communist protesters anywhere outside the Soviet Union in the communist era. Although Kadar declared in 1961 a process of national reconciliation, on the basis that `whoever is not against us is with us', millions of people affected by the crimes of 1956 and by the repression of 1956-60 refused to forgive and forget.

Recognising by the late 1980s that the communist party's legitimacy had been critically undermined by the events of 1956, reformist communist party leaders resolved to transform the party's image before facing the electorate. In January 1989 the reformist Pozsgay leaked the controversial finding of a party historical commission under his chairmanship, rejecting the official line that the 1956 uprising constituted a `counter-revolution', and describing it instead as a "popular uprising...against an oligarchic system of power which had humiliated the nation". As a gesture of national reconciliation, Imre Nagy and other leaders of the 1956 uprising executed in 1958 were given a state funeral in June 1989. Some 200,000 people attended the re-burial.

Although these gestures went some way to appease Hungarians, there remained strong pressure to introduce tough policies to administer justice at least to those guilty of the worst excesses of 1956. Many of the new generation of conservative politicians elected in 1990 were former dissidents with vivid memories of the violence and subsequent repression. Nevertheless attempts to legislate to allow for prosecution quickly ran into constitutional difficulties.

In February 1992 the Constitutional Court rejected legislation designed to facilitate the prosecution of those suspected of serious "crimes" committed in the communist era but then permissable under the constitution. The Court ruled that "laws must be made in advance of a crime, not afterwards". When the legislature approved a law exempting crimes including treason and murder from the 20-year statute of limitations, the Constitutional Court narrowed the exemptions to include only war crimes or crimes against humanity. Prosecutions were duly launched in 1994, and in January 1995 two former militiamen became the first to be convicted for their brutal part in the events of 1956; they were found guilty of crimes against humanity for their part in the killing of up to 200 unarmed demonstrators at Salgotarjan.

In February 1992 legislation was passed declaring null and void sentences for "crimes committed against the state" between 1963 and 1989, even if they had been committed in association with a foreign power; the law effectively pardoned former spies, whatever their motives.

The issue of the role of the secret police and its alleged former collaborators has played a less significant role in post-communist Hungarian politics than in Poland, Czechoslovakia or East Germany. The state security service was abolished in 1990. In 1991 rumours circulated about the alleged past involvement of leading members of the Smallholders with the communist-era secret police, and 13 FKgP leaders voluntarily underwent a security check. All but FKgP leader Torgyan then chose to release the findings, while Torgyan filed a civil suit against Antall and the security ministers accusing them of slanderously claiming that he had worked for the security service.

In March 1994 parliament passed legislation under which some 15,000 high ranking officials were to be screened for collaboration with the communist-era secret police or involvement in suppressing the 1956 uprising. The law applied to parliamentary deputies, ministers, senior civil servants, others in the military, police, national bank and diplomatic service and editors of newspapers and periodicals. Opposition leaders claimed that the law, passed just weeks before the 1994 general elections, was designed to remind the electorate of the worst excesses of the communist party, in order to discredit its successor the MSzP.

Justice issues under the MSzP

In the 1994 general election campaign, MSzP leader Gyula Horn called for a national reconciliation. Horn himself had personally experienced the brutality of the events of 1956, his own brother having been murdered by anti-communist rebels, and he himself having been a young member of an armed communist militia; he vigorously denied allegations that he had beaten rebel prisoners.

In June 1994 Horn and Nagy's daughter visited Nagy's grave to pay their respects; Horn urged that Hungary should eschew "divisive opposition and past grievances" and instead unite for "the future and common goals". The call appealed to the growing number of Hungarians, particularly younger people, who regarded the preoccupation with the events of almost four decades before as counter-productive.

Horn was clearly unwilling to support continued state efforts to identify those responsible for the events of 1956, and later in 1994 his government abolished the Historical Fact-Finding Committee established that spring. The committee, which consisted of lawyers and historians, had been given a brief to report on the political crimes of the communist era. The government also failed for some time to release secret police documents essential for the implementation of the March 1994 screening law. The government was forced to comply when the Constitutional Court approved the law in December 1994.

MEDIA

In common with other central European states the press in Hungary has boomed since 1989. The number of titles on the market expanded rapidly but the overall size of the market eventually contracted and many titles folded. Concern has focused on the often polemical nature of Hungarian journalism, with its sometimes meagre factual content.

On the other hand the broadcast media, which remained in state hands, have been highly controversial, perhaps more so than in any other country in the region. State supervision of the broadcast media had been officially authorised by a 1974 decree. Although in June 1992 the legislature declared this decree unconstitutional, a new law on the mass media was delayed. The MDF repeatedly claimed that the broadcast media favoured the opposition, particularly the MSzP, while the opposition in turn protested that the MDF consistently interfered in the editorial freedom of state broadcasters. In summer 1992 a constitutional clash blew up over President Goncz's refusal to comply with Antall's repeated requests to replace the heads of state radio and TV. Although the Constitutional Court supported Goncz, the two broadcast chiefs eventually resigned in January 1993. Meanwhile, in December 1992 the parliament voted to put state radio and TV finances under the control of the prime minister's office.

In autumn 1993 the broadcast of several radio programmes deemed critical of the MDF was suspended, prompting 10,000 people to rally in Budapest against government control of the media. As the 1994 general elections approached, parliament passed a highly controversial screening law in March 1994 under which public officials and newspaper editors were to be screened for past collaboration with the communist-era secret police. In the same month 129 Hungarian radio journalists were sacked ostensibly on economic grounds. Opposition claims, backed by rallies of to 30,000 protesters, that the dismissals were actually a political purge of anti-government journalists, were borne out by broadcast officials after the elections. During the election campaign itself the state broadcast media had demonstrated bias against the MSzP, giving prominence to allegations that MSzP leader Horn had personally participated in beating of prisoners during 1956 revolution.

Under Horn as prime minister the controversy continued. In July 1994 President Goncz dismissed the MDF-nominated heads of state TV and radio, but the coalition and opposition failed to agree on new candidates, and the Horn government appointed its own nominees. Conservative journalists found their access to air time restricted.

In October 1994 the Constitutional Court ruled that state interference in the media was illegal; it therefore ruled out direct government financing, requiring the passage of legislation on the media. In December 1995 the long-delayed media bill was finally passed. Public service broadcasters were to function as public foundations under the supervision of boards of trustees appointed by parliament. Two television channels and a radio station were to be privatised. The law therefore set out the terms for a legal distancing of the government from the editorial content of state TV and radio broadcasts.

ETHNIC AND NATIONAL RELATIONS

Hungary is one of the most ethnically homogeneous countries in the region, being almost 97 per cent ethnically Hungarian. In September 1992 parliament passed a bill of rights to protect ethnic identities and languages, including self-government at local and national level, while in February 1995 Hungary signed the Council of Europe's Convention on the Protection of National Minorities.

Despite Hungary's minority rights legislation, representatives of the 300,000-strong Romany community have frequently protested of widespread racial prejudice against Roma. Historically high rates of illiteracy, poverty and crime among Romanies have persisted.

Pursuing his theme of reconciliation after the socialist victory in the 1994 general elections, in July 1994 Horn wrote to Hungary's Chief Rabbi Robert Schweitzer to concede that Hungary shared partial responsibility for the death of Jews during the Second World War, and to offer an official apology.

FOREIGN AFFAIRS

European integration

In common with its central European neighbours Poland and Czechoslovakia, Hungary's emergence from communist rule and from Soviet domination in 1989-90 was regarded by Hungarians as a return to the country's rightful place as part of the European political and cultural mainstream. Hungary's new centre-right government immediately looked for confirmation of this status by declaring its intention to join the EC (EU) and NATO at the earliest possible opportunity. Hungary later risked worsening its fragile relations with the rump Yugoslavia, which was host to an ethnic Hungarian community of several hundred thousand, by allowing NATO bombers to use Hungarian airspace as part of their operations in the former Yugoslavia.

Hungary's early prospects for rapid integration into Western institutions were significantly improved by its image in the West as the most liberal of the Soviet bloc states and the most prepared for radical economic reforms. The stability of domestic politics in 1990-94, which contrasted with the frequent changes of government in Poland and the breakdown of the federation in Czechoslovakia, encouraged continued high levels of foreign investment. The Hungarians keenly backed attempts at a co-ordinated approach to European integration by the Central European states, the so-called Visegrad countries.

Despite the return to government of the ex-communist MSzP in 1994, there was continuity in Hungary's policy towards NATO and the EC (EU). Indeed the relative failure of the nationalist parties in 1994 allowed Horn a degree of latitude in the making of foreign policy not enjoyed by many Eastern European leaders.

Nevertheless opposition leaders remained vigilant for signs of a weakening of the Hungarian commitment to an expansion of NATO. In November 1994 Horn commented that Hungary and others should persuade Russia that their prospective membership of NATO posed no threat; he was immediately criticised as having implied a Russian veto on NATO membership.

Russia

Hungary retained better relations with Russia than did Poland or Czechoslovakia. Russia remained an important trading partner. The 52,000 Soviet troops previously stationed in Hungary had withdrawn by 1991 under the terms of a 1990 agreement. Most outstanding issues between Russia and Hungary had been solved by 1995. The two sides had compromised over Hungarian claims for compensation for the environmental damage caused by Soviet troops, and counter-claims from Russia for the military infrastructure it had been forced to abandon. The Soviet trade debt to Hungary of some $1.7bn, accrued in 1989-91, was cancelled in 1993-4 in exchange for 28 Russian MiG-29 fighters, arms and spare parts. In November 1992 Russian President Boris Yeltsin visited Hungary, publicly condemning the 1956 Soviet invasion and visiting the grave of Nagy. Relations have been more sensitive, however, since the rise of nationalism in Russia and consequent increasing Russian opposition to the expansion of NATO.

The Hungarian diaspora

Hungary's relations with several neighbours have been affected by the fundamental issue of the large ethnic Hungarian minorities lying outside Hungary's borders. Only two thirds of the estimated 15 million ethnic Hungarians actually live within Hungary, at least three million being in Romania and some 600,000 in Slovakia. In August 1992 prime minister Antall, addressing a congress of Hungarian peoples, stressed the Hungarian government's duty to protect the interests of Hungarians living beyond Hungary's borders. Antall's comments revived deep-rooted suspicions in Slovakia and Romania that Hungarian leaders nursed irredentist ambitions towards Hungary's historic territories.

Horn's approach, in contrast, was to declare himself the prime minister only of Hungarian citizens, and to seek a "historic reconciliation" with Romania and Slovakia: to renounce all territorial claims in exchange for guarantees on the civil rights of Hungarian minorities. In March 1995 Hungary struck precisely such a deal with Slovakia; a historic basic treaty. Negotiations with Romania on a similar basic treaty proved more complicated. (*See also Foreign Relations and Ethnic and National Relations sections of Romania and Slovakia chapters.*)

CONSTITUTION

Hungary's constitution is an extensively amended version of the communist-era basic law passed in 1949.

The Round Table agreement of April 1989 led to the passage in October 1989 of a "transitional constitution" (in reality a package of constitutional amendments) introducing a multi-party democratic system. Hungary officially renounced its status as a people's republic. In November 1989 a referendum narrowly endorsed the view of radical opposition parties that the president should be chosen by a democratically elected parliament, rather than elected directly.

In September 1992 a new Bill of Rights was introduced, including provision for the rights of national and ethnic minorities; the Bill included measures designed to protect ethnic identities and languages and self-government at local and national level.

Negotiations on a comprehensive new basic law have been problematic. The new government in office after May 1994, controlling more than the two-thirds of the legislature necessary to pass constitutional legislation, had a better prospect than its predecessor of getting such a document approved.

Hungary's Constitutional Court, composed of ten judges, began operating on 1 January 1990. The Court has broad prerogatives: to examine both existing legislation and bills under consideration by parliament. Aware of the sweeping potential of their powers, the Court's judges have acted with prudence lest they be regarded as intruding into the legislative process.

The Court has nevertheless made a series of highly significant rulings. In September 1991 it ruled that the presidency was not a merely ceremonial office but should have limited powers. In 1992 it ruled that the statute of limitations could not be suspended to enable prosecutions for the atrocities of 1956, and that such prosecutions could therefore only be brought on charges of war crimes or crimes against humanity. The Court has also played a significant role in the long-running argument over legislation on the media, while in a series of rulings in the second half of 1995 it declared unconstitutional important elements of the government's economic programme, partly on the grounds that reasonable notice should be given for major changes in social security.

PRINCIPAL PERSONALITIES

The communist era

Matyas **Rakosi** (1892-1971). Party leader 1945-56, closely identified with Stalinism and with Hungary's show trials and brutal purges of this period. As a communist activist Rakosi participated in the bolshevik government of Bela Kun in 1918. He was imprisoned in 1925-40 by the Horthy regime, then exiled. He spent the Second World War in Moscow, returning with the Red Army to lead the communists, who dominated "coalition" governments even before the single-party regime was formalised in 1949. Identified with the "Muscovites", he conducted a series of purges of rival party factions, condemning the "home" former resistance leader Laszlo Rajk in 1949 and ousting "revisionist" prime minister Imre Nagy in 1955. When de-Stalinisation got under way with Khrushchev's Secret Speech in 1956, Rakosi found himself isolated and in July 1956 he resigned.

Imre **Nagy** (1896-1958). Prime Minister in 1953-5 and the reformist premier during the 1956 revolution. A Russian prisoner in 1917, Nagy fought in the Russian civil war as a communist party member, returning to Hungary in the 1920s but then going back to the Soviet Union, and working there until the Red Army liberated his native country in 1944. He was briefly agriculture minister, then interior minister (until February 1946), but became a critic of the agricultural collectivisation programme, and was expelled from the politburo in 1949. Nagy escaped further punishment in the purges, however; he returned to government in 1951, and was made prime minister in July 1953 at the urging of the Soviet leadership, charged with improving living standards in an attempt to modify the unpopularity of the Rakosi regime. Ousted in April 1955, he retired to write and then advocate a "revisionist" alternative to the Stalinism of Rakosi. In the dramatic conditions of October 1956 he was recalled to office by a hardline leadership hoping to harness his popularity. His declaration of Hungarian neutrality hastened the Soviet invasion. With his arrest, secret trial and June 1958 execution, Nagy became and remained the most potent of martyr figures. His ceremonial reburial in June 1989 was attended by some 200,000 mourners.

Janos **Kadar** (1912-1989). Party first secretary for over three decades (1956-88) and the dominant figure of what became known as the "Kadar era". A youthful communist opponent of the Horthy regime and an active wartime resistance leader, he emerged after the liberation as party secretary in Budapest, then (1948-50) as minister of the interior. In the party's factional disputes he turned against his close friend Laszlo Rajk, who was executed in 1949, but was himself purged in turn in 1950, and then imprisoned from 1951 to 1954. Rehabilitated in 1954, he was soon identified with Imre Nagy and the reformism of 1956, but swiftly changed horses when Soviet troops moved to crush the Hungarian uprising. The Soviet authorities left Kadar in charge, as prime minister (1956-58) as well as party leader, of pursuing the repressive process of "normalisation". In the 1960s Kadar launched a new experiment; "whoever is not against us is with us" on the ideological front, and the "new economic mechanism" (introduced in 1968) which encouraged a "regulated market" to deliver material benefits which would win public support. It was only in the 1980s, when Hungary's economic situation deteriorated, that Kadar came seriously under challenge, and he became entrenched in a sterile defensiveness against calls for "reform of the reform". The May 1988 party conference provided the occasion for the reformers to oust him, designating him as party president but without a politburo seat. Seriously ill, he died in hospital on July 6, 1989.

Miklos **Nemeth** (b. 1948). The last communist prime minister (November 1988 to May 1990), and one of the principal party reform leaders together with Rezso Nyers and Imre Pozsgay. From a peasant background, Nemeth joined the party in 1968. He studied and worked as an economist, in academia, in government and, from 1981, within the party apparatus. In 1988, coinciding with the fall of Kadar, he emerged quite suddenly as a key figure, promoted to the politburo in May and appointed to succeed the new party leader Karoly Grosz as prime minister in November. His attention was devoted primarily to the management of the rapid programme of economic change and to piloting through an IMF-backed austerity package. The party, reconstituted as the Hungarian Socialist Party, refused to back this programme. Nemeth's endorsement of the transition to multi-party democracy was summed up in his memorable assessment: "The revolution happened not only because people did not want to live in that way, but also because the government did not want to govern in that way." In early 1991 he was appointed to the new European Bank for Reconstruction and Development (EBRD), as a vice-president in charge of personnel and administration, and vacated his seat in the Hungarian parliament.

Imre **Pozsgay** (b. 1933), one of the four-member party presidium in June-October 1989, and politically pre-eminent among the reform communists in the transition to multi-party democracy. A career party official in the MSMP, he first marked out his reformist credentials as minister of culture in 1975-82. Out of favour with Kadar thereafter, he commissioned the influential 1987 "Change and Reform" document, which helped open the floodgates with its advocacy of fundamental political as well as economic change. After Kadar's departure, he set up the round table talks of 1989 and supported the reappraisal of 1956, then worked to make the new MSzP a contender for office in a multi-party democracy. He was disappointed in his hopes of winning the presidency, however, when in November 1989 a referendum rejected the constitutional proposal for early direct presidential elections, in favour of letting a new parliament choose. His popularity waned rapidly thereafter: he finished only third in his Budapest constituency in the March 1990 general election, although he did obtain a seat in parliament on the MSzP national list. In November 1990 he left the party, sitting as an independent, and in May 1991 he was instrumental in forming, with Zoltan Biro, a new National Democratic Federation, an apparently unsuccessful attempt to launch a national centrist movement.

Principal personalities of the post-communist era

Jozsef **Antall** (1932-1993). The leader of the Hungarian Democratic Forum (MDF) and prime minister from May 1990 until his early death in December 1993. Antall was the son of a founding leader of the original Independent Smallholders' Party. Banned from teaching history because he had been active in youth organisations supporting the 1956 uprising, he became an archivist and later museum director. He was a founder member of the MDF in September 1987, on the liberal democratic wing. As MDF president from October 1989, he was charged with forming a coalition after the party's success in the 1990 elections, and became the dominant figure in the post-communist government from 1990, despite the increasingly debilitating symptoms of lymph gland cancer. Antall moulded the MDF into a centre-right conservative party and brought relative stability to Hungarian politics over a three-year period. His political objective was to oversee fundamental changes with minimum upheaval; he therefore favoured a social market approach rather than economic shock therapy. Antall's style was serious and reserved rather than charismatic. He was sometimes accused of a donnish aloofness which failed to communicate government policy to the Hungarian electorate.

Arpad **Goncz** (b. 1922). President of Hungary since 1990. A lawyer and personal secretary to one of the Smallholders' Party leaders before 1947. Under communist rule Goncz worked as a welder and then served six years of a life sentence for his involvement in the 1956 uprising. He then became a literary translator, playwright and dissident intellectual in the Budapest "democratic opposition" from which the Alliance of Free Democrats ultimately emerged in late 1988. He became president of the writers' union in 1989. At the 1990 general election he entered parliament, and was elected as its Speaker and thus as interim President, with the approval of the MDF. On 3 August 1990 the parliament re-endorsed the choice of Goncz as President in an unopposed election. Whilst in office Goncz worked to extend the powers of the formally ceremonial presidency. He clashed with the MDF over other constitutional issues, notably the party's attempt to appoint new heads of the state broadcast media (*see Constitution and Media sections*). Goncz became a popular and respected figure and was re-elected as president for a further five-year term in June 1995; having been nominated as a conciliatory gesture by the MSzP, he defeated a single rival by a margin of more than three to one.

Gyula **Horn** (b. 1932). Leader of the Hungarian Socialist Party (MSzP) and Prime Minister from 1994. Horn came from a poor family in a working class district of Budapest; his father, a communist, was killed by the police during the Second World War. Having left school at 11, Horn studied accounting in the Soviet town of Rostov in 1950. During the 1956 revolution, in which his brother was killed by anti-communist rebels, he was a member of a communist militia. In 1959 he joined the Foreign Affairs Ministry; he became a diplomat, then (from 1985) deputy foreign minister and (from 1989) Minister of Foreign Affairs. Having joined the ranks of the reform communists in the early 1980s, Horn earned a place in history on 2 May 1989, when he and Austrian Foreign Minister Alois Mock symbolically severed the iron curtain by cutting the barbed wire on the Austro-Hungarian border, precipitating the mass exodus of East Germans to the West which led to the fall of the Berlin wall. Horn was a founder of the MSzP in October 1989. He became a parliamentary deputy in spring 1990 and MSzP chairman in May 1990. Although Horn repeatedly stressed his commitment to a technocratic government pursuing economic reform and economic integration, and called for reconciliation and social peace in Hungary, some suspected his apparent conversion to be an act of political expediency motivated from a desire for power rather that a genuine ideological commitment.

POLITICAL PARTIES

The communist party and successors

The **Hungarian Communist Party** was founded in November 1918. Rapidly attracting the support of demobbed soldiers restive over the anticipated loss of historic Hungarian territory, the party merged with the socialists in March 1919, and the communist leader Bela Kun formed a government. Kun's pro-Bolshevik regime introduced a series of radical measures but rapidly lost popularity, eventually being forced from office by the disastrous failure of an irredentist military adventure against Romania in summer 1919. Under the Horthy regime thousands of communist activists perished in the white terror, and the communist party was banned until after the Second World War. In 1948 the reconstituted communist party merged with the social democrats to form the **Hungarian Workers' Party**, which became the sole legal party. During the turmoil of 1956 the party was formally dissolved and reformed as the **Hungarian Socialist Workers' Party** (MSMP). In October 1989 the party went through its latest metamorphosis, recreating itself as the **Hungarian Socialist Party** (MSzP) under a reformist leadership. The MSzP declared its commitment to a multi-party system and free market economy, marking its transformation into what Pozsgay called a new democratic socialist party in the European tradition. The MSzP voluntarily renounced most of the MSMP's assets. There was no attempt to ban ex-communist parties by the new post-communist regime. In the 1990 general election the MSzP came fourth with 10.89 per cent of the party list vote. Shortly after these elections Gyula Horn became MSzP leader. MSzP membership haemorrhaged, but by 1991 it had stabilised; the MSzP remained the largest and best organised of Hungary's parties. During four years in opposition Horn worked hard to present the MSzP as genuinely committed to democracy and the free market and technically the team most competent to govern Hungary. The MSzP returned to power in 1994, winning nearly a third of the vote and achieving a majority in the legislature. Having stressed the theme of national reconciliation and social justice in the general election campaign, the MSzP then formed a coalition with the liberal SzDSz. Divisions within the MSzP over the pace and extent of economic reform became apparent, with several ministers unwilling to implement drastic spending cuts.

The other successor party to the communists was the rump MSMP, backed by unreconstructed communists, which itself changed its name to the **Workers' Party** in December 1992. The party scored under 4 per cent of the vote in both 1990 and 1994, winning no seats in either election. The **National Democratic Federation** (NDSz), a centrist party formed by former leading reform communists Pozsgay and Zoltan Biro in September 1992, also failed to make a significant political impact.

Other parties

The fate of hardline leftist parties is outlined above, while right-wing extremism also met with indifference; in April 1993 anti-extremist legislation banned the wearing or display of Nazi or communist symbols.

The **Hungarian Democratic Forum** (MDF). Hungary's principal conservative party and the major force in the centre-right coalition which governed Hungary from 1990-94. The MDF was founded in September 1987 and officially constituted as a political party one year later. The MDF had at least three strands: populist-nationalist, Christian-democratic and liberal-democratic. Drawing its support principally from provincial and rural areas, the MDF achieved a dominant position in the 1990 elections and formed a coalition government with two other rightist parties, the FKgP and KDNP. Under MDF leader Jozsef Antall the government steered a broadly centre-right course. Elements in the nationalist-populist wing of the MDF soon became restive over the government's liberal economic policies and approach to post-communist justice issues (*see also Justice section*). In summer 1993 a breakaway group of ten deputies formed the nationalist right-wing Hungarian Justice and Life Party (MIEP--*see below*). The split left the MDF's centre-right leadership in a stronger position within the party, but facing growing unpopularity with the electorate. Despite four years of stability under the MDF-led government, many Hungarians regarded themselves as losers in the economic transition process, and the MDF was heavily defeated in the 1994 elections by the ex-communist MSzP. The party was punished for its poor communication of policy and its preoccupation with ideology. One example of this was its repeated attempt to curb what it regarded as the bias of the broadcast media (*see Media section*). The death of Antall in December 1993 also affected the result. The charismatic Lajos Fur, the Defence Minister in the Antall government, succeeded Antall as MDF leader and faced the difficult task of rallying the right-wing parties and effectively re-launching the MDF to a sceptical electorate.

Hungarian Justice and Life Party (MIEP). Hard-right nationalist party formed by disgruntled former MDF members in summer 1993. The MIEP leader Istvan Csurka was a former MDF vice president, whose political creed was a blend of aggressive nationalism, anti-Semitism, populism, and etatism, with emphasis on strong state control of the economy. In August 1992 Csurka had published a pamphlet alleging a conspiracy to undermine Hungary between MDF moderates, Jews, the IMF, liberals and the former communist elite. Having unsuccessfully challenged Antall for the MDF leadership in January 1993, Csurka left the MDF in summer 1993, anticipating his formal expulsion, and taking with him nine other deputies. The MIEP was crushed in the 1994 elections, winning less than 2 per cent of the vote.

The **Alliance of Free Democrats** (SzDSz). Liberal party in opposition from 1990-4 and in coalition with the MSzP from 1994. Founded in November 1988, by urban intellectuals from the dissident tradition, particularly liberals associated with the *samizdat* journal *Beszelo*. Among them was Janos Kis, who had been active as a critic and opponent of the Kadar regime since the mid-1970s, and who became SzDSz leader. The SzDSz's first assembly of delegates, in April 1989, adopted a radical programme of liberal and free market principles. Anticipating a triumph in the coming elections, the SzDSz became increasingly assertive in the latter stages of the 1989 round-table talks. The 1990 general election result came as a disappointment. Kis resigned in 1991, taking responsibility for declining party membership and the discouraging evidence of opinion polls. The party's leaders were widely regarded as well-meaning but remote intellectuals. The party leadership changed repeatedly over the following two years; the populist Peter Tolgyessy (1991-2) was too anti-communist while in contrast Istvan Peto (1992-3) was too zealous an advocate of cooperation with the MSzP. Gabor Kuncze became party leader in 1993 and marshalled support for the party, so that although it finished the 1994 elections with a reduced share of the vote, it was now placed second. The SzDSz leadership's decision to enter a coalition with the MSzP was accepted by the membership, illustrating the party's political pragmatism and distaste for dogma; SzDSz leaders negotiated a favourable coalition agreement giving the party an effective veto over the policy of the Horn government.

The **League of Young Democrats** (FIDESz). Minor centre-right party. The radical students who formed FIDESz in March 1988 imposed an age limit of 35 on party members. Although originally closely linked to the SzDSz the two parties gradually drifted apart. FIDESz's youthful image and proclaimed distaste for traditional politics helped it to achieve a surprise success in the general elections of 1990, winning nearly 9 per cent of the vote. The party's popularity grew in 1991-3, by which time opinion polls rated FIDESz as the clear front-runner in the coming election. In April 1993 the FIDESz congress reformed its "collective leadership", elected Viktor Orban as the new party chairman and abolished the age limit for party members. But by the end of 1993 divisions were apparent as several leading members protested that Orban was moving FIDESz too far to the right. The FIDESz leadership's strong anti-communist stance was subsequently blamed for the party's disappointing performance in the 1994 elections, when its share of the vote actually fell. Orban resigned but was re-elected as FIDESz chairman in July. FIDESz was renamed Fidesz-Hungarian Civic Party (Fidesz-MPP) in April 1995. It announced itself prepared to co-operate with the right in parliament.

The **Independent Smallholders' Party** (FKgP). Minor right-wing agrarian party which formed part of the conservative coalition in 1990-4 and then entered the opposition. The FKgP was reactivated in February 1988, claiming direct descent from the party of the same name which had been forced out of power in the immediate postwar period despite its success in the 1945 elections. The FKgP mounted virtually a single-issue campaign in 1990, demanding the restitution of property to its pre-1947 owners or the payment of compensation. The FKgP was also noted for its anti-communist stance. The FKgP emerged as the third largest party and obtained four cabinet posts in Antall's coalition government. FKgP leader Jozsef Torgyan proved to be a controversial figure, tainted by rumours of his alleged past association with the communist-era secret police. In February 1992 Torgyan unilaterally decided to withdraw from the coalition over the government's failure to restore property systematically to former owners. Only 11 of the FKgP's 44 deputies followed Torgyan in what was subsequently re-named the **Independent Smallholders' and Peasants'**

Party (also FKgP); most of the remainder continued to back the MDF-led government and eventually formed the **United Historical Smallholders' Party** (EKGP-TT) under Janos Szabo. Of the two parties, only Torgyan's won seats in 1994, taking just under 9 per cent of the vote.

ELECTIONS

Legislature

Under the communist regime candidates for the National Assembly were required to accept the programme of the official mass movement, the Patriotic People's Front (PPF), which was completely dominated by the MSMP. At the last such elections, in June 1985, voters were offered a choice of candidates under an electoral law passed in 1983.

The multi-party electoral system introduced under the law of 20 October 1989 contained highly complicated arrangements for electing the National Assembly (*Orszaggyules*) for its fixed four-year term. 176 members were elected in single-member constituencies, by overall majority in the first round or by simple majority in a second round run-off. The election of a further 210 members, by proportional representation, used a dual mechanism based on Hungary's 19 counties.

In elections on 25 March and 9 April 1990, the former communist MSzP was swept from power, winning less than 10 per cent of seats in the legislature. The MDF, with almost a quarter of the popular vote, won enough seats to dominate the parliament in coalition with other centre-right and conservative parties. Of the 43 registered parties, 28 took part in the election, 12 of them at national level.

In the election on 8 and 25 May 1994 the MDF vote plummeted while the MSzP won over half of the legislature's contested seats. The revival of the MSzP's electoral fortunes in the mid-1990s mirrored similar developments elsewhere in East-Central Europe.

| | March-April 1990 | | May 1994 | |
	%*	seats	%*	seats
MDF	24.71	164	11.73	37
SzDSz	21.38	92	19.76	70
FKgP	11.76	44	8.85	26
MSzP	10.89	33	32.96	209
FIDESz	8.94	21	7.00	20
KDNP	6.46	21	7.06	22
Agrarian association	3.15	1	2.10	1
Independents, others	12.71	10	10.64	1
**Reserved	n/a	8	n/a	8
Total	100.0	394	100.0	394

* Percentage of votes cast for party lists
** Fixed minority representation

MDF=Hungarian Democratic Forum; SzDSz=Alliance of Free Democrats; FKgP=Independent Smallholders' Party; MSzP=Hungarian Socialist Party; FIDESz=Federation of Young Democrats; KDNP=Christian Democratic People's Party.

Presidency

Under the communist regime the Assembly elected a figurehead national President. The proposal to change to direct presidential elections was overturned by a referendum on 26 November 1989. Arpad Goncz was proposed by the MDF and elected overwhelmingly by the Assembly on 2 May 1990 as interim President, having resigned his membership of the SzDSz. He was confirmed in office for a five-year term by an election in the Assembly on 3 August 1990, and elected for a second term on 19 June 1995. He had been proposed on this occasion by the MSzP and supported by the SzDSz, and attracted 259 votes, while Ferenc Madl, a former culture minister and law professor, won 76 votes, including the combined support of the MDF (Goncz's erstwhile allies), the KDNP and FIDESz-MPP.

CHRONOLOGY

9th Century. The Hungarian Kingdom is established by Magyars invading from the east.

1000. Stephen is crowned as the first Hungarian king and Hungary embraces Christianity. Over the next five centuries an empire evolves in alliance with Habsburg Austria against the Turks.

1867. The Dual Monarchy is created, giving Hungary formal autonomy within the Habsburg empire.

1914-18. Hungary participates in the First World War as an ally of Germany.

1919. A communist regime led by Bela Kun survives for six months before being ousted by Romanian troops. Kun is replaced by Adml. Horthy; in the ensuing "white terror" thousands of communists, intellectuals and entrepreneurs, including many Jews, are murdered.

1920. Treaty of Trianon: historic Hungary loses two thirds of its territory in the postwar settlement. Horthy becomes Regent (head of state). The Smallholders win elections.

1921. Count Istvan Bethlen begins a decade as Prime Minister, during which he combines political and social conservatism with state support for industry.

1932. Right-Radical leader Gyula Gombos become Prime Minister, introducing an increasingly fascist regime.

1936. Gombos dies, and Horthy engineers a retreat from full Nazism, but retains close links with Nazi Germany.

1938. The *Anschluss* makes Nazi Germany a direct neighbour. Hungary introduces anti-Semitic laws.

1938-41. Hungary is re-assigned territory from Slovakia, Romania and Ruthenia and, in November 1940, formally allies itself with the Axis powers. Hungarian troops participate in the German invasion of Yugoslavia, reclaiming further territory from Serbia, and in the German invasion of the Soviet Union.

18-19 March 1944. Germany occupies Hungary.

15 October 1944. Horthy signs an armistice treaty with the Soviet Union, whose forces are poised to invade Hungary. He is arrested by the Germans and replaced by Ferenc Szalasi, leader of the pro-Nazi Arrow Cross movement.

December 1944. Formation in Soviet-liberated Debrecen of a broad-based anti-fascist provisional government.

February 1945. Liberation of Budapest by the Red Army, which by 4 April has driven the last German troops out of the country.

March 1945. A land reform act expropriates the feudal estates which had hitherto accounted for the greater part of the nation's land.

November 1945. General elections, in which the Smallholders emerge as by far the largest party in the parliament, with 245 out of 409 elective seats, and head a broad coalition government.

June 1947. Smallholder prime minister Ferenc Nagy leaves the country, as the most prominent victim of `salami tactics' under which the communist party eliminates its opponents one by one.

August 1947. The Communists emerge as the largest single party in Hungary's second post-war general election.

June 1948. The Social Democrats are forcibly merged with the Communists to form the Hungarian Workers' Party (MMP).

May 1949. The third post-war general election completes the communist takeover, as a single list is put forward by the People's Independence Front, a communist-dominated bloc with four smaller participating parties. The minor parties in the Front are effectively eliminated by 1954, when the Front is renamed the People's Patriotic Front.

1949. Hungary becomes a People's Republic under its new Constitution.

1949. The "Muscovite" (pro-Soviet) party general secretary Matyas Rakosi purges Laszlo Rajk from the top leadership as a `Titoist', replacing him as interior minister by Janos Kadar. Rajk is executed on 15 October. In 1950-51 Kadar in turn is dismissed, then purged and imprisoned.

July 1953. Following Stalin's death, Rakosi's rival Imre Nagy becomes premier with the support of the new Soviet leadership; Nagy's `New Course' reduces political terror and political prisoners are released, while peasants may gain permission to leave collective farms, and workers' conditions are improved.

1955 Rakosi condemns Nagy as a `right deviationist' and deposes him, reinstituting an increasingly unpopular hardline regime.

February 1956. Following Khrushchev's denunciation of Stalin, Rajk is posthumously rehabilitated.

18 July 1956. Rakosi surrenders the party leadership to Erno Gero.

6 October 1956. Some 200,000 people attend the re-burial of Rajk's corpse, in a demonstration against Stalinism and in favour of Titoism and democratisation.

23 October 1956. A student-led demonstration in Budapest, inspired by the loosening of Soviet control over Polish affairs, demands the reinstatement of Imre Nagy and the withdrawal of Soviet forces. The demonstration becomes a popular uprising; the militia's vain attempt to control the protests is overwhelmed despite the arrival of Soviet tank support. A revolution appears to be developing as the Soviet authorities withdraw their tanks.

24-25 October 1956. Nagy becomes prime minister again, with Kadar as first secretary. The party is soon reformed as the Hungarian Socialist Workers' Party (MSMP). Nagy announces the disbanding of the hated secret police, authorises the restoration of multi-party democracy and, on 1 November, announces that Hungary is to leave the Warsaw Pact.

30 October 1956. Nagy forms a multi-party government.

4 November 1956. The Soviet Army crushes the Hungarian uprising, launching a massive tank offensive against violent resistance particularly in Budapest. Nagy is arrested, and Kadar is chosen by the Soviet leadership to re-establish communist control. Casualty figures vary from 2,500 to 60,000 killed.

16 June 1958. Imre Nagy is executed in the Soviet Union for treason, along with his defence minister Pal Maleter and two others, after a major show trial.

1961. After five years of repressive "normalisation" Kadar moves towards policies of national reconciliation, on the basis of his 1959 statement to the party congress that 'whoever is not against us is with us'.

January 1968. The Kadar regime introduces the 'New Economic Mechanism' (NEM), an attempt to combine elements of a market economy with central planning.

August 1968. Hungarian forces participate in the suppression of Czechoslovakia's 'Prague Spring'.

12 November 1968. The Soviet party leader Leonid Brezhnev, speaking at the PZPR congress in Warsaw, presents the Brezhnev doctrine, an ideological justification for the armed interventions in Hungary in 1956 and in Czechoslovakia in 1968. Under the doctrine, socialist states are declared to have limited sovereignty, and under extraordinary circumstances they have an "internationalist obligation" to intervene in each other's affairs.

November 1972. The party central committee signals a retreat from the market economy experiments of the NEM, by returning to a policy of subsidising uneconomic enterprises. The ensuing increase in centrally-disbursed subsidies is so rapid that the regime recognises in 1979 the necessity to control it.

1977. The underground democratic opposition begins to organise. *Samizdat* publications increase, especially after 1982.

1983. Kadar declares that there will be "no reform of the reform".

March 1985. Mikhail Gorbachev becomes general secretary of the Soviet communist party.

June 1985. Parliamentary elections are held, offering voters a choice of candidates under a 1983 law; many independent candidates voice support for democracy and human rights.

1985. Figures from both the reform wing of the party and the democratic opposition combine to publish the *Social Charter* in the *samizdat* journal *Beszelo*, advocating "constitutional communism" or a system of checks and balances to restrain the power of the party, and calling for the resignation of Kadar.

15 March 1986. Several thousand people in Budapest mark the anniversary of the 1956 uprising, and police break up a demonstration on a bridge over the Danube; student-led pro-democracy marches thereafter become an annual event.

November 1986. The Writers' Union Congress repudiates party control and asserts that the deteriorating situation in Hungary is of concern to all responsible intellectuals.

November 1986. Influential economists issue a call for radical change in the document *Turning-point and Reform*.

September 1987. Reformers within the party, led by Imre Pozsgay, participate in a meeting at Lakitelek near Budapest organised by one of the proliferating discussion groups which marks the emergence of a strongly populist current of opposition.

30 March 1988. The Federation of Young Democrats (FIDESz) is formed as a student group independent of the official Communist Youth Union.

May 1988. Kadar is replaced as general secretary of the MSMP by Premier Karoly Grosz; the special party conference also replaces the majority of the politburo.

3 September 1988. The populists, having effectively taken the political initiative, formally constitute the Hungarian Democratic Forum (MDF) as a conservative opposition movement at Lakitelek.

12 September 1988. Environmentalists mount a demonstration of some 30,000 people in Budapest against the grandiose Gabcikovo-Nagymaros power scheme. The Hungarian government orders the suspension of work on the Nagymaros dam in May 1989.

13 November 1988. The liberal Alliance of Free Democrats (SzDSz) is formally constituted as a political party.

11 January 1989. Parliament passes a law allowing the formation of independent political parties. The MSMP on 11 February votes in favour of the establishment of a multi-party system.

28 January 1989. Pozsgay leaks the controversial finding of a party historical commission under his chairmanship, describing the events of 1956 as a "popular uprising...against an oligarchic system of power which had humiliated the nation".

5 April 1989. In a new departure in Central-Eastern Europe, the round table talks in Poland end with the announcement of partially free, multi-party elections.

2 May 1989. Hungary begins the dismantling of the fences along its Austrian border, the first step in tearing down the `Iron Curtain'.

16 June 1989. The remains of Imre Nagy and other leaders of the 1956 uprising are given a state funeral.

6-18 June 1989. The communists are heavily defeated in the Polish elections.

6 July 1989. The death of Kadar coincides with the full legal rehabilitation of Nagy.

July 1989. Gorbachev addresses an assembly of Warsaw Pact leaders in Bucharest to renounce the Brezhnev doctrine.

22 July 1989. A joint opposition candidate wins a parliamentary by-election, the first time an opposition deputy has been elected since 1947.

22 August 1989. Effectively acknowledging the power struggle within the party, Karoly Grosz announces his intention to step down as MSMP general secretary.

11 September 1989. Hungary lifts the restrictions on travel by East Germans enforceable under a 20-year-old bilateral East German-Hungarian treaty, thereby allowing thousands to pass through the country as an escape route to the West. This action, effectively breaking ranks with the rest of the communist bloc over freedom of travel, is denounced by East Germany but, significantly, the Soviet Union describes it only as "a very unusual step".

18 September 1989. Round table talks between the MSMP, the opposition groups and communist-led social organisations, end in agreement on the framework for introducing multi-party democracy. The MDF signs, while the more radical opposition SzDSz and FIDESz refuse.

6-10 October 1989. The MSMP holds its historic 14th extraordinary congress, reconstituting itself as the Hungarian Socialist Party (MSzP), electing moderate reformer Reszo Nyers as party president, and backing Pozsgay as its candidate for the state presidency.

17-23 October 1989. Parliament approves the introduction of a multi-party democratic system and renounces Hungary's "people's republic" status.

9 November 1989. The Berlin wall is breached, marking the symbolic end of Soviet domination of the "satellite states".

21 December 1989. Parliament votes to dissolve itself in March 1990 to make way for multi-party elections.

1 January 1990. A new Constitutional Court formally begins to operate.

21 January 1990. The government orders the disbanding of the State Security Service after opposition parties reveal evidence that it has been continuing its covert surveillance of their activities.

10 March 1990. An agreement is signed with the Soviet Union on the withdrawal by July 1991 of the 52,000 Soviet troops based in Hungary.

14 March 1990. The IMF announces approval of a standby credit agreement to support Hungary's emergency economic plan for 1990.

25 March and 8 April 1990. Multi-party elections are held, marking the defeat of the MSzP and the victory of the opposition parties, particularly the MDF.

6 May 1990. Antall announces the formation of a cabinet led by the MDF and including the right-wing Independent Smallholders (FKgP), the Christian Democratic People's Party (KDNP) and non-party technocrats.

29 July 1990. A referendum, proposed by the MSzP, attracts a negligible turnout and therefore fails to institute a system of direct presidential elections.

3 August 1990. Parliament elects the SzDSz's Arpad Goncz as Hungarian President.

18 September 1990. Parliament approves a privatisation programme.

3 October 1990. The Supreme Court rules that the government's plans to return confiscated land to its pre-1947 owners, as demanded by the Smallholders' Party, are unconstitutional.

26-28 October 1990. A steep fuel price increase prompts a strike and blockade of Budapest streets by taxi drivers; the government backs down and halves the increase.

20 December 1990. Cabinet changes reflect government disagreements about the speed of economic change to a free-market economy.

30 December 1990. A controversial austerity budget for 1991 is passed after prolonged argument; it cuts subsidies, removes many price controls, and continues privatisation measures, while striving to avoid the "shock treatment" approach by retaining generous social services and welfare provision.

15 February 1991. Antall hosts a meeting with the Czechoslovak and Polish presidents which declares the three countries' "total integration into the European political, economic, security and legislative order".

24 April 1991. The National Assembly approves legislation on compensation for land and property expropriated under the communist regime since June 1949; former owners are to be given vouchers to buy into the government's privatisation programme.

29 May and 26 June 1991. The Constitutional Court rules that the legislation on compensation for expropriated property is unconstitutional; the Assembly then passes a modified law, lowering the ceiling for compensation but extending its applicability to expropriations dating back to May 1939.

9 June 1991. The last Soviet soldier leaves Hungary, but disputes continue about the cost of environmental damage caused by Soviet troops since the 1956 uprising.

26 June 1991. Passage of legislation designed to partially compensate some 1.5 million people whose property, or that of their relatives, had been expropriated since 1939.

28 June 1991. The nine-member Comecon organisation is formally dissolved at a meeting in Budapest.

1 July 1991. The Warsaw Treaty Organisation or Warsaw Pact is formally dissolved.

31 October 1991. A law is passed to compensate those imprisoned or deported for political reasons between 1939 and 1989, and to compensate the families of those executed.

4 November 1991. Parliament passes legislation to allow murder and treason charges against those responsible for crimes under the communist regime. The constitutional court rules on 3 March 1992 that the legislation is retroactive and therefore unconstitutional.

16 December 1991. Hungary, together with Czechoslovakia and Poland, signs association agreements with the European Community, providing for the introduction of free trade over a ten-year period.

11 February 1992. The last remaining restrictions on food prices are lifted.

19 February 1991. Legislation quashes sentences imposed by the communist regime for "crimes against the state".

5 May 1992. The second phase of the privatisation programme is launched.

28 August 1992. The government announces that state firms in strategic sectors will remain under state control.

10-11 November 1992. Russian President Boris Yeltsin visits Hungary; he condemns the 1956 Soviet invasion and visits the grave of Nagy. The two sides strike an agreement to cancel mutual claims for compensation over Russian military bases in Hungary.

17 December 1992. Legislation imposes strict criteria for allowing abortions.

6 January 1993. The presidents of state radio and TV resign alleging an attempt by the MDF to control the broadcast media.

14 April 1993. Parliament bans the use of extremist political symbols.

21 June 1993. Hard-right nationalist Csurka leaves the MDF to form the Hungarian Justice Party (MIP).

7 July 1993. A law on minority rights protects national and ethnic groups; guarantees such groups education in their mother tongue; and establishes cultural and heritage organisations and "local and national self-governments".

6 October 1993. Antall is hospitalised for the treatment of cancer; Interior Minister Boross becomes acting Prime Minister.

19 October 1993. Parliament approves legislation lifting the statute of limitations in the case of war crimes or crimes against humanity. The legislation is designed to facilitate the prosecution of those responsible for atrocities in 1956.

12 December 1993. Antall dies. Boross formally succeeds him on 21 December.

4 March 1994. Over 100 journalists are dismissed from state radio, just weeks before parliamentary elections. Mass protests follow.

8 March 1994. Parliament passes legislation under which high ranking officials are to be screened for collaboration with the communist-era secret police or involvement in suppressing the 1956 uprising. The law applies to MPs, ministers, senior civil servants, other public officials and senior journalists. Opposition politicians claim the law is designed to affect the outcome of elections.

8-29 May 1994. Parliamentary elections. The MDF is beaten into third place by the MSzP, which almost triples its share of the vote over 1990. The SzDSz finishes second. The campaign is marked by controversy over allegations made in the state broadcast media that during the 1956 revolution MSzP leader Gyula Horn personally beat rebel prisoners. The MSzP campaign, in contrast to the MDF's, stresses national reconciliation and competence.

24 June 1994. The MSzP and SzDSz strike a coalition deal which gives the latter only three cabinet posts but an effective veto on cabinet decisions. The two parties together

control more than the two thirds of seats in the parliament necessary for passing constitutional legislation.

15 July 1994. Formation of the MSzP-SzDSz coalition cabinet under prime minister Horn.

18 October 1994. A supplementary budget introduces austerity measures designed to arrest the growth of the budget deficit.

29 January 1995. Finance Minster Laszlo Bekesi resigns, citing Horn's alleged reluctance to implement pro-market reforms.

31 January 1995. Two former militiamen are convicted of crimes against humanity for their part in the massacre of civilian demonstrators on the town of Salgortarjan in 1956.

12 March 1995. The government introduces a second austerity package, known as the stabilisation programme.

9 May 1995. A new law is designed to hasten privatisation and takes preparatory steps toward the sale of public utilities.

22 May 1995. Goncz is re-elected as president for a further five-year term by the parliament, having been formally nominated by the MSzP.

30 June, 13 September and 23 November 1995. In separate rulings the constitutional Court declares unconstitutional elements of the March stabilisation programme.

1 December 1995. Labour Minister Magda Kosa Kovacs resigns in protest at social security cuts proposed in the stabilisation programme.

December 1995. The first scale large privatisation proceeds with the sale of the energy sector.

21 December 1995. Approval of a long-delayed media bill establishing a new mechanism for supervision of the broadcast media.

CZECHOSLOVAKIA

The country's official name was the Czechoslovak Socialist Republic (*Ceskoslovenska Socialisticka Republika*) from July 1960, a nominal federation comprising the Czech and Slovak Republics. It was renamed after the 1989 revolution, becoming the Czech and Slovak Federative Republic on 20 April, 1990. The federation was dissolved on 1 January 1993, to create two independent states, the Czech Republic and the Slovak Republic.

A land-locked country in central Europe, Czechoslovakia covered a total area of 127,881 sq. km (somewhat smaller than East Germany), of which the Czech Lands comprised nearly 79,000 sq. km and Slovakia just over 49,000. The Czechoslovak population was some 15,600,000, about two thirds of whom lived in the Czech Republic.

The Czech Republic comprises the historic Czech Lands of Bohemia and Moravia. In the west and north the mountains of the Bohemian Massif form an imposing natural frontier. Fertile lowlands constitute much of the remainder of the Czech lands. Slovakia is a mountainous region dominated by the north-western portion of the Carpathian Mountains; in the south are lowlands along the Danube. The eastern province of Ruthenia was ceded to the Soviet Union after the Second World War.

Pre-war Czechoslovakia was flanked by Germany to the north and west, Poland in the north-east, Romania, Hungary and Austria in the south. Post-war, it had borders with East Germany, West Germany, East Germany, Poland, Soviet Ukraine, Austria and Hungary. Prague (Praha), the federal and Czech capital, is by far the largest city in either republic; its population of at least 1,200,000 is about three times that of the Slovak capital Bratislava. Other main towns are: in the Czech Republic, Ostrava and the Moravian city of Brno; in Slovakia, the eastern city of Kosice. Three quarters of the Czechoslovak population was defined as urban, with the concentration of towns and cities in the Western and northern Czech lands, while Slovakia remained to a significant extent an agrarian society.

In ethnic terms the Czechoslovakia founded in 1918 was the most heterogeneous of the new states of Central and Eastern Europe. Almost a quarter of the population were German-speakers concentrated in the mountainous border areas contiguous with Germany. Of the 8.8 million people (65 per cent of the total) described in the 1921 census as "Czechoslovaks" by mother tongue (both Czechs and Slovaks groups spoke related West Slavic languages), probably less than a quarter were Slovaks. There were also communities of Hungarians (6 per cent, predominantly in southern Slovakia), Ruthenians (3 per cent, mainly in eastern Slovakia) and Jews (3 per cent). Most of the Jews perished in the Nazi holocaust. After the Second World War virtually all German-speakers were expelled from the country and Ruthenia was ceded to the Soviet Union.

By 1991 Czechs comprised some 63 per cent of the population, Slovaks about 31 per cent. There were 600,000 ethnic Hungarians, mostly concentrated in southern Slovakia; between 300,000 and 500,000 Romanies (gypsies), up to two thirds of whom were based in Slovakia; small minorities of remaining Germans and Poles, and some Ukrainians (Ruthenians) in eastern Slovakia.

The Roman Catholic Church is by far the largest denomination in Slovakia. It is also the principal church in the Czech Republic, but the Czechs have in addition a strong tradition of non-conformism and secularism; Czechoslovakia's population thus included 400,000 Hussites, most of them living in what is now the Czech Republic.

HISTORICAL NARRATIVE

The first Czech sovereign state was the medieval Kingdom of Bohemia. The Kingdom was bounded by clear natural frontiers; its subjects shared a distinct Slavic identity which contrasted with the surrounding German communities. The Czech state came to an end with defeat by Austria-Hungary at the Battle of the White Mountain in 1620.

Administered for the next three centuries within the relatively enlightened Austrian portion of the Habsburg Empire, which set up an efficient although largely German-staffed bureaucracy, the Czech Lands became the most economically developed part of that Empire. By the late nineteenth century Czech society had developed along West European lines, becoming relatively complex and sophisticated. In this period there was a surge of interest in the history, language, traditions and culture of the Czechs, inspired by a new wave of Czech writers and composers. Czechs of all classes increasingly regarded themselves as a nation. This national identity drew on the legacy of the 15th century Hussite rebellion, which had established a tradition of anticlericalism, modernism and secularism.

Slovakia, in contrast, had no history of sovereignty, having for centuries formed part of the Kingdom of Hungary. The Hungarian portion of the Habsburg Empire was both more authoritarian and more reactionary. Its rigid structure had changed little over the centuries, and Slovaks had remained a poor, religious, ill-educated and largely agrarian people in awe of their Hungarian masters. Upwardly-mobile Slovaks tended to become assimilated into the Hungarian elite. Most Slovak peasants had little national consciousness. By the nineteenth century elements in the small Slovak intelligentsia began to discuss Slovak ethnic identity, and some became pan-Slavists. Tomas

Masaryk, a Moravian Slovak, opposed pan-Slavism, but began to argue late in the century that linguistic similarities in particular made Czechs and Slovaks kindred peoples. Masaryk demanded the establishment of an autonomous, Western-oriented union of Czechs and Slovaks within the Habsburg Empire.

During the latter stages of the First World War, as the collapse of the Habsburg Empire became imminent, Masaryk and his supporters began to urge the Western allies to back the creation of a Czechoslovak state. Despite the lack of support in Slovakia for the concept of a Czechoslovak nation, his arguments were accepted.

The new state was geographically rational, being a central area of lowlands protected on three sides by mountains, and with Slovakia representing a considerable eastern hinterland of mountainous and forested territory. Its longest continuous frontier was with Germany in the north and west.

Democracy in interwar Czechoslovakia is widely regarded as having been the most stable and effective in a volatile region, due largely to the relatively sophisticated political culture of the Czech Lands and to Slovak intellectual leaders. Civil rights were respected and the constitution upheld. Masaryk, the president for 16 years, was held in high regard and was an important unifying figure until 1935, when he stepped down in favour of his disciple Eduard Benes.

Czechoslovakia's central problem was its ethnic heterogeneity. Czechs constituted only about a half of the population and Slovaks probably little more than 15 per cent (although their share of the population subsequently increased with a markedly higher birth rate), while ethnic Germans, mainly in the Sudetenland, comprised some 25 per cent. The concentration of minorities in border areas discouraged recourse to arrangements allowing them real autonomy, and not only Germans but Slovaks too were resentful of this, although most Slovaks did approve of Slovakia's having been separated from Hungary

Despite the investment of considerable Czech resources in improving education, bureaucracy and communications in Slovakia, many Slovaks came to regard the new Czech elite as parasitical. Slovakia suffered particularly severely during the depression of the early 1930s and the economic gap between the Czech lands and Slovakia actually widened. The Slovak Populist Party provided a focus for Slovak discontent, becoming increasingly radical in arguing for Slovak links to Nazi Germany and eventually advocating full Slovak independence. Meanwhile the German minority also radicalised, as demonstrated by the strong support for the Nazi Henleinist party in 1935.

The *Anschluss* unifying Nazi Germany and Austria in 1938 left the Czech lands surrounded on three sides by the hostile forces of Hitler's Reich. The capitulation of the Western allies to Hitler's demands at Munich in 1938 and the subsequent German annexation of the Sudetenland brought to a close the first chapter of Czechoslovak history. Czechoslovakia was dismembered, with the economic muscle of the Czech economy being harnessed for the German war effort and Slovakia gaining notional independence for the first time, although clerical fascist leader Jozef Tiso was widely regarded as a Nazi puppet. The Slovak Populists participated in the regime.

Post-war Czechoslovakia - The communists in power

Czechoslovakia emerged from the Second World War having incurred relatively little material damage compared to neighbouring Poland, partly because of the decision not to resist the Nazis (although there was an unsuccessful Slovak rebellion in August-October 1944 and a Prague Uprising in May 1945). It was principally the Red Army which liberated Czechoslovakia, although the US army entered the country from the West to liberate Plzen. Within six months both Soviet and US troops had withdrawn. The German minority was expelled in 1945-6, but similar plans for the Hungarian minority were not fully implemented.

Before the war ended, Benes, the leader of the London-based government-in-exile, had met Klement Gottwald, the leader of the Czechoslovak Communist Party (KSC), to drive a bargain in establishing the programme for a coalition National Front government. Gottwald had secured a favourable deal. The programme included commitments to nationalise key industries and finance, and to expand welfare provision, as well as to adopt a Soviet-oriented foreign policy. In postwar territorial changes the Soviet Union gained a common border with Czechoslovakia for the first time, Carpathian Ruthenia being ceded to Soviet Ukraine.

At the time of the general elections in May 1946, the stock of the Communists was riding high; they won 38 per cent of the vote, doing particularly well in the more industrialised Czech lands, and became the largest party. Elsewhere in Central and Eastern Europe communist successes at the polls were influenced by Soviet occupation and strong-arm tactics. In the case of Czechoslovakia the polls were peaceful. Instead the communist success reflected the fact that the Western liberal democracies had betrayed the country in 1938, whereas the Soviet Union had liberated it in 1945. Moreover, despite its proscription during the war years, the KSC was the strongest communist party in Europe with the exception of the Soviet party, and attracted considerable support from the Czech Lands' sizeable industrial proletariat. More widely, the communist success reflected what Benes himself identified as a European tide running towards socialism, which flowed from the retrospective judgment that the depression of the 1930s had discredited liberal capitalism, from the experiences of the war and from the need for state intervention to repair shattered economies.

Following the communist election victory Gottwald became prime minister. When friction grew in the Communist-led coalition, and non-communist ministers threatened to resign as a group, Moscow precipitated the February 1948 "Prague coup", in which the communists seized all power.

Gottwald, who took over from Benes as President after single-list elections in June 1948, introduced a hardline Stalinist regime. Surviving political parties were reduced to mere ciphers within a subservient National Front, and a new constitution defined the country as a people's democracy. Gottwald used show trials, purges and executions to tighten his grip on the KSC in the early 1950s; party members were charged with bourgeois nationalism (particularly Slovaks), and with Titoism, Trotskyism and treason; Zionism was added to the charge sheet for dealing with the party's Jewish intellectuals.

Gottwald's death in March 1953, just days after that of his mentor Stalin, did not mark a change of direction. Although Gottwald's successor Antonin Novotny repudiated the Gottwald personality cult, he resisted de-stalinisation until well into the 1960s.

Novotny's major achievement was the completion of agricultural collectivisation in the late 1950s. A new, Soviet-style constitution introduced in 1960 adopted the title Socialist Republic, thus claiming to have advanced further in building socialism than the rest of Central and Eastern Europe.

The "Prague Spring" of 1968 - Clampdown and "normalisation"

Czechoslovakia's 20-year experience of Stalinism, which was peculiarly ill-suited to a country with strong liberal and democratic roots, made the "Prague Spring" seem a particularly attractive alternative. Economic stagnation prompted the beginnings of reform in the mid-1960s. Reform gathered pace from 1967, as economist Ota Sik's "socialist market economy" inspired economic decentralisation.

Throughout the postwar period Slovak communists had been growing increasingly dissatisfied over the centralisation of power in Prague. As a concession to Slovak opinion, the hitherto low-profile Slovak communist leader Aleksander Dubcek was chosen to replace Novotny as KSC first secretary in January 1968. (Ironically, the one significant reform to survive Dubcek was the introduction of a federal system, with devolution of powers to Czech and Slovak republican governments.)

Dubcek's receptiveness to liberal reforms encouraged excitement to spread about a "third way", market socialism in conditions of political pluralism and greater individual freedom. The loosening of press controls in the Prague Spring of 1968 stimulated an energetic public debate on reform, the heady prospect of what Dubcek dubbed "socialism with a human face" inspiring Czechs and Slovaks alike beyond the limits of cautious prudence.

Fearing popular pressure to concede similar reforms, the Soviet regime and most of the Warsaw Pact allies saw the Czechoslovak experiment as potentially destabilising. Their usually effective warning, military manoeuvres, went unheeded in June, and in August the tanks arrived in Prague.

"Normalisation" began in earnest with Dubcek's April 1969 replacement as KSC first secretary by Husak. Most of the reforms of the Prague Spring were reversed. Normalisation offered a carrot and a stick: higher living standards, but no tolerance of dissent. Normalisation imposed a rigid orthodoxy; dissident opponents were vengefully pursued and humiliated. Its leaders persisted in the falsehood that the crackdown had been necessary to "save socialism" rather than to protect Soviet geopolitical interests.

Despite the harassment, dissidents continued to organise and publish underground literature. Vaclav Havel and several prominent figures from the Prague Spring were among the signatories to Charter 77, which attracted international attention to the civil rights abuses in the country.

With economic stagnation setting in during the early 1980s, normalisation began slowly to unravel. Czechoslovakia's relative consumer affluence had been achieved only by ruthless exploitation of the country's natural resources, with little thought to the long-term consequences, not least environmental costs. With the resources thus generated ploughed straight back into consumer goods, little was invested in restructuring the country's outmoded industrial base. By the second half of the 1980s, Czechoslovakia had begun to borrow abroad - not as heavily as Poland and Hungary, but with increasing urgency as trade within Comecon became more problematic.

A limited version of Gorbachev's perestroika, notably featuring the increased devolution of managerial powers, was attempted from 1987. There was however no accompanying Czechoslovak version of *glasnost*. Any admission of criticism was bound to mean giving expression to critics of the 1968 invasion. The KSC's ageing hardline leaders could not themselves recant on the invasion as so many of them had been personally implicated. By 1989 the threat hung over these figures that the Soviet Union would rehabilitate the Prague Spring and condemn the invasion.

The "velvet revolution"

Within the KSC in 1989 there were some figures apparently open to reform ideas; Adamec, the prime minister since October 1988, was the most prominent of these, but was in a minority. Milos Jakes, the KSC general secretary since December 1987, represented stagnation not change in the leadership, since Jakes had been a key figure in "normalisation". Others, such as Prague party chief Miroslav Stepan, were thought prepared to use force to crush the opposition, as the Chinese did at Tiananmen Square in June 1989.

The opposition, launched on its mass defiance by huge popular protests against police repression on 17 November 1989, showed skill in using the network of contacts built up from the start of Charter 77, and in negotiating at the highest political level, despite having very little experience to call on. They also showed courage in the face of the danger of a violent crackdown. In this they were of course encouraged by Gorbachev's renunciation of the Brezhnev doctrine in June, and the gathering revolution in East Germany, which had led to the breach of the Berlin Wall on 9 November. The signs were that the Soviet Union would not intervene to protect the hardliners in Czechoslovakia.

Conspiracy theorists have pointed to evidence that Soviet intelligence actually encouraged the police brutality on 17 November. These theorists argue that the object was to provoke opposition protests leading to the removal of the hardline leadership and its replacement by a new communist elite of younger reformers. Gorbachev had, after all, apparently connived in the "palace coup" to topple Zhivkov in Bulgaria the week before. However, the Czechoslovak opposition proved too tenacious to settle for minor change, with huge protests greeting Adamec's proposal on 3 December of a new communist-dominated government. A crucial factor was the massive support of workers for the "velvet revolution", as shown in a two-hour general strike on 27 November. Although the protest rallies in Prague in the preceding ten days had been attended by hundreds of thousands of people, and not all of the protesters were the intellectuals, students, artists and actors who had formed the opposition's core for years, it was this strike which gave opposition leaders the direct evidence that working people stood with them.

The "velvet revolution" was brief, euphoric, and quite remarkably thorough in levering the communists from power. Before the end of 1989 a non-communist government under Marian Calfa was in office and Havel, a former dissident, had been installed as head of state. Within seven months the Soviet Union had agreed to withdraw all troops, free and democratic elections had been held, the communist-era secret police had been abolished, and legislation guaranteeing civil rights had been approved; by March 1992 Czechoslovakia had become the first ex-communist state in Central and Eastern Europe to ratify the European Convention on Human Rights.

The victory of the former dissident Civic Forum (OF) and its Slovak counterpart Public Against Violence (VPN) in the elections of summer 1990 marked the vanquishing of the communist party. Uniquely in the region, the party remained relatively conservative, even opting to retain its name.

Meanwhile, the post-communist government emphasised a return to Czechoslovakia's pre-war status as a Western-oriented European democracy. As the old communist-bloc economic and security organisations wound up, so Czechoslovakia forged new links with Western-oriented institutions such as the Council of Europe, the EC and NATO. Havel promoted Czechoslovak interests vigorously in a flurry of state visits, capitalising on his country's excellent new international.

Economic reform in Czechoslovakia initially proceeded at a cautious pace. The reforms, masterminded by the radical former banker Vaclav Klaus gathered momentum only with the launch of mass privatisation in 1991-2. This programme was designed to transform ownership rapidly, whilst at the same time giving the largest possible number of people a stake in the process.

The secession issue - Elections in 1992

The broad opposition movements of 1989 had split by 1991, largely over the pace of economic reform. Also of significance was the emergence of a Slovak populist strand in the VPN, led by Meciar, which had become increasingly nationalistic. The Slovak parliament in October 1990 passed a law making Slovak the republic's official language, and in December 1990 the Slovaks secured increased autonomy under a power-sharing law, but a comprehensive constitutional package had yet to be agreed.

In March 1991 the leaders of the principal Czech and Slovak parties agreed that the two republics should combine voluntarily in a federative state. Slovak leaders, meanwhile, began to argue for a voluntary union between sovereign republics, with any federal entity established only by a treaty between them. Slovak Prime Minister Meciar's growing nationalism contributed to his ousting as Slovak Prime Minister in spring 1991, but with the subsequent establishment of his Movement for a Democratic Slovakia (HZDS), the campaign for Slovak sovereignty gathered pace.

In July a federal law permitted either a republican parliament or the Federal Assembly to order a referendum on secession, but by autumn 1991 the talks over constitutional change were deadlocked. Havel suggested a compromise package of constitutional amendments, including (i) the reform of the second chamber of the Federal Assembly to comprise deputies from the republican parliaments; (ii) a republican veto on constitutional proposals; and (iii) a presidential power to call referendums on the constitution. Havel's proposals failed to find favour and were rejected by the Federal Assembly in early 1992.

As parliamentary elections loomed in mid-1992, it became clear that the political situation in each of the republics was polarising. In the Czech Republic the former dissident leaders of the OF were losing ground to technocrats, like Klaus, who favoured liberal economic policies. In Slovakia populist leaders like Meciar backed continued state support for industry. This polarisation reflected the contrasting economic situation in the two republics. While unemployment in both fell in 1992, the Slovak rate was some three times higher at some 12 per cent. Slovaks feared that the federal privatisation programme, the first round of which got under way in 1992, was ill-suited to the Slovak economy, and suspected that Czech leaders paid scant regard to Slovak interests in framing economic reforms. They noted the disparity in economic investment: by 1992 the Czechs had attracted more than three quarters of foreign funds coming into the country.

Even before the elections, on 7 May 1992, the Slovak National Council voted for a declaration of sovereignty, but the majority fell short of the necessary three-fifths.

The election results confirmed the emergence of antagonistic political forces in the Czech and Slovak Republics. In the Czech Republic Klaus's right-wing conservative ODS was the clear winner; Slovaks, in contrast, chose the HZDS on the strength of a campaign which had promised Slovak sovereignty and prosperity through state intervention.

Despite seven decades of unity, and the uniformity imposed by more than four decades of communist rule, historical factors had bequeathed the Czechs and Slovaks significantly different political cultures. These factors were rooted both in the differing experiences of empire and in the interwar period. The Czechs' historic tolerance of dissent and approbation of bargaining and compromise, respect for the law, and their faith in the market as the principal generator of wealth, placed them firmly in the mainstream of Western European political culture. Slovaks, on the other hand, demonstrated support for strong, charismatic leaders; a dominant role for the state, particularly in the economy; and a vigorous assertion of Slovak national interests in the face of perceived threats from neighbours and minorities.

The 1992 elections effectively gave the Slovak nationalist parties a veto on decisions taken at both Slovak republican and federal levels. It became clear that a viable governing coalition at federal level was unlikely.

Czech leaders quickly grasped the historical momentum behind Slovak independence. Rather than seek to save the federation in a weakened form, Klaus chose to negotiate for the best possible terms for a dissolution of the federation. He therefore rejected as impractical Slovak suggestions of a monetary and defence union, and even derided an HZDS proposal for confederation as "a joke". Klaus's tough tone in the talks took Meciar aback, and he appeared to suffer a loss of nerve over independence in August 1992, musing publicly that Slovakia was unready to bear the economic costs, including the sudden cessation of Czech subsidies. But by autumn 1992 the two republics had signed more than 30 draft treaties governing their relations after dissolution, including a customs union, treaties on the freedom of movement between the two republics, and on common borders and defence cooperation.

The "velvet divorce", whereby the country was divided peacefully and legally into two republics, was virtually without historical precedent. The orderly nature of the partition was disturbed only by Slovak churlishness in refusing to support the re-election of Havel, a prominent federalist, to serve as federal president until dissolution.

Havel continued to support the federation in principle but recognised that with the leaders of virtually all the main parties opposed, dissolution was inevitable. Ironically, opinion polls continued to show that a majority of both Czechs and Slovaks also favoured the preservation of the union in some form.

ECONOMY

The gap in economic performance between the Czech and Slovak republics widened in the last three years of the federation. Although both republics faced a sharp recession, unemployment and inflation were both higher in Slovakia, while the Czech economy showed earlier signs of recovery, having attracted considerably more foreign investment, particularly from Germany.

In the immediate aftermath of the velvet revolution, Czechoslovakia had adopted a cautious approach to economic reform. The supporters of "shock treatment" on the Polish model had been in a minority, with many Czech politicians, such as Havel, favouring a pragmatic "social market" approach. Meanwhile Slovak leaders, including Meciar and Carnogursky, had been concerned that without continued state intervention, Slovakia's outmoded heavy industries would collapse; they therefore expressed considerable scepticism toward radical pro-market reforms. Slovakia's relatively poor economic performance added to the perception among Czechs that continued federation would act as a brake on Czech economic aspirations. The uncertainty over the future of the federation discouraged foreign investment, particularly in 1992, and delayed economic recovery. Gradually the Czech radical liberals--notably federal Economy Minister Klaus--gained ground. With a major privatisation programme introduced in 1992, divisions over economic policy came to play a significant role in the dissolution of the federation later that year.

Privatisation

The sale of small enterprises began in 1991. The process accelerated rapidly from May 1992 with the mass privatisation programme; citizens applied for vouchers which were exchangeable for shares in some 1,500 state firms comprising 40 per cent of state property. Some 8.5 million people participated and most chose to lodge their vouchers with private investment funds rather than to invest them directly. The "voucher" scheme had two principal virtues: it could work rapidly, and give citizens a perceived vested interest in the process. Although several other post-communist countries imitated the voucher scheme, it was not an unqualified success. The private investment funds, which by 1993 numbered over 400, eventually bought most of the vouchers, reducing the level of public participation in the process. A lack of state regulation of the funds led to accusations of corruption and unethical conduct: for instance many funds attracted investors by making unsustainable promises of a tenfold return on investments within a year (*see also section on the economy of the Czech Republic*).

Restitution

The drafting of restitution measures was complicated by the legislators' anxiety to return property to Jews, Czechs and Slovaks whilst avoiding the same legal requirement vis a vis the former Sudeten German minority. Restitution measures were confined to the return of property confiscated after 1948, when German property had already been seized by the state.

In October 1990 Parliament passed legislation on the restitution of an estimated 70,000 houses, shops and small businesses confiscated between 1955 and 1962. In February 1991 further legislation covered property seized after the 1948 coup. The restitution of agricultural land--again, that confiscated from 1948--was introduced under legislation including the Soviet Union and Yugoslavia, collapsed in turmoil following the end of the cold war.

The end of Czechoslovakia was however infinitely more orderly and amicable, and for this reason the process became known as the "velvet divorce". The separation was conducted in an atmosphere of compromise, and with each side pledging to maintain good relations. There were no major recorded instances of intercommunal violence between Czechs and Slovaks. Indeed, opinion polls up to dissolution and afterward showed that majorities in both republics favoured continued federation.

The large Czech and Slovak minorities in each other's respective states can expect to be treated with respect. (*See also Czech and Slovak sections on Ethnic and National Relations*.)

FOREIGN AFFAIRS

Czechoslovakia's 40-year isolation from the West ended on 17 December 1989, with the ceremonial cutting of the wire fence marking the frontier with Austria. Within ten weeks the Soviet leader Gorbachev had agreed with President Havel to withdraw all Soviet troops by July 1991; he went on to express regret over the "unfounded invasion" in 1968. With the dissolution of both Comecon and the Warsaw Treaty Organisation within four days in the summer of 1991 Czechoslovakia's formal military and economic links to the Soviet Union were severed. Relations with Russia were good.

Czechoslovakia initially sought a high profile. President Havel and Foreign Minister Dienstbier travelled widely, implicitly promoting the idea of Czechoslovakia's return to its rightful place as a sophisticated country with a cultural history in the Western European tradition. In early 1991 Czechoslovakia joined the Council of Europe; in March 1992 an association agreement with the European Community took effect, and later that month Czechoslovakia became the first ex-communist state in eastern Europe to ratify the European Convention on Human Rights. The Czechoslovak regime also favoured links to NATO.

Czechoslovakia suffered no major problems with neighbours in 1990-2, although there were areas of sensitivity in relations with Germany (*see Czech Republic Foreign Affairs section*) and Hungary (*see Slovakia Foreign Affairs section*).

The orderly and legal manner of the dissolution of the Czechoslovak federation reflected great credit on both newly independent states, in stark contrast to the violence in Yugoslavia, and the chaos of the Soviet disintegration. It was however the Czech Republic which inherited much of the international good will accumulated by its federal precursor, since the West regarded the rise of nationalism in Slovakia with considerable suspicion.

CONSTITUTIONAL ISSUES

The Czechoslovak Socialist Republic was renamed the Czech and Slovak Federative Republic in April 1990, as a gesture to Slovak nationalists. Also in 1990 civil rights legislation was introduced and autonomy devolved to the republican parliaments. A constitutional court was established in Brno in January 1992. Other major constitutional changes became bogged down by growing Slovak demands, initially for passed in May 1991, when former owners and their descendants were offered the return of "fixed assets" and an interim ownership stake in agricultural co-operatives farming their land, pending further reforms to settle the fate of the co-ops.

POST-COMMUNIST JUSTICE ISSUES

The legal search for a just resolution to the transgressions of the communist era rapidly turned from senior communist leaders to those who had been tainted by their past collaboration with the communist regime. As the debate on decommunisation got under way in 1990, a parliamentary commission was formed to investigate rumours that some former dissidents had acted as double agents during the communist era.

Some regarded former collaborators as morally tainted and unworthy of holding state office. Others stressed that former collaborators could be subject to blackmail either by former StB agents (*see Czech Republic Justice section*) or by other politicians (fears apparently born out when Meciar was deposed as Slovak Prime Minister in 1991 accused of using secret police files to gather information on his political rivals). Suspicions were exacerbated when in March 1991 the parliamentary commission named ten deputies as former secret police collaborators, including Jan Kavan, the former dissident leader. Kavan vigorously protested his innocence.

In June 1991 the federal parliament passed a law on "lustration" or purification, designed to screen public office-holders for links with the communist-era secret police. The lustration law, signed reluctantly by Havel in August 1991, forbade former collaborators from holding state offices for a period of five years. It proved highly controversial, with many protesting that it infringed human rights. Critics cast doubt on the reliability of the primary source of evidence - the secret police files - which they argued could be incomplete, forged, or falsely compiled by the original investigating agent. Moreover some of those accused had collaborated under duress. There was no proper legal process by which the accused could publicly put their case. Besides, some questioned the fairness of a law which punished the collaborators rather than the agents who had recruited them.

In an attempt to reduce unease over lustration, in March 1992 the parliament approved legislation permitting citizens access to StB files on themselves. Later in the same month Czechoslovakia became the first ex-communist state in Central and Eastern Europe to ratify the European Convention on Human Rights.

In the autumn of 1992 a military court convicted three former senior officials for their role in the repression of the anti-communist demonstrations of 1988-9. Former Interior Minister Frantisek Kincl, his deputy Alojz Lorenc, and former Counterintelligence chief Varle Vykypel were sentenced to terms of between three and four years imprisonment for ordering the unlawful arrest of protesters.

ETHNIC AND NATIONAL RELATIONS

The attempt to create a unified Czechoslovak nation from two linguistically similar groups failed. Historical and cultural factors proved insuperable. The dissolution of the Czechoslovak federation at the end of 1992 confirmed a historic trend in Central and Eastern Europe, as multi-ethnic states created in the wake of the First World War, more autonomy, then for sovereignty, and finally for independence. The constitution as it stood in late 1992 was therefore an amended version of the communist-era basic law dating from 1960. This constitution established a federation comprising two republics, the Czech Republic and Slovakia. Each had a legislature or National Council, the Czech chamber including 200 seats and the Slovak 150. The Federal Assembly comprised the Chamber of People (with 101 Czech deputies and 49 Slovaks) and the Chamber of Nations (with 75 deputies from each republic). The Federal Assembly appointed the President, who in turn appointed the Federal government. The federation was dissolved at midnight on New Year's Eve 1992.

PRINCIPAL PERSONALITIES

The communist era

Klement **Gottwald** (1896-1953). General secretary of the Czechoslovak Communist Party (KSC) from 1929, Gottwald stood unsuccessfully against Masaryk in the 1934 presidential election. As recommended by the Comintern, he subsequently led the party's switch to a popular front policy, supporting Benes as Masaryk's successor. Gottwald went into exile in the Soviet Union after the 1938 Munich debacle. He negotiated the creation of the National Front with Benes in 1945. When the KSC emerged from elections in 1946 as the largest party, Gottwald became prime minister of the National Front government. Loyally following Soviet orders, Gottwald implemented the takeover of all government power in February 1948 and the launched the Stalinist purges of the party. He became President in 1948, and from 1951 he resumed the party leadership. Gottwald died in a Moscow sanatorium in March 1953, nine days after the death of Stalin.

Antonin **Novotny** (1904-75). Novotny was noted for maintaining a Stalinist line from 1953, when he succeeded Gottwald as first secretary of the KSC, until the mid-1960s, when he accepted some hesitant steps towards reform. A domineering character, he was especially unpopular in the party with Slovaks, whose leading figures, including Husak, he had imprisoned in the 1950s for "bourgeois nationalist" deviations. It was a Slovak, Dubcek, who replaced Novotny in early 1968.

Aleksander **Dubcek** (1921-1992). The communist party leader during the 1968 "Prague spring", who attempted to abandon Stalinism in favour of "socialism with a human face". When Dubcek replaced Novotny as KSC leader in January 1968 his name was not widely known, despite his role as leader of the Slovak communists. His appointment was regarded as a bid to placate disgruntled Slovaks in the party. The reforms introduced under Dubcek's leadership won him wide popularity. When Warsaw Pact forces invaded in August 1968 Dubcek was arrested but released after effectively abandoning his reform policies. By April 1969 he had been ousted as KSC leader. After a brief spell as ambassador to Turkey, Dubcek was expelled from the KSC in 1970. He returned to obscurity as an administrator in the Slovak forestry service. During the November 1989 revolution Dubcek was ecstatically received at mass pro-democracy rallies. Although suggested as a possible figurehead president, he stood aside in favour of Havel, and instead became speaker of the federal parliament. Dubcek joined the Public Against Violence movement, switching to Meciar's Movement for a Democratic Slovakia in July 1991 but strongly opposing the dissolution of the federation. In March 1992 he was elected as chair of the small Social

Democratic Party in Slovakia. The party performed poorly in the 1992 elections and Dubcek resigned as speaker of the federal parliament. In September 1992 Dubcek suffered grave injuries in a car crash and he died on 7 November 1992. Thousands of mourners attended his funeral. Some three years after the accident the Slovak parliament opened an investigation into the circumstances surrounding Dubcek's death.

Gustav **Husak** (1913-91). The party leader charged with "normalising" Czechoslovakia following the turmoil of 1968. Although Husak had been part of the Dubcek leadership he subsequently became known principally for establishing a neo-Stalinist regime. Husak had first made his name in the Communist Party of Slovakia and had helped to lead the 1944 Slovak uprising against the German occupation. He was imprisoned in 1954-60 as a Slovak "bourgeois nationalist". He replaced Dubcek as party leader in April 1969 and held that office until his replacement by Jakes in 1987. He was also head of state from 1975 until he was forced to resign by mass pro-democracy rallies on 10 December 1989, a moment which marked the triumph of the "velvet revolution". Husak was expelled by the KSC in February 1990 and died on 18 November 1991.

Milos **Jakes** (b. 1922). A key figure in the hardline, post-1968 regime. Jakes was a friend and contemporary of Dubcek from the 1950s, when both had attended the Higher Party School in Moscow. He joined the Dubcek leadership in March 1968 as chair of the KSC central control and auditing commission. Jakes retained this post after the Warsaw Pact invasion and became, with Husak and Vasil Bilak, one of the key leaders of "normalisation". In December 1987 Jakes succeeded Husak as party general secretary. Jakes' harsh rule made him the most despised of the communist leaders. His resignation on 24 November 1989 was received ecstatically by pro-democracy demonstrators. The KSC expelled him on 7 December, and he was subsequently detained for criminal investigation.

Post-communist leaders

Vaclav **Havel** (b. 1936). The leading communist-era dissident and playwright who served as Czechoslovak president from 1989-92 and as Czech president from 1993. Havel came from a wealthy Czech family and under the anti-bourgeois regulations of the 1950s he was forbidden a higher education. He turned to the theatre, working first as a stage hand and then gaining fame as a playwright. He was politically active during the Prague Spring and as a result he was banned from public life during the normalisation era. Supporting himself by working in a brewery, he became a prominent and frequently-detained dissident. He drafted large parts of Charter 77, and co-founded the Committee for the Defence of the Unjustly Persecuted (VONS) in 1978. His most recent arrest, in February 1989 for "incitement and obstruction", helped attract international attention to the opposition's grievances against the hardline regime. Released in May, he was one of Civic Forum's founders and its unofficial leader through the November 1989 revolution. From his election as Czechoslovak president in December 1989 he enjoyed a high international profile and considerable prestige. At home, he backed radical economic reforms but his concern over social justice acted as a brake on the more zealous free marketeers within the government. A fervent federalist, Havel struggled to frame a constitutional settlement acceptable to both the Czech and Slovak republics, and was bitterly disappointed at the dissolution of the federation. In January 1993 Havel was elected to the mainly ceremonial Czech presidency for a five-year term by the Czech parliament. Since 1993 he has campaigned for a deepening of Czech democracy, expressing concern that the government has concentrated too narrowly on economic reforms.

Vaclav **Klaus** (b. 1941). A key figure in the Czechoslovak government from 1989-92 and Czech Prime Minister from July 1992. A Czech born in Prague, Klaus had identified with the 1968 reformists as a young economist, but took a low profile under the Husak regime, working in the state bank. He joined Civic Forum in December 1989 and served as Czechoslovak Finance Minister from December 1989 until June 1992. Klaus was a remarkable success in this post, masterminding the mass privatisation scheme. He earned a reputation for arrogance but also for efficiency and competence. He describes himself as a Thatcherite and has been the leading Czech advocate of free market principles. Klaus's views on economic policy hastened the split in Civic Forum, of which he became chair in October 1990. He co-founded the right-wing liberal Civic Democratic Party (ODS) in February 1991 and became its leader. The ODS scored a striking success in the Czech Republic in the 1992 elections. Klaus became Czech Prime Minister in July 1992 and, grasping that the federation was doomed, he resolved to end it on terms as favourable as possible to the Czechs. On this and other issues, his relations with Havel thereafter became sensitive. The new Czech constitution passed in autumn 1992 gave the presidency a limited, mainly ceremonial role, making the prime minister the dominant political figure in the republic. Since independence in January 1993 Klaus has concentrated on transforming the Czech economy and takes considerable credit from its position as the most economically promising of all the postcommunist states, and for its remarkable political stability.

Vladimir **Dlouhy** (b. 1953). A minister in the federal cabinets of 1989-92 and in the Czech Cabinet appointed in 1992. Dlouhy was an economist and colleague of Klaus before the revolution. Unlike Klaus, Dlouhy was also a communist party member, and remained so until after the revolution, when he joined Civic Forum. He was appointed to the first post-communist federal cabinet as a deputy prime minister and served as federal Economics Minister in 1990-92. With the disintegration of Civic Forum Dlouhy joined the right-wing Civic Democratic Alliance (ODA), which became a minor partner in the Czech governing coalition from 1992; Dlouhy was appointed as Trade and Industry Minister. Despite his recent communist past, Dlouhy has a reputation for honesty and competence which has consistently made him the most trusted and popular Czech politician, according to opinion polls.

Jiri **Dienstbier** (b. 1937). The foreign minister from December 1989 until June 1992. Dienstbier was a friend, ally and fellow Chartist with Havel, and a co-founder of Civic Forum in November 1989. His foreign experience dated from his days as a radio correspondent in the 1960s. Dismissed as a journalist in 1970 during normalisation, Dienstbier went on to suffer the typical dissident fate, working as a stoker and then spending three years in prison from 1979. Dienstbier's Civic Movement founded in 1991 appealed rather narrowly to centre-right intellectuals and despite Dienstbier's personal prestige the party failed to win seats in the 1992 federal and republican parliamentary elections.

Petr **Pithart** (b. 1941). Premier of the Czech republic from February 1990 until June 1992. A signatory of Charter 77, Pithart had been a law lecturer and Oxford scholar but was relegated to labouring and clerical work under "normalisation" from 1970. He was prominent in co-ordinating Civic Forum's activities in the "velvet revolution".

Vladimir **Meciar** (b. 1942). The nationalist leader and Slovak Prime Minister for three terms in 1990-1, in 1992-4, and from December 1994. Despite a series of scandals Meciar has retained his position as the dominant figure in Slovak politics since the velvet revolution. Meciar was a boxer who worked in the communist youth movement; he was expelled from the party under "normalisation" and then studied law. He joined the VPN movement and became Slovakia's interior minister in December 1989; from June 1990 he was Slovak prime minister. Meciar's populist Slovak nationalist course and leadership style split the VPN and in April 1991 he was dismissed as prime minister, accused of incompetence and of abusing information gathered by the communist-era secret police. Meciar and his supporters formed the Movement for Democratic Slovakia (HZDS). Meciar's popular touch swept him back to power in 1992, effectively mandating him to seek a dissolution of the federation. He negotiated the "velvet divorce" with the Czech leader Klaus. His highly controversial leadership style, coupled with his centre-left economic policies, divided the HZDS. In September 1993 Meciar was reported to have described Romanies as "mentally backward" and in November he made a vitriolic attack on opposition politicians and international institutions. Although in both cases Meciar subsequently denied having made the comments attributed to him, they probably struck a chord with parts of the Slovak electorate. Concern that the privatisation process was being harnessed for the direct financial benefit of the HZDS led to a breakaway under HZDS Foreign Minister Jozef Moravcik which eventually brought down Meciar's second cabinet. Meciar's third term as Slovak prime minister, following the HZDS success in the parliamentary elections of 1994, was marked by a protracted dispute with President Michal Kovac, whom Meciar had resolved to depose. The tone of Meciar's leadership has occasionally concealed a kind of pragmatism; he has shown some tolerance for limited economic reform, agreed to minority rights legislation as part of a basic treaty with Hungary, and given pledges, albeit admittedly lukewarm, on future Slovak membership of the EU and NATO.

Michal **Kovac** (b. 1930). Slovak President from February 1993, whose struggle with Vladimir Meciar has dominated the politics of independent Slovakia. Michal Kovac was nominated by Meciar in 1993 as a compromise candidate for the presidency. Despite fears that he would merely obey Meciar's will, he gradually asserted himself to become a significant check on the acquisition and exercise of power by Meciar. On taking up the presidency in February 1993 Kovac resigned his membership of the HZDS and appointed staff from all parties; by autumn 1993 Kovac claimed to be non-partisan. His struggle with Meciar became public in November 1993 with his rejection of the prime minister's candidate for privatisation minister. Kovac effectively caused the downfall of Meciar's cabinet in March 1994 with a speech accusing Meciar of incompetence, undemocratic practices and populism. He supported Jozef Moravcik, who had led a moderate breakaway from the HZDS, as Prime Minister. Meciar, when he returned to office in late 1994, resolved to strip the presidency of its powers and duly removed the president's function as head of the armed forces and supervisor of the secret services. The kidnapping in August 1995 of Kovac's son, who was wanted on fraud charges by the German police, was widely linked to the HZDS.

Jozef **Moravcik** (b. 1945). Leading Slovak moderate. A law professor, Moravcik entered the Czechoslovak parliament as a VPN deputy in February 1991. He switched to Meciar's HZDS in April 1991 and was elected as an HZDS federal deputy in June 1992. From July to December 1992 Moravcik served as Czechoslovakia's last federal foreign minister and following the dissolution of the federation he became Slovak foreign minister in March 1993. Moravcik was influential in persuading the West that Slovakia would retain its Western orientation, in particular promising that the republic would pass minority rights laws in securing Slovak membership of the Council of Europe in mid-1993. The nationalistic Meciar clashed with Moravcik and in February 1994 the latter formed a new faction in the HZDS, the Alternative of Political Realism (APR), which subsequently evolved into the Democratic Union (DUS). Within weeks he had been expelled from the HZDS and had resigned from the government. When Meciar's cabinet fell in March, Moravcik was appointed prime minister at the head of a five-party coalition. Under Moravcik's moderate rule there was a brief period of political stability and the economy began to revive. However, the DUS polled under 10 per cent of the vote in early elections in autumn 1994, and Moravcik was replaced by Meciar in December, when he took a seat in the Slovak parliament.

Marian **Calfa** (b. 1946). Calfa, a Slovak communist, was interim federal prime minister from December 1989, leading the first cabinet for more than four decades without a communist majority, until mid-1992. He formally left the KSC in January 1990 to join Public Against Violence, winning a seat in federal parliament in the June 1990 elections. He continued as prime minister at the head of a mainly Civic Forum/Public Against Violence government until his resignation following the general elections of June 1992. The son of a railway worker, Calfa had been a legal official and had held a government post, as minister without portfolio, for only 18 months before becoming prime minister.

Jan **Carnogursky** (b. 1944). Premier of the Slovak Republic from April 1991 until June 1992. A lawyer with a reputation for defending dissidents, Carnogursky was himself arrested in August 1989 for dissident activity, and released only in the midst of the November revolution. He was brought into Calfa's interim federal government in December, as a deputy premier. When Carnogursky's right-wing Christian Democratic Movement (KDH) came second in the Slovak elections of June 1990, he left federal office and devoted himself to Slovak affairs. The KDH entered a coalition with Public Against Violence in which Carnogursky served as deputy premier. With the split of the VPN Carnogursky was appointed as Prime Minister to replace Vladimir Meciar in April 1991. Noted for favouring a moderate course on autonomy amid the increasing populist clamour for secession, he was swept from office by the victory of Meciar's HZDS in 1992. Although the KDH returned to government under Prime Minister Moravcik, Carnogursky did not join the cabinet.

POLITICAL PARTIES

The broad coalitions of opposition forces that united to sweep the communists from power in the velvet revolution quickly began to divide on fundamental issues by 1991.

The **Communist Party of Czechoslovakia** (KSC) was formed in 1921 and dissolved at the end of 1992 following the termination of the federation. Despite some discussion in 1990-1 on the proposed proscription of the party, action against it was limited to the seizure of most assets acquired by the KSC during its period in power. Old guard leaders, notably Husak, had been expelled from the KSC in 1989-90; but this had been balanced by the resignation of members of the pro-reform wing, notably Calfa. The rump party remained one of the most conservative of East-Central Europe's former ruling communist parties, and resisted the adoption of Western European-style social democracy. In both federal elections of 1990 and 1992 the KSC finished second but with under 15 per cent of the vote. Although KSC membership haemorrhaged from 1990, halving in the first six months of that year alone, the party retained a core of members and an organisational structure that no other party could match. The KSC's successor parties were the KSCM in the Czech Republic and the SDL in Slovakia, both of which had existed as entities within the KSC prior to 1993.

Civic Forum (OF) was formed as a broad alliance of Czech pro-democracy groups in November 1989, and unofficially led by Havel until his assumption of the presidency in December. Its sister movement in Slovakia was **Public Against Violence** (VPN). Founded mainly by dissident intellectuals, the OF/VPN rapidly also attracted reform-communists such as Calfa and technocrats such as Klaus. The 1990 round table talks and the June 1990 elections led to the formation of a primarily OF/VPN federal government, while Pithart led an OF-dominated Czech government and VPN deputy Meciar became Slovak Prime Minister. The OF and the VPN contained members with widely disparate views. Although they preserved their unity on democratisation and civil liberties, arguments over economic policy and Meciar's increasing Slovak nationalism divided the movement. When the radical liberal Klaus was elected as OF chairman in October 1990, the division became unsustainable, and the OF divided amicably in April 1991, giving rise to the ODA, ODS and OH (*see Czech Republic parties section*). The split in the VPN, which also took place in April 1991, was more acrimonious, with Meciar being dismissed as Slovak Prime Minister and expelled from the VPN. His new party, the HZDS (*see Slovakia parties section*), attracted many former VPN members.

The (Czechoslovak) **Christian Democratic Movement** (KDH), a conservative centre-left Catholic party, was the junior partner in the federal government formed in June 1990. Its main constituency was in Slovakia and in 1992 the party's Slovak wing, under Jan Carnogursky, broke away to form the (Slovak) KDH. In the Czech lands, where clericalism had much less historical significance, there were smaller Catholic groups, the Christian Democratic Party and the Christian Democrat Union.

ELECTIONS

Legislature

The communist-era bicameral Federal Assembly comprised a 200-seat Chamber of the People and 150-seat Chamber of Nations. The Czech and Slovak republics each had a National Council or parliament elected in the same way. There was a single-candidate electoral system in which the KSC, notionally working within the Fatherland Front structure, recorded almost 100 per cent of the vote in turnouts of over 99 per cent. About 80 per cent of the seats in parliament went to the KSC under this arrangement and the remainder to its four nominally separate partners. The KCS majority was removed in January 1990 as a result of the decision of the round table talks and the co-option of non-communist MPs.

The legislatures elected in 1990 and 1992, under interim arrangements pending completion of the constitution-making process, were (i) a bicameral Federal Assembly, with the 150 seats in the Chamber of the People and the Chamber of Nations, each with

150 seats, and (ii) separate Czech and Slovak National Councils, of 200 and 150 seats respectively. The system adopted for all these chambers was proportional representation, with a minimum threshold for representation of 5 per cent (the single exception being the 1990 Slovak National Council elections of 1990, when a 3 per cent threshold applied).

(*For results of Republican elections in 1992 see Czech Republic elections section and Slovakia elections section.*)

The June 1990 general election resulted in a victory for Civic Forum and People Against Violence, but with unexpectedly strong residual support for the communists. The June 1990 election was dominated by the ODS in the Czech lands and the HZDS in Slovakia.

8-9 June 1990	Chamber of the People				Chamber of Nations	
	total %	total seats			total %	total seats
OF/VPN	46.6	87			45.9	83
KSC	13.6	23			13.7	24
CDU/CDM	12.0	20			11.3	20
MSD-SMS	5.4	9			3.6	9
SNS	3.5	6			6.2	7
Coexistence	2.8	5			2.7	7
Others	16.1	0			16.6	0

5-6 June 1992	Chamber of the People			Chamber of Nations		
	Czech %	Slovak %	total seats	Czech %	Slovak %	total seats
ODS	33.9	4.0	48	33.4	3.7	37
HZDS	-	33.5	24	-	33.9	33
Left Bl.	14.3	-	19	14.5	-	15
SDL	-	14.4	10	-	14.0	13
CSSD	7.7	-	10	6.8	-	6
SPR-RSC	6.5	0.4	8	6.4	0.3	6
KDU-CSL	6.0	-	7	6.1	-	6
LSU	5.8	-	7	6.1	-	5
SNS	-	9.4	6	-	9.4	9
KDH (Sk)	-	9.0	6	-	8.8	8
Hungarian	-	7.4	5	-	7.4	7
SDSS	*5.0	-	0	-	6.1	5
Others	25.9	17.2	0	26.7	16.5	0
Total			100			150

*All figures have been rounded up to the nearest 0.1 per cent; the SDSS's precise score was 4.98 per cent, just under the 5 per cent hurdle for representation.

Presidency

Under the communist regime from 1948 the president of the republic was elected at five-yearly intervals by the Federal Assembly. Communist Czechoslovakia's five presidents were Gottwald (1948-53), Zapotocky (1953-7), Novotny (1957-68), Svoboda (1968-75) and Husak (1975-1989).

Havel became interim President on Dec. 30, 1989, his election having been declared unanimous by the Federal Assembly after other candidates had all stood down. Re-elected for a further interim period of two years on July 5, 1990, he was again the sole candidate (after others had been disqualified as not properly nominated). Requiring a three-fifths majority in each 150-member chamber of the Federal Assembly, he received 114 to 25 in the Chamber of the People, and 120 to 25 (nine of the Czech section and 16 of the Slovak section) in the Chamber of Nations.

On 3 July 1992 Havel failed to secure re-election as Federal President, despite being the sole candidate, after Slovak deputies withdrew their support. Under changes in the presidential election procedure enacted in April 1992 Havel was obliged to withdraw to clear the field for new candidates. Further attempts to elect a federal president on 16 and 30 July and 6 August also failed. In the meantime Havel resigned and his presidential duties were transferred to the Federal Prime Minister on 20 July.

CHRONOLOGY

1618-48. The Thirty Years' War results in the defeat of the medieval Kingdom of Bohemia and its absorption into the Habsburg empire, the decisive reverse having taken place at the Battle of the White Mountain in 1620.

19th century. A revival of Czech culture helps to establish and strengthen Czech national identity. Tomas Masaryk, a Slovak professor of philosophy, begins late in the century to argue that Czechs and Slovaks constitute one national group; he urges Austria to make the Czech Lands and Slovakia an autonomous province of the Habsburg empire.

1914-18. The First World War severely weakens the Habsburgs and creates a power vacuum in Central Europe.

30 May 1918. Masaryk, now the principal exponent of a unified Czech-Slovak state, signs the Pittsburgh agreement with emigre Czech and Slovak groups in the USA on the future structure of a Czech-Slovak state, under which Slovakia is apparently guaranteed autonomy.

28 October 1918. Declaration of an independent Czechoslovak state.

21 December 1918. Masaryk becomes the first Czechoslovak President.

1919. The Paris peace settlement confirms the creation of Czechoslovakia.

29 February 1920. A new constitution establishes a unitary state; Czechoslovakia becomes a parliamentary democracy with a strong, centralised executive. Neither Slovakia nor the three million ethnic Germans based mainly in the border area known as the Sudetenland are granted autonomy.

October 1921. Foundation of the Communist Party of Czechoslovakia (KSC).

November 1925. The KSC reaches a prewar peak in legislative elections, finishing second in a fragmented field.

May 1935. The pro-Nazi National Front Party wins over 60 per cent of the German vote in legislative elections. By 1936 its leader Konrad Henlein is demanding federalisation of the state into racially-based units.

1935. Masaryk steps down as president in favour of Eduard Benes.

March 1938. Anschluss: Nazi Germany annexes Austria.

September 1938. The Munich agreement: Czechoslovakia is abandoned by its Western allies and forced to cede the Sudetenland to Germany.

22 October 1938. Benes resigns the presidency and flees to London.

1939. Germany annexes the rest of Czechoslovakia without facing armed resistance. Bohemia and Moravia are made a protectorate under Reinhard Heydrich, while Slovakia is given nominal independence under clerical fascist Jozef Tiso. Czech and Slovak Jews are deported en masse to Nazi concentration camps. Nazi repression in other respects does not compare to the brutality in Poland, although the assassination of Heydrich by the Czech resistance is followed by ruthless reprisals, and in 1944 a Slovak rebellion is put down.

March 1945. In Moscow, Benes, now head of the London-based Czechoslovak government-in-exile, agrees with Klement Gottwald, the leader of the Communist Party of Czechoslovakia (KSC), to form a National Front or coalition of six pre-war political groups. The National Front's programme includes nationalisation of industry, a Soviet-oriented foreign policy, and the expulsion of Germans and Hungarians -- a fate which the latter group largely escapes.

April-May 1945. The liberation of the country by the Red Army and by US troops in the far west. Both armies have withdrawn by the end of 1945.

May 1946. The KSC wins 38 per cent of the vote in general elections; Gottwald, as leader of the largest party, is invited to head the National Front.

July 1947. A decision to accept Marshall Plan assistance is rescinded under pressure from the Soviet Union.

25 February 1948. After an effective coup in Prague, Gottwald's new communist-dominated cabinet is reluctantly sworn in by President Benes.

March 1948. The death of Jan Masaryk, which is officially described as suicide, removes the last leading opponent of communist power.

April 1948. The social democrats are merged into the Communist Party.

9 May 1948. Under a new constitution, Czechoslovakia is declared a people's democracy.

30 May-2 June 1948. The communist-dominated National Front is victorious in single-list elections; Benes resigns the presidency and is succeeded by Gottwald.

October 1949. The arrest of "bourgeois elements" begins on a large scale.

March 1950. Religious leaders are put on trial for treason.

October 1950-March 1951. Political show trials reach their height.

September 1951. Gottwald becomes general secretary of the party.

November 1952. An anti-Semitic purge of senior communist officials ends with the execution of 11, including former KSC general secretary Rudolf Slansky.

5 March 1953. The death of Stalin is followed nine days later by that of Gottwald.

June 1953. A workers' protest over price rises and currency reform is vigorously repressed.

September 1953. State and party leadership is divided with the appointment of Antonin Zapotocky as President and of Antonin Novotny as party leader. Industrial planners place new emphasis on consumer goods, but any political "deviation" is met with repressive measures.

April 1954. Gustav Husak is convicted of Slovak separatism and given a life prison sentence.

November 1957. The offices of head of state and party leader are unified once again as Novotny succeeds Zapotocky as president.

June-September 1963. Novotny ousts the leading Stalinists in the party following the rehabilitation of Slansky and other victims of the Stalinist show trials. The modesty of Novotny's subsequent reforms, and his autocratic style, frustrate the proponents of change.

January 1968. The "Prague Spring" begins when Novotny is replaced as party leader by Aleksander Dubcek; in March Novotny is replaced as President by Ludvik Svoboda.

April 1968. The "Prague Spring" leadership puts forward the Action Programme proposing comprehensive political and economic reforms.

June 1968. Intellectuals publish the "2000 words" statement advocating liberalisation. There is a popular surge of support for reforms.

June 1968. Warsaw Pact manoeuvres in Czechoslovakia underline the threat to the reform leadership.

21 August 1968. A massive invasion by Warsaw Pact forces crushes the "Prague Spring"; the tanks are met by thousands of unarmed protesters in Prague.

27 August 1968. Dubcek and other leading reformers return from a week in effective detention in Moscow, having been forced to reverse their reforms.

September 1968. Soviet party leader Leonid Brezhnev sets out the "Brezhnev doctrine" in a *Pravda* article; he declares that socialist states have limited sovereignty and argues that their socialist allies have an "internationalist obligation" to intervene in the defence of socialism.

January 1969. A student, Jan Palach, becomes a martyr for the dissident movement when he commits suicide by self-immolation in Wenceslas Square, in protest at the Warsaw Pact invasion. There are anti-Soviet riots in March.

April 1969. Dubcek is ousted and replaced by Husak.

September 1969. A "loyalty drive" or purge of reformers begins; Husak reports in December 1970 that 326,817 people have been expelled from the party, including Dubcek in June 1970.

July 1972. Trials begin of former Dubcek supporters.

1 January 1977. Charter 77 is published by intellectual opponents of the Husak regime, including dissident playwright Vaclav Havel and former reform communists; the charter concentrates on the regime's poor human rights record. Dissidents continue to be harassed and imprisoned.

June 1983. Police break up an anti-government demonstration in Prague.

March 1986. The KSC congress in Prague reacts with extreme caution to the radical proposals for reforms in the Soviet Union, put forward by the new Soviet leader Mikhail Gorbachev.

April 1987. Gorbachev is enthusiastically welcomed by the public during a visit to Prague, but despite support from Husak other voices within the party publicly express reservations over the Soviet reforms.

17 December 1987. Husak retains the post of state President but is replaced as KSC general secretary by the hardliner Milos Jakes.

21 August 1988. Demonstrations in Prague, on the anniversary of the Warsaw Pact invasion in 1968, begin a period of increasing public protest by students and others.

October 1988. Ladislav Adamec is appointed as prime minister and soon announces that planned economic reforms will be brought forward to early 1990.

January 1989. Protests over human rights abuses are followed by the arrest of over 800 dissidents, including Havel, who is imprisoned until May. Also in January, Adamec returns from Moscow speaking of the party's desire for dialogue with critics, and restrictions on travel to the West are eased.

October 1989. The mass opposition rallies in East Germany encourage the Czechoslovak opposition, but riot police attack a demonstration, using clubs to break up a crowd estimated at over 10,000.

17 November 1989. The "velvet revolution" begins with an officially sanctioned student march in Prague to mark the 50th anniversary the death of a student murdered by the Nazis. The rally develops into a pro-democracy demonstration and the crowd swells. Afterwards, riot police near Wenceslas Square beat a group of students with clubs, injuring 140 and making many arrests. False reports that one demonstrator has been killed increase outrage over police brutality and help to rally huge demonstrations in succeeding days.

19 November 1989. The opposition organises itself around the Civic Forum (OF) coalition in Prague and its Slovak sister movement Public Against Violence (VPN). The Socialist Party and the People's Party, hitherto both part of the KSC-dominated National Front organisation, issue a joint resolution with Civic Forum urging dialogue and demanding the resignation of communist hardliners.

21 November 1989. Adamec opens discussions with the protesters.

24 November 1989. Dubcek joins Havel to address over 250,000 cheering demonstrators in Prague. In extensive changes in the party leadership Jakes is replaced as KSC general secretary by Karel Urbanek.

26 November 1989. Adamec leads a party and government delegation in discussions with Civic Forum, and tells a crowd of nearly 500,000 that he will convey protesters' demands to the party.

27 November 1989. Workers show massive support for the opposition, mobilising 60 per cent support nationwide for a two-hour general strike.

28-30 November 1989. The KSC concedes the abolition of its "leading role".

1 December 1989. The 1968 Warsaw Pact invasion is reassessed by the KSC as "unjustified and mistaken".

3 December 1989. Adamec proposes a government with a large Communist majority; huge protests resume.

7 December 1989. Adamec resigns, and the new KSC leadership expels Jakes and hardline former Prague party leader Miroslav Stepan.

10 December 1989. A government with a non-communist majority is formed under communist Marian Calfa, and President Husak resigns.

17 December 1989. The border with Austria is opened ceremonially by the cutting of the wire fence.

20-21 December 1989. The KSC congress apologises for "unjustified reprisals" against dissidents; Adamec becomes party chairman and Vasil Mohorita is elected to the new post of first secretary; hardliner Vasil Bilak is expelled.

30 December 1989. Havel is elected unanimously by the Federal Assembly as Federal President; Dubcek becomes Federal Assembly President (Speaker).

January-February 1990. The political parties hold round-table talks, agreeing on arrangements for the forthcoming elections, and on reducing the Communist presence in the existing parliament.

1 February 1990. The *Statni Bezpecnost* (StB, the security police) is abolished.

17 February 1990. Husak and 21 other leaders are expelled from the KSC.

26-27 February 1990. Havel and Gorbachev meet in Moscow to sign an agreement on a complete Soviet troop withdrawal by July 1991; Gorbachev expresses regret over the "unfounded invasion" in 1968.

27-28 March 1990. New laws are approved on freedom of association, of assembly and of the press.

20 April 1990. In a compromise designed to satisfy Slovaks, the country is renamed the Czech and Slovak Federative Republic.

8-9 June 1990. The first free multi-party elections since 1946 end in victory for Civic Forum and Public Against Violence, with a combined overall majority in both chambers of the Federal Assembly. The KSC does unexpectedly well by beating the Christian Democrats to finish second.

27 June 1990. A new government is formed under Calfa (now a VPN member) and consisting of VPN, Civic Forum, the Christian Democrats and unaffiliated experts. In Slovakia VPN heads a coalition government led by Vladimir Meciar, while in the Czech Republic Civic Forum dominates a new coalition under Petr Pithart.

5 July 1990. Havel is re-elected as president by the Federal Assembly for a two-year term.

20 September 1990. Czechoslovakia joins the IMF.

2 October 1990. Parliament passes legislation on the restitution of an estimated 70,000 houses, shops and small businesses confiscated between 1955 and 1962.

25 October 1990. A language law adopted by the Slovak National Council (parliament) makes Slovak the official language there; nationalists protest that it fails to restrict the use of other languages sufficiently.

16 November 1990. A law on confiscation of Communist Party assets is passed by the Federal Assembly.

12 December 1990. The Federal Assembly passes a power-sharing law, devolving more power to the Czech and Slovak republican parliaments.

1 January 1991. A programme of economic reforms includes the abolition of price controls on most goods and the privatisation of small businesses.

9 January 1991. A Bill of Rights guaranteeing individual freedoms and political pluralism is passed by the Federal Assembly.

21 February 1991. Legislation is passed on the restitution of property seized after the 1948 coup.

4 March 1991. The framework for a new constitution, linking the two republics voluntarily in a federative state, is agreed by the leaders of the principal parties.

22 March 1991. The controversy about links between politicians and the former state security police (StB) is fuelled when a special commission names as former

collaborators ten current members of parliament, among them the prominent former dissident Jan Kavan.

23 April 1991. Meciar is dismissed by the presidium of the Slovak National Council and is succeeded as Slovak premier by Jan Carnogursky. Meciar stands accused of incompetence and of abusing access to secret police files; he has alienated many former colleagues in VPN by his strident Slovak nationalism.

April 1991. Splits are formalised both in Civic Forum--with the formation of Klaus's Civic Democratic Party (ODS) and of Dienstbier's Civic Movement (ODA)--and in Public Against Violence, from which Meciar leads a breakaway group formally named the Movement for Democratic Slovakia (HZDS) on 22 June.

21 May 1991. The Federal Assembly passes legislation on the restitution of land confiscated from private owners by the state after 1948. The former owners and their descendants are offered (i) the return of "fixed assets" and (ii) an interim ownership stake in agricultural co-operatives farming their land, until further reforms settle the fate of the co-ops.

13 June 1991. A privatisation programme is launched for large nationalised industries.

19 June 1991. Soviet troops complete their withdrawal from Czechoslovak territory.

28 June 1991. Comecon is formally dissolved after its 46th session in Budapest.

1 July 1991. Prague hosts the final meeting at which the Warsaw Treaty Organisation or Warsaw Pact is formally dissolved by its remaining members.

18 July 1991. A Referendum Law is passed, allowing either a republican parliament or the Federal Assembly to propose a referendum on secession.

4 October 1991. The Federal Assembly passes a law on screening state office-holders for connections with the former security services. The law bans former StB members and former StB collaborators from holding state offices for a period of five years. Havel reluctantly signs the law on 17 October.

17 November 1991. In a television broadcast Havel puts forward ideas for constitutional changes intended to end the deadlock between federal and republican parliaments. They include linking the republican parliaments to the federal legislature through a second chamber, the Federal Council; the concession of a republican veto on constitutional proposals; and the presidential power to call referendums on the constitution. In January 1992, however, the Federal Assembly rejects Havel's constitutional proposals.

12 February 1992. The Milovy agreement, struck by a joint commission from Slovak and Czech National Councils, sets out a possible compromise formula under which the Slovak and Czech peoples "express [their] wills to live in a common state" but "[recognise] each other's sovereignty". According to the agreement the federation is to have responsibility for defence and foreign policy; the two republics are to be accorded equal representation in federal bodies; and republics may secede after a referendum on independence. The Milovy agreement is provisionally accepted by the presidium of the Czech National Council, but is rejected by its Slovak counterpart as containing too many concessions.

4 March 1992. The Federal Assembly approves legislation permitting citizens access to StB files on them.

18 March 1992. Czechoslovakia becomes the first ex-communist state in eastern Europe to ratify the European Convention on Human Rights.

7 May 1992. A majority in the Slovak National Council votes for a declaration of sovereignty (73-59), but not the 60 per cent it has previously agreed is necessary.

5-6 June 1992. Parliamentary elections at federal and republican level expose the increasing polarisation between the Czech and Slovak republics; in the former the CDU is the main victor, while in the latter the HZDS is the clear winner.

8 June 1992. ODS and HZDS officials hold talks, after which Klaus remarks that views are "fundamentally different". Four days later Klaus declares that "if we cannot form a reasonable state, we shall opt for a reasonable and quiet separation".

20 June 1992. Following more talks Klaus and Meciar agree that they "preferred to split Czechoslovakia" than continue talks on a compromise. Both sides agree that new constitutional arrangements must be drafted by 30 September 1992.

24 June 1992. Meciar takes office as Slovak prime minister, replacing Carnogursky and leading a cabinet dominated by the HZDS.

25 June 1992. Havel argues that uncertainty should be dispelled and that if the federation is to be dissolved a decision should be taken quickly; he again backs a referendum.

1 July 1992. A transitional federal cabinet takes office headed by Jan Strasky of the ODS. In the Czech Republic a cabinet dominated by the ODS and led by Klaus takes office.

3 July 1992. The Federal Assembly fails to re-elect Havel as federal president after Slovaks withdraw their support. Havel is obliged to withdraw from subsequent contests. Further attempts to elect a federal president, on 16 and 30 July and 6 August, also fail.

17 July 1992. The Slovak National Council proclaims Slovak Republican sovereignty. Havel announces his resignation as federal president with effect from 20 July, from when federal prime minister Strasky assumes presidential powers.

23 July 1992. Klaus and Meciar strike an agreement on the procedure for dissolution of the Czechoslovak state: a 60 per cent majority is to be required in both republican parliaments.

27 August 1992. A timetable for the partition of Czechoslovakia is agreed, despite opinion polls showing that majorities in both republics favour continued union.

1 October 1992. The Federal Assembly rejects the bill on separation and instead approves proposals for a Czech-Slovak Union, put forward by Czech leftists and Slovaks. On 6 October both Klaus and Meciar reject the idea of continued union as "unrealistic".

10 October. Meciar and Klaus agree to the establishment of a Czech-Slovak customs union.

13 November 1992. The Federal Assembly approves a bill on the procedure for division of the federation's assets.

17 November 1992. The Czech and Slovak National Councils issue resolutions authorising the dissolution of the federation and assuming from 1 January 1993 "full responsibility for the continuity of state power".

25 November 1992. The Federal Assembly reluctantly approves constitutional amendments formalising the dissolution of the federation on 1 January 1993, and abrogating the constitutional requirement for a referendum on dissolution.

31 December 1992. The Czech and Slovak Federative Republic is dissolved at midnight. Relations between the two states are to be governed by 25 inter-state treaties and various inter-governmental agreements signed since the autumn.

8 February 1993. The currency union between the Czech and Slovak republics ends with the introduction of separate currencies.

8 March 1993. Despite Slovak opposition, the Czech Republic introduces new frontier regulations under which Slovak citizens must be in possession of a valid passport to cross the border.

17 March 1993. In a dispute over continued delays in the division of former federal assets Klaus announces the suspension of Slovak participation in the continuing mass privatisation scheme. The Czech government reverses its decision in mid-May following progress in talks. By end-1993, agreement has been reached on the division of some 95 per cent of federal assets.

1 July 1993. Kovac and Havel agree on border controls: identity cards are henceforth sufficient for transit across the Czech-Slovak border.

December 1993. Officials reveal that the apportionment of 95 per cent of federal assets and liabilities has been agreed in negotiations.

CZECH REPUBLIC

After gaining independence on New Years' Day 1993 the Czech Republic consolidated on the reforms of the preceding three years. The Republic's political stability and rapid economic progress in 1993-5 were exceptional.

The occasionally tense relations in the ruling coalition may have been due as much to personal friction as to genuine policy differences. The ruling ODS retained its popularity, according to opinion polls, making it the front runner for legislative elections due in 1996.

The Czech Republic continued its policy of assimilation into the European mainstream. The government grew increasingly confident that the country could earn EU membership on purely economic criteria, and so its enthusiasm waned for a co-ordinated political campaign with the other members of the Visegrad Group. The republic also vigorously supported early NATO membership. Although relations with Germany have generally been good, German pressure to restitute property to ethnic Germans expelled from the Czech Lands after 1945 has soured matters. A Constitutional Court ruling of March 1995 upholding the deportations enraged former Sudeten Germans.

President Havel retained a high level of prestige both at home and abroad, but appeared to be frustrated by the limited powers of the presidency. His principal criticism of the conduct of government since 1993 has been of the alleged failure to consolidate Czech democracy by weaving democratic values into the social fabric. Havel argues that the state should withdraw from its position of pre-eminence and encourage the development of a thriving "civil society". By this Havel means a highly participatory system in which interest groups proliferate, forming a democratic counterbalance to the centralising and oligarchic tendencies of the state. He regards the government as complacent and lacking vision, in concentrating on the economy and the technical matters of governance. Klaus, on the other hand, dismisses the very notion of a civil society, and argues that democratic values are strengthened through the practice of democratic government.

Although trade with Slovakia dropped temporarily following the dissolution of the federation, the Czech economy suffered relatively little disruption. Indeed, dissolution ended a period of uncertainty and made the Czech Republic an even more attractive prospect to Western investors. The prestige of the reforms has suffered, however, from scandals surrounding the privatisation process, notably from the conviction for bribery of the senior privatisation official, and the unethical conduct of certain private investment funds.

Despite the upturn, many Czech citizens had yet to experience dramatic improvements in living standards. There was also growing unease over the standard of state education and health provision. Major demonstrations in 1995 against the low level of social support coincided with the emergence of the Social Democrats as a potential front runner for the 1996 parliamentary elections.

ECONOMY

Since independence, the economy of the Czech Republic has improved, and by the mid-1990s it was widely regarded as the strongest of the post-communist countries in the region. The Czech economy came out of recession in 1994 and in the early autumn of 1994 such was the buoyant level of hard currency reserves that the Czech National Bank chose to repay outstanding IMF loans, worth $471 million, up to five years ahead of schedule.

The Klaus government has taken a firm hand to the economy, introducing strict wage controls, and its tough fiscal policies contributed to budget surpluses in 1994 and 1995. A new currency, the Czech crown, was introduced in February 1993 and became fully convertible in autumn 1995. The inflation rate in 1994-5 was among the lowest recorded by a post-communist state.

Paradoxically the low level of unemployment has caused some concern, with Trade and Industry Minister Dlouhy convinced by 1995 that despite privatisation (*see below*) many firms remained inefficient and overstaffed, and that this had affected productivity and hence profitability and investment levels. Application of a strict bankruptcy law passed in 1993, which would have necessitated radical restructuring, has been deferred until economic conditions are deemed suitable.

Mass privatisation has continued: some six million people participated in a second wave of voucher sales beginning in October 1993. By end-1994 over 80 per cent of firms were either in the private sector or planning to transfer to it. Despite strong public support for privatisation, the process has been tainted by controversy. There has been suspicion over the role of private investment funds, the largest of which, the Harvard Capital and Consulting Co (HC&C), has claimed more than one million investors. Its president Viktor Kozeny was damaged by allegations in 1993 that he requested secret service information with which to blackmail Czech politicians. The arrest in autumn 1994 of the director of voucher privatisation, Jaroslav Lizner, and his conviction 12 months later on bribery charges, also dented the reputation of the process.

Restitution

Legislation on the restitution of property has been hampered by the difficulty of framing legislation that would exclude claims by German families deported after the Second World War (*see also Foreign Affairs section*).

In March 1995 the Constitutional Court upheld the 1945 decrees stripping Czechoslovakia's 2.5 million Germans of their property and authorising their deportation. The court was ruling on the case of a German citizen, Rudolf Dreithaler, who had applied for the restitution of his parents' former home in Liberec. Former Sudeten Germans were enraged by the ruling.

In April 1992 the Czech parliament had approved legislation on the restitution of property confiscated in 1945-8 - affecting 25,000 people. In April 1994 legislation approved the restitution of property to those - mostly Jews - who had lost it under the Nazi regime from 1938 because of their racial identity.

JUSTICE ISSUES

The Czech Republic continued to implement "lustration" legislation passed by the Czechoslovak parliament in 1991. In September 1995 the Czech parliament renewed the legislation, extending its term by a further four years, despite Havel's warning that lustration ran contrary to the rule of law.

Under legislation passed in July 1993 the Czech parliament declared the communist-era regime to have been illegal. Anti-communist activity--even when conducted "in co-operation with a foreign democratic power"--was declared to have been legitimate. In contrast communist-era crimes committed from ideological (i.e. pro-communist) motivation were exempted from the statute of limitations to clear the way for prosecutions. In early 1995 the parliament established an Office for the Investigation of Communist Crimes (UDV), and in August of that year the UDV brought charges of high treason against ten former communist leaders in connection with the invasion of Czechoslovakia by Warsaw Pact troops in 1968. The ten included Milos Jakes, the former KSC general secretary, and Jozef Lenart, the Czechoslovak Prime Minister from 1963-8.

The UDV's inquiries had been facilitated by Russian co-operation: in summer 1992 Russian President Boris Yeltsin presented to his Czechoslovak counterpart documents dating from 1968, in which leading Czechoslovak communists had requested military intervention by their Warsaw Pact allies.

Secret service

The FBIS, the federal successor to the communist-era StB, gave way in turn to a Czech counterpart, the Bureau of Intelligence and Security (BIS).

A series of scandals and unsubstantiated allegations have magnified public concern over the activities of former secret police agents. In summer 1993 the Czech media were dominated by the "Wallis Affair". A former StB and FBIS agent, Vaclav Wallis, was accused of having sold compromising information on the private lives of senior politicians, including Klaus and Havel, allegedly to Viktor Kozeny, the head of the Czech Republic's largest investment fund. Czech TV alleged that the Wallis affair was part of a concerted campaign by elements in the BIS to discredit democracy and the market economy.

In July 1994 the Czech parliament passed legislation reforming the security services and improving their accountability to the government, presidency and parliament. The reformed BIS was permitted to gather information from individuals on a voluntary basis and under a guarantee of anonymity. In January 1995 Klaus dismissed claims revived by Jan Kalvoda, the leader of the minor coalition party the ODA, that the BIS was spying on mainstream political parties, and Kalvoda's subsequent failure to substantiate his allegations embarrassed the ODA.

ETHNIC AND NATIONAL RELATIONS

The Czech Republic's population is relatively homogeneous, with the largest minorities being Slovaks and Romanies. In the first year of independence there was a rise in the number of attacks on minority groups. The number of Romanies in the Czech Republic increased as many had crossed from Slovakia in advance of the dissolution of the federation. In summer 1993 Czech Prosecutor Jiri Setina was forced to resign after proposing a law to combat "unrest caused by undisciplined migrants", remarks clearly aimed at Romanies. Under a Czech citizenship law passed in 1993 and effective from June 1994, thousands of Roma became stateless because they did not satisfy citizenship criteria, not least the requirement that applicants should have a clean criminal record for five years prior to application.

(For relations with Germany over former minority of ethnic Germans, see below under Foreign Affairs.)

FOREIGN AFFAIRS

Czech foreign policy since independence has emphasised the Czech "return to Europe". The confidence with which the republic approached the question of assimilation into Western institutions resulted from the Czechs' conviction that their culture formed a historic part of Western civilisation.

Initial co-operation on a joint approach with the Republic's Central European neighbours, the Visegrad Group, stalled in 1993, due mainly to Czech scepticism. Czech leaders are aware that the country's economic progress and political stability have made the country the best qualified for membership of European and international security and economic structures. The rise of nationalism in Russia, however, has had an unsettling effect on Central Europe, encouraging a renewal of links between the four Visegrad states. Notwithstanding this, Czech leaders probably regard their country as more secure at least than Poland, and therefore feel the pressure less.

An EU association agreement struck in October 1993 took effect on 1 February 1994. The government announced that it would apply for full EU membership in 1996, by when it expected to be able to meet most of the economic criteria without asking for special exemptions.

Relations with Germany have been generally good. Trade has increased rapidly and German investment has poured into the country. In February 1992 Havel and Kohl signed a Czechoslovak-German Treaty of good neighbourliness and co-operation, although this faced criticism both in Germany, for the lack of provisions on restitution of Sudeten Germans' property, and in Czechoslovakia, for the failure explicitly to annul the 1938 Munich agreement. Since Czech independence there have been a number of bilateral agreements including a May 1993 military co-operation deal providing for the regular exchange of security information and military expertise. As with Poland, Germany has supported the Czechs' bid for NATO membership.

The most significant problem in Czech-German relations has been the question of the ethnic Germans deported mainly from the Czech Lands following the Second World War. The Sudeten Germans have demanded the repeal of the 1945 decrees which stripped Czechoslovakia's 2.5 million Germans of their property and authorised their deportation. Although President Havel, visiting Germany in April 1993, revealed that both sides were considering compensating each other's citizens for the transgressions of the Second World War and its aftermath, the Czech government continued to veto direct talks with Sudeten German representatives. In autumn 1993 German government officials threatened that this failure to negotiate would delay Czech reintegration into European institutions. By 1995 the Czech position had hardened, with Havel arguing in February that "the evil of expulsion was just a sad consequence of the evil that preceded it" and that "the time of apologies and of sending bills for the past should end". In March the Constitutional Court upheld the 1945 decrees and in August Klaus ruled out legislation on a "right of return" for Sudeten Germans.

The generally good relations with Austria have been affected by the February 1993 decision to proceed with the construction of the Temelin nuclear power station in southern Bohemia. The 2,000 megawatt station would relieve the Czech Republic's reliance on "dirty" brown coal-fired power stations in the north of the country. Austria, however, has consistently raised concerns over the safety of the plant and its effect on the environment. In spring 1994 Klaus rejected an offer from his Austrian counterpart Franz Vranitsky of $50 million to abandon the project.

CONSTITUTIONAL ISSUES

The Czech constitution was passed in December 1992, shortly before the dissolution of the Czechoslovak Federation, by the republican legislature, the Czech National Council.

The constitution established a parliamentary democracy under a presidency with a mainly ceremonial role; a presidential veto may be overturned by parliament. The president is elected for a five-year term by the bicameral parliament. Under interim arrangements the existing Czech National Council was designated as the new, 200-seat lower house, the Chamber of Deputies, while the establishment of an upper house, the Senate, was not settled until the passage of legislation in September 1995. The Senate was to comprise 81 seats, elected on the US model: with one third of seats being re-elected every two years, senators were to serve fixed six-year terms. The Senate was to oversee the legislative process in the lower house, and to take interim legislative powers during elections to the lower house. Elections to both houses were scheduled for 1996.

A 60 per cent majority in both chambers is necessary for constitutional amendments. In June 1993 Parliament voted to establish a Constitutional Court to review constitutional legislation and a Supreme Control Office to provide independent auditing of government finances.

The constitution also requires the sub-division of the country into regions, but despite pressure for the passage of early legislation from President Havel, prime minister Klaus succeeded in delaying legislation on the matter even beyond local elections in 1994. The matter has been complicated by pressure from Moravia and Silesia for administrative autonomy.

POLITICAL PARTIES

The Czech Republic has gained a reputation as one of the most committed to liberal, centre-right policies in East-Central Europe. The left has been damaged by internal divisions, but may perform better in elections scheduled for 1996.

Communist Party of Bohemia and Moravia (KSCM). The KSCM was formed within the KSC in 1990. In alliance with other leftist groups as the Left Bloc the party won some 14 per cent of the vote in the 1992 Czech parliamentary elections. Internal divisions have increasingly marginalised the party. KSCM leader Jiri Svoboda was frustrated in his attempt to liberalise the party and led a breakaway to form the **Party of the Democratic Left** in July 1993. He was succeeded as KSCM leader by the more conservative Miroslav Grebenicek.

Czech Social Democratic Party (CSSD). Centre-left party led since March 1993 by Milos Zeman, a left wing economist. The CSSD won 6.5 per cent of the vote in the 1992 Czech elections. In 1993 the CSSD ruled out collaboration with the communists and instead combined with the LSU and the Christian Social Party to form the Realistic Bloc. By 1995 the CSSD parliamentary faction had swollen to 21 after a series of defections, mainly from the KSCM. According to opinion polls, the party had become the most popular of the leftist parties and a potential threat to the centre-right hegemony in the Czech Republic.

Liberal Social Union (LSU). A centre-left bloc which won some 6.5 per cent of the vote in the 1992 Czech elections. The LSU, CSSD and Christian Social Union operated together as the Realistic Bloc from July 1993.

Civic Democratic Party (ODS). Liberal right-wing party, founded within Civic Forum by Klaus in February 1991. The party's strong leadership, clear pro-market ideology and technocratic credentials secured it a decisive victory in the 1992 Czech elections, when it won almost 30 per cent of the vote. Following these elections the ODS leadership quickly abandoned its federalist stance and backed the dissolution of the federation. With Klaus as prime minister the ODS dominated the governing coalition and was the driving force behind the radical economic reform programme. The party's confidence and firm management of the ruling coalition has contributed to the remarkable political stability in the Czech Republic.

Civic Democratic Alliance (ODA). Centre-right party with a similar economic stance to the ODS but which takes a more pragmatic line on social policy. The party's technocratic leadership appeals strongly to right-wing intellectuals. The ODS polled under 6 per cent of the Czech vote in 1992 and joined the governing coalition as a minor partner. Trade and Industry Minister Vladimir Dlouhy, a former communist, is one of the country's most popular politicians.

Christian Democratic Union-Czechoslovak People's Party (KDU-CSL). A centre-right Catholic party led by Josef Lux. The KDU-CSL has a strong local organisation particularly in Catholic areas of Moravia and in rural districts, but has suffered from being the successor of the CSL, which participated in the communist-era National Front. The party attracted less than 7 per cent of the vote in the 1992 Czech elections.

Association for Moravia and Silesia (SMS). The SMS was formed by provincial activists who feared increasing domination by Bohemia and advocated autonomous government within the Czech Republic for the territories of Moravia-Silesia. Competing as the **Movement for Self Administered Democracy** (HSD) the party won 22 seats in the Czech National Council in 1990, slipping to 14 in 1992. The SMS failed to persuade legislators to re-name the country the Czecho-Moravian Republic in 1992, but has succeeded in making local government reform a political hot potato on which legislation has been considerably delayed.

The **Civic Movement** (OH) was constituted formally on April 27, 1991, from the nucleus of the Liberal Club within Civic Forum, and advocated a "social market" approach. Despite having respected leaders in the form of Federal Foreign Minister Jiri Dienstbier and Czech Prime Minister Petr Pithart, and the tacit support of Havel, the party narrowly failed to win seats in 1992.

Association for the Republic-Republican Party of Czechoslovakia (SPR-RSC). A xenophobic, extreme right-wing party led by Miroslav Sladek. The party SPR-RSC won 14 seats in the Czech National Council in the elections of 1992. Sladek's controversial leadership led to a series of defections until the parliamentary caucus numbered only six. In August 1995 several former deputies of the SPR-RSC merged with others to form the **Patriotic Republican Party** (VRS).

ELECTIONS

The legislative elections of 5-6 June 1992 represented the first major test for many of the Republic's political parties, which had only recently been formed in the wake of the fragmentation of Civic Forum. The clear winner was Klaus's technocratic ODS, whereas former dissident Dienstbier's OH failed to pass the 5 per cent threshold for representation.

	% of vote	seats
ODS	29.73	76
*Left Bloc	14.05	35
+CSSD	6.53	16
LSU	6.52	16
KDU-CSL	6.28	15
SPR-RSC	5.98	14
ODA	5.93	14
HSD-SMS	5.87	14
OH	4.59	0
Others	14.52	0
Total	100	200

Turnout 85.0 per cent.
*Including the KSCM   +Competed as Czechoslovak Social Democracy

CHRONOLOGY

16 December 1992. The Czech National Council adopts a constitution for the Czech Republic, to take effect on 1 January 1993.

1 January 1993. The Czech Republic becomes an independent state after the "velvet divorce" with Slovakia. Czech Prime Minister Klaus promises to maintain close links with Slovakia.

26 January 1993. The Czech parliament elects Vaclav Havel as President of the Czech Republic for a five-year term. Havel is sworn in on 2 February 1993.

8 February 1993. The Czech Republic introduces its own currency, the koruna.

17 June 1993. Legislation establishing a constitutional court is passed and signed by Havel.

30 June 1993. The Czech Republic is admitted to the Council of Europe.

9 July 1993. The Chamber of Deputies declares the former communist regime to have been illegal, and permits the suspension of the statute of limitations in cases of ideologically-motivated crime.

4 October 1993. The Czech republic signs an association agreement with the European Community (EC/EU).

1 January 1994. Havel uses his new year address to begin a campaign for the construction of an authentic "civil society".

10 March 1994. The Czech Republic joins NATO's Partnership for Peace programme.

4 October 1994. EU foreign ministers agree to begin "structured dialogue" with associate members in East-Central Europe, including the Czech Republic, with a view to eventual full membership.

31 October 1994. Jaroslav Lizner, the director of the voucher privatisation agency, is arrested on bribery charges. He is sentenced to seven years imprisonment in October 1995.

January 1995. The Office for the Investigation of Communist Crimes (UDV) is established under Vaclav Benda.

8 March 1995. The Constitutional Court upholds decrees made in 1945 by Czechoslovak president Benes, which stripped Czechoslovakia's 2.5 million Germans of their property and authorised their deportation. Former Sudeten Germans are enraged by the ruling.

25 March 1995. An estimated 60,000 to 90,000 people demonstrate in Prague in a rally against insufficient social provision, organised by trade unions.

27 September 1995. Legislation establishes an 81-seat upper house, the Senate, to be elected in 1996.

9 October 1995. Health workers force the resignation of Health Minister Ludek Rubas, after threatening strike action. Rubas had been widely criticised by health workers and politicians for failing to reform the service or to protect its employees' salaries.

18 October 1995. The Chamber of Deputies renews lustration legislation, extending its term by four years to 2000, and thus overriding a presidential veto earlier in the month.

1 November 1995. In the first major strike since 1989, hospital doctors stop work for 24 hours in protest at the poor state of the health service.

18 November 1995. The ODS and KDS vote to merge from March 1996. The KDS's parliamentary faction had been halved in September 1995 when several deputies defected to the KDU-CSL in protest at the planned merger.

SLOVAKIA

Newly independent Slovakia was a tiny country, barely bigger than Estonia. Much of its territory was remote, heavily forested and mountainous. Of its population of five million a high proportion was scattered throughout rural areas. Some 600,000 were ethnic Hungarians, concentrated in the southern lowlands adjacent to Hungary.

Slovakia's industrial base had been developed rapidly in the communist era, with the typical over-emphasis on heavy industry such as engineering, armaments, metals and chemicals. Many Western economists regarded such industries as white elephants.

Prior to independence leaders of some Slovak parties, notably Meciar of the HZDS, had demonstrated a tendency to authoritarianism and an inconsistent approach to the rule of law. Voters, meanwhile, had appeared to disregard evidence of grave misconduct by some politicians, preferring to trust in charismatic leaders such as Meciar.

Divisions within the HZDS over Meciar's leadership were evident from the outset. His favoured candidate for the Slovak presidency, Roman Kovac, was rejected by parliament, and a compromise figure in Michal Kovac was chosen instead. By March 1993 Meciar's government had lost its majority after several HZDS deputies defected to the opposition and the junior coalition partner, the ultra-nationalist SNS, withdrew from government. The price for the return of the SNS in November, which proved highly controversial with the ethnic Hungarian minority, was the key education portfolio. A more serious split in the HZDS occurred in 1994, with the defection of Foreign Minister Jozef Moravcik and his supporters in February bringing the government down the following month. Moravcik, whose principal complaint was the claim that Meciar had harnessed the privatisation process for the financial benefit of the HZDS, formed a new party, the Democratic Union of Slovakia (DUS).

Moravcik's eight-month term as prime minister was characterised by remarkable political stability; for most of this period Slovak parties prepared for the early parliamentary elections in autumn 1994. Moravcik successfully held together a broad coalition including the DUS, the SDL, the SKDU and a breakaway from the SNS. The coalition succeeded in improving the budget deficit, in securing the passage of legislation on mass privatisation and ethnic minority rights, and in restoring IMF support.

Despite the scandals surrounding Meciar's leadership, he returned to power after the 1994 elections, having secured a share of the vote only slightly down on 1992. The new government comprised the HZDS, the SNS and the leftist ZRS, and was dubbed by the opposition the "red-brown" coalition. The appointment of a ZRS deputy as privatisation minister was a clear signal of the future direction of economic policy and the government quickly halted Moravcik's mass privatisation scheme.

In the meantime, the most significant political conflict in the period after the 1994 elections was the struggle between Meciar's HZDS and President Kovac, which had been incipient since Kovac's December 1993 call for the resignation of Meciar's cabinet. Kovac had played a crucial role in deposing Meciar in March 1994, accusing him of incompetence, of inhibiting democracy and of populism. The following month Kovac had cautioned that a further Meciar term "could be considered dangerous for Slovakia" and warned of a "personality cult" surrounding the HZDS leader.

Meciar's response, once back in office as prime minister, was to begin a campaign to strip Kovac of his powers, with the aim of eventually prompting the president to resign. In April 1995 Kovac reluctantly agreed to hand over control of the secret service to the government, whilst denying Meciar's claim that the service had been used to spy on him. In June 1995 the National Council transferred the function of head of the armed forces from the presidency to the cabinet.

In late August 1995 President Kovac's son was kidnapped and delivered to the Austrian police, who wanted him in connection with an alleged company fraud in Germany. Slovak police later uncovered strong evidence of secret service involvement in this kidnapping. The continuing struggle between Kovac and the Meciar government further undermined political stability in Slovakia and damaged the country's reputation in the West.

ECONOMY

As predicted, the performance of the Slovak economy worsened after independence, but despite conflicting signals over the long-term direction of economic policy there were signs of recovery by 1994.

With the abolition of the joint Czech-Slovak currency, and a sharp fall in mutual trade between the two newly independent states, Slovakia experienced sharp recession in 1993. The rates of unemployment and inflation rose rapidly. By 1994, however, a slow recovery had begun as trade with the Czech Republic picked up.

The populist stance of the HZDS has sent contradictory signals about Slovak economic policy. Although Meciar emphasised in the weeks before independence that he favoured a market economy, the HZDS has demonstrated ambivalence toward foreign investment, international financial institutions, and structural reform such as privatisation. Indeed, Meciar and the HZDS have favoured continued state control of large parts of the economy.

Meciar's two spells as prime minister since independence have been marked by a reluctance to introduce the tough budgetary regime required by the IMF as a precondition for aid. The Moravcik government, in contrast, passed a tough budget restricting spending in line with IMF guidelines, but its apparent deference to international institutions may have cost it votes in the parliamentary elections of 1994.

Privatisation

Privatisation since independence has made extremely slow progress, and has been tainted by allegations of corruption. In 1993 the Meciar government rejected continued large-scale voucher privatisation, opting instead for conventional methods including direct sales, which slowed to a trickle. There were persistent allegations from the opposition and from dissident elements within the HZDS of a conflict of interest within the privatisation agency, the National Property Fund.

One of the first acts of the Moravcik government was to halt several allegedly corrupt sales; it then reshuffled the directors of the National Property Fund and secured the passage of a law on large-scale voucher privatisation.

Meciar's return as Prime Minister in December 1994 threw into confusion a privatisation process now to be directed by a leftist ZRS privatisation minister. Implementation of Moravcik's voucher privatisation scheme was quickly halted and under legislation passed in July 1995 it was scrapped. Further legislation excluded from the privatisation process "strategic" firms in the gas, power, railways, post office, telecommunications, arms, agriculture, forestry and water management sectors.

Property restitution

Property restitution in Slovakia has been limited to an October 1993 law on returning property to churches and religious communities. The law concerned buildings, farmland, forests and vineyards confiscated under communist rule from 1948, and similar property confiscated from Jews after 1938. Property confiscated and subsequently transferred to private hands was exempt, thus protecting so-called nomenklatura privatisation.

JUSTICE ISSUES

The question of administering justice for the crimes of the communist era has been eclipsed by controversy over the alleged abuse of StB files and political manipulation of the postcommunist intelligence service, the SIS. In early 1995 Meciar claimed that President Kovac had ordered the SIS to spy on him. Kovac responded with counter-accusations that Meciar was constructing a shadow intelligence service, but in April 1995 reluctantly signed legislation transferring control of the SIS from the presidency to the government. The suspected involvement of the SIS in the kidnapping of Kovac's son in late August 1995 raised fears that Meciar and the HZDS had harnessed the service for their own interests.

MEDIA

Slovakia's media have been subject to consistent political interference since the velvet revolution, and particularly after the 1992 elections. The issue has contributed to Slovakia's image abroad as the least democratic of the Central European states.

HZDS leader Meciar, angered by the media response to the series of scandals surrounding him since 1991, has repeatedly acted to support the pro-HZDS press and extend control over the editorial content of the state-run broadcast media.

In the run-up to the 1992 elections Meciar warned the press that newspapers which "did not tell the truth" would face punishment. Soon after independence several senior media figures were dismissed, including the editor and director of the state-owned *Smena*, Slovakia's leading newspaper. Most *Smena* editorial staff subsequently founded a new privately-owned daily, *Sme*, which continued to take an independent line. In 1995 *Sme* published evidence of secret service involvement in the kidnapping of

President Kovac's son; soon after *Sme* editor Peter Toth was beaten by unknown assailants. On the other hand, the loss-making pro-HZDS daily *Republika* received financial subsidies from the state news agency TASR until, in spring 1994, the Moravcik government sacked the TASR director and transferred ownership of *Republika* to a private company.

Meciar also moved to increase HZDS influence over the broadcast media by making a series of appointments in 1992-4 to Slovak TV and radio, and to the broadcasting supervisory councils. Attempts by the Moravcik government to appoint less biased officials were reversed by parliament following the HZDS victory in the 1994 elections, prompting Roman Kovac, the outgoing Deputy Prime Minister, to claim that the state broadcast media were no longer "public institutions" but "directed by [the HZDS]".

The extent of political bias at state TV was demonstrated in May 1995 by Slovak State TV Director Jozef Darmo, an HZDS appointee, in dismissing a request from President Kovac to broadcast a television address to the nation. Kovac, who had been defeated in a parliamentary motion of no confidence, was told by Darmo that his planned address comprised mere "tabloid invective".

ETHNIC AND NATIONAL RELATIONS

Slovakia's largest ethnic minority, the ethnic Hungarian community, reacted to the dissolution of the Czechoslovak federation with some concern. Slovak Prime Minister Meciar had repeatedly accused the Hungarians of undermining Slovak territorial integrity. Hungarian deputies had criticised the failure to include guarantees on minority rights in the constitution passed in autumn 1992. Despite sharing some of these concerns, Hungary agreed in June 1993 not to veto Slovak membership of the Council of Europe, having received assurances from Slovak officials that legislation on minority rights was imminent. This legislation was however heavily delayed, and indeed the situation appeared to deteriorate with the appointment of an SNS deputy as education minister in November 1993, and cuts to the training programme of Hungarian-language teachers.

In January 1994 some 3,000 representatives of the ethnic Hungarian minority assembled at Komarno. Despite fears that the assembly would demand secession, it merely called for administrative autonomy.

Minority rights legislation was eventually passed by the Moravcik government, permitting minorities to register their names in their native language and ordering the erection of bilingual road signs in districts where minorities comprised at least 20 per cent of the population.

The return of Meciar as Prime Minister in late 1994 marked a renewal of ethnic tension. The junior coalition partner, the SNS, had announced in May that only ethnic Slovaks would be granted party membership. To the chagrin of the Hungarian communities, SNS deputies were appointed to the defence portfolio and reappointed to the Ministry of Education.

Nevertheless the new Meciar cabinet backed the signature in March 1995 of a historic basic treaty with Hungary, in which both states pledged to protect minority rights (*see Slovak Foreign Affairs section*).

The Romany minority

In September 1993 Meciar allegedly called for cuts in family benefits to discourage Romany families from reproducing. He subsequently denied having described the Roma minority as "mentally backward" and "socially unadaptable". Following a series of attacks on Romanies by skinheads in Ziar na Hronom in central Slovakia in July 1995, SNS leader Jan Slota condemned the resort to violence but pointedly noted the high rate of crime among the Romany population. In September 1995 the Union of Romany Political Parties of Slovakia combined several Romany parties under leader Mikulas Horvath.

FOREIGN AFFAIRS

Adopting a pro-Western orientation in the first year or so of Slovakia's independence, the government emphasised its commitment to long-term membership of both the EU, striking an association agreement in October 1993, and NATO, signing up to the Partnership for Peace in February 1994. However, with the formation in late 1994 of the coalition of leftist and nationalist parties, which included an SNS deputy as Defence Minister, the government exhibited growing ambivalence towards the West. Instead relations with Russia warmed considerably. According to reports in September 1995, the Slovak government had chosen to accept a $150 million loan from Russia to complete the controversial Mochovce nuclear power station, and to refuse a conditional $300 million loan from the EBRD. The Austrian government strongly opposed the Mochovce project, arguing that it was based on outdated technology and therefore posed a considerable safety and environmental threat to Austria.

Slovakia enjoyed good relations with the Czech Republic, despite arguments in 1993-4 over the division of federal assets, the status of the frontier between the two states, and the Czech rejection of Slovak joint citizenship proposals.

Hungaro-Slovak relations

There has been considerable argument between Hungary and Slovakia over the controversial Gabcikovo-Nagymaros dam project. This grandiose project, originally conceived in the communist era, involves diverting the course of the Danube, which forms the border between the two countries. Hungary pulled out of the project in 1989 citing financial and environmental considerations, and in May 1992 Hungary renounced the original 1977 agreement on construction of the dam. Work on the Slovak side proceeded regardless, and in October 1992 Slovakia began damming the Danube.

In November 1992, however, Slovakia agreed to halt the project pending an inquiry by a special commission from the EC. Thenceforth the main issue of sensitivity was Slovakia's treatment of its ethnic Hungarian minority (*see also Slovakia: Ethnic and National Relations*).

Hungary's Prime Minister from 1990-93, Jozsef Antall, had declared himself the Prime Minister of all Hungarians. His concern for ethnic Hungarians outside Hungary's political borders was regarded by Slovak nationalists as barely-concealed irredentism. Hungarian policy changed significantly in 1994 with the appointment of Gyula Horn as Hungarian Prime Minister. Horn called for a "historic reconciliation" between Hungary

and its neighbours. The result was the landmark Hungaro-Slovak Treaty of Friendship
and Co-operation signed in March 1995. Under this treaty minority rights were to be
regarded as fundamental human rights; minorities were designated as "integral parts of
the society and state" and their "ethnic, religious and language identity" were to be
protected; and the Hungaro-Slovak border was declared "inviolable". Extreme Slovak
nationalists opposed the treaty but it was approved comfortably by the parliament.

CONSTITUTIONAL ISSUES

The Slovak constitution, adopted in September 1992, established a parliamentary
democracy with a unicameral 150-seat legislature, the National Council. The president
is elected by the parliament and plays a mainly ceremonial role: the presidential veto
may be overturned by a simple majority of parliament. A constitutional court can block
parliament's decisions. A three-fifths majority is required to remove the president or
shorten his term, but this can only be done on the grounds that the president's conduct
endangers "the sovereignty and territorial integrity of Slovakia" or undermines the
"democratic constitutional system". From 1994 Prime Minister Meciar, arguing that the
presidency was insufficiently accountable, led a campaign to strip it of its powers,
removing the president's functions as commander of the armed forces and chief of the
intelligence service. Meciar's campaign was directed at the incumbent Michal Kovac;
he favoured Kovac's removal and then a new presidential constitution.

POLITICAL PARTIES

Slovak politics have been dominated since 1991 by the HZDS. Although the party has
become increasingly nationalistic, it has left-wing roots. (In Slovakia, as elsewhere in
the region, the traditional Western left/right division is in some ways misleading, with
notionally right- and left-wing parties all offering nationalist policies combined with
state-interventionist economics.)

Party of the Democratic Left (SDL). Socialist party led by Peter Weiss; the successor
of the **Communist Party of Slovakia** (KSS), which had been part of the KSC since
1948. The SDL abandoned the hard-left stance of the KSC and moved towards social
democracy, participating in the broad coalition under Jozef Moravcik which governed
Slovakia for eight months in 1994. This helped to precipitate a split, with Jan Luptak
leading a breakaway labourist faction in April 1994, the **Association of Workers of
Slovakia** (ZRS). In consequence the SDL performed less well than expected in the
elections of 1994, polling 10.4 per cent of the vote (as part of the Common Choice
Bloc) compared to the ZRS's 7.3 per cent. The ZRS then entered the "red-brown"
coalition with the HZDS and SNS, while the SDL joined the opposition.

Movement for a Democratic Slovakia (HZDS). Nationalist centre-left party led by
Vladimir Meciar, which has dominated Slovak politics since its formation in spring
1991. The HZDS was formed by Meciar following his expulsion from the VPN. In
adopting an agenda combining nationalism and scepticism towards economic reform
the party was widely accused of populism. In 1992 it won over 37 per cent of the vote
in the Slovak elections, and although the party had campaigned for sovereignty rather

than independence, Meciar quickly pressed for the latter. The HZDS dominated the cabinet which supervised Slovakia's transition to independence but from March 1993 a string of senior government officials resigned and set up rival political factions, including Moravcik's **Democratic Union**. Most accused Meciar of practising an authoritarian leadership style and of delaying economic reform. With President Kovac also losing patience with him, Meciar was deposed as prime minister in March 1994. Despite warnings from Kovac of a personality cult around Meciar, more than one third of voters again endorsed the HZDS in the elections that autumn, and Meciar formed a government again in December 1994.

Slovak National Party (SNS). Extreme right-wing nationalist party. After an impressive showing in the Slovak elections of 1990, when the party took 19 seats, the SNS has lost support to the HZDS. It has however benefitted from holding the balance of power in parliament. The party served as a junior coalition partner to the HZDS in June 1992 to March 1993; in November 1993 to March 1994; and again from December 1994. To the chagrin of liberals and of the Hungarian minority, the party's portfolios have included the ministries of education and defence. The party leadership has moved further to the right following the expulsion of former chairman Ludovit Cernak in February 1994 and his replacement by Jan Slota. In May 1994 the SNS decided to refuse party membership to those from ethnic minorities.

Slovak Christian Democratic Movement (SKDH). Founded in 1992 as a breakaway from the federal Christian Democratic Movement and led by Jan Carnogursky. The SKDH is more nationalistic and left-wing than its federal precursor. Its support was relatively stable from 1992-4 at between 9 and 10 per cent.

The Hungarian coalition comprises the **Hungarian Christian Democratic Movement**, the **Hungarian Independent Initiative**, and the **Coexistence** movement representing Romany and other smaller ethnic minorities. It won some 7.4 per cent of the vote in 1992, and following its participation in the Moravcik government it improved its performance in 1994, winning over 10 per cent.

ELECTIONS

The 1992 Czechoslovak federal and republican legislative elections marked the beginning of the end of the federation. The election results of 1994 in independent Slovakia showed a high degree of continuity with the 1992 republican poll, with leftist and nationalist parties together taking about 60 per cent in both cases, and Meciar's nationalist HZDS emerging as by far the largest party.

Turnout was respectively 84.0 per cent on 5-6 June 1992 and 75.7 per cent on 30 September-1 October 1994.

Slovakia's electoral law imposes hurdles of 5 per cent for parties and 10 per cent for coalitions of four or more groups.

Slovak National Council elections, June 1992 and September-October 1994

| | Percentage of votes | | Seats | |
	1994	1992	1994	1992
*HZDS	34.96	37.26	61	74
+Common Choice (SDL)	10.41	14.70	18	29
#Hungarian coalition	10.18	7.42	17	14
SKDH	10.08	8.88	17	18
DUS	8.57	-	15	-
ZRS	7.34	-	13	-
SNS	5.40	7.93	9	15
Others	13.06	23.81	0	0
Totals	100	100	150	150

*In coalition with the small Slovak Farmers' Party (RSS)
+An electoral bloc comprising the SDL, the Farmers' Movement, the Social Democratic Party of Slovakia and the Green Party; 1992 figures refer to votes won by the SDL standing alone
#Comprising the Hungarian Christian Democratic Movement, the Hungarian Independent Initiative and Coexistence (for Romanies and others)

CHRONOLOGY

17 July 1992. The Slovak National Council proclaims Slovak Republican sovereignty.

1 September 1992. The National Council adopts a new Slovak constitution, which is signed by Prime Minister Meciar and National Council Chair Ivan Gasparovic in a televised ceremony two days later. The constitution establishes a parliamentary democracy with limited presidential powers.

1 January 1993. Slovakia formally becomes an independent state. Meciar warns that independence will bring economic difficulties, necessitating austerity measures.

26-27 January 1993. Meciar's favoured candidate for the Slovak presidency, Roman Kovac, fails to secure the necessary 60 per cent majority in the National Council.

8 February 1993. Slovakia introduces its own currency, the koruna.

15 February 1993. Michal Kovac of the HZDS, a compromise candidate, is overwhelmingly elected as Slovak President.

18 March 1993. SNS leader Ludovit Cernak resigns as Economy Minister, taking his party into "constructive opposition", in protest at the appointment of a former federalist as defence minister.

19 March 1993. Milan Knazko is dismissed as Foreign Minister and resigns from the HZDS in late March; in April he founds an "independent deputies' caucus", drawing with him a handful of HZDS deputies, thus leaving the government in control of only 66 of the National Council's 150 seats.

22 April 1993. The government's programme is approved with the support of the Party of the Democratic Left (SDL).

30 June 1993. Admission to the Council of Europe.

7 September 1993. Meciar allegedly remarks that Slovakia's Roma minority is "mentally backward" and "socially unadaptable". He later insists that he has been misquoted.

4 October 1993. Slovakia strikes an association agreement with the European Community.

18 November 1993. The SNS, having agreed to re-join the governing coalition, secures three portfolios, including--controversially--the ministry of education. President Kovac for the second time rejects Ivan Lexa, Meciar's close ally, as candidate for the privatisation ministry.

28 November 1993. Meciar makes a vitriolic attack on leading political figures and international institutions, notably the IMF, in a speech in the town of Zlata Idaka. Meciar later claims his comments have been manipulated by the press.

3 December 1993. President Kovac requests Meciar's resignation and formation of a new government. In subsequent weeks a split emerges in the SNS, and the defection of several deputies leaves the government in a minority.

9 February 1994. Slovakia accedes to NATO's Partnership for Peace programme.

10 February 1994. The HZDS splits again, this time over allegedly corrupt privatisation; a new faction, the Alternative of Political Realism (APR), is formed by Foreign Minister Jozef Moravcik and Deputy Prime Minister Roman Kovac. The APR is subsequently reconstituted as the Democratic Union of Slovakia (DUS).

9 March 1994. In his annual televised "Report on the State of the Slovak Republic", President Kovac expresses "serious reservations about the style and ethics" of Meciar's leadership. He accuses Meciar of incompetence, of inhibiting democracy and of populism, and claims that Meciar has backed corrupt privatisation practices.

11 March 1994. Meciar is defeated in a vote of no confidence in the National Council; the cabinet resigns three days later.

16 March 1994. A new cabinet takes office, comprising a broad array of five parties under Jozef Moravcik as Prime Minister. They are the leftist SDL, the right-wing Christian Democratic Movement, and three centrist groups formed by breakaway factions from the HZDS and the SNS: Moravcik's DUS; Knazko's new, liberal, right-of-centre party, the Alliance of Democrats of the Slovak Republic (ADSR); and Cernak's right-wing conservative National-Democratic Party (NDS). The cabinet immediately halts 13 privatisation projects suspected of being corrupt.

6 April 1994. The Moravcik government replaces eight of the nine officials at the National Property Fund (the privatisation agency).

13 April 1994. The government programme is announced, and includes a pledge to accelerate the pace of economic reform.

23 April 1994. Knazko's ADSR is merged into Moravcik's DUS.

14 May 1994. The SNS introduces new party regulations permitting only ethnic Slovaks to join, and thus excluding Jews, Romanies, Hungarians and other minorities.

22 July 1994. The IMF approves loans worth $263 million.

30 September to 1 October 1994. Independent Slovakia's first general elections. The HZDS wins a major victory, capturing over one third of the vote, while Moravcik's

DUS wins under 10 per cent. The ex-communist SDL fails to match expectations, while a splinter group from the SDL, the Association of Workers of Slovakia (ZRS), performs relatively well.

3 November 1994. The Moravcik cabinet submits its resignation, remaining in office pending the appointment of a successor. The National Council cancels plans to privatise 38 state enterprises.

4 November 1994. A parliamentary commission of inquiry is established to investigate the dismissal of Prime Minister Meciar in March 1994.

13 December 1994. A new cabinet with Meciar as Prime Minister takes office; the cabinet, known as the "red-brown coalition", comprises the HZDS, the nationalist SNS and the leftist ZRS. The SNS takes defence and education and the ZRS privatisation and three other portfolios.

14 December 1994. The Cabinet postpones the second wave of voucher privatisation.

5 April 1995. The National Council debates a draft law transferring control of the secret service (SIS) from the presidency to the government. Meciar claims that President Kovac has used the SIS to gather information on him. Kovac counters that Meciar is constructing a "shadow" intelligence service, and protests that Meciar plans to strip the presidency of its powers. The National Council approves the law and Kovac reluctantly signs it on 8 April.

18 April 1995. Ivan Lexa, a close ally of Meciar, is appointed SIS director.

5 May 1995. President Kovac is defeated in a motion of no confidence, which nevertheless fails to secure the three-fifths support of the National Council constitutionally necessary to dismiss him from office. The vote follows a report by the 5-member Separate Control Commission (OKO) established in November 1994 to monitor the SIS, which alleges that Kovac and Moravcik have manipulated the SIS to discredit the HZDS.

11 May 1995. In the Church's first significant intervention in Slovak politics since 1989, the Conference of Bishops of Slovakia writes to parliament to warn that political instability is "endangering the foundations of the state".

16 May 1995. Up to 25,000 people demonstrate support for Kovac at an opposition rally in Bratislava.

23 June 1995. The National Council votes by a narrow majority to strip the presidency of its function as head of the armed forces, transferring this prerogative to the cabinet.

12-13 July 1995. The National Council passes privatisation legislation scrapping the mass voucher privatisation scheme and excluding from privatisation "strategic" sectors of the economy, including the public utilities, railways, telecommunications, arms and agriculture.

31 August 1995. The son of President Kovac is kidnapped by unknown persons and delivered to police in Austria, where he is charged with fraud.

7 September and 18 October 1995. Successive police investigators are dismissed from the kidnapping case after pursuing evidence of involvement by the SIS. Although SIS Director Lexa accuses the police of using "criminal methods", prosecutors clear the dismissed investigators of criminal charges in mid-November.

7-10 October 1995. The pro-Meciar daily *Slovenska Republika* prints evidence, subsequently proved as fake, that President Kovac has Austrian bank accounts containing millions of dollars.

12-13 October 1995. During a visit to Germany, Kovac describes the SNS as "a chauvinistic and nationalistic party": the SNS responds on 25 October by accusing Kovac of treasonous activities.

15 November 1995. The National Council approves a new language law restricting the use for official purposes of languages other than Slovak. The law meets with protest from the ethnic Hungarian parties and from the Hungarian government. President Kovac signs the law on 28 November, having received government assurances that legislation on minority languages is imminent.

EAST GERMANY

The eastern part of Germany used as its official title the German Democratic Republic, GDR (*Deutsche Demokratische Republik, DDR*) from 1949 until the unification of Germany on 2-3 October 1990.

The GDR, which ceased to exist upon unification, had occupied a total area of 108,333 sq. km (excluding West Berlin, an area of 480 sq. km which was under joint Allied control). It lay mainly in the North German plain, with the Elbe river crossing the country from south-east to north-west, the Harz mountains rising in the south-west and the Erzgebirge in the south. The GDR's longest border was the "inner German border" which separated it from West Germany. The northern border was the Baltic coast; to the south-east lay Czechoslovakia, and, to the east, Poland, whose border with the GDR followed the line of the Oder and Neisse rivers.

The 1990 population of 16,434,000 was only just above a quarter that of West Germany (the Federal Republic of Germany, FRG or BRD). The GDR had slightly more inhabitants than Czechoslovakia, but less than half as many as Poland, and the combination of emigration and a low birthrate meant that the population fell during its 41-year history (having been calculated at 17,314,000 in the 1946 census for the Soviet zone excluding Berlin). Three quarters of its people lived in urban areas. East Berlin, i.e. the Soviet sector of divided Berlin, was by far the largest city and also the GDR's capital; the second city was Leipzig, south of Berlin in Saxony, and the most urbanised (and polluted) part of the country was the southern industrial belt around Leipzig, Dresden and Karl-Marx-Stadt (the GDR name for Chemnitz). The main Baltic port was Rostock.

Ethnically, the GDR was homogeneous; 99.7 per cent of the population (excluding *gastarbeiter*, foreign workers from Vietnam and elsewhere) were German, and the only surviving indigenous ethnic minority of any numerical significance were the Sorbs, a Slavic people, some 110,000 of whom lived mainly around Cottbus . As a consequence of the holocaust there were estimated to be only 5,000 Jews in the GDR. The predominant religious faith was Christianity (mainly Lutheran protestant, but with a significant Roman Catholic presence in the south-west); rather under one-third of the total population belonged to one or other of the Christian churches as of the late 1980s.

HISTORICAL NARRATIVE

In the Europe of the Reformation, the states of Saxony and Brandenburg were part of the German heartland of Lutheran protestantism. At the time of the Peace of Westphalia, which ended the 30 Years War in 1648, these two were the largest of a mosaic of war-ravaged German electorates, dukedoms and city states in the area which would eventually comprise East Germany. Saxony in the south included Leipzig and Dresden, and was the wealthiest and most economically developed. Brandenburg was centred on the region's largest city, Berlin, with Mecklenburg and West Pomerania (the latter under Swedish rule) in the north.

In Napoleonic Europe, the eastward extension of the Confederation of the Rhine briefly incorporated Saxony and Mecklenburg, while Brandenburg was incorporated fully into Prussia as part of that rising power's westward expansion and consolidation. Prussia was the dominant force in the eventual unification of Germany in the nineteenth century. The power of Saxony, however, was already on the wane by 1815, to the extent that Prussia gained part of its territory in the Congress of Vienna settlement. Briefly Saxony stayed outside the Prussian customs union, until its extension to form the wider *Zollverein* in 1834. The German Reich (Empire) as established by Bismarck in 1870 had Berlin as its capital; with Prussian lands stretching far to the east, the area which later became the GDR was very much the central rather than eastern swathe of this Reich.

Defeat in the First World War precipitated the abdication of Kaiser Wilhelm on 9 November 1918 and the declaration of the Weimar Republic; constituent assembly elections took place in January 1919 and the following month the socialist Friedrich Ebert became the republic's first president.

The postwar settlement under the 1919 Versailles treaty changed the geographical balance of Germany. The new Weimar Republic was compelled to accept a major transfer of territory to Poland, the return of Alsace-Lorraine to France, the demilitarisation of the Rhineland, the surrender of all the German colonies as well as some more minor territorial adjustments, curbs on its armed forces, the acceptance of war guilt and a huge bill for reparations. This enforced settlement provided a territorial focus as well as other grounds for nationalist resentment and economic burdens, which contributed to destabilising the Weimar Republic.

Weimar was Germany's first experience of a liberal democratic parliamentary system, but it was not one which strengthened the roots of the democratic institutions which were subsequently destroyed by totalitarianism. The parties which participated in the Weimar system were tainted from the outset with the opprobrium of having accepted Versailles, however reluctantly. Thereafter, they proved unable to unite to offer strong government or cope with the economic crises of hyper-inflation in 1923 and mass unemployment in the post-1929 world recession. The resentments and fears thus engendered provided fertile ground for the rise of the irredentist and revanchist Nazi party, which came to power in 1933 with Adolf Hitler as Chancellor.

Proclaiming a Third Reich, Hitler pursued a policy geared to reasserting the dominant position of Germany in central Europe. A series of escalating confrontations included rearmament, the reoccupation of the Rhineland in 1936, the March 1938 *Anschluss* (union) with Austria, and the annexation of the Sudetenland from Czechoslovakia in October 1938 and of Bohemia and Moravia the following March. Eventually, having concluded the 1939 Nazi-Soviet Pact to ensure that the Soviet Union would be co-aggressor rather than adversary, Hitler pushed Britain and France into war in September 1939 by the invasion of Poland. Thereafter, in 1940 and 1941, the success of the German armies extended the dominance of the Third Reich far beyond central Europe, to the Atlantic coast with the defeat of France, as well as north through Scandinavia, and south-east through the Balkans as Germany overran Yugoslavia and Greece.

In June 1941, repudiating the 1939 Nazi-Soviet pact, the Germans launched an offensive which took their armies through Soviet-held territory in the Baltic states, Poland and Bessarabia, across Soviet Ukraine and deep into Russia. These military successes extended still further the reach of the Nazi racial "final solution", a vast system of subjugation of Slavic "subject races" and an extermination programme directed against Jews and gypsies. The death of six million Jews in the Nazi holocaust and the elimination of whole communities across central and eastern Europe profoundly affected the ethnic and social-political composition of the countries of the region in the postwar era.

The tide of war in Europe ran strongly in Germany's favour until it was turned, at enormous cost in Russian lives, by the eventual failure of this invasion of the Soviet Union, made manifest by the German Sixth Army's surrender at Stalingrad in January 1943. Thereafter, the Red Army slowly drove back the Germans into and across Poland, as well as advancing into Hungary and Romania. In gaining the ascendancy in the east, the Soviet Union was assisted by Allied landings in Italy in early 1944 and, crucially, by the opening of the main Western front with the Normandy landings in June 1944. The Soviet offensive launched in January 1945 swept towards Berlin, while Anglo-American forces crossed the Rhine in March; as Hitler's Reich collapsed, the lines of respective Soviet and Western occupation of Germany were set by the speed of the advance of their troops.

The perpetuation of this division of Germany dated from the wartime decisions of the allies, at Yalta and Potsdam, that a defeated Germany should be placed under an occupation regime consisting of Soviet, US and British zones. (To add a French zone, the US and British reallocated some territory from their zones.) In a 'partition within a partition', Berlin, an enclave 150 km inside the Soviet zone, was divided into a Soviet sector and three Western sectors (US, British and French), all under joint four-power control.

For Soviet policy under Stalin, it was a fundamental geopolitical imperative that German might should never again threaten the awful destruction of the Second World War. The Soviet hold over eastern Germany, a heavy military occupation reinforced by territorial changes and the exaction of crippling reparations, provided some guarantees in this respect. However, as the powers who had been wartime allies against Germany rapidly became Cold War adversaries on a global scale, the protection of the Soviet bloc's front line, on the "inner-German border", became the central concern around which its European alliance system and military dispositions were organised. The Warsaw Pact, set up in May 1955 essentially as a counterpart to NATO, included the GDR as a founder member (while West Germany formally joined NATO in the same month).

All formerly German territory to the east of the Oder-Neisse line was given to Poland in 1945, while the Soviet Union itself took northern East Prussia (as well as pre-war eastern Poland and part of Czechoslovakia). The redrawing of the map was accompanied by the enforced migration westwards of millions of ethnic Germans, settling mainly in West Germany. The eastern boundaries of what was to become East Germany were regarded as definitive by the Soviet side, but seen by the Western Allies as provisional pending a formal peace treaty with Germany.

The Soviet side resisted Western plans for economic integration and self-government in Germany. The 1947 Marshall Plan, a co-ordinated European recovery programme for Europe financed by US aid, was denounced by Stalin as American imperialism; it was applied in the Western zones of Germany, but not in the Soviet zone. When the Western powers included West Berlin in their 1948 West German currency reform, the Soviet authorities reacted by blockading road and rail access in a bid for overall control of the whole city. The West in turn responded with a massive operation to keep West Berlin supplied with basic essentials by air from July 1948 to May 1949. The Berlin airlift provided a potent symbol of the Cold War, which was already in a state of high tension (the US President having made his "Truman doctrine" commitment to resist "totalitarianism", and implemented it in Greece, while the Communist takeover in Czechoslovakia was forced through in February 1948). The hardening of the Cold War division of Europe (NATO itself was formed during the period of the Berlin airlift, in April 1949), with East and West Germany straddling the frontier, in turn hastened the political division of Germany into two states, one a free-market democracy aligned with the West and the other a communist-ruled state within the Soviet bloc.

Formation of the West and East German states

The process of building a political structure in Germany moved forward in the three Western zones, where the *Land* governments elected in 1946 had come together in an economic council by mid-1947, and had begun drafting a federal constitution in mid-1948. Their Basic Law was produced in May 1949 and was swiftly ratified by the Western *Länder*, where federal elections took place in August. The Federal Republic of Germany (FRG) formally came into being on 21 September 1949.

The following month, on 7 October 1949, the German Democratic Republic was proclaimed in the Soviet-occupied zone (five *Länder* and East Berlin, which became the GDR capital). It was regarded by the West as having no legal basis.

The political background of the GDR regime

The failure of the democratic institutions of the Weimar Republic, the rise to power of Hitler, and the experience of Nazi totalitarian rule, defeat and destruction in the Second World War, was the historical context in which the GDR regime was constructed. To create a political apparatus within their zone of occupation, the Soviet authorities turned initially to the remnants of the pre-Nazi German left, relying principally on communists brought back from their Moscow exile. The establishment of communist rule in East Germany essentially took the form of the creation of structures under the control of the occupying Soviet authorities; by comparison with other Central and East European countries which experienced a "takeover" of greater or lesser brutality, in East Germany little had survived the Nazi regime and the war in the way of political structures to take over.

Nazi totalitarian repression had all but eliminated internal communist resistance. The Communist Party of Germany (KPD), revived in 1945, had been founded in 1918 as the DKP by left-wing Social Democrats, and was in effect the heir to the intellectual tradition of the Spartacus League. After the crushing of the Spartakist rising in Berlin in early 1919, the DKP veered between ultra-leftism (launching unsuccessful uprisings again in 1921 and 1923) and attempts to co-operate with the Social Democrats within the parliamentary structure of the Weimar Republic. Ernst Thälmann, its leader from 1925, followed in 1928 the Communist International line of regarding the Social Democrats not as potential allies but as "social fascists". This stance ruled out any possibility of a united front against the rising threat of Nazism. It greatly swelled the ranks of communist militants, confirming the DKP as the largest communist party in the world apart from the CPSU, but the Nazi movement on the streets, and the manoueverings of its leaders among nationalist political leaders and industrialists, ultimately proved too potent a combination to be withstood by communist confrontation. The DKP, with almost 17 per cent of the vote in the November 1932 elections and over 12 per cent the following March even after Hitler had become Chancellor, became the object of ruthless Nazi suppression. The party was outlawed on the pretext of being blamed for having set fire to the Reichstag building and for planning an uprising; its leading members were murdered and thousands sent to concentration camps, while a number of those who escaped to the Soviet Union were later killed in Stalin's purges.

The Social Democrats (SPD) had been the largest political party in the pre-Hitler Weimar period, but could neither command a majority itself, nor for the most part could it agree to join coalitions with right-centre governments, whose existence it could thus only "tolerate" or disrupt. Drawing like the communists on the continent's largest industrial working class, the strength of the Social Democrats had lain in the trade unions (which Hitler had subsequently destroyed), although 40 per cent of SPD members had been white-collar rather than blue-collar workers. With a pacifist and anti-clerical tradition, the SPD under Weimar had limited its appeal among the middle classes by retaining the Marxist rhetoric of class interest, and had failed to attract support from a younger generation whose socialists were more inclined to identify with the more vigorous DKP. Dissolved in 1933 under the Nazi regime (which in December of that year bound the Nazi party and state together), it could do nothing to preserve working-class loyalty, while the Nazis claimed credit for full employment and appeased key workers over wage limits while clamping down to prevent any organised opposition.

In April 1946 the Socialist Unity Party (SED) was formed by a merger of the revived KPD and the SPD in the Soviet zone (a fate which the socialists of Berlin resisted). The initial idea of the KPD and revived SPD being jointly represented in the SED leadership (the social democrat Otto Grotewohl and the communist Wilhelm Pieck were its joint chairmen) survived only until 1947 when it was declared that the Russian road to socialism was the only model. Backed by the Soviet administration, the SED dominated the political scene and the communists dominated the SED. In September 1946 the SED topped the poll in all five provincial (*Land*) elections; thereafter, elections were conducted on a single-list basis, first used for the People's Council election in May 1949 (when two-thirds were recorded as approving and one-third as opposing the single list).

The SED took half the ministerial portfolios in its first coalition government, with Grotewohl as prime minister while Pieck became President. The SED's partners (Christian Democratic Union-CDU, Liberal Democratic Party-LDP, National Democratic Party-NDPD and the Democratic Peasants' Party-DBD) were progressively reduced in significance within the National Front, the umbrella organisation formed in 1950.

Walter Ulbricht, a KPD leader who had been in exile in the Soviet Union since 1933, became the GDR's dominant leader in its first two decades. Coming to power as an obedient Stalinist, he was SED general secretary from 1950 (the post was restyled first secretary in 1953), and head of state as well from 1960. He systematically purged his opponents in 1950, targeting alleged Titoists; in 1953-54, after the Berlin riots; and again after liberal hopes inspired in Hungary had been crushed by Soviet tanks in 1956.

The SED was a mass membership "Marxist-Leninist party of the working people in town and country". The single-list parliamentary elections under the communist regime allowed the division of seats between the SED, other National Front parties, and mass organisations, to be predetermined. In comparison with other such Front arrangements elsewhere in Eastern Europe, the National Front formula in the GDR allocated only a modest proportion of the parliamentary seats to the SED (127 out of 500 in the *Volkskammer* in 1986), but nonetheless gave it complete dominance in policy terms. The fundamental units of organisation of the SED were residential and grouped by district, while control in the workplace was exercised principally through the communist-dominated unions, the Confederation of German Free Trade Unions (FDGB) being the sole legal formation. The SED also controlled workers' militia groups in factories throughout the GDR.

Stalinisation - The Berlin Wall

In October 1950, when it joined the Council for Mutual Economic Assistance (Comecon), the GDR was incorporated formally within the Stalinist conception of an international economic system designed to make policies and production capabilities more coherent within the Soviet-led bloc. In practice, the exaction of war reparations continued to drain resources out of East Germany to the benefit of the Soviet Union, while the GDR regime under Walter Ulbricht was required to implement the two main planks in the Stalinist approach to "building socialism", namely the rapid development of heavy industry and the collectivisation of agriculture.

The SED party machine created under Ulbricht was harnessed to the central planning of the economy, in an effort to match the economic progress of the capitalist West, with an emphasis on the heavy industrial base, and a determination to extract maximum effort from the workforce (with problems of labour shortage exacerbated by a continuing flight to the West). When the workers of East Berlin and other cities came out on the streets in protest over demands for a higher work rate in June 1953 they were ruthlessly suppressed with assistance from the Soviet occupation forces; 21 people were killed and thousands arrested. Perturbed by the strength of dissent, the Soviet authorities (in the new climate following Stalin's death in March) ended the exaction of reparations and the Soviet High Commission insisted that a reluctant Ulbricht should appease the workers by pursuing a temporary "new course", relaxing the drive for socialisation of the economy and producing more consumer goods. The following year this gave way to a further push to fully centralised planning, nationalisation of industry, and collectivisation of farming.

From the 1960s, however, the GDR's economic planners placed a continuing emphasis on consumer goods, attempting to satisfy the demand for improved living standards, and on social policy, education and welfare provision. They could (and did) claim partial success. The GDR reached by some way the highest standard of living of the Comecon countries, but some of its achievements were later revealed as no more than the manipulation and falsification of statistics for propaganda purposes. And no propaganda could obliterate the message which could be drawn from measurements on the other yardstick, the comparison with a much more affluent West Germany. This comparison was all too glaring when it could be seen on television, as was possible almost everywhere in the East except in the area around Dresden.

Throughout the 1950s there had been a continuing exodus of East Germans to the West. This serious drain of manpower (and strain on the pride of the regime) was one of the factors which provoked the building in August 1961 of the ultimate symbol of divided Germany and divided Europe, the Berlin Wall (later extended along the whole length of the border with West Germany, ostensibly to prevent Western subversion). The decision to build the wall was taken by the Warsaw Pact, and also reflected the growth of tension over Berlin between the Soviet and the three Western administering powers, after the Soviet side had in 1958 begun moves to integrate the whole of Berlin into the GDR.

Resistance to political reform

When Warsaw Pact forces moved in to crush the reform communist experiment in Czechoslovakia in August 1968, German troops were among them. The "Prague Spring" ideas of political pluralism had found no echo within the SED, but the Soviet ideological justification for intervening, the Brezhnev doctrine of "internationalism" for the defence of socialism, was clearly full of import for the future of the GDR. Its 1968 constitution, describing itself as 'a socialist state of the German nation', had referred to the goal of unification 'on the basis of democracy and socialism', was significantly amended by 1974, dropping the words 'of the German nation' to leave simply the description "a socialist state", and replacing wholesale the article about eventual unification. Henceforth, the GDR proclaimed itself 'an inseparable part of the socialist community' linked 'irrevocably and for ever' to the Soviet Union.

An East-West German treaty which guaranteed the inviolability of the intra-German border (December 1972) enabled both states to become members of the UN the following September 1973. Meanwhile, tensions in Berlin had been eased by a new Quadripartite Agreement (September 1971) specifying that the status quo could not be changed unilaterally. In 1975 both the GDR and the FRG signed the Final Act of the Conference on Security and Co-operation in Europe (CSCE), in which the existing borders of all European states were declared to be inviolable.

These international developments were pursued under the leadership of Erich Honecker, who had succeeded Ulbricht on the latter's resignation in 1971. This was, however, apparently the measure of his experimentation, a limited openness to change in external policy, encouraged by the West German abandonment of the policy of "maintaining tension" in favour, from the late 1960s, of a policy of improving "inner-German" contacts and establishing normal relations with Soviet bloc countries. The advent of Mikhail Gorbachev's reformist regime in the Soviet Union in 1985 put Honecker under added pressure to find an East German reformist response. Relations between the two Germanies also suffered in the 1970s and 1980s from high-profile political scandals which accompanied the uncovering of evidence of the extensive spy networks which each side was using against the other.

Internally, the Honecker regime was one of the most conservative in the Soviet bloc, in tune with the Brezhnev line, and quite unprepared for the challenge of reform. By 1985, the East German economy had been in serious trouble for at least five years, although the systematic falsification of statistics under economy secretary Günter Mittag concealed some of the extent of this problem. Industry was in need of large-scale investment, in technology which could make it possible to increase productivity. The response was, in part, large-scale foreign borrowing (running up a hard currency debt of over $20 billion by the end of 1989); there were also cuts in spending on housing and social welfare programmes. Honecker and his associates maintained, however, that the example of the *perestroika* reform programme in the Soviet Union was not applicable in the GDR. The Soviet leader's visit for the SED's 11th congress in April 1986, and the embarrassment caused by his references to the Soviet party's spirit of self-criticism and efforts to overcome stagnation, set the tone of his difficult relationship with Honecker.

The East German response was essentially two-fold; to censor, if possible, the information on policy changes in the Soviet Union, and to seek to divert attention (and get more Western money) by arranging the first-ever visit to Bonn (the West German capital) by an East German leader. Honecker's visit to West Germany eventually took place in September 1987, but not before it had been made abundantly clear that

Gorbachev would not welcome such a visit giving another lease of life to the GDR's elderly hardline leadership. The coming of *glasnost* would ultimately expose the luxury in which Honecker, official trade union leader Harry Tisch and his associates had isolated themselves from the realities of East German life; these revelations, however, were to follow rather than to precede the collapse of the regime.

Exodus and popular protest - The replacement of Honecker

Freedom of travel was a major issue in the period leading up to the fall of the communist regime, with thousands defying the strict rules preventing them going to the West.

One precipitating factor in the collapse of the GDR was this defiance, which transformed itself into a sudden wave of refugee emigration. Most of those who abandoned East Germany in this way were the young, often the well-educated, people whom the GDR could least afford to lose. They left at first legally, on visa-free trips to Czechoslovakia, and then took refuge in Western embassies across Central and Eastern Europe. Many began going through Hungary, escaping into Austria. There was a marked absence of decisive action from Berlin to stop the departures, and on 11 September the Hungarians opened the border to Austria, letting the East Germans out. A breach of communist solidarity which had previously seemed unthinkable, this decision brought down no Soviet retribution or condemnation; the Soviet Union under Gorbachev's leadership was finding its way towards a post-Cold War accommodation with the West which effectively ruled out the recourse to the interventionist approach which had characterised the Brezhnev doctrine.

In consequence, thousands of East Germans drew the conclusion that the floodgates had opened. More people poured into Western embassies in Prague and Warsaw, then across the border from Czechoslovakia to West Germany after 4 November, and finally through Berlin when the Wall itself was breached five days later.

A third of a million East Germans left for West Germany in 1989, compared with under 40,000 the previous year. Even larger numbers became demonstrators on the streets of Leipzig, Dresden, East Berlin and other cities. The first signs of public protest came in May 1989, when church-based pro-democracy groups arranged to observe the local election process and then denounced the cynical fraud of the officially-announced near-unanimous vote for the approved National Front list. The protest demonstrations centred on Leipzig, and were firmly suppressed. Leipzig's Catholic church of St Nicholas, however, became a centre for Monday meetings of pro-democracy and civil rights groups, and it was from this initial nucleus that the massive-scale demonstrations of October developed and spread across the country. When the crowds reached many tens of thousands, the security forces could no longer disperse them, without recourse to army action on the scale of China's Tiananmen Square massacre in June. Honecker drew this parallel himself on 10 October (and indeed his regime had been one of the few to congratulate the Chinese leadership, whom Egon Krenz had visited in June). The demonstrations, however, continued to grow, demanding reform, demanding dialogue.

Within the SED leadership, Honecker's position had been weakened both by his chronic ill health and by the pressure for reform which was coming from the Soviet leadership. Gorbachev had visited Berlin as recently as 6-7 October, for the GDR's 40th anniversary celebrations, and warned Honecker that leaders who failed to respond to popular pressures "put themselves in danger". Demonstrators in Leipzig, clearly identifying the Gorbachev line as offering positive hope for reform in the GDR, had chanted "Gorby, Gorby" and "we want to stay"; but, within hours of his departure, the East German police had broken up demonstrations in Berlin and Dresden. On that anniversary day, for those who looked back over the history of the GDR, there was a striking contrast with 1953, when it had been Soviet troops who put down the country's previous large-scale popular protests.

As in Hungary, and as would soon be the case in Bulgaria and Czechoslovakia, the fall of the old leadership in the GDR (Honecker resigned on 18 October and was replaced by Egon Krenz) apparently offered a brief moment for reformists within the ruling party to regain the initiative. In this respect, however, East Germany was to be like Czechoslovakia, in that the initiative had already passed to the democratic opposition.

New Forum, the first of the opposition groups to apply for recognised association status (unsuccessfully, in September 1989), had grown by mid-October to a membership of over 25,000, drawn mainly from among the artists, students and intellectuals who dominated the demonstrations early on. Groups of the leftist "citizens' movement", like New Forum, Democracy Now, the Peace and Human Rights Initiative and the Greens, had been associated closely with the churches, particularly the St Nicholas church in Leipzig. They were joined, as the SED's hardline grip was loosened, by rejuvenated non-communist parties which for 40 years had disappeared or been subservient within the National Front. The Social Democrats, the Liberal Democrats and (more cautiously) the Christian Democrats took up critical positions; in this they were sustained by the renewal of links with their West German counterparts, a factor which later contributed to the impetus towards unification.

The fall of the Berlin Wall and the collapse of the GDR

Restrictions on travel to Czechoslovakia were lifted on 1 November 1989, and two days later it was made clear that those wishing to leave would not have to renounce their East German citizenship. The dramatic announcement followed, on 9 November, that East Germans were free to travel abroad as they wished, requiring only to have their identity documents stamped with an exit visa (which could readily be obtained). This allowed them to cross the Berlin Wall, and the intra-German border, which they did in huge numbers in the ensuing days, to the extent that the exit visa requirement was waived because it was impossible to administer. Television carried footage of people who, crossing the open checkpoints in the Wall, embraced security guards who had hitherto been under orders to shoot to kill at anyone trying to escape. A new law on the right to foreign travel, removing the threat of the deprivation of citizenship, was approved by parliament in December 1989 to take effect in February.

The collapse of the GDR after the fall of the wall was spectacularly rapid and, within a year, quite unexpectedly complete.

For all Krenz's concessions (and they were many and major; it was Krenz who opened the Wall, who agreed to open elections, and who conceded on ending the SED's "leading role"), he cut an implausible figure in his new reformist garb, and was swept aside within seven weeks. Few believed his claim that he had prevented violence in early October, by countermanding Honecker's orders for the use of force. As Honecker's own chosen successor, and as the former head of the hated *Stasi* security police, Krenz could not win support as a leader capable of setting the SED on a genuinely new and democratic course. The most credible candidate for such a task,

Hans Modrow, the reform-minded SED leader from Dresden, now took over the government from Honecker's long-serving prime minister Willi Stoph.

With free elections promised, Modrow formed a new government in mid-November. This consisted of the SED and the four other parties of the National Front which had previously been subservient to it, but which were now given much greater participation (the CDU, the Liberal Democratic Party--LDPD, the National Democratic Party-- NDPD and the Democratic Farmers' Party--DBD). The Christian Democrats in particular were given a real role.

The SED's emergency congress on 8-9 December confirmed that the party was following somewhat hesitantly the lead given by the reformists within its leadership. The congress adopted an action programme on restructuring the economy, and committed itself to democratic pluralism, but at this stage took only a half new name, styling itself Socialist Unity Party-Party of Democratic Socialism (SED-PDS).

From January 1990 Modrow sought to broaden the basis of his government further. By this time the important policy decisions were being made not in the government, but in the round-table talks under way with opposition groups since early December. On 5 February a "government of national responsibility" was formed with the addition of eight opposition party representatives. The GDR had its first-ever government with a non-communist majority. Elections were brought forward from May to 18 March .

Free elections and the momentum of unification

The unification of Germany, scarcely on the agenda when the Wall was first opened on 9 November, had become the dominant issue by the time of the March 1990 elections. Indeed, so far had the picture changed that the main arguments concerned when and how, not whether, to unite. Relegated to the fringe (as the results confirmed) were those, perhaps expressing a majority view only three months before, who stressed positive aspects in the old GDR, distinguishing it from capitalist West Germany, and seeking the continuation of a distinct East German state, which should be democratic, certainly, and respectful of civil rights, but egalitarian, preserving the best achievements of the East's social and welfare system.

The election left the CDU and its Alliance for Germany partners in a position of unexpected strength. The figure who loomed largest in its campaign was not an East German at all but the West German CDU leader and Federal Chancellor Helmut Kohl. The Social Democrats, also reliant on their Western sister party for weight in their campaign, trailed behind in second place. Third, with a solid core of support even now, were the former communists of the SED, having completed their name change to become simply the Party of Democratic Socialism (PDS).

After the March 1990 elections, it took four weeks to form the first fully post-communist government in East Germany, sworn in on 12 April. A "grand coalition" with the Christian Democrat Lothar de Maizière as prime minister, it included the CDU-dominated Alliance for Germany, the Free Democrats and Social Democrats, but excluded the PDS. Principal government members included Peter-Michael Diestel of the DSU as Deputy premier and minister of internal affairs: Markus Meckel (SPD) as foreign minister and Rainer Eppelmann (Democratic Awakening) in charge of defence and disarmament.

The process of forming a government was complicated by an issue which was to become a recurring feature of the political scene; allegations against leading figures (now focusing on SPD leader Ibrahim Böhme) about working for, or at least informing to, the hated *Stasi*. It had already been decided, in December, to disband the *Stasi*, and its East Berlin headquarters building had been ransacked in January. The compromising entries in its files, kept on more than one East German in three, went on leaching out in the ensuing years, even after unification, ultimately ruining the political career of de Maizière himself and prompting the government to propose (but then abandon) the idea of an amnesty.

The FDP left the coalition in July and the SPD in August, and the government itself ceased to exist with German unification on 2-3 October. During its six-month existence, it was heavily preoccupied with the economic, political and external dimensions of the unification issue (this last, however, being worked out principally between the Soviet Union on the one side and the NATO allies including West Germany on the other).

First to be decided were the terms of economic union (which took effect on 1 July). This agreement, and the accompanying programme of privatisation administered by the *Treuhand*, in effect defined the nature and the speed of the transition to free market economics. The package was costly for the West in immediate terms. Only gradually did it also become apparent how severe the dislocation would be in the East, in a society where the inefficiencies of outmoded industrial production had been concealed behind state ownership, guaranteed employment and public subsidy.

More debated at the time than economic union was the form and timing of political union. The uneasy relationship between the parties in the broad coalition government broke down first in July 1991, over a question of essential interest for future party political advantage: de Maizière's proposal that unification should follow, rather than precede, all-German elections, which would avoid the application of existing West German rules in those elections. The Free Democrats (who left the coalition in protest on 24 July), and the Social Democrats, saw this as favouring the CDU's ally the DSU, which could be eliminated from parliament if the West German 5 per cent minimum threshold were applied.

The SPD left the coalition the following month (raising the question of whether the government would still be able to get a two-thirds majority for a unification treaty), protesting over the dismissal of SPD finance minister Walter Romberg and other cabinet members whom de Maizière held responsible for poor economic management.

The unification of Germany took effect at midnight on 2-3 October 1990. In effect it involved the disappearance of the East German state, its merger into the existing structure of the Federal Republic, and the holding of all-German elections on 2 December. These elections returned to power the CDU-led coalition under Helmut Kohl, who could claim them as his triumph. More than anyone, he had identified and ridden the tide of German unification in the past twelve months.

The reality of unification for the east

For many Germans, however (and for non-Germans too), the celebrations of unification were clouded with concern, in a way that had not been the case on the euphoric day the Wall came down. In rebuilding the economy, large-scale unemployment had already emerged as a heavy price, even though the East started from a higher point, and had far better chances of attracting investment, than the post-communist regimes elsewhere in the region. Many individuals found themselves paying for involvement with the old system; not just the corrupt top party officials and the secret police informers, but others such as border guards who faced prosecution for shooting to kill would-be escapers, and many thousands of teachers, debarred from teaching if they were too heavily implicated in the indoctrination of the "*Stabu*" lessons in "citizenship studies". The emergence of racism and crude Nazi-style violence among skinhead gangs, hitting the headlines with attacks on immigrant workers, was the response of a fringe minority. An indicator of wider discontent could be found in persistent electoral support around the 20 per cent mark for the PDS, arguing for more state protection for those whom "freedom" had left jobless, exposed and vulnerable.

Unification essentially involved the takeover of the east by the west, and the creation of a market economy based on privatisation, assisted by large-scale transfers of public funds over a much longer period than the one or two years which was initially envisaged.

The allocation of blame for the crimes and corruption of the GDR regime caused controversy repeatedly in the five years following unification. An even more pervasive issue for the country's political culture was how to come to terms with the extent to which the citizens of the GDR had been made complicit by the control exercised by its surveillance and political police network.

However, it was the consequences of the dismantling of the failed state planned economy, the acute problems of unemployment and lost social protection, and above all the feeling of insecurity, which loomed largest among the still small but significant minority five years on who apparently regretted the collapse of the GDR. On the fifth anniversary of unification, 15 per cent gave answers in opinion polls showing that they felt they were worse off economically, and 25 per cent said that their lives overall had changed for the worse.

ECONOMY

Chancellor Kohl's West German government made a major miscalculation over the likely costs of unification. Motivated by the desire to reinforce the momentum, it encouraged the belief that unification could be achieved economically, with the expected attendant rapid rise in living standards in the east, without major costs to taxpayers in the west.

The calculation (or at least the hope) was that unification would produce an economic boom in the east, sufficient to pay for the expensive decision to boost consumer spending power among East Germans by exchanging their Ostmarks one for one against the deutschemark in the currency union which took place on 1 July 1990. Warnings about the dangerous inflationary impact of this measure proved unfounded. However, while the west enjoyed a shortlived unification boom, the uncompetitiveness of outmoded industries in the east was ruthlessly exposed by the shift to a much-overvalued exchange rate, and output plummeted.

A flood of factory closures followed, entailing high costs to the government in unemployment and social security benefits, on top of the costs of much-needed environmental improvements, construction, and investment.

Kohl's belated recognition of the need for sustained public sector aid to restructure the east was translated into the imposition in 1991 of a special surcharge on income and corporation tax. Introduced as a one-off measure, this idea was revived in September 1992 as the German government ran into a major crisis over the funding of the east.

The so-called "solidarity pact" of 13 March 1993 provided for the reintrodution of the "solidarity surcharge" with effect from January 1995, at 7.5 per cent, and although there were plans to phase it out, the likelihood of this happening in the near future receded as the pressures on the budget deficit became more acute in the run-up to Germany joining a common EU currency. The net value of public funds transferred from western to eastern Germany from July 1990 to the end of 1995 was in excess of 700 billion deutschemarks.

Part of these transfers did finance investments which helped to promote economic output, increasing per capita GDP from 30 per cent to 50 per cent of the western German level, with growth (seriously negative at -31.4 per cent in 1991) taking hold at 7.8 per cent in 1992, 5.8 per cent in 1993, 9.9 per cent in the housing boom year of 1994 and 5.3 per cent in 1995. The main area of expansion, however, was in the services sector; indeed, of some 500,000 companies set up in the five years after unification, only 14,000 operated in the industrial sector.

Kohl's optimism about a five-year transformation remained unfulfilled; despite the creation of new infrastructure, roads, a merged railway system from 1994, modern telecommunications and a cleaner energy industry. Economic union, which had to a large extent consisted of the takeover of the east by the vastly wealthier west, had by 1995 still not achieved the creation of a truly self-sustaining market economy in the former eastern *Länder*. Unemployment remained obstinately above 15 per cent, and the closure of the Bremer Vulkan shipyards in Rostock in late 1995 underlined the extent to which some of the surviving heavy industry remained unviable without continuing public subsidy.

Privatisation

Once committed to economic union in 1990, the GDR government moved rapidly to set up in March 1990 the agency which was to oversee the transfer of the thousands of state-owned enterprises to private ownership, under the supervision of the Finance Ministry. Known as the *Treuhandanstalt*, this body began by reviewing the possibilities for privatising the enterprises thus placed under its control (which also included agricultural land and forests). Its initial decisions concentrated as much on liquidating the unviable concerns (over 300 of which, with 80,000 employees, had been closed down by April 1991, the month in which *Treuhand* president Detlev Rohwedder was assassinated).

However, privatisation gathered pace once the initial problems over ownership of land and buildings had been resolved - the legal uncertainties arising from the existence of different East and West German legal systems having been overcome with unification. The number of companies privatised had topped 2,000 by May 1991. Few (46 at this stage) had gone to foreign investors, however, and the strong impression had been created that the process was organised to favour the interests of investors from the western part of Germany, promoting resentment among easterners about the nature of this apparent wholesale takeover.

Any such resentment had insufficient force to slow the privatisation process, however, with the German government fully committed to the creation of a market economy system. By the end of 1944 only 65 firms remained unprivatised, and the *Treuhand* was wound up, its task officially completed. It had privatised over 14,000 enterprises, 25,000 restaurants and other service businesses, and 41,000 properties. It had however recorded an overall loss in the process, of some 275 billion deutschemarks, in view of the high costs of capital injections needed to conclude sales, and the expenditure on repairing environmental damage. Whereas the state holdings placed under the *Treuhand* in 1990 had employed some 4,000,000 people, over 60 per cent of these jobs had disappeared as a result of privatisation or the liquidation of unviable concerns.

A report published by the Organisation for Economic C0-operation and Development (OECD) in March 1996 noted that, alone of the former Soviet bloc countries, East Germany had virtually completed its privatisation; the Czech Republic had privatised or liquidated 81 per cent of its large state-owned enterprises, Hungary 75 per cent, Estonia 74 per cent, Lithuania 57 per cent, Latvia 46 per cent, Slovakia 44 per cent, Poland 32 per cent, Romania 13 per cent and Bulgaria 10 per cent.

Restitution

The 15 June 1990 agreement, subsequently incorporated in chapter IX of the 1990 unification treaty, established, against the opposition of the SDP, that there should be full restitution, or compensation, for the owners or heirs to property confiscated under the GDR regime in 1949-90. Where east Germans were tenants in such property their tenure would be secured, notwithstanding the reversion of title to ownership. In the case of property expropriated under the occupying Soviet administration in 1945-49, however, there would be no restitution or compensation, and ownership would instead pass to the German federal authorities.

Moreover, a strip of land 165 km long, along the eastern side of the Berlin Wall, which had been controlled by the GDR defence ministry, was transferred to federal ownership--a decision contested on behalf of its former owners. The ensuing protracted "wall property dispute" placed a continuing blight over redevelopment of the land in question, much of which was prospectively of high commercial value as money poured in to the reconstruction of central Berlin.

In a move designed to prevent the restitution principle from becoming an obstacle to economic development and investment in the east, the federal government subsequently made a provision that a new investor could gain title, and the original owner be required to accept compensation rather than restitution, if the investor's plans met certain criteria notably on the creation of jobs.

Legislation approved by the *Bundestag* on 20 May 1994, set the amount of compensation available as DM12 billion for those expropriated under the GDR, with DM 2 billion for those who suffered under Nazism but had not been compensated under the GDR. This legislation also provided for limited compensation for Soviet seizures in 1945-49 (the constitutional court having upheld in April 1991 the position established in the unification treaty that there would be no restitution in such cases).

POST-COMMUNIST JUSTICE ISSUES

The Stasi

The decision to disband the *Stasi*, the Ministry of State Security, was taken by the Modrow government on 14 December 1989, but it was not until 12 January, and as a result of much pressure, that Modrow agreed not to set up any replacement, pending the holding of elections and formation of a democratically-elected government. It was revealed at this time that there had been 85,000 *Stasi* personnel, of whom 25,000 had already been dismissed, and on 15 January Modrow promised that disbanding would be completed within 10 days. Meanwhile direct action in a number of cities gave protesters a degree of temporary control over the huge number of files, which the *Stasi* had kept on one GDR citizen in three. The Leipzig offices of the *Stasi* were occupied on 4 December 1989 and the East Berlin *Stasi* headquarters was ransacked on 15 January.

The state treaty on unification stipulated that the files would remain for the time being in East Germany, where a commission under pastor Joachim Gauck was set up on 28 September 1990 by parliament to supervise them, following further occupations of the Berlin headquarters in that month by demonstrators demanding access to their files. In November 1991 the federal parliament approved legislation allowing people the right of access to their own files, but leaving Gauck's commission to decide on the publication of any records, thereby seeking to control the spread of rumours and allegations about politicians having been informers. Gauck said in October 1995 that his commission was dealing with files on around 91,000 full-time *Stasi* officials and 175,000 unofficial assistants, as well as records concerning a much larger number of victims of *Stasi* surveillance; some 930,000 people had applied to see their files, and parliaments and public authorities had asked to see files in 1,760,000 cases. As of end-1995, Barbel Böhley was prominent among those pressing for compensation from the German state for those who had suffered oppression and discrimination under the GDR.

A suggestion to screen all members of parliament was rejected in March 1990. Those who resigned over the issue of *Stasi* connections, while in many cases denying that allegations about them had any substance, included Democratic Awakening's first leader Wolfgang Schnur in March 1990; the SPD leader Ibrahim Böhme, also in March 1990 (he was eventually excluded from the party over this issue in July 1992); the Free Democrat construction minister Axel Viehweger in September 1990 (after the publication of a list of 68 government members and parliamentarians with alleged *Stasi* links); and Lothar de Maizière, by now minister without portfolio in the all-German government and CDU deputy chairman, in December 1990.

De Maizière resumed the post of CDU deputy chair on the strength of having been exonerated by a government inquiry in February 1991, but resigned again in September 1991. In the neighbouring *Land* of Saxony-Anhalt, the minister-president, Gerd Gies, resigned in July 1991 amid accusations that he had sought political advantage by accusing rivals of *Stasi* involvement.

The Gies affair highlighted a growing recognition that it was not always straightforward to establish the culpability or the motives behind particular instances of contact with the *Stasi*. The following spring the SPD head of the *Land* government in Brandenburg, Manfred Stolpe, a former lawyer for the Evangelical church in the GDR, lost his Green/Alliance 90 coalition partners in a controversy over his having had meetings with the *Stasi*, but ultimately he withstood this challenge and retained popular support. On the other hand Gerhard Riege, a PDS member of the federal parliament committed suicide in February 1992 rather than face media publicity about *Stasi* connections.

Trials of former leaders - The "shoot-to-kill" prosecutions

Proposals to bring former GDR leaders to justice moved quite rapidly away from the idea of any kind of general indictment for treason. Such a charge would raise intractable problems, including the fundamental question of whether the leaders of the East German state could be condemned on the grounds of its having had no legal basis for existence.

Prosecutions were brought, however, for corruption, for electoral fraud (in connection with the controversial 1989 local elections), and, above all, against those held responsible for deciding, maintaining and implementing a "shoot-to-kill" policy against those trying to escape from the GDR by crossing the Berlin Wall. Ultimately, Honecker himself and several of the main other leaders of the pre-1989 period were deemed too old and ill to face trial, and, although charges against Egon Krenz and others were being prosecuted as at the end of 1995, relatively few cases had been brought to a conclusion except for the prosecutions of border guards who actually carried out shootings.

The main exceptions were the former East German union leader and SED politburo member Harry Tisch, who was sentenced in June 1991 to 18 months' imprisonment for corrupt misappropriation of union funds (but released immediately, having served nearly a year on remand), and former defence minister Heinz Kessler, who along with his deputy and a regional SED official were convicted on 16 September 1993 of complicity in the shoot-to-kill policy and violating human rights; he received a sentence of 7½ years and they got shorter terms.

Honecker, former state security minister Erich Mielke and former GDR president Willi Stoph and three others had originally been charged together with Kessler in May 1992, but when the trial began in November of that year Stoph and Mielke were ruled too ill to stand trial, and on 12 January 1993, the prosecution of Honecker too was abandoned on the grounds of age and infirmity. Having been brought back from the Chilean embassy in Moscow to face trial, he was released and allowed to join his wife in Chile, where he died the following year. Mielke's trial was abandoned at the end of 1994 after another attempt, again because he was too ill.

On 9 January 1995, manslaughter charges were brought against Egon Krenz, Harry Tisch and five other former SED politburo members over the "shoot to kill" policy. Related charges were brought against eight senior generals, whose trial began in August 1995. Some 200 investigations had originally been launched, and some 30 border guards brought to trial, commencing in late 1991; these trials ended variously with minor prison sentences, suspended sentences or acquittals, although in October 1993 a guard got 10 years for murder, for shooting someone who had already surrendered..

With regard to the controversy over fraud in the May 1989 East German local elections, city-level officials received suspended sentences and fines in February 1992. Hans Modrow, who had been SED party secretary in Dresden, was charged in March 1992, but eventually let off with a caution; his case was retried after a prosecution appeal, and on 8 August 1995, he received a nine month prison sentence for electoral fraud .

Markus Wolf, who had been the GDR head of intelligence in 1958-87, was arrested in 1991 and charged in September 1992 with treason, espionage and corruption; at the end of a seven-month trial he was sentenced on 6 December 1993 to six years' imprisonment.

FOREIGN AFFAIRS

With the issue of German unification following so rapidly upon the removal of the GDR regime, questions of foreign relations were never really addressed separately by de Maizière's government.

The redefinition of Germany's relationships as a whole, with the four powers which had occupied it in 1945 and within European alliances, were discussed in a "two-plus-four" structure formulated in February 1990, involving the Federal Republic of Germany, the GDR, the USA, the UK, France, and the Soviet Union. Negotiations took place between May and September. The suggestion that there might be some form of non-NATO status for East Germany was overtaken by the momentum of German unification, and Gorbachev, having initially held out for such an arrangement, accepted in his talks with Kohl in mid-July 1990 that united Germany could be part of NATO. The so-called "two-plus-four" treaty, formally known as the "Treaty on the Final Settlement with respect to Germany", was signed on 12 September 1990; its ratification was completed by the Soviet Union, as the last of the Four Powers to do so, in March 1991.

The Federal Republic of Germany signed a good neighbourliness, partnership and co-operation treaty with the Soviet Union on 13 September 1990; and Germany agreed to provide aid amounting to some DM 12 billion towards resettling Soviet troops to be withdrawn from Germany by 1994. The last of the occupying troops left in 1994; the departure of the last Russians was marked by a ceremony in Berlin on 31 August 1994, and the remaining British, French and US contingents left Berlin the following month.

A border treaty with Poland, signed by the foreign minister of unified Germany and his Polish counterpart in Warsaw on 14 November 1990, confirmed the position already accepted by the GDR in 1950, that Germany formally abandoned any territorial claims dating from the end of World War II. A treaty of good neighbourliness and co-operation was also signed with Czechoslovakia on 27 February 1992, although there continued to be friction over lobbying for property restitution among ethnic Germans expelled from the Sudetenland after World War II.

CONSTITUTIONAL ISSUES

The introduction of pluralism within the GDR constitution

A key phrase in article 1 of the constitution of the GDR specified that the GDR was led by "the working class and its Marxist-Leninist party". This was deleted on 1 December 1989, with the almost unanimous support of the *Volkskammer*.

Thereafter, there were a series of changes necessary for the holding of free elections, and the round table discussed a draft for a new constitution for East Germany, agreeing at its final session on 12 March 1990 that this should be discussed by the new parliament and then put to a referendum. This never took place, as the general consensus for unification made it irrelevant. However, changes were made in April 1990 by the new *Volkskammer*, removing the description of the GDR as "a socialist state of workers and peasants" and abolishing the State Council (whose chairman had been head of state), with the speaker of the *Volkskammer* becoming head of state in an acting capacity.

A social charter, the product of the work of the round table, was approved by the East German parliament on March 7, 1990, guaranteeing the right to work and the right to strike. Unification under the Basic Law of the Federal Republic automatically extended its guarantees of other rights and freedoms to citizens from the former East Germany.

Unification under the existing constitution of the Federal Republic

The state treaty on unification, signed on 31 August, determined that the two Germanies would be united, on 3 October, by means of the GDR ceasing to exist, and five *Länder*, recreated on the territory of the GDR, joining the Federal Republic under the provisions of Article 23 of its Basic Law. It was agreed that any further matters arising from unification, which required settlement by amendment of the constitution, should if possible be regulated within two years from that date. This would apply in particular on the issue of abortion, where West German law had been much more restrictive than that of East Germany, and where both sets of legislation would remain operative pending a compromise. However, the abortion issue in particular proved more difficult to reconcile than this timetable allowed. A relatively liberal law to apply throughout the country gained parliamentary approval in June-July 1992 but was struck down by the constitutional court the following year, being eventually replaced by more restrictive legislation in 1995.

It was only in 1994 that the *Bundestag* (in June) and the *Bundesrat* (in September) completed parliamentary approval of a series of other minor constitutional amendments under discussion since unification, on implementing the existing right to equality between the sexes, and on environmental protection and non-discrimination against the handicapped.

PRINCIPAL PERSONALITIES

The communist leaders of the GDR

Walter **Ulbricht** (1893-1973), a Weimar Republic Communist from Leipzig who had fled to Moscow in 1933, became an SED politburo member in January 1949 and general secretary in July 1950, and over the next two decades (from 1960 as head of state as well as party leader) imposed rigid Stalinism, both in terms of party terror and in terms of economic nationalisation and the collectivisation of agriculture. Ousted from the party leadership by his former protégé Honecker in 1971 (although still head of state until his death), his dominance was subsequently played down.

Willi **Stoph** (b. 1914). A Communist in his youth, and a prominent SED member with a politburo seat from 1953 onwards, he was prime minister for nine years under Ulbricht, then his successor as President, then again prime minister from 1976 to 1989, as a loyal number two to Honecker. He resigned on 7 November 1989, and was arrested in May 1991 to face charges of responsibility for murder over the GDR's "shoot to kill" policy against would-be escapers. By the time his trial began in November 1992, however, he was ruled too ill to face the charges, and the trial was discontinued the following August.

Erich **Honecker** (1912-1994). A communist organiser from the Saar, he was imprisoned in 1935-45 by the Nazi regime, then rose rapidly within the SED, and joined the politburo in 1958. It was on his initiative that the Berlin Wall was built in 1961. He was regarded as Ulbricht's chosen successor, but ousted him early, with

Soviet support, in 1971, and was the dominant figure of GDR politics for the next two decades (adding to the party leadership, in 1976, the role of head of state). Keen to promote his own and his country's international image, he found himself quite out of step with the changes of the late 1980s. The growing perception of his inadequacy was compounded by his serious illness, and he was ousted from power in October 1989 in what was in effect a bid by the SED to give itself a new lease of life in power. The discovery of his corruption and use of funds for personal luxury helped inflame the public against him and his regime, but he was found to be too ill to stand trial. Arraigned again, in 1990, this time for responsibility for the "shoot-to-kill" policy against would-be escapers from the GDR, he was moved in March 1991 from a Soviet military hospital to Moscow, and in December he took refuge in the Chilean embassy there to avoid extradition. The German government eventually succeeded in having him brought to Berlin in July 1992, but in January 1993, after the court ruled he was too ill to stand trial on the manslaughter charges, he was allowed to join his wife in Chile, where he died on 29 May 1994.

Günter **Mittag** (1926-94). A politburo member from 1966 and SED secretary for the economy, Mittag was principally responsible for the mismanagement, under-investment and corruption of the latter years of the GDR. He was also blamed by his own colleagues in the SED old-guard leadership for his failure to deputise effectively in the summer of 1989, when Honecker was ill and a firm line was needed over the exodus of young East Germans. After Honecker's resignation, the fate of his hardline associate Mittag provided an index of the party's efforts to show a genuine commitment to change. Dropped from the politburo on 18 October, he was expelled from the central committee on 10 November and from the party itself on 23 November, and arrested on 3 December. Proceedings against him on corruption charges were dropped in 1993 because of his ill health and infirmity, and he died in March 1994 in Berlin.

Egon **Krenz** (b. 1937). Rising through the SED youth movement, with a seat in the party politburo from 1983 and responsibility for security policy, Krenz was often seen as Honecker's chosen successor. He followed the hard line of his mentor's regime until mid-1989, making it unlikely that reformists would subsequently dissociate him from the rigging of the local elections in May, and the congratulations which he offered to the Chinese party leadership for dealing with their pro-democracy demonstrators in Tiananmen Square. Ultimately, convinced of the need for changes by the attitude of Gorbachev, the exodus of asylum-seekers and the size and tenacity of the demonstrations of early October, he engineered the ousting of Honecker. Taking over himself as SED general secretary and then head of state, but lasted only seven weeks at the top. Unable to present himself as a credible reformer (although he put through such crucial changes as allowing freedom of travel, opening the Wall, and renouncing the party's leading role), he disappeared from the stage almost as soon as he had resigned his party and state posts (on 3 and 6 December respectively); in the following month the party expelled him, as part of the process of making its break with the Honecker regime. Eventually he was charged in January 1995, along with other party leaders, over the "shoot-to-kill" policy used by guards against would-be escapers from East Germany.

Hans **Modrow** (b. 1928). Brought into full membership of the SED politburo as an indication of its commitment to change on Nov. 8, 1989, Modrow, the party secretary from Dresden with a good name for personal honesty, had managed to sustain a real dialogue with the pro-democracy demonstrators. He was charged later the same month with heading what would be the GDR's last communist-led government, in which capacity he put forward his own plan for a unified but neutral Germany. At the March 1990 elections his reputation as a genuine reform leader was credited with helping his party (now renamed the PDS) retain a significant vote and finish third. He remained as caretaker prime minister until the new government was formed, and then stood, unsuccessfully, as the PDS candidate for the post of *Volkskammer* speaker. Brought to trial in 1992 for electoral fraud over the controversial May 1989 communal elections, he was let off in 1993 with a caution, but the prosecution appealed successfully and he was eventually sentenced to nine months' imprisonment on 8 August 1995.

Post-communist political leaders in the period prior to German unification

Ibrahim **Böhme** (b. 1944). Elected as SPD party chairman in late February 1990 as a figure whose dissident credentials apparently represented a clear break with the party's role within the SED (from which he had himself resigned, as a young historian in his early 30s, and been imprisoned and then banned from teaching history), Böhme came under attack immediately after the March elections as an alleged *Stasi* informer; he denied any such connection, but nevertheless stood down, formally resigned the East German SPD leadership on 1 April 1990, and was excluded from the party in July 1992.

Gregor **Gysi** (b. 1948). A lawyer, long-standing SED party member and son of one of Honecker's government ministers, Gysi was not himself in tune with the hardline stance of the Honecker regime, and was known for defending dissidents; the party brought him in as its new leader in December 1989 to signify the break with the past, and, under its new name of PDS, he led it to respectable performances in the multi-party elections of 1990. The PDS re-elected Gysi as its leader in January 1991 and again in December. In mid-1992 he was a leading figure behind the cross-party moves to create "committees for justice" to try to defend east Germans against humiliation and the destruction of their jobs and livelihoods in industry and agriculture. Although replaced as PDS party president in January 1993, he remained its most influential figure as leader of the parliamentary party.

Lothar **de Maizière** (b. 1940). Once a professional viola player, he was a lawyer with no real political experience when the CDU chose him as its new leader in November 1989. Associated with the pro-unification drive of West German Chancellor Kohl, the CDU and its allies won a strong enough position in the March 1990 to make its leader the obvious choice as the prime minister who would lead the GDR out of existence. De Maizière became a deputy chairman of the merged all-German CDU in October 1990, and a minister without portfolio in Kohl's government, but was then exposed to allegations that he had been a *Stasi* informer. He resigned, resumed his party post after the announcement in February 1991 that an inquiry had exonerated him, but resigned again in September, and gave up his parliamentary seat, as the allegation persisted.

POLITICAL PARTIES

The name **Socialist Unity Party of Germany** (SED) was used from 1946, denoting the merger of the Social Democrats in the Soviet zone with the German Communist Party (founded as the DKP in 1918 by left-wing Social Democrats from the underground wartime Spartacus League, and revived as the KPD in 1945 after having been banned and persecuted under the Hitler regime). The SED's "leading role" was abolished as of 1 December 1989, and many of its leaders expelled (and in some cases subsequently prosecuted).

At the emergency party congress on 8-9 December 1989 the SED redefined itself as a socialist party committed to democratic pluralism, adopting an action programme agreed by the central committee a month earlier (including the restructuring of a socialist planned economy guided by market conditions), and taking the half-new name Socialist Unity Party-Party of Democratic Socialism (SED-PDS). The decision to drop the first half was announced the following February, the name **Party of Democratic Socialism** (PDS) being confirmed at an election congress on 24-25 February 1990.

The main plank of the PDS election campaign in March 1990, and its subsequent principal concern as an opposition party, was the effort to preserve as far as possible within a free market context the level of social welfare and employment protection which had been built up under the communist regime. The PDS deputies in the *Volkskammer* voted against the terms of both the treaty on economic and monetary union, and the unification treaty. The *Land* government of Bavaria took the decision (not followed by other *Land* governments) in 1991 to put the PDS under surveillance as a possible danger to the constitution. By 1995 PDS party membership across Germany stood at some 120,000, of whom 90 per cent had reportedly been communist party members.

Legislation introduced by the East German government on 31 May 1990 allowed it to investigate and establish the value of party assets, and provided for expropriations of funds and property acquired by parties by the misuse of their position under the communist regime. As of October 1990 the PDS declared its assets to be worth DM4,000 million. Allegations that the PDS was transferring funds abroad illegally in that month led to police raids on the party headquarters, and charges against its treasurer and other officials. The *Treuhand* agency, set up to handle privatisation, took control of all PDS property and froze its bank accounts in June 1991, preventing it from spending money without permission. This followed the problems experienced by an independent commission which had been set up by the federal government to audit the funds and property of all the former GDR's ruling parties, to establish how it had been acquired and what parts of it could be retained by the parties concerned.

In the multi-party East German legislative elections in March 1990, the PDS did unexpectedly well, finishing third with 16.4 per cent (30 per cent in East Berlin) and 66 out of 400 *Volkskammer* seats. It scored 14.6 per cent in local elections on May 6, and between 9.7 and 15.7 per cent in the elections for the five reconstituted *Land* parliaments in the East on 14 October.

In the all-German elections in December 1990 the PDS, clearly disadvantaged in comparison with the other major parties in that it had no powerful counterpart organisation in the West, nevertheless still won 17 seats in the *Bundestag*, on the basis of its 11.1 per cent of the poll in the East; in the elections for a unified Berlin parliament at the same time the PDS won nearly a quarter of the votes in what had been East Berlin. In the succeeding years support for the PDS in the eastern part of the country showed a significant if gradual increase, reaching 19.8 per cent in the October 1994 federal elections. Four months earlier, its 19.9 per cent in the Saxony-Anhalt *Land* elections had given it sufficient representation to make the subsequent SPD-Green coalition there dependent upon its support.

Principal parties in the post-communist East

The **Christian Democratic Union** (CDU) in East Germany, which had been for over 40 years a subordinate part of the communist-dominated National Front, became the dominant element in the Alliance for Germany which won nearly half the total vote in the March 1990 elections. Its campaign and pro-unification programme were dominated by the influence of its West German counterpart led by Federal Chancellor Helmut Kohl, under whose leadership the CDUs of West and East merged on 1 October 1990. The East German CDU leader Lothar de Maizière was prime minister of the last East German government, from April 1990 until unification in October. The post-unification disillusionment caused by economic problems in the East led to a marked falling-off in CDU popularity there in 1991, as did the conviction of its 1966-89 leader Gerald Götting in July 1991 for diverting party funds into his own holiday home, and the discrediting, over alleged *Stasi* connections, of de Maizière himself. He had taken over the CDU leadership on 10 November 1989, as the party distanced itself from the SED (although participating in the Modrow government), and he led its participation in the subsequent round-table talks. The CDU's programme of pluralism, democracy based on Christian values, and the creation of a market economy with encouragement for Western investment, was set out at an extraordinary conference on 15-16 December 1989. The party dominated the elections to the parliaments of the former east German *Länder* everywhere save Brandenburg in October 1990, and repeated this performance in the polls held between June and October 1994, as well as confirming its position as the leading party in Berlin in 1991 and 1995.

Also part of the Alliance for Germany (set up on 5 February 1990) were the **German Social Union** (DSU) and the centre-right **Democratic Awakening** (DA). The DSU had been founded on 20 January 1990, with a right-wing former Christian Social Party leader, the Leipzig pastor Hans-Wilhelm Ebeling, as its first chairman. Both Ebeling and Peter-Michael Diestel, who became de Maizière's deputy premier, left the DSU on 2 July 1990, after which the party retained no real significance. The DA was formally constituted as a party in Leipzig on 16 December 1989, led first by the lawyer Wolfgang Schnur and, after his disgrace over *Stasi* connections, by pastor Rainer Eppelmann.

The Free Democrats / Liberals in the East consisted of (i) the **Liberal Democratic Party** (LDPD), one of the four non-communist parties in the ruling National Front, which had begun to take a much more independent and pro-democracy line after Honecker's departure in October 1989, under the leadership of Manfred Gerlach and Rainer Ortleb, and which on 3 November joined the calls for the resignation of the government of prime minister Willi Stoph; (ii) a separate **Free Democratic Party**, critical of the LDPD for its history of collaboration with the communists, and set up later in November; (iii) the **German Forum**, and (iv) the **National Democratic Party** (NDPD), which like the LDPD had been one of the parties which existed under the communist-dominated National Front umbrella and then tried to reassert its separate identity. The Free Democrats / Liberals came together on 12 February 1990 (with the NDPD joining in March), as the **League of Free Democrats** (BfD) to avoid splitting the centre vote in the March elections. This was the first group to merge formally with its West German counterpart, on 11 August 1990; the FDP leader in the West, Otto Graf Lambsdorff, continued as party chairman and the BfD and Eastern FDP leaders were added as deputy chairmen. In only two of the former east German *Länder* did the FDP hold any parliamentary seats in 1990-94, and in both of these (Saxony-Anhalt and Thuringia) the were eliminated in elections held respectively in June and October 1994.

The **Social Democratic Party** was reformed as a separate entity illegally on 1 October 1989. It sought to symbolise its return to its pre-1946 independence by adopting at its first national conference on 12-14 January 1990 the name Social Democratic Party of Germany (i.e. SPD, like its counterpart in the West) rather than Social Democratic Party of the GDR (SDP). The same conference confirmed its conversion to the objective of German unification. The allegation of *Stasi* connections made against Ibrahim Böhme, who was elected as party chair at the 22-25 February party congress, affected its performance in the March 1990 elections, and he resigned thereafter, giving way initially to Markus Meckel. Meckel then took on the role of foreign minister in the coalition government, until the SPD left the government in the crisis over economic policy management in September. The party merged in late September 1990 with its Western counterpart, and its then current chairman Wolfgang Thierse became a deputy chairman of the all-German party. In the former east German *Länder* the SPD was strongest in Brandenburg, increasing its dominance of the state parliament and raising its share of the vote from 38 to 54.1 per cent in the September 1994 elections. Elsewhere it was the second party behind the CDU, albeit only very narrowly behind in Saxony-Anhalt where it formed a coalition with the Greens (dependent also on PDS support) after the June 1994 election.

Alliance 90 was the electoral alliance formed on 7 February 1990 for the March 1990 East German elections by three groups which had first emerged as authentic voices of the democratic opposition in 1989: the left-wing citizens' movements Democracy Now, whose leading figure was the documentary film-maker Konrad Weiss; New Forum, co-founded in September by the Berlin painter and activist Bärbel Böhley and the biologist Jens Reich, and legalised on 8 November; and the Peace and Human Rights Initiative. The revival of mainstream parties linked closely to their respective West German counterparts, and the rapid change of focus on to the issue of unification rather than that of changing East Germany, meant that the Alliance 90 platform (although it did accept, in the face of some dissent, the idea of gradual unification, leading to a demilitarised Germany) won only 2.9 per cent of the vote and 12 *Volkskammer* seats in March 1990. Its deputies subsequently agreed to form a joint parliamentary group with the **Greens** (who had formed a party on 24 November 1989). In the December 1990 all-German elections, campaigning jointly with the Greens in the East, they increased their joint vote and narrowly passed the 5 per cent minimum threshold now applicable there, securing six Alliance 90 and two Green seats in the *Bundestag*; they did better in former East Berlin, winning nearly 10 per cent there in the December 1990 election of a unified city government. In September 1991 at a meeting in Potsdam the three movements within the Alliance 90 merged formally into a single organisation of that name, with statutes in line with federal party laws; part of New Forum opposed this merger.

Alliance 90 and the Greens agreed to merge on 16-17 January 1993, and won 7.3 per cent of the vote in the 1994 federal elections, thus being the third largest grouping in the *Bundestag*. In Berlin the Greens/Alliance 90 won 13.2 per cent of the vote in elections in October 1995, but of the former east German *Länder* only Saxony-Anhalt had Green representatives in parliament after elections in the course of 1994, the October 1994 poll in Thuringia having eliminated the Greens there. In Saxony-Anhalt the Greens became junior partners in a coalition with the SPD.

ELECTIONS

Legislature

Under Communist rule, the legislature, the 500-member unicameral *Volkskammer* (People's Chamber), designated as the highest state authority and nominally responsible for electing the Council of Ministers, was itself elected by universal suffrage from a single list of candidates for a term of five years, most recently in 1986.

A new unicameral *Volkskammer* of 400 members was elected on 8 March 1990 (and dissolved on 2 October, immediately prior to the unification of Germany; 144 of its members were then delegated to sit in the *Bundestag* pending the December 1990 all-German elections). The system used in March 1990 was proportional representation with no minimum threshold for representation.

Electoral regulations for the first all-German elections (on 2 December), as approved by the *Volkskammer* on 22 August, would have adopted the West German system, i.e. proportional representation in the 662-member *Bundestag* within the unit of the *Land*, and with 5 per cent of the overall national vote as the minimum threshold for party representation. Its only real concession to the smaller Eastern groups would have been to allow for "piggy-back" arrangements, in which parties of similar outlook might aggregate their votes for the purpose of calculating the 5 per cent, provided that they had not put up lists in competition with each other.

After unification, however, the rules were changed because the Federal Constitutional Court had found this system to be unfair to smaller parties in the East with no counterpart in the West. For the 1990 elections only, the minimum threshold was 5 per cent in either the former West or the former East.

For the next federal *Bundestag* elections, in 1994, there were 328 single-member constituencies, whose representatives were elected by simple plurality; a party winning three constituencies in a given *Land* would also qualify for a proportion of that *Land*'s party list deputies in the federal parliament, even if it did not achieve the overall national threshold of 5 per cent, a circumstance which applied on this occasion to the PDS.

The allocation of seats in the *Bundesrat*, the upper federal house, was reorganised upon unification to allow each *Land* to send between three and eight members.

General election results

18 March 1990: elections to *Volkskammer* in East Germany

	%	seats
CDU	40.82	163
DSU	6.31	25
Democratic Awakening	0.99	4
Free Democrats	5.28	21
SPD	21.88	88
PDS	16.40	66
Alliance 90	2.91	12
Others		21
Total		400

The turnout was given as 93.4 per cent.

2 December 1990: elections to *Bundestag* in united Germany

	% in West	% in East	seats
CDU	35.5	41.8	268
CSU	8.8	-	51
Free Democrats	10.6	12.9	79
SPD	35.7	24.3	239
PDS	0.3	11.1	17
Alliance 90/Greens	4.8	6.1	8
Others			0
Total			662

The turnout was 74.7 per cent in the East and 77.8 per cent overall.

16 October 1994, elections to *Bundestag*

	% overall	% in East	seats
CDU	34.2	38.5	244
CSU	7.3	-	50
FDP	6.9	3.5	47
SPD	36.4	31.5	252
Greens	7.3	4.3	49
PDS	4.4	19.8	30
Others	3.5	2.4	0
Total			672

The turnout was 79.1 per cent.

Presidency

Under communist rule the head of state was the Chairman of the 25-member Council of State, elected by the *Volkskammer* (Honecker until 18 October 1989, then Egon Krenz briefly on 26 October-6 December, then Manfred Gerlach pending election of a new *Volkskammer*.

On 9 April 1990 the new *Volkskammer* abolished the Council of State, provided that the state presidency should be a directly elected post, and meanwhile approved the appointment of its new speaker, Sabine Bergmann-Pohl, as acting head of state. She discharged the duties of this office until unification on 2-3 October 1990, when East Germany became part of the Federal Republic with federal President Richard von Weizsäcker as its head of state.

Local and state elections

Local elections were held throughout East Germany on 6 May 1990 (when the CDU won some 35 per cent, the SPD 21 per cent, the PDS 14.6 per cent and the Free Democrats 6.7 per cent; the SPD came first in East Berlin and the PDS second).

Elections for five reconstituted *Land* parliaments took place on 14 October 1990 giving the CDU control in Mecklenburg-Western Pomerania, in Saxony, in Saxony-Anhalt and in Thuringia, while the SPD emerged as the leading party in Brandenburg and came second everywhere else. This basic result was repeated in each case in 1994. The

PDS was third in four *Länder* but fourth behind the FDP in Saxony-Anhalt in 1990; in 1994 they finished third everywhere, in each case increasing their share of the vote.

Berlin held its first elections for a unified city parliament at the same time as the all-German legislative elections on 2 December 1990. The CDU emerged in first place overall, although behind the SPD (and only narrowly ahead of the PDS) in the former East Berlin. The October 1995 elections in Berlin again saw the CDU win the highest number of votes ahead of the SPD, with the PDS third and the Greens/Alliance 90 fourth.

CHRONOLOGY

January 1871. German unification and the proclamation of the Second Reich under Kaiser Wilhelm I.

1914-18.The First World War, ending with the defeat of Germany.

November 1918. Abdication of Kaiser Wilhelm II.

January 1919. Failure of the left-wing Spartakist rising in Berlin.

February 1919. Friedrich Ebert is elected as the first President of the new Weimar Republic.

June 1919. Harsh terms are imposed on Germany by the Versailles peace treaty, signed under protest by the Weimar leaders.

1923.Hyper-inflation and the collapse of the currency wipes out savings and profoundly undermines the security of middle-class Germans.

1929. The beginning of a world recession which results in mass unemployment in Germany.

May 1932. Nazi street violence reaches a peak.

November 1932. Elections are held, in which the Nazis win just under one third of the vote, less than the combined share of the (bitterly divided) socialist and communist parties.

January 1933. Hitler is appointed as Chancellor.

March 1933. The Nazi party wins 43.9 per cent of the vote in elections held under intimidatory emergency regulations; centre-right parties thereupon vote through an Enabling Act under which Hitler gains the authority to establish one-party Nazi rule. The unions are suppressed.

1935. Promulgation of the Nuremberg Laws, depriving Jews of citizenship, confirming the Nazis on a course which leads to the application of policies of racial extermination across central and eastern Europe; six million Jews die in the holocaust by 1945.

1936-38. Hitler systematically attacks the foreign policy constraints placed on Germany by the Versailles settlement, merges Austria into Germany in the March 1938 *Anschluss*, and annexes the Sudetenland from Czechoslovakia.

August 1939. Signature of the Nazi-Soviet pact.

September 1939. The Second World War begins with the German invasion of Poland.

June 1941. Having already overrun much of France, Scandinavia and the Balkans, the Germans invade the Soviet Union, where the tide of war turns against them in late 1942.

8 May 1945. Nazi Germany surrenders to the Allies, and the areas liberated by the Red Army in the eastern part of the country become the Soviet-occupied zone.

1 July 1945. The Western allied forces arrive in Berlin, which, like Germany as a whole, is divided into zones occupied and administered by the USA, Britain and the Soviet Union. (The French zones are subsequently carved out of the US and British zones.)

1946. Elections are held.

April 1946. The Social Democrats and the Communists are merged to form the Socialist Unity Party (SED) led initially by Otto Grotewohl and Wilhelm Pieck, and from 1950 by Walter Ulbricht.

January 1949. Poland officially incorporates the territories formerly part of Germany; mass expulsions of Germans to the west follow in March 1950.

May 1949. The end of the Berlin blockade.

7 October 1949. The German Democratic Republic is proclaimed officially.

February 1950. Creation of the Ministry of State Security, the *Stasi*.

June 1950. East Germany formally accepts the Oder-Neisse line as its border with Poland.

July 1950. A new constitution is adopted by the Socialist Unity Party.

17 June 1953. Riots begin in Berlin and spread to other cities but are then suppressed by Soviet forces.

September 1955. A treaty is signed with the Soviet Union, which formally recognises the sovereignty of the GDR.

13 August 1961. The Berlin Wall goes up.

November 1968. Soviet party leader Leonid Brezhnev articulates the doctrine that socialist states have limited sovereignty and that other socialist countries may have an "internationalist obligation" to intervene in the defence of socialism.

March-May 1970. Meetings between Premier Willi Stoph and West German Chancellor Willy Brandt lead to recognition of the GDR by West Germany, and an agreement on access to Berlin from the West.

August 1970. West Germany signs a treaty with the Soviet Union recognising postwar border arrangements.

May 1971. Erich Honecker takes over from Ulbricht as party leader.

September 1971. The Four-Power Agreement is signed on the status of Berlin; the final protocol to this treaty is signed in June 1972.

December 1972. A treaty is signed with West Germany to normalise relations, although it falls short of full diplomatic recognition.

February 1973. The GDR is recognised by Britain and France.

September 1974. Diplomatic relations are established with the USA.

January 1982. As part of a sustained peace campaign primarily focused around the Lutheran and Evangelical churches, the so-called Berlin Appeal is launched by 35 activists including Pastor Rainer Eppelmann. It calls for a pacific alternative to military service and, in its wider aims, for the removal of all foreign troops from Germany as a whole and the creation of a nuclear-free zone.

April 1986. Gorbachev visits East Germany during the SED congress, but Honecker fails to get Soviet backing for his already-postponed plan to be the first East German leader to visit West Germany.

September 1987. Honecker finally visits West Germany.

May 1989. Local elections are held. The usual declaration of almost unanimous support for the National Front's sole list is challenged by church organisations who have observed the count; demonstrations against widespread rigging are suppressed by police in Leipzig.

11 September 1989. East Germans who have left the country in large numbers in recent weeks effectively as refugees, are allowed to cross the border from Hungary into Austria, marking a critical breach in the solidarity of the East European regimes against the free movement of their citizens.

9 September 1989. Opposition groups come together to form a broad alliance known as New Forum.

7 October 1989. The 40th anniversary of the founding of the GDR is marked by official celebrations at which Gorbachev, the principal guest, makes no secret of having pressed the East German leadership to implement a programme of reforms.

7 October 1989. A meeting at Schwante near Potsdam decides on the refounding of a separate SPD, with Ibrahim Böhme as its first leader.

9 October 1989. Some 70,000 people attend the largest yet of Leipzig's regular Monday demonstrations at the St Nicholas Church, focus of opposition protest. Whereas these demonstrations have hitherto been countered violently by the security forces, on this occasion the police do not attack, local SED party leaders having joined in an appeal for a "free exchange of views about the further development of socialism in our country". The SED politburo holds an emergency meeting on 10-11 October to discuss its response, with a split evident between hardliners and the more liberal-minded leaders from Leipzig and Dresden. By the following Monday the demonstration in Leipzig has swollen to some 120,000 and there have been large-scale demonstrations elsewhere, notably in Dresden and Halle.

18 October 1989. Honecker resigns and is succeeded as party leader by Egon Krenz, who becomes head of state on 24 October. Others leaving the politburo include Honecker's hardline lieutenant, Günter Mittag.

23 October 1989. Mass demonstrations call for free elections; Leipzig again witnesses by far the largest protest, numbering some 300,000.

27 October 1989. The Council of State announces an amnesty for those who have gone abroad illegally, and those accused of criminal acts during demonstrations, in an attempt by the Krenz regime to recover some control over the situation. Plans to liberalise travel laws are announced in the succeeding days.

4 November 1989. More than half a million people demonstrate in East Berlin, while in Dresden a pro-democracy demonstration is joined by the reform-minded local SED leader Hans Modrow.

7 November 1989. The government headed by long-serving prime minister Willi Stoph resigns.

8 November 1989. The entire SED politburo resigns at a plenum of the central committee; its short-lived successor includes Hans Modrow. New Forum is legalised.

9 November 1989. The decision to open the Berlin Wall is announced, and the night ends in popular euphoria.

10 November 1989. The SED under Krenz's leadership produces an "action programme" which includes a commitment to free elections. Mittag, blamed for the regime's failure to respond to the growing emigration exodus in August while he was deputising for the ailing Honecker, is expelled from the SED central committee. Lothar de Maizière is elected chairman of the CDU.

17 November 1989. Modrow forms a new government, with an SED majority membership, and announces the reorganisation and renaming of the *Stasi* (Ministry of State Security), the hated secret police.

18 November 1989. The first legal meeting of Neues Forum, in Leipzig, is attended by over 50,000 people.

28 November 1989. Proposals for a German confederation are put forward by West German Federal Chancellor Helmut Kohl.

3 December 1989. Krenz, who has been unable to contain the demand for the abolition of the communist regime, resigns the SED leadership, and the whole SED politburo and central committee also resign, on the day that some two million people form a human chain across the country, demanding democracy and the punishment of corrupt former leaders. *Stasi* offices are stormed in Leipzig the following day, and then in several other cities, and pro-democracy activists begin searching their files.

6 December 1989. Krenz resigns as head of state.

7 December 1989. The first meeting is held of the Round Table, effectively an alternative government embracing groups across the political spectrum, from the SED, its former National Front partners and the "mass organisations", to the churches, newly-founded independent parties and pro-democracy citizens' movements. The first meeting agrees on holding democratic elections, initially scheduled for 6 May 1990.

7-17 December 1989. The SED extraordinary congress is held, electing Gysi as its leader and ending by deciding to adopt the name SED-Party of Democratic Socialism (further changed, to just the PDS, on 4 February 1990).

14 December 1989. The government decides to disband the *Stasi* altogether, replacing it with a smaller intelligence service and a special body for the protection of the constitution.

15 January 1990. The *Stasi* headquarters in Berlin is occupied and ransacked by protesters denouncing the police state system.

21 January 1990. Krenz and 13 other former SED politburo members are expelled from the party; Honecker, leaving hospital eight days later, is considered too ill to be arrested.

1 February 1990. The conservative Alliance for Germany is formed for the forthcoming elections, bringing together the CDU, the German Social Union and Democratic Awakening.

1 February 1990. Modrow puts forward proposals of his own for the unification of Germany, but with a precondition of military neutrality, reflecting the Soviet concern that the strategic balance would be upset if a united Germany were part of NATO.

5 February 1990. Modrow's temporary "government of national responsibility", whose formation has been agreed on 28 January pending elections now scheduled for 18 March, brings in eight opposition leaders to place the communists in a minority for the first time.

6 February 1990. West German Chancellor Helmut Kohl calls for immediate negotiations on economic and monetary union.

13 February 1990. Agreement is reached that the "external aspects" of German unification, including wider military and security issues, will be negotiated under the "two-plus-four" formula by the two Germanies and the four World War II allies, Britain, France, the USA and the Soviet Union.

18 March 1990. Elections result in an unexpectedly convincing victory for the right-wing Alliance for Germany.

9 April 1990. Lothar de Maizière becomes prime minister at the head of a "grand coalition" which is sworn in on 12 April.

23 April 1990. The West German government announces that the East German Ostmark will be exchanged at parity with the deutschemark upon monetary union for personal wages and savings up to 4,000 marks.

5 May 1990. The first round of "two-plus-four" talks takes place in Bonn; subsequent rounds are in Berlin (22 June), Paris (17 July) and Moscow (7 September).

18 May 1990. The state treaty on economic and monetary union is signed by the finance ministers of the two Germanies; it is approved by both parliaments on 21-23 June.

1 July 1990. German economic and monetary union is declared and East Germany is brought within the European Communities customs union, becoming subject to EC agricultural regulations one month later.

16 July 1990. Soviet President Mikhail Gorbachev, at a meeting in Stavropol with West German Federal Chancellor Kohl, concedes that a united Germany can decide freely whether to join NATO.

24 July and 20 August 1990. Free Democrats and Social Democrats pull out of de Maizière's government, the former opposing his proposal that German unification should not take place until immediately after the all-German elections on 2 December, and the latter objecting to his making cabinet changes against their wishes.

23 August 1990. The *Volkskammer* reaches a compromise over the date for unification, which is brought forward to 3 October. The CDU has abandoned (on 9 August) a plan to bring forward the all-German elections, and the *Volkskammer* has agreed (on 22 August) to use the West German electoral system almost unchanged.

31 August 1990. The second state treaty, on unification, is signed in East Berlin; it is approved by both parliaments on 20-21 September.

12 September 1990. The "Treaty on the Final Settlement on Germany", the outcome of the "two plus four" talks, is signed in Moscow (its ratification being concluded on 4 March 1991). It confirms the existing German borders (providing for a further bilateral treaty between Germany and Poland to confirm their Oder-Neisse border), stipulates the withdrawal of the 370,000 Soviet troops currently in East Germany by the end of 1994 (with Germany paying for their upkeep, as accepted by Kohl to resolve the last obstacle outstanding after the final round of two-plus-four talks on 7 September), accepts Germany's right to decide on its alliances (and thus to join NATO) while debarring alliance forces from the territory of former East Germany, and ends the "rights and responsibilities" of the wartime allies with respect to Germany and Berlin.

13 September 1990. Bilateral treaties are initialled (with ratification being completed on 2 April 1991) under which Germany and the Soviet Union pledge good-neighbourliness, partnership and co-operation; agree that neither will assist in aggression against the other; and agree on the stationing, upkeep and withdrawal by 1994 of Soviet troops.

24 September 1990. East Germany leaves the Warsaw Pact.

3 October 1990. German unity, effective from midnight on 2-3 October and taking the form of the merger of the former East Germany into the Federal Republic, is celebrated nationwide, although some protests are recorded over the rising unemployment in the East.

14 October 1990. Elections are held for the five *Land* parliaments in the East; the CDU wins control of four, with the SPD heading the poll only in Brandenburg.

14 November 1990. The border treaty with Poland is signed by the German and Polish foreign ministers in Warsaw, formally abandoning German territorial claims dating from the end of World War II, a position which the GDR had already accepted in 1950.

2 December 1990. The all-German elections, for the chancellorship and an enlarged *Bundestag*, produce a victory for Kohl and his CDU-led governing coalition; the CDU also wins elections for a unified city parliament in Berlin.

10 December 1990. The latest in a line of former East German politicians affected by allegations of having been a *Stasi* informer, de Maizière denies giving any information except that which, as a lawyer, he felt might have assisted his clients; he nevertheless resigns his government post (as minister without portfolio) and the CDU deputy leadership which he has held since the merging of the eastern and western parties in October. He is exonerated by a government inquiry in February, and resumes the CDU deputy leadership, but the allegations persist and in September 1991 he resigns and also gives up his seat in parliament.

January 1991. Departments of Marxism-Leninism are closed in universities and institutes across the East, as are many other history, philosophy and social science departments.

11 January 1991. The separate constitutions of West and East Berlin are suspended at the first meeting of Berlin's new unified parliament.

27 January 1991. The PDS holds a congress in Berlin and re-elects Gysi as its chairman.

29 January 1991. In the first case of an East German leader to come to trial, former trade union leader Harry Tisch is charged in Berlin with diverting funds for holidays, a holiday home and a hunting lodge; convicted and sentenced on 6 June to 18 months' imprisonment, he is then released, having served nearly a year in detention already and with the benefit of a reduction of sentence for good behaviour.

8 March 1991. The federal government agrees to a one-year surcharge on income and corporation tax as part of a package of funding for reconstruction in the east.

9 March 1991. Plans for an amnesty for former *Stasi* agents are dropped by the government.

25 March 1991. A demonstration in Leipzig, with 60,000 participants, is the largest in a series of protests over unemployment.

1 April 1991. Detlev Rohwedder, the head of the *Treuhand*, the agency which has become increasingly unpopular in the East as it implements its responsibilities for privatising industries formerly in GDR state ownership, is assassinated in Düsseldorf in a shooting for which the Red Army Faction claims responsibility.

8 April 1991. The growth of racism among "skinhead" gangs in the East, raising the spectre of a rebirth of Nazism, is highlighted by attacks on Poles, who can now enter the country without visas.

20 June 1991. The *Bundestag* votes to move the seat of government from Bonn to Berlin; the *Bundesrat*, however, votes on 5 July to stay in Bonn. Chancellor Kohl subsequently announces (in October 1993) that the government's move to Berlin is to be completed by the year 2000.

14 November 1991. The *Bundesrat* approves legislation allowing individuals to have access to files which had been kept on them by the *Stasi* (and which are now administered by a special commission set up under pastor Joachim Gauck), but restricting press publication without authorisation.

12 March 1992. A commission of enquiry is set up by the federal parliament, headed by pastor Rainer Eppelmann, and charged with investigating the former GDR regime to produce "a judgment of communism and its methods".

17 June 1992. Legislation provides for the rehabilitation and compensation of those prosecuted for political reasons under the GDR regime..

29 July 1992. Honecker is brought back from Moscow to face trial over the shoot-to-kill policy, but is subsequently deemed unfit to stand trial.

22-24 August 1992. There is serious rioting in the depressed city of Rostock, formerly a shipbuilding centre, in one of the most high-profile of a spate of cases in which neo-Nazis exploit resentment against foreigners seeking asylum.

14-15 December 1992. Chancellor Kohl, visiting Moscow, agrees to write off claims for Soviet debts to the former GDR, while Russia agree not to pursue compensation for military property and installations there.

13 March 1993. The federal government and the *Länder* reach agreement on a "solidarity pact" to fund the continuing transfer of resources for reconstruction in the east, the main feature being the reintroduction from January 1995 of the 7.5 per cent "solidarity surcharge" on income tax.

16 September 1993. The first senior figure of the former GDR regime to receive a lengthy prison sentence, former defence minister Heinz Kessler gets 7½ years for complicity in the shoot-to-kill policy and for violating human rights; his deputy and a former regional SED official get slightly shorter sentences.

24 March 1994. A Lübeck synagogue suffers the first of two arson attacks.

20 May 1994. Legislation is approved on compensation (but not restitution) for property expropriated under Soviet occupation in 1945-49 as well as under the GDR regime to 1990.

29 May 1994. Honecker dies in Chile, where he was allowed to go to join his wife in January 1993.

31 August 1994. A ceremony in Berlin marks the departure of the last Russian troops.

16 October 1994. Federal elections return the CDU-FDP coalition to power, demonstrating the political ascendancy of Chancellor Kohl.

31 December 1994. The *Treuhand* is wound up, having effectively completed the privatisation process.

9 January 1995. Charges are brought against Egon Krenz and six other former SED politburo members for manslaughter for approving the "shoot-to-kill" policy. The trial begins on 13 November.

8 August 1995. Modrow receives a nine month prison sentence for electoral fraud over his role in the May 1989 communal elections; he was originally charged in March 92, and let off with a caution, but his case was retried after a prosecution appeal. City-level officials had received suspended sentences and fines in February 1992 for their role in the fraudulent poll.

December 1995. Germany faces the problem of rising unemployment, which topped four million in February 1994 and now stands at 16.8 per cent in the east compared with 9.4 per cent in the west.

ROMANIA

The official name of the country was the Romanian People's Republic from December 1947 until 1965, and thereafter the Socialist Republic of Romania (*Republica Socialista Romania*) until Dec. 28, 1989, when it was renamed simply Romania. Romania's land area of 229,000 sq. km is slightly smaller than that of the UK and more than twice as large as Bulgaria to the south or Hungary to the north-west. In the communist era the 23 million population made Romania the third most populous communist state in Central and Eastern Europe, excluding the Soviet Union.

Present-day Romania has three principal historical regions: Walachia, Moldavia and Transylvania. Walachia, the southern third of the country, formed the core Romanian

territory known as the Old Kingdom or Regat. Agriculturally rich, low-lying land, Walachia is bounded by the Transylvanian Alps in the north, and by the Danube in the south, which marks the border with Bulgaria. Bucharest, the Romanian capital, is Walachia's major centre of population. Moldavia in the east is rural but densely populated in the north near the border with Ukraine. Moldavia is divided from the former Romanian territory of Bessarabia in the east, which was annexed by the Soviet Union in 1941, and which now comprises the independent republic of Moldova. Transylvania, which was part of historic Hungary for the millennium before the First World War, now forms a mountainous hinterland in Romania's north-west occupying more than a third of the country's territory. Romania's Dobruja territory borders the Black Sea coast in the south-east.

Bucharest is a city of some two million inhabitants, apart from which the largest urban centre is Brasov (350,000). Only four other towns have populations above 300,000, namely Constanta, Timisoara, Iasi and Cluj. Nevertheless the population is officially classified as over 50 per cent urban.

In ethnic terms something under 90 per cent are Romanian, speaking a Romance language written with the Latin script. The Hungarian minority is variously given as 1,700,000 (in Romanian census figures) and over two million (Hungarian estimates), and is concentrated in Transylvania. Romania's other large minority is the Roma (Gypsy) community, which officially numbers just a few hundred thousand but which may actually be as large as two million. Many of the Roma speak the Romany language. There are also small minorities of German-speaking Saxons, Ukrainian-speakers, Serbs, Croats, Russians and Turks.

The main religion is Christianity. There are only about 15-30,000 Jews (most of the 400,000-strong post-war Romanian Jewish community having emigrated from 1953 onwards) and 40,000 Muslims. Most of the Christians belong to the Romanian Orthodox church. Uniate Catholics were banned in 1948 and required to join the Romanian Orthodox church. The Roman Catholic church is identified with the Hungarian minority. There are smaller Calvinist, Lutheran and Baptist churches.

HISTORICAL NARRATIVE

Modern Romania is the product of the fragmentation of a series of empires in the region. Romania first achieved independence in 1877, in territory comprising the former Ottoman territories of Walachia and Moldova. Romania acquired the Black Sea region of Dorogea from the Turks in 1878, and Bessarabia from Russia in 1917. The following year, in the peace settlement at the end of the First World War, the great powers favoured Romania by more than doubling its pre-war territory and population, with the award of Transylvania (formerly part of historic Hungary) and Bukovina (which had been Austrian since 1775). The new territories of Greater Romania (*Romania Mare*) included substantial ethnic minorities, so that 28 per cent of the country's overall population in the interwar period was non-Romanian. The most significant was the ethnic Hungarian minority, concentrated mainly in Transylvania.

In 1918 Romania was one of the poorest and most backward countries in Europe. Almost 80 per cent of the population lived in rural areas. Agricultural productivity levels were generally low, rural poverty high and public education very poor. There were, however, considerable regional variations within this profile, a legacy of the historically different experience of regions hitherto under Ottoman, Hungarian, Austrian or Russian rule.

The Liberal governments of the 1920s supported the development of Romania's previously tiny industrial sector, and by the 1930s, stimulated by the high demand for Romanian petrol and agricultural products, industrial production was increasing rapidly. The economy continued to improve in the early war years, but the increasing prosperity of entrepreneurs failed to trickle down to peasants, whose standard of living remained stagnant.

The entrepreneurial class, which was heavily dominated by Jews, was despised by the peasants as corrupt, cosmopolitan and "foreign". Their suspicions were shared by Romania's rulers and from the 1920s anti-Semitic laws restricted Jewish access to university places and some professions.

Although democracy was nominally introduced after the First World War, and a parliament was elected in 1919, most elections were comprehensively rigged, commencing with the poll of March 1920.

The Romanian monarchy had been instituted in 1881. Under a new, étatist constitution in place from 1923, the extensive Royal prerogatives were confirmed, basic civil liberties were heavily curtailed, and Romania's natural resources were declared to be state property. A highly centralised system of administration was introduced, so that many of Romania's new regions enjoyed less autonomy even than under the earlier imperial regimes.

Romanian politics in the 1930s were dominated by King Carol, who deliberately undermined his governments, appointing 18 different prime ministers in that decade, and in 1938 imposing a Royal dictatorship under which political parties were banned and many rivals were assassinated. Carol deployed nationalist rhetoric to gain popular legitimacy, and gradually grew closer to Nazi Germany.

Carol's reputation was destroyed in 1940, when he deferred to pressure from Germany by agreeing to cede Bessarabia to the Soviet Union, Bukovina to Bulgaria and Transylvania to Hungary. The subsequent uproar forced him to flee the country in disgrace, and Carol was replaced by the 19-year old King Michael, while the right-radical Iron Guard movement formed a government.

Throughout the 1930s the Iron Guard had gained in popularity, initially among the peasants and later among the urban working class, by espousing a semi-mystical creed combining anti-Semitism, anti-modernism and Christian Orthodoxy. Once in power the Guard launched a harsh campaign of terror against political opponents and Jews. Its regime was short-lived, however, and by 1941 Marshal Ion Antonescu, ostensibly supported by King Michael, had deposed the Iron Guard; it was replaced by a brutal and even more pro-Nazi dictatorship. Romania joined the war on the side of the Axis and contributed considerable forces to the German invasion of the Soviet Union. Antonescu's government sent many Romanian Jews to their deaths in Nazi concentration camps.

By 1944 the tide of war had turned against the Axis powers, and Soviet troops had reached the Romanian border; King Michael, having been promised the return of Transylvania by the Western Allies in return for defection to the anti-Nazi cause, dismissed Antonescu and changed sides, a major blow to the retreating Germans in south-east Europe. The country had lost over 300,000 men in the cause of the Axis, and a further 110,000 Romanians were now killed fighting against it in 1944-5.

A peace treaty concluded in September 1947 restored Transylvania to Romania, but both Bessarabia and northern Bukovina remained in Soviet hands, while Southern Dobruja was retained by Bulgaria under the 1946 Paris settlement.

Romania had barely a decade's experience of (flawed) democracy. The country's political culture was characterised by the anti-modern and xenophobic values typical of peasant agrarian-dominated societies; with these values prevalent, Romanian leaders relied on authoritarian and étatist political structures. The communist party, which took up the reins of power after the war, drew on these traditions in imposing a rigid national-communist dictatorship.

Communist takeover

With Soviet troops in occupation from the summer of 1944, the immediate postwar political scene was dominated by the Romanian Communist Party (PCR). Nowhere in Eastern Europe, with the exception of Poland, was the Soviet role in imposing communism more open.

The PCR had been included in a coalition government appointed by King Michael to replace the Antonescu regime in 1944. PCR influence grew rapidly, its proposals for agrarian reform winning support among the peasantry, many of whom began seizing land in anticipation of a communist government. Fascists were arrested and anti-Semitic legislation repealed. In March 1945 a Soviet-backed communist regime was set up and by December it had been recognised by the Western allies. The National Democratic Front, of which the PCR was a leading component, claimed a comprehensive victory in the much-criticised 1946 elections. In December 1947 Michael was forced to renounce the throne and go into exile; the official title of the country became the People's Republic of Romania. The communist victory was completed in 1948, as the communists became the sole legal party, having banned rivals or coerced them into mergers. (In October 1947 the communist party merged with the Socialists to become the Romanian Workers' Party, which it remained until it reverted to its original name in 1965.)

By the late 1940s, when other communist regimes in the region were launching bloody purges to consolidate Stalinism, such was the extent of the Romanian communists' domination that there were relatively few targets for purge and show trials. Nevertheless, the paraphernalia of the police state, already in place in Romania since the interwar period, had been put at the disposal of the party. A spate of show trials of alleged Zionists exposed anti-Semitism within the party.

The Romanian party contained a strong nationalist faction, prominent among which was party first secretary Gheorghe Gheorghiu-Dej. Unusually, during the purges it was the Muscovite group in the party leadership (some of whom were Jews) which suffered at the hands of the nationalists. The party's subsequent advocacy of "national communism" was reflected initially in its economic policy. While the party rapidly implemented a Stalinist programme, commencing agricultural collectivisation and the nationalisation of major industries in 1948, it defied Soviet plans for Romania to take a primarily food-producing role in the international socialist division of labour. Instead the party operated a "Romania first" economic policy which stressed the importance of rapid industrialisation and economic autarky. Then in 1953 the party was one of the first in the region to signal a shift of resources towards the provision of consumer goods.

In other respects, before 1956 the party leadership was relatively orthodox; it refused to contemplate liberalising political or economic reforms, with the result that even after Khrushchev's Secret Speech there was no de-Stalinisation programme in Romania. Indeed Gheorghiu-Dej regarded the events of 1956, when the disturbances in Romania were the most serious in the region after Hungary and Poland, not as a cue to liberalisation, but as a means of asserting Romanian autonomy vis à vis the Soviet Union, particularly in foreign policy. In the midst of the Hungarian uprising Gheorghiu-Dej publicly argued against foreign intervention there, and by 1958 he had persuaded the Soviet leadership to withdraw the Red Army from Romanian territory.

The Ceausescu years

When Gheorghiu-Dej died in March 1965, Nicolae Ceausescu became party leader and by December 1967 he was also President of Romania. Ceausescu made a play of pursuing "national communism" with even greater vigour than his predecessor.

Over most of his 25 years in power, the Ceausescu regime cultivated the good opinion of the West. This was achieved on the basis of a maverick foreign policy, an anomaly in the otherwise monolithic stance of the "Soviet bloc" countries. Romania retained links with China, and with Israel after the 1967 war. Even more striking, Romania refused to participate in the 1968 invasion of Czechoslovakia, which Ceausescu condemned, as he later denounced the Soviet invasion of Afghanistan. This critical independence was probably tolerated by Moscow only because of Romania's relative strategic insignificance; nevertheless in 1968, and again in 1971, there were fears in Romania of Soviet intervention.

Domestically, however, Ceausescu maintained perhaps the most repressive and centralised regime in Eastern Europe, ruthlessly suppressing any hint of dissent. Only the miners' strike of 1977, which demonstrated that industrialisation had created a growing and potentially powerful working class, stood out as a moment of mass protest. There was also some dissent within the party. In 1978 Constantin Pirvulescu stood against Ceausescu for the post of general secretary, only to be denounced and expelled. In the 1980s, there continued to be quixotic opposition to Ceausescu within the PCR leadership, but the highly centralist organisation of the party worked in the leader's favour. Beyond the narrow clique close to the leader, which included Ceausescu's wife Elena, the government and party leadership was frequently reshuffled in the classic ploy to prevent the emergence of powerful rivals. Meanwhile, a personality cult of monumental proportions was constructed around Ceausescu, and the leader remained in firm control throughout most of his quarter-century in power.

No major economic reforms were introduced in the 1960s; although workers' participation was formally initiated in 1968, in practice there was little substance to this and other changes, which are best regarded as mere modifications of the system. Nevertheless Ceausescu's popularity in Western capitals facilitated Romania's admission as a member of the international financial community from the early 1970s. Foreign funds flowed in, and were used for investment in the continuing development of a heavy industrial base, to improve the provision of consumer goods, and to fund several grandiose projects which, although utterly irrational in economic terms, provided patriotic inspiration for the regime's propagandists. [They included the Danube-Black Sea canal project, a vastly expensive white elephant which lay virtually idle after its completion, and the redevelopment of Bucharest, including the construction of the Xanadu-like "Palace of the Republic" which was unfinished in 1989.] In consequence Romania acquired a chronic foreign debt, and with the downturn in the international economy in the mid-1970s found itself unable to find markets for its exports.

In 1982 Ceausescu again demonstrated his ability to find a peculiarly Romanian path when he announced that the foreign debt was to be paid back, to avoid compromising the country's independence. To do this, a large export surplus was necessary; agricultural output, already affected by under-investment in the drive to industrialise, was therefore to be diverted from meeting internal food needs to sale on the external market.

The debt was successfully cleared by 1989, a unique achievement in the communist bloc, but in the preceding decade the Romanian people had been exposed to tremendous hardship, with food rationing and shortages of electricity even for basic heating in winter. As the price of Ceausescu's economic policies had become more apparent, the regime had relied increasingly on its huge security police apparatus, whose elite *Securitate* divisions were inculcated from their youth with the doctrine of unswerving loyalty to Ceausescu. (Recruitment from orphanages was a characteristic technique, to ensure maximum psychological bonding to the leader-figure.) Wage demands and protests were vigorously suppressed; when in 1987 workers in Brasov demonstrated against shortages and the imposition of a seven-day working week, troops were sent in. Amidst this harsh landscape, the regime, with crass insensitivity, proclaimed a "golden age", and continued to channel scarce resources into its grandiose projects, earning Ceausescu the bitter resentment of the working classes.

The repression also took the form of the withdrawal of individual freedoms in social policy. In order that Romania could reach a 30 million population "target", abortion had been criminalised and women were required to use no birth control unless they already had five children. Ironically, the regime's failure during the austerity regime of the 1980s to provide opportunities for Romania's young population born from the mid-1960s onwards was a further cause of discontent.

Another social policy priority, the Romanisation campaign, was an attempt to alter the ethnic balance of Transylvania by encouraging ethnic Romanians to settle there; in practice many of the new arrivals backed anti-Hungarian policies. The systematisation policy, launched in earnest in March 1988, ostensibly sought to impose a more rational and "modern" pattern of habitation in rural areas, but marked a new low in the brutality and extremity of the regime. Under the programme half of the country's 13,000 villages were to be demolished by the end of the century, and their inhabitants resettled in agro-industrial centres. In practice this meant the bulldozing often of historic majority-Hungarian villages and the forcible resettlement of their populations in often bleak accommodation in the towns. For obvious reasons, both policies were extremely unpopular in neighbouring Hungary, which by the late 1980s was travelling in an ideologically opposite direction, toward liberalisation.

Hungary had taken its cue for reform from the Soviet Union, which by the mid-1980s had begun to liberalise. Highly suspicious of Gorbachev's *perestroika* and *glasnost*, the Romanian leadership on the other hand had censored reformist ideas from the Soviet Union. Whereas Romania's independent foreign policy had earned Western praise during an era of Soviet conservatism, by the 1980s Romania's opposition to Soviet-style reforms, coupled with the growing repression and human rights abuse, marked the Romanian government out for Western censure. The Ceausescu regime became increasingly isolated.

Revolution in 1989

By July 1989, when Bucharest played host to a meeting of the Warsaw Pact, the wave of revolution had begun to break over Central and Eastern Europe. Hungary had begun to dismantle its section of the "iron curtain", with destabilising consequences for East Germany, while the Polish communist party had been defeated by Solidarity in partially free elections. At the Warsaw Pact meeting, Ceausescu performed a volte face: having effectively resisted the Brezhnev doctrine for most of his political career, the dictator now demanded its confirmation in the form of Warsaw Pact military intervention to restore communist authority in Poland, a demand which contrasted starkly with his 1968 condemnation of the invasion of Czechoslovakia. Ceausescu's stance merely succeeded in confirming the Romanian leader's Canute-like isolation. Indeed Gorbachev had travelled to Bucharest to deliver the contrary message: effectively to declare the Brezhnev doctrine dead, and to release the satellite states from the Soviet orbit. Accordingly, throughout the succeeding late summer and autumn one after another of the region's communist regimes fell; so that by December Romania was the last remaining hard-line regime in the Soviet bloc.

Despite the pacific nature of the last of these upheavals - Czechoslovakia's "velvet revolution" in Prague from 17 November to 10 December - observers predicted that any uprising in Romania would be met with highly repressive measures. When the Romanian revolution came, it did indeed prove to be the most violent in the region; subsequent estimates put the total number of dead at 1,033. The revolution also occurred with exceptional speed; only ten days elapsed from the first demonstrations in mid-December to the execution of Ceausescu by the victorious rebels.

The origins of the Romanian revolution, incongruously, lay in unrest among the Hungarian minority. The detention of an ethnic Hungarian pastor, Father Laszlo Tokes, in western Transylvania's main town of Timisoara, prompted his supporters to rally on 15 December 1989. When the Hungarian protesters were joined by others chanting anti-Ceausescu slogans, security forces attacked the crowd, beating many protesters. A second rally in Timisoara on 17 December was fired on by security forces, killing many people. Subsequent estimates put the figure at 72 dead, but rumours spread in Bucharest that a massacre had taken place on the scale of the atrocity in Peking's Tiananmen Square six months before. Television viewers in western Transylvania were angered by Western pictures purporting to show the bodies of dozens of the dead, including women and children. (It subsequently transpired that the bodies thus depicted had been taken randomly from the Timisoara hospital morgue, having died from quite different causes.)

Ceausescu blamed the Timisoara unrest on foreign agents and traitors; a dismissive response which merely inflamed public opinion. On 20 December Ceausescu made the grave error of continuing plans to deliver a speech, televised live, to a mass crowd at the party headquarters in Bucharest. In one of the most dramatic episodes in the collapse of communism in the whole region, the address was interrupted by loud chanting from the crowd. The television pictures showed the dictator falter and fall silent, apparently bewildered at the protests, before television officials cut transmission. Ceausescu now appeared indecisive and weak. Crowds gathered once more, later that evening, to demand his resignation. *Securitate* troops opened fire, and buried their many victims secretly.

The revolution was completed with astonishing suddenness on 22 December. When further mass demonstrations took place to demand the overthrow of the regime, the Defence Minister Gen. Vasile Milea refused to order the army to open fire on the demonstrators. Ceausescu's close entourage began to panic, and Milea was summarily executed, his death being reported as suicide. Milea's murder prompted the army to change sides. Armed rebels, backed by some military units, took the television station and then stormed the presidential palace; with *Securitate* and other elite units no longer able to guarantee his safety, the beleaguered Ceausescu and his wife fled the palace by helicopter. The *Securitate* fought back desperately over the succeeding days, implementing long-established plans to defend the republic from "counter-revolution". Even after the capture and execution on 25 December of Ceausescu and his wife, *Securitate* snipers continued to take lives in Bucharest; relative calm was eventually restored in the city by the new year.

In the interim, the rebels had been broadcasting under sniper fire from the television station in Bucharest. Many of those who gathered there, including senior figures from the army and communist party, formed the National Salvation Front (FSN), which they described as an interim opposition movement designed to restore peace and stability to Romania and to establish democracy. Although they further pledged to dissolve the FSN prior to elections, the FSN and its successors came to dominate post-communist Romanian politics.

Most of the revolutions of 1989-90 occurred either "from above", as the outcome of negotiation between communist elites and opposition leaders, or "from below", as the outcome of mass unrest. The Romanian case is a controversial one; whilst some point to the mass rallies in Timisoara and Bucharest as the driving force behind the revolution, others claim that institutional elites were the real agents of change, and argue that the Romanian case is not a genuine revolution but merely a coup d'état, replacing an autocracy with an oligarchy.

Prior to the events of December 1989, there had been very few signs of serious discontent within the nomenklatura, such was the extent of Romanian totalitarianism. Yet in March 1989 six prominent party members, including former foreign minister Corneliu Manescu and party newspaper editor Silviu Brucan, had jointly accused Ceausescu of having discredited socialism, ruined the economy, and earned international condemnation over human rights issues. Meanwhile other institutions felt aggrieved by the conduct of the administration. The army had lost ground to the *Securitate*, to which Ceausescu had increasingly assigned both status and resources. A younger, "second echelon" of ambitious officials was frustrated with the paralysis of a system in which aged and incompetent leaders clung to power.

Among those who claimed that the revolution had been planned by a coalition of otherwise conservative figures in the nomenklatura were Brucan and Gen. Nicolae Militaru, two founder members of the FSN who resigned in August 1990. Whether or not there was a conspiracy, the FSN did indeed represent the former nomenklatura. Almost all of its leading figures were current or past officials of the communist party or of the communist state. The party did also include some reformists, including academics and technocrats from the old communist party, and some of the few dissidents who had achieved publicity during the dictatorship.

Consolidation in power of the National Salvation Front

For decades Romanian society had been dominated by the monolithic party-state. Unlike some Central European states it had no historical experience of pluralist democracy, the interwar state having been authoritarian and despotic. Amidst the violence and turmoil of 1989, the FSN had emerged rapidly as the only viable successor to the communist party. Crucially, the party had the firm support of the military. The short interim between the revolution and the elections of May 1990 gave ambitious political activists little time to organise new parties capable of rivalling the FSN. When the election campaign began in the spring, the FSN waved the banners of democracy and the free market, the standards behind which people across the region had rallied during the revolutionary upheavals of the autumn and winter. The FSN won the overwhelmingly support of Romanian voters.

The FSN's dominance quickly began to cause concern among reformist elements of the intelligentsia. Despite the blood spilt in the campaign for change, Romania remained under the control of an ideologically conservative communist elite. Most of the former *Securitate* agents, far from being called to account for the repression of the communist era, were recruited to the new state police machinery, and inadequate sentences were handed down to former associates of Ceausescu. Student-led protesters sustained an eight-week demonstration, before and after the 1990 elections, complaining that former communists in the FSN had "stolen" the revolution and demanding their removal.

The government's brutal reaction to this criticism seriously damaged its credibility. With the tacit support of the government, thousands of miners armed with clubs were brought from the Jiu Valley to Bucharest in mid-June 1990. The miners terrorised the city, beating anyone who resembled a student or intellectual, and dispersing the protests. President Ion Iliescu of the FSN, who had denounced the students as fascists, thanked the miners for their intervention. The episode confirmed the new government's intolerance of dissent and willingness to use violence and intimidation to silence its opponents, as well as Iliescu's position as one of the party's leading conservatives. In the West, the episode badly tarnished the reputation of the Romanian revolution, and appeared to confirm that Romania's political culture was better suited to authoritarianism than to democracy. It appeared that behind the pluralist facade of Romanian democracy, the FSN intended to entrench itself, immovable, in the foundations of Romanian public life.

Nevertheless, within the FSN was a more liberal faction associated with the Prime Minister in 1990-1, Petre Roman. During Roman's period in office the conservative and liberal factions of the FSN grew apart. The divisions were aggravated by personal rivalries, and by Roman's leadership style, which his critics alleged was high-handed and authoritarian.

The FSN had won the 1990 elections by promising economic reform with minimal social costs. In practice the party's conservative faction was very reluctant to commence radical reforms. However, in common with other governing parties in the former communist bloc, the Roman government had found that without key reforms, crucial Western financial assistance was hard to attract. The liberalisation of prices in the spring of 1991 was Roman's first major economic reform, and the passage of a privatisation law in August his last: in between, he piloted through parliament a land law and a new constitution (which was eventually approved by referendum in December 1991).

The price liberalisation in particular proved unpopular. Industrial discontent was almost continuous throughout 1991, as workers protested at the falling value of their wages. Industrial production declined sharply, spreading fear of redundancies. When the Jiu Valley miners again arrived en masse in Bucharest, this time it was to protest against the declining standards of living. There were violent clashes with security forces, and the cabinet office was attacked and fire-bombed. Roman, conceding that the government had presented its arguments for austerity poorly, offered his resignation; to his consternation, Iliescu accepted it with alacrity. Immediately there were claims from the reformist camp that the miners' rampage had been organised by yet more shadowy figures in the former nomenklatura, anxious to protect their interests by undermining economic reforms.

Roman was replaced by Theodor Stolojan, whose interim government served for over a year until the 1992 elections. Stolojan had actually resigned from the Roman government in March 1991 in protest at the slow pace of economic reform, and following his appointment as Prime Minister he insisted that he would continue his predecessor's reformist economic course. Indeed, Stolojan introduced internal convertibility of the leu (which Roman had regarded as the third major step, following price reform and privatisation, toward the market economy). Overall, however, progress toward the free market remained relatively slow, and Romania fell even further behind its former Soviet bloc allies. Nevertheless, Stolojan worked hard to improve Romania's international image, especially by establishing contacts with NATO and the EC (EU).

Meanwhile, the split in the FSN was confirmed in the run-up to the 1992 elections. The conservative faction, supported by Iliescu, formed the Democratic National Salvation

Front (FSND, from May 1993 the Democratic Party-FSN or PD-FSN), while Roman's reformist faction retained the FSN name until July 1993, when it was renamed the Social Democracy Party of Romania (PDSR). Roman, freed of restraints, excoriated Iliescu for neo-communism, for obstructing democratic and economic reforms, and for protecting former *Securitate* agents.

Despite this vehement criticism, conservatives and extremist parties claimed success in the 1992 parliamentary elections at the expense of the reformists. Roman's FSN had become closely associated with the harsh costs of the limited reforms already in place, and took only just over 10 per cent of the vote. The FSND, in contrast, became the largest party in the legislature, winning more than a quarter of the vote, including strong support from rural areas, and taking one third of the seats in the lower house. The runner-up was the Democratic Convention of Romania (CDR), a centre-right bloc of 18 parties which included the National Peasant Party-Christian Democratic (PNT-CD). The Romanian National Unity Party (PUNR) and the Greater Romania Party (Romania Mare or PRM), both of which combined ultra-nationalist policies with neo-communism, took a combined total of over 11 per cent of the vote, while the leftist Socialist Party of Labour (PSM) and Agrarian Democratic Party (PDAR) took a combined 6.5 per cent of Senate seats.

Iliescu was victorious in the presidential elections, winning over 60 per cent of the vote in a run-off in October. He had openly campaigned as a conservative, accusing his main rival Emil Constantinescu of the CDR of backing radical reforms which would increase unemployment and create a "wild east" of unfettered capitalism. Constantinescu's campaign, meanwhile, had been hampered by his hitherto low political profile and poor campaign organisation and strategy.

Following the elections, Nicolae Vacariou, an independent, formed a minority coalition. Vacariou's cabinet was dominated by the FSND but also included non-party technocrats; among them were prominent figures from communist-era governments, notably the Industry Minister Dumitru Popescu. Vacariou was initially regarded as a pragmatist, but despite pledging to continue economic reforms his government's programme announced shortly after taking office was conservative.

Indeed by 1993 Vacariou had come to be firmly associated with the conservative faction of the PD-FSN, which controlled most of the key portfolios overseeing economic reform. Vacariou did place considerable emphasis on two key reforms implemented in 1993, namely the last round of price liberalisation and the introduction of value added tax, and on a four-year economic programme announced in March 1993 which pledged to privatise some 20 per cent of state owned firms. Overall progress in economic reform, however, was extremely slow. Despite the institutional and legal preparations for privatisation, few sales took place (prompting the resignation in September 1993 of the privatisation minister Aurelian Dochia) while massive state subsidies to vulnerable industries continued, to stave off mass unemployment. Even Iliescu began to gain a reputation for relative pragmatism over economic reform, exemplified in his successful campaign for the appointment of the radical Mircea Cosea as Minister of State for Economic Reform in 1993. Iliescu was nevertheless at this stage careful to avoid a confrontation with the increasingly influential national-communist parties, the PSM, PRM and PUNR.

Although the economic decline had halted by 1993, unemployment had reached 9.2 per cent of the workforce, and real wages were only some 60 per cent of their level in October 1990. Social strife worsened as unease grew over the declining standard of living. Major strikes took place in May and August 1993 and the demonstrations of November and December were the largest since 1989.

As the minority Vacariou government grew increasingly vulnerable, the prime minister turned to the national-communist parties to protect its position in parliament. In June 1993 the governing coalition had announced a parliamentary alliance with the PRM and the PUNR. In February 1994 a formal agreement was struck with the PUNR, the PRM and the two leftist parties, the PSM and PDAR. When two PUNR nominees formally join the cabinet in August 1994, it emerged that two other ostensibly independent ministers appointed in the spring were in fact PUNR members, leaving the PUNR with a total of four portfolios.

Although the precise nature of the compromise between the PD-FSN and the national communists was not revealed, from the government's record in 1994-5 it became clear that the PUNR and PRM had agreed not to block economic reforms in exchange for a more assertive policy toward Romania's ethnic minorities [*see also below and Ethnic and National Relations section*]. While many major economic reforms remained firmly off the agenda (there being, for instance, no political will to restructure large state-owned enterprises), in February 1994 parliament did finally pass an IMF-approved economic austerity package after two months of fierce debate. The package included privatisation, tax reform and budget controls. The passage in April 1994 of a land tax as part of the austerity package drove the PDAR from the ruling coalition. This political loss was more than compensated by the renewal of IMF support in May 1994, when Romania was granted credits totalling some $450m, and by the new austerity policy's success in reducing the inflation rate from 300 per cent in 1993 to 70 per cent in 1994. While 1994 also marked the first year of significant growth since the revolution, this had a negligible impact on standards of living. Nevertheless, by June, when the government struck an agreement with the Alfa cartel trade union to increase the minimum salary, industrial unrest had died down, reflecting in part the increasing divisions within the labour movement.

In 1995 a mass privatisation scheme finally got under way with the public distribution of vouchers in a programme designed to sell off some 3,000 state enterprises by spring 1996. In November 1995 restitution legislation was passed providing for compensation to the former owners, or their descendants, of some 200,000 properties confiscated by the communist state in the late 1940s and 1950s.

Aside from the economic situation, the most pressing issue facing the Romanian government in 1992-5 was the status of the sizeable ethnic Hungarian minority and relations with Hungary. In March 1993 the government had established a forum for the discussion of ethnic relations issues, the Council of National Minorities. By July 1993 talks between the government and Hungarian minority leaders had produced an agreement to improve Hungarian-language education and to erect bilingual road signs, but by September the Hungarian minority party, the Hungarian Democratic Union of Romania (UDMR), had withdrawn from the council, followed shortly by Romany community leaders. Prospects for a settlement were boosted in 1994 by events in Hungary, where the nationalist government was replaced by a socialist prime minister calling for a "historic reconciliation" between Hungarians and Romanians, but on the other side the ultra-nationalist PUNR and PRM formally joined Romania's governing coalition in the same year, and by August 1994 leaders of the Hungarian minority had responded to the government's increasingly nationalist tone by becoming more radical themselves. Their demand for "special status" was in turn interpreted by the Romanian nationalists as a demand for autonomy, which they regarded as veiled Hungarian irredentism.

The Hungarians were upset by two further developments in 1995. In July a new education law came into force, under which Romanian became the compulsory language of higher education, and in September new legislation banned the public display of foreign flags and the singing of foreign national anthems. Despite protests, the Romanian government received the influential backing in August of Max van der Stoel, the OSCE's national minorities commissioner, who argued that doubts over the education law were "unjustified" and insisted that "the situation of national minorities in Romania [had] substantially improved". During van der Stoel's visit to Romania, Iliescu deliberately echoed the words of the Hungarian prime minister in insisting that the "international climate [offered] Romania and Hungary a unique chance for a historic reconciliation".

In foreign policy, Romanian diplomats impressed Western governments by their enthusiasm for links with Western-oriented economic and security organisations, and moved quickly in 1993 to secure associate membership of the EC (EU), and participation in NATO's Partnership for Peace programme. The inclusion in government from 1994 of the national-communist parties initially appeared to have relatively little effect on this foreign policy. Nevertheless, as the next round of elections neared, those parties began to seek increasing influence over government policy. In consequence the tensions within the coalition grew throughout 1995.

By autumn 1995 President Iliescu was leading a counter-attack on behalf of the social democratic elements in the PD-FSN, against the nationalists. In October 1995, Iliescu denounced the leaders of the PUNR and PRM, respectively Gheorghe Funar and Corneliu Vadim Tudor, as "little Zhirinovskys", a reference to the ultra-nationalist Russian demagogue Vladimir Zhirinovsky, who was regarded by most Romanians as both sinister and absurd. Tudor retaliated by denouncing Iliescu as a "brash dictator" and "a protector of impertinent Zionists".

Despite these arguments within the coalition, Vacariou succeeded in bringing a degree of stability to Romanian politics in 1992-5. Relations with the West and with neighbours improved, while key changes in economic and ethnic minority policies provided a basic minimum to satisfy international institutions. However there was the strong impression that Vacariou and the PD-FSN lacked a coherent vision of Romania's future. Economic reform proceeded exceedingly slowly. The standing of democracy was diminished by the government's growing reputation for corruption and the widespread perception that the *nomenklatura* had been the principal beneficiaries of the "revolution". Vacariou's decision to admit to the coalition two xenophobic and anti-Semitic neo-communist parties, both of which occasionally displayed contempt for democracy, the rule of law, and for the free market, lent credibility to the type of parties which in Western democracies tend to operate at the margins. Opposition parties appeared poorly positioned to take electoral advantage of flaws in the ruling coalition, partly due to internal conflicts sometimes based more on personal loyalties than on issues of substance.

ECONOMY

Economic reforms were begun by the Roman government in the spring of 1991. The dropping of public subsidies on basic goods led to a doubling of prices. Although the impact of the reform was mitigated by increased social security benefits and compensation payments to workers and pensioners, the reform rapidly eroded living standards and provoked serious industrial discontent. The trade unions established themselves as powerful political players. The conservative ex-communists who dominated the FSN concluded that economic reform was dangerously destabilising.

Roman conceded that the government had presented its arguments for austerity poorly but remained convinced of the necessity of reform. Roman's technocratic successor Stolojan insisted that he would continue the reformist course. Despite the introduction of internal convertibility of the leu, progress toward the free market remained relatively slow, and Romania fell even further behind its former Soviet bloc allies.

Iliescu's victory in the presidential elections of 1992 owed much to his criticism of his rivals whom, he claimed, planned to create a "wild east" of unfettered capitalism. The new Prime Minister, Vacariou, a pragmatist by reputation who pledged to continue the reforms, nevertheless appointed PD-FSN conservatives to most of the key economic portfolios and announced a conservative economic programme.

The economic decline had halted by 1993, but with unemployment increasing and real wages declining industrial unrest grew. Despite a final round of price liberalisation and the introduction of value added tax, and the announcement of a four-year economic programme which included privatisation, the economic reforms proceeded extremely slowly. Even Iliescu pressed for the appointment of a more radical economic team, with limited success.

In 1994-5 major economic reforms remained firmly off the agenda, and large state-owned enterprises escaped re-structuring. Although IMF support had been withheld in July 1993 for this reason, in February 1994 the parliament did pass an IMF-approved economic austerity package. Once Romania had pledged to make progress with restructuring and privatising state-owned companies, to maintain convertibility of the leu, and to reduce inflation to below 100 per cent by end-1994, Romania was granted credits totalling some $450m. Although Romania fulfilled its pledge on inflation, reducing the rate from 300 per cent in 1993 to 70 per cent in 1994, privatisation failed to get properly under way until late 1995.

1994 marked the first year of significant growth since the revolution. Although living standards remained stagnant, industrial unrest died down, reflecting in part the increasing divisions within the labour movement. When in April 1995 legislation was approved linking public sector pay rises to increases in productivity and improved economic efficiency, the protests were relatively muted.

In November 1995 the Bucharest stock exchange was re-opened after 50 years, but this symbolically significant development was eclipsed by the slide in the value of the leu, which reflected the Western markets' loss of confidence in the Romanian reform process.

Romania's economic situation has been affected by short-term problems, notably the effect on the regional economy of the Balkans of the sanctions on the rump Yugoslavia in place since 1993. A number of long-term, historical factors also affected economic policy and performance in 1989-95, and shaped Romania's medium- to long-term economic prospects.

Traditionally the Romanian state has played a significant role in the economy. The 1923 constitution designated the country's natural resources as state property, a clause which foreshadowed the "national-communism" of the Ceausescu era. Many Romanians continue to look to the state for a solution to the country's economic problems. The strong state role in the economy has generated the problems typical to large bureaucracies. According to liberal critics, nepotism and corruption have thrived in the post-communist elite which has evolved from the communist-era nomenklatura.

The Ceausescu-era strategy of rapid modernisation was implemented with little thought to the long-term preservation of the country's resources. Much of the country's oil and other assets were squandered by the communist regime, and are now close to exhaustion.

Whilst other countries benefited from the persistence of a latent but strong entrepreneurial tradition, this is weak in Romania. The entrepreneurial class during the interwar period had been smaller than that of any of the Central European states, and it had also been dominated by Jews. This had the effect of limiting the social penetration of the liberal values that entrepreneurs typically endorse. With the death of many Romanian Jews during the Second World War and the emigration of most of the remaining community after the war, any vestiges of a pre-communist entrepreneurial class were almost eliminated.

The xenophobia which caused such hostility to Jews in the pre-communist period, and which subsequently found expression in national communism, persists. Many politicians portray Romania as being confronted by a dread conspiracy of rapacious foreigners, spearheaded by the Western banks and the IMF (both of which are regarded as Jewish-dominated by many Romanians), ruthlessly to exploit Romanian resources. The low levels of foreign investment in Romania since 1989 have been in part a reaction to this hostility. They also reflect the fact that with the paying-off of Romania's large foreign debt in the 1980s, foreign investors ironically no longer have a vested interest in the Romanian economy, and have devoted more attention and resources to the chronic debtors such as Hungary. If the mutual mistrust between Western capital and Romanians continues, the Romanian economy is unlikely to integrate itself quickly into the West, and development will continue to proceed slowly.

Privatisation

State-owned companies still comprised 90 per cent of Romanian industry in May 1994, and sales into private sector ownership began in earnest only in 1995.

In August 1991 President Iliescu had signed a law on privatisation of the non-agricultural sector of the economy. In a concession to nationalists, 30 per cent of shares was to be set aside for acquisition by Romanian nationals. The scheme was launched in June 1992. Privatisation vouchers were distributed to the public and managed by private investment funds. Although 6,200 enterprises were earmarked for participation in the scheme, only 30 per cent of the equity in each company was to be sold in the first year. The remaining 70 per cent stake in the companies was to be managed by a "State Investment Fund", which was to release a further 10 per cent stake for sale each year until 1999.

In Romania's first full privatisation, a majority stake in the Vranco textile factory was sold to the Italian firm Incom in August 1992, while the remaining 49 per cent equity stake was sold to a management consortium. Vranco was the first of 30 enterprises earmarked for sale under a programme financed by the EC (EU).

In September 1993 privatisation minister Aurelian Dochia resigned in protest at delays in the privatisation process. Although in February 1994 parliament passed an IMF-approved economic austerity package including privatisation, by March 1995 only 900 small-scale enterprises had been fully privatised.

In March 1995 a new mass privatisation law was passed, under which some 3,904 state enterprises were to be privatised by spring 1996. Accordingly, in August 1995 all Romanian citizens received privatisation vouchers worth about $500. There were considerable doubts over the quality of the companies included in the scheme; nearly a quarter of those companies scheduled for sale made losses in 1994.

Restitution

In February 1991 a land law was passed, leading to the nominal restoration of land to some six million people by the end of 1992. There was bureaucratic confusion surrounding the reform, with the legal status of new owners unclear.

In November 1995 restitution legislation was passed providing for compensation to the former owners, or their descendants, of some 200,000 properties confiscated by the communist state in the late 1940s and 1950s.

POST-COMMUNIST JUSTICE ISSUES

The Romanian events of 1989 yielded the most spectacular and notorious example of revolutionary justice of all the upheavals of 1989-90. On 25 December 1989, only four days after his televised humiliation before a massed, jeering crowd, Ceausescu and his wife Elena were given a summary trial at the military garrison near Tirgoviste. Indignantly, they refused to be held accountable to their accusers. As heavily armed *Securitate* agents continued their desperate struggle against the revolution in Bucharest, a firing squad executed Nicolae and Elena Ceausescu. The trial and execution were recorded on video and broadcast on state television later the same day. The Ceausescus were buried in a falsely marked grave, which has since become a place of pilgrimage for their admirers.

The execution was not the act of local military commanders but, according to subsequent reports, was secretly the decision of three leaders of the FSN, Iliescu, Silviu Brucan and Dumitru Mazilu. In the fevered atmosphere of the revolution, with *Securitate* snipers continuing to take lives on the streets of the capital, many Romanians supported the executions as the quickest way of ending the violence. Many also regarded the killing of the dictator as natural justice. Nevertheless, it raised several questions. Many observers stressed that it had shown an absolute disregard for the law and for the most basic civil rights. Others speculated that Ceausescu's rapid execution served the interests of Romania's new leaders, by avoiding lengthy court proceedings which might throw unwelcome light on their own communist pasts. In this interpretation, Ceausescu was made a scapegoat by a communist elite anxious to distance itself from its responsibility for the communist era, and as quickly as possible to stake its claim to power and prestige in the post-communist era.

The post-communist regime in other respects, however, has demonstrated a degree of compassion towards former leading communists that has made many Romanians uneasy. Few criminal charges were brought successfully against senior communists. Charges and sentences were frequently altered, the legal situation was in considerable doubt, and the net was not cast widely; instead a relatively few officials were convicted. Again, many suspected that those convicted were scapegoats.

In September 1990 the former dictator's son Nicu Ceausescu was sentenced to 20 years in prison for incitement to murder, in connection with the resistance by *Securitate* forces. In June 1991 his sentence was reduced to 16 years, and in November 1992 he was released from prison on health grounds.

In March 1991, charges of complicity in genocide against 13 former politburo members were dropped in favour of the lesser charge of having supported the violent and criminal suppression of the December 1989 demonstrations in Timisoara and Bucharest. In December 1991 the appeal court overturned the convictions on these lesser charges.

Also in December 1991 eight officials and former *Securitate* officers were imprisoned for the "aggravated murder" of the demonstrators at Timisoara in December 1989. The eight included former *Securitate* chief Colonel-General Iulian Vlad and former propaganda minister Ion Totu. In April 1992 the Higher Court of Justice ruled that they were instead guilty of the lesser charges of complicity in aggravated murder or attempted murder, but confirmed their prison sentences. Totu hanged himself, but in March 1994 the eight were formally pardoned by President Iliescu.

The government has attempted to bring belated justice to some of the high-profile victims of the communist era. The 1987 Brasov rioters, who attained heroic status after the 1989 revolution, had their convictions for "hooliganism" annulled and finally, in March 1991, they were reclassified as having been political prisoners.

Bishop Laszlo Tokes, the key figure in the Timisoara events and subsequently a leading figure in the UDMR, became a high-profile campaigner demanding "justice in the name of the victims of post-communism". Tokes was particularly incensed that former *Securitate* agents, far from being brought before a post-communist justice system or even screened for their past behaviour (*see Czechoslovakia chapter*), were actually being re-employed by Romania's new intelligence service. In February 1993 former *Securitate* agents even formed the National League of Honesty, Dignity, Democracy and Justice to fight discrimination against fellow former agents.

The Romanian intelligence service itself provided convincing evidence in July 1994 that it is best regarded as the successor to the *Securitate*, rather than an accountable and democratic security agency. Its provisional report on the 1989 revolution accused "foreign interests", in particular Soviet intelligence, of having provoked the revolution by inciting demonstrations, spreading seditious rumours and other sabotage. The report thus cleared senior Romanian communists of the accusation that they had been behind the revolution, whilst leaving the impression that the revolution had been negative for Romania.

ETHNIC AND NATIONAL RELATIONS

The potency of the ethnic relations issue was amply demonstrated in 1989. The catalyst for the revolution was, after all, unrest among the two million-strong ethnic Hungarian community, based mainly in the Western region of Transylvania.

Hungarian minority rights had been gradually eroded since the effective abolition of the Hungarian autonomous region in 1968. By the late 1980s Hungarians were under pressure from the systematisation campaign [*see narrative section*], which many regarded as targeted against Hungarian villages, and from the relocation of ethnic Romanians, many of whom were nationalists, to areas where Hungarians were concentrated. Events in Hungary over two decades had contrasted with those in Romania; the Hungarian government had achieved a reputation as East-Central Europe's most liberal regime.

The December 1989 demonstrations in Timisoara, from which the revolution grew, were initially a protest by ethnic Hungarians against the deportation of the ethnic

Hungarian pastor Tokes, and reflected the growing unease within the minority. This unease was not assuaged by the revolution, despite the inclusion of minority rights guarantees as part of a batch of constitutional amendments passed in late December 1989. In March 1990 ethnic Hungarian demonstrations in the Transylvanian town of Tirgu Mures degenerated into serious riots, resulting in the death of several people. Evidence emerged later that ethnic Romanian peasants armed with clubs and other improvised weapons had been bused into Tirgu-Mures by extreme nationalists. The riots sent a clear signal to post-communist leaders that the ethnic tension in Transylvania could be exploited by nationalist politicians.

When free legislative elections were held in May 1990, ethnically-based parties were permitted to register. The well-organised Hungarian Democratic Union of Romania (UDMR) won some 7 per cent of the vote. The UDMR demanded the award of special status to the ethnic Hungarian community, including extensive guarantees on ethnic minority rights.

With the new democratic freedoms, nationalist parties quickly became active, particularly in Transylvania. Their rapid progress was confirmed in February 1992 when Gheorghe Funar of the ultra-nationalist Romanian National Unity Party (PUNR) was elected as mayor of the ethnically mixed Transylvanian town of Cluj-Napoca. Within weeks Funar had outraged Hungarian opinion by ordering the removal of all bilingual signs from the town. Funar argued that special status for the Hungarian minority was a Trojan horse for Hungarian irredentists.

In the elections of 1992 the PUNR and the like-minded Greater Romanian Party (PRM) won over 10 per cent of the vote. These two xenophobic parties came to occupy a strategically important position in parliament.

Over the next three years prospects for a deal between the government and minority leaders ebbed and flowed. The government's forum for the discussion of ethnic relations issues, the Council of National Minorities, yielded an agreement in July 1993 on Hungarian-language education and the erection of bilingual road signs, but by September relations had again deteriorated; representatives of the Hungarian and Romany communities withdrew from the council and the agreement was not implemented. Fresh impetus for a deal was provided with the election of a socialist government in Hungary [see Foreign Affairs section], but in 1994 the two ultra-nationalist parties joined the governing coalition, winning a degree of political respectability. In contrast the UDMR was increasingly portrayed even by moderate opposition parties as an extremist organisation.

In February 1995 government officials and UDMR representatives jointly proclaimed their commitment to dialogue on minority rights issues following two days of talks in Atlanta Georgia attended by former US President Jimmy Carter. Progress remained extremely slow, however, and the passage of controversial legislation later in 1995 further chafed on ethnic Hungarian leaders. Under one law Romanian was designated as the official language of higher education, and under another foreign flags and national anthems were banned. The laws provoked big protest rallies in Transylvania, but the Romanian government won a degree of support over the education law from the international community.

By autumn 1995 Iliescu was vigorously defending Romania's record, insisting that the country had introduced "generous provision" for its ethnic minorities. He added that prospects for a "global" settlement between Hungary and Romania, including a minority rights package, were good.

Hungary's other ethnic minority of significant size is the Romany (Gypsy) community, which may number up to two million (census data are unreliable on this point). The Romanies are only partially integrated into Romanian society, and poverty, illiteracy and crime rates are relatively high. Roma representatives are guaranteed seats in the Romanian legislature through the allocation of 13 seats to ethnic minorities. [Note: the Hungarian community is deemed to be of sufficient size to win representation without special arrangements.]

Many prominent Roma, including Roma leader Gheorghe Raducanu, complain bitterly of racial prejudice by ethnic Romanians. In one notorious incident, in a village near Tirgu Mures in September 1993, three Roma men were lynched by a mob of ethnic Hungarian and Romanian villagers following the alleged murder of an ethnic Romanian. A government statement subsequently blamed "mounting social tension" in the area and pledged that official efforts would be made "to encourage the process of social integration".

Although Romania's Jewish community had dwindled to between 15,000 and 30,000 by the 1990s, anti-Semitism remains a feature of public life. During the early communist era Romania experienced a wave of anti-Semitism as leading members of the Jewish community were tried for Zionism. However, by the late 1950s, the communist regime had adopted perhaps the most liberal policy in communist Central and Eastern Europe towards its Jewish community. Rabbi Moses Rosen, the Chief Rabbi for forty years from 1954, was the flamboyant figure instrumental in persuading the regime to permit free emigration for Jews, which most took up, and to grant religious freedom to those that remained. After the revolution of 1989 and the rise of Romanian nationalism, Rosen warned in 1993 of an "escalation of anti-Semitism", prompting Iliescu to call for the prosecution of extreme right-wing parties and media for anti-Semitism. The leader of one ultra-nationalist party denounced Iliescu in 1995 as "a protector of impertinent Zionists".

FOREIGN AFFAIRS

Following the revolution Romania severed its formal security and economic links with the Soviet Union. Nevertheless, relations with the Soviet Union and Russia remained relatively stable. By 1993 the prospects had receded for early reunification with the main part of the territory lost to the Soviet Union in 1941, which had secured independence in 1991 as the republic of Moldova. To the consternation of Romanian nationalists, Moldovan enthusiasm for reunification had waned. The shelving of this issue, however, improved Romanian-Russian relations considerably.

From 1990 the new regime sought to improve links with the West as the first priority of its foreign policy. Despite Romania's lack of progress in economic reform and democratisation, the involvement of extremist parties in government from 1994, the poor state of ethnic relations in the country, and a poor image as a impoverished and politically immature Balkan state, Romania made considerable progress in relations with the West.

The result of the 1992 elections, the defeat of reformists and centre-right parties and the success of the left and the national-communists, briefly appeared to threaten this process. When Teodor Melescanu took over as Foreign Minister after the elections, he struck a xenophobic note, asserting that Romania's "independence and sovereignty" was his top priority, and thus implying that they had hitherto been endangered by Western and international institutions and interests. The election result was met with consternation in the USA, where the House of Representatives blocked a package on mutual trade. But despite Melescanu's rhetoric, in February 1993 Romania signed an association agreement with the EC (EU), and Romanian officials insisted that early membership was a priority. Whilst the tardiness of Romanian economic reform placed the country firmly in the "slow track" to full EC membership, Romania was among the first countries to join NATO's Partnership for Peace programme in 1993, indicating its diplomatic ambitions to be regarded as intrinsic to any new, Western-oriented security structure which might emerge from the ashes of the Cold War.

Admission to the Council of Europe was delayed until October 1993, making Romania the last former Soviet bloc country in the region to join; securing membership at all was nevertheless a minor diplomatic success, bearing in mind the considerable doubts over Romania's human and ethnic rights record, expressed most vocally by Hungary.

Relations with Hungary have presented Romanian diplomats with their biggest political challenge. The existence of a large ethnic Hungarian community resident mainly in Transylvania, which was part of historic Hungary for a millennium before 1918, is at the root of the problem. When Hungarian Prime Minister Antall declared in 1990 that he was Prime Minister of all Hungarians, Romanian suspicions of Hungarian irredentism were apparently confirmed. Negotiations on a basic treaty between Hungary and Romania made little progress. The situation looked unlikely to improve following the election of extreme nationalist parties to the Romanian parliament in 1992. The formal inclusion of these parties within the Romanian coalition from early 1994 was a further setback. However the socialist victory in Hungarian elections in 1994 has changed the climate. Hungary's socialist leader and new prime minister Gyula Horn called for a "historic reconciliation" with Romania and Slovakia, proposing that Hungary renounce all territorial claims in exchange for guarantees on the civil rights of ethnic-Hungarian minorities. In the highest-level diplomatic contact for four years, Romanian foreign minister Melescanu visited Hungary in September 1994 to welcome Hungarian progress in recognition of the permanence of the mutual border. By the late summer of 1995, as the PD-FSN appeared to be distancing itself from the nationalist parties, the momentum behind a settlement seemed to be increasing. In August 1995 Iliescu echoed Horn in declaring that the "international climate [offered] Romania and Hungary a unique chance for a historic reconciliation", while Hungary signalled that there could be no deal without the settlement of "contentious issues".

After relations with Hungary, perhaps the toughest diplomatic test for Romania was set by the economic blockade imposed on the rump Yugoslavia in 1993. Romania has effectively succeeded in escaping punishment for its failure to implement the sanctions, after Western diplomats tacitly accepted that Romania should not be expected to bear the burden of policing the sanctions, as well as the knock-on cost to its own economy in disrupted trade.

CONSTITUTIONAL ISSUES

The FSN acted quickly after the revolution to introduce new constitutional measures. In a series of decrees on 28-29 December 1989 the 1965 constitution was amended to drop the country's official title of Socialist Republic, to guarantee the rights of national minorities, to allow freedom of worship, and to provide for conversion to a free market economy. Other announcements included abolition of the ban on abortion and birth control, abolition of the death penalty, and the promise of free elections in spring 1990.

The civil rights situation improved rapidly when on 5 January 1990 all political prisoners imprisoned since 1947 were released under an amnesty.

A referendum on 8 December 1991 approved a new constitution, which then took effect on 13 December. The constitution gave substantial powers to an executive presidency and included guarantees of pluralism, respect for human rights and a free market economic system. Constitutional matters have since been relatively uncontroversial in Romania, which has successfully avoided major confrontations between political institutions over constitutional prerogatives.

There is some support in Romania for the institution of a constitutional monarchy. However Romanian governments have been strongly opposed, and Ex-King Michael has been persistently refused entry to Romania. In October 1994 he was turned back at Bucharest airport, on the grounds that he posed a threat to the republican constitution. Twelve months later the Royal succession was thrown into doubt when a Romanian Court accepted the long-standing claim to the succession of Crown Prince Lambrino, King Carol's son by his first marriage.

Romania's human rights situation has been subject to considerable scrutiny. Whilst human and civil rights have improved dramatically since the Ceausescu era, there has been particular concern over ethnic minority rights.

Another measure controversial with civil rights activists was the passage in November 1994 of legislation providing prison sentences of up to five years for some categories of behaviour by homosexuals.

PRINCIPAL PERSONALITIES

Gheorghe **Gheorghiu-Dej** (1901-65). The first leader of the Romanian communist regime, Gheorghiu-Dej was a party activist in the 1930s. He was imprisoned under the wartime Iron Guard regime. As party first secretary in the immediate postwar period, he was the dominant figure in the Front government and thereafter tightened his grip on power by the intimidation of opponents outside the party, and merciless purges of rivals within it. His control of the party machinery, and his adeptness at playing on strong Romanian nationalistic sentiments, enabled him to use these purges to remove the pro-Moscow faction in the party, whereas elsewhere in Eastern Europe it was the "nationalists" like himself who faced denunciation in the late 1940s and early 1950s. He launched Romania on the independent foreign policy pursued by his successor Ceausescu, securing the removal of all Soviet troops from Romania by 1958. His stance of "Romania first" also involved insisting that Romania must modernise and develop its own heavy industrial base, rather than be food supplier to the Soviet bloc. After his death from cancer there was a brief and rather half-hearted attempt to discredit him; his brutal purges were criticised, and some of his surviving victims were rehabilitated.

Nicolae **Ceausescu** (1918-89). The Romanian party leader from 1965 until his violent overthrow in December 1989, and head of state for all but two of those years. He began his political life as a teenage communist activist from a peasant family, and was imprisoned under King Carol and again by the Iron Guard during the war. Associated closely with Gheorghiu-Dej's nationalist group in the party, he succeeded his mentor as general secretary, and played the patriotic card riskily but successfully. Besides maintaining contacts with China and Israel, he condemned the Warsaw Pact's 1968 invasion of Czechoslovakia, and declared all-out resistance against the threat of Romania suffering the same fate. Although he kept Romania within the Warsaw Pact, he offered Western governments the possibility of an intermediary, and enjoyed the attention and foreign honours which he (and his high-profile wife Elena) received in return. His economic schemes were geared to notions of Romania's grandeur, and a pride in what modern man could do to his environment, but his lifestyle was remote from the hardship which such policies entailed for ordinary people. The Ceausescu nepotism was unpopular in the upper echelons of the party, but strict censorship and a pervasive personality cult stifled dissonant voices as he proclaimed his rule to be the "golden age", and he seemed genuinely astonished to encounter protest and even hatred from his people in December 1989, when he and Elena were overthrown, captured and shot. Some national-communist politicians, including Corneliu Vadim-Tudor of the Greater Romania Party, have called for Ceausescu's rehabilitation as a national hero who protected Romania from Soviet domination.

Ion **Iliescu** (b. 1930). The President of Romania since May 1990, and previously the head of the FSN and of its interim administration. Iliescu, an engineer by profession, was the son of a communist railway worker. His political career began as a communist youth leader, and during the communist era he rose to ministerial rank before becoming party propaganda secretary. In 1971, having offended superiors with his lack of enthusiasm for the burgeoning Ceausescu personality cult, he was sidelined first to regional party leadership in Timisoara and Iasi, and then to lesser technical postings. Visible from early on in the December uprising as one of the FSN leaders, he had become its dominant figure by early January 1990. Iliescu won an overwhelming victory in the May 1990 presidential election, but subsequently his image was badly tarnished by his dependence on the violent intervention of pro-government miners to break up pro-democracy student protests. Iliescu himself, although no longer officially part of the FSN once he became President, was a powerful influence among those who wanted to cushion free market reforms with maximum social protection; to this end prime minister Roman was abandoned in September 1991, and Iliescu's supporters formed a conservative breakaway from the FSN, the DFSN (subsequently renamed the PD-FSN), which emerged as the largest single party in parliament after the 1992 legislative elections. The introduction of a new constitution in December 1991 having enhanced presidential powers considerably, Iliescu convincingly secured re-election as President in 1992.. He had campaigned on a conservative platform against radical reforms which would create a "Wild East" of unfettered capital. As Iliescu's presidency progressed, he adopted an increasingly pragmatic and social-democratic line, encouraging the government to continue moderate economic reforms. He also tolerated the presence within the coalition from 1994 of two ultra-nationalist parties, the PUNR and the PRM, although by the autumn of 1995--perhaps anticipating the next legislative elections--he had moved to distance himself and the PD-FSN from their coalition partners.

Silviu **Brucan** (b. 1928). A former diplomat and editor of the communist party newspaper *Scienteia*, Brucan became identified as a reformist and was detained after signing the March 1989 critical letter to Ceausescu. When the December uprising began he immediately emerged as an FSN leader, its chief spokesman and foreign affairs expert, but became one of its most vocal critics when it transpired that the FSN intended to consolidate its own political power by contesting the elections. He retired from politics himself, but later added his voice to the charge that the December revolution was really a form of coup, plotted in advance by figures within the Ceausescu regime.

Marian **Munteanu** (b. 1964). A student leader in Bucharest and participant in the December 1989 uprising, he then became the most visible anti-communist opponent of the FSN, leading the University Square occupation in May-June until the miners arrived, when he was beaten up and arrested. Released six weeks later after sustained protests, he became chairman in December 1990 of the Civic Alliance. Munteanu became a key figure in the centre-right CDR bloc, of which the Civic Alliance Party was a member. He won a seat in parliament as a CDR deputy in 1992.

Petre **Roman** (b. 1944). The prime minister of the FSN regime until the miners compelled his resignation by their opposition to economic austerity measures in September 1991. Roman, a professor of engineering in Bucharest, was the son of a veteran communist activist and was himself a long-standing communist party member until he became involved in the December 1989 uprising. He became interim prime minister and succeeded Iliescu as FSN leader when the latter became president. Roman led the FSN to its victory in the May 1990 elections but his austerity measures--introduced in 1991--caused a rift with conservative elements in the FSN, notably Iliescu. Confronted by a violent anti-government demonstrations by miners, Iliescu abandoned Roman in autumn 1991 and the president's supporters formed a breakaway from the FSN, the DFSN. Roman's rump FSN performed poorly in the 1992 elections, having set out its stall as a pro-reform, social-democratic party. Roman had by this time become an implacable opponent of Iliescu and the DFSN, and was bitterly critical of the inclusion in coalition with the DFSN (now renamed the PD-FSN) of ultra-nationalist parties from 1994.

Nicolae **Vacariou** (b. 1943). Romanian prime minister from November 1992. Vacariou was a former economist who had served as a junior finance minister. An independent, he initially formed a notionally technocratic government which was nevertheless dominated by the FSND and included former communist-era officials, notable Industry Minister Dumitru Popescu. Vacariou proved a colourless political personality, eclipsed by more charismatic figures. Despite declaring that continued reform was "an absolute priority" he pledged the government to "assume special care for the social costs of the process". His style was cautious pragmatism, illustrated in his willingness to admit extreme right-wing parties to his government. With economic reform progressing only extremely slowly, Vacariou was increasingly regarded as a conservative.

Theodor **Stolojan** (b. 1943). The prime minister from October 1991 until November 1992, at the head of the coalition government formed following the resignation of Roman, Stolojan was chosen as a non-party figure with a commitment to economic reform; he had been finance minister under Roman until April 1991 and then director of the privatisation agency. Since 1992 he has been an economist at the World Bank.

Emil **Constantinescu** (b. 1939). Leader of the centre-right opposition bloc, the CDR. A university lecturer involved with the 1989-90 protests, he became rector of Bucharest University, and was chosen as CDR candidate for the 1992 presidential elections, finishing runner-up to Iliescu after a campaign hampered by his inexperience and relatively low political profile. As CDR President from November 1992 Constantinescu had a difficult act to follow in succeeding the popular and able Corneliu Coposu, but his lack of party affiliation assisted him in establishing authority over the bloc.

POLITICAL PARTIES

The Communist Party and successors

The **Romanian Communist Party** (PCR) was originally founded in 1921. Romanian communists had a relatively low profile during the limited democracy of the interwar period, especially after King Carol assumed the throne in 1930. The Soviet Union effectively imposed communist rule after the Second World War, although some peasants supported the new regime because of promised land reforms. From 1948 (when it formally absorbed the Social Democratic Party) until 1965 the party was titled the **Romanian Workers' Party**, before reverting to its original name. The PCR claimed a membership of approaching four million in 1989, making it the largest communist party in Central and Eastern Europe (outside the Soviet Union). Under communist rule the party-dominated broad front organisation monopolised Assembly seats and claimed over 97 per cent support.

In the immediate aftermath of the overthrow of Ceausescu, the ruling FSN announced the banning of the party, but retracted this decision almost immediately. The PCR's assets were nationalised in January 1990. It was not active during the legislative elections of May 1990, although other leftist parties did win a handful of seats. Nevertheless a new law forbade the registration of communist and other extremist parties (*see below*). Although in May 1994 a Bucharest Court ruled that the PCR should be registered as a legal party, this decision was soon reversed on appeal. By 1994 the party had only 4,000 members and was led by Victor Hancu, who insisted in one breath firstly that the party had radically transformed itself, and secondly that Ceausescu should be rehabilitated as a national hero.

Leaders of the FSN repeatedly denied that their party was the principal successor to the communist-era PCR, despite the fact that most of them were former communist officials. The FSN nevertheless gained a reputation as the party of the former nomenklatura.

A self-proclaimed successor party to the PCR, the **Socialist Party of Labour** (PSM), emerged in November 1990. A former prime minister, Ilie Verdet, was confirmed as the SLP leader in August 1991. Constantin Pirvulescu, a veteran dissident communist, was the PSM's honorary president. The party secured some 3 per cent of the vote in the 1992 elections and joined the coalition government of Vacariou, though it failed to gain seats in cabinet.

The **Agrarian Democratic Party of Romania** (PDAR) has its roots in communist-affiliated agrarian organisations. The PDAR was politically close to the FSN in 1990-2, and subsequently to the FSND. It won a handful of parliamentary seats in 1990 and 1992. In November 1993 it joined the national-communist PUNR in the National Unity bloc. The PDAR then joined the grand coalition of the PDSR plus the national-communists formed in early 1994; but it quickly withdrew in protest over the passage of a land tax in the spring of 1994.

Other parties

The legacy of authoritarian rule dating back to the interwar period had significant implications for the nascent Romanian democracy. The Ceausescu-era limitations on the freedom of speech and of association, which far exceeded those of most other communist bloc states, had atomised Romanian society, breaking down the formal and informal bodies combining people. In 1990 only the FSN was sufficiently organised to contest the elections effectively, benefiting in organisational terms from the party's common past experience of communist party membership. Since 1990 other parties have emerged, but with only one election since the revolution having been contested by a plurality of serious parties, it is difficult to make generalisations about Romanian voting behaviour. The parties that have emerged, however, have tended to be populist in the sense that they attempt to appeal to the Romanian people as a whole, rather than seeking to represent a class or social cross-section, as many Western parties do. The only group they do not seek to represent is the Hungarian minority, which has its own political party.

Legislation passed after the revolution bans the registration of parties supporting totalitarianism, extremism, fascism or communism. Nevertheless two parties have prospered in Romania which by Western standards are extreme, namely the PUNR and the PRM, which combine ultra-nationalism with neo-communism. Together they won some 11 per cent of the vote in 1992. In contrast centrist or reformist parties have fared poorly relative to similar parties in Central Europe.

The **National Salvation Front** (FSN) dominated the political scene in the aftermath of the overthrow of Ceausescu. The FSN was set up during the revolution as a temporary rallying point for diverse opponents to the regime, but former communists and senior military men quickly came to dominate the FSN leadership. The initial declared intention of its leaders to pilot the country toward democratic elections, and then to disband, was soon rescinded. As early as January 1990, those few people with longer-standing dissident credentials, like Doina Cornea, had broken with the FSN and accused its leadership of past collaboration with the Ceausescu regime; these critics alleged that the former nomenklatura had "stolen" the revolution. The FSN's first national conference was held on April 7-8, 1990. The conference elected a 71-member council, which in turn elected as party leader Ion Iliescu. When Iliescu became Romania's President in June 1990, Petre Roman replaced him as FSN leader. The FSN's programme for the May 1990 elections called for "a complete and irreversible break with the communist system and its ideology", and defined the FSN as a centre-left party, advocating a gradual transition towards a market economy, while preserving a minimum wage and unemployment benefits and retaining much state ownership in industry and agriculture. Despite its overwhelming victory, public confidence in the FSN fell. Iliescu and Petre Roman, the Prime Minister from summer 1990, soon became known as the champions of two rival factions within the party. While Roman argued for severe austerity measures, thereby gaining a reputation as a reformist, Iliescu and others became noted for their conservatism by insisting on continued social support and state-subsidies for industry. The government also failed to bring to justice the worst offenders of the Ceausescu era.

In March 1991 Roman won the overwhelming backing of an FSN national convention for a social democratic programme, A Future for Romania. But by the late summer Roman's limited economic reforms had become extremely unpopular, and when miners violently protested at the government's "attack" on their living standards Roman unwillingly left office. The episode sealed the antipathy between Roman and Iliescu, which by the next national convention, in March 1992, had split the party. Iliescu's supporters formed the **Democratic National Salvation Front** (FSND), becoming the **Democratic Party-FSN** (PD-FSN) in May 1993, while Roman's faction retained the name FSN until becoming the **Social Democracy Party of Romania** (PDSR) in July 1993. Despite Roman's vehement criticism of the conservatives, Iliescu and his cohorts were vindicated in the 1992 elections and formed a minority government. The PD-FSN's lack of an economic programme was increasingly exposed in office, and its willingness to collaborate in coalition with the neo-communist and ultra-nationalist parties cast further doubt on its own democratic credentials. Iliescu's attack on these parties in autumn 1995 appeared to herald a distancing of the PD-FSN from the extremist parties, with a view to the next legislative elections.

The **Democratic Convention of Romania** (CDR) was formed in November 1991 as a centre-right bloc of more than a dozen parties, of which the **National Peasant Party-Christian Democratic** (PNT-CD) was the most significant. Also included was the **Civic Alliance Party**, which cut its teeth in organising a series of protest demonstrations in 1990 against both the austerity measures and the continued presence of ex-communists in high office. The **National Liberal Party** left the bloc in April 1992 and failed to win seats in the elections the following month. In these elections the CDR finished second with over 20 per cent of the vote. The PNT-CD took over half of the bloc's 82 seats in the Chamber of Deputies. Emil Constantinescu, the CDR's unsuccessful candidate in the 1992 presidential elections, who was not at that time a member of any party, became the CDR leader in November 1992, replacing the veteran dissident Corneliu Coposu (who was also the PNT-CD leader). Coposu's death in November 1995 robbed the bloc of its best-known and most respected figure.

The **Romanian National Unity Party** (PUNR) is the political wing of the anti-Hungarian organisation Vatra Romaneasca (Romanian Cradle). The PUNR is a national-communist party advocating continued state control of the economy and an ultra-nationalist foreign and domestic policy. In February 1992 PUNR member Gheorghe Funar was elected as mayor of the ethnically mixed town of Cluj in Transylvania. Funar stood as a candidate in the 1992 presidential elections, polling some 1.3 million votes; in October 1992 he was elected as chair of the PUNR, replacing Radu Ceontea. In 1994 the minority Vacariou government struck a coalition deal with the PUNR and several other parties, and by August the PUNR had four nominees in ministerial office. Once in government the PUNR conceded ground on economic reform in return for a tough line on ethnic minority rights. Tensions within the coalition grew in 1995, when Iliescu denounced Funar as a "little Zhirinovsky".

The **Greater Romania Party** (*Romania Mare* or PRM) is ideologically similar to the PUNR; it has demonstrated even greater xenophobia, and its leaders have frequently denounced Romanies, Jews and the West in general, although Hungarians are still its principal target. Corneliu Vadim Tudor, who was confirmed as party leader at the PRM's first congress in March 1993, has claimed that Hungarian minority leaders have plotted a bloody ethnic division of Romania on Yugoslav lines. Tudor has also described Ceausescu as a patriot and has called for his rehabilitation.

The **Hungarian Democratic Union of Romania** (UDMR) represents the interests of Romania's ethnic Hungarian minority. To this end it has demanded extensive guarantees on ethnic minority rights, especially on Hungarian language education, local autonomy, and cultural matters. Under writer and publisher Geza Domokos the UDMR in 1990-2 formed the most effective and cohesive group in parliament apart from the FSN itself, achieving a position of relative respectability and cooperating with opposition parties. In January 1993 the moderate writer Bela Marko was elected UDMR leader. The UDMR's radical wing is led by Bishop Laszlo Tokes, a prominent public figure who was a key figure in the events of 1989. Since the rise of the ultra-nationalist parties, the UDMR has become a pariah party. The UDMR leadership's denial that it seeks autonomy for ethnic Hungarian areas is given short shrift by the ethnic-Romanian parties. The UDMR applied to join the centre-right CDR in June 1995, but CDR grandee Coposu denounced it as "extreme nationalist".

ELECTIONS

Legislature

Under communist rule the 1965 constitution nominally designated the 369-member unicameral Grand National Assembly as the principal political authority. This body was elected for a five-year term from a list of party-approved candidates of the communist-dominated front organisation, which was known successively as the National Democratic Front, the People's Democratic Front, the Socialist Unity Front and finally the Socialist Democracy and Unity Front. A choice of candidates was offered in some seats from 1975 onwards. Turnouts were regularly given as nearly 100 per cent, with over 97 per cent voting for the official candidates. The most recent such elections took place in 1985.

Interim constitutional arrangements and an electoral law, approved on 17 March 1990, provided for a multi-party democratic election using modified proportional representation in 41 multi-member constituencies. A number of seats were allocated to national minorities. Free legislative elections, the first since December 1928, were held on 20 May 1990, and resulted in an overwhelming FSN victory. A direct presidential election was held simultaneously. The newly elected assembly was charged with the responsibility of passing a new constitution.

Legislative elections on 20 May 1990

| | National Assembly | | Senate | |
	%	seats	%	seats
FSN	66.3	263	67.0	92
UDMR	7.2	29	7.2	12
NLP	6.4	29	7.1	9
PNT-CD	2.6	12	2.5	1
Ecological Movement	2.6	12	2.5	1
Ecological Party	1.4	8	1.4	1
Romanian Unity Alliance	2.2	9	2.2	1
PDAR	1.6	9	1.6	0
Others & independents	9.7	5	8.5	12
Allocated to minorities & others	-		-	11
Total	100.0	400	100.0	119

Changes to the electoral law before the September 1992 legislative elections reorganised the legislature, reducing the size of the lower house and increasing the upper. Election was by party lists based on proportional representation; a minimum 3 per cent threshold applied, increasing by one percentage point for each additional party in any given electoral coalition. The FSND, a conservative successor party to the FSN, emerged as the largest party. The rump FSN itself won only just over 10 per cent of the vote. The PSM, a successor to the PCR, won a handful of seats, and the extreme nationalist PUNR and PRM were also successful. The defeated runner-up, the CDR, alleged that large-scale electoral fraud had taken place, pointing to the electoral commission's own data, which revealed that as many as 3,000,000 votes had been declared invalid, and that a further 1,500,000 votes had been cast by people outside their places of residence.

Legislative elections on 27 September 1992

	Chamber of Deputies % of vote seats		Senate % of vote seats	
FSND*	27.71	117	28.29	49
CDR**	20.01	82	20.16	34
FSN***	10.18	43	10.38	18
PUNR	7.71	30	8.12	14
UDMR	7.45	27	7.58	12
PRM	3.89	16	3.85	6
PSM	3.03	13	3.18	5
PDAR	-	-	3.30	5
Others	20.02	-	15.14	-
Reserved seats+	-	13	-	-
Total	341		143	

*Renamed the Democratic Party-FSN (PD-FSN) in May 1993.
**The CDR was a centre-right bloc of 18 parties, of which the PNT-CD was the most significant; this party was allocated some 42 of the CDR's 82 seats in the Chamber of Deputies. Other parties in the CDR were the Civic Alliance Party; the National Liberal Party-Youth Wing; and the Romanian Social Democratic Party (which merged with the PD-FSN in January 1996).
***Renamed the Social Democracy Party of Romania (PDSR) in July 1993.
+Set aside for representatives of Romania's smallest 13 ethnic minorities.

CDR=Democratic Convention of Romania; FSND=Democratic National Salvation Front; FSN=National Salvation Front; NLP=National Liberal Party; PCR=Communist Party of Romania; PDAR=Democratic Agrarian Party of Romania; PNT-CD=National Peasant Party-Christian Democratic; PRM=*Romania Mare* or Greater Romania Party; PSM=Socialist Party of Labour; UDMR=Hungarian Democratic Union of Romania.

Presidency

Under the 1965 constitution the President of the Republic was elected by the Assembly and also presided over the 21-member Council of State (again elected by the Assembly). Ceausescu held this post himself from 1967.

Under interim constitutional arrangements direct elections to the moderately powerful presidency were held concurrently with the parliamentary elections on May 20, 1990, and were won by Ion Iliescu of the FSN with 85 per cent of the vote in an 86 per cent turnout. The two defeated contenders were returning exiles who represented "historic" parties of the pre-communist period, Radu Campeanu of the NLP (10.2 per cent) and Ion Ratiu of the PNT-CD (4.3 per cent). The electoral law provided that, once elected, the President could not be a member of a political party. Iliescu duly resigned as FSN leader, and was sworn in as President on 20 June 1990.

Iliescu, as the nominee of the FSND, faced more significant competition for the presidency in 1992, his political rivals having improved their organisation, and the constitution of December 1991 having increased the executive powers of the post. Despite the stronger challenge, he almost achieved a majority in the first round on 27

September, winning 47.34 per cent against 31.24 per cent for Emil Constantinescu (who was not a member of a political party, but was the nominee of the CDR bloc). The extreme nationalist candidate Gheorghe Funar of the PUNR received some 1.3 million votes, 10.88 per cent of the total, and finished in third place. Caius Dragomir (FSN) was fourth with 4.75 per cent, ahead of Ion Manzatu (RP) with 3.05 per cent and independent Mircea Druc with 2.75 per cent. In the second round run-off on 11 October Iliescu took 61.43 per cent against 38.57 per cent for Constantinescu.

CHRONOLOGY

1859. The principalities of Walachia and Moldova, which since the sixteenth century have been under Turkish rule, are unified, forming the core of the modern Romanian state.

1877. Independence from Ottoman rule.

1881. Romania becomes a kingdom.

1917-21. Legislation is passed breaking up the largest estates and redistributing the land to peasants. The land reform is fully implemented by 1927.

1914-18. Romania participates in the First World War on the Allied side.

1918. In the peace settlement following the First World War, Romania's territory and population are doubled with the award of Transylvania from Hungary, Bessarabia from Russia and Bukovina from Bulgaria.

November 1919. Romania's first parliamentary elections by universal male suffrage.

March 1920. Fresh elections are held and the results rigged, setting a precedent for the interwar period.

1923. A new, étatist constitution restricts freedom of association, designates the country's natural resources as state property, centralises the administration, and confirms the extensive Royal prerogatives.

1927. King Ferdinand dies. The official heir to the throne, Crown Prince Michael, is deemed too young to succeed, and Royal prerogatives pass to a committee.

1928. Formation of National-Peasant government. Restrictions on free speech are lifted; other liberalising measures are taken; genuinely free elections take place in December 1928.

1930. Carol, father of Crown Prince Michael, returns from exile to declare himself King and quickly establishes an authoritarian regime which dominates the political parties.

February 1938. King Carol formally establishes a royal dictatorship.

1940. At the insistence of Nazi Germany, Carol cedes over one third of Romanian territory to Hungary, Bulgaria and the Soviet Union; the consequent uproar forces him to flee the country. King Michael replaces him and the right-radical Iron Guard institutes a fascist dictatorship. There is a series of pogroms against political opponents and Jews.

1941. Hitler backs the ousting of the unstable Iron Guard in favour of army chief Gen. Ion Antonescu, who introduces a brutal military dictatorship. Romania enters the war on the Axis side and participates in the genocide against Jews.

23 August 1944. With Soviet troops poised to invade central Romania, King Michael launches a coup d'etat, deposing Antonescu. Romania changes sides in the war, allying with the advancing Soviet forces.

31 August 1944. The Red Army arrives in Bucharest prior to the occupation of Romania as a whole.

6 March 1945. A Soviet-backed regime is set up under Petru Groza.

May 1946. Paris peace conference.

November 1946. The communist-dominated National Democratic Front claims to have won over two thirds of the vote in a disputed general election.

September 1947. The postwar peace settlement confirms the return of Transylvania, but Southern Dobruja remains Bulgarian, and the Soviet Union retains northern Bukovina and Bessarabia.

October 1947. The merger of the social democrats into the Communist Party lays the basis for the Romanian Workers' Party.

30 December 1947. King Michael is forced to abdicate, the monarchy is abolished and the Romanian People's Republic proclaimed.

1948-50. Major industries are nationalised and a programme of agricultural collectivisation commences. There is a Stalinist emphasis on heavy industrial development; paradoxically this conflicts with Soviet plans for Romania to be primarily a food producer.

1953-54. Leading members of the Jewish community are tried for Zionism.

1956. In the midst of the Hungarian uprising, Gheorghiu-Dej argues against foreign intervention in Hungary.

July 1958. Soviet troops are withdrawn from Romania under a Warsaw Pact agreement.

19 March 1965. Gheorghiu-Dej dies, and is succeeded by Nicolae Ceausescu as party first secretary.

1965. A new constitution is introduced, and the RWP reverts to its pre-1947 name, the Romanian Communist Party (PCR).

May-June 1966. Ceausescu attacks the Soviet annexation of Bukovina, further distancing his regime from the Soviet line in international affairs.

January 1967. Romania becomes the first East-Central European country to grant West Germany formal recognition.

1968-71. A short-lived experiment in economic liberalisation results in little substantive change, despite the nominal introduction of "workers' participation".

August 1968. Romania condemns the Warsaw Pact invasion of Czechoslovakia.

August 1969. US President Nixon visits Romania, where huge crowds turn out to greet him; Ceausescu visits the USA the following year.

1971-72. Romania becomes a member of GATT, the IMF and the World Bank.

March 1975. The USA grants most favoured nation trading status to Romania.

April-July 1978. Ceausescu becomes the first communist head of state from Eastern Europe to visit London.

March 1980. Romania and the UK issue a joint statement criticising the Soviet invasion of Afghanistan.

December 1982. Ceausescu resolves to pay off the country's foreign debt by the end of the decade, by means of a sustained export drive. A series of harsh austerity measures are introduced including rationing of food (much of which is now earmarked for export) and of energy.

September 1983. US Vice-President Bush visits Romania and afterwards describes Ceausescu as "one of Europe's good communists".

October 1985. A state of emergency is declared in the energy industry.

15 November 1987. Major riots in Brasov mark the most serious challenge to the Ceausescu regime; the trouble is forcibly suppressed.

5 April 1988. Plans are announced for the forcible "systematisation" policy, to impose a more "modern" pattern of agro-industrial centres by demolishing half of Romania's villages by the year 2000. Hungary expresses concern that systematisation will be targeted against Romania's ethnic Hungarian minority and on April 19 accuses Romania of a policy of forcible assimilation. The plan also marks a shift in international perceptions of the Romanian regime.

March 1989. Six formerly prominent communist figures, all still party members, accuse Ceausescu in an unprecedented open letter of discrediting socialism, ruining the economy, and earning international condemnation over human rights issues. The six include former foreign minister Corneliu Manescu and party newspaper editor Silviu Brucan (the latter already marked out as a critic since the Brasov riots of 1987).

April 1989. The completed repayment of foreign debt is announced proudly in Bucharest.

June 1989. The Polish communists are humiliated by Solidarity in partially free elections.

July 1989. A fence which the Romanians had begun to construct along the northern border, to prevent the departure of ethnic Hungarians, is dismantled after international criticism.

July 1989. The Warsaw Pact meets in Bucharest. Ceausescu proposes military intervention in Poland; his call merely confirms his isolation.

9 November 1989. German anti-communist demonstrators breach the Berlin Wall.

20-24 November 1989. The 14th party congress records the regime's "achievements" over the past five years. The Soviet communist party sends a message calling for an "exchange of experiences" among socialist countries, implying that the PCR should consider its own version of "perestroika".

10 December 1989. The communist regime in Czechoslovakia falls, leaving Romania as the only remaining hard-line Soviet-bloc regime.

15-17 December 1989. A demonstration in Timisoara, called to protest over the removal of the ethnic Hungarian priest Father Laszlo Tokes, swells to a march of several thousand chanting "Down with Ceausescu!". Although the army commander refuses to shoot unarmed protesters, when the demonstrators return in defiance on 17 December, troops do fire on the crowd; although some 70 people are killed, rumours spread in Bucharest of a massacre of thousands.

21 December 1989. Ceausescu appears at midday to address a crowd which has been called to hear his speech from the balcony of the party headquarters in Bucharest, and is bewildered when demonstrators shout him down. A large crowd, including many students, reassembles in the evening and the *Securitate* forces open fire.

22 December 1989. Ceausescu, having once again tried to address the crowd, is overthrown when the armed forces change sides in Bucharest and join the demonstrators; he flees Bucharest.

23 December 1989. An ad hoc "National Salvation Front" (FSN) put together by the army and the opposition protesters, based at the television station, declares its authority and calls for free elections. Elite units of the *Securitate* forces fight back, killing indiscriminately, in an effort to preserve the Ceausescu regime.

25 December 1989. Ceausescu and his wife Elena, having been captured at Tirgoviste to the north west of Bucharest, are given a summary trial, sentenced to death, and shot repeatedly.

26 December 1989. A video recording showing Ceausescu's corpse is broadcast on television. The fighting in Bucharest and elsewhere begins to subside. Ion Iliescu is declared President of the FSN and a government is formed under Petre Roman, both men being former communists.

28-29 December 1989. The country's official title of Socialist Republic is dropped, and the new regime guarantees the rights of national minorities, promises freedom of worship, and commits itself to the creation of a free market economy. Other announcements include the legalisation of abortion and birth control, abolition of the death penalty, and the promise of free elections in April 1990.

5 January 1990. All political prisoners imprisoned since 1947 are released under an amnesty.

12-13 January 1990. Demonstrators at a day of national mourning shout down Iliescu and Roman with cries of "down with the communists" and "death for a death". In response the FSN announces the dissolution of the communist party. Iliescu, however, almost immediately lifts the ban, announcing that the issue should be decided by a referendum, which is never held.

24 January 1990. Leading dissident Doina Cornea resigns from the FSN, claiming that it is dominated by former communists.

26 January 1990. Dumitru Mazilu, the FSN's first vice-president, resigns after a campaign against him, based on the allegation that he had been closely involved with the *Securitate*.

1 February 1990. Pending the election of a legislature, a Provisional Council of National Unity is formed, on which the FSN has 105 seats and the 35 registered political parties three each.

2 February 1990. Four former communist leaders are sentenced to life imprisonment with hard labour for "co-authorship of genocide".

19-20 March 1990. Demonstrations by ethnic Hungarians in the mainly-Hungarian town of Tirgu Mures in Transylvania to demand minority rights are challenged by a Romanian mob; several people are killed in the resulting riots. The Tirgu Mures events arouse fears of an inter-ethnic conflict in Romania.

May 1990. Diplomatic relations are restored with the Vatican following the legalisation of the Catholic church in Romania.

20 May 1990. The FSN wins an overwhelming victory in legislative elections while Iliescu wins 85 per cent of the vote in the presidential election.

May 1990. Petre Roman is named as prime minister. Demonstrators led by students and intellectuals for weeks sustain a protest in Bucharest, claiming that the revolution has been "stolen" by former communists in the FSN.

15-16 June 1990. Miners arrive en masse in Bucharest, employing great brutality to break up the anti-FSN demonstrations. While Iliescu welcomes the miners' intervention, the international community is shocked and the reputation of the new Romanian democracy is damaged.

20 July 1990. Roman presents legislation on the legal framework for a free market economy and the development of the private sector, initially involving small and medium-sized enterprises.

August 1990. Former FSN leaders Silviu Brucan and Gen. Nicolae Militaru claim that the overthrow of Ceausescu had been plotted by opponents within his regime.

21 September 1990. The former dictator's son Nicu Ceausescu, 39, is sentenced to 20 years in prison for incitement to murder, in connection with the attempted

counter-revolution by *Securitate* forces; in June 1991 his sentence is reduced to 16 years.

November-December 1990. Some prices rise dramatically as subsidies are removed in line with the Roman government's economic reform policy; protesters mount large demonstrations, union leaders demand social protection measures, and continuing strikes force the government on 11 December to defer further price liberalisation.

February 1991. Passage of a land law. The law leads to the restoration of land to some six million people by end-1992, but there is bureaucratic confusion surrounding the reform.

13 February 1991. Romania applies formally for associate membership of the European Community.

16-17 March 1991. The FSN at its first national convention endorses Petre Roman as its leader, approves new party statutes and backs Roman's "A future for Romania" programme for a market economy on social democratic principles.

18 March 1991. Former *Securitate* chief Col.-Gen. Iulian Vlad is convicted of illegally ordering the arrest of demonstrators on 21 December, 1989, and sentenced to three and a half years.

1 April 1991. In what is regarded as the first significant economic reform, a second wave of price liberalisation doubles the prices of many basic goods; attempts are made to mitigate the impact of the liberalisation through compensation payments to workers and pensioners and social security increases.

14 August 1991. Iliescu signs a law on privatisation of the non-agricultural sector of the economy. Opposition to the sell-off of industry to foreign capital is partially countered by a requirement that 30 per cent of shares be set aside for acquisition by Romanian nationals, to whom free ownership certificates will be allocated.

3 September 1991. The Romanian parliament supports Moldova's declaration of independence from the Soviet Union, and Iliescu later suggests readiness to consider unification.

27 September 1991. Petre Roman resigns as prime minister, after three days of rioting in Bucharest by miners from the Jiu valley, protesting against the austerity policies identified with Roman. Roman describes himself as the victim of "those who want to maintain the old system".

October 1991. Theodor Stolojan, a non-party technocrat and former finance minister, becomes prime minister. Despite professing a commitment to free market economic reforms, he announces a six-month delay in the price liberalisation programme.

21 November 1991. A new constitution receives parliamentary approval, giving substantial powers to an executive presidency and enshrining guarantees of pluralism, respect for human rights, and a free market economic system. A referendum on 8 December approves the new constitution, which takes effect on 13 December.

9-12 December 1991. Eight officials and former *Securitate* officers are imprisoned for the "aggravated murder" of the demonstrators at Timisoara in December 1989. They include former *Securitate* chief Col.-Gen. Iulian Vlad and former propaganda minister Ion Totu (who hangs himself in April 1992 when his 16-year sentence is confirmed).

February 1992. Gheorghe Funar of the ultra-nationalist Romanian National Unity Party (PUNR) is elected as Mayor of the ethnically mixed Transylvanian town of Cluj.

March 1992. The FSN splits, with conservatives leaving to form what becomes the Democratic National Salvation Front (FSND). The rump party under Roman retains the FSN name.

25-27 April 1992. The first visit by ex-King Michael since the revolution.

1 June 1992. Beginning of mass privatisation scheme designed to sell off 6,000 enterprises over an eight-year period, with the distribution of vouchers to the public.

3 August 1992. Romania's first privatisation, with the sale of a textile firm to an Italian company.

27 September 1992. Legislative and presidential elections. The FSND wins a quarter of the vote and over a third of the seats in the lower house. Only two other parties win more than ten per cent of the vote: the centre-right Democratic Convention of Romania (CDR) bloc, and the FSN. Iliescu is comfortably re-elected in a second round in October, and re-affirms his commitment to pluralism and a free market economy.

4 November 1992. Nicolae Vacariou, an independent, forms a minority government dominated by the FSND but also including non-party technocrats and former communist-era ministers. Although Vacariou promises to continue economic reforms his programme is widely regarded as conservative.

17 November 1992. Romania initials an association agreement with the EC (EU), the fourth ex-communist state to do so after Poland, Hungary and Czechoslovakia.

March 1993. The government presents to parliament a modest four-year economic programme including the abolition of subsidies for staple goods and services and the privatisation of 20 per cent of state-owned firms.

12 April 1993. Striking workers demonstrate against the declining standard of living.

7 May 1993. The strikers achieve their goals, securing a considerable increase in the minimum wage. The government agrees to link wages to the cost of living and to productivity.

May 1993. Roman's FSN becomes the Social Democracy Party of Romania (PDSR).

25 June 1993. The governing coalition announces a parliamentary alliance with the ultra-nationalist and neo-communist parties, the Greater Romania Party and the PUNR. The small leftist parties in parliament subsequently add their tacit support to the governing coalition.

6 July 1993. Three government officials, including Interior Minister Danescu and Finance Minister Gheorghescu, are accused of corruption by a parliamentary commission of inquiry.

10 July 1993. The ruling FSND becomes the Democratic Party-FSN (PD-FSN).

18 July 1993. Talks between the government and Hungarian minority leaders end with agreement to improve Hungarian-language education and to erect bilingual road signs.

8 September 1993. Privatisation minister Aurelian Dochia resigns in protest at delays in the privatisation process.

18 and 29 November 1993. Major demonstrations take place in Bucharest and elsewhere to protest at the falling standards of living.

17 December 1993. The Vacariou government survives a motion of no confidence by only 13 votes; over the next four days there is a series of anti-government demonstrations by students and trade unionists.

28 January 1994. Over one million workers participate in a one-day strike called by the three major trade unions to demand improved wages and social security payments.

2 February 1994. The ruling PDSR-dominated government strikes a provisional coalition deal with the national-communist PUNR and PRM, and the two leftist parties, the Socialist Party of Labour (PSM) and Agrarian Democratic Party (PDAR).

9 February 1994. The Senate passes an IMF-approved economic austerity package after two months of fierce debate; it includes privatisation, tax reform and budget controls.

28 February and 1 March 1994. Some 750,000 workers participate in a general strike to protest at poor wages and to demand an acceleration of economic reforms.

6 March 1994. A government re-shuffle is influenced by the PUNR; although the latter does not formally take place in cabinet, two new, ostensibly independent ministers are in fact PUNR members, and two more join in August.

25 March 1994. President Iliescu formally pardons eight former communist officials convicted in December 1991 of aggravated murder.

14 April 1994. The passage of a land tax as part of the February austerity package provokes the withdrawal of support of the PDAR.

11 May 1994. In a move conferring significant credibility on Romania's reforms, the IMF approves credits totalling some $450m.

5-6 September 1994. In the most high-level diplomatic contact for four years, the Romanian foreign minister Melescanu visits Hungary and welcomes Hungarian progress in recognition of the permanence of the mutual border.

7 October 1994. Ex-King Michael is barred from entry to Romania on arrival at Bucharest airport, on the grounds that he poses a threat to the republican constitution.

17 February 1995. Government officials and representatives of the ethnic Hungarian minority jointly proclaim their commitment to dialogue on minority rights issues. The announcement follows two days of talks in Atlanta Georgia attended by former US President Jimmy Carter.

21 March 1995. Passage of a law designed to privatise 3,000 state enterprises by spring 1996.

6 April. Legislation links public sector pay rises to increases in productivity and improved economic efficiency. On 11 April some 10,000 people rally in Bucharest to protest the law.

28 June 1995. The passage of an education law, subsequently signed into law by President Iliescu on 24 July; the law makes Romanian the compulsory language of higher education, but permits the continued use of minority languages for tuition in specified subjects at primary and secondary level.

1 August 1995. Distribution of vouchers for the mass privatisation scheme commences.

28-31 August 1995. Max van der Stoel, the OSCE's national minorities commissioner, visits Romania, commenting that "the situation of national minorities in Romania has substantially improved" and referring to "unjustified doubts" over the education law.

30 August 1995. Iliescu declares that the "international climate offers Romania and Hungary a unique chance for a historic reconciliation".

2 September 1995. Large demonstrations are held by ethnic Hungarians in Transylvania against the education law.

20 September 1995. Passage of new legislation banning the public display of foreign flags and the singing of foreign national anthems.

October 1995. During a visit to the USA Iliescu denounces the leaders of the far right-wing coalition partners, the PUNR and PRM.

19 October 1995. The PD-FSN announces a severing of ties with the PRM; the following day the leftist PSM announces its intention to leave the coalition.

24 November 1995. Passage of restitution legislation concerning some 200,000 properties confiscated by the communist state in the late 1940s and 1950s.

BULGARIA

The official name of the country was the People's Republic of Bulgaria (*Narodna Republika Bulgaria*) from 1947 until 1990. It was renamed as simply the Republic of Bulgaria on 15 November 1990.

Geographically Bulgaria is a south-eastern outpost of Slav habitation in Europe. It lies to the east of Yugoslavia, and in between Romania, across the Danube to the north, and Greece and Turkey to the south. Although Bulgaria has a sense of closeness to Russia,

it does not share a common border except in that it lies on the Black Sea coast. Bulgaria covers an area of 110,912 square km (less than half the size of Romania or Yugoslavia); its population of some 9,000,000 (static or falling) is likewise dwarfed by that of Romania and Yugoslavia (both over 23 million) and is slightly smaller than that of Hungary. The most populated areas are in the fertile lowlands of the Danube plain, around the capital Sofia, the Black Sea coast around the fast-growing city of Varna, and from Plovdiv south-eastward into Upper Thrace. Most mountainous is the Rhodope massif dividing south-western Bulgaria from Greece and Macedonia; the Balkan Mountains run in a line from north of Sofia to north of Stara Zagora. Sofia, with a population of 1,100,000, is by far the largest city, three times as big as Plovdiv or Varna. Officially nearly two-thirds of the population is classified as living in urban areas, the consequence of rapid migration to the main towns since 1945.

According to official 1992 figures, the population comprised 85.8 per cent ethnic Bulgarians, 9.7 per cent ethnic Turks and 3.4 per cent Gypsies. Bulgarians speak a South Slavic language written in the Cyrillic script; they share common ethnic features with Serbs and Russians. Few Bulgarians live outside the country's borders (setting aside the question of the kinship of Macedonians with Bulgarians) and the main minorities issue, an important one, concerns Bulgarian Turks. There are approximately three quarters of a million Turkish speakers (a difficult figure to assess reliably in historical terms in view of the controversial programme to "assimilate" the Turkish population in the mid-1980s, and the repression of mid-1989 which provoked a huge wave of emigration to Turkey). There are also about a quarter of a million gypsies in Bulgaria. The retention of the Pirin Macedonia district meant that there were some 200,000 Macedonian-speakers in the far west of the country as recorded in the 1946 census, but their language was officially classified as a Bulgarian dialect and their sense of distinct identity discouraged strongly in the assimilation campaign of the 1960s. The Bulgarian government continues to deny the existence of a separate Macedonian language as distinct from Bulgarian.

Muslim ethnic Bulgarians, known as Pomaks, were compelled to abandon Muslim names in an assimilation campaign in the early 1970s; most Bulgarians with religious affiliations are Eastern Orthodox Christians, although atheism was officially encouraged under the communist regime.

HISTORICAL NARRATIVE

Bulgaria was under the rule of the Ottoman Empire for almost five centuries, until Bulgarian forces drove out their Turkish occupiers in the 1870s. The Treaty of Berlin in 1878 founded Bulgaria as an autonomous principality. Bulgarian leaders were frustrated by the great powers' decision not to apportion more territory to the new state; they were particularly jealous of Macedonian territory, whose Slavic population they regarded as ethnically kindred.

Bulgaria had no indigenous nobility; its Turkish landlords had been expelled and their estates redistributed among the indigenous peasantry. In consequence Bulgaria became one of Central and Eastern Europe's most egalitarian societies. An effective education system was put in place which increased social mobility. The bureaucracy which assimilated educated peasants and artisans was however corrupt and inclined to act arbitrarily.

In the early years of the Bulgarian state, Bulgarian nationalism was as yet ill-defined. There was even some debate in the 1880s on the possibility of voluntary absorption into the Russian empire (an idea revived in a different form by the communist regime decades later). But by the turn of the century Bulgarian society had generated a vigorous nationalism which supported its leaders' increasing assertiveness in regional affairs. Bulgaria declared itself an independent kingdom in 1908 and from 1912 plunged into a series of conflicts designed to expand its regional power. In the Balkan wars of 1912-13 Bulgaria gained a foothold in Macedonia, taking the Pirin region, and seized the agriculturally rich Southern Dobruja region in the north. Then in 1915 Bulgaria entered the First World War on the side of the Central powers, taking more Macedonian territory and giving it access to the Aegean.

By 1918 the country had borne a terrible human cost for its bellicosity, with as many as two thirds of the male population between 20 and 50 years either wounded (400,000) or killed (155,000). The sacrifice proved futile; with defeat by the Western Allies, Bulgaria was forced to hand back most of its captured territory, with the exception of some ten per cent of Macedonia. In addition, under the terms of the 1919 Treaty of Neuilly, Bulgaria was required to pay reparations, and significantly to limit the size of its standing army.

The interwar period

Bulgaria's increasingly unpopular participation in the war had ultimately been brought to an end by a mutiny of peasant troops, the Radomir rebellion, which had also resulted in the abdication of Tsar Ferdinand in favour of his son Boris. A key figure in the rebellion was Aleksandur Stamboliski, the leader of the peasantist Agrarian Union (BZNS). As the two principal anti-war parties, the agrarians and the Communists emerged victorious from the legislative elections of 1919. In autumn 1919 Stamboliski formed an Agrarian-led coalition.

Bulgaria remained an overwhelmingly agrarian society, with urban dwellers comprising just one fifth of the overall population throughout the interwar period. Unlike the peasantry in many other Central and East European states, in Bulgaria this class was not trenchantly conservative and anti-modern, being relatively well-educated and amenable to innovation in both agronomy and politics.

Stamboliski's regime, although short-lived, was one of the most extraordinary in the whole region during the interwar period, marking a deeply flawed experiment in agrarian democracy. An agrarian radical who was prone to demagoguery, Stamboliski derided cities as "Sodoms". He embarked on an ideological mission to usurp the urban classes - the intelligentsia, entrepreneurs and bureaucrats - as the dominant political caste, in favour of the peasantry. Accordingly, members of the intelligentsia were excluded from the Agrarian leadership and the state bureaucracy was packed with Agrarian Union members. State control over grain prices was intended to eliminate the role of merchants.

The regime celebrated peasant values. It was egalitarian, a radical land reform limiting the size of peasant properties and expropriating surplus land. (A successor government in August 1924 almost completely reversed this reform.) It was also collectivist, obliging men aged between 20 and 40 years to engage in an eight-month term of physical labour for the state. (Subsequent governments retained this measure, but scrapped a similar requirement for women; the scheme achieved a number of significant public works, including the improvement of communications links.) Stamboliski also held an ambitious strategic vision of unifying Balkan states under the Agrarian banner, and for this reason proposed the foundation of a Green International comprising the region's peasantist parties. Stamboliski thus eschewed the irredentist fervour over Macedonia in favour of what he regarded as higher aims, which however were considered by many Bulgarians as unpatriotic and hopelessly utopian. This position earned him the bitter opposition of the terrorist Internal Macedonian Revolutionary Organisation (VMRO), which regarded any rapprochement with Yugoslavia - which occupied most of Macedonia - as treason.

In April 1923 fresh elections were held in an atmosphere of intimidation. The thuggery of the Agrarians' paramilitary force, the Orange Guard, helped the Union to achieve an overwhelming parliamentary majority, but the Agrarian victory proved the final straw for the regime's enemies.

The nationalist forces which combined to oust Stamboliski were an alliance of the bourgeois parties, the military, and the intelligentsia, backed by VMRO, and quickly endorsed by Tsar Boris. The coup d'état was the earliest of the spate of putsches in Central and Eastern Europe from the mid-1920s, which one by one dislodged many of the region's faltering democracies. The new regime was led by Aleksandur Tsankov and comprised virtually all the leading parties except for the communists and peasantists, under the Democratic Concord umbrella. Characteristically of interwar Bulgarian politics, the coup was marked by the utmost brutality; Stamboliski was tortured, dismembered and beheaded, and a belated communist insurrection in September was ruthlessly put down; a White Terror was then launched which claimed the lives of thousands of agrarians and communists in 1923-6. Amidst the violence, some peasantists and communists were allowed to compete in the (admittedly rigged) polls of November 1923, in which the Democratic Concord won a clear majority. By the mid-1920s the Agrarian Union had fragmented into several factions, while the Communist Party had been banned and several of its leaders executed. The communist party nevertheless continued to operate underground and remained Bulgaria's most effectively organised party and the strongest communist movement in the Balkans, rivalled in Central and Eastern Europe possibly only by the communist party of Czechoslovakia. Elements of the communist party confronted the government with a terror campaign, the most spectacular attack being the bombing of Sofia cathedral in April 1925, when government ministers were among some 128 people killed.

Eventually even Boris quailed at the cycle of violence and the Tsankov cabinet was replaced with a relatively relaxed regime. The communists even founded a front Labour Party which although banned from campaigning in the partially free parliamentary elections, increasing its share of the vote from 2 per cent in 1927 to a remarkable 12.5 per cent in 1931. By then the depression had struck Bulgaria, removing the foreign market for food exports on which the economy depended. At a time of grave hardship for the majority, the conspicuous corruption of the government caused widespread anger. Capitalising on this discontent, the communists launched a wave of unrest in the form of strikes and riots, which was met with a new state crackdown. The government prudently introduced reforms designed to ameliorate the situation of the peasantry, including the cancellation of debts and guaranteed high state purchase prices for their produce. In combination, these measures staved off widespread peasant unrest during the depression.

Nonetheless, Bulgarian politics remained unstable and violent, and two more coups followed in the mid-1930s. In May 1934 army officers and technocrats seized power in a bloodless putsch design to forestall a similar takeover by peasantist factions or by former premier Tsankov, who was by this time an open Nazi. Although Kimon Georgiev became prime minister at the head of an authoritarian, modernising government, the coup's *eminence grise* was Col. Damian Velchev. The Georgiev-Velchev regime suspended the constitution of 1879, banned opposition newspapers, trade unions and political parties; de-politicised and emasculated the legislature and subordinated the cabinet to the monarchy. In January 1935 Tsar Boris himself launched a third coup d'état. Boris's regime retained many of its predecessor's authoritarian innovations.

From the 1923 coup onward, Bulgaria had become increasingly isolated from its neighbours. Until the military coup of 1934, VMRO had been tolerated, despite atrocities at home and abroad - particularly in Yugoslavia, whose King Alexander was assassinated by VMRO agents in 1934. The Georgiev-Velchev regime banned VMRO and from the mid-1930s Boris ended Bulgarian isolation by engineering closer relations with the emerging European powers of Nazi Germany and fascist Italy. Although the Bulgarian regime increasingly adopted fascist trappings, this did not reflect purely ideological considerations, but a cold calculation of Bulgarian strategic interests. There were economic dividends, as Germany purchased Bulgarian agricultural produce in bulk and industrial production began to recover rapidly from the effects of the depression. There were also territorial gains, once the Second World War had begun; despite being technically neutral until 1941, Bulgaria was assigned considerable territory, including the Southern Dobruja from Romania. Bulgaria allowed the German army to deploy on its territory in February 1941, then formally joined the Axis powers in March, but Boris contrived to make a minimal contribution to the German war effort. Although Bulgarian troops were deployed in Yugoslav Macedonia, they were not involved in its conquest. Boris also refused to deport Bulgarian Jews to the concentration camps. Crucially, he never declared war on the Soviet Union. Even so, opponents of Bulgaria's alliance with the Axis powers had become increasingly restive. Political opposition was organised by the communist-dominated Fatherland Front. The communist party was also the focus of armed resistance and in spring 1943 a partisan movement was launched which, although poorly armed, targeted both German forces and the pro-German regime. Ruthless government reprisals included the public display of partisans' corpses.

Boris died at the age of 49 in 1943, shortly after a summit meeting with Hitler, and in mysterious circumstances. Although the German army pulled out of Bulgaria at the end of 1943, and Stalin called on Bulgaria to switch sides in the war, it did so only after the communist insurrection of September 1944, even as the Red Army crossed its northern borders. Bulgaria's subsequent sacrifices in the Allied war effort were greater than those it had sustained for the Axis, as over 30,000 Bulgarian troops died assisting the Red Army and the Yugoslav Partisans in driving the Germans from the Balkans.

The communist takeover

The communist party was in a position of great strength at the end of the war. It had been a major political player throughout the interwar period; it had an extensive organisation; it had won popular legitimacy by leading political and military resistance to the pro-Nazi regime; and its principal rivals for power were weakened, the peasantist movement by its internal divisions and the monarchy by its association with Nazism (a referendum in September 1946 confirmed the abolition of the monarchy). Moreover, it was able to capitalise on long-standing pro-Russian fraternalism among Bulgarians, which identified the Soviet Union as an ally. Finally, the communists claimed credit for negotiating a relatively generous postwar settlement for a former Axis power: although they lost Macedonia and access to the Aegean Sea, they retained Southern Dobruja in the north.

The shape of the postwar settlement was of course the result of bargaining between the postwar regional superpowers. Regardless of its citizens' Russophilia, the Great Powers had already assigned Bulgaria to a postwar Soviet bloc - Churchill and Roosevelt having been content, under the terms of the Yalta agreement on the future division of Europe into spheres of interest, to allow Bulgaria into the Soviet orbit in exchange for guarantees from Stalin not to interfere in the pro-Western orientation of Greece.

The communists consolidated their position in 1944-5 by eliminating the historical parties of the centre and right. They did so in reprisals against the wartime regime which were the worst in Central and Eastern Europe; at least 30,000 officials of the former regime were tried and on one day in February 1945 100 senior figures were shot. There followed a two-year hiatus in the communist takeover, with the Allies continuing formally to control Bulgarian affairs by virtue of the country's status as a former Axis power. During this period, elections were held in which - although the communist-dominated Fatherland Front won a convincing victory - Nikola Petkov's Agrarians took a substantial 22 per cent of the vote.

It was not until the Allies formally released their grip on Bulgaria in 1947 that the communist takeover was completed. The ruthless Prime Minister Georgi Dimitrov, a veteran Comintern leader who had spent 20 years in Moscow, launched a second violent campaign to dispose of the opposition through "salami tactics". In September 1947 Petkov was executed after a show trial in which he was accused of treason. The Social Democrats were merged into the communist party in 1948. Other smaller parties were dissolved, and from 1949 onwards the Fatherland Front comprised only the Bulgarian Communist Party (BKP) and a newly subservient Bulgarian Agrarian National Union (BZNS).

In the late 1940s the BKP followed the rest of the Soviet bloc in launching a series of show trials aimed at eliminating dissident elements within the party. Dimitrov's Muscovite faction targeted leaders of the party's wartime resistance, who had forged strong links with the Partisans in Yugoslavia, where the maverick leadership was now regarded with hostility by Moscow.

Stalinisation

From 1947 the Bulgarian communist leadership implemented a classic Stalinisation programme, demonstrating an alacrity in toeing the Soviet line that was to become characteristic of the regime until the 1990s.

Bulgaria was bound economically to the Soviet bloc, becoming a founder member of Comecon in 1949. Under Comecon's plans for a division of labour between the socialist states, Bulgaria was initially given the only role which suited its predominantly agrarian economy, as a food producer. Whilst private enterprises were nationalised in 1947, and a five-year plan completed the socialisation of the economy in 1949-54, the collectivisation of agriculture was not pushed through until the late 1950s. Seeking to expand its economic base, the leadership in 1959 launched a programme of rapid industrialisation. Sustained and rapid growth was the pattern until the mid-1970s.

Dimitrov had died in mid-1947, to be replaced as party leader by another Stalinist, Vulko Chervenkov. Following Stalin's death in 1953, the reformists in the Soviet and Bulgarian leadership gained strength; in 1954 Chervenkov stood aside to become prime minister and was succeeded as party first secretary by Todor Zhivkov, who increasingly became an advocate of Khrushchevite de-Stalinisation. A protracted power struggle followed, which was resolved only in 1961-2 with the final defeat of Chervenkov.

The Zhivkov era

Zhivkov was one of the most durable of all European communist leaders. Under his 35-year rule, Bulgaria distinguished itself as the most stable and docile of all Soviet bloc states. The regime was characterised by a remarkable dearth of dissident activity, and hence there was little need for totalitarianism. Nevertheless there was repression: Zhivkov's Bulgaria was a police state in which convicted dissidents were dispatched to forced-labour camps.

Zhivkov exercised power through a regional and local network of party barons, each of which presided over a clannish party elite on an almost feudal model. This *nomenklatura* structure, being composed of a hierarchy of élites all anxious to preserve their privileges, was rigidly conservative. Zhivkov tended to suppress initiative and intellectual purpose within his leadership coterie. Although he had a fondness for the rhetoric of reform, Zhivkov often shelved his own proposals, or had them passed only to reverse them or simply not to implement them at all.

Whilst economic growth rates remained high, there seemed little need to tinker with the system. By the mid-1970s, however, structural problems with the Bulgarian economy had become increasingly apparent. Investment had been misdirected to industrial white elephants. In the rush for growth, safety and the environment had been all but disregarded and the consequent pollution and damage to health was acute. Much of Bulgaria's industry relied on artificially cheap raw materials imported from the Soviet Union. Growth rates slowed and as financial crisis loomed, Zhivkov initially sought to conceal the extent of the problem by selling on the world market the oil which Bulgaria was able to buy at concessionary rates from the Soviet Union. A policy response came at the beginning of the 1980s in the form of a Bulgarian version of Hungary's New Economic Mechanism, which gave some official encouragement to a limited experiment in market socialism, but this failed to kick-start the economy.

From the mid-1980s, it became increasingly clear that the Soviet Union under its new leader Mikhail Gorbachev would not continue to support a stumbling Bulgarian economy. Ironically, Zhivkov was the first East European leader to pay lip service to the Gorbachev reforms, issuing the "July Conception" in 1987 which initiated campaigns against bureaucracy, corruption and inefficiency, while decentralisation was a theme of the party congress of January 1988. Parliamentary elections in February 1988 for the first time allowed voters a choice between candidates, although all were approved by the Fatherland Front. In reality, though, Zhivkov remained implacably opposed to radical change, and later in 1988 there were the familiar signs of retreat from reform as two prominent party reformists were dismissed. Zhivkov regarded both Gorbachev's "big ideas" as carrying grave political risks; *glasnost* allowed criticism, which was potentially destabilising; whilst *perestroika* would necessitate unpopular austerity measures.

Rather than restructure the Bulgarian economy, the regime from the mid-1980s had begun to borrow heavily from foreign banks in an attempt to finance recovery. The economy again failed to respond and by the end of the decade Bulgaria, like many of its communist bloc allies, was saddled with a crushing burden of foreign debt which it could not afford to service, still less to repay.

By 1989, as the economic situation deteriorated and the regime's popularity waned, Zhivkov was ready to resort to a blatantly chauvinist tactic to rally support. Already in the mid-1980s he had courted nationalist favour by targeting the Turkish minority, launching an assimilation campaign requiring Turks to adopt Slavic names. Now Zhivkov tried again to stress the nationalist credentials of his regime, playing on the widespread fears and resentments rooted in a five hundred year history of oppressive Ottoman rule. Effectively without consulting colleagues, he clamped down hard on demonstrations against assimilation in May 1989, and in June he challenged those who regarded themselves as Turks to go to Turkey. Over 300,000 did so before Turkey closed the border. The anti-Turkish campaign was a disaster for Bulgaria's international image, and a setback for food production, since many of the ethnic Turks were effective producers on fertile land, but it was extremely popular among many Bulgarian nationals, not least those who seized the abandoned property and possessions of the émigrés.

The palace revolution

Dissident groups had slowly begun to emerge in the latter 1980s, often based around environmental groups. The popularity of the anti-Turkish measures gave Zhivkov the confidence to challenge these emerging opposition forces. In October 1989 police cracked down on human rights and environmentalist demonstrations in Sofia, even as delegates to the CSCE were gathered in the city to hold a conference on the environment.

It was reputedly this episode which drove foreign minister Mladenov to the point of preparing his "palace coup" on 9 November. With Gorbachev having been briefed by Mladenov in advance, a majority of the politburo agreed that Zhivkov should go, much to the dictator's astonishment. Large crowds gathered spontaneously in Sofia to celebrate Zhivkov's fall and press for further reform.

Unsettled by these demonstrations, reformist elements in the BKP now worked rapidly to reverse the party's recent excesses and to alter the party's ideological basis before facing the electorate. Many of the anti-Turkish measures were abandoned and minority rights restored, encouraging many Turks to return. By the end of January 1990 the communists' constitutional monopoly had been scrapped in favour of a pluralist system; free elections to a Grand National Assembly charged with writing Bulgaria's new constitution had been called; round table talks with the newly formed opposition Union of Democratic Forces (SDS) had begun; and the postcommunist justice process had commenced with the arrest of Zhivkov for alleged abuse of power, embezzlement, and inciting racial hatred.

By spring 1990 the BKP had reconstituted itself as the Bulgarian Socialist Party (BSP) under the leadership of Zhivkov's former ideologist, Aleksandur Lilov. The party explicitly clung to its Marxist roots, remaining more conservative than many of its counterparts elsewhere (such as the Polish or Hungarian former ruling parties), but nominally committing itself to a market economy and democratisation.

Bulgaria's first democratic elections since the early 1920s took place in October 1990. The SDS, with insufficient time to organise, performed poorly in the polls. The reformed BSP, on the other hand, secured an unprecedented victory for a former communist party by winning an absolute majority. Only after the June 1990 elections did the BSP begin to suffer a mauling at the hands of the opposition. A heavy blow was dealt within a month of the polls when Mladenov was forced to resign the presidency following the emergence of videotaped evidence that he had called for the use of tanks against pro-reform demonstrators in December 1989. He was replaced as president by SDS leader and former dissident Zhelyu Zhelev. Over succeeding months the public was gradually mobilised in the anti-communist cause. There were anti-BSP riots in Sofia; industrial unrest grew as the economy worsened (food rationing was extended to Sofia in September 1990). The SDS refused to participate in a grand coalition. In the face of continuing economic collapse, the BSP was unable to govern effectively, weakened by a sustained campaign of demonstrations and of strikes organised by a growing independent trade union movement. Lukanov's BSP-dominated cabinet collapsed in the face of a general strike in November 1990 after only two months in office. Little legislation was passed by his successor Dimitur Popov, but the Assembly did promulgate a new constitution in mid-year, following which it dissolved itself, having performed its primary function.

Fall of the BSP

The first truly revolutionary events occurred in Bulgaria in autumn 1991, with the defeat of the BSP in fresh elections and the formation of the first non-communist government since 1944. The opposition victory, however, was far from convincing. Although the SDS emerged as the largest party in the new parliament, the National Assembly, it was short of an overall majority, and was forced to form a minority government with the support of the ethnic-Turkish Movement for Rights and Freedoms.

The SDS government, under Filip Dimitrov, came to power promising substantial and rapid reforms. In the end it served for only 12 months, during which time its increasingly confrontational anti-communist stance alienated even its former leader, President Zhelev. During its short tenure, the SDS government took the first steps toward a Bulgarian version of Polish-style "shock therapy", including land reform, the dissolution of agricultural co-operatives, price liberalisation and the passage of privatisation legislation. Many of the government measures, however, were poorly drafted, causing subsequent legal and technical problems (this problem particularly affected the privatisation process, which subsequent governments were able to delay). The technical deficiencies of the government coupled with its over-politicisation were shortcomings similar to those of other parties in the region, notably Hungary's MDF and Lithuania's *Sajudis*.

The SDS's fall from power was followed by a two-year hiatus under two BSP-backed "governments of experts", those of Lyuben Berov and Reneta Indzhova. During this period, there was considerable acrimony and mutual recrimination in the opposition camp. Zhelev was the target of considerable invective, accused at least of acquiescing in the re-communisation of Bulgaria. By the elections of 1994 Zhelev had become perturbed at the BSP's conservatism and his presidency had become more politicised, as a rallying point for the anti-communist opposition.

The Berov/Indzhova hiatus did feature Bulgaria's first privatisation, in May 1993, but further sales were few and far between. Despite Indzhova's rhetoric, both regimes failed to introduce significant reforms. For two years in 1993-4, whilst Central and Eastern Europe was galvanised by revolutionary economic change, Bulgaria marked time.

The return of the BSP

In October 1994 the BSP won a convincing election victory and in January 1995 BSP leader Zhan Videnov formed a government. One of the most conservative ex-communist parties in the former communist bloc had been returned to office with a significant majority. The BSP had won back power by posing as the party of technocracy, and Videnov duly appointed eight non-party "experts" to the cabinet.

In May 1995 the government's "Action Programme" set out its policy goals for 1995-8. They included commitments to develop democracy, constitutionality and civil society; to introduce market economic reforms, and to reduce inflation and unemployment; and to integrate Bulgaria into Western economic and security institutions. Ironically the government on 15 May stressed that the "burdensome legacy" of the communist past was a significant impediment to progress in these areas.

The BSP's likely ideological direction was not clear after one year in office; the 1995 budget, for instance, cut social spending but increased state subsidies to industry. At the end of the year, however, came a highly significant development, with the finalisation of mass privatisation legislation in December 1995, designed to sell off over 1,000 enterprises using the Czech voucher model. Bulgaria's application in the same month for full membership of the EC (EU) was a significant symbolic commitment to retain a pro-Western policy orientation.

ECONOMY

One inheritance of the Zhivkov era was an economy in a parlous state. So serious was the crisis that in this predominantly agrarian country food rationing was introduced in Sofia in September 1990. On top of the disruption caused by the collapse of the Soviet Union, the economy suffered further from the knock-on effect of international sanctions on its former major trading partners Serbia-Montenegro and Iraq, the costs of which were estimated by finance officials at $11 bn. Another major problem was the unreliability of energy supplies, with Russian provision intermittent and provision from Bulgaria's dangerously antiquated nuclear power stations subject to interruption.

The Zhivkov regime had borrowed heavily from foreign banks in an attempt to kick-start the economy from the mid-1980s. The result was chronic indebtedness with no balancing benefits. The Bulgarian economy was still dominated by Stalinist white elephants: large-scale industries that could not survive without continued Soviet support in the form of cheap raw materials which were no longer forthcoming. Nevertheless post-Zhivkov governments (with the exception of the SDS interlude in 1991-2) postponed radical reforms, fearing the mass unemployment that would flow from industrial restructuring (unemployment nevertheless tripled to 350,000, or 8 per cent of the workforce, by the end of 1991). Although price liberalisation in 1991 brought food queues to and end, the reform proved unpopular with those whose spending power diminished as inflation reached 338 per cent in 1991 (it then fluctuated between 80 and 60 per cent in 1992-5). Political leaders had noted the growing influence of Bulgaria's trade union movement, which had effectively demonstrated the potentially devastating impact of industrial unrest. The independent Confederation of Labour, *Podkrepa*, was the largest with membership growing at 600,000 in late-1992; there was also the Confederation of Independent Trade Unions in Bulgaria (CITUB), a successor to the official trade unions of the communist era, which increasingly asserted its independence. Notwithstanding the brief SDS flirtation with economic "shock therapy", post-communist governments therefore generally sought to maintain high levels of employment and continued to fund generous social security budgets; the Berov cabinet even reinstated some price controls. This relaxation of financial discipline inevitably led to increases in the budget deficit in 1993.

Although progress in economic reform was unusually slow, Bulgarian leaders post-Zhivkov had initially engineered a reorientation of economic policy from East to West. Comecon was formally dissolved in June 1991, the IMF disbursed its first loan in March 1991, and by the end of 1995 parliament had approved a Bulgarian application for EU membership. Forging new trading links with the West was hampered by the disruption caused by the war in the former Yugoslavia. Foreign investment remained very low. By the time the BSP returned to power in 1995 it had become clear that Bulgaria's left-wing favoured a renewal of economic links to the east. In May 1995 Prime Minister Videnov agreed with his visiting Russian counterpart Viktor Chernomyrdin to increase economic co-operation, particularly between the two countries' moribund defence industries. The government was keen to emphasise that it would still promote links with Western economies, and in October 1995 legislation was passed with the aim of creating a relatively favourable foreign investment regime in strategic sectors of the Bulgarian economy.

Despite the failure to introduce reforms, and the disappointingly modest growth of private enterprise, the Bulgarian economy came out of recession in 1994 and modest growth was again recorded in 1995. This was a relatively favourable climate for the new BSP government to set out in May 1995 its "Action Programme" establishing policy goals for 1995-8. They included commitments to introduce market economic reforms and to reduce inflation and unemployment. Earlier in May a relatively tight budget for 1995 had been passed in which although social spending was reduced, state subsidies to industry were actually increased. The BSP government's attempt to cultivate a pro-market image was soon dented by a June 1995 Constitutional Court ruling that BSP-sponsored amendments to the Land Act were unconstitutional, principally by denying the right to private ownership.

Privatisation

Bulgaria's privatisation process was repeatedly delayed. In May 1992 Bulgaria was the last country in central and eastern Europe outside the former Soviet Union to pass privatisation legislation. Bulgaria's first major privatisation took place in May 1993. The privatisation agency created by the SDS government in April 1992 privatised only five enterprises in 1992-4. Other sales were organised by the Trade ministry. Four times parliament legislated on mass privatisation schemes which failed to get off the ground. In December 1995 the parliament finalised legislation to privatise over 1000 firms in the tourism, agriculture, machine engineering and transport sectors from March 1996. The scheme was based on the Czech model of voucher privatisation; the state was to retain a share of one third of enterprises and majority control of some strategic enterprises, especially in the energy sector.

Restitution

Restitution laws on 11 December 1991 and 5 February 1992 covered a range of property including small businesses, shops and housing.

The SDS government of 1991-2 passed amendments to the Land Reform Law designed to abolish collective farms and restore up to 30 hectares of land to former owners. While some 80 per cent of arable land had been claimed by the end of 1992, only 10 per cent had been handed back. In 1994 parliament amended the legislation to extend by three years the deadline by which properties had to be returned.

POST-COMMUNIST JUSTICE ISSUES

Justice campaigners targeted Bulgaria's ex-communist leaders over an unusual number of issues including corruption; economic and environmental damage; state-sponsored terrorism (notably the 1978 murder of the BBC journalist Georgi Markov and alleged links to the 1981 attempted assassination of Pope John Paul II); the racist anti-Turkish campaign; and gross civil rights violations.

The justice process quickly claimed prominent figures. In July 1990 President Mladenov was forced to resign with the emergence of videotaped evidence that he had urged the use of tanks against demonstrators in December 1989. The opposition also suffered, with the December 1990 resignation of SDS leader Petar Beron amid claims that he had worked for the communist-era secret police. Investigators were subsequently hampered by the discovery that significant parts of the secret police archive had been removed.

With the country in crisis, in March 1991 the BSP leadership released a document acknowledging "the political responsibility of the party and the personal guilt of its leaders". Then in June 1991 the BSP-dominated parliament passed legislation on financial compensation for the victims of the communist police state.

Despite these conciliatory measures, senior SDS leaders demanded justice. In 1991 SDS Finance Minister Ivan Kostov accused the communists of having misappropriated 1.8 billion leva between 1949 and 1990. In October 1991 the Supreme Court froze BSP assets, and the following month the BSP agreed to relinquish control over its holdings in state companies worth two billion leva. The SDS justice campaign brought it to the edge of constitutionality. A draft 1992 banking law forbade former top communists from holding senior posts in the financial sector but was revoked by the Constitutional Court. Although the Court upheld another law purging the management of higher educational institutions of former communists, when the SDS regime tried to use its influence to reshuffle the religious leadership implicated in collaboration with the communist regime, the Court warned the government not to interfere in religious affairs.

Ivan Tatarchev, the prosecutor general from February 1992, sought the prosecution of former senior communists with a zeal which unsettled the BSP. In July 1992 the parliamentary immunity of former prime minister Andrei Lukanov was lifted; he was then arrested on charges linking him to the alleged secret diversion of state funds to Third World communist states. In October 1992 former ministers Georgi Atanasov and Stoyan Ovcharov were convicted of grand larceny and sentenced to prison terms of ten and nine years respectively.

Todor Zhivkov was Tatarchev's most prominent target and faced a wide range of charges brought in several tranches from 1992. In September 1992 he was sentenced to seven years in prison for embezzling 21.5 million leva from the state; he faced other charges relating to the labour camps in which hundreds of detainees died amid extreme brutality, and the anti-Turkish campaign.

ETHNIC AND NATIONAL RELATIONS

Bulgaria's ethnic Turkish community is concentrated in south-central and north-eastern agricultural areas . The Pomaks generally occupy similar areas.

Zhivkov's chauvinist assimilation campaign compulsorily Bulgarised the names of 820,000 ethnic Turks between 1984-9. The assimilation campaign gathered pace towards the end of the 1980s with legislation restricting the practice of Islam and banning Turkish-language teaching. When the Zhivkov regime opened the Turkish border in May 1989, 350,000 Turks fled this persecution. Most of their homes and property were sold or expropriated.

The post-Zhivkov government was therefore confronted with an extremely tense inter-ethnic situation, which had caused serious damage to Bulgaria's international reputation. Zhivkov's successor as BKP leader, Petur Mladenov, quickly realised that whatever the domestic popularity of the assimilation campaign, the BKP's bid to win credibility as a democratic party would be hampered by its continuation. The government's January 1990 decision to restore minority rights to ethnic Turks drew large protest demonstrations, but persuaded many Turks to return home to Bulgaria.

Turks were allowed to revert to their real names and religious rights were restored. Turkish-language teaching was supposed to resume in January 1991 but the measure was postponed, drawing mass protests and hunger strikes by ethnic Turks. In October 1991 the BSP-dominated legislature upheld the ban; nevertheless the newly appointed SDS Education Minister declared in November 1991 that the "extracurricular" teaching of Turkish language was admissible. Meanwhile the 1991 constitution had designated Bulgarian as the country's sole official language.

The 1991 constitution also banned ethnic or nationally-based political parties, apparently ruling out DPS participation in elections; but later in 1991 the Supreme Court, whilst refusing to register DPS as a political party, nevertheless allowed it to contest the 1991 elections.

In 1991-3 ethnic Turks and Roma bore the brunt of recession, their hardship worsened by the absence of substantial property restitution measures. The DPS's role as power broker in the legislature has been extremely useful in preventing the two major parties from playing the national card.

FOREIGN AFFAIRS

Unusually in a former Soviet satellite state, anti-Russian sentiment during the mass opposition rallies of 1989-90 was minimal. This was in keeping with the tradition of cordiality in Russo-Bulgarian relations. Nevertheless, post-Zhivkov, Bulgarian leaders moved to sever links with the Soviet Union. Comecon was formally dissolved in June 1991 and the Warsaw Pact in July 1991. The country established a Western orientation, in March 1993 becoming an associate member of the EC (EU), before agreeing an application for full membership in December 1995. EU membership nevertheless remained a distant prospect as Bulgaria formed a place at the back of the queue with Romania and Albania. Bulgaria acceded to NATO's Partnership for Peace programme in February 1994 and to associate membership of the Western European Union (WEU) later in the same year. Strong US links abide, having been forged soon after the fall of Zhivkov when US advisers were appointed to assist the SDS campaign for the 1991 elections. US officials praised the post-Zhivkov reversal of the anti-Turkish campaign and Bulgaria's diplomatic contribution in the attempt to stabilise the volatile Balkan region.

By the mid-1990s Bulgarians' long-standing Russophilia had begun to revive as the years of Soviet domination receded into the past and hopes for Western-generated prosperity faded. In May 1995 Prime Minister Videnov and his visiting Russian counterpart Viktor Chernomyrdin agreed to increase economic co-operation, particularly between defence industries, while Russian Foreign Minister Andrei Kozyrev declared that Russia's good relations with Bulgaria were based on "largely identical interests". A major oil pipeline construction deal was designed eventually to link Bulgaria with Russia and other Balkan and Black Sea states in a gas provision grid.

Like their Romanian counterparts, Bulgarian officials lobbied strongly for the lifting of UN sanctions against the former Yugoslavia, which they claimed had the effect of unfairly penalising Bulgaria. In early 1993 Bulgaria won international praise for its attempts, despite these criticisms, strictly to implement the sanctions by controlling traffic on the Danube. Threats by Serbian skippers to pollute the river deliberately in retaliation allegedly led Bulgarian officials and international monitors thenceforth to turn a blind eye to the continuing trade.

The issue of greatest sensitivity in Bulgaria's relations with neighbours has been the emergence of the independent republic of Macedonia from the ruins of the former Yugoslavia. In the interwar period, Bulgarian irredentism towards Macedonia had soured relations with both Greece and Yugoslavia. The Bulgarian communist regime was also given to emphasising the country's ancient Thracian cultural antecedents in such a way as to suggest that Bulgaria had a historical, cultural and ethnic claim to Macedonia as a whole. The situation had contributed to the periodic revival of tension with communist Yugoslavia.

Despite the declared intention of post-Zhivkov leaders to establish equally friendly relations with all Bulgaria's neighbours, the Macedonian issue soured relations with Greece. Bulgaria persisted in refusing to recognise a distinct Macedonian nation or even language, which officials argued was merely a dialect of Bulgarian; they were nonetheless strongly supportive of a Slavic Macedonian state beyond Serbian or Greek control. Bulgaria's 1992 recognition of Macedonia was denounced by Greece as "an error that [threatened] Balkan stability". Bulgarian officials grew increasingly sceptical about Serbian and Greek regional policy. President Zhelev even alleged that he had vetoed secret Greco-Serb proposals for a three-way partition of Macedonia with Bulgaria.

The reversal of the anti-Turkish campaign, and the participation in government of the mainly Turkish DPS, facilitated much improved relations with Turkey.

CONSTITUTIONAL ISSUES

The country was governed from April 1990 until mid-1991 under interim constitutional arrangements. The Grand National Assembly was charged with drafting a new constitution, and opposition leaders argued that its BSP majority following the June 1990 elections would allow unfair protection of the party's interests. A number of dissident SDS deputies, however, supported the final document, which was ratified with support from 309 out of 400 deputies.

On 12 July 1991 this new constitution was promulgated. It established a parliamentary republic in which the president, although directly elected, had no legislative veto power and was confined to security concerns and ceremonial duties. The constitution defined Bulgaria as a "democratic, constitutional and welfare state"; it guaranteed equal rights and freedoms; but banned parties based on religious or national interests (although the Supreme Court subsequently ruled against blocking DPS participation in the 1991 elections). Bulgarian was designated as the country's sole official language. Constitutional changes required a two-thirds legislative majority; since 1991, both major parties have had sufficient representation in parliament to veto constitutional proposals.

Despite ambiguities in the framing of the 1991 constitution, particularly on the role of the presidency (which President Zhelev has successfully extended whilst in office), the Constitutional Court has taken a low profile. In mid-1995 the court began to become more influential, ruling in June that amendments to the Land Act passed by the BSP-dominated legislature were unconstitutional on 20 counts, principally by denying the right to private ownership.

PRINCIPAL PERSONALITIES

Todor **Zhivkov** (b. 1911). Bulgarian communist leader for 35 years until 1989. A printer and son of a peasant, Zhivkov won respect as a partisan fighter and organised the coup of September 1944 by which the Fatherland Front took power. Brought into the top party leadership by Chervenkov in 1954, he became the dominant figure by exploiting his position as first secretary and his talent for convincing the Soviet leadership of his malleability. By 1962 he was prime minister as well as party leader, and made the next three decades the Zhivkov era in Bulgaria, playing off or cutting down possible rivals, while always remaining a loyal follower of the Moscow line. Gorbachev, however, he apparently failed to convince, especially when, with the economy deteriorating and with few real results from his grand reforming projects, he clamped down on any Bulgarian *glasnost* and launched the fierce anti-Turkish campaign of mid-1989. Apparently astonished by the "palace coup" which toppled him that November, he believed at first that he would go into honourable retirement. This hope was soon dashed by the vehemence with which demonstrators denounced him. Zhivkov has faced a wide range of charges brought in several tranches from 1992. In

September 1992 he was sentenced to seven years in prison for embezzling 21.5 million leva from the state; he faced other charges relating to the labour camps in which hundreds of detainees died amid extreme brutality, and the anti-Turkish campaign.

Georgi **Dimitrov** (1882-1949). A unionist, revolutionary socialist, and member of parliament from the age of 21, Dimitrov was involved with the Comintern from 1919. Forced to flee Bulgaria after the abortive 1923 insurrection, he exemplified the international revolutionary activist of the 1920s. Arrested by the Nazis in 1933 and charged with involvement in the *Reichstag* fire, he made himself a celebrity by his defiant defence and acquittal. He was Comintern executive secretary from 1934 and based in Moscow until his return to Bulgaria to lead the Fatherland Front in 1944. In this role, and as prime minister from 1946, Dimitrov was the founding father of the communist regime, and ruthless in his elimination of opponents and possible rivals, giving way to Stalinists of lesser stature only because of his illness two months before he died in a Moscow sanatorium in 1949. Venerated by the regime and placed in a mausoleum in Sofia, Dimitrov's body was removed and cremated in July 1990, when an unexpectedly large crowd turned out.

Petur **Mladenov** (b. 1936). Born into a peasant family in Toshevtsi in 1936, Mladenov (whose father died fighting with the partisans) went to Sofia University in the late 1950s and then to the Moscow State Institute of International Relations. As foreign minister from 1971 until 1989, he became acutely conscious of how Bulgaria's international reputation was suffering from Zhivkov's nationalistic repression of ethnic Turks in mid-1989. He prepared the way carefully, both with Gorbachev and with fellow reformists in the party, for a surprise "palace coup" which ousted Zhivkov on 9-10 November. Mladenov himself then took on temporarily both the party leadership and the chairmanship of the State Council, resigning the former post (and thereby denoting the separation of party and state) before the party congress the following January. In April 1990 he secured election as interim state president, but resigned in disgrace when opponents produced video evidence that he had suggested using tanks against a December 1989 pro-democracy demonstration.

Zhelyu **Zhelev** (b. 1935). Bulgarian President since August 1990. Zhelev, a sociologist, had first come to prominence in the 1970s as one of the country's few dissidents. In late 1989 he was a founder of the SDS and in early 1990 he became its first leader. His conciliatory style won him joint SDS-BSP backing as a compromise candidate for the Bulgarian presidency and Zhelev was confirmed in this office in Bulgaria's first direct presidential elections in 1992. Meanwhile, having resigned SDS membership, Zhelev had sought to operate above the political fray, and disdained the SDS's increasingly confrontational anti-communism. His decision to oust the SDS government of Filip Dimitrov drew accusations of treachery from his erstwhile allies and the resignation of his Vice-President Blaga Dimitrova. The BSP victory in the 1992 elections, combined with the slow pace of reforms under Videnov's BSP government, awoke fears of re-communisation and Zhelev turned to a more politicised style as the effective leader of the opposition in 1993-5.

Filip **Dimitrov**. A former lawyer, academic and vice-president of the Greens within the SDS, Dimitrov became SDS chairman in December 1990 and prime minister, at the age of 36, after the October 1991 elections. An Orthodox Christian on the right wing of the SDS, he had conducted an energetic campaign, and set out his priorities as economic stabilisation, the control of inflation, more rapid privatisation, and the confiscation of BSP party property. His cabinet's confrontational approach alienated President Zhelev and he remained in office for just 12 months. He railed against what he described as the "re-communisation" of Bulgaria and his party adopted an increasingly vitriolic anti-communist tone. Dimitrov resigned in December 1994 after disappointing election results.

Andrei **Lukanov** (b. 1938). The reform communist appointed as prime minister in the first post-Zhivkov government in 1990, Lukanov had backed Mladenov's "palace coup" the previous November, and was seen as a down-to-earth political operator as well as a well-educated technocrat and linguist. The son of a former politburo member, he was born in the Soviet Union, educated at the Moscow State Institute for International Relations, elected to parliament in 1976, and appointed by Zhivkov in 1987 as minister of foreign economic relations. It was to Lukanov that the responsibility fell, after the 1990 elections, to try to bring the opposition into a governing coalition under his leadership; an attempt which he eventually abandoned to form another short-lived and hamstrung BSP-based government in the autumn of 1990. At the December 1991 party congress he was dropped from the party's supreme council. Lukanov faced corruption charges dating from his period as prime minister.

Aleksandur **Lilov** (b. 1933). BSP leader in 1990-1. A Moscow-educated literature graduate from a poor peasant family, Lilov had been appointed to the BKP politburo in 1974, becoming Zhivkov's ideology chief. As BSP leader Lilov withstood a challenge from more radical reformers and even continued to embrace Marxism. After handing the party leadership to his disciple Videnov, Lilov operated as the BSP's ideologue and *eminence grise*.

Zhan **Videnov** (b. 1959). The successor to Lilov as BSP leader in December 1991, Videnov was elected with his predecessor's second-round support as a younger generation representative of the left socialist wing, against the challenge from Georgi Pirinski of the more reform-minded social democratic wing. He was a graduate of the Moscow Institute of International Relations and a specialist in foreign economic relations. Following the 1994 election victory, in January 1995 Videnov took office as prime minister. His government demonstrated a pragmatic commitment to market reforms including privatisation.

Ahmed **Dogan**. A philosophy professor in his mid-30s, Dogan became leader of the Movement for Rights and Freedoms, the political voice of Bulgaria's embattled ethnic Turkish minority. Dogan also proved an especially vocal advocate of "putting the whole BSP in the dock" for the crimes of the Zhivkov era. He subsequently persuaded his party to tolerate cooperation with the BSP in government.

Lyuben **Berov** (b. 1925). Economic historian and presidential adviser to Zhelev who became prime minister of a caretaker cabinet of experts in late December 1992. The Berov cabinet introduced some key reforms in 1993-4 but is best regarded as a hiatus between the SDS cabinet of 1991-2 and the BSP cabinet of 1995 onwards.

POLITICAL PARTIES

The **Bulgarian Communist Party** (*Bulgarska Komunisticheska Partiya--BKP*) went through a succession of name changes from its inception at the turn of the century. From 1903-19 it was the Bulgarian Workers' Social Democratic Party (Narrow Socialists); from 1919-24 the BKP; from 1924-48 the Bulgarian Workers' Party; and from 1948, when it absorbed the Social Democrats, the BKP again. After its proscription in 1924, the communists also operated a legal front Labour Party in 1927-34. The **Fatherland Front** of the communist era was a nominal alliance of the communists, the BZNS and "independents", with a common list presenting the only candidates for election. Party numbers under Zhivkov fluctuated, as a consequence of the various purges, generally somewhere in excess of one million.

The constitutional right to a "leading role" was renounced by the BKP on 13 December 1989 and confirmed in constitutional amendments by the legislature in January. The BKP's congress in January-February 1990 changed the party's name to the **Bulgarian Socialist Party** (BSP) after a referendum among party members. (A small rump BKP, comprising hardline communists, kept the red flag flying but achieved minimal electoral support.) In October 1991 the Supreme Court froze BSP assets.

The BSP advocated pluralism and a "socially oriented market economy", acknowledged "the political responsibility of the party and the personal guilt of its leaders" for their part in the economic crisis confronting Bulgaria and eschewed Leninism. Despite its claim to make a clean break with the past, however, the BSP also explicitly re-stated its commitment to Marxism as "a modern left-wing socialist party". The brain behind this limited ideological reorientation was Aleksandur Lilov, Zhivkov's former chief ideologist and BSP leader in 1990-1. His successor and disciple was Zhan Videnov from December 1991. Videnov consolidated control over party and purged leading reformists from the party leadership, such as former PM Andrei Lukanov.

The BSP proved remarkably resilient, almost equalling the SDS share of the vote in 1991 elections, and winning an outright majority in 1994. In February 1993 the party claimed that its membership had stabilised at the high level of 380,000. In power, it demonstrated a growing pragmatism by introducing privatisation reforms in late 1995. Despite predictions of reversion to a Russophile foreign policy, the BSP regime maintained an even approach.

The **Bulgarian Agrarian National Union** (BZNS) was the only other legal party during the communist era; its roots go back to the turn of the century and it played a prominent role in interwar politics. In 1990 it severed its links with the communists, established links with the SDS and contested the legislative elections, winning 16 seats. The BZNS joined the interim coalition government. In July 1990 Zhelyu Zhelev was the party's compromise choice as leader. In keeping with the factional differences that had riven the BZNS during the interwar period, by 1991 anti-communist agrarians had formed the breakaway **BZNS-*Nikola Petkov*** (BZNS-NP), named after the prominent agrarian leader who was liquidated in the postwar Stalinist purges. Both the BZNS and the BZNS-NP left the SDS to contest the 1991 elections separately, and both failed to win seats. The BZNS was reunified in 1992 under the leadership of Anastasia Moser-Dimitrova, a daughter of former agrarian leader Georgi Dimitrov and leader of the BZNS-NP since February 1992. The party strongly advocated land restitution. The BZNS jointly contested the 1994 elections with Stefan Savov's **Democratic Party** (DS) as the **People's Union** (PS) and won a modest 6.5 per cent of the vote. A small leftist agrarian faction, the *Aleksandur Stamboliski*-**BZNS** (AS-BZNS), contested the elections in alliance with the BSP.

The **United Democratic Front** (SDS) was formed in December 1989 as an anti-communist umbrella movement, drawing on the (admittedly weak) tradition of dissident activity under the Zhivkov regime. It was unprepared for the 1990 elections, and proved unable to mount a sufficient challenge to the BSP outside urban areas. In the second half of 1990, however, it firmly took the political initiative. The agrarians and social democrats rallied to its banner and SDS chairman Zhelyu Zhelev was elected interim President by the parliament in August 1990. In December 1990 Green leader Filip Dimitrov became SDS leader. Divisions soon became apparent as the agrarians contested the 1991 elections separately. The SDS nevertheless won a narrow victory in these polls and Dimitrov formed a minority government, which favoured radical pro-market policies and a pro-Western foreign policy. It lost power in 1992 due to internal divisions and a highly politicised approach. President Zhelev played a key role in replacing the Dimitrov regime with the non-party administration of Berov, provoking SDS accusations of acquiescing in the re-communisation of Bulgaria. In March 1993 19 SDS deputies, weary of the increasingly virulent anti-communism of the SDS leadership, defected to support the Berov cabinet. Thereafter the SDS shifted further to the right, exemplified in the increasing influence of its monarchist faction. In December 1994 Dimitrov resigned after the poor election results that year; he was replaced by the former Finance Minister Ivan Kostov.

The **Movement for Rights and Freedoms** (DPS) was a mainly ethnic Turkish party formed to lobby for equal rights and end forced assimilation in the face of the Bulgarian nationalist feeling whipped up in the latter years of communist rule. It put on a strong showing in the elections of 1990, 1991 and 1994, while having to counter the repeated suggestion that it should be debarred as an ethnic-based and militarised body. Having supported the SDS government in 1991-2, the DPS established a new alliance with the BSP in late 1992. DPS leader Ahmed Dogan was largely successful in quelling internal party opposition to co-operation with the ex-communist BSP.

The **Bulgarian Business Bloc** (BBB) was dominated by its charismatic leader Georges Ganchev, a former Olympic fencing champion and subsequently émigré businessman, who won third place as an independent candidate in the 1992 presidential elections (a feat echoing that of Poland's Stanislaw Tyminski). The party was the smallest in parliament after the elections of 1994 and appeared to have a malleable ideological orientation depending on the whim of its leader.

ELECTIONS

Legislative elections

Elections to the Grand National Assembly on 10 and 17 June 1990 were Bulgaria's first genuine multi-party polls since the early interwar period, to create an interim legislature charged with drafting a new constitution. Half of the 400 seats in this legislature, the Grand National Assembly, were elected in single-member constituencies and half were distributed among the parties on a proportional representation basis, with a 4 per cent minimum threshold. Turnouts were recorded as 90.8 per cent in the first round and 84 per cent in the second.

For the legislative elections on 13 October 1991, the new constitution (of July 1991) had established a new 240-seat National Assembly, with all candidates elected on a proportional representation basis. A total of 38 parties and groups put up candidates, but only three cleared the 4 per cent minimum threshold. Turnout was 83.87 per cent.

Legislative elections on 18 December 1994 were contested by 50 parties or blocs, of which only five cleared the 4 per cent threshold necessary to win parliamentary seats.

BBB=Bulgarian Business Bloc; BSP=Bulgarian Socialist Party; BZNS=Bulgarian Agrarian National Union; AS-BZNS=*Aleksandur Stamboliski* Bulgarian Agrarian National Union; BZNS-NP=Bulgarian Agrarian National Union-*Nikola Petkov*; DAR=Democratic Alternative for the Republic; DPS=Movement for Rights and Freedoms; DS=Democratic Party; PS=People's Union (a bloc comprising the DS and BZNS); SDS=Union of Democratic Forces.

Legislative election results, 1990, 1991 and 1994

	1990 seats	1991 %	seats	1994 %	seats
BSP*	211	33.14	106	43.50	125
SDS	144	34.36	110	24.23	69
DPS	23	7.55	24	5.44	15
BZNS	16	3.86	0	-	-
PS**	-	-	-	6.51	18
BBB	-	-	-	4.72	13
Others	5	21.09	0	14.44	0
Total	400		240		240

*The BSP in 1991 contested elections in a bloc with nine small parties, including nationalists. In 1994 it stood in formal alliance with two minor parties, the AS-BZNS and the *Ecoglasnost* Political Club.
**Comprising Moser's unified BZNS and the Democratic Party.

Presidential elections

The 1971 constitutional arrangements provided for the National Assembly to elect a State Council, whose president was in effect head of state. On 17 November 1989 Mladenov was elected to this office in place of the deposed Zhivkov. In the interim pending agreement on a new constitution, Mladenov was elected President by the Grand National Assembly on 3 April 1990. His resignation in July 1991 necessitated a new contest and required the victorious candidate to win a two-thirds parliamentary majority. Following five inconclusive rounds of voting on 24-30 July 1991, the parties agreed on a compromise candidate in the person of SDS chairman Zhelev; unopposed, he won 284 of the 389 votes cast.

The July 1991 constitution provided for direct presidential polls, and Bulgaria's first direct presidential elections took place on 12 and 19 January 1992. Zhelev emerged as the front runner with 45 per cent of the first round vote; Velko Valkanov, an independent with BSP endorsement, won 30 per cent and Georgi Ganchev, an independent, 17 per cent; there were 19 other candidates. In the second round Zhelev was confirmed as President for a further five-year term, with 53 per cent of the vote to Valkanov's 47 per cent.

CHRONOLOGY

14th century. Bulgaria comes under Ottoman rule.

1870s. The Ottoman occupiers are driven from Bulgaria.

1878. Bulgaria is created as an autonomous principality in the Treaty of Berlin which follows the Russo-Turkish war of 1877-8.

1908. Bulgaria declares full independence.

1912-13. Second Balkan War; Bulgaria acquires Southern Dobruja to the north.

1915. Bulgaria opts to support the central powers and gains access to the Aegean Sea.

September 1918. Radomir rebellion; peasant troops mutiny, forcing an armistice on 29 September and the abdication of Tsar Ferdinand on 3 October in favour of his son Boris.

17 August 1919. Bulgaria's first postwar elections are won by two anti-war parties, the peasantist Bulgarian Agrarian National Union (BZNS, 31 per cent) and the Communist Party (18 per cent).

6 October 1919. Aleksandur Stamboliski, leader of the BZNS, forms a coalition government.

27 November 1919. Peace Treaty of Neuilly: Bulgaria loses less than ten per cent of its prewar territory but has to relinquish most of its wartime gains including Southern Dobruja and most of Macedonia. In addition Bulgaria must pay reparations and limit its armed forces to 20,000 troops.

1919-20. A general strike called by the communists is crushed by Stamboliski with the assistance of the BZNS paramilitary wing the Orange Guard.

28 March 1920. In fresh elections, the BZNS increases its share of the vote to 38 per cent, and rigs the results to give itself a parliamentary majority.

December 1922. The Orange Guard enters Sofia and seizes the offices of opposition parties.

April 1923. Amid an atmosphere of Orange Guard intimidation, the BZNS wins 53 per cent of the vote in legislative elections.

9 June 1923. Nationalists backed by the ultra-nationalist VMRO launch a coup against Stamboliski, who is captured, tortured and beheaded on 14 June. Prof. Aleksandur Tsankov becomes prime minister.

19-28 September 1923. A communist uprising is defeated. Thenceforth Agrarians and communists are targeted in a ruthless "white terror".

4 April 1924. The communist party is banned, but continues as a popular underground organisation.

4 January 1926. Tsankov is replaced as prime minister by the more moderate Andrei Lyapchev.

21 June 1931. The governing Democratic Concord loses elections, polling only 30 per cent of the vote to 47 per cent for a coalition of moderate agrarian and bourgeois parties; the communist front Labour Party wins 12.5 per cent.

13 May 1934. A second coup d'etat, this time bloodless, is launched by army officers and technocrats anxious to avert a takeover by peasantists or Tsankov's Nazis. The constitution of 1879 is suspended and a highly authoritarian regime introduced.

22 January 1935. In a third coup d'etat, Tsar Boris seizes power. Increasingly close links are forged with Nazi Germany and fascist Italy.

7 September 1940. Southern Dobruja is transferred back from Romania to Bulgaria at Germany's behest. Later territorial acquisitions include large parts of Macedonia, again giving Bulgaria access to the Aegean Sea.

February 1941. Bulgaria permits the deployment of German forces on its territory.

March 1941. Bulgaria formally joins the Axis powers.

December 1941. Tsar Boris declares war on the Western Allies.

July 1942. Establishment of the Fatherland Front, a communist-dominated opposition movement including Nikola Petkov's Agrarians.

Spring 1943. Foundation of the communist-dominated People's Liberation Insurgent Army to resist Nazi occupation.

28 August 1943. Death of Tsar Boris at the age of only 49.

7-9 September 1944. The Fatherland Front seizes power in Sofia. In the midst of the revolution, the Red Army invades on 8 September. Bulgaria follows Romania in changing sides in the war.

March 1946. The Fatherland Front forms a new government.

May 1946. Bulgaria retains the territory of southern Dobruja, previously annexed by Romania, in the settlement agreed at the Paris peace conference and confirmed in a peace treaty in September 1947. It loses Macedonia however.

8 September 1946. Bulgaria votes to become a republic in a referendum which overwhelmingly rejects restoration of the monarchy; the People's Republic constitution is adopted formally in December of the following year.

October 1946. Elections for the Grand National Assembly produce a victory for the ruling Fatherland Front, with the communists taking 277 out of 465 seats and the Front as a whole winning 364; the following month Georgi Dimitrov forms a new government. Nikola Petkov's BZNS nevertheless takes 22 per cent of the vote.

23 September 1947. Petkov is executed as a traitor after a show trial.

December 1947. Soviet forces withdraw from Bulgarian territory under the terms of the peace settlement.

August 1948. The Social Democrats are merged into the Communist Party (BKP).

April 1949. The party is purged of "nationalist deviationists" led by Traicho Kostov, who is tried and hanged in December allegedly for plotting with Tito; he is posthumously rehabilitated in 1956 following the first criticisms of Stalinism by the Soviet leadership under Khrushchev.

2 July 1949. Death of the veteran communist leader Georgi Dimitrov.

March 1954. Todor Zhivkov becomes party first secretary, with his predecessor Vulko Chervenkov as premier.

January 1959. Plans for full agricultural collectivisation are announced.

1961-62. Zhivkov confirms his supremacy with the expulsion from the party of Chervenkov, who has already lost the premiership and whose declared admiration for communist China has become a liability now that the Sino-Soviet dispute has developed. Zhivkov takes over as prime minister from another rival, Anton Yugov, who is accused of responsibility for the execution of Kostov in 1949.

April 1965. Elements within the army attempt unsuccessfully to mount a coup apparently directed simply at the removal of Zhivkov from the leadership.

1971. Zhivkov takes over the state presidency (Chairman of the State Council), Stanko Todorov becomes prime minister and Petur Mladenov foreign minister.

June 1980. The first laws are introduced to permit the formation of joint ventures with foreign capitalists.

January 1982. The New Economic Mechanism requires state enterprises to be guided by market pressures, with the objective of becoming financially self-supporting, with a minimum of central planning (although in practice the economy remains largely directed by the centre).

July 1987. Zhivkov's "July Conception" sets out new ideas on the liberalisation and decentralisation of the economy. At least on paper, this seems more far-reaching than the Soviet programme propounded by Gorbachev, but it causes a measure of administrative confusion and remains largely unimplemented.

16 January 1988. The dissident Independent Society for Human Rights is formed.

February 1988. Elections allow a choice between candidates for the first time, but all need approval from the Fatherland Front.

July 1988. Two prominent reformists, Chudomir Aleksandrov and Stoyan Mikhailov, are dismissed from the politburo and party secretariat respectively.

February 1989. *Podkrepa* ("Support") is formed as the first independent trade union.

May-August 1989. The "assimilation" programme, in reality an anti-Turkish campaign, drives hundreds of thousands of ethnic Turks across the border into Turkey.

10 November 1989. Zhivkov is persuaded to resign, following careful manoeuvring by his opponents on the BKP central committee; he is replaced as party general secretary by foreign minister and Gorbachev ally Petur Mladenov.

18 November 1989. Large crowds demonstrate in Sofia, celebrating the fall of Zhivkov and pressing for further reform.

December 1989. Formation of the opposition United Democratic Front (SDS).

11 December 1989. The communist government puts forward proposals for free elections. On 15 January 1990 parliament votes to repeal constitutional provisions guaranteeing a leading role to the communist party.

January 1990. Despite SDS support for the measure, there are large demonstrations against the government decision to restore minority rights to ethnic Turks. Zhivkov is arrested.

16 January 1990. Round table talks begin, in which the SDS delegation is led by Zhelyu Zhelev and Petur Beron.

30 January to 2 February 1990. The BKP holds its first party congress since the fall of Zhivkov, reaffirming its Marxist roots, but committing itself to a reformist programme and electing Aleksandur Lilov as its chairman.

8 February 1990. The SDS having refused to join a broad coalition government, a new interim communist government is formed and headed by Andrei Lukanov.

25 February 1990. The biggest opposition rally in Sofia to date attracts some 200,000 participants, demanding postponement of the proposed elections to give time for the SDS to organise itself as an effective political party.

3 April 1990. Mladenov is elected formally as interim President by the parliament, which then dissolves itself pending summer polls. The communists adopt the new name of Bulgarian Socialist Party (BSP).

10 and 17 June 1990. The first free multi-party elections leave the BSP with a majority in the Grand National Assembly. The BSP is unable to bring the opposition into a broad alliance, and no government is formed for over three months.

6 July 1990. Mladenov is forced to resign as President, when even the BSP repudiates him on the basis of videotape evidence that he urged the use of tanks against demonstrators on 14 December 1989.

1 August 1990. Compromise candidate Zhelyu Zhelev of the SDS is elected as President.

26 August 1990. Rioting in Sofia ends with the burning of the BSP party headquarters.

September 1990. Food rationing is extended to the capital.

20 September to 29 November 1990. Andrei Lukanov's BSP-dominated cabinet lasts just two months as opposition protests mount, culminating in November with a general strike, called by *Podkrepa* and endorsed by CITUB. In December an interim coalition government is formed under the non-party leadership of Dimitur Popov.

15 November 1990. Parliament changes the country's name from People's Republic to simply Republic of Bulgaria.

1 February 1991. Subsidies are removed and prices increase dramatically for basic foodstuffs, fuel and transport, under a pro-market economic reform programme endorsed by parliament and the IMF.

25 February 1991. Parliament passes a land reform law stipulating the return of communist-expropriated land and property to its former owners. Zhivkov's trial begins.

9 June 1991. Parliament passes legislation on financial compensation for the victims of communist rule.

28 June 1991. The nine-member Comecon organisation is formally dissolved at a meeting in Budapest.

1 July 1991. The Warsaw Treaty Organisation is formally dissolved.

12 July 1991. A new constitution is approved by the Assembly and comes into effect the following day.

13 October 1991. Legislative elections leave the SDS as the largest single group in the Grand National Assembly; the BSP is narrowly beaten into second place.

8 November 1991. Filip Dimitrov forms the first government without communist representation since 1944, an SDS minority administration with DPS support.

14-19 December 1991. The BSP, holding its 40th congress but the first since its relegation to opposition status, rejects reformist proposals for a social-democratic orientation and elects a new leadership headed by the young conservative Zhan Videnov.

8 January 1992. Hundreds of thousands of people participate in a general strike called by CITUB to demand improved wages and job security.

12-19 January 1992. Zhelev is victorious in the second round of Bulgaria's first direct presidential election, taking 53 per cent of the vote to beat the BSP-backed, notionally independent candidate Velko Valkanov.

20 March 1992. Legislation is passed under which all agricultural co-operatives are to be dissolved on 1 November 1992.

5 February 1992. A government decree orders the restitution of property nationalised by the communist regime in 1947-62 including shops, small businesses and houses.

28 April 1992. Bulgaria is the last ex-communist country outside the Soviet Union to pass privatisation legislation.

9 July 1992. Arrest of former PM Lukanov on charges of misappropriating state funds.

4 August 1992. Russian President Boris Yeltsin visits Bulgaria, signing a ten-year treaty of friendship and cooperation.

4 September 1992. Todor Zhivkov is convicted and jailed for misappropriation of state funds and embezzlement.

28 October 1992. The government is defeated in a vote of confidence after the DPS sides with the opposition BSP.

30 December 1992. Formation of "Government of Experts" under 67-year old economist Lyuben Berov and with BSP and DPS support. Several ministers are defectors from the SDS; they are backed by a breakaway faction of the SDS in March 1993.

May 1993. Bulgaria's first major privatisation takes place, but although over 200 other sales are slated for 1993, only a handful actually take place.

June 1993. The SDS holds a series of rallies to demand the resignation of Zhelev, whose willingness to cooperate with the BSP they regard as treachery. On 30 June Vice President Blaga Dimitrova resigns over differences with Zhelev.

8 March 1994. Berov suffers a heart attack and is ill until late April; he is replaced in the interim by Deputy Prime Minister Evgeni Matinchev.

2 April 1994. Zhelev announces his withdrawal of support from the cabinet; he calls for the formation of a new cabinet with SDS participation.

4 May 1994. Over 800,000 people take part in a strike called by CITUB to demand higher wages and lower prices.

2 September 1994. Resignation of Berov cabinet.

17 October 1994. Dissolution of the legislature pending fresh elections; on 18 October Zhelev appoints an interim cabinet under Bulgaria's first woman prime minister, Reneta Indzhova, who is associated with the SDS and is a former head of the privatisation agency.

18 December 1994. The BSP wins parliamentary elections, taking an overall majority in the legislature, while the SDS is disappointed with less than a third of the seats.

26 January 1995. A new BSP-led coalition takes office with Zhan Videnov as prime minister. The cabinet includes eight independents, while two seats are given to the AS-BZNS and one to the *Ecoglasnost* Political Club.

15 May 1995. The government's "Action Programme" sets out its policy goals for 1995-8. They include commitments to develop democracy, constitutionality and civil society; to introduce market economic reforms; to reduce inflation and unemployment; and to integrate Bulgaria into Western economic and security institutions.

23 June 1995. The directors of state radio and television are removed by parliament for alleged bias against the BSP; the opposition alleges that the BSP is attempting to control the media.

August 1995. The privatisation head is sacked for his failure to introduce the mass privatisations by the original summer 1995 deadline.

3 October 1995. Assassination attempt on Macedonian President Kiro Gligorov; suspicion falls on the revived VMRO among others.

December 1995. Parliament approves formal application for EU membership. Final parliamentary approval of voucher privatisation legislation designed to sell off 40 per cent of shares in 1063 enterprises by distributing vouchers to the public on the Czech model.

ALBANIA

The official name of the country was the People's Republic of Albania from 1946 and the Albanian People's Socialist Republic (*Republika Popullore Socialiste Shqiperise*) from 1976 until 1991. It was renamed as the Republic of Albania on 29 April 1991.

Albania's land area, of 28,748 sq. km, made it by some way the smallest of the eight independent European countries under Communist rule in the post-1945 period. Located on the western flank of the Balkan Peninsula, Albania is moun-tainous in the centre and east; there are lowlands in the west along the Adriatic coast. Albania shares borders with the Yugoslav republics of Montenegro and Serbia to the north, with the former Yugoslav republic of Macedonia to the east, and with Greece to the south.

Albania's population of some 3,100,000 is principally concentrated in the western lowlands. Years of rapid population growth and low life expectancy have resulted in a very young society where the average age in 1990 was only 28 years. In the post-communist era population growth may have reversed, as the birth rate has declined and up to 400,000 Albanians have emigrated.

Tirana, the capital, is the only substantial city, with a population of about 225,000; other main towns, with 60-80,000 inhabitants, are the port of Durres and Elbasan, Shkoder, Vlore and Korce. Since 1991 there has been considerable migration from rural to urban areas, which by 1995 accounted for some 40 per cent of the population.

Significant numbers of Albanian-speakers live beyond the borders of the Albanian state. Some 1.3m ethnic-Albanians form the majority population in the neighbouring Serbian province of Kosovo, and there are at least 440,000 in the former Yugoslav republic of Macedonia, comprising some 22.9 per cent of the population there according to official figures. There is an emigré community of some 600,000 in the USA.

Albania is relatively homogeneous in ethnic terms. The largest minority group, ethnic Greeks, officially numbers 50,000, but the Greeks insist that their community numbers up to 400,000. There is also a Slav minority.

Albania's majority religion is Islam, although many self-declared Muslims do not practice. There are substantial Roman Catholic and Orthodox Christian minorities; the Greek minority practices Greek Orthodoxy. Religion was banned under the communist regime. Mosques and churches were allowed to reopen from late 1989 onwards.

The Albanians are an indo-European people who migrated to the Balkans in around 1,000 BC. Their history as a distinct, self-identified ethnic group pre-dates the Slav nations that now surround them. The Albanian language comprises two dialect groups, the dominant one (Tosk) being associated with the south and lowlands and the other (Gheg) with the mountainous north.

HISTORICAL NARRATIVE

Overshadowed by a succession of greater regional powers, from the Romans to the Bulgarians and Serbs, Albania then came under Ottoman rule, exercised in a relatively lenient form in part because of shared Muslim religious beliefs. Albania was the last Balkan country to sever its links with the Ottoman empire, attaining nominally independent status in 1912 during the Balkan Wars, and thus becoming the only country in Europe with a Muslim majority. From the outbreak of the First World War until 1920 the country was under military occupation by Italy, Greece and Yugoslavia. Albania's independence was restored in 1920, within boundaries fixed in 1921.

Albania in the early 1920s was the least developed European country. Since there was virtually no industry, some 80 per cent of the population depended for their living on the land, which was itself a meagre resource, since two thirds of it was either woodland or completely unproductive. Some 90 per cent of Albanians were illiterate. So backward was Albanian political culture that the usual twentieth century European political categories did not apply. Albanian society was best characterised as feudal in the lowlands and tribal in the mountainous north. Power was diffused between rural, regionally-based clans. Ahmed Zogu, a conservative warrior-chieftain from the north, made himself ruler of the country by conquest in 1924 and took the title of King Zog four years later. In terms of state-building Zog's achievements were not inconsiderable, in the context of inter-war Albania. Imposing an authoritarian regime, he successfully disarmed rival clans and brought a degree of order and social stability to the country after centuries of internal conflict. Although some liberalising reforms were introduced in 1936, allowing a degree of freedom of expression, there was no democracy or pluralism in interwar Albania. There was some slow progress in economic and cultural modernisation; literacy rates improved slightly and the economy developed modestly, benefitting from Italian investment.

Although Albanians resented Italian domination, Albania depended on Italian money and Italian military support against Greek and Yugoslav irredentism. Distracted by higher diplomatic and strategic priorities, Mussolini delayed action against Albania, but the Zog regime eventually collapsed when the Italian military invaded in April 1939.

The Italian campaign in the Balkans fared poorly and by 1943 Italian troops had been replaced by German forces. Albanian resistance was initially led by the nationalist Bali Kombetar army. The various Albanian communist groups, hitherto deeply divided, unified in 1941 under the supervision of the Yugoslav communists to form the Albanian Communist Party, which organised an effective partisan force. Again under Yugoslav direction the Albanian party 1944 effectively proclaimed executive and legislative power for itself and a Provisional Democratic Government was formed under communist leader Enver Hoxha. In autumn 1944 Tirana was liberated from the German army.

The communist party was Albania's first organised political party, and the first to appeal above clan interests. By the time Soviet officials arrived in Albania in the late summer of 1944, the Albanian party had established control over the principal levers of state power, and had achieved this position without Soviet help. Instead, Albania had become virtually a client state of Yugoslavia. Tito's barely concealed desire to annex Albania led Hoxha to sever Albanian links with Yugoslavia in 1948, and leading pro-Yugoslav "traitors" were executed in 1949. Over the next four decades the Albanian regime became increasingly isolationist, rejecting all other communist states.

Isolation and Enverism

Hoxha established a close personal bond with Stalin, which lasted until the Soviet dictator's death in 1953. He regarded Stalin's reformist successor Nikita Khrushchev with barely concealed distaste. Relations with the Soviet Union became hostile after Albania supported China during the Sino-Soviet split in 1961. Although Albania had joined the Warsaw Treaty Organisation in 1955, it played no real part and formally withdrew in 1968 following the Pact invasion of Czechoslovakia. Albania was never a member of Comecon. In 1977-78 Albania cut its last links to international Marxist-Leninist solidarity and aid when it split with China, accusing it of revisionism and of attempting to dominate the small Balkan state. Hoxha sought to glorify Albania's isolation as a mark of its integrity in pursuing the one true road to socialism; even foreign economic assistance was renounced. Illegal migration from Albania was defined as treason and hundreds of people were shot by border guards whilst attempting to leave the country. Even within the communist bloc, Albania was regarded as a barbarous backwater.

Hoxha's ideology, known as Enverism, was a modified Stalinism. Although Enverism designated the industrial proletariat as the principal focus of the revolution, it laid an unusual emphasis on agriculture and the peasantry, and contained pastoral elements exemplified in the banning of private cars and motorcycles. Enverism was imposed in typically totalitarian fashion; an overweening cult of personality glorified Hoxha's name, image and works, which became all-pervasive. The state extended control into all areas of personal life to create a highly collectivist system in which personal freedoms were utterly subordinated. Religion was officially abolished, and on a more absurd level the state outlawed some Western fashions, including the wearing of beards (this being a manifestation of the xenophobia behind the isolationist policy). Opponents of Hoxha were dealt with in ruthless purges. The last of several leading party members to commit suicide (as the official accounts described it) was Mehmet Shehu, in 1981 after 27 years as prime minister. Some 100,000 Albanians were arrested and internally exiled, while many more were the victims of imprisonment without trial, police harassment, and extra-judicial or summary execution.

Before Hoxha died in April 1985, he groomed his protégé Ramiz Alia for the succession, installing him as President. Alia's apparently smooth takeover seemed to hold out only the most limited prospect for reform. The country's international isolation, even if it was now slightly relaxed in respect of contacts with the West, provided a barrier against any spread of the epidemic of *glasnost* and *perestroika*. Rumours suggested that the main internal challenge to Alia might still be from a hardline faction around Hoxha's widow Nexhmije, and although the first demonstrations were held in the northern town of Shkoder in 1989, the tide of change had not yet reached Albania.

The emergence of opposition - Concessions to pluralism

In January 1990 Alia professed to see no parallels between the situation in Albania and the demise of the "revisionist" regimes of Eastern Europe, whose ruling cliques had "compromised and soiled the legitimacy of the socialist state". In reality the Albanian leadership was increasingly nervous. As demonstrations and industrial unrest began to multiply in 1990, the first significant shift occurred within the PPS as opponents of the hardline leadership and young party reformers gained the upper hand. In the first half of the year the ban on religion was lifted and limited political and economic liberalisation was permitted. When demonstrations spread to the capital, the government avoided a crackdown, lest it provoke an outraged popular reaction. Students and workers now mobilised in mass demonstrations to demand multi-party elections.

The real turning point for Albania came in summer 1990, when thousands of young men began to seek asylum abroad by taking refuge in the West German, French and Italian embassies. Although the regime chose to regard these first asylum-seekers as "anti-patriotic elements", and to allow them to leave, in reality the exodus was a heavy blow to the regime's legitimacy. Thousands more began pouring over the southern border with Greece and across the Straits of Otranto to Italy. The Albanian people, in their poverty and desperation, were voting with their feet, and against the way of life imposed by a regime with little popular credibility.

Opposition groups, having been vigorously suppressed during the communist era, took some months to emerge and initially lacked political focus. By the end of 1990 new political forces had grown in confidence and purpose, calling for liberal-democratic and free market economic reforms, although many Albanians, particularly in rural areas, were bewildered by the political changes and suspicious of these new urban-based liberal movements.

The elections of March-April 1991 revealed the extent of support in urban areas for the newly-formed opposition Democratic Party of Albania (PDS), although rural areas remained stubbornly conservative. For Alia there was personal humiliation when he was roundly defeated in a Tirana constituency, and the election soon proved a hollow victory for his party.

A general strike in May 1991 compelled the regime to concede the formation of a "pluralist" government. In June 1991 opposition parties, notably the PDS, were brought into government. The coalition survived for six months of repeated disagreements over economic reform and the remaining power of the communist elite, until the withdrawal of the opposition, which was by then anxious to prepare for fresh elections.

In June 1991 the PPS had re-launched itself as the Socialist Party of Albania (PSS), styling itself as a social democratic party in the Western mould, and under a new leader in the young economist Fatos Nano. Despite its new programme, the party's electoral prospects were wrecked by the gathering economic and social chaos. By the end of 1991 the economy had ground to a standstill, the country was dependent on foreign food aid, and order had broken down as crowds looted and rioted. Albania, the poorest country in Europe, now faced the continent's most desperate economic crisis, and the vestigial legitimacy of the regime disintegrated.

The anti-communist PDS in power, 1992-95

In the March 1992 elections, the PSS vote collapsed, and the PDS swept to power with a large majority of the legislature. The resignation of President Alia in early April marked a definitive end to the communist era. Alia's successor as President was PDS leader Sali Berisha, who immediately stressed his commitment to the creation of a constitutional state on the West European model, and a free market economy. A PDS-dominated government was formed, also in April 1992, with Aleksander Meksi as prime minister.

The government's principal achievement in 1992-5 was in economic reform. The PDS-led government introduced a series of radical measures, including social security changes, price liberalisation and privatisation. Following catastrophic negative growth rates in 1991 and 1992, by 1995 Albania was recording Eastern Europe's highest growth rate (at 6 per cent) and had brought inflation down to single figures. Despite the consequent improvements in the standard of living, the upturn failed to win the government popularity. Many Albanians were concerned at the extent of unemployment, which stubbornly remained at about one third of the workforce between 1993 and 1995.

More controversially the PDS launched Eastern Europe's most sweeping postcommunist justice policy, involving the prosecution of a whole generation of senior former communist leaders, of whom Nexhmije Hoxha, Ramiz Alia and Fatos Nano were but the most prominent. The Socialists claimed that the PDS had launched a wave of show trials designed to discredit the PSS. As the 1996 elections approached, the PDS stance actually hardened, with the passage of laws preventing former communist leaders even from holding public office.

The PDS's justice policies contributed to growing disquiet over the human rights situation in Albania. Controversial and restrictive media legislation signed into law in October 1993 was a further cause for concern. Voters' suspicions that the PDS harboured authoritarian tendencies lay behind their rejection in November 1994 of a draft presidential constitution. Concerns grew further in 1995, with mounting evidence that the PDS had established a dominant position over the judiciary.

The PDS achieved a number of foreign policy successes, establishing fruitful relations with the West, notably Italy, the EC (EU) and the USA. These new relationships won Albania considerable aid and a measure of stability, membership of NATO's Partnership for Peace being in this respect a particular advantage. While Albania's conspicuously moderate nationalism made the country more attractive to Western leaders, concern grew in the international community in 1995 over perceived human rights abuses, giving the impression that the diplomatic capital assiduously accrued over the preceding three years could easily be squandered.

Relations with Albania's most significant neighbour, Greece, improved in 1995 after three years of tension. From 1992 Albania accused Greece of irredentist designs on southern Albania, whilst Greece repeatedly accused Albania of persecuting its ethnic Greek minority. An OSCE investigation cleared Albania of the latter charge in early 1995, and the passage in mid-1995 of legislation recognising ethnic minority rights facilitated Albanian accession to the Council of Europe.

ECONOMY

When Albania began to shrug off communism from 1991, it did so as Europe's poorest country. Figures from 1990 recorded that only 29 per cent of the labour force were employed in industry, while 57.5 per cent were employed in agriculture. By late 1991 Albania was confronted with the worst economic crisis in the region, as industry virtually ground to a standstill. GDP fell by over 27 per cent in 1991 and by almost 10 per cent in 1992. Despite the introduction of food rationing, food shortages caused the mass exodus of tens of thousands of Albanian economic refugees, and a wave of strikes and disorder. Italy, the EC (EU) and the USA were the prime movers in an emergency food aid programme from 1991 which helped to restore order and economic stability.

The same foreign powers were also behind some considerable aid programmes to revive Albanian industry and modernise Albanian agriculture. The Italian government, for example, agreed an $800m loan for agricultural development in 1992. Investment and business know-how from neighbouring Greece was likely to make an increasing impact in Albania, particularly after the improvement in relations between the two countries in 1995.

Albania's relative lack of development dated from its experience of Ottoman domination for centuries prior to independence in 1912. Despite the modest growth of industry during the interwar period, most were concerned with raw materials extraction. Although Albania had a mercantile and trading tradition, it failed to establish a strong entrepreneurial tradition.

A dramatic illustration of Albanian naivete in dealing with the market had been provided in 1990, when officials at the State Bank of Albania lost $200m in a disastrous experiment in currency trading. Even today the losses account for a high proportion of the country's foreign debt. Despite this disastrous economic start to the post-communist era, the Albanian economy has made a remarkable recovery since 1992. The economic achievements of the Meksi government's radical reform programme included the highest economic growth rates in Central and Eastern Europe; a discernable improvement in average living standards; a dramatic reduction in the inflation rate from 226 per cent in 1992 to single figures in 1995; and the rapid privatisation of agriculture and much industry (see below).

There were social costs to the reforms, however, which have damaged the popularity of the government. Unemployment was extremely high at some 450,000 or more than a third of the workforce in 1993-5. Unpopular social security changes included the IMF-inspired phasing out from 1992 of rules under which the unemployed received 80 per cent of their former salary in state benefits; the government's long-term commitment to improving the level of social provision was mitigated by the pressing need to reduce the budget deficit and to invest in the improvement of supplies of water and electricity. The need for the latter was amply demonstrated in December 1994, when severe energy shortages compelled the government to introduce rationing of electricity, exempting only mines, hospitals and state bakeries.

The 1995 Dayton peace agreement on the former Yugoslavia, and the consequent lifting of sanctions on the rump Yugoslav state, has deprived Albanian traders of a major immediate source of revenue, through the illegal but lucrative smuggling of oil and other goods. Nevertheless a compensatory increase in other trade with the former Yugoslav republics was expected. The lifting of Greece's trade embargo on neighbouring Macedonia in 1995 was also expected to have a positive knock-on effect on Albania.

Privatisation

Agricultural reforms began in August 1991, with the programme of breaking up agricultural cooperatives and handing back land to peasants. The programme was surrounded by some bureaucratic confusion over whether the peasants legally owned the land they had been awarded.

The private sector grew rapidly, with 50,000 small businesses having been established by 1993. In September 1991 a package of economic reforms introduced by the coalition government included the creation of a national privatisation agency. Slow progress over privatisation in 1992-4 led sceptics to conclude that the PDS-led government was less than enthusiastic about ownership transformation. However a programme of privatisation launched in early 1995 made rapid progress; 20 state enterprises were sold in October 1995 to over one million holders of privatisation vouchers in the first round of mass privatisation auctions. A further group of 30 companies was scheduled for privatisation in early 1996.

POST-COMMUNIST JUSTICE ISSUES

Justice for the victims

The postcommunist justice process arguably began during the last months of the communist era, when a pardon was approved on 5 January 1991 for 202 people serving prison sentences for "agitation and propaganda against the state" and for "attempted defection abroad". A general pardon was announced on 12 March 1991, and on 2 July 1991 Alia signed a further decree pardoning the last political prisoners.

Many of the thousands of Albanians who had survived political persecution during the communist era joined a group based in Shkoder, the increasingly assertive Association of the Formerly Politically Persecuted, led by Kurt Kola. A hunger strike by Kola's group persuaded parliament to approve a law in February 1993 retroactively declaring innocent those convicted in the communist era of political crimes, those who died in custody, victims of execution without trial, and Albanians killed whilst attempting to cross the border (a crime which had been classified as treason). Not content with this victory, Kola's group launched a mass hunger strike of 2,500 former political prisoners in August 1994 to demand compensation for past injustices; despite a court ruling that the protest was illegal, and police brutality and mass arrests, the government eventually agreed to pay out compensation of 50,000 lek ($530) to each from December 1994.

In May 1991 the *Sigurimi* (the communist-era secret police) was replaced by a new state body, the Albanian Security Service (SHIK). Critics subsequently claimed that SHIK had established itself as a powerful political force, and had been used on a partisan basis by the government.

Justice for the perpetrators

Albania has witnessed perhaps the most sweeping action against the alleged perpetrators of communist-era injustices seen in any former communist state.

The question of bringing to justice those responsible for the repression of the communist era had become highly politicised by the mid-1990s. The PDS-dominated government from 1992 onwards launched a series of trials of former communist leaders on a range of charges from corruption to homicide. The reformed communist party, the PSS, claimed that the court proceedings were unfair and politically motivated, chiefly to damage the electoral credibility of the PSS. Former President Ramiz Alia, who was convicted in 1994 of abuse of power, denounced the proceedings against him as a "show trial". Other prominent former communists convicted of various crimes included virtually all of the last communist-era cabinet, and in January 1993 Nexhmije Hoxha, the elderly widow of Enver Hoxha. In June 1995 Enver's son Ilir Hoxha was sentenced to one year under house arrest for "inciting national hatred" purely for criticising the PDS in a newspaper article.

Perhaps the most controversial conviction was that of Fatos Nano, the leader of the PSS, who in April 1994 was sentenced to 12 years in prison for corruption, although no evidence was presented that he had personally benefitted from the alleged theft. The arrests continued into late 1995, when 14 former leading communists, including former President Haxhi Lleshi (aged 82 years), were charged with responsibility for the policy of internal exile.

The September 1995 Law on Genocide facilitated the prosecution of the perpetrators of crimes committed during the communist era "for political, ideological or religious motives". It also introduced highly controversial measures designed to drive senior former communists from public life completely. All those who had held senior office during the communist era were barred from public office until 2002. The law thus disqualified many senior figures in the PSS from contesting the elections or, if victorious, from serving as cabinet ministers. The law was followed in November by legislation requiring the screening of senior public officials for past involvement with the *Sigurimi*. A seven-member parliamentary committee appointed by the government was to use *Sigurimi* archives to screen parliamentary candidates, central and local government officials, and media staff; those found to have collaborated would also be barred from public office until 2002. Files on other citizens were to be closed for thirty years. Socialist and other opposition parties expressed the fear that the law would be implemented on a partisan basis, used to target senior opposition figures.

MEDIA

In October 1993 media legislation was signed into law which declared that the press was free, but introduced a number of restrictions, forbidding publication of "state secrets" or material deemed to threaten the public good, democracy, national peace or the "morals of the youth". Journalists' groups and the opposition claimed that this law would prevent the press from reporting allegations of government corruption and they criticised the vague terms of the law and the punishments available under it, including the seizure of offending publications, the imposition of heavy fines, and imprisonment. In February 1994 two journalists for the PSS daily *Koha Jone* were sentenced to prison terms, respectively of 18 months and four years, for publishing a relatively minor military document forbidding the carrying of weapons by off-duty soldiers.

The opposition argued that these convictions were symptomatic of the PDS-led government's growing intolerance of criticism, manifested in attempts to intimidate or silence perceived opponents in the media. In August 1994 ten opposition newspapers suspended publication in protest at crippling new taxes and at tariffs on the import of essential materials. Throughout 1995 opposition journalists reported increasing harassment and violence against media staff; incidents included the firebombing of the *Koha Jone* offices. Some accused SHIK, the secret police, of responsibility.

CHURCH-STATE RELATIONS

The communist regime abolished religion in 1967, proclaiming Albania as the world's first atheist state. This was explicitly confirmed in the 1976 constitution. The ban on "religious propaganda" was lifted in May 1990 and was soon followed by the first services. In November 1990 a Catholic mass was held in Shkoder, while the first legal Islamic service took place in Tirana in January 1991. Relations with the Vatican were restored in September 1991, and Pope John Paul II visited Albania in April 1993.

Although religious faith survived the period of prohibition, particularly among older people, religious practice was weakened by neglect. Most Muslims do not observe even the taboos on the consumption of pork and alcohol, while the Albanian Orthodox Church has relied heavily on clerics from its Greek counterpart for assistance in re-establishing its ministry. Similarly, Arab states have funded a considerable Mosque-building programme.

ETHNIC AND NATIONAL RELATIONS

Albania's only major ethnic minority is the Greek community concentrated mainly in the country's south. Whilst official figures put the size of the community at only 50,000, the Greeks themselves claim to number between 300,000 and 400,000. Albanian nationalists regard them as a Trojan horse for Greek irredentism, while Greek nationalists call Albania's southern third Northern Epirus, which they regard as historically Greek territory. The militant pro-Greek separatist group Northern Epirus Liberation Front was responsible for a number of terrorist attacks in 1992-5, including the April 1994 killing of two Albanian border guards.

Moderate ethnic-Greeks supported the Omonia ("Concord") movement, which won five seats in the 1991 elections. Under a February 1992 electoral law, however, ethnically-based organisations were effectively banned from registering as political parties. Most ethnic Greeks instead backed the Human Rights Union (EAD), which won two seats in parliament in 1992. Thenceforth Omonia was increasingly demonised in the Albanian right-wing press as extremist and separatist. The conviction of five prominent Omonia activists in September 1994 for a range of anti-constitutional activities, including "treason for carrying out the orders of a foreign secret service" and illegal possession of weapons, was widely criticised in the international community as unsafe and politically motivated. In February 1995 the Appeals Court ruled that procedural violations had taken place, and freed the activists.

By 1994 Greek officials were claiming that Albania was responsible for "unprecedented and continuing persecution" of the ethnic Greek minority, and in the early summer Omonia leader Thomas Kyriakou claimed that his community was being "terrorised" by a wave of arrests. Despite the repeated and grave claims about Albanian persecution, in February 1995 the OSCE suspended its investigation into the allegations, having found no evidence to substantiate them. The passage in June 1995 of legislation recognising the rights of ethnic minorities to separate languages and customs facilitated Albania's admission to the Council of Europe in July 1995.

FOREIGN AFFAIRS

Albania's relationship with the West

The Albanian regime formally abandoned isolationism in April 1990, and by 1991 the country had adopted a pro-Western stance.

Italy, which had played such a dominant role in Albania in the interwar period, quickly re-established a role as postcommunist Albania's main link to the West. The relationship was initially forged from necessity, as tens of thousands of Albanian migrants poured across the Straits of Otranto in the spring of 1991 seeking asylum in Italy. To stem the flow, Italy launched a major aid programme, becoming over the next four years Albania's principal donor. In September 1991 Italian troops arrived in Albania for the first time since 1943 to deliver emergency food aid under Operation Pelican. On completion of the operation in December 1993, Albania impatiently required Italian forces to leave immediately. Negotiations have since taken place on the long-term deployment of Italian troops in Albania. Albania has also developed links with the European Communities (EC, subsequently EU), and the EC has become another major aid donor.

As the 1990s progressed, Albania developed a closer relationship with the USA. US Assistant Defence Secretary Stephen Nye in February 1995 praised Albania's "responsible position toward its neighbours" and its "major contribution to stability in the Balkan region" (a description Greek officials met with raised eyebrows). A series of joint US-Albanian military exercises took place in 1995. In autumn 1995, with the Albanian elections barely eight months away, Berisha made a prestigious visit to the White House. The USA was, however, disappointed by the deterioration in the human rights situation in Albania, and the dismissal of Supreme Court Chair Brozi appeared to ring some alarm bells in the White House. Despite increasing concern in the international community over growing human rights abuses in the country, in July 1995 Albania was admitted to the Council of Europe.

Mindful of its location in the unstable Balkans, Albania was the first ex-communist country to apply for associate membership of NATO under the Partnership for Peace (PfP) initiative; the country was admitted in February 1994. Joint exercises took place in 1994-5 with NATO forces from Germany, Greece, Italy, Turkey, the UK and the USA.

Membership of the Islamic Conference

Although Albania had a Muslim majority, most did not practice, and strongly favoured the West over the Arab world. Berisha has nevertheless been anxious to exploit the economic advantage of a closer association with Muslim states, and to this end Albania joined the Organisation of the Islamic Conference (OIC) in 1993. In April 1993 the People's Assembly ratified a treaty of Friendship and Co-operation with Turkey.

Relations with Balkan neighbours

Albania has sensitive relations with all of its Balkan neighbours. Its problems derive from mutual suspicions of irredentism, and are complicated by the ethnic map of the region, which overlaps political frontiers.

Greece is potentially Albania's most important external relationship, not least economically. Relations were extremely poor in 1991-4, the principal problems being mass Albanian migration to Greece and the alleged mistreatment of the Greek minority in Albania.

With the new freedom of movement, tens of thousands of Albanian migrants began crossing the southern border from 1991, looking for work in Greece. Many migrants alleged systematic brutality by Greek border guards. In early 1993, with the total number of Albanians in Greece thought to have reached 200,000, the Greek government cracked down with the mass expulsion of illegal immigrants. The rate of repatriations became an effective barometer of the state of relations between the two Balkan neighbours, reflecting principally the tension over the ethnic Greek minority in Albania. In April 1994 Greek Foreign Minister Papoulias furiously denounced Albania for "unprecedented and continuing persecution" of this minority. By May 1994 Papoulias was warning grimly of "drastic measures" to protect the rights of the Greek minority. In the late summer some 50,000 Albanian migrants were repatriated, their total numbers having reached as many as 400,000, and Greece announced further border controls. Residents of the border region reported that Greek border guards had begun opening fire on Albanian migrants without warning. In a related development Berisha accused Greece of launching a "cold war" against Albania.

In February 1995 an OSCE investigation into allegations of Albanian persecution of the Greek minority was suspended, its officials having found no evidence to substantiate the claims. In the same month five prominent ethnic Greeks controversially jailed in 1994 were released. Thenceforth relations between Albania and Greece quickly improved. Talks in Tirana in March 1995 between the Greek and Albanian Foreign Ministers were described as "extremely positive", but major sticking points remained, notably over the Greek demand for the opening of independent Greek-language schools in southern Albania. The growing economic links made it likely that Greek-Albanian relations would continue to improve gradually; this would also be important in Albania's campaign to join European institutions.

The **Kosovo** issue has dominated relations with the Federal Republic of Yugoslavia (FRY) to the north. A nominally autonomous province of the Republic of Serbia, Kosovo is regarded by Serbian nationalists as the crucible of the Serbian nation [*see also Yugoslavia chapter*], but has for some decades had an ethnic-Albanian majority. From the early 1990s Serbia imposed an increasingly repressive regime in Kosovo. In September 1991 Kosovo followed Slovenia, Croatia and Bosnia-Hercegovina in declaring independence. The Albanian decision to recognise Kosovan independence was regarded with hostility by the Serbian and Yugoslav authorities; Albanian support for the Bosnian Muslims in their war against the Serbs further antagonised them. Albania subsequently shifted its stance on Kosovo, pressing for generous autonomy rather than independence. The shift implicitly conceded that whatever its territorial ambitions to the north, Albania lacked any offensive military capability to impose them. Nevertheless relations with Serbia deteriorated still further when the latter launched a programme in 1995 to resettle ethnic-Serb refugees in Kosovo. Berisha's attempts to resolve the Kosovo question within the framework of the Dayton peace talks of late-1995 failed, and Kosovo remained a potential future flashpoint.

Relations with **Macedonia** were somewhat uneasy, again due to the presence of a significant ethnic Albanian minority in northern Macedonia. The Macedonian authorities again suspected the Albanian minority of irredentism, and in a disputed verdict, ten leaders of the minority were convicted in June 1994 of organising a separatist army.

CONSTITUTIONAL ISSUES

Albania in the Hoxha period had two constitutions: that of January 1946, under which the monarchy was formally abolished and the People's Republic of Albania proclaimed; and that of December 1976, which renamed the country as the People's Socialist Republic of Albania and designated the PPS as the "sole leading political force".

In April 1991 a new interim constitution renamed the country simply as the Republic of Albania. The new political system was defined as "democratic and juridical, based on social equality, the defence of freedom and the rights of man, and political pluralism". The balance of power between executive institutions was divided fairly evenly. The President was commander-in-chief of the armed forces, appointed the government as a whole and had powers to dissolve the People's Assembly or to declare a state of emergency. Constitutional amendments passed in April 1992, immediately before Sali Berisha's presidential term, allowed the president to call, attend and chair cabinet meetings, and to issue orders to cabinet ministers.

A new draft constitution strongly favoured by President Berisha and the PDS was completed in 1994. Controversially, the document laid out strong presidential powers, including the appointment of cabinet ministers, judges and state media officials, and powers to influence criminal investigations. The draft constitution prompted the resignation of three constitutional court judges, who claimed that colleagues in the court had demonstrated bias toward the PDS in delaying examination of the document.

In October 1994 the draft constitution failed to secure the necessary two-thirds support in the People's Assembly and in November it was rejected by voters in a referendum, but in 1995 Berisha announced plans to put a substantially unmodified document to the electorate once more.

In March 1993 the People's Assembly adopted a charter of Human Rights. Despite this move, there was increasing concern throughout 1994-5 over alleged government abuse of basic freedoms, notably in relation to freedom of speech, freedom of assembly, and the basic rights of the ethnic Greek minority.

Claims that Berisha sought undue influence over the judiciary were given substance in 1995, when Supreme Court Chair Brozi was sacked. Brozi had criticised the PDS's approach to constitutional issues on a number of fronts, not least with the allegation that the PDS was gradually packing the judiciary with inexperienced but loyal officials. He claimed that the constitutional court was compliant to the PDS.

PRINCIPAL PERSONALITIES

Communist era

Enver **Hoxha** (1908-85). A southern Albanian from Gjirokaster, Hoxha joined the communist party in the 1930s while at university in France. Returning to Albania in 1936 as a French teacher after abandoning his studies in law, he joined a Marxist group in Korçë to organise against the regime of King Zog. In 1941 Hoxha was chosen as first secretary-general of the newly-constituted Albanian Communist Party. It was the resistance struggle which brought this small group to prominence through the National Liberation Movement and National Liberation Army, thanks in part to Hoxha's charismatic leadership and ruthlessness. In power from 1944 (he formally relinquished in 1954 his government post as prime minister, but not the first secretaryship of the renamed Party of Labour of Albania), he consolidated his personal supremacy in a series of purges beginning with the "pro-Yugoslav" faction (Hoxha himself having always been associated with the rival Albanian nationalist standpoint). Hoxha oversaw the creation of a Stalinist centralised power structure and command economy, but fell out with the Soviet leadership over the Sino-Soviet split in 1960-61, whereupon Khrushchev denounced the "bloody atrocities" of his purges. Ever more xenophobic in the cocoon of his personality cult after the break with China in the late 1970s, Hoxha in 1982 denounced his long-time associate Mehmet Shehu (who had died in mysterious circumstances the previous December) for having been a US, Yugoslav and Soviet agent since the war; further purges were reported in the succeeding years. When Hoxha died in April 1985 his personality cult remained intact and his widow Nexhmije continued to wield much influence as a hardliner in the party central committee, chairing the umbrella Democratic Front until December 1990. The violence of attacks on the statues and symbols of Hoxha all over Albania in 1991 underlined the extent to which the communist period had been defined by his omnipresence; Nexhmije was expelled from the party in June, and she and other hardliners were arrested in December 1991.

Ramiz **Alia** (b. 1925). Alia was born in Shkoder to poor Muslim parents. In his late teens, with Albania under German occupation, Alia joined the communist partisans and fought in Albania and Yugoslavia. His war record and responsibilities led to a prominent position in the party youth movement; he was a leading proponent of Albania's "cultural revolution" in the 1960s, and became Hoxha's chosen successor after the death of Mehmet Shehu. A full member of the politburo from 1961 and Head of State from 1982, he assumed real power as PPS first secretary after Hoxha's death in 1985. His approach was initially to proceed with cautious reforms, while preserving the Hoxha cult. Persuaded only in the course of 1990 that a desperate economic situation and growing popular protest required more rapid change, he effectively marginalised the hardline elements in the party, and took the gamble of allowing other parties to contest the 1991 elections. The PPS's overall success in those polls in March-April, securing a two-thirds majority in an Assembly which duly re-elected him as President, disguised a collapse of support in the towns (Alia himself lost humiliatingly in a Tirana constituency). As President he was debarred under the new interim constitution from holding party leadership posts, which he duly resigned in early May. The PPS went on to reform itself under the leadership of Fatos Nano, renaming itself the Socialist Party of Albania (PSS). On 1 January 1992 Alia survived a heart attack. After the defeat of the PSS in March legislative elections, he resigned the presidency, and by September 1992 he had been placed under house arrest. Alia denounced the proceedings against him as a politically-motivated show trial, but in July 1994 he was convicted of sanctioning a variety of crimes whilst president, including the killing of Albanians illegally crossing the border, the use of summary executions, and the embezzlement of state funds. Despite his ill health, he began a nine-year prison sentence in September 1994, but was released in July 1995 under the terms of a 1994 amnesty.

Adil **Carcani** (b. 1922). A party member from wartime resistance days and a politburo member from 1961, he was Shehu's successor as prime minister from 1982, and was identified with the early, cautious reform moves under the Alia regime in 1985-90. Given responsibility for forming a government with a fresh "reformist" image in December 1990, he was replaced two months later in the immediate pre-election turmoil.

Post-communist era

Sali **Berisha** (b. 1945). Albanian President from 1992 and former leader of the PDS. Born to a peasant family near the Kosovo border, Berisha studied medicine in Tirana, qualifying as a cardiologist. He was allowed to study in Paris in 1978 and to conduct research in Copenhagen in the 1980s. Berisha was a PPS member in the communist era but never held high office in the party. He rose to prominence in 1990, when student demonstrations swept Tirana to demand the introduction of a multi-party system. Berisha was a co-founder of the first major opposition party to emerge, the PDS, and was elected as PDS leader at its first national congress in September 1991. The victory of the PDS in legislative elections in 1992 paved the way for his election to the presidency. As head of state he rapidly came to dominate Albanian politics. The PDS-led government introduced radical economic reforms and controversial justice policies which led to the trial of dozens of former communist officials, including Berisha's principal rival, PSS leader Fatos Nano, who was imprisoned in April 1994. Although Berisha had won considerable popularity during his first year as President, his aggressive style began to antagonise former allies as well as opponents. Suspicious that he harboured authoritarian tendencies, voters inflicted a major personal defeat on him by rejecting his draft constitution in a referendum in November 1994. Throughout the following year Berisha began to use increasingly undemocratic methods, extending his control over the judiciary and backing legislation that effectively disqualified the leaders of the PSS from parliament. Many Albanians regarded the campaign as a bid to weaken the opposition in advance of the scheduled 1996 elections.

Fatos **Nano**. Socialist leader and former prime minister. As a young economist, Nano was brought into the communist government by President Alia in December 1990. Within months Nano was prime minister, leading the provisional government formed immediately before the March 1991 elections. Nano committed his government to the free market economy. He was re-appointed following the elections, but after a wave of anti-communist strikes his government fell within a month. When the PPS was renamed the Socialist Party of Albania (PSS) at its June 1991 congress Nano was elected party chairman, and he remained party leader despite the poor showing of the PSS in the 1992 elections. By the summer of 1993 the party had recovered by reshaping itself in the mould of a Western European-style social democratic party and mounting an effective opposition campaign against the populism of the governing PDS. In July 1993 Nano was arrested in connection with the disappearance during his term as prime minister of some $8m of Italian aid money. Although no evidence was offered in court that Nano had personally benefitted from the alleged fraud, he was given a 12-year prison sentence in April 1994 for misappropriating state funds, dereliction of duty and falsifying official documents. Human rights groups backed Nano's claim that the trial was a politically motivated show trial to discredit the PSS. Doubts over the conviction appeared to be shared by the Albanian people; despite his incarceration he remained socialist leader, and his political stature and popularity rating increased.

POLITICAL PARTIES

The communist party and successors

The **Albanian Communist Party**, formed in Autumn 1941, unified the various Albanian communist factions. The party was renamed the **Party of Labour of Albania** (PPS) in 1948, and was led until his death in 1985 by Enver Hoxha.

The PPS was renamed the **Socialist Party of Albania** (PSS) in June 1991, and adopted a Western European-style social democratic programme. The new party leadership was composed of young reformists, including the overall leader Fatos Nano, and noted opponents of the old guard, such as Dritero Agolli. Most of the property of the former PPS was nationalised by government decree in November 1991. Despite its heavy defeat in the 1992 legislative elections, and a series of show trials of former communist leaders, including Nano, the party recovered in 1993-5, apparently shrugging off the legacy of the past. The party retained as many as 110,000 members.

In late 1991 the **Albanian Communist Party** was reconstituted by the conservative rump of the PPS. It was banned under July 1992 legislation (*see below*), and leader Hysni Milloshi was arrested on a legal technicality.

Principal non-communist parties

In February 1992 a new electoral law effectively banned ethnically-based organisations from registering as political parties. In July 1992 an amendment to the law on political organisations banned "fascist, anti-national, chauvinistic, racist, totalitarian, communist, Marxist-Leninist, Stalinist" or "Enverist" organisations. The principal targets of these two laws were, respectively, the Omonia organisation (*see below*) and the Albanian Communist Party (*above*).

The nationalist right performed poorly in Albania's first two free elections. As commonly happened across Eastern Europe, voters favoured social democratic parties committed both to reform and to social protection. Public opinion has reacted against the authoritarianism apparent in the PDS-led government attempts to discredit and weaken its rivals in advance of legislative elections due in 1996.

The **Democratic Party of Albania** (PDS). Centre-right party; the first to be legally formed, on 12 December 1990, after the communist regime permitted rival parties. The PDS emerged as the leading opposition force in the 1991 elections, winning support principally in the capital and major towns. Although its platform included private land ownership and "shock therapy" for a rapid transition to a market economy, it also included social democratic elements, with pledges to maintain adequate social provision. The PDS's main leaders were the charismatic anti-communist Sali Berisha, who was elected chairman by a large majority at the first PDS national assembly in Tirana in September 1991, and Gramoz Pashko. The party entered the pluralist "national stability government" in June 1991, withdrawing in December to prepare for fresh elections. On Berisha's assumption of the presidency in April 1992, he was succeeded as PDS leader by Edouard Selami, a 30-year old lawyer. The party's electoral victory in 1992 was extremely popular, but it soon faced criticism from the PSS for failing to fulfil the extravagant promises made during its campaign, and for the allegedly authoritarian tendencies of the PDS leadership. The PDS-dominated government has however achieved some considerable successes, notably in economic reform. Selami was dismissed by a special conference on 5 March 1995 for opposing Berisha's plans to repeat a referendum on the draft constitution; he has become a prominent critic of the President. Despite qualms over Berisha's authoritarian style, the party appeared likely to rally behind its leader for the 1996 elections.

Democratic Alliance. Centre-right party formed in November 1992 when senior PDS leader Gramoz Pashko, a leading economist and former finance minister, broke away from the PDS with five other deputies. Pashko criticised Berisha for allegedly back-pedalling on economic reform. He described the new Democratic Alliance as liberal and committed to institutional, economic and cultural reforms. Selami Ceka was elected as Democratic Alliance leader.

Republican Party of Albania (PRS). Right-wing party formed in 1991. In common with other right-wing parties the PRS had irredentist tendencies, supported a vengeful justice campaign against former communist leaders, and backed the rights of former landowners. PRS deputies held three posts in the coalition government from June to December 1991. The PRS was a minor partner in the PDS-led coalition from 1992-4, but withdrew to "constructive opposition" in December 1994.

Omonia ("Concord"). The party of the ethnic Greek minority. Omonia was permitted to compete in the 1991 elections, and won five seats. It was denied registration for the 1992 elections, and was thereafter increasingly marginalised, depicted by Albanian parties and press as extremist and terrorist. It was led by Thomas Kyriakou.

Human Rights Union (EAD). A party supported principally by ethnic Greeks unable to support the Omonia party in the 1992 election, in which the EAD won two seats.

ELECTIONS

Legislature

Communist era elections. A unicameral People's Assembly, with 250 members, was elected every four years from a single list of candidates, by universal suffrage of those over 18 (with turnouts generally recorded as at or near 100 per cent). The last two such elections were in November 1982 and February 1987.

1991 elections. Candidates in the multiparty elections of March-April 1991 contested single-member constituency elections. The first round of ballots took place on 31 March. Where no candidate had secured an overall majority, which was the case in 19 constituencies, second round run-off elections were held on April 7 or 14. The PPS won a resounding victory, taking more than two thirds of the seats in the Assembly. The opposition PDS took a disappointing 75 seats, but secured its position as the only serious rival to the PPS.

	1st round	2nd round	Total
PPS	162	7	169
PDS	65	10	75
Omonia	3	2	5
National Veterans' Committee	1	-	1
Total	231	19	250

According to Western observers, the conduct of the 1991 elections was largely fair. Opposition parties nevertheless criticised PPS control over the state media and highlighted reports that local socialist officials had intimidated some rural constituencies. In Shkoder in early April, opposition demonstrations against alleged electoral fraud developed into anti-communist riots during which the police headquarters was destroyed and four people were killed.

1992 elections. An electoral law approved by People's Assembly in February 1992 reduced the size of the People's Assembly to 140 seats. Of this number, 100 were directly elected by single-member constituencies on the same basis as 1991. In a device to compensate for disproportionality in the results from the direct elections, the remaining 40 seats were distributed to parties according to their aggregated national vote in the first round of voting; a 4 per cent threshold applied.

The law also defined the terms under which political parties could register for participation in elections. Controversially, it effectively excluded ethnically-based political parties including the ethnic Greek Omonia party (although Omonia candidates were free to run in single-member constituencies).

At the March 1992 election the PDS exploited mounting economic chaos to reverse the results of the previous year and take a two thirds majority of the legislature, sufficient to pass constitutional legislation. The ex-communist PSS was thus swept from power. The Albanian Social Democratic Party (PSDS) established itself as the third largest party, whereas the right again performed poorly, with the PRS taking only one seat.

	Single-member constituencies first round %	seats	Party list seats	Total seats
PDS	62	90	2	92
PSS	25	6	32	38
PSDS		1	6	7
EAD		2	0	2
PRS		1	0	1
Total	100	100	40	140

Presidency

Under the communist regime the People's Assembly elected the Presidium whose president (Omer Nishani from 1946 to 1953, Maj.-Gen. Haxhi Lleshi from 1953 to 1982, then Ramiz Alia) was nominal head of state.

Under the interim constitution adopted on April 29, 1991, the newly-elected People's Assembly on April 30 elected Ramiz Alia to the new post of President of the Republic; a token PPS opponent, Namik Dokle, received two votes against 172 for Alia, while 71 votes (corresponding to the entire opposition) were ruled invalid.

Following the defeat of the PSS in legislative elections in March 1992, Alia resigned the presidency on 3 April.

Sali Berisha was elected on 6 April 1992 for a five-year term as Albania's new President by 96 votes to 35, exceeding by two votes the minimum two-thirds support of the People's Assembly necessary for election. He resigned as leader of the PDS, complying with the post-communist convention that party and state leadership should be divided.

Referendum

In a referendum on 6 November 1994, 53.9 per cent of voters rejected the proposed draft constitution and 41.7 per cent expressed approval. Turnout was 84.43 per cent.

CHRONOLOGY

1912. Albania declares independence after centuries of domination by the Ottoman Empire.

1914-20. Albania is divided between three greater powers, Italy, Greece and Yugoslavia.

1920. Independence is restored with the withdrawal of foreign armies, at US insistence; the following year the state's borders are confirmed.

November-December 1923. Legislative elections.

1924. Warrior-chieftain Ahmed Zogu seizes power.

1926-7. Successive treaties with Italy promote political and military cooperation.

1928. Zogu establishes a monarchy, becoming King Zog I. He cracks down on internal conflicts, disarming many of Albania's feuding clans and bringing relative internal stability to the country.

1935-6. Zog liberalises his regime, relaxing press controls.

7-10 April 1939. Italian troops occupy Albania, forcing King Zog into exile.

Spring 1941. Germany launches its invasion of the Balkans, displacing Italy as the occupying power in Albania. Over the next three years Germany doubles Albania's size and population by awarding territory formerly part of Greece and Yugoslavia.

Autumn 1941. The various Albanian communist factions unify into the Albanian Communist Party. The Yugoslav communists play a key role.

September 1943. Establishment of the communist-dominated National Liberation Council, which in May 1944 declares itself the "supreme executive and legislative organ".

August 1944. A Soviet military mission arrives in Albania, too late to usurp the Yugoslav communists' pre-eminence in Albanian affairs.

October 1944. Formation of a Provisional Democratic Government under communist leader Enver Hoxha.

November 1944. Liberation of Tirana.

November 1945. The Allies recognise the Hoxha government (although the USA and UK subsequently break off diplomatic relations).

2 December 1945. In legislative elections only the communist-dominated Democratic Front is allowed to stand, and is rejected by only 7 per cent of voters.

January 1946. Proclamation of a republic, with Enver Hoxha as its leader.

1948. The Albanian Communist Party renames itself the Albanian Workers' Party (PPS).

1948. Albania's quarrel with Yugoslavia is followed by purges of alleged "Titoists". In May 1949, following the first anti-Titoist show trial in Eastern Europe, former Interior Minister Koci Xoxe is executed for backing political union with Yugoslavia.

1961. Criticism of the Soviet policy of peaceful coexistence with the West, articulated at the PPS congress in February, indicates Albania's support for China in the developing Sino-Soviet dispute. Purges of pro-Soviet elements begin in May; diplomatic relations with the Soviet Union and East European countries are broken off by the end of the year, leaving Albania with a single diplomatic ally in distant China.

1967. Religion is officially abolished.

1968. Albania formally withdraws from the Warsaw Treaty Organisation, having played no real part since its foundation in 1955.

1974-76. Widespread purges are directed against party dissidents who back the Soviet line in East-West detente.

January 1976. A new constitution enshrines the PPS's isolationist and inward-looking approach.

July 1978. Albania's complete isolation is confirmed with the halting of Chinese aid after Hoxha accuses China of seeking hegemony.

December 1981. The death of prime minister Mehmet Shehu is officially described as suicide. More purges in the top party leadership are reported over the next three years.

April 1985. Hoxha dies and is succeeded by Ramiz Alia.

June-December 1989. Communist regimes topple across the Soviet bloc, from the Polish elections in June to the execution of Romanian hard-line dictator Ceausescu on 25 December.

January 1990. Despite the first reports of internal unrest, the PPS leadership asserts that there will be no pressures for change in Albania. Nevertheless, Alia puts forward a package of economic and political liberalisation measures, including production incentives to workers and the idea of limited choice between PPS-approved candidates in elections.

17 April 1990. The regime abandons isolationism as Alia calls at a party plenum for "friendly relations with all countries". The plenum also approves limited economic reforms.

7-8 May 1990. Reforms of the legal system and penal code are approved by parliament; the ban on "religious propaganda" is lifted.

7-9 July 1990. Reformists displace hardliners in the party politburo and government. Alia stresses gradualism in economic reform; later in the month artisans are permitted a degree of "free enterprise" trading, and restrictions on foreign investment are modified.

9-13 July 1990. Thousands of asylum-seekers who have taken refuge in foreign embassies are given passports and allowed to leave Albania.

30 July 1990. Diplomatic relations are restored with the Soviet Union.

16 November 1990. Albanian Catholics hold their first legal service since the proscription of religion in 1967. Muslims follow suit in January 1991.

11 December 1990. As pro-democracy demonstrations spread from Tirana to other towns, five hardliners are dismissed from the party leadership and Alia announces that opposition parties will be permitted.

12 December 1990. Formation of the Democratic Party of Albania (PDS).

23 December 1990. The official trade union federation declares its independence from the communist party. Strike activity increases.

9 February 1991. Amid a growing exodus, thousands of people are prevented by police from leaving the port of Durres on ferries to Italy.

22 February 1991. In a pre-election concession to the opposition, Fatos Nano, an economist, replaces Carcani as Prime Minister.

22-24 February 1991. Student-led protesters chanting "Hoxha-Hitler" tear down the giant statue of Enver Hoxha in Tirana. Tanks are called in to the capital to restore order; Alia orders troops to fire on demonstrators if necessary. Attacks on monuments to Hoxha continue in succeeding days. On 24 February pro-Hoxha forces or "Enverists" clash with opponents, leading to four deaths; there are rumours, not discouraged by Alia, that an Enverist coup is imminent. A mass exodus of refugees to Italy begins.

15 March 1991. Diplomatic relations are restored with the USA (and, on 29 May, with the UK).

31 March 1991. In the first round of multi-party elections, the PPS dominates rural areas; the opposition Democratic Party (PDS) is heavily defeated despite its strong showing in the main towns.

2-10 April 1991. Anti-communist rioting breaks out in Shkoder; the police HQ is destroyed; four people are shot dead and 57 injured by security forces. The PDS is outraged and boycotts the opening session of the new People's Assembly.

29 April 1991. A new interim constitution supersedes that of 1976; the country no longer bears the official title of "Socialist People's Republic" but is simply the Republic of Albania.

30 April 1991. The new People's Assembly elects Ramiz Alia as President. Alia resigns from the PPS leadership, observing a clause in the draft constitution placing the presidency above party politics.

9 May 1991. A new PPS government is sworn in, again under Fatos Nano. On 10 May Nano announces his programme, committing his government to the free market economy.

4 June 1991. A general strike prompts the resignation of the Nano government.

11-13 June 1991. The PPS holds its congress in Tirana, criticises Hoxha, expels old guard leaders and renames itself the Socialist Party (PSS). Fatos Nano is elected as the new party chairman.

12 June 1991. Ylli Bufi, named as prime minister on 5 June, announces the formation of an interim "government of national salvation" in which the communists will for the first time share power with opposition parties, the PDS and PSDS.

5 August 1991. The government begins its programme of breaking up agricultural co-operatives and handing back land to peasants. Further reforms announced in September include the establishment of a privatisation agency.

25 August 1991. Anti-communist demonstrations resume in Tirana; a sustained campaign focuses on control of the media by ex-communists. Throughout the summer there is chronic industrial unrest and widespread disorder.

September 1991. The mainly ethnic-Albanian province of Kosovo in neighbouring Serbia declares independence; only the Albanian government recognises the declaration.

1 September 1991. With the economy in chaos and the country facing a humanitarian crisis, Italian troops arrive in Albania for the first time since 1943 to administer an emergency food aid programme, Operation Pelican. Italy also agrees to provide $800m toward Albanian agriculture. Italian troops leave in December 1993.

4 December 1991. Hoxha's widow Nexhmije is arrested.

6 December 1991. Ylli Bufi resigns as prime minister after the withdrawal of the PDS from his government. On 16 December an interim government under Vilson Ahmeti is sworn in, pending the organisation of fresh elections.

January-March 1992. Dozens of people are killed as security forces crack down on looters and rioters caught raiding foreign aid depots and other premises in search of food and other goods. Industry reaches a virtual standstill as the social paralysis and disorder worsens.

4 February 1992. A new electoral law effectively bans ethnically-based organisations from registering as political parties, to the consternation of the Greek minority and of the Greek government.

18 February 1992. Albania seals an agreement with the EC (EU) on trade and economic cooperation.

22 and 29 March 1992. Legislative elections: the PDS wins 62 per cent of the vote and 92 of the 140 seats in the new People's Assembly, while the PSS vote collapses.

3 April 1992. Alia resigns as President. Parliament passes a series of constitutional amendments augmenting presidential power over the cabinet.

6 April 1992. Berisha is elected by the People's Assembly as Albanian President, and takes office on 9 April. He stresses his commitment to human rights, privatisation and market reforms, and the creation of a constitutional state on the West European model.

13 April 1992. A new cabinet dominated by the PDS and led by Aleksander Meksi takes office; the new government's economic reform programme includes price liberalisation and the privatisation of farmland, state enterprises and housing.

19 May 1992 A cabinet decree orders the phasing out of social security rules under which the unemployed receive 80 per cent of their former salary in state benefits, after pressure from the IMF.

16 July 1992. An amendment to the law on political organisations bans extremist organisations, including communist parties.

3 November 1992 The PDS splits, losing its two-thirds majority in the Assembly as senior figure Gramoz Pashko and five other deputies form the Democratic Alliance and call for faster economic reforms.

27 December 1992. Five former PSS and police officials get long prison sentences for ordering the shooting of demonstrators in Shkoder in April 1991.

27 January 1993. Nexhmije Hoxha, now 72, is sentenced to nine years in prison for misuse of government funds in 1985-90. The Court of Appeal increases her sentence to 11 years in May 1993.

January-February 1993. Greece expels thousands of illegal Albanian immigrants, a small proportion of the estimated 200,000 Albanian migrants in Greece.

25-27 March 1993. Up to ten Albanians are killed by Yugoslav border guards in a series of incidents.

June 1993. A senior Greek Orthodox cleric is deported by the Albanian authorities, accused of sponsoring ethnic Greek separatism; in retaliation the Greek authorities expel tens of thousands more illegal Albanian immigrants.

16 June 1993. The government fails to present a completed draft constitution to the People's Assembly; the PSS and PSDS begin a boycott of the parliament in protest.

11 October 1993. Controversial and restrictive media legislation is signed into law.

15-16 November 1993. Karolos Papoulias, foreign minister in Greece's new socialist government, visits Albania for wide-ranging talks with Prime Minister Meksi.

27 February 1994. Two journalists for the socialist daily *Koha Jone* are sentenced to prison terms for publishing a relatively minor military document. The opposition criticises the move as an attempt to intimidate the opposition press.

3 April 1994. Socialist leader Fatos Nano is convicted of misappropriating state funds, dereliction of duty and falsifying official documents during his short term as Prime Minister in 1991. The charges concerned the disappearance of Italian aid worth $8m. Three other former communist officials are convicted of related offenses.

10 April 1994. Two Albanian border guards are killed by raiders at their training camp near Gjirokaster. Although the militant pro-Greek group Northern Epirus Liberation Front claim responsibility, the Albanian government blames Greece.

2 July 1994. Ramiz Alia is convicted of abuse of power and conspiring to violate the rights of citizens, and is sentenced to nine years in prison. Ten other former senior communist officials are sentenced to between three and eight years in prison (several sentences being suspended). In late November Berisha orders a reduction in Alia's sentence to five years in prison, and he is eventually released in the summer of 1995.

5 August 1994. 2,500 former political prisoners begin a hunger strike to demand compensation for past injustices; despite police brutality and arrests, the government eventually agrees to pay compensation from December 1994.

7 September 1994. Five leaders of the Omonia ethnic Greek organisation are convicted of a range of anti-constitutional activities, including treasonably "carrying out the orders of a foreign secret service" and illegal possession of weapons. Four of those

convicted claimed that confessions they had made in custody had been extracted under torture. Greece denounces the convictions as "a very strong provocation".

6 November 1994. Albanian voters reject the draft constitution. The referendum result is a major blow to Berisha and the ruling PDS.

4 December 1994. Berisha accuses the government of corruption and inefficiency and implements a major reshuffle. The PSDS quits the coalition.

17 December 1994. Severe energy shortages compel the government to introduce rationing of electricity, exempting only mines, hospitals and state bakeries.

9 February 1995. The Omonia activists remaining in prison are released by the Court of Appeals, which rules that procedural violations had taken place.

26 February 1995. An OSCE investigation into alleged persecution of the ethnic Greek minority is suspended, having found no evidence to substantiate the claims.

13 March 1995. Talks between the Greek and Albanian Foreign Ministers in Tirana are described as "extremely positive" and plans for joint military exercises are announced.

8 June 1995. Ilir Hoxha, son of the late Enver, is sentenced to one year under house arrest for "inciting national hatred" following his vitriolic criticism of the PDS in a newspaper article.

21 June 1995. Passage of legislation recognising the rights of ethnic minorities to separate languages and customs.

July 1995. Albania is admitted to the Council of Europe.

7 July 1995. The Court of Appeals orders the immediate release of Alia under the terms of a November 1994 amnesty.

17 August 1995. Launch of the voucher privatisation scheme; citizens can exchange their vouchers for shares in any of 20 enterprises.

21 September 1995. Supreme Court Chair Zef Brozi is dismissed after a constitutional crisis between executive and competing judicial organs. Brozi had resisted PDS pressure in calling for the re-examination of the conviction of PSS leader Nano. Attempts to arrest Brozi are thwarted by the USA, which organises his flight into exile.

22 September 1995. The People's Assembly passes the highly controversial and partisan Law on Genocide, which Berisha signs five days later. The law facilitates the prosecution of the perpetrators of crimes committed during the communist era "for political, ideological or religious motives". More controversially, it also bars from public office until 2002 senior communist-era office-holders and collaborators with the former secret police.

YUGOSLAVIA

The Yugoslav state which disintegrated in 1991 was founded as a federal republic under Tito's leadership in the aftermath of the second world war. Its official name since 1963 had been the Socialist Federal Republic of Yugoslavia (SFRY), comprising the six republics of Bosnia-Hercegovina, Croatia, Macedonia, Montenegro, Serbia and Slovenia. In April 1992 the "rump" state, comprising Serbia and Macedonia, took the name Federal Republic of Yugoslavia (FRY).

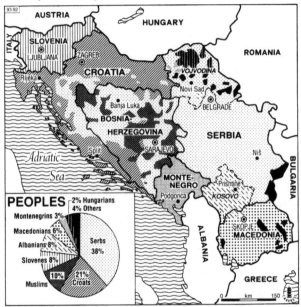

Yugoslavia, meaning land of the south Slavs, was the largest country in the Balkans. It was somewhat bigger than Romania both in terms of population (nearly 24 million) and land area (255,800 sq. km.). Three quarters of the country was mountainous, with the highest peak in the Slovenian Alps in the north, and with rugged terrain extending parallel with the Adriatic coast to the Albanian border and across into southern Serbia, Kosovo and Macedonia. The main lowland areas, including fertile arable land, were the Sava valley from Zagreb to Belgrade, the narrower valley of the Morava valley which flowed north to join the Danube downstream from Belgrade, and, most importantly, the Danube plain itself, extending north and north-west of Belgrade to the Romanian and Hungarian borders. (The western Danube plain was part of Slavonia in Croatia; the eastern plain was in Vojvodina, an autonomous province within Serbia.)

There was a pronounced trend of population movement from rural to urban areas, with some 47 per cent of the population classified as urban in 1990. Belgrade, the federal and Serbian capital, was by some way the largest city with a population of about 1,500,000.

Yugoslavia conducted its full censuses every ten years, but that of April 1991 was badly affected by boycotts by disaffected nationalities. According to the 1981 figures, the total population was 22,425,000 of whom over nine million or 40 per cent lived in Serbia; 20 per cent in Croatia, 18 per cent in Bosnia-Hercegovina, 8.5 per cent each in Slovenia and Macedonia, and 2.6 per cent in Montenegro.

Distribution by ethnic groups is shown on the accompanying map. Linguistically, Serbo-Croat was most widely used, officially as a single spoken language, although many Serbs wrote it using the Cyrillic script while Croats and Bosnian Muslims used the Roman script. Other official languages of Yugoslavia were Slovene and Macedonian. The largest minorities were concentrated in Serbia's two autonomous provinces: Kosovo, which had a rapidly increasing community of 1.7 million Albanians, and Vojvodina, with some 400,000 Hungarians.

The Federal Republic of Yugoslavia (FRY, comprising the republics of Serbia and Montenegro) was founded in April 1992 following the secession of Bosnia-Hercegovina, Croatia, Macedonia and Slovenia. Its area was 102,173 sq. km (about 40 per cent of the SFRY) and its population 10,407,000 (to which Montenegro contributed respectively 13,812 sq. km. and 616,000 people). Belgrade was once again the federal and Serbian capital.

HISTORICAL NARRATIVE

The state founded in 1918, ethnically the most complex of the new states to emerge from the peace settlement following the First World War, was until 1929 officially titled the Kingdom of Serbs, Croats and Slovenes, and included minorities of Albanians, Bosniaks (Muslims), Italians, Germans, Romanies (Gypsies), Turks, Jews and others. Despite their ethnic similarities the two largest ethnic groups, Croats and Serbs, had deep-rooted cultural and religious differences. The Serbs had for centuries been dominated by the extra-European traditions of the Ottoman Empire, of which Serbia was formally a part until 1878. Under this tyrannical and highly conservative regime, high taxes were exacted, but not invested in infrastructural or educational improvements; the economy therefore remained predominantly agrarian. The bureaucracy and justice system were venal and arbitrary. Whilst the Catholic Church was persecuted, the Ottoman Empire and the Eastern Orthodox Church practised a mutual tolerance.

The dominant influence for Croats, on the other hand, had been the essentially European traditions of the Austro-Hungarian or Habsburg Empire, which absorbed most Croat land in 1699. Austria-Hungary invested in the economic infrastructure, including communications, and established an education system and a relatively efficient bureaucracy. Although this too was an authoritarian regime with a developed secret police apparatus, it permitted a greater degree of intellectual freedom. Catholicism was predominant.

The idea of "Illyria", a Balkan union of the South Slavs, was not a mass phenomenon among either Serbs or Croats. Its original proponents in the nineteenth century were Croat intellectuals weary of the oppressive Habsburg Empire and inspired by a Pan-

Slavism which placed emphasis on the common linguistic heritage with Serbs. Union with their Serb "cousins", they calculated, would afford an independent Croatia vital protection from predatory Italian expansionism.

The Serbian leadership began to favour union with Croat and Bosnian territory to the West only in the latter years of the First World War, and then not from genuine "Yugoslavism" but as compensation for the country's exceptional war losses. This was reflected in the constitutional arrangements effectively imposed by the Serbs in 1920, which awarded the Yugoslav monarchy to the Serb royal house. The Serbs dominated the interwar regime, the office of prime minister being held by Serbs for all but five months of that 22-year period.

Croat leaders, initially resigned to Serb hegemony, were stirred by the demagogic Peasant Party leader Stijepan Radic. By 1925 Radic had publicly abandoned Croatian secessionism but continued to demand autonomy. His assassination by a Serb on the floor of the parliament in 1928 ushered in a crisis that culminated in the declaration of a Royal dictatorship in 1929. Despairing of the Yugoslav ideal, the King even offered Croat leaders independence, but the fear of Italian and Hungarian irredentism prompted them to reject the offer.

The experiment with democracy was a failure, characterised by fractiousness and instability: there were 24 cabinets between 1918 and 1928. The post-1929 dictatorship gave Yugoslavia the appearance of stability until the assassination of King Alexander in France in October 1934. In reality the underlying political problems worsened. Throughout the 1930s no member of the royal house even visited Zagreb. There was no constructive attempt to solve the national problem until the *Sporazum* of 1939; and even this was a result of the imperative to unite the country before the impending European war. Neither democracy nor dictatorship successfully tackled the problems of Yugoslavia's outmoded economy. At the outbreak of the second world war some three quarters of the population remained dependent on agriculture, and yet only 1 per cent of the state budget was spent on that sector.

Wartime Yugoslavia experienced appalling violence. Following the invasion by Axis forces in April 1941, the *Ustasa* set up a Croat state under Nazi patronage, whose genocidal campaign against Serbs was the most horrific aspect of a desperate war in which all sides deliberately used terror against civilian communities. Despite the political changes after the war, many communities never forgave their wartime adversaries; thus in 1991, adding to the increasingly frenzied atmosphere of ethnic hatred, enraged villagers on both sides of the divide disinterred from their mass graves the bodies of ethnic kin murdered in wartime pogroms.

Paradoxically, "Yugoslavism" was actually strengthened by the horrors of the war. The communists' emergence as the strongest political force in 1945 was based in part on its status as the only genuine supranational Yugoslavist party, pledged to end inter-ethnic violence. Two other factors gave the communists a legitimacy which underpinned their rule throughout the postwar period. The first was the prestige of the Partisans, who had emerged victorious from two wars, defeating the Serb nationalists and fiercely resisting the Axis powers; the second was the leadership of Josip Broz Tito.

The party's popularity allowed Tito to resist Soviet hegemony, and this in turn further strengthened the communists' popular credibility. Unlike most other Central and East European countries (*but see also Romania*), it was the "Cominformists" rather than the "bourgeois nationalists" who fled or were purged. Yugoslavia retained control over military and economic policy: it remained outside the Warsaw Pact and at arm's length from Soviet economic planning (although it did become an associate member of Comecon).

Although the breach with the Soviets in 1948 and the blockade which followed deprived Yugoslavia of much-needed assistance with its ambitious first five-year plan for economic centralisation and industrialisation, by the mid-1950s the communist regime had provided a measure of prosperity. The communists stimulated rapid industrialisation, invested in the communications infrastructure, and dramatically improved educational provision. Yugoslavia's distinctive contributions to socialist practice, from the late 1940s, were participatory and decentralising reforms such as workers' self-management. This idea was progressively extended from industrial workers' councils to broader social and administrative self-management. Making the system responsive to market signals, a specific objective from the mid-1960s, involved in practice a high level of reliance on the directors of the individual enterprises.

Communist Yugoslavia was also characterised by exceptional constitutional and institutional flexibility, in which Edward Kardelj played a key role. A series of constitutions established a state structure designed to withstand the mutual suspicions of the component republics. The last Titoist constitution, promulgated in 1974, was the leadership's response to the upsurge of Croatian nationalism three years before. Its complex arrangements on the delegation of powers and the rotation of federal posts created cumbersome procedures and bureaucracies which impeded change. Crucially, the constitution gave Serbs a growing sense of grievance against the federation. In the late 1970s Tito and Kardelj had reputedly been considering further reforms designed to address these complaints.

Economic problems in the 1980s provided the context in which the political crisis developed at the end of the decade. Since 1974, when constitutional amendments had given the republics more economic power, the gap had widened between the prosperous and relatively modern northern and western parts of the country and the impoverished south, particularly Kosovo and Macedonia. Slovenia and Croatia in particular had increasingly pursued economic autarky and had come to resent the flow of resources to the south (where many federal subsidies were squandered on "prestige" projects with no long-term economic value). As economic growth began to slow across the country, increased foreign borrowing appeared the only available means of sustaining living standards. The federal government in 1989-90 made what turned out to be a last attempt to grapple with the economic situation, as prime minister Ante Markovic declared war on hyperinflation. A currency reform pegged the new dinar to the deutschemark, wages were held down and prices allowed to rise, a balance of payments surplus was achieved to reduce the foreign debt, and a package of reform measures was pushed through to try to encourage a more genuine free market. The effect on inflation was dramatic in 1990, but it did not change the fact that so many of Yugoslavia's economic units were operating in an unrealistic environment, behind the protection of a web of special interests.

Such was Tito's prestige as a unifying figure that his death in 1980 immediately gave rise to grave predictions of civil war. Within a year developments in Kosovo, Serbia's southern autonomous province, which was regarded as the cradle of Serb nation, had set in motion a revival of militant Serbian nationalism that was to be the driving force behind the disintegration of the federation.

Kosovo's ethnic-Albanian community had grown rapidly in the post-war period. Increasingly, it came to dominate the province's political and economic life. Complaining of discrimination, Kosovar Serbs had migrated from the area in growing numbers from the 1960s. By 1981 the Kosovar Albanians were demanding republican status within the Yugoslav federation. Their mass protests were bloodily suppressed by the Army. The sensational publication in September 1986 of the *Memorandum of the Serbian Academy of Arts and Sciences* galvanised Serbian nationalism, principally on the Kosovo issue. Slobodan Milosevic, the leader of the Serbian Socialist Party, was one of the first to grasp the political significance, and rapidly established his credentials as a Serb nationalist during a visit to Kosovo in 1987. He was the force behind amendments to the Serbian constitution, introduced just prior to his assumption of the Serbian Presidency in 1989, which effectively scrapped the province's autonomous status, to the outrage of the Kosovar Albanians.

The revival of Serbian nationalism rekindled similar sentiments among the Croats and Slovenes in the late 1980s. Serbia's unilateral amendment of its republican constitution in 1989 was a decisive moment. Other republican leaders could follow Serbian precedent in amending their own constitutions to protect themselves from Serbian domination. This was the rationale behind Slovenia's claim to the right of secession in September 1989. (*See sub-chapters on Croatia and Slovenia for more details.*)

Leaders of the three main republics sensed a vacuum at the centre. The legitimacy of the federal communist party, the League of Communists of Yugoslavia (SKJ), had been critically undermined. The party appeared unable to respond to the rise of nationalism; the younger generation cared little for the party's wartime exploits; Tito had been dead for almost a decade; and the economy was failing. When the SKJ convened for its extraordinary 14th congress on 20 January 1990, it did so in the context of revolutionary upheaval across Eastern and Central Europe. Amid the turmoil, the Slovene and Croatian parties had abandoned their monopoly on power and called multi-party elections. Although the fractious congress endorsed similar elections for all the republics, it rejected further devolution. This prompted the Slovene walk-out that marked the effective end of the federal party.

With or without the SKJ, Markovic said, "Yugoslavia continues to function"; but, as preparations went ahead for changing the federal Constitution, it was in the republics that the key decisions were being made. Although Markovic had won some respect with the impact of his austerity measures, his federal government ceased to have a real role beyond overall economic administration. His federal party, the Alliance of Reform Forces, was launched in mid-1990 but the federal elections for which it was intended never took place.

Instead, in the elections held in all six republics in 1990, republican and nationalist parties were the victors. In Serbia, Milosevic's ex-communist Socialist Party (SPS) won convincingly. Elsewhere, only in Slovenia did the ex-communist party perform respectably, having established its reformist and nationalist credentials. Otherwise voters opted for nationalist parties. In Croatia the HDZ swept to power and its leader Franjo Tudjman became republican President, while 90 per cent of Bosnian voters opted for ethnic parties. The republican election results led to the final paralysis of federal civil institutions, culminating in the Serbian refusal in May 1991 to countenance the scheduled assumption of the Presidency by the Croat nominee, Stipe Mesic.

By the summer of 1990 most of the parties had begun to make secret preparations for war. The JNA ordered the secret disarmament of Slovene territorial forces, while Croatia launched a covert arms procurement programme. By early summer 1991, the momentum behind Croatian and Slovene independence was unstoppable. The two republics jointly proclaimed their "dissociation" from the Yugoslav federation in June 1991.

The federation's one remaining fully functioning institution was the JNA or federal army, the federation's last defender, which demanded intervention in Slovenia. The JNA failed to use overwhelming force and was humiliated by the Slovene militia; when it demanded full-scale intervention, Serbia vetoed the idea. The Slovene debacle marked the death of Yugoslavism; henceforth the JNA served Serbian strategic objectives. Thus when Vukovar fell to Serb-JNA forces in November 1991, exposing Croatia's eastern flank to attack, the JNA offensive was halted, because the Serbian leadership had no desire to reverse Croatian secession, instead deploying the JNA to protect majority-Serb areas (even this aim being qualified; see below on defeat of Croatian Serbs).

In March 1991 Milosevic told a student meeting that he aimed to create a state for all Serbs. That month, he and Tudjman met secretly to discuss the partition of Yugoslavia. Although both agreed to divide Bosnia-Hercegovina, Croatian-Serbian co-operation was ultimately confounded by the political pressures caused by war in Croatia.

The Croatian Serbs, who had suffered genocide at the hands of the wartime Independent State of Croatia, had refused to accept the authority of Zagreb and had declared their secession from Croatia. They were better prepared for war than the Croatian government, and with the backing of the JNA, quickly established dominance over several enclaves together comprising some 30 per cent of Croatian territory. In April 1992 they established the Republic of Serbian Krajina (RSK).

By April 1992 Bosnia-Hercegovina, Croatia, Macedonia and Slovenia had seceded from the federation. The rump Yugoslavia, consisting of Serbia and the tiny republic of Montenegro, reconstituted itself as the Federal Republic of Yugoslavia (FRY), with the father of Serbian nationalism, the intellectual Dobrica Cosic, as President. The new federal regime was dominated by the Serbian leadership; its reduced powers were reflected in its budgets, three quarters of which were devoted to military expenditure.

JNA involvement in Bosnia-Hercegovina was less overt than that in Slovenia and Croatia. One month after the outbreak of war in Bosnia in April 1992, a JNA "withdrawal" was ordered. The 80,000 JNA troops who nevertheless remained in Bosnia-Hercegovina were no longer formally under federal command, but stayed on the federal payroll. The arrangements allowed federal and Serbian authorities to disavow responsibility for the appalling excesses of the Serb forces in Bosnia-Hercegovina committed over the next three-and-a-half years. This nice distinction could not prevent Serbia from becoming an international pariah state, and in June 1992 the UN imposed economic sanctions on the rump Yugoslavia.

The role of the international community in the first months of the "Wars of the Yugoslav Succession" had been only marginal. European diplomats were bewildered by the parties' resort to force, which they regarded as folly bordering on insanity. Some European critics blamed EC recognition of Croatia, Slovenia and Bosnia-Hercegovina for the failure to find a peaceful settlement, but war had in fact been inevitable since the 1990 elections. Fighting persisted as long as the principal parties continued to regard war as actually or potentially the most effective way of achieving their ends.

By spring 1993, with international sanctions beginning to bite in Serbia and the establishment of a UN War Crimes Tribunal, Milosevic had begun to weary of the war. He appeared confident that the partial military victory achieved by Serb and JNA forces could be completed through political means in a post-war context. The Bosnian Serb rejection of the Vance-Owen plan was a turning point, and thenceforth Milosevic applied increasing pressure on his Bosnian allies to accept terms for peace. It remained unclear to what extent Milosevic's displeasure with Karadzic had been manufactured in order to distance the Serbian leader from events in Bosnia-Hercegovina. By August 1994, though, Serbia had imposed an economic blockade on the Bosnian Serbs, and in early October the international sanctions on the rump Yugoslavia were partially lifted after monitors were permitted on the Serbian-Bosnian border.

Milosevic subsequently also failed to assist the RSK in its disastrous defeat by overwhelming Croatian forces in August 1995. The Croatian victory, combined with the improved organisation of the mainly Muslim Bosnian government forces and the massive NATO bombing campaign against Bosnian Serb targets, turned the tide of the war in Bosnia-Hercegovina. Under severe pressure, the Bosnian Serbs agreed to allow Milosevic to represent them at the Dayton peace talks. At Dayton, Milosevic made a series of concessions. Notably, he abandoned the Serb demand for control of Serb suburbs of the Bosnian capital Sarajevo, thus effectively removing the power base of Bosnian Serb leader and potential rival Radovan Karadzic. The question of prosecuting Milosevic for war crimes in Croatia and Bosnia-Hercegovina was shelved.

Milosevic thus positioned himself for relative international respectability as leader of a peacetime Serbia.

During the war period, Milosevic had consolidated his control over the rump Yugoslavia. Federal President Cosic and his Prime Minister Milan Panic had launched a significant challenge to Milosevic, designed to bring peace to Bosnia-Hercegovina and establish a more liberal regime in the FRY. Milosevic defeated his federal rivals by calling and winning early Serbian elections in late 1992, easily defeating Panic in the Serbian presidential contest. By June 1993 Cosic had been removed from the federal presidency. Thereafter, Milosevic's control of federal institutions was complete. Milosevic also succeeded in neutralising a revived Orthodox church as a political threat.

In the political sphere, the Milosevic regime was assisted by its gradual assumption of control over the media, taking control of the last independent newspaper, *Borba*, and ensuring positive coverage in the state-owned broadcast media. No doubt assisted by his grip on the media, Milosevic demonstrated an uncanny ability to lead public opinion, whereas the opposition showed a knack of moving in the opposite direction. When nationalism was electorally profitable, the opposition took a moderate stance; when the Serbian people had become war-weary, the opposition moved to militancy.

Admittedly, the quality of opposition leadership was poor, exemplified in the erratic Serbian Renewal Movement leader Vuk Draskovic. Milosevic's use of extremist proxies such as the SRS, for example in the removal of Cosic, enabled him to position his own party toward the centre, allowing it manoeuvrability when circumstances demanded a change of policy direction.

The opposition never succeeded in attaching blame to the SPS for the disastrous economic situation. Instead blame was successfully turned on to the international community, so that even as inflation reached a monthly rate of over one million per cent in December 1993, the SPS was returned to parliament with an increased number of seats. Pressure on the economy was eased somewhat by the qualified success of the new currency, the so-called super dinar introduced in early 1994 and pegged to the deutschemark. This currency reform ended hyperinflation virtually overnight. Despite the scepticism of the international markets, the currency proved relatively stable in 1994-5. Thus Milosevic retained his popularity with a pragmatic blend of nationalism and bread-and-butter issues; he was careful never to let the Bosnian Serb tail wag the Serbian dog, offering only qualified support for the Bosnian Serbs from 1993 and abandoning the Croatian Serbs in 1995.

Thereafter, Milosevic's main challenge was to rebuild an economy shattered by the dissolution of the federation, the direct and indirect costs of the war, and the effect of international sanctions. Essential structural economic reforms postponed during the war years were by 1995 inescapable.

By 1995 Milosevic's formidable wife, Mirjana Markovic, had emerged as a political leader and ally; her party, the Yugoslav United Left, although without parliamentary representation, had secured a place in cabinet.

PRINCIPAL PERSONALITIES

Josip Broz **Tito** (1894-1980). Communist Yugoslavia's leader for 35 years. Although a Croat, Tito's heroic status as a leader of Partisan resistance to the Nazis won popularity with all Yugoslav nations and rally the country behind the communist regime. The communist party leader from 1937, Tito had initially been an orthodox Stalinist, but turned to his own brand of Marxism-Leninism, causing an irreparable rift with Moscow by the late 1940s. Titoism included Yugoslav neutrality, workers' self-management, economic decentralisation and the concept of social ownership. Tito showed great flexibility in adapting Yugoslav institutions in an attempt to solve the many structural problems which confronted the state. Under his stewardship Yugoslavia developed rapidly, as measured by both economic and educational indexes. His death was immediately followed by predictions of resurgent nationalism and the break-up of Yugoslavia.

Edward **Kardelj** (1910-1979). The principal architect, with Tito, of communist Yugoslavia. Kardelj, a Slovene, was a graduate of the Lenin Institute in Moscow, a wartime Partisan, and close associate of Tito from that time onwards. A leading theorist of self-management, he was the legal brain behind the many postwar constitutional and institutional reforms introduced by the Tito regime. He had been regarded as Tito's natural successor until his death one year before Tito's.

Milovan **Djilas** (1912-95). A prominent leader of the Partisans during the Second World War, Djilas then became Tito's effective number two as agitation and propaganda chief. Noted for his stinging criticism of Soviet-style communism, he was expelled from the League of Communists in 1954 amid attempts to effect a Yugoslav-Soviet rapprochement. Undeterred, he elaborated his theories in his highly influential 1957 book, *The New Class*, arguing that any party or bureaucracy with a monopoly of power will harden into a self-serving elite, and calling for democratisation. The book earned him a seven-year prison sentence for revisionism. In his latter years he became an eloquent critic of Serbian nationalism and of the Milosevic regime which fostered it.

Slobodan **Milosevic** (b. 1941). Serbian President since 1989 and the *eminence grise* of the wars of the Yugoslav succession. Milosevic was born to Montenegrin parents in Pozaravec. Both parents committed suicide before Milosevic reached adulthood. In 1964 Milosevic obtained a law degree from Belgrade University, and there established a lasting friendship with Ivan Stambolic, the future President of Serbia. Milosevic was appointed director general of Technogas, the state-owned gas company, in 1973, and served as head of the Bank of Belgrade from 1978-83. Although he had joined the SKJ in 1959, Milosevic did not enter politics until 1984, when he became an SKJ official in Belgrade. By 1986 Milosevic had become Serbian communist party chief. The following year he established himself as a Serb nationalist hero during a visit to Kosovo. Having engineered the fall of his old friend Stambolic, in May 1989 Milosevic was appointed Serbian President by the Serbian parliament. He received democratic mandates in 1992 and 1993. Milosevic dominated the Serbian Socialist Party from its inception. He also came to dominate the Yugoslav federal institutions, particularly after defeating federal prime minister Milan Panic in Serbian presidential elections in 1992. Thereafter, Milosevic cracked down on the opposition and the independent media, and his grip on Serbia-Montenegro became even tighter. Such was his position of strength that he was able to implement an economic blockade against the Bosnian Serbs and late to abandon the Croatian Serbs. Milosevic insisted that he did not control the Bosnian Serb military and was not therefore responsible for their excesses. From 1995 Milosevic was increasingly associated with Yugoslav United Left, led by his formidable wife Mirjana Markovic.

Vuk **Draskovic** (b. 1946). Leader of the opposition Serbian Renewal Movement. Early in his political career Draskovic was a hawkish nationalist. As the wars of the Yugoslav Succession worsened, the demagogic Draskovic adopted a new role: that of democrat and pacifist. A series of mass rallies were held in Belgrade to demand the resignation of the Milosevic regime. When in June 1993 Draskovic was arrested, severely beaten and incarcerated, human rights groups and prominent figures such as Danielle Mitterrand were attracted to his romantic image and lobbied for his release. He was freed in July after a hunger strike which reportedly brought him close to death. By December 1993, he had performed a *volte face* which embarrassed many of his Western supporters: in the campaign for Serbian elections Draskovic called for Serbian annexation of Bosnian Muslim areas including Mostar and Sarajevo. The naked expediency of this manoeuvre failed to impress Serbian voters.

Dobrica **Cosic** (b. 1921). Writer widely regarded as the spiritual leader of the Serb nation. From peasant roots, Cosic became cultural commissar under Tito, successfully resisting the imposition of socialist realism on Yugoslav literature and art. In 1968 Cosic was dismissed from the Central Committee for accusing ethnic Albanians of anti-Serbianism and separatism. From the 1970s Cosic was a prominent member of the Serbian Academy of Sciences and Arts. His popularity protected him from arrest as he held a series of meetings with other intellectuals to discuss democratic reforms. The publication in 1986 of the Academy's Memorandum, which served as an agenda for Serb nationalism, was publicly defended by Cosic. In June 1992 Cosic was elected as President of the FRY by the Federal Assembly. Although widely expected to act as a figurehead for the Milosevic regime, Cosic soon demonstrated his discomfort with the FRY's status as a pariah state. His Prime Minister Milan Panic attempted to stop the war in Bosnia-Hercegovina and to dislodge Milosevic. Despite his popularity, Cosic was removed from office in June 1993 for exceeding his constitutional powers, notably by conducting foreign policy without the approval of the federal parliament.

Ratko **Mladic** (b. 1943). Commander of Bosnian Serb forces during the Bosnian war. Mladic was born in south-eastern Bosnia; his partisan father was killed in a clash with the *Ustasa*. As commander of the Knin garrison of the JNA from summer 1991, he established his Serb nationalist credentials in playing a key role in the ejection of Croatian forces and civilians from the *Krajina*, during which "ethnic cleansing" was deployed for the first time in the war. Mladic was appointed JNA commander in Bosnia-Hercegovina in May 1992, after the army's formal withdrawal; he went on to become commander of the Bosnian Serb Army. Mladic supervised a war of the utmost brutality against the poorly armed Muslims and became a politically powerful figure. Despite sharing his aims, Serb leaders cynically distanced themselves from him; Karadzic even described him as mad. Undeterred, Mladic personally supervised the infamous assault on Srebrenica in summer 1995. When the Bosnian Serb defences crumbled later that year, Mladic was in hospital, thus preserving part of his reputation; Karadzic's attempts to dismiss him were foiled by a rebellion among the Bosnian Serb general staff. As part of the Dayton peace agreement, Mladic was to be barred from holding senior political office, and faced eventual arrest and trial for crimes against humanity at the UN War Crime Tribunal in the Hague.

Radovan **Karadzic** (b. 1945). Bosnian Serb leader from 1990, elected as "President" of the *Republika Srpska* by its assembly in December 1992. Born in Montenegro, Karadzic moved to Sarajevo as a teenager, and subsequently became a psychiatrist. His status as a protege of Dobrica Cosic helped him to the leadership of the Serbian Democratic Party (SDS) in July 1990. He played a key role in the outbreak of war in Bosnia-Hercegovina, warning that a declaration of Bosnian sovereignty could result in the annihilation of the Bosnian Muslims. Karadzic argued that the Muslims wanted to establish an Islamic state and that the Croats were Ustasa bent on genocide of the Serbs. Karadzic repeatedly denied responsibility for ethnic cleansing, even claiming that Muslims were the principal perpetrators of war crimes. In July 1995 UN War Crimes Tribunal in The Hague charged Karadzic with genocide and crimes against humanity and issued international warrants for his arrest. Milosevic's concession of Sarajevo to Bosnian Government control as part of the Dayton peace agreement neutralised Karadzic's power base. Dayton also barred Karadzic from holding senior political office.

Alija **Izetbegovic** (b 1925). President of Bosnia-Hercegovina from 1990 and leader of the SDA. Izetbegovic was a veteran Muslim nationalist who, as a member of the nationalist *Mladi Muslimani* (Young Muslims), was arrested and jailed in a crackdown by the Partisans in the 1940s, in which a number of his colleagues were executed.

Throughout the post-war period, as Izetbegovic became a lawyer and intellectual, he was under police surveillance. In 1973 he wrote the Islamic Declaration, which appeared to call for a Muslim state, although rejecting the use of violence for this end. Ten years later, amid a new wave of repression by a Bosnian regime rendered insecure by the death of Tito, Izetbegovic was convicted of counter-revolution and conspiring to create a Muslim state; he served five years of a 14-year prison sentence. In July 1989 Izetbegovic explicitly rejected the notion of a Bosnian Islamic state as unrealistic, because of the ethnically mixed character of the republic. Izetbegovic was the only president of a Yugoslav republic elected in 1990 not to have been a communist. He was temperamentally ill-suited to his role as a war leader, initially bewildered by the brutality of the conflict, but impressed observers with his sincerity, dignity and lack of vanity. He made peace with the Serbs in 1995 against the advice of his military leaders, who had urged a complete victory over the Bosnian Serbs.

Franjo **Tudjman** (b. 1922). President of Croatia since 1990. Tudjman served with distinction in the communist partisans and initially pursued a military career, reaching the rank of general at a remarkably young age. He entered the postwar communist government, but his support for Croatian nationalism led to his dismissal as Political Commissar in 1967 and to terms in prison in the 1970s and 1980s. During this time, Tudjman established himself as a historian. His controversial *Wastelands of Historical Reality* celebrated the wartime *Ustasa* regime for achieving statehood for Croatia and claimed that *Ustasa* crimes were grossly exaggerated by communist propagandists. Despite his dissident status, Tudjman was permitted foreign travel and in the 1980s became the effective leader of the nationalist opposition among the wealthy emigre communities who later bankrolled the 1990 election campaign. In power, Tudjman moved quickly toward Croatian independence. He was reelected as president in 1992, thereafter establishing an increasingly authoritarian regime, with a Tito-like cult of personality attaching to himself. The sweeping military gains of 1995, when the rebel Serb forces of the Krajina were heavily defeated and Croatian troops advanced with their Muslim allies in Bosnia, brought him another decisive election victory in October 1995. By the end of 1995, Tudjman had established Croatia as a regional power to counterbalance an emerging Greater Serbia.

Milan **Kucan** (b. 1941). The Slovene President from 1990, Kucan had been a reformist leader of the Slovene League of Communists (ZSK) since 1986. A pragmatic, prudent leader, Kucan was not an instinctive nationalist, but concluded in November 1988 that the revival of Serb nationalism spelt the end of Yugoslavia. Kucan was behind the reforms of the ZSK in 1989. He was elected president in April 1990, soon renouncing ZSK membership to stand above party politics, and was instrumental in preparing Slovenia for the independence declaration of 1991. Kucan acquiesced in the covert re-arming of his country and when the time came, he led Slovenia decisively into war with the JNA. He portrayed Slovenia as the diminutive but plucky victim of aggression by a neighbouring bully, deliberately recalling the example of Czechoslovakia in 1968. Following independence Kucan's popularity as the leader of one of the Central and Eastern Europe's most stable and prosperous states was confirmed with his convincing re-election in 1992 for a five-year term. By December 1994 Kucan was proclaiming that Slovenia had "no problems and no enemies".

Kiro **Gligorov** (b. 1917). Macedonian President since January 1991. The popular Gligorov was convincingly re-elected in direct polls in 1994. As a veteran of the communist era, Gligorov was associated with the Titoist policy to cultivate a distinct Macedonian nationality. Gligorov's principal achievement as Macedonia's president was to retain domestic and foreign support during the long dispute with Greece, despite the growing economic crisis. Although Gligorov made a show of clinging defiantly to the republic's name and symbols, he frequently signalled his willingness to compromise, a major factor in obtaining the eventual settlement with Greece in 1995. Gligorov paid the price for this flexibility in the form of serious injuries sustained in an assassination attempt.

POLITICAL PARTIES

The **Communist Party of Yugoslavia**, which from 1952 was named the **League of Communists of Yugoslavia** (SKJ), was originally organised in 1919. As the only party to appeal above ethnic or regional loyalties, the party emerged as the third strongest in the 1920 parliamentary elections. The following year it was banned after an assassination plot against the Prince Regent Alexander. When the party launched its People's Liberation Struggle against the occupying Axis powers in June 1941, under the leadership of Josip Broz Tito, it was an orthodox Stalinist organisation. The communist army, the Partisans, nevertheless won British support for its ferocious campaign against the Nazis. The Partisans also engaged in a ruthless civil war against the Serb nationalist Chetnik movement. Its status as a supranational Yugoslavist party won it widespread support among a war-weary population. By 1948 the Yugoslav party had been expelled from the Cominform for "nationalist deviation" and the rift with the Soviets deepened with the elaboration of Titoism to include workers' self-management and other reforms. The SKJ's leaders, particularly Tito and Edward Kardelj, demonstrated a remarkable facility for constitutional innovation to meet the difficulties posed by the centrifugal tendencies of the federation. The party was severely weakened by the death of both leaders in 1979-80. It effectively disintegrated at its Extraordinary 14th Congress in January 1990, when the Slovene delegation walked out; by 1991 the SKJ had effectively broken up into republican leftist parties, notably the Serbian SPS. The SKJ's federalist successor parties, including the JNA-dominated **League of Communists-Movement for Yugoslavia** (SK-PJ) and the **Alliance of Yugoslav Reform Forces** (SKRJ, led by Ante Markovic), were heavily defeated by nationalist and republican parties in the republican elections of 1990.

The **Socialist Party of Serbia** (SPS) was established in July 1990 as the successor to the League of Communist of Serbia (SKS). Led by Serbian President Slobodan Milosevic, it won an overwhelming majority in republican elections in 1990 and repeated its success in the 1992 and 1993 Serbian and federal elections, due to its exceptional skill in adopting a nationalist agenda. The party leadership was nevertheless careful to allow other parties to form the nationalist vanguard, thus allowing itself to retreat to the centre when expedient; thus a temporary ally, the SRS, was by 1993 exposed as extremist, while the SPS posed as moderate. By 1995 the SPS leadership, with one eye on "winning the peace", had returned to the politics of the left. Milosevic, however, had by now distanced himself from the party, appearing to favour the **Yugoslav United Left** party led by his wife, Mirjana Markovic.

The **Serbian Democratic Movement** or **Depos** was an opposition coalition formed in May 1992. Its controversial leader Vuk Draskovic was also leader of a principal constituent member of Depos, the **Serbian Renewal Movement** (SPO). Depos and its demagogic leader initially attempted to mobilise mass opposition to the Milosevic regime by adopting a dovish stance and calling for democratic reforms. Despite large demonstrations in Belgrade and other urban centres, Depos failed to achieve wide popularity in the provinces. Depos was extremely divided, and the internal contradictions within it proved its undoing. Having posed as a democrat and a peacemaker, by 1994 Draskovic had become a belligerent nationalist strong-man. In September 1994 two senior leaders of Depos, Vlad Gajic and Mihajlo Markovic, resigned in protest at Draskovic's contempt for the party's "code of practice and democratic principles". Depos's attempts to manoeuvre itself into an electorally profitable position discredited the bloc, and even during Serbia's economic crisis Depos failed to make up significant electoral ground.

The **Serbian Radical Party** (SRS) was an ultra-nationalist formation which had become Serbia's second largest party by 1992. Its military wing, the Chetniks, was responsible for some of the worst atrocities of the wars in Croatia and Bosnia-Hercegovina. Led by Vojislav Seselj, the SRS backed the creation of a Greater Serbia through ferocious tactics and defended Serbian expansionism with a creed based on chauvinistic peasant values. In 1992-3 Milosevic used the SRS in an unholy parliamentary alliance to help him depose FRY President Cosic, but then launched a campaign to discredit the SRS. Prior to the 1993 elections, he published the first press allegations of Chetnik war crimes, and backed a rival ultra-right wing group, the **Serbian Unity Party** (SSJ). Despite these tactics, the SRS performed surprisingly well to retain 39 seats in the Serbian legislature. Seselj was jailed in September 1994 after a series of violent altercations in the Serbian legislature, following which several deputies broke away to form the SRS-Nikola Pasic.

ELECTIONS

Serbian legislative elections

	9-23 Dec 1990	20 Dec 1992	20 Dec 1993
SPS	194	101	123
SRS	-	73	39
SPO	19#	-*	-*
Depos	-	49**	45
DZVM	8#	9	5
DS	7#	7	29
DSS	-	-	7
Others	22	11+	2
Total	250	250	250

\# Competing as United Opposition bloc
* Competing as Depos member
** Including DSS
+ Of which five were members of the Group of Citizens of Kosovo-Metohija

SPS=Serbian Socialist Party; SRS= Serbian Radical Party; SPO= Serbian Renewal Movement; Depos=14 party coalition including the SPO and DSS; DZVM=Democratic Community of Vojvodina Hungarians; DS=Democratic Party; DSS=Democratic Party of Serbia

The results of republican elections in Montenegro in 1990 and 1992, and of elections to the FRY legislature in 1992 and 1993, are not reproduced here, nor are the Serbian elections of 31 May 1992 which were boycotted by the opposition, allowing the SPS to win an artificially high share of the vote.

Serbian presidential elections

Slobodan Milosevic of the SPS was elected president of Serbia in 1989 by the Serbian republican legislature. He received his first popular mandate in the first round of presidential elections in December 1990, winning 64.34 per cent of the vote against 20 per cent for Vuk Draskovic. Milosevic was re-elected on 20 December 1992, with 56.3 per cent of the vote; his nearest rival was Milan Panic, with 34.0 per cent.

CHRONOLOGY

1389. Serbia suffers a major defeat by the Ottoman Empire in the Battle of the Field of the Black Crows at Kosovo. Serbia eventually succumbs to Ottoman rule in 1459.

1526. The Ottomans drive the Austro-Hungarian Empire from most of Croatia.

1699. Croatia re-joins the Austro-Hungarian Empire.

1878. The Congress of Berlin recognises Serbia and Montenegro as independent states (Serbia having enjoyed autonomy within the Ottoman Empire since 1815).

28 June 1914. The First World War begins with the assassination in Sarajevo of Archduke Ferdinand of Austria by Gavril Princip, a supporter of a South Slav state. The conflict exacts a withering toll on the Serbs; in their war against the central powers, they suffer greater per capita losses than any other single country at some 20 per cent of the population.

1 December 1918. Foundation of the Yugoslav state as the Kingdom of Serbs, Croats and Slovenes, a state five times the size of pre-war Serbia.

28 June 1921. The Vidovdan constitution establishes a unitary state under the Serb Royal house. Croatian Peasant Party leader Stijepan Radic leads protests at the absence of decentralisation or federalisation.

2 August 1921. The communist party is banned after an assassination plot against Prince-Regent Alexander.

18 March 1923. Elections are conducted by universal male suffrage. Serbian deputies win a majority. Radic's Croatian Peasant Party takes nearly 22 per cent of the vote.

March 1925. Whilst in prison, Radic formally abandons demands for Croatian independence.

July 1925 to January 1927. The Serbian Radicals form a coalition with the Croatian Peasant Party, in a short-lived experiment in joint rule by Croats and Serbs.

20 June 1928. Radic is one of three Croat deputies fatally wounded in the parliament by a Serb Radical deputy. Croat deputies subsequently boycott the parliament.

July 1928. Despairing of the Yugoslav ideal, the King offers the Croats secession, but the offer is refused by Croat leaders, who fear Italian and Hungarian irredentism.

6 January 1929. King Alexander dissolves parliament and suspends the 1921 constitution, instituting a royal dictatorship. Trade unions and ethnically- and regionally-based parties are banned. No senior Croat or Slovene leader is included in the regime.

January 1929. Ante Pavelic founds the Croat right-radical *Ustasa* ("Insurgency") movement with covert Italian and Hungarian support. The *Ustasa* and the Internal Macedonian Revolutionary Organisation (VMRO) launch a terror campaign against the regime.

3 October 1929. The country is formally renamed as the Kingdom of Yugoslavia.

9 October 1934. King Alexander is assassinated in Marseilles by Croat fascists and Macedonian extremists. The new King Peter being just 11 years old, royal powers are exercised by Paul, the new Prince Regent.

1937-39. The regime of prime minister Milan Stojadinovic shows increasingly dictatorial tendencies and adopts fascist trappings; Yugoslavia establishes close economic and diplomatic relationships with Nazi Germany and fascist Italy.

6 February 1939. Stojadinovic is dismissed by Prince Paul and replaced with Dragisa Cvetkovic.

26 August 1939. Cvetkovic strikes a major constitutional deal with the Croats, the *Sporazum*, creating a consolidated Croatian *banovina* (administrative unit) comprising 30 per cent of Yugoslavia's territory and population. Institutionally the *banovina* is to be virtually separate, responsible only to the monarch; Belgrade retains responsibility only for Croatia's defence, foreign affairs, and communications policies.

25 March to 6 April 1941. Under overwhelming pressure, Yugoslavia joins the Tripartite pact, provoking a military coup, whereupon Axis forces invade Yugoslavia.

10 April 1941. The *Ustasa* declares the Independent State of Croatia (NDH), a clerical fascist regime under Nazi patronage and controlling much of Bosnia-Hercegovina; the NDH is the first (nominally) independent Croatian state. The *Ustasa* launches a genocidal campaign against the Serb community. Most of Slovenia is annexed to the German *Reich* and the rump of Serbia is occupied by German forces.

June 1941. The communist Partisan army under the leadership of Josip Broz Tito launches the People's Liberation Struggle, against the occupying Axis powers and against the rival Yugoslav Army of the Fatherland, better known as the Chetniks, a Serb nationalist and royalist movement led by Draza Mihailovic.

29 November 1943. The Partisans proclaim their own government in areas they control.

March 1945. Formation of a Government of National Unity with Tito as Prime Minister.

11 November 1945. Elections to a Provisional Assembly are won by the communists.

29 November 1945. Proclamation of the Federal Republic of Yugoslavia; abolition of the monarchy. The government subsequently displays classic Stalinist strategy in launching a programme of rapid industrialisation and agricultural collectivisation.

March 1946. Mihailovic is convicted of collaboration with the German occupiers and is subsequently executed, the most prominent victim of a purge of rival political leaders.

January 1946. A new, Soviet-type constitution establishes a federation comprising six republics; Bosnia-Hercegovina, Croatia, Macedonia, Montenegro, Serbia and Slovenia. Each is to have its own republican communist party.

June 1948. The rift with the Soviet Union begins: the Cominform, meeting in Budapest, denounces Titoism as a nationalist deviation and expels Yugoslavia.

June 1950. Workers' councils are established in industry, the first step in "workers' self-management".

May 1951. New measures allow farmers to sell produce on the free market.

November 1952. The Sixth Congress of the Yugoslav Communist Party changes its name to the League of Communists of Yugoslavia (SKJ) and declares that "the [SKJ] is not and cannot be the direct operative manager and commander in economic, state or social life"; accordingly, the congress further decentralises economic decision-taking and devolves more power to the workers' councils.

14 January 1953. Tito is elected as President of Yugoslavia.

1955-6. Despite progress in summer 1955 towards a Soviet-Yugoslav rapprochement, including a visit by Khrushchev to Belgrade, relations again deteriorate in 1956, when the "Yugoslav model" becomes a focus of attention for pro-reform and anti-Soviet demonstrators in Poland and Hungary. Tito condemns the Soviet invasion of Hungary.

August 1957. Milovan Djilas, Tito's former number two, publishes *The New Class*, in which he argues that Yugoslav socialism is creating powerful and self-serving elites among party cadres and managers. By October Djilas has been sentenced to seven years in prison for propaganda.

1961. Belgrade hosts the first conference of the Non-Aligned Movement. Constitutional changes allow Muslims to identify themselves as members of a distinct national group in census returns.

April 1963. A new constitution re-titles the country the Socialist Federal Republic of Yugoslavia (SFRY), bolsters judicial independence, and introduces limited choice in some elections.

1969-71. The Croatian Spring: a faction of the Croatian communist leadership, Maspok (*Masorni Pokret* or "mass movement") experiments in reform communism and moderate nationalism, to the consternation of conservative Serbs in the republic. Tito brings a halt to the process with a purge of the Croatian leadership.

July 1971. In an attempt to ensure equal representation for Yugoslavia's principal ethnic groups, Tito introduces a system of collective leadership under which senior federal posts are to rotate between officials from each of the republics.

February 1974. The promulgation of the fourth constitution since the war is an attempt to address fears of Serb domination following the Croatian Spring. The constitution allows each of the six republics to establish its own central bank, police force, judiciary and education system. The two provinces within Serbia, Vojvodina and Kosovo, are given the same powers, and awarded seats in the federal collective presidency; Serbia thus has only one vote on an eight-member collective presidency. The constitution also introduces further economic decentralisation, increasing the powers of workers' councils and in practice encouraging economic autarky in the larger republics.

4 May 1980. Tito dies. Chairmanship or "Presidency" of the federal collective Presidency thenceforth rotates annually between representatives of each republic.

March-April 1981. Widespread unrest among ethnic Albanians demanding republican status for Kosovo; several people are killed and a state of emergency is declared.

24 September 1986. Publication of a sensational document subsequently regarded as a manifesto for Serbian nationalism: the *Memorandum of the Serbian Academy of Sciences and Arts*. The document warns of the country's coming disintegration, claiming that Serbs face political and economic discrimination by Croats and Slovenes

and that the Serbs of Kosovo face genocide. Dobrica Cosic, a Serb nationalist writer, is widely regarded as the Memorandum's author.

24 April 1987. Slobodan Milosevic, leader of the Serbian League of Communists (SKS). establishes himself as a Serb nationalist hero during a visit to Kosovo.

14 December 1987. Dismissal of Ivan Stambolic as Serbian President after intrigues against him by his former friend Milosevic.

March 1989. A new federal government takes office under Ante Markovic and concentrates on the country's economic crisis, especially its persisting hyper-inflation.

28 March 1989. Adoption of a new Serbian constitution; the autonomous status of Serbia's two provinces, Vojvodina and Kosovo, is effectively abolished. The move gives Serbia direct control of the provinces' seats in the eight-strong federal collective presidency; with the support of loyal Montenegro, Serbia can now command half the seats on that body. In Kosovo 22 civilians and two policemen are killed during protests against the changes.

May 1989. Slobodan Milosevic becomes Serbian President.

28 June 1989. Milosevic tells one million Serbs, gathered in Kosovo to mark the 600th anniversary of the Battle of the Field of Black Crows: "Six centuries later again we [Serbs] are in battles and quarrels. They are not armed battles, though such things cannot be excluded yet." The address is another key moment in the re-awakening of Serbian nationalism.

27 September 1989. The Assembly in Slovenia approves constitutional changes which include the republic's right, as an "independent, sovereign and autonomous state", to secede from Yugoslavia.

December 1989. The assemblies of Slovenia and Croatia legalise opposition parties and call multi-party elections for spring 1990.

20-23 January 1990. The federal League of Communists of Yugoslavia (SKJ) convenes for its 14th extraordinary congress, gives up its monopoly on power, and approves a multi-party system. However the Slovene delegation walks out when the congress rejects its proposals for further devolution to the republics, and the federal party subsequently withers away.

8 April 1990. Yugoslavia's first multi-party elections for more than four decades are held in Slovenia; they are won by the centre-right DEMOS coalition. Milan Kucan, the popular reformist leader of the Slovene League of Communists (renamed ZSK-Party of Democratic Renewal), is elected as Slovene President on 22 April.

22 April-7 May 1990. Croatian multi-party elections: victory for the nationalist Croatian Democratic Community (HDZ); on 30 May the Croatian parliament elects Franjo Tudjman, leader of the HDZ, as President.

2 July 1990. The Slovene parliament formally proclaims Slovene sovereignty.

November-December 1990. Multi-party elections in Bosnia-Hercegovina, Macedonia, Montenegro, and finally Serbia, complete the process begun with spring polls in Slovenia and Croatia. Nationalist victories in Bosnia-Hercegovina and Macedonia confirm the trend towards disintegration of the federal state. Serbia returns the incumbent hardline President Milosevic with a large majority and Montenegro likewise elects a communist president and a communist-dominated assembly.

21 December 1990. The Croatian Assembly promulgates the republic's new constitution, including the assertion of Croatia's sovereignty and right to secede.

9 January 1991. The Federal Presidency orders the Slovene and Croatian territorial defence forces to surrender their arms within ten days. The Yugoslav People's Army (JNA) is placed on alert on 23 January to enforce the order, but on 25 January the federal presidency backs down from a military confrontation with Croatia and Slovenia, despite heavy pressure from the JNA, and televised evidence of Croatia's arms procurement programme.

25 January 1991. The Macedonian assembly declares the republic's sovereignty and right to secede.

March 1991. The war in Croatia begins with an assault by Croatian Serb irregulars on the Croatian police station at Plitvice.

9 March 1991. Milosevic orders tanks into Belgrade to crush pro-democracy demonstrations.

16 March 1991. Milosevic declares that "Yugoslavia is dead", renounces the authority of the federal presidency, and orders a general mobilisation. The Krajina Serbs declare independence from Croatia; on 18 March Milosevic tells a student meeting that his objective is to create a state for all Serbs.

23 March 1991. Milosevic and Tudjman meet secretly at Karadjordjevo to discuss the partition of Bosnia-Hercegovina.

15 May 1991. Serbia effectively vetoes the election of Croat Stipe Mesic as president of the collective state presidency, in defiance of the principle of annual rotation between representatives of the constituent republics.

19 May 1991. A referendum in Croatia records a 94 per cent majority for independence, but in the Serb-inhabited areas, where unrest and violence are increasing, a vote the previous week has called for separation from Croatia and union with Serbia. (A similar referendum in Slovenia on 21 December had also approved independence.)

25 June 1991. Croatia and Slovenia proclaim their independence and "dissociation" from the Yugoslav federation.

25 June - 4 July 1991. The ten-day war in Slovenia; the JNA attempts to take control of the republic in the name of securing Yugoslavia's borders, and is humiliated by Slovene defenders. A ceasefire is declared on 4 July, with the official death toll at 67. A troika of EC foreign ministers persuades Croatia and Slovenia to make the gesture of postponing for three months their declarations of independence.

18 July 1991. The Federal Presidency agrees to withdraw the JNA for a "temporary" period within three months; the agreement is an effective recognition of Slovene secession.

22-31 July 1991. Widespread Croat-Serb violence breaks out in Croatia, Croatian Serb irregulars are supported by JNA units in running battles with Croat security forces.

26 August 1991. The ethnically Croat village of Kijevo in Serb-held Croatia is the first town to fall victim to "ethnic cleansing" in the war, as Croatian Serb irregulars backed by JNA artillery drive the town's Croat minority from their homes.

7 September 1991. An EC-sponsored peace conference, chaired by former UK foreign secretary Lord Carrington, opens in the Hague.

14 September 1991. JNA barracks in Croatia are surrounded by Croatian militia. Croatian Serb irregulars, backed by JNA heavy artillery, begin their assault on the strategic town of Vukovar in eastern Slavonia.

15 September 1991. Macedonia declares independence, one week after a referendum in which 95 per cent back secession.

25 September 1991. The UN Security Council imposes an embargo on arms sales to Yugoslavia.

15 October 1991. The parliament of Bosnia-Hercegovina declares the sovereignty of the republic, clearly a prelude to the declaration of independence. Ethnic Serb deputies walk out.

18 November 1991. The fall of Vukovar to Serb forces, who murder hundreds of captured Croat men.

23 December 1991. Germany recognises Croatian and Slovene independence.

2 January 1992. The 15th ceasefire, but the first to hold, between Croatia and the Federal authorities.

8 January 1992. The UN Security Council authorises the deployment in Croatia of a force of 10,000 UN peacekeepers; the Serb-held areas, known as the Krajina, are to become a demilitarised zone patrolled by the peacekeepers. The first Unprofor troops arrive on 19 March 1992.

15 January 1992. The EC recognises Slovene and Croatian independence, despite the fact that Croatia's minority rights provision does not meet the EC's own criteria. Germany has forced through recognition despite the opposition of the UK and the Netherlands. Bosnia-Hercegovina's application for recognition fails; Macedonia's is vetoed by Greece.

12 February 1992. Serbian and Montenegrin officials meeting in Titograd agree to remain within "a common state which would be the continuation of Yugoslavia".

26 March 1992. JNA forces withdraw from Macedonia.

4 April 1992. The Croatian Serbs' National Council establishes the Republic of Serbian Krajina (RSK), comprising 30 per cent of Croatian territory.

5-6 April 1992. The civil war in Bosnia-Hercegovina begins as Serb paramilitaries open fire on peace demonstrators in Sarajevo. The JNA denies involvement.

6-7 April 1992. EC states and the USA formally recognise the independence of Bosnia-Hercegovina.

27 April 1992. The Federal Republic of Yugoslavia (FRY, comprising the republics of Serbia and Montenegro) comes into existence with the passage of a new constitution by the Yugoslav Federal Assembly. The new federal entity comprises a presidency, government and legislature.

4 May 1992. The FRY Presidency orders the formal withdrawal of the JNA from Bosnia-Hercegovina. However, some 80,000 JNA soldiers who hold Bosnian or other citizenship remain; although formally no longer under federal command, they continue to be paid by the federal authorities. On 20 May the Bosnian Government declares the remaining JNA troops in Bosnia-Hercegovina an "occupying force" and announces plans to form a Bosnian Army.

22 May 1992. Bosnia-Hercegovina, Croatia and Slovenia become UN members.

24 May 1992. Elections in Kosovo, declared illegal by Belgrade, are won by the Democratic Alliance of Kosovo (DSK), whose leader Ibrahim Rugova is elected President. Rugova advocates non-violent protest.

31 May 1992. The SPS wins a comfortable majority in Serbian elections, due in part to an opposition boycott of the poll. On the day of the elections, tens of thousands rally in Belgrade in anti-war demonstrations organised by the opposition.

1 June 1992. UN-imposed economic sanctions come into effect in the FRY; later in June petrol rationing is introduced.

15 June 1992. Dobrica Cosic is elected as President of the FRY by the Federal Assembly.

23 June 1992. Serbian police close the Kosovar parliament.

14 July 1992. Milan Panic, a Serbian-born US businessman, is elected as FRY Prime Minister in a "government of experts".

10 August 1992. In the first official visit to Albania by a senior Yugoslav leader since 1948, Panic announces plans to lift the state of emergency in Kosovo.

26-7 August 1992. At the London Conference, Panic prevents Milosevic from speaking and offers to demilitarise Bosnia-Hercegovina, facilitate the provision of aid, and allow the deployment of UN observers on the Serbian-Bosnian border to verify allegations of Serbian support for the Bosnian Serb rebels.

3 September 1992. Opening of the Permanent Conference on Yugoslavia in Geneva by Cyrus Vance and Lord Owen, the mediators respectively of the UN and the EC.

16 September 1992. The Bosnian Serb parliament backs union with the FRY.

20 December 1992. Panic is defeated by Milosevic in early Serbian presidential elections; the incumbent wins 56 per cent of the vote. In simultaneous elections to the Serbian and Federal legislatures gains are made by Milosevic's SPS and the ultra-nationalist SRS.

10 February 1993. Nikola Sainovic forms a Serbian cabinet supported by a new SPS-SRS alliance.

28 February 1993. Amid continuing reports of ethnic cleansing in Kosovo, US President Bill Clinton warns that "the USA is ready to send a military force against the Serbs in Kosovo and further afield in Serbia".

2 March 1993. Radoje Kontic, a Montenegrin, forms a new federal government, restoring the hardline Serb nationalist Vladislav Jovanovic to the Foreign Affairs portfolio.

25-6 April 1993. The Bosnian Serb assembly rejects the Vance-Owen peace plan for Bosnia-Hercegovina, despite strong pressure from Serbia-FRY.

17 April 1993. The UN Security Council approves further UN sanctions against the FRY, effective from 27 April. They include tougher controls on vessels entering FRY waterways or ports and a ban on the provision of all but essential food, medicine and other humanitarian goods and services.

28 April 1993. Serbia's parliament approves the Vance-Owen plan.

1 June 1993. Cosic is removed from office for having exceeded his powers.

2 June 1993. Opposition demonstrations in Belgrade lead to the death of one police officer; Draskovic is arrested, severely beaten and incarcerated. He begins a hunger strike which leads to his release on 9 July.

25 June 1993. Milosevic's grip on the FRY tightens with the appointment of his close ally Zoran Lilic as the FRY's new President.

2 September 1993. The SRS withdraws support from the Serbian government.

4-5 November 1993. 40 members of the SRS paramilitary wing, the Chetniks, are arrested; detailed allegations of Chetnik atrocities in Bosnia-Hercegovina and Croatia appear in the Serbian press for the first time.

19 December 1993. The SPS wins early Serbian elections, despite the economic crisis and hyperinflation, but narrowly fails to secure an overall majority. Opposition parties fare poorly despite a dramatic move to the nationalist right, exemplified in Draskovic's call for the annexation of Bosnian Muslim areas including Mostar and Sarajevo,. The SRS defeats the challenge of an ultra-nationalist rival Serbian Unity Party (SSJ), the party of war criminal Zeljko Raznjatovic.

19 January 1994. Jovanovic and Tudjman sign a joint declaration on normalising FY-Croatian relations; Bosnian Croat leader Milan Boban and Bosnian Serb leader Radovan Karadzic sign a parallel document.

24 January 1994. The FRY introduces a new currency, the new dinar or "super dinar", in a successful bid to conquer hyperinflation.

17 March 1994. Appointment of Serbian "Cabinet of Economists" under Mirko Marjanovic.

18 March 1994. The Washington Accords: the renewal of the Muslim-Croat alliance in Bosnia-Hercegovina is a dramatic U-turn for Tudjman, who has previously supported the partition of Bosnia-Hercegovina. This represents a turning of the tide in the Bosnian war.

5 August 1994. Serbia imposes an economic blockade against the Bosnian Serbs; only humanitarian supplies of food and medicine are to be allowed to cross the Serbian-Bosnian border. The blockade is Milosevic's retaliation for the "senseless and absurd" Bosnian Serb rejection of the Contact Group peace plan (see Bosnia chronology).

14 September 1994. The FRY government approves the deployment of international observers on its borders with Bosnia-Hercegovina.

5 October 1994. UN observers having accepted the authenticity of the FRY blockade of the Bosnian Serbs, some sanctions are lifted for a trial period: Belgrade airport is reopened for international flights, the port of Bar to maritime traffic, and sporting and cultural links are resumed.

11 July 1995. Srebrenica in eastern Bosnia, a UN-designated "Safe Area" which is of critical strategic importance in the security of a Greater Serbia, falls to the Bosnian Serbs.

4-6 August 1995. Operation Storm: the RSK falls to Croatian forces, driving some 150,000 Serbs from Croatia; Milosevic refuses to intervene.

30 August 1995. The Bosnian Serbs agree to join a combined Serb delegation headed by Milosevic in peace talks.

30 August - 14 September 1995. Operation Deliberate Force: a massive campaign of NATO air strikes against Bosnian Serb military and communications targets.

8 September 1995. The FRY, Croatia and Bosnia-Hercegovina achieve an "agreement on basic principles" toward settling the conflict.

18 September 1995. Bosnian Serb forces crumble before a joint offensive by Croatian, Bosnian Croat and Bosnian Government forces.

12 October 1995. A 60-day ceasefire takes effect in Bosnia-Hercegovina, and is subsequently extended.

1 November 1995. Peace talks open at the Dayton air base in Ohio.

21 November 1995. The leaders of the warring parties initial the Dayton peace agreement.

22 November 1995. The UN Security Council suspends all sanctions on the FRY. It also votes to end the arms embargo against the former Yugoslavia in stages, commencing in 1996.

14 December 1995. Formal signature of the Dayton accords at a ceremony in Paris.

CROATIA

Croatia proclaimed independence in June 1991. It won recognition as an independent state from the EC in January 1992 and from the USA in April 1992, and was admitted to the UN in May 1992.

Croatia consists of a northern band of territory (Slavonia, extending from below the Slovene alps in the west to the River Danube in the east), which is connected by a narrow hinge of land to a southern strip of coastal territory (Dalmatia, which tapers gradually from its widest point, below the Istrian peninsula in the north, to Montenegro in the south). Off the coast lies an archipelago comprising dozens of islands.

Croatia shares land borders with Slovenia, Hungary, Serbia and Montenegro, but by far the longest is with Bosnia-Hercegovina. Croatia's land area of 56,538 sq. km. makes it somewhat larger than Bosnia-Hercegovina but still among the smallest of East-Central European states.

Croatia's population in 1991 was 4,760,300, of whom 900,000 lived in the capital Zagreb. Other major cities are the ports of Rijeka and Split, the Dalmatian capital; the historic city of Dubrovnik lies at the southernmost reach of Dalmatia. Ethnically, in 1991 Croatia was 77.9 per cent Croat, with a community of 500-600,000 Serbs forming 12.2 per cent of the whole. Many Serbs lived in urban areas, particularly Zagreb; others were spread through rural areas in the hinterland beyond Croatia's coastline. Since the last census in 1991 war has wrought major demographic changes, including an influx of Bosnian Croats and Bosnian Muslims fleeing the conflict in their republic, and an exodus of Serbs, leaving only about 100,000.

HISTORICAL NARRATIVE

Croatia was part of Austria-Hungary for most of the nine centuries before the creation of Yugoslavia in 1918. As a result the Croats were primarily influenced by Germanic and Italian cultures. Despite the linguistic similarities, the legacy of the separate development of Croats and Serbs under different empires gave rise to religious, cultural and social factors which divided the two peoples. In keeping with the religious practice of Austria-Hungary, Croatia was overwhelmingly Roman Catholic.

Serbs had settled in numbers in Croatia centuries before, many having been driven north and west by the invading Ottoman armies. Their settlements occupied the front line between Austria-Hungary and the Ottoman Empire; one area known as the *Krajina* ("borderlands") was the site of a cluster of such settlements. The Croatian Serbs developed a reputation as fierce defenders of Christian orthodoxy from the Islamic hordes, and were employed in large numbers as soldiers in the Austro-Hungarian army. After the withdrawal of Ottoman forces, the Serb settlements remained, now as ethnically isolated pockets many miles from major concentrations of fellow Serbs. The Serbs' distinct ethnic identity was not assimilated by the majority Croat community; indeed there remained remarkable contrasts even as Yugoslavia entered the Second World War.

The Krajina Serbs' first experience of a nominally independent Croatia was a catastrophic one. The *Ustasa* regime of 1941-5 launched a genocidal campaign against their "inferior" Serb cousins, in which one third of Serbs were to be liquidated, one third expelled and one third compulsorily converted to Catholicism. The Krajina Serbs who survived this onslaught became pathologically suspicious of Croatian nationalism, regarding any revival of it as fascist and necessarily anti-Serb. Despite the apparently peaceful co-existence of the communist era, when the Croatian Spring reached its peak in 1971 Serb conservatives successfully insisted on a tough crackdown on moderate Croatian nationalism.

The HDZ, the Croat nationalist movement formed in 1989, was portrayed by Krajina Serb propagandists as crypto-fascist, little more than a revived *Ustasa*. The HDZ merely confirmed this reputation with a series of crassly insensitive decisions in 1990-2: firstly, in failing to offer substantial minority rights guarantees to the Serbs, even abolishing their status as a constituent nation of Croatia; secondly, in reviving nationalist symbols which, whilst actually pre-dating World War II, were nevertheless associated in Serb minds with the *Ustasa* regime; and thirdly, in attempting to rewrite history to reassess the reputation of the *Ustasa* regime. The principal exponent of this revisionist history was Franjo Tudjman, HDZ leader and Croatia's president from 1990.

Despite the nationalist bluster of the hawks in the HDZ, and a secret armament programme, Croatia was ill-prepared for war when it broke out in summer 1991. Croatian Serb irregulars, with the direct assistance of JNA units and heavy artillery, were better organised; by early 1992, in fighting which cost up to 50,000 lives, they had established control over several areas known collectively as the Krajina (although Serb areas extended well beyond the historical Krajina area). The Republic of Serbian Krajina (RSK), declared in April 1992, comprised some 30 per cent of Croatia. In securing this territory, Serb forces drove some 500,000 Croats from their homes, practising the first "ethnic cleansing" of the war (although the term was not to enter common usage until 1992) and using appalling violence against Croat civilians at Kijevo, Vukovar and elsewhere. At the vanguard of Serb forces were several militias, including the notorious ultra-nationalist Tigers paramilitary group led by former Serbian intelligence agent Zeljko Raznjatovic (widely known by his *nom de guerre* "Arkan"). The Krajina Serb irregulars were reinforced by JNA units and backed by JNA heavy artillery, which often targeted civilian areas. Unsurprisingly the war provoked the growth of ethnic hatred in other parts of Croatia; in Zagreb the considerable Serb minority kept a low profile but many were dismissed from state jobs, expelled from state universities or evicted from state-owned homes.

The loss of the Krajina deprived Croatia of energy facilities and severed vital communications links, virtually cutting off the land link between Croatia's north and the Dalmatian coast in the south. Only the Bosnian Government foothold in the north-western Bosnian enclave of Bihac, a major route centre, prevented the whole of northern Bosnia-Hercegovina and Krajina from coming under Serb control.

Despite the military successes of the RSK, and JNA support in achieving them, there is evidence that even at an early stage Serbian President Milosevic regarded long-term Serbian military support for the Krajina as unviable, on the grounds that their communities were too distant from any defensible borders of a Greater Serbia.

Meanwhile hawks in the Croatian regime were increasing their influence. They believed in guaranteeing Croatian security through military means. They were therefore resolved not only to reclaim the Krajina but to annex parts of Bosnia-Hercegovina. Within the HDZ these hawks were known as the Hercegovina lobby and were led by Gojko Susak, the Defence Minister. Susak was instrumental in a military build-up which, despite the arms embargo against former Yugoslavia, gave Croatia the most organised, well-equipped and effective army in the region. There were persistent rumours of covert US and German military assistance.

Tudjman was sympathetic to the Hercegovina lobby. He was obsessed with his historical role as the founder of the first fully independent Croatia after the false dawn of the *Ustasa*'s Nazi client NDH. Restoring the new state's territorial integrity was his first priority. He therefore insisted on limiting the UN peacekeepers in Croatia, the UN Protection Force or Unprofor, to six-month mandates. During the 32 months before the Croatian offensive of Operation Storm in August 1995, Tudjman frequently engaged in sabre-rattling over Unprofor's failure to disarm rebel Serbs, insisting that the presence of peacekeepers in buffer zones would lead to an unacceptable Cyprus-style *de facto* partition of his republic. The Croatian Army also launched several exploratory operations against the RSK, the last and largest of which was Operation Lightning in May 1995, which was the first evidence that the Croatian Army had developed an overwhelming superiority over the RSK.

The most controversial policy outcome of Tudjman's flirtation with the Hercegovina lobby was war against the Bosnian Muslims until February 1994. This strategy, a disastrous failure, was born from Tudjman's grandiose ambition to create a Greater Croatia from the ruins of Bosnia-Hercegovina. Tudjman had discussed partition of the republic with Milosevic in secret talks from 1991.

Tudjman committed 30,000 regular Croatian Army troops to Bosnia-Hercegovina and publicly defended Croatia's "right" to intervene there. He eventually abandoned his tactics and made common cause with Bosnian Muslims, but only having caused immense damage in human and economic terms in Hercegovina. The volte face on Bosnia-Hercegovina was a tactical not a strategic change: a decision to use political rather than military means to achieve the same long term goal - a close relationship with Hercegovina (the exact outcome, be it annexation, suzerainty or condominium status being undefined). Progress on establishing the Muslim-Croat federation in Bosnia-Hercegovina was halting; plans for the Bosnian-Croatian confederation remained ill-defined.

Argument within the HDZ over the intervention in Bosnia-Hercegovina had caused serious divisions within the ruling party. When it was formed in 1989, the HDZ had included a spectrum of nationalist opinion from liberals to ultra-conservative Christian democrats, but over the years in government the right wing of the HDZ had become increasingly dominant. Democratisation stalled as the right-wing imposed an authoritarian regime. The press came under government control and the state broadcast media were dominated by the HDZ. A Tito-like cult of personality developed around Tudjman, whose every move was documented by the television news. He acquired smart military uniforms and many of Tito's former country retreats, including on the idyllic Adriatic island of Brioni. In 1995 he appointed his own son as chief of military intelligence.

The HDZ's rightward drift allowed it to eclipse the ultra-nationalist right and Dobroslav Paraga's *Ustasa*-style Party of Rights (HSP) was vigorously repressed. The strategy worked: Croatia was a right-wing country; the left had performed very poorly there in 1990 and had failed to recover. The strategy also allowed the HDZ to take on the regional parties which emerged after 1990, and which Tudjman darkly accused of centrifugalism. The regional press in Dalmatia and Istria was cajoled into pursuing Zagreb's line.

However, the rightward direction of government policy alienated the HDZ's centrists and liberals. In April 1994 the party's liberal wing, lead by the chairs of the parliament's two houses, Stipe Mesic and Josip Manolic, broke away to form the Croatian Independent Democrats (HND). They argued for democratisation, participatory reforms, economic liberalisation, and compromise in peace negotiations. The HND showed promisingly in opinion polls in 1994.

Meanwhile, the Krajina Serbs had become preoccupied with their own factional splits and were ill-prepared for the inevitable Croatian campaign which eventually came in August 1995. The Croatian Army demonstrated its new prowess in an operation praised by Western military commanders for its efficiency. Only eastern Slavonia remained in Serb hands.

The recapture of the Krajina drove 300,000 Serbs into Bosnia-Hercegovina and Serbia. There were many ugly clashes as tens of thousands of vengeful Croat returnees confronted departing Serb families. Elderly Serbs who remained in their homes were systematically murdered by Croatian troops and many Serb homes were razed to the ground. Whilst the Croatian government initially claimed that the Serbs were welcome to stay, Tudjman soon declared that those who had left could not all return.

The newly powerful Croatia appeared likely to dominate Bosnia-Hercegovina. The Croatian military played a key role in vanquishing the Bosnian Serbs in September 1995, and the decision to halt the Muslim-Croat northward advance was Zagreb's not Sarajevo's. Whilst this decision was in part designed to avoid provoking direct Serbian intervention, it was also calculated to ensure that the Muslim-dominated federation controlled only a rump of central territory, ensuring its long-term dependence on its western neighbour. Almost immediately Tudjman demonstrated Croatian strength by enfranchising Croat emigrés, including the 300,000 Bosnian Croats, to take part in the 1995 Croatian elections; this move was regarded by the Bosnian government as a blatant challenge to Bosnian sovereignty. With Bosnian Croat areas still using the Croatian currency, a *de facto* annexation of Hercegovina appeared to be on the Croatian agenda.

For all his tactical errors, Tudjman had achieved a major strategic victory, reflected in the results of the 1995 elections. The liberal challenge of the HND was brushed off; the left was heavily defeated; and the extreme right fell away. Regional parties showed reasonably well. Tudjman dominated the campaign, portraying himself as a military hero with the momentum of history behind him: a Croatian patriarch.

The ageing Tudjman faced considerable challenges in his second elected term as president. The authoritarian right had prospered during the war but its peacetime role was less clear. The ruling HDZ claimed to be a modern Christian democratic party, but in several key respects the regime more resembled the last years of Franco's Spain. Its intolerance of opposition was evinced in its controls on the media and its tendency to seek the complete defeat of rivals through ethically dubious political tactics. Secondly, the HDZ showed enthusiasm for étatist solutions which allowed the state to extend its role even further from its communist base. A strong, unitary state necessarily denied the aspirations of regionalists, particularly in Istria and Dalmatia, whose leaders Tudjman and the HDZ all but accused of trying to break up the nascent Croatian Republic. Thirdly, the state was identified with the Croat nation, and the nation with the leader, with a tendency to venerate personalities which was rarely seen in the West .

FOREIGN AFFAIRS

By end-1995 Croatia had established itself as a power in the region to rival Serbia. German support had played a crucial role early in the conflict, in persuading an uncomfortable EC to recognise Croatia in January 1992, despite Croatia's failure to meet the EC's own pre-conditions on human and minority rights. Some European diplomats regarded recognition as having fanned the flames of war, particularly in Bosnia-Hercegovina. They privately accused Germany of attempting to expand a sphere of influence to include Croatia, claiming that Germany was anxious for an outlet into the Adriatic. Over the succeeding years, Germany took a much lower profile, partly due to its inability (until constitutional changes in 1994) to commit ground troops beyond NATO territory.

Croatian nationalism in general was regarded by many European diplomats as having opened a European can of worms. The central role of Serbian nationalism in the disintegration of Yugoslavia was poorly understood in many Western European capitals. As accusations of war crimes increased from 1991, many were initially reluctant to acknowledge that Serb extremists were the principal culprits. Reports of atrocities by Bosnian Croats, and of Croatian military intervention in Bosnia-Hercegovina, appeared to confirm suspicions of Croatia's rightward drift and marked the low point in Croatia's relations with the West; Croatia risked becoming a pariah state. Croatia came back from the brink when, at US insistence, the Muslim-Croat alliance was renewed in 1994. Croatia was rewarded with unofficial US assistance (the US ambassador to Croatia Peter Galbraith was subsequently to face allegations that he had co-operated in the illegal provision of arms to Croatia in violation of the international arms embargo and of stated US policy).

However, potentially Croatia's most important international partner, the EC, remained cautious. Future relations depended on Croatian progress in pro-market economic reforms and democratisation. On these grounds Slovenia and Bosnia-Hercegovina were more likely to receive EC co-operation, with Croatia likely to be ranked in a second group with the FRY and Macedonia.

POLITICAL PARTIES

In contrast to many other former communist countries in the region, left-wing parties have fared poorly in Croatia since 1990.

The Croatian (communist) Party renamed itself the **Party of Democratic Renewal** for the 1990 republican elections, and subsequently became the **Social Democratic Party** (SDP). In 1990 the party had pledged to work for Croatian statehood; although it won almost one million votes, Croatia's electoral system gave it only 73 of the 356 seats in both chambers of the parliament. By 1995 its popularity had declined and it took less than 9 per cent of the vote in legislative elections. Attempts to unite the fragmented leftist parties had been largely unsuccessful.

The **Croatian Democratic Community** (HDZ) was formed in February 1989 and legalised in December that year. It was led by the former communist Franjo Tudjman. The HDZ began life as a nationalist umbrella movement which attracted conservatives, hard-line chauvinists, democrats and liberals alike. By February 1990 its membership stood at 200,000. Clear links to emigrés, who funded the 1990 election campaign to the tune of up to $4m, alienated Serbs, who regarded overseas Croats as chauvinists and *Ustasa* war criminals. Although the party's overt goals were initially limited to Croatian self-determination and sovereignty, the 1990 electoral slogan having been "We'll Decide Our Fate for Ourselves", the HDZ soon began to press for independence. The party won 205 out of 356 seats in both chambers of the Croatian legislature in 1990. A sister party was established in Bosnia-Hercegovina in summer 1990 and became the predominant political force in the Croat areas of Hercegovina. The "Hercegovina lobby", notably Susak, became influential in the HDZ, in advocating the effective or actual annexation of Croat-majority areas in southern Bosnia-Hercegovina. In October 1993 a special HDZ congress defined the party as Christian democratic. The leadership's increasingly authoritarian policies alienated the HDZ's liberal wing, led by Stipe Mesic and Josip Manolic, which broke away in April 1994 to form the **Croatian Independent Democrats** (HND). The military victories of 1995 won the HDZ its most impressive victory in early elections in October 1995.

The **Joint List** was a bloc of five centrist, centre-right and regional opposition parties, including the **Croatian People's Party** (HNS), which contested the 1995 elections, coming second with under 20 per cent of the vote.

ELECTIONS

Legislative elections

(NOTE: results of elections to the upper house, the Chamber of Districts, held on 7 February 1993 and won by the HDZ, have been omitted for brevity.)

Elections for the lower house of the Croatian National Assembly were held on 22 April - 6 May 1990, and on 2 August 1992. In September 1995 an electoral law redesignated the legislature's lower house as the Chamber of Deputies, and reformed it by reducing the number of seats to 80; allowing nearly half a million emigré Croats to vote in elections, thus enfranchising 300,000 Bosnian Croats; and reducing the fixed Serb minority representation in parliament from 13 to three. Polling took place on 29 October 1995 and the HDZ won an overall majority of seats.

Seats won in elections in April-May 1990 and August 1992

	1990	1992
HDZ	171	85
SDP *	48	11
HNS**		6
HSP**		5
HSLS**		14
Croatian Farmers' Party**		3
Serbian Democratic Party	5	3
Others, including regional parties & independents	45	11
Total	269	138

* Formerly the Croatian (communist) Party and standing in 1990 as the Party of Democratic Renewal.
** No separate results available for 1990.

Results of elections in October 1995

	% of vote	seats
HDZ	45.23	42
Joint List bloc	18.26	16
HSLS	11.55	10
SDP	8.93	8
HSP	5.01	4
Others	11.02	0
Total	100.00	80

HDZ=Croatian Democratic Community; HND=Croatian Independent Democrats; HNS=Croatian People's Party; HSLS=Croatian Social-Liberal Party; HSP=Croatian Party of Rights; Joint List bloc=five parties, including the HNS and regional parties; SDP=Social Democratic Party

Presidential elections

Franjo Tudjman of the HDZ was elected as Croatian President by the legislature immediately after the 1990 elections, and took office on 30 May 1990.

Direct presidential elections took place on 2 August 1992, when Tudjman was re-elected overwhelmingly, winning 1,519,100 votes to 585,535 for Drazen Budisa of the HSLS. Savka Badcevic-Kucar (HNS) was third with 161,242 votes, and there were five other candidates.

CHRONOLOGY

1526. The Ottomans drive back the frontiers of the Austro-Hungarian Empire and occupy most of Croatia.

1699. Croatia rejoins the Austro-Hungarian Empire.

1 December 1918. Foundation of the Yugoslav state as the Kingdom of Serbs, Croats and Slovenes.

20 June 1928. Croatian Peasant Party leader Stijepan Radic is murdered by a Serb Radical deputy.

9 October 1934. King Alexander is assassinated in Marseilles by the extreme Croatian nationalist *Ustasa*.

26 August 1939. The *Sporazum* creates an autonomous Croatian *banovina* comprising 30 per cent of Yugoslavia's territory and population.

1941-5. After the invasion of Yugoslavia by Axis forces, Croatia becomes for the first time a nominally independent (but Nazi puppet) state, the NDH under the genocidal *Ustasa* regime.

1969-71. The Croatian Spring: the Croatian (communist) Party experiments with moderate nationalism.

1974. A new constitution devolves power to the republics, leading on the economic front to increasing autarky.

December 1989. The assemblies of Slovenia and Croatia legalise opposition parties and call multi-party elections.

20-23 January 1990. The federal League of Communists of Yugoslavia (SKJ) effectively breaks up.

22 April-7 May 1990. Multi-party elections: victory for the nationalist Croatian Democratic Union (HDZ).

30 May 1990. The Croatian parliament elects HDZ leader Franjo Tudjman as Croatian President.

25 July 1990. Approval of constitutional changes, notably on the republic's name, presidential system, symbols (including the controversial readoption of the *sahovnica* or chequerboard used most recently by the *Ustasa*); the Serbs are no longer recognised as a constituent nation of Croatia.

1 October 1990. The "Serbian National Council" formed by Serbs in Croatia declares the existence of an "autonomous region" in areas of majority-Serb population, and Serbian President Milosevic calls for federal intervention to defend them from Croatian repression.

8-11 October 1990. In a single consignment, some 20,000 Kalashnikov rifles are smuggled over the Hungarian border as part of a secret operation to arm Croatia in preparation for civil war.

21 December 1990. The Croatian Assembly promulgates the republic's new constitution, including the assertion of Croatia's sovereignty and right to secede.

20-21 February 1991. The parliaments of Slovenia and Croatia call for the dissolution of the federal state of Yugoslavia.

1 March 1991. The war in Croatia begins with an assault by Croatian Serb irregulars on the Croatian police station at Plitvice.

23 March 1991. Milosevic and Tudjman, meeting secretly at Karadjordjevo, strike a secret deal to give a new Croatian *banovina* some 30 per cent of Yugoslav territory, including much of Bosnia-Hercegovina. Milosevic later reneges on the deal.

19 May 1991. A referendum in Croatia records an 83 per cent turnout and a 94 per cent majority for independence, but in the Serb-inhabited areas, where unrest and violence

are increasing, a vote the previous week has called for separation from Croatia and union with Serbia.

25 June 1991. Croatia and Slovenia proclaim their independence and dissociation from the Yugoslav federation.

July-August 1991. In majority-Serb areas, JNA units join Serb militants in running battles with Croat security forces, and over 100 people are killed.

26 August 1991. The ethnically Croat village of Kijevo in Serb-held Croatia is the first town to fall victim to "ethnic cleansing" in the war, as Croatian Serb irregulars backed by JNA heavy artillery drive the Croat population from their homes.

14 September 1991. Serb irregulars begin their assault on the strategic town of Vukovar in eastern Slavonia.

1 October 1991. The JNA begins its assault on Dubrovnik.

18 November 1991. The fall of Vukovar is followed by atrocities against the remaining Croatian soldiers and civilians. By the end of 1991 the Serbs control 30 per cent of Croatian territory and have displaced 300,000 Croat refugees.

23 December 1991. Germany recognises Croatian and Slovene independence.

2 January 1992. A 15th ceasefire between Croatia and the federal authorities comes into effect. Under the terms of a new peace plan, a considerable contingent of UN peacekeepers known as the UN Protection Force (Unprofor) is to patrol four UN Protected Areas (UNPAs) or buffer-zones between Croatian and rebel Serb forces. The Krajina are declared "demilitarised zones" and Unprofor is tasked with disarming Croatian Serb forces, a function it never fulfills. In February Tudjman accepts the peace plan, but agrees only to a six-month mandate, which is subsequently extended. The first Unprofor troops arrive in Croatia in March and complete their deployment in June.

15 January 1992. The EC recognises Croatia.

14 February 1992. Helsinki Watch demands Croatian investigation of allegations of the mass murder and torture of unarmed civilian and military detainees.

4 April 1992. Declaration of the Republic of Serbian Krajina (RSK), including parts of Eastern and Western Slavonia, the Baranja, the Krajina and Western Srem.

7 April 1992. US recognition of Croatia.

8 May 1992. Passage of human and minority rights legislation providing special status to Serb-majority districts, namely Knin and Glina.

22 May 1992 Croatia becomes a UN member.

30 September 1992. FRY President Cosic and Tudjman sign an agreement on the withdrawal of the JNA from positions on the Croatian coast, including from Dubrovnik.

2 August 1992. President Tudjman and his HDZ party win simultaneous presidential and legislative elections boycotted by most Serbs.

8 September 1992. Greguric is replaced by Hrvoje Sarinic as prime minister in a major government reshuffle.

22-9 January 1993. Croatian forces seize a number of key infrastructural facilities from RSK forces. Under heavy pressure from Germany and the EC, Tudjman orders the offensive to halt.

2 March 1993. Some 420,000 workers participate in a "warning strike" to protest at low wages and rising prices.

12 March 1993. The government acquires a majority stakeholding in Croatia's only independent daily newspaper, *Slobodna Dalmacija*, and assumes editorial control.

29 March 1993. Resignation of the Sarinic cabinet after some six months in office. The government's popularity has been weakened by financial scandal and the introduction of economic austerity measures.

3 April 1993. A new cabinet is sworn in under Prime Minister Nikica Valentic.

19-20 June 1993. In a referendum repudiated by Zagreb, Serbs in the RSK vote overwhelmingly for unification with the *Republika Srpska* and "other Serbian lands".

9 September 1993. A major Croatian offensive is aimed at Serb villages bordering the RSK.

2 November 1993. Tudjman presents a peace plan offering local political and cultural autonomy to Croatian Serbs. Tudjman demands similar measures to protect the Croat minority in Serbia, and Serbian recognition of Croatian sovereignty and territorial integrity.

28 December 1993. Defence Minister Susak admits that Croatia has "helped" the Bosnian Croats, and threatens full-scale intervention if the Bosnian Government offensive against Bosnian Croat positions continues. The USA warns Croatia that continued military involvement in Bosnia-Hercegovina could lead to the imposition of international sanctions.

19 January 1994. FRY Foreign Minister Jovanovic and Tudjman sign a joint declaration on normalising relations; the leaders of the Bosnian Croats and Bosnian Serbs, respectively Boban and Karadzic, sign a parallel document. The agreement meets opposition in Croatia, where HDZ and opposition deputies call for a renewal of the Croat-Muslim alliance against the Serbs.

23 January 1994. Milan Martic, Milosevic's favoured candidate, is victorious in elections to the "presidency" of the RSK, defeating the incumbent leader Babic.

1 March 1994. The Washington Accords create a Muslim-Croat Bosnian Federation; the agreement represents a dramatic U-turn for Tudjman and a temporary defeat for the annexationist ""Hercegovina lobby". The accords also include tentative plans for a loose confederation of Croatia and Bosnia-Hercegovina.

30 April 1994. The liberal wing of the HDZ breaks away to form the Croatian Independent Democrats (HND). The new party is led by Stipe Mesic and Josip Manolic, who accuse Tudjman of attempting to establish a one-party state.

24 May 1994. The opposition begins a boycott of parliament (which lasts until 19 September) in protest at irregularities in the elections to replace Mesic and Manolic as the Speakers of the lower and upper houses of parliament.

19 October 1994. A "Mini-Contact Group", also known as the Zagreb Group or Z-4, and comprising the USA, Russia, and two EC representatives, is formed; it proposes the reintegration of the RSK into Croatia, including the return of Croat refugees to their former homes, in exchange for Croatian guarantees of extensive autonomy.

2 December 1994. Croatia signs an economic co-operation agreement with the RSK on the mutual restoration of communications and services. By 21 December the E-70 motorway linking Zagreb with Lipovac in eastern Croatia, which traverses Serb-held areas in the UNPA Sector West, has reopened.

12 January 1995. Tudjman gives formal notice that Unprofor's mandate in Croatia will be terminated on 31 March.

30 January 1995. The Z-4 presents a peace plan under which the RSK would return some 50 per cent of the territory it controlled in exchange for extensive autonomy, including control over education, taxation, and law enforcement. The plan is rejected by both Croatia and the RSK.

8 February 1995. The RSK suspends implementation of the December 1994 economic agreement with Croatia, and on 20 February establishes a military alliance with the Bosnian Serbs.

6 March 1995. Croatia, Bosnia-Hercegovina and the Bosnian Croats agree to establish a military alliance.

12 March 1995. Tudjman agrees to extend the UN peacekeepers' mandate in Croatia for a further six-month period, but under radically revised terms; a drastically reduced UN force of 5,000 peacekeepers, renamed the UN Confidence Operation in Croatia (UNCro), is to fulfill three tasks: (i) to deter the passage of arms to the RSK from neighbouring Serb-held areas in Bosnia-Hercegovina and the FRY; (ii) to facilitate the passage of aid from Croatia to Bosnia-Hercegovina; and (iii) to support the implementation of existing agreements.

24-9 April 1995. RSK irregulars in Sector West close the Zagreb-Lipovac E-70 motorway and allegedly murder five Croatians travelling on the road.

1-2 May 1995. Operation Lightning. In the biggest engagement with Croatian Serb forces since September 1993, the Croatian Army advances into Sector West. Within 48 hours Croatian troops have complete control of the area, including the E-70 motorway. The Croatian Army claims to have sustained only 33 fatal casualties, whilst putting Serb deaths at 350-450. Serb media allege that Croatian forces have committed dreadful atrocities against Serb civilians and unarmed, retreating irregulars. By 18 May only 1,800 of the 15,000 Serbs previously in the area remain.

2-3 May 1995. Croatian Serb forces retaliate by firing rockets at Zagreb, killing six people and injuring 175.

21 May 1995. The RSK Assembly votes for unification of Croatian Serb and Bosnian Serb territories.

9 June 1995. Tudjman warns that unless the Croatian Serbs accept Croatian sovereignty, military action will be taken to recover Serb-held territory.

15 June 1995. Tudjman appoints his son Miroslav as Director of the Croatian Intelligence Service.

27 July 1995. Thousands of Croatian Army troops reinforce the HVO in central Bosnia-Hercegovina, and advance northward.

4 August 1995. Operation Storm. In a crucial turning point for the wars in former Yugoslavia, the Croatian Army launches a massive offensive against the RSK. Croatian troops, backed by helicopters, rocket launchers and tanks, meet little resistance. They enter Knin on 5 August and force an effective Serb surrender on 9 August. Almost all of the 150,000 Croatian Serbs in the area flee to Bosnia-Hercegovina and Serbia, some burned out by Croatian forces. Only Sector East, including Vukovar and bordering the FRY, still remains under Serb control.

22 August 1995. Tudjman calls early elections for October.

18 September 1995. Passage of an electoral law allowing emigré Croats to vote in elections; the law effectively enfranchises Bosnian Croats, angering the Bosnian

Government. The law also reduces the fixed Serb minority representation in parliament from 13 to three, reflecting the dwindling numbers of Serbs in the republic.

30 September 1995. EC monitors allege a campaign of terror against Croatian Serbs during and after the Croatian offensive against the RSK.

29 October 1995. The HDZ, with Tudjman presenting himself as a military hero, wins a major victory in legislative elections, taking more than 45 per cent of the vote. The opposition Joint List bloc, comprising five right-wing and centre-right parties, wins under 20 per cent and the liberal HND fails to clear the 5 per cent threshold necessary for representation. In contrast to many other former communist countries, left-wing parties fare poorly. There is controversy over media bias toward the HDZ.

7 November 1995. Zlatko Matesa is appointed Prime Minister at the head of a new HDZ government.

12 November 1995. The Croatian Serbs agree to relinquish control over the last remaining Serb-held enclave in Croatia, Eastern Slavonia, following talks at Dayton between Tudjman and Milosevic. Under the agreement the region is to be under UN administration for a transitional period of up to two years. The agreement averts the threat of Croatian military action, as Croatian troops and armour have massed on the borders of the enclave over the preceding days.

BOSNIA-HERCEGOVINA

The Republic of Bosnia-Hercegovina declared sovereignty on 15 October 1991. A majority of voters backed Bosnian independence in a referendum boycotted by ethnic Serbs the following February. On 7-8 April 1992 Bosnia-Hercegovina was granted recognition as an independent state by EC states and the USA, and in May it became a UN member. With an area of 51,129 sq. km., Bosnia-Hercegovina is one of the smaller states in East-Central Europe, of comparable size to Slovakia or Estonia.

Bosnia-Hercegovina formed the mountainous core of the former Yugoslavia. Its only outlet to the sea was south of Ploce on the Dalmatian coast. It was flanked in the north and west by Croatia, and in the east by Serbia and Montenegro - which now comprise the rump Yugoslavia or FRY.

Bosnia-Hercegovina's population in 1991 was 4,365,000, spread mainly through scattered rural communities. Its capital Sarajevo had a population of 470,000; its second city was the ethnically mixed northern settlement of Banja Luka. The war of 1992-5 caused considerable demographic changes, as two million people were driven from their homes and fled the conflict to settle elsewhere in Bosnia-Hercegovina, in Croatia or beyond.

The republic was ethnically the most diverse in the SFRY. No one group formed a majority. The Bosnian Muslims or *Bosniaks* were the most populous, forming 43.7 per cent of the population; the Serbs comprised 31.4 per cent and the Croats 17.3 per cent. Such was the inter-mixing of ethnic groups that ethnic maps of the republic resembled a patchwork quilt; speaking broadly, Serbs tended to predominate in the east, Croats in the Hercegovina region in the south, and Muslims in some central areas.

HISTORICAL NARRATIVE

The rivalry between the two principal agents in the Wars of the Yugoslav Succession, the Croats and the Serbs, made the spread of war from Croatia to Bosnia-Hercegovina inevitable. Serbian President Slobodan Milosevic and his Croatian counterpart Franjo Tudjman were both pledged to protect the interests of the large minorities of their ethnic kin in Bosnia-Hercegovina. In March 1991 the two met secretly at Karadjordjevo to discuss the partition of Bosnia-Hercegovina between their two republics, paying scant regard to the interests of the Bosnian Muslims.

The Bosnian Muslims were ethnic Slavs whose ancestors were converted to Islam during the long occupation by the Ottoman Empire. They spoke Serbo-Croat, and both Croats and Serbs had claimed them as their own ethnic kin. Throughout their history, they had demonstrated a pragmatic ability to co-operate with the dominant force in the region, whichever that might be. They were not noted for the aggressive assertion of their own interests. Islamic religious practice had largely lapsed by the 20th century: even taboos on the consumption of pork and alcohol were widely ignored. They were not recognised as a distinct national group within Yugoslavia until 1961, when "Muslim" was included as an official nationality in census returns. From the 1960s onward the Bosnian Muslims developed a stronger sense of their distinct ethnic identity, drawing as much on cultural and social factors as on religion, and defined to some extent in negative ("not-Croat", "not-Serb"). By the 1980s, the most salient such factors were tendency to concentrate in urban areas, making them generally more educated, liberal and cosmopolitan than other ethnic groups in Bosnia-Hercegovina.

Fearing the destabilisation of the republic, the communist regime had vigorously subdued any stirring of Muslim nationalism. In the 1940s the Partisans had bloodily suppressed the *Mladi Muslimani* or "Young Muslims", of which Alija Izetbegovic had been a member. In the most recent crackdown in the 1980s, Izetbegovic was again among those jailed. With the communist retreat in 1989-90, nationalist parties made immediate advances. In the 1990 republican elections, Bosnian Muslim voters, sensing an impending crisis caused by the growth of Serbian and Croatian nationalism, opted for the SDA, led by the now freed Izetbegovic.

Bosnia's other ethnic groups were deeply suspicious of the SDA, which they regarded as militant-Islamicist. The demagogic leaders of the Bosnian Serbs, keen to stimulate Serb secessionism, played on Serbs' historic antipathy toward the Ottoman Empire, deliberately overlooking ethnic similarities and instead referring to the Bosnian Muslims as "Turks". Izetbegovic's July 1991 decision to apply for Bosnian membership of the Organisation of the Islamic Conference (OIC) handed Serb nationalists a useful propaganda weapon.

In fact the SDA leadership was largely true to the Bosnian Muslim tradition of pragmatism. In 1989, Izetbegovic himself explicitly rejected the notion of a Bosnian Islamic state as unrealistic, because of the ethnically mixed character of the republic. Instead, throughout the 1992-5 war, the Bosnian Muslims were the champions of a multi-ethnic, unified Bosnia-Hercegovina. For this they won the support of a minority of Croats and Serbs who favoured a multi-national Bosnian state; the Bosnian Government, the Bosnian Collective Presidency and the Bosnian Army all included non-Muslims. When Izetbegovic declared in February 1991 that he was "prepared to sacrifice peace for a sovereign Bosnia-Hercegovina", he was not asserting a militant secessionism but, in view of the impending secession of Croatia and Slovenia, identifying the choice for Bosnia-Hercegovina as one between independence and absorption by a Greater Serbia. When war actually broke out in April 1992, Izetbegovic appeared to exemplify his people's shock and indecision in the face of Serb and later Croat violence.

If Bosnian Muslims were poorly prepared psychologically for the conflict, their militarily preparations had been even more tentative. Whereas the Serbs and the Croats had access to considerable weapons supplies, the Muslims had no army, few small arms, virtually no heavy weapons or motorised armour, and no military aircraft. The arms embargo which was one of the first acts of the international community in attempting to calm the conflict hindered the Bosnians still further, while barely affecting their enemies. The Muslims were unable to mount a significant military response until 1994-5, and then they were dependent on the support of the Croatian Army.

Militant Bosnian Serb resistance to Bosnian independence had got under way in the summer of 1991 with the establishment of several Serb Autonomous Regions (SAOs) guarded by armed irregulars. Bosnian Serb leaders made clear that they would not accept an independent Bosnia-Hercegovina. In a parliamentary debate in October 1991, Bosnian Serb leader Radovan Karadzic threw down the gauntlet to the Bosnian government, warning that the Bosnian Muslims faced annihilation in the event of war. His threat could not prevent the parliament from declaring the republic's sovereignty; Karadzic led a Serb walk-out from the Bosnian parliament, marking an official Serb withdrawal from inter-ethnic institutions in the republic (although "pro-Bosnian" Serbs continued to serve on the collective presidency). In January 1992 the Bosnian Serbs established the Serbian Republic of Bosnia-Hercegovina (which later became the *Republika Srpska*). The Bosnian Serbs' aims were clear: to carve out as much Bosnian territory as possible through military means, to create a contiguous area of ethnic Serb habitation, and to unify with fellow Serbs in a Greater Serbia. They consolidated control over parts of eastern Bosnia-Hercegovina adjoining Serbia and established a secure corridor linking this territory with their other stronghold in the north west.

The Serbian leadership shared the Bosnian Serbs' strategic objectives. Throughout the early stages of the war the Bosnian Serb military campaign received considerable unofficial support from Serbia and the FRY. Military materiel, fuel, food, and other basic goods poured over the border. The wages of many Bosnian Serb soldiers were paid out of the federal budget.

The Serbian leadership nonetheless repeatedly denied any role in operational matters. It had good reason to distance itself from the Bosnian Serb campaign. The coalition of Serb forces in Bosnia-Hercegovina, from the Serbian paramilitary Tigers group led by the notorious Zeljko Raznjatovic (alias "Arkan"), to Bosnian Serb irregulars and the JNA units officially on paid leave, had conducted a ferocious onslaught against both Muslim and Croat civilians. The systematic use of terror - mass murder, rape, and the destruction of Muslim and Croat homes - was deployed to ethnically "cleanse" or "purify" Serb-inhabited areas. The most notorious of dozens of "detention centres" across Bosnia-Hercegovina, Omarska, was exposed in summer 1992. Over three years the campaign drove hundreds of thousands of people from their traditional homes. In the northern Banja Luka-Prijedor area, for example, of a pre-war population of 500,000 Muslims only 20,000 or so remained by 1995. In the strategically crucial eastern third of Bosnia adjoining Serbia, Muslims fled from their rural settlements to seek shelter in several small towns; these became besieged enclaves, subject to repeated attack by the surrounding Bosnian Serb forces, who consistently refused to allow the UN to provide humanitarian aid. Sarajevo too was surrounded and placed under siege, terrorised by Serb gunners who targeted civilians from the hills above the city.

The Bosnian Serbs denied the existence of an ethnic cleansing programme, protested that related crimes were grossly exaggerated, and insisted that Muslims had committed worse crimes against Serb civilians. Despite these claims, in March 1995 the UN Commission on Human Rights blamed Serbs in Bosnia-Hercegovina and Croatia for the worst abuses of the war and accused them of having pursued a "systematic policy of ethnic cleansing and genocidal acts". Investigation and prosecution of the perpetrators was the responsibility of the UN War Crimes Tribunal in the Hague, which opened in November 1993. There was considerable speculation as to whether the Tribunal would be able to find evidence to link the leadership of Serbia and the FRY to war crimes committed in Bosnia-Hercegovina. In July 1995 the Tribunal indicted Karadzic and Bosnian Serb military commander Gen. Ratko Mladic on charges of genocide and crimes against humanity; further charges were filed in December 1995.

Muslim hopes for international military intervention in the campaign to resist Serb aggression were in vain. Limited, covert assistance came from the USA (in the form of training by ex-US Army specialists) and from Islamic governments (in the form of illegal arms drops), but crucially Croatia chose to enforce the UN arms embargo against Bosnia-Hercegovina even during its periods of military alliance with Bosnia. The UN declared six besieged Muslim enclaves "Safe Areas" in May 1993, but failed to offer more than token forces to defend them from Serb assault (*see below*). Despite these disadvantages, the Bosnian Army gradually improved its performance throughout the war, first demonstrating this in the war against the Bosnian Croats in 1993. By January 1994 Izetbegovic was claiming that the Bosnian Army numbered some 200,000 combat personnel.

Where the Bosnian Serb campaign was systematic, Croatian tactics in Bosnia-Hercegovina were opportunistic. Initially the Croatian regime and its Bosnian Croat proxies made common cause with the Bosnian Muslims, launching a joint military campaign against the Bosnian Serbs. After just a few months of war, however, the Croatian leadership altered its policy.

The Bosnian Croat leadership was demonstrably more closely controlled by Croatia than was the Bosnian Serb leadership by Serbia. The dominant political party in Bosnian Croat areas was the Croatian Democratic Community (HDZ), notionally the "sister" organisation of Tudjman's HDZ, but in practice effectively the same party. Within the HDZ was an influential body of hardline nationalists, known as the Hercegovina lobby, which including Croatian Defence Minister Susak. This lobby advocated the annexation of the Croat-dominated southern region of Bosnia-Hercegovina, overlooking the fact that a majority of Bosnian Croats lived elsewhere in Bosnia-Hercegovina. Under the prompting of this lobby and with the support of Tudjman, the Bosnian Croats soon began to assert their "rights" in Hercegovina. In July 1992 Bosnian Croat leader Milan Boban illegally declared the Croatian Community of Herceg-Bosna, and by August 1992 war between the Muslims and Croats had begun. Initially Bosnian Croat forces (the Croatian Defence Council or

HVO) proved superior and by October 1992 the regional capital of Mostar, previously an ethnically mixed town, had fallen to the HVO. By summer 1993, however, Bosnian government forces had improved their performance, prompting direct Croatian intervention of up to 30,000 troops in support of the HVO campaign. In November Tudjman defended Croatia's "right" to intervene "to defend the Croat nation in Bosnia-Hercegovina".

By February 1994, Tudjman had again reversed his policy. Croatian leaders feared UN sanctions and wanted to avoid being implicated in war crimes allegations against the HVO. Moreover both military advisers and public opinion strongly favoured a renewal of the alliance with Muslims against the Serbs.

On 18 March 1994 Bosnian Government and Bosnian Croat officials signed the Washington Accords, a landmark agreement on the creation of a Muslim-Croat federation. The accords envisaged a Federation divided into eight cantons - four Muslim, two Croat, and two multi-ethnic. A strong federal government was to be responsible for defence, foreign affairs and the economy. The offices of President and Prime Minister (of which the latter was probably to be more powerful) were to rotate annually between Muslim and Croat leaders. The Washington Accords also included a preliminary agreement between Bosnian Government and Croatian officials on linking Bosnia-Hercegovina and Croatia in a loose confederation with common policies on defence, crime, education, and culture.

The federation was formally established in late May 1994. In July Mostar, the scene of the most bitter Muslim-Croat conflict, was placed under EC administration. But progress in implementing the Washington Accords was extremely slow. On the expiry of his six-month term as federation president, Bosnian Croat leader Kresimir Zubak refused to relinquish the post, arguing that so flimsy was the institutional structure of the federation that the presidency had been powerless; he demanded an extension of his term and the provision of a sound institutional and legal base for the federation. By April 1995 the situation had improved with Zubak and the federation vice-president Ejup Ganic, a Muslim, agreeing a package of measures on the establishment of federation institutions, notably a police force.

Although the renewal of the Muslim-Croat alliance was a significant step towards the end of the war in Bosnia-Hercegovina, the military situation in spring 1995 still appeared strongly to favour the Bosnian Serbs. The Serbs still controlled up to 70 per cent of Bosnian territory and they had the best-equipped and best-led army. In reality, however, their position had been steadily weakening since 1993. Crucial tactical differences with Serbia had emerged; Milosevic appeared content with the military gains in Bosnia and regarded the potential benefits of continued military action as being outweighed by the growing burden of international sanctions imposed since 1991-2. The Bosnian Serbs, however, continued to press for complete victory, which would give them an outlet into the Adriatic, half of Sarajevo, and guarantees on secession from Bosnia-Hercegovina and unification with the FRY. Relations between the two worsened sharply with the Bosnian Serb rejections of the Vance-Owen plan in 1993 and of the Contact Group plan in 1994 (*see below*); the latter rejection was denounced as "senseless and absurd" by Milosevic, who blamed the "mad political ambitions and greed" of the Bosnian Serb leadership. Thus, by spring 1995 the Bosnian Serbs were more isolated than ever and lacking essential supplies, notably fuel for their mechanised army.

Throughout that spring and early summer the Bosnian Army made gains, particularly in the north. More significant was an advance northward from Hercegovina by the HVO and the Croatian Army, which thus began to close a loop around Serb-held territory in Croatia. When Croatia launched its devastating assault on its own rebel Serbs in August 1995, hundreds of thousands of Serb refugees poured into Bosnia-Hercegovina. The victories of the reorganised Croatian Army demoralised Bosnian Serb troops and caused chaos on northern Bosnia's roads. The next major blow was dealt by NATO, which in late August launched a massive aerial bombing campaign, supported on the ground by the NATO Rapid Reaction Force, against Bosnian Serb military targets (*see below for more on the international context of the war*). The Bosnian Serbs' mechanised army, which depended for its strength on mobility, was undone; supply lines were severed and telecommunications links went dead. On 11 September came the final decisive push, a joint Bosnian Army-HVO-Croatian Army offensive, which immediately made gains which appeared the more spectacular after three years of war by attrition. Even the Serb stronghold of Banja Luka was being threatened by the advance when it was halted in early October. The war was effectively over, and a comprehensive peace settlement had been struck by year-end.

Unsuccessful international mediation 1992-4 - UN and NATO involvement

International attempts to find a peace settlement in 1992-94 were confounded by the lack of good faith on the part of all parties in the process. The first ceasefire brokered by EC mediator Lord Carrington in April 1992 was broken within hours, setting a precedent for the rest of the war. Croatian and Serbian negotiators consistently denied direct involvement in the war or in any atrocities; at the London Conference in August 1992, Bosnian Serb leader Karadzic even condemned ethnic cleansing, claiming that Serbs had been its principal victims.

The London conference marked the first attempts by Serbian leaders to call a halt to the war. FRY prime minister Milan Panic attempted to sideline Milosevic, offering major concessions toward peace, but within months of the conference he and federal president Cosic had been dismissed and their pledges ignored. By 1993, however, the hawkish Milosevic had also begun to cultivate the image of a peacemaker.

On 2 January 1993 the Vance-Owen plan, the first comprehensive attempt to solve the crisis, was presented to the warring parties (*for more detail see chronology below*). Direct talks between the leaders of the parties took place for the first time since the beginning of the war. Under heavy pressure from Milosevic's Serbia, the Bosnian Serb leadership provisionally accepted the plan, but it was undermined by veiled US opposition, based on the grounds that it rewarded Serb aggression. Karadzic then ordered a referendum of Bosnian Serbs which overwhelmingly rejected the plan.

The summer of 1993 was dominated by proposals for a "Union of Three Republics", in which three ethnically-based republics were to be loosely linked under a weak federal body. The plan collapsed in September 1993 after the failure of talks on the British warship *Invincible* in the Adriatic; a signing ceremony planned for the next day was cancelled. Izetbegovic said the proposals had offered Bosnia-Hercegovina a choice between "a just war and an unjust peace". Talks in Geneva in November 1993 were the last between senior officials of all three warring parties until the final settlement at Dayton in late 1995.

The last and equally ill-fated peace plan before Dayton was proposed in July 1994 by the Contact Group of countries, comprising France, Russia, the UK, the USA and Germany. The Contact Group plan envisaged the award of 51 per cent of Bosnian territory to the Bosnian Federation, but in the process accepted the results of ethnic cleansing, including the concession of Banja Luka-Prijedor to the Serbs; the plan was effectively rejected by the Bosnian Serb assembly on the grounds that it left unresolved several key issues, including the fate of Sarajevo.

In the absence of a peace deal, and with no international will to impose a settlement on the former Yugoslavia, in June 1992 the UN Security Council had mandated the deployment of the first 1,000 peacekeepers on operational duty in Bosnia-Hercegovina. The United Nations Protection Force (Unprofor) eventually grew to some 17,000 by 1995. Its aim was initially confined to the provision of aid to besieged communities. In so doing, Unprofor was undermining a central military tactic used by all sides in the conflict - siege; its convoys were therefore subject to intimidation and repeated attack. Aid provision was frequently suspended. By August 1992 a UN Security Council resolution had authorised the use of "all measures necessary" to ensure the delivery of humanitarian aid, giving Unprofor a mandate to defend itself when attacked. In June 1993 Unprofor troops were empowered to call air strikes in their defence, but in practice so cumbersome and circuitous was the chain of command involved, and so strict were the rules of engagement, that such strikes rarely took place.

The UN's role in Bosnia-Hercegovina frequently displayed a glaring gap between noble intentions and modest deeds. In October 1992 the UN Security Council established a "No-Fly Zone" or ban on military flights in Bosnian airspace. Only in spring 1993, however, did NATO begin to enforce the zone. Despite Bosnian Government claims of frequent air raids by Bosnian Serb forces, the first major engagement did not take place until February 1994, when four Bosnian Serb aircraft were shot down by NATO jets.

Shortly after the creation of the No-Fly Zone, international media pressure over the plight of the besieged enclaves mainly of eastern Bosnia led to the creation of six UN "Safe Areas": Sarajevo, Bihac, Gorazde, Srebrenica, Tuzla and Zepa. However the international community committed only a fraction of the estimated 35,000 peacekeepers needed to defend the enclaves. Sporadic Serb shelling continued to terrorise the Safe Areas, often killing dozens of people every week; the international community made little response beyond condemnation. In February 1994 a mortar shell, probably fired from behind Serb lines, struck a crowded Sarajevo market place killing dozens of people in one attack. Although Karadzic denounced the bombing as "a stage-managed fraud" perpetrated by Muslims to win international sympathy, an international outcry over the incident spurred the UN to take action to protect Sarajevo. With UN approval, NATO - using the threat of air strikes - imposed a 20-km. heavy weapons exclusion zone around the city. Heavy weapons within the area had either to be removed or surrendered to the UN at weapons collection points, where they were supervised by Unprofor.

The events of February 1994 appeared to rescue some prestige for the UN, after its attempts at peacekeeping had been ridiculed in the world's media. The organisation's constant humiliations at the hands of the forces of the warring parties had badly damaged the UN's reputation. But by April 1994, the UN had once more been undermined, as a massive Serb assault on the Gorazde Safe Area began; eventually several air strikes, and the threat of a wider bombing campaign, caused the Serbs to suspend the advance, but only after considerable loss of life.

The UN's credibility was further damaged by the events of the seven weeks from late May 1995. When Serb shelling of Sarajevo resumed after a four-month ceasefire, the UN - under US influence - was determined to make a decisive response. NATO aircraft launched the first attacks on the Bosnian Serb military infrastructure, destroying eight weapons dumps near Pale. Bosnian Serb parliamentary chair Momcilo Krajisnik claimed that "with this attack NATO and the UN have finally buried their impartiality and destroyed our trust in them". Bosnian Serb forces began taking hundreds of UN personnel into custody as hostages; television pictures of manacled Unprofor peacekeepers, placed at the likely locations of air strikes, were shown around the world. Under Serbian pressure, the hostages were released in mid-June, but the UN had learned that it could no longer deploy peacekeepers and aid workers in Serb-held areas; they were duly withdrawn, abandoning UN weapons-collection centres and allowing the Bosnian Serbs to recover hundreds of heavy weapons.

Then on 11 July the UN operation in Bosnia-Hercegovina reached its nadir. As a token force of 150 Dutch UN peacekeepers stood by, the enclave of Srebrenica fell to a massive Bosnian Serb assault under the personal direction of Bosnian Serb military commander Mladic. In the worst single atrocity in Europe since the Second World War, at least 8,000 captured Muslim men were massacred. Soon afterwards another Safe Area, Zepa, also fell to the Bosnian Serbs. Despite their vehement condemnation of the Bosnian Serbs, the international community, including the Unprofor leadership, appeared resigned to the loss of the beleaguered and indefensible eastern Safe Areas. French President Jacques Chirac was the only major Western leader to call for the use of force to eject the Serbs from Srebrenica.

The US role in Bosnia-Hercegovina had been inconsistent, often sending contradictory signals to the warring parties. The guiding thread of US policy was a reluctance to press the Bosnian Muslims to settle for what Izetbegovic called "an unjust peace" in which the results of ethnic cleansing were officially accepted and the Muslims were left with an unviable rump state. Much US dissatisfaction with the international approach to the conflict rested on the UN arms embargo, which denied the Bosnian Muslims the means to defend themselves. In November 1994 the USA announced that its forces in the Balkans would no longer enforce the embargo. Russia and the USA's European allies, who after all had troops on the ground, regarded this approach as irresponsible.

Throughout the war, Russian leaders - with one eye on the nationalist lobby at home - adopted the most sympathetic possible approach to the Bosnian Serbs, to the exasperation of the Western powers. The Bosnian Serbs, however, demonstrated a knack of outraging international opinion at critical moments, allowing Russia to fall in behind international action.

The Unprofor withdrawal from Bosnian Serb areas allowed NATO to target the Bosnian Serb military with relatively little fear of reprisals. In July 1995 NATO commanders had been given the means to do so, as the first units of the Rapid Reaction Force were deployed in Bosnia-Hercegovina. The force was under direct UK and French command, avoiding the diffusion of responsibility which had caused such problems for Unprofor commanders in the past.

With these measures in place, the USA eventually succeeded in persuading its European partners effectively to side with the Muslim-Croat Federation against the Bosnian Serbs. In two weeks in late August 1995, NATO bombers, in combination with the gunners of the Rapid Reaction Force, laid waste to Bosnian Serb military and communications targets, dramatically disrupting the Serbs' ability to wage effective war. Bosnian Serb defences crumbled in the face of a joint Muslim-Croat attack. Under heavy US pressure, it was Croatia which privately called a halt to the advance before it took Banja Luka, the capture of which would almost certainly have drawn the FRY into direct intervention in Bosnia-Hercegovina. In the end, international intervention had played a critical role, but the credit went to the USA and NATO rather than to the UN and the European powers, despite their commitment of men and resources to the region for the preceding three years.

The Dayton accords

When peace talks opened at the Wright-Patterson airbase in Dayton, Ohio, on 1 November 1995, Izetbegovic, Milosevic and Tudjman were all present for the first time since November 1993. Neither Karadzic nor Mladic attend the talks, having been indicted on war crimes charges. Instead Milosevic represented both the Bosnian Serbs and the FRY, although his delegation included leading Bosnian Serbs such as Krajisnik.

Several crucial bilateral deals were the early results of the talks. At the mid-way point, Izetbegovic and Tudjman signed a deal to strengthen the Muslim-Croat Federation, under which the Croat mini-state of Herceg-Bosna was to be dissolved and Mostar was to become the federation's capital. Then Milosevic agreed to relinquish the last remaining Serb-held enclave of Croatia, Eastern Slavonia, although continuing disagreement over a timetable for reintegration ultimately scuppered plans to include mutual recognition between the FRY and Croatia in the Dayton accords.

As the deadline for the conclusion of talks approached, brinkmanship on all sides appeared to have wrecked projects for a settlement. But on 21 November 1995 the leaders of the warring parties initialled the Dayton peace agreement, envisaging a loose political structure to join essentially two entities, the Muslim-Croat Federation, comprising 51 per cent of Bosnian territory, and the Bosnian Serb Republic, with 49 per cent.

Under the agreement, each entity was permitted to form special relations with neighbouring countries, on the condition that such arrangements did not challenge the sovereignty and territorial integrity of Bosnia-Hercegovina. The country was to have a single, elected collective presidency and parliament based in Sarajevo, and a single monetary system. Indicted war criminals were to be barred from office. The agreement further guaranteed freedom of movement throughout Bosnia-Hercegovina and the right of displaced people to return to their properties and reclaim lost assets. Sarajevo was to be under Federation control and a land corridor was to link the Bosnian capital with the Gorazde enclave, but Srebrenica and Zepa were to remain in Serb hands. In an effective exchange for Serb withdrawals from territory near Dubrovnik, Croatia was to cede the Bosnian Serb Republic land in the Bay of Kotor, giving the Bosnian Serbs access to the Adriatic. One major outstanding territorial issue was submitted for international arbitration, with the Bosnian Government rejecting Bosnian Serb demands that the Posavina corridor linking Serb-held eastern and Western Bosnia should be widened and secured.

The Dayton accords were officially signed at a ceremony in Paris on 14 December 1995. Under the terms of the accords, the parties were required to withdraw their forces from zones of separation within 30 days from 14 December; to exchange territory within 45; and to move all heavy weapons to designated places within 120.

An international Implementation Force (I-For) under NATO command was to implement the Dayton Accord. The force of 60,000 troops would replace Unprofor, which was to "withdraw" by 31 January 1996. I-For was given complete freedom of movement and the tasks of resettling refugees, settling border disputes, and establishing "secure conditions" for free elections. I-For commanders were given strong powers to control communications and regulate military movements.

Despite the settlement there appeared to be an irreparable rift between the Muslim-Croat federation and Bosnian Serbs. There were considerable doubts over Bosnian Serb goodwill towards the deal, despite Karadzic's pledge that the Bosnian Serb leadership would implement the settlement in full. Bosnian Serb anger initially focused on the handing-over to Federation control of Sarajevo's Serb-majority suburbs. In December Sarajevo's 120,000-strong Serb community voted by over 98 per cent against the Dayton settlement.

The human costs of the Bosnian war were heavy. About 250,000 people had been killed in the war and two million displaced. The physical and psychological damage to Bosnians wrought by ethnic cleansing, including mass rape, added to the country's peacetime burdens.

In December 1995 the World Bank estimated the cost of reconstruction at $51 billion. The international community pledged a major aid programme. A positive post-war role could not, however, repair the damage done to the prestige of the UN and the Europeans by the failure of their policy in Bosnia-Hercegovina.

POLITICAL PARTIES

The **Party of Democratic Action** (SDA) was formed on 26 May 1990 in Sarajevo. It declared itself a "political alliance of Yugoslav citizens belonging to Muslim cultural and historical traditions". Veteran Muslim nationalist Alija Izetbegovic became the SDA leader. Bosnian Muslims opted overwhelmingly for the SDA in the 1990 republican legislative elections, and Izetbegovic became President of the Bosnian Presidency. Despite accusations of militant Islamicism, the SDA remained for the most part a pragmatic party favouring a multi-national Bosnia-Hercegovina.

The **Serbian Democratic Party** (SDS) was formed in summer 1990 as a branch of the Croatian Serb SDS. Radovan Karadzic was elected as the party's president. Another senior figure was Momcilo Krajisnik, who was to become chair of the Bosnian, and then of the Bosnian Serb, parliaments. The Bosnian Serbs overwhelmingly backed the SDS in the 1990 republican elections and the party took more than a third of the seats. The SDS leadership refused to contemplate an independent Bosnia-Hercegovina and immediately made preparations for war. The SDS was noted throughout the ensuing conflict for its belligerent, uncompromising nationalism, in seeking a complete victory which would have allowed Bosnian Serb secession, access to the Adriatic Sea, partition of the Bosnian capital Sarajevo, and over half of Bosnian territory.

The **Croatian Democratic Community** (HDZ) was formed in the summer of 1990 as the Bosnian Croat sister of Croatia's ruling party. In practice the Bosnian HDZ leadership acted as virtual proxies for their colleagues in Zagreb.

ELECTIONS

Legislative elections, 9 November 1990

SDA	87
SDS	71
HDZ	44
League of Reform Forces	13
Reformed communists	18
Others	7
Total	240

In simultaneous elections to the collective **presidency**, two places were reserved for each of the principal ethnic groups and one for a "Yugoslav"; Izetbegovic became President of the Presidency despite finishing runner-up to the controversial Muslim entrepreneur Fikret Abdic (by some one million votes to 850,000); Muslim Ejup Ganic, a nationalist, took the "Yugoslav" seat.

CHRONOLOGY

1878. The Austro-Hungarian empire occupies Bosnia-Hercegovina, ending four centuries of Ottoman rule. Formal annexation takes place in 1908.

28 June 1914. The First World War begins with the assassination in Sarajevo of Archduke Ferdinand of Austria by Gavril Princip, a supporter of a South Slav state.

1 December 1918. Foundation of the Yugoslav state, which includes Bosnia-Hercegovina.

26 August 1939. The *Sporazum* effectively divides Bosnia-Hercegovina between the Croats and Serbs.

1941-5. The Croatian *Ustasa* regime controls much of Bosnia-Hercegovina.

January 1946. Tito's victorious communist regime promulgates a new Soviet-type federal constitution in which Bosnia-Hercegovina is one of six republics. Islamists are targeted in a purge in the late 1940s.

1961. Constitutional changes allow Muslims to identify themselves as members of a distinct national group in census returns.

1973. Alija Izetbegovic's *Islamic Declaration* calls for a Muslim state in Bosnia, but rejects the use of violence for this end.

February 1974. A new constitution devolves considerable powers to the republics.

26 May 1990. Foundation of the Party of Democratic Action, with Alija Izetbegovic its leader. Two months later the Serbian Democratic Party (SDS) is founded, and Radovan Karadzic is elected as its leader.

9 November 1990. Multi-party elections to the Bosnian parliament: parties based on the three main ethnic groups win nearly 90 per cent of the vote. In simultaneous elections to the collective presidency Izetbegovic becomes President of the Presidency, and under a power-sharing arrangement Croat Jure Pelivan becomes prime minister and Bosnian Serb Momcilo Krajisnik parliamentary chairman.

27 February 1991. Izetbegovic declares that he is "prepared to sacrifice peace for a sovereign Bosnia-Hercegovina".

23 March 1991. Milosevic and Croatian counterpart Tudjman meet secretly at Karadjordjevo to discuss the partition of Bosnia-Hercegovina.

July 1991. Izetbegovic seeks Bosnian membership of the Organisation of the Islamic Conference (OIC), apparently confirming Serb and Croat fears that the Muslims favour an Islamic regime.

15 October 1991. The parliament of Bosnia-Hercegovina declares the sovereignty of the republic. Bosnian Serb deputies walk out. In the preceding debate Karadzic has warned that in prompting war, Izetbegovic could be responsible for "[making] the Muslim people disappear".

9 January 1992. Establishment of the Serbian Republic of Bosnia-Hercegovina (subsequently renamed *Republika Srpska*).

15 January 1992. Bosnia-Hercegovina's application for EC recognition fails.

29 February - 1 March 1992. In a referendum boycotted by Bosnian Serbs, 99.4 per cent of voters opt for independence. Bosnian Serb leader Radovan Karadzic declares that "we are not going to accept an independent Bosnia-Hercegovina".

3 March 1992. Izetbegovic proclaims the independence of Bosnia-Hercegovina. Later in March inter-ethnic clashes take place in Sarajevo and Bosanski Brod.

18 March 1992. Leaders of the Bosnian Serbs, Muslims and Croats sign an agreement on cantonisation, but Izetbegovic subsequently re-states the Muslim commitment to a unitary state.

1 April 1992. The Serb ultra-nationalist Tigers militia commence "ethnic cleansing" in the Bijelina area of north-western Bosnia. On 4 April Izetbegovic issues a general mobilisation of the Bosnian territorial defence, and Serb members of the collective presidency resign.

5-6 April 1992. The Bosnian Serbs declare independence; the civil war in Bosnia-Hercegovina begins as Serb irregulars open fire on peace demonstrators in Sarajevo. In the following fortnight Serb forces seize two suburbs of Sarajevo, and begin the military campaign to open a corridor between the two main Serb-dominated areas in the republic's East and West. The JNA denies involvement.

6-7 April 1992. On consecutive days, Bosnia-Hercegovina is recognised by EC states and the USA.

8 April 1992. Zvornik is the first town to fall to Bosnian Serb forces backed by the JNA. Muslim civilians are deliberately targeted.

21 April 1992. The Serb siege of Sarajevo begins.

23 April 1992. A ceasefire brokered by EC mediator Lord Carrington is broken within hours, setting a precedent for the rest of the war.

4 May 1992. The FRY Presidency orders the formal withdrawal of the JNA from Bosnia-Hercegovina; nevertheless, some 80,000 mainly Bosnian JNA soldiers remain.

On 20 May the Bosnian Government declares the remaining JNA troops an "occupying force" and announces plans to form a Bosnian Army.

22 May 1992. Bosnia-Hercegovina becomes a UN member.

15 June 1992. Tudjman and Izetbegovic declare their commitment to joint military action against the Serb "common enemy".

29 June 1992. The UN Security Council mandates the deployment of 1,000 peacekeepers at Sarajevo airport. This initial complement grows to reach some 17,000 by 1995.

4 July 1992. Bosnian Croat leader Milan Boban declares the Croatian Community of Herceg-Bosna, comprising approximately 18 per cent of Bosnian territory in the south-west. The Bosnian Government repudiates the declaration as illegal.

14 July 1992. Serb forces launch fierce bombardments of Gorazde and other eastern Bosnian towns where large numbers of Muslim refugees have gathered.

6 August 1992. The Serb concentration camp at Omarska in northern Bosnia is exposed to international attention in a television report by ITN.

13 August 1992. A UN Security Council resolution authorises the use of "all measures necessary" to ensure the delivery of humanitarian aid to civilians in isolated enclaves.

26-7 August 1992. The London Conference, co-chaired by the UN Secretary-General and UK Prime Minister and attended by representatives of 20 countries plus the EC and CSCE.

16 September 1992. The *Republika Srpska* "parliament" backs union with the FRY.

7 October 1992. The northern town of Bosanski Brod falls to Serb forces, which thus consolidate their grip on a narrow land corridor linking Serb-held areas of North-Western and Eastern Bosnia-Hercegovina.

9 October 1992. The UN Security Council adopts a resolution imposing the "No-Fly Zone", a ban on military flights in Bosnian airspace. Only in spring 1993, however, does NATO begin to enforce the zone; even then some helicopter flights are permitted.

9 October 1992. Karadzic and Boban agree a ceasefire between Bosnian Serb forces and the Bosnian Croat HVO. Within days the HVO is fighting the mainly Muslim Bosnian Army, and by 25 October Mostar has fallen to the HVO.

2 January 1993. The Vance-Owen plan envisages a decentralised Bosnian state with a nine-member central presidency (three from each ethnic group) and 10 autonomous provinces. Each ethnic group is effectively to control three provinces, with Sarajevo under joint control. The plan requires the Serbs (currently in control of 70 per cent of Bosnian territory) to relinquish ground, allocating them only some 50 per cent of the total.

4-12 January 1993. Direct talks between the leaders of the warring parties take place for the first time since the beginning of the war.

11 March 1993. Bosnia's Unprofor commander Gen. Philippe Morillon promises international protection for the beleaguered eastern enclave of Srebrenica.

17 April 1993. The UN Security Council approves tougher UN sanctions against the FRY, effective from 27 April.

25-6 April 1993. The Bosnian Serb assembly rejects the Vance-Owen peace plan, despite strong pressure from Serbia-FRY, and is overwhelmingly backed in a referendum on 15-16 May.

6 May 1993. UN Security Council resolution 814 declares Sarajevo, Bihac and the eastern enclaves of Gorazde, Srebrenica, Tuzla and Zepa to be "Safe Areas" and orders the warring parties to ensure that they are not subject to "armed attacks or any hostile act".

9 May 1993. The HVO, covertly backed by up to 30,000 Croatian Army troops, launches a major military offensive against the Bosnian Army around Mostar.

4 June 1993. UN Security Council resolution 836 authorises Unprofor "to take the necessary measures, including the use of force, in reply to bombardments against the Safe Areas" and in defence of humanitarian aid convoys. Acceptable force is defined as "close air support", i.e. the targeting of forces in the act of engaging Unprofor troops.

28 August 1993. Proclamation of the Croat Republic of Herceg-Bosna.

20 September 1993. The Geneva Conference's Union of Republics plan fails, as talks on the British warship Invincible founder on the Bosnian Muslims' insistence on an outlet into the Adriatic.

27 September 1993. Maverick Bosnian Presidency member and Muslim entrepreneur Fikret Abdic announces the secession of his north-western power-base, the strategic enclave of Bihac, a UN Safe Area.

25 October 1993. Haris Silajdzic, a Muslim, is appointed prime minister, violating the convention that the office goes to a Croat.

9 November 1993. Mostar's Old Bridge, the structure built in 1566 and a symbol of Bosnian multi-ethnicity, is destroyed by HVO gunners.

17 November 1993. Opening of the UN War Crimes Tribunal in the Hague, to investigate and try those accused of war crimes since 1991 in the former Yugoslavia.

29 November 1993. Talks between leaders of the warring parties, held in Geneva, are the last to take place before the final settlement at Dayton.

5 February 1994. 68 people are killed and 197 injured when a single mortar bomb strikes a crowded Sarajevo market place; Serbs are held responsible for the atrocity.

9 February 1994. NATO ambassadors issue an ultimatum to the Bosnian Serbs, imposing a 20 km heavy artillery exclusion zone around Sarajevo with effect from midnight on 20-21 February. Fearing punitive air strikes, the Serbs comply at the last minute.

17 February 1994. Kresimir Zubak is elected as Bosnian Croat leader, replacing the hardline nationalist Boban.

24 February 1994. The Muslim-Croat war ends.

18 March 1994. The Washington Accords: Bosnian Government and Bosnian Croat officials sign an agreement on the creation of a Muslim-Croat federation, with preliminary agreement on linking this in a loose wider confederation with Croatia. On 30 March the Assembly of Bosnia-Hercegovina ratifies a new constitution based on the Washington Accords.

10-11 April 1994. Serb targets near the UN Safe Area of Gorazde are bombed by NATO planes in the first UN-requested air strikes in former Yugoslavia.

30 May 1994. Constituent session of the Assembly of the (Muslim-Croat) Bosnian Federation. Bosnian Croat leader Zubak is elected as Federation President, Muslim Ejup Ganic becomes Vice-President, and Silajdzic becomes Federation Prime Minister.

The institutions of the Republic of Bosnia-Hercegovina continue to operate in parallel. On 14 June Tudjman visits Sarajevo.

9 June 1994. A ceasefire takes effect between all three parties, hailed by Unprofor commander Lt.-Gen. Rose as "the beginning of the end of the war".

6 July 1994. The Contact Group (comprising France, Russia, the UK, the USA and Germany) unveils a proposed "Map" (actually a peace plan), awarding 51 per cent of Bosnian territory to the Bosnian Federation.

19 July 1994. The Bosnian Serb assembly fails to accept the Contact Group's Map on the grounds that three issues remain unresolved: the Bosnian Serbs' future relationship with the FRY, Bosnian Serb access to the Adriatic and the status of Sarajevo.

5 August 1994. Angered at Bosnian Serb intransigence, Milosevic imposes an economic blockade against the Bosnian Serbs, allowing the transit only of humanitarian supplies of food and medicine. In mid-September the FRY approves the deployment of international observers on the Serbian-Bosnian border.

5 October 1994. International sanctions against the FRY are selectively suspended for a trial period, UN observers having accepted the authenticity of the FRY blockade.

January 1995. A four-month "total cessation of hostilities", signed by all the warring parties, comes into effect; it expires on 30 April.

6 March 1995. Croatia, Bosnia-Hercegovina and the Bosnian Croats agree to establish a military alliance.

19 March 1995. A Bosnian Army offensive begins in the Tuzla area. From early April a joint Croatian-Bosnian Croat advance makes gains in southern Bosnia-Hercegovina.

May 1995. Fighting intensifies in the Sarajevo area.

25-6 May 1995. In response to renewed Bosnian Serb shelling of Sarajevo, NATO aircraft launch the first attacks on the Bosnian Serb military infrastructure, destroying eight weapons dumps near Pale. Bosnian Serb forces retaliate by bombarding Tuzla, killing some 48 civilians, and by taking UN personnel as hostages, subsequently placing some of them near potential NATO targets to form a human shield.

3 June 1995. NATO and European Defence Ministers agree to create a heavily armed Rapid Reaction ground force force under direct UK and French command.

13 June 1995. Karadzic declares the hostage crisis over.

18 June 1995. Unprofor troops are withdrawn from Bosnian Serb-held territory.

11 July 1995. Srebrenica, the eastern enclave and UN Safe Area sheltering some 40,000 Muslims, falls to Bosnian Serb forces supervised by Gen. Mladic. Dutch UN peacekeepers based in the enclave offer no resistance, and Bosnian Serb forces massacre up to 8,000 Muslim men in the worst single atrocity of the Bosnian war.

25 July 1995. Another "Safe Area", the eastern enclave of Zepa, falls to the Bosnian Serbs. The UN War Crimes Tribunal indicts Karadzic and Mladic on charges of genocide and crimes against humanity; further charges follow in November in relation to the Srebrenica massacre.

4-9 August 1995. In Croatia, government forces retake most of the territory held by the Croatian Serbs since 1991, thereby fundamentally altering the military balance in Bosnia-Hercegovina; the besieged Bosnian Fifth Army in Bihac is relieved and Abdic's rebel army there is defeated. On 12 August the Bosnian Army and the HVO jointly launch an offensive in central Bosnia.

28 August 1995. A single mortar blast kills 37 people in Sarajevo's Markale market place; the UN identifies the Bosnian Serbs as the perpetrators.

30 August 1995. NATO launches Operation Deliberate Force, a massive aerial campaign, supplemented by the gunners of the Rapid Reaction Force on the ground, against Bosnian Serb military and infrastructure targets. Its aims are to halt Serb shelling of the four remaining UN Safe Areas, to open routes into Sarajevo, and to drive heavy weapons from the exclusion zone around the capital. Russian President Boris Yeltsin denounces the operation as a "cruel bombardment".

31 August 1995. The Bosnian Serbs agree to join a combined Serb delegation headed by Milosevic in peace talks.

8 September 1995. Senior officials of the conflict's main protagonists meet in Geneva, for the first time for 18 months, for talks mediated by Richard Holbrooke, architect of the recent US initiative. The Foreign Ministers of Bosnia-Hercegovina, Croatia and the FRY sign an "agreement on basic principles", including the retention of a single state of Bosnia-Hercegovina sub-divided into two entities, the Muslim-Croat federation and a Serb Republic, controlling respectively 51 and 49 per cent of the territory.

11 September 1995. A major offensive by the combined forces of the Bosnian Army, the HVO and the Croatian Army begins in central and western Bosnia-Hercegovina and makes rapid advances into Serb-held territory. On 13 September the siege of Sarajevo ends as the Bosnian Serbs begin to withdraw heavy weapons from the 20-km exclusion zone around Sarajevo, and on the following day Operation Deliberate Force is suspended.

18 September 1995. Bosnian Serb forces crumble before a joint offensive by Bosnian Army, Croatian Army and Bosnian Croat forces which threatens the Serb stronghold of Banja Luka in northern Bosnia.

5 October 1995. US President Bill Clinton announces a 60-day ceasefire, following the signature of an accord (mediated by Holbrooke) which includes guarantees on freedom of movement designed to allow "ethnically cleansed" refugees to return to their homes.

12 October 1995. The ceasefire takes effect, having been delayed by 48 hours ostensibly due to the Serbs' failure to restore utilities to Sarajevo, but in fact to allow further Muslim-Croat military gains.

14 October 1995. The Muslim-Croat share of Bosnian territory stands at to 52.26 per cent.

24 October 1995. Izetbegovic denounces the extension of the franchise in Croatian elections to the Bosnian Croat community.

1 November 1995. Peace talks open at the Dayton air base in Ohio. For the first time since November 1993 Izetbegovic, Milosevic and Tudjman are all present. Milosevic represents both the FRY and the Bosnian Serbs.

21 November 1995. The leaders of the warring parties initial the Dayton peace agreement, envisaging a loose political structure joining the Muslim-Croat Federation, with 51 per cent of Bosnian territory, and the Bosnian Serb Republic, with 49 per cent. Displaced people will have the right to return to their properties and reclaim lost assets.

23 November 1995. Karadzic pledges that the Bosnian Serb leadership will implement the Dayton settlement in full "despite certain painful clauses".

12 December 1995. Sarajevo's 120,000-strong Serb community votes by over 98 per cent against the Dayton settlement.

14 December 1995. Formal signature of the Dayton accords at a ceremony in Paris. The signature requires the parties to withdraw their forces from zones of separation within 30 days; to exchange territory within 45; and to move all heavy weapons to designated places within 120.

20 December 1995. Formal transfer of power from Unprofor to a 60,000-strong international Implementation Force (I-For) under NATO command which is given a wide range of powers to implement the Dayton Accord.

22 December 1995. The Bosnian presidency declares an end to the state of war.

SLOVENIA

The Republic of Slovenia officially declared independence on 7 October 1991, received EC recognition on 15 January 1992, and won a seat at the UN on 22 May 1992. At just 20,251 sq. km, Slovenia formed less than 10 per cent of the Yugoslav land area. Less than half the size of Estonia, it is the smallest ex-communist state in central and eastern Europe. Its population is 1,962,000 (rather more than Estonia's) and its only major city is the capital Ljublijana, a settlement of some 300,000 people.

Geographically, Slovenia is part of alpine central Europe and not a Balkan state. It shares borders with Austria, Hungary, Croatia and Italy, whose major port of Trieste is barely 65 km from Ljublijana. Slovenia itself has an outlet into the Adriatic at the port of Koper.

Ethnically Slovenia is relatively homogeneous, being 87.6 per cent Slovene; minorities include Croats (2.7%), Serbs (2.4%) and Muslims (1.4%). The minority populations have been swelled since the last census in 1991 by the influx of refugees from the wars in neighbouring Croatia and Bosnia-Hercegovina. There are ethnic Slovene minorities in Italy and Croatia. The Slovenes are separated by language from other south slavs (a language group arguably comprising Serbs, Croats, Bosnian Muslims, Macedonians and Bulgarians). Slovenes are traditionally Catholics.

HISTORICAL NARRATIVE

The lands of the Slovenes were historically part of the core territories of the Austro-Hungarian Empire from the 14th century and are therefore steeped in the bureaucratic and essentially European political and cultural traditions of the Habsburg lands; unlike Serbia, Bosnia-Hercegovina and parts of Croatia they escaped long centuries of domination by the tyrannical and intolerant Ottoman Empire. Traditionally, Slovenia was an agrarian society of devout Catholics. In interwar Yugoslavia the Slovenes reached a *modus vivendi* with the dominant Serbs, allowing Slovenes a relatively privileged position in the kingdom. During the Second World War the Slovenes provided staunch opposition to Italian and German occupiers. Slovenia then became a loyal constituent republic of communist Yugoslavia.

The rise of moderate Slovene nationalism in the second half of the 1980s flowed from three developments: (i) the reaction against growing nationalism among Serbs, who seemed ready to assert their own interests within the federation using the aggressive methods exemplified in the crackdown on the Albanians of Kosovo; (ii) widening cultural differences, the Slovenes regarding themselves increasingly as part of the European mainstream whereas the southern republics appeared mired in reactionary "eastern" cultural and political values; and (iii) the widening economic gap between the modernised Slovene economy and the struggling southern republics, which increasing the Slovene desire for autarky.

Slovenia was the most developed of the former Yugoslav states. Almost one half of the labour force was engaged in industry. Thus, although Slovenia accounted for a mere 8.4 per cent of Yugoslavia's population, it generated as much as 20 per cent of GNP and 30 per cent of exports (although this performance was due in part to the cheap raw materials and labour in neighbouring Yugoslav republics, and to the captive markets there).

The Slovene President from 1990, the ex-communist Milan Kucan, initially delayed direct confrontation with the federal authorities over Slovene independence. Instead he pressed for increasing autonomy and, with Defence Minister Janez Jansa, made detailed and secret military, legal and political preparations for independence. At secret meetings with Milosevic in January 1991, Kucan secured Serb acquiescence in Slovene secession; although the Serbian leadership publicly gave the opposite impression, it had already abandoned the idea of defending the entire federation and looked instead to protect only majority-Serb areas, of which there were none in Slovenia. When Slovenia declared its dissociation from Yugoslavia in June 1991 the JNA intervened in defence of a federal Yugoslavia, but without Serbian support the JNA "invasion" of Slovenia quickly failed.

Since independence Slovenia has enjoyed remarkable political and economic stability. In December 1994 President Kucan even declared that Slovenia had "no enemies and no problems". He clearly regarded as relatively minor the disputes with Croatia (over the mutual border and the division of federal assets) and with Italy (over compensation to ethnic Italians dispossessed by the Yugoslav state in the postwar period - an argument which delayed talks on associate Slovene membership of the EC). Slovenia's liberal regimes tolerated a free press; Slovenian nationalism remained moderate; and there was progress in integration with Europe, as Slovenia established itself in the "fast track" to EC membership with the Czech Republic, Hungary and Poland.

Independence had remarkably little economic impact on Slovenia. By mid-1994 some 90 per cent of Slovenia's trade had been reoriented westwards; standards of living were relatively stable; and by 1994 the growth rate stood at some 4.5 cent.

Slovenia had only two prime ministers in 1990-5, presiding over a series of centre-right coalitions. Christian Democrat Lojze Peterle, apparently preoccupied with his historical role in re-establishing Christian traditions, presided over a poorly organised cabinet of 27 portfolios, which made slow progress in economic reform. Janez Drnovsek, in office from April 1992, turned to pressing bread-and-butter issues, but also made limited progress with structural reform and privatisation. Drnovsek's Liberal Democrats (LDS), a successor to the Socialist Youth Organisation, became the leading party following the December 1992 elections.

The coalitions formed since 1990 all included a range of political parties; Slovenia has been refreshingly free of serious disputes between the right and the ex-communist parties, due in part to the fact that the Slovene communists led the country to independence. There are some personal grudges, however; Jansa, for example, still reputedly suspects Kucan of having connived in his arrest by the JNA in 1988. A controversial figure, Jansa's shifting ideological position now places his Social Democrats (SDSS) firmly on the right; his party withdrew from the coalition in March 1994 and by 1995 was performing well in opinion polls.

POLITICAL PARTIES

The **Slovene League of Communists** (ZSK) was renamed the **ZSK Party of Democratic Reform** in December 1989 under the slogan "Europe Now!". Reformist Milan Kucan, the party leader since 1986, was the driving force behind the modernisation. The party performed disappointingly in 1990, taking only 17 per cent of the vote. Although Kucan was elected President, he renounced his party membership The party formed the main element of a new bloc, the **United List for Social Democracy** (ZL), to contest the elections of 1992; its poll rating slipped further to under 14 per cent. The bloc was subsequently reconstituted as a political party under the ZL name. It participated in the LDS-led coalition government in office from January 1993.

Demos, a diverse coalition of seven opposition parties, won 55 per cent of the vote in the 1990 elections before dissolving itself in December 1991. Demos included the **Christian Democratic Party** (SKD), which has been ever-present in Slovene governments since independence and whose leader Lojze Peterle served as Slovene Prime Minister from 1990-2, and the LDS.

The **Liberal Democratic Party of Slovenia** (LDS) emerged as the leading party in the 1992 elections, and formed a coalition government. Party leader Janez Drnovsek, Slovenia's prime minister since April 1992, was reappointed in January 1993. The LDS's roots were in the Socialist Youth Organisation and particularly in a group of journalists associated with the Organisation's publication *Mladina*. The party supported faster pro-market reform, democratisation and closer European links. In March 1994 the LDS absorbed the Greens (ZS) and the Democrats (DS) to become the **Liberal Democracy of Slovenia** (LDS).

ELECTIONS

Legislature

The 90-seat lower chamber comprised 38 members elected directly; 50 awarded proportionately to parties passing a 3 per cent threshold; and two seats reserved for representatives of the Italian and Hungarian minorities. The 40-seat upper chamber, the State Council, comprised 22 members elected directly and 18 nominated on a corporatist basis to represent various professions and interest groups.

In elections to the lower house on 8 April 1990 the centre-right DEMOS coalition won 55 per cent of the vote and 47 of the 80 seats, while the ex-communist ZSK-Party of Democratic Reform took only 17 per cent and 14 seats. The Liberal Party took 12 seats, the Socialist Alliance five and others two.

In the 6 December 1992 elections the LDS, formerly a constituent party of Demos, finished in first place, winning 22 seats in the lower house from just under 24 per cent of the vote; the SKD and the ZL both won a share of the vote in the low teens, to gain 15 and 14 seats respectively; a further five minor parties won seats, ranging from the xenophobic Slovene National Party (SNS) on 9.9 per cent to the Social Democratic Party of Slovenia (SDSS) on 3.3 per cent.

Presidential elections

Milan Kucan, the popular reformist leader of the ZSK, won direct presidential elections on 8-22 April 1990 with 52 per cent of the second round vote, defeating Joze Pucnik of Demos. Kucan resigned his leadership of the ZSK to serve as an independent president. On 6 December 1992 Kucan was emphatically re-elected in the first round with 64 per cent of the vote; Ivo Bizjak of the SKD won 21 per cent, and Jelko Kacin of the DS was most successful of five other candidates with 7 per cent.

CHRONOLOGY

13th century. The Austro-Hungarian Empire takes control of Slovene-populated areas, there having been no tradition of a sovereign Slovene state. Slovene bureaucrats prosper in the Habsburg administration.

1 December 1918. Foundation of Yugoslav state, the Kingdom of Serbs, Croats and Slovenes.

Early 1980s. Liberalisation in Slovenia; the proliferation of cultural, political and other interest groups marks the beginnings of pluralism in the republic.

February 1987. A group of Slovene nationalist intellectuals publishes *Contributions to the Slovene National Programme*, which argues for a return to traditional Slovene Christian values, thereby outraging the JNA.

Summer 1988. Arrest of the Ljubljana Four for involvement in the publication of a string of allegations against the JNA in the Slovene weekly *Mladina*; the four, who include activist Janez Jansa, are jailed for between six months and four years. The Slovene opposition is galvanised as unprecedented protest demonstrations of up to 100,000 people take place in Ljublijana.

27 September 1989. The Assembly in Slovenia approves constitutional changes which include the republic's right, as a "sovereign and autonomous state", to secede from Yugoslavia.

December 1989. The Slovene League of Communists is renamed the ZSK Party of Democratic Reform under the slogan "Europe Now!". Opposition parties are legalised by parliament and multi-party elections called for the following spring.

20-23 January 1990. The federal League of Communists of Yugoslavia (SKJ) convenes for its 14th and final extraordinary congress; Slovene proposals for further devolution to the republics are rejected and the Slovene delegation walks out for good.

8 April 1990. Slovenia holds the first multi-party elections in Yugoslavia since the beginning of the communist period. The elections for the republican Assembly are won by the centre-right DEMOS coalition, while a direct presidential election (completed in a second round on April 22) is won by Milan Kucan, the popular reformist, who then resigns his leadership of the ZSK-Party of Democratic Renewal.

16 May 1990. A Slovene government is formed under the leadership of Christian Democrat Lojze Peterle. The new Defence Minister is Social Democrat leader Janez

Jansa (one of the Ljublijana Four). The JNA commences a secret programme to disarm the Slovene Territorial Defence.

2 July 1990. The assembly in Slovenia issues a formal proclamation of the republic's sovereignty.

23 December 1990. A referendum overwhelmingly approves plans to declare full independence, in the absence of an agreement on constitutional reform within six months.

24 January 1991. Milosevic, in a secret meeting with Kucan, signals Serbian acquiescence in Slovene secession.

25 June 1991. Slovenia proclaims its dissociation from the Yugoslav federation.

25 June - 4 July 1991. The ten-day war. The JNA attempts to take control of the republic in the name of securing Yugoslavia's borders. On 27 June Kucan denounces the JNA movements as an invasion and orders a military response. The ferocity and organisation of the Slovene army startles the JNA. Many JNA troops are pinned down in their barracks and JNA armoured columns are halted by Slovene ambushes.

4 July 1991. A ceasefire is declared. The official death toll is 67. Both Slovenia and Croatia are persuaded to suspend for three months their declarations of independence.

18 July 1991. The Federal Presidency agrees to withdraw the JNA for a "temporary" period within three months; the agreement is an effective recognition of Slovene secession.

7 October 1991. Formal declaration of independence.

25 October 1991. JNA forces complete their withdrawal.

23 December 1991. Adoption of a new constitution. Demos dissolves itself into its constituent parties.

15 January 1992. The EC recognises Slovene and Croatian independence.

22 April 1992. Peterle resigns as prime minister following a vote of no confidence by the parliament, which has become restless with the poor organisation of government and the slow pace of economic change, notably privatisation. His Christian Democratic government is replaced by a Liberal Democratic (LDS) cabinet under LDS leader and former federal presidency member Janez Drnovsek.

22 May 1992 Slovenia becomes a UN member.

6 December 1992. Presidential and parliamentary elections; Kucan is re-elected on the first ballot with 64 per cent of the vote; while the LDS is the strongest party in parliament although short of a majority.

12 January 1993. Drnovsek is re-elected as prime minister by the parliament, heading a coalition comprising the LDS, SKD and three smaller parties, the ex-communist United List bloc (ZL), the Greens (ZS) and Jansa's Social Democrats (SDSS).

23 July 1993. A cache of 120 tonnes of arms is discovered at the Maribor airport; Defence Minister Jansa is implicated in the transit of arms to Bosnia-Hercegovina, in violation of the UN arms embargo against former Yugoslavia.

12 March 1994. The LDS merges with three minor parties, the DS, ZS and Socialists, to form the Liberal Democracy of Slovenia (also LDS), under Drnovsek.

28 March 1994. Dismissal of Defence Minister Janez Jansa after allegations that his agents had been involved in beatings; his SDSS withdraws from the coalition.

December 1994. On a visit to Slovakia, Kucan declares that Slovenia has "no problems and no enemies". Rumbling disputes with Croatia and Italy nevertheless continue over, respectively, disputed borders and compensation for ethnic Italians dispossessed after the Second World War.

4 March 1995. Italy lifts its veto on the holding of talks between the EC and Slovenia on associate membership.

MACEDONIA

Macedonia unilaterally declared independence from Yugoslavia on 15 September 1991, but international recognition was delayed. Greece objected that the republic's name implied a territorial claim on Greek Macedonia. In April 1993 Macedonia took a seat at the UN under the compromise name Former Yugoslav Republic of Macedonia (FYROM): it won recognition as FYROM by six EC states in December 1993 and by the USA and Russia in February 1994.

Macedonia's territory comprises only 25,713 sq. km., making it the second smallest East-Central European former communist state (after Slovenia). Its capital and only major town is Skopje. Mountainous and landlocked in the centre of the Balkan peninsula, it shares borders with Serbia, Bulgaria, Greece (which affords the republic its only relatively easy access to the sea, by road to the port of Salonika) and Albania.

Macedonia has one of the most ethnically complex societies in the region. According to the 1991 census, Macedonia's population of 2,038,047 was 64.5 per cent Macedonian, 21.1 per cent Albanian, 4.8 per cent Turk, 2.7 per cent Romany, 2.5 per cent Muslim and 2.2 per cent Serb. These figures are hotly disputed by the minorities; the Albanians claim to comprise 40 per cent of the population and the Serbs 12.5 per cent. (An EC-sponsored census held in 1994 was, like that of 1991, disrupted by an Albanian boycott, shedding doubt on the results, which had recorded a total population of 1,940,000, of which 66.5 per cent were Macedonian, 22.9 per cent Albanian, 2 per cent Serb and 8.6 per cent others.) According to official figures two-thirds of the population are Orthodox Christians and 30 per cent are Muslims.

Perhaps the most fundamental ethnic problem faced by the Macedonian state is an external one: the refusal of neighbouring states even to recognise the validity of a distinct Macedonian nationality.

During the communist era Macedonian leaders began a campaign to define a Macedonian nationality distinct from that of neighbouring national groups. As part of this campaign efforts were made to establish the Macedonian vernacular as a separate language. Most Serbs and Bulgarians, however, continued to regard Macedonian as merely a dialect of their own closely related languages and viewed Macedonian nationality as artificial.

Greece, meanwhile, claimed the name and history of Macedonia as part of an exclusively Hellenic heritage. Greece's northern province was also named Macedonia, and with the collapse of Yugoslavia, Greece began seriously to fret over Macedonian irredentism. These concerns were reinforced by fears that northern Greece's

"Slavophonic" minority might find common cause with the Macedonian Republic. (Greece's extreme sensitivity to centrifugal pressure is exemplified in its refusal to admit the existence of national minorities on its territory; its Turkish minority is described as "Greek Muslims".)

Macedonia was the least economically developed of all the Yugoslav republics, with the exception of Montenegro. Despite its considerable deposits of metals and minerals, Macedonia relied heavily on agriculture.

HISTORICAL NARRATIVE

Macedonian territory has been under dispute since the Ottoman Empire's grip on the Balkans began to weaken in the nineteenth century. It was eventually incorporated into Yugoslavia in 1918. With the creation of the communist Yugoslav Federation after the Second World War, Macedonia achieved republican status within Yugoslavia. Although a tiny militant-nationalist group, the Internal Macedonian Revolutionary Army (VMRO), had operated during the interwar period, by the 1940s Macedonian nationalism was still embryonic. The new Macedonian leadership deliberately nurtured it as a means of establishing the tiny republic as a political force within the federation, and of answering the Serb tendency to regard the republic as "Southern Serbia".

Despite the rise of Macedonian nationalism, exemplified in the eventual emergence of the VMRO-DPMNE as the largest single party in the 1990 elections, the republic's secession from the Yugoslav federation was not an act of zealotry but of rational calculation, faced with the alternative of effective annexation by its dominant northern neighbour Serbia.

From the beginning of the wars in former Yugoslavia the Western powers were concerned at the possibility that the conflict might spread beyond the borders of the old federation. There were rumours that Greece and Serbia were keen to partition Macedonia between themselves and Bulgaria, and fears that a land-grab in Macedonia could prompt Albanian and Turkish intervention. Militarily Macedonia was extremely weak, with no air force and no armoured vehicles save two Second World War-era T-34 tanks.

These concerns led to the preventive deployment of UN peacekeepers in 1992-3, including the first commitment to the Balkan theatre of US ground forces. Due mainly to their symbolic presence, the situation in Macedonia's border regions was remarkably peaceful in 1993-5.

Macedonia's most fundamental problem has been relations with its southern neighbour Greece (for Greek objections to the republic's name, see above). One of President Gligorov's principal achievements was to retain the support and sympathy of Western leaders during the long dispute with Greece. Gligorov clung defiantly to the republic's name and symbols, in the knowledge that any concession on these fundamentals could undermine the state's legitimacy in the minds of its own citizens, particularly when Macedonian nationality was a relatively recent phenomenon defined "from above". Although Macedonia won the vital support of Bulgaria, Turkey and the USA, its international recognition was delayed by Greek opposition until late 1993. Thenceforth, Greece exerted leverage on Macedonia by economic means, in the form of a trade blockade in place from February 1994 until October 1995.

Macedonia was already confronted by severe economic problems, caused not least by the imposition of international sanctions on its northern neighbour Serbia. The trade blockade helped encourage a black economy under which a relative few, often with criminal roots, prospered while the majority suffered increasing hardship. In the long term, the emergence of wealthy and powerful criminal clans may well be the most damaging and destabilising legacy for Macedonia of the wars to the north.

Gligorov's second major achievement was to keep a lid on internal tensions. Despite several crises in relations with the ethnic Albanian community, notably the conviction in June 1994 of ten prominent Albanians on charges of organising a secessionist army, the PDP (the principal Albanian party) participated in the coalition government throughout most of 1990-5 (although the party split at its 1994 congress, with a minority faction favouring a move into opposition). Conversely, Macedonian nationalism was kept in check, with the militant VMRO-DPMNE losing ground to the centre-left governing parties. Gligorov demonstrated a readiness at least to turn a blind eye to authoritarianism when the 1994 elections were partially rigged to deny the VMRO a single seat in parliament (although even on official figures the VMRO presidential candidate had polled over 14 per cent).

The settlement of the dispute with Greece in autumn 1995 paved the way to Macedonia's full membership of the international community. The cost to Macedonia was accepting the probable long-term official use of the FYROM name, and dropping from the national flag the Star of Vergina, an ancient symbol found at the grave of Alexander the Great, the ruler of ancient Macedonia.

The settlement with Greece was Gligorov's crowning achievement, but he was unable to attend the signing ceremony; instead he was recovering in hospital from serious injuries sustained in an assassination attempt just days before. Whether the culprits were a foreign power, Macedonian nationalists, Albanian separatists or organised criminals remained unclear. Gligorov's absence, even if only temporary, led to question marks over the continued stability of the republic.

POLITICAL PARTIES

The **Social Democratic Alliance of Macedonia** (SDSM), a bloc of reformist ex-communists, formed the main party of government from the 1990 elections onwards; it was led by the youthful Branko Crvenkovski, the prime minister from 1992-5. The special political and economic circumstances since 1990 have tended to conceal its ideological direction, apart from moderate nationalism and a tendency to authoritarianism.

The Internal Macedonian Revolutionary Organisation-Democratic Party for Macedonian National Unity (**VMRO-DPMNE**) is an ultra-nationalist party which bears the name of an interwar Macedonian-Bulgarian terrorist group. Despite winning the 1990 republican elections, the VMRO-DPMNE was kept out of government by an unholy alliance of ethnic Albanian parties and the left. The VMRO-DPMNE withdrew midway through the 1994 elections alleging massive electoral fraud and failed to win a single seat. They opposed the 1995 compromise with Greece under which Macedonia agreed to alter its national flag. The party denied any part in the assassination attempt on President Gligorov.

The **Party of Democratic Prosperity** (PDP), the principal ethnic Albanian party, was a junior coalition partner from 1990. Despite divisions within the party over continued co-operation with the SDSM in government, the pragmatic PDP leadership calculated that the alternative - government by the chauvinist VMRO - was worse. In April 1995 the PDP renamed itself the **Party of Democratic Prosperity of Albanians in Macedonia** (PDPSM).

ELECTIONS

Legislative elections

The VMRO-DPMNE became the largest single party in a fragmented parliament in legislative elections on 11 November - 9 December 1990, taking 37 of the 120 seats. The SDSM took 18, the League of Communists 31 and the PDP 25.

The SM, an alliance of the SDSM, the Liberals and the Socialists (formerly the rump League of Communists), won 95 seats in the 120-seat *Sobranie* in legislative elections on 16-30 October 1994. The PDP took 10, the ethnic Serb People's Democratic Party (NDS) four and others 11. Having boycotted the second round alleging massive electoral fraud, the VMRO-DPMNE failed to win a single seat. The party demanded the nullification of the elections.

Presidential elections

Kiro Gligorov was elected as president by the legislature and inaugurated in that office on 6 January 1991. In direct presidential elections on 14 October 1994 Gligorov was re-elected, winning over 50 per cent of the poll in the first round and easily defeating his main rival Ljubisa Georgievski, the nominee of VMRO-DPMNE.

CHRONOLOGY

1912-18. The Balkan Wars conclude in 1913 with the division of Macedonia between Greece, Bulgaria and Serbia (victors over the Ottoman Empire, which had been the dominant force in Macedonia for the preceding four centuries). During the First World War Macedonia is occupied by Bulgaria.

1 December 1918. Foundation of the Yugoslav state as the Kingdom of Serbs, Croats and Slovenes; northern Macedonia is absorbed by the new state and is dominated by Serbs in the interwar period.

1929. The Internal Macedonian Revolutionary Organisation (VMRO), an extreme Macedonian-Bulgarian nationalist group, launches a terrorist campaign against the Serbs.

9 October 1934. The Yugoslav King Alexander is assassinated in Marseilles by an *Ustasa*-VMRO squad.

January 1946. Macedonia is designated as a constituent republic of the Yugoslav federation. "Macedonian" becomes a recognised nationality.

November-December 1990. Legislative elections result in a fragmented parliament. The revived VMRO-Democratic Party for Macedonian National Unity (VMRO-DPMNE) becomes the largest single party but does not participate in government;

instead an alliance of the ethnic Albanian PDP and the ex-communist Social Democratic Alliance of Macedonia (SDSM) takes office.

6 January 1991. Kiro Gligorov, a veteran communist, is elected President of Macedonia by the republican legislature.

25 January 1991. The Macedonian legislature declares the republic's sovereignty and right to secede.

8 September 1991. In a referendum, 95 per cent of voters support secession.

15 September 1991. Macedonia declares independence.

20 November 1991. The legislature promulgates a new constitution.

6 January 1992. Constitutional amendments formally renounce territorial claims on other countries, in a bid to appease Greece, which fears Macedonian irredentism.

14 February 1992. Greek demonstrators in Salonika insist that the name Macedonia is part of Greece's own historical identity and cannot be appropriated by the new state.

26 March 1992. JNA forces complete their withdrawal from Macedonia.

4 September 1992. Appointment of a new cabinet under the 31-year old leader of the SDSM, Branko Crvenkovski.

6 November 1992. Four people are killed in inter-ethnic riots in Skopje.

10 December 1992. Over one million Greeks demonstrate in Athens against international recognition of Macedonia under its existing name.

11 December 1992. The UN Security Council authorises the dispatch of 700 UN peacekeepers to Macedonia.

8 April 1993. Macedonia becomes a full member of the UN under the name Former Yugoslav Republic of Macedonia (FYROM).

24 June 1993. The first of 300 US troops arrive in Macedonia to reinforce Unprofor (the UN peacekeepers). The troops are the first commitment of US ground forces to the Balkans during the wars in the former Yugoslavia.

16 December 1993. Recognition by six EC states: Denmark, France, Germany, Italy, the Netherlands and the UK.

3-9 February 1994. Russian and US recognition.

16 February 1994. Greek Prime Minister Papandreou announces the immediate imposition of a trade ban on Macedonia; only humanitarian supplies are to be permitted across the Greco-Macedonian border.

30 April 1994. Crvenkovski claims that Greece intends to destabilise Macedonia and thereafter to partition the country between itself and Serbia.

27 June 1994. Ten ethnic Albanians are convicted of setting up a 21,000-strong "All-Albanian Army" with the aim of fighting a war to unify Western Macedonia with Albania. The ten include the prominent Husein Haskaj, the former Deputy Defence Minister, and Methad Emini, honorary president of the PDP. On 3 July ethnic Albanian deputies begin a boycott of parliament in protest.

14 October 1994. Gligorov is re-elected as President.

16-30 October 1994. The ruling Alliance of Macedonia bloc wins a majority of parliamentary seats in disputed legislative elections.

9 February 1995. The PDP and other ethnic Albanian deputies begin a boycott of the legislature in protest at the passage of a law banning the use of the Albanian language in official documents. The PDP nevertheless remains in the governing coalition.

15 February 1995. Ethnic Albanians establish a university at Mala Recica, near Tetovo; in clashes with the police on 17 February, one ethnic Albanian supporter of the university is shot dead.

22 April 1995. The PDP becomes the Party of Democratic Prosperity of Albanians in Macedonia (PDPSM).

14 July 1995. The PDPSM abandons its parliamentary boycott.

13 September 1995. The Greek and Macedonian foreign ministers sign an interim accord in New York after four weeks of talks mediated by Cyrus Vance. Each side proclaims mutual respect for each other's sovereignty and territorial integrity, including the existing border. Macedonia agrees to drop the Vergina Sun symbol, claimed by Greece as part of its heritage, from its national flag, while Greece agrees to end the trade blockade.

3 October 1995. Gligorov is seriously injured in an assassination attempt, when a bomb explodes damaging his car and killing his driver and a passer-by.

5-10 October 1995. The Macedonian parliament approves changes to the national flag and overwhelmingly ratifies the New York accord.

12 October 1995. Macedonia is granted full membership of the OSCE.

15 October 1995. The Greek trade embargo is lifted with the final signature of the New York accord at a ceremony in Skopje.

THE BALTIC STATES

The independent Republics of Estonia, Latvia and Lithuania were annexed by the Soviet Union in 1940 and were subsequently designated constituent Soviet Socialist Republics (SSRs) of the Union. The international community never formally recognised the annexations. The three states declared independence from the Soviet Union in 1990-1; this was recognised by the Soviet Union itself on 6 September 1991 and the three states were admitted to the UN on 17 September 1991.

Estonia, Latvia and Lithuania are situated on the eastern shores of the Baltic Sea. Their territory covers much of the Baltic Plains. Estonia, at 45,100 sq. km., is less than one fifth the size of the UK. Latvia and Lithuania are both somewhat larger, being 64,600 and 65,200 sq. km. respectively.

Estonia is flanked in the north by the Gulf of Finland; its capital, Tallinn, which is home to half a million people, is on the northern coastline some 50 miles from Helsinki. In the west lies the Gulf of Riga and in the east, Russia; Estonia's eastern border town of Narva is only 150 km. from St. Petersburg. Beyond Estonia's southern border lies Latvia, which is dominated by its coastal capital Riga, a city of some 900,000 people. Its second city is Daugavpils. In the east Latvia borders Russia and Belarus; Latvia's southern neighbour is Lithuania. The latter's capital, Vilnius, is in the country's south and is populated by some 590,000 people. Lithuania is flanked by Belarus in the south-east, by a short frontier with Poland in the south, and in the south west by the tiny coastal enclave of Kaliningrad, which is under Russian sovereignty.

At 1,565,000, Estonia's population is the smallest of any former communist state in Eastern and Central Europe. Latvia is home to 2,576,000 people and Lithuania to 3,751,000. Large communities of non-indigenous predominantly Slavic peoples, mainly Russians, Belorussians ("White Russians") Ukrainians and Poles, comprise some 38 per cent of the Estonian population and 48 per cent of the Latvian.

None of the three Baltic nationalities are Slavic. Estonians speak a Finno-Ugric language related to Finnish and Hungarian and are descended from Asiatic tribes. Latvians and Lithuanians speak languages of a Scandinavian type and are part of the indo-European group. All three use the latin rather than cyrillic script.

The principal religions of Estonia are Lutheranism and Russian Orthodoxy; Latvia has Lutherans, Russian Orthodox and Roman Catholics, while Roman Catholicism predominates in Lithuania.

HISTORICAL NARRATIVE

In the centuries prior to their absorption into the Russian Empire, the peoples of the eastern shores of the Baltic Sea were dominated by German, Swedish and Polish rulers. Only Lithuania, in union with Poland in the 15th and 16th centuries, had been a major European power, its territory extending south to the Black Sea. But by the late eighteenth century Lithuania, along with Estonia and Latvia, had become a province of Tsarist Russia. Germans and Poles remained landowners and burghers, while the mercantile and commercial classes were dominated by Germans and Jews; the indigenous peoples mainly comprised the peasantry.

A policy of vigorous Russification was practised most assiduously in Lithuania, Russia having identified the Roman Catholic Church as a potent symbol of Lithuanian aspirations for statehood. Even so, by the nineteenth century the mainly Lutheran Estonian and Latvian churches, as well as the Lithuanian church, had begun to generate an indigenous intelligentsia capable of articulating the growing national consciousness of the Baltic peoples.

Economic and social change underscored the religious and ethnic divide between the Baltic nations and Russians. Rapid industrial growth in the early 20th century left Russia's Baltic provinces economically among the most developed in the Empire. National consciousness among the emerging working class was significantly stronger than it had been among the previous generation of peasants. When discontent within the Russian Empire erupted into revolution in 1905, some of the worst disturbances were in the Baltic provinces, where the implicit desire for national self-determination combined with the malaise caused by a failing economy.

The First World War fatally weakened the Tsarist state by destroying the last vestiges of the Tsar's popular legitimacy and by eroding the state's capacity to impose its rule. The October 1917 Bolshevik revolution swept away imperial power and brought an end to Russian involvement in the First World War. With the former empire's centre now weakened by military defeat, the beginnings of civil war, and the emergence of indigenous independence movements, and in the face of a continued German offensive, the Bolshevik regime was forced to withdraw the Russian military from the empire's periphery.

Making a virtue of necessity, the Bolsheviks in November 1917 issued the Declaration on the Rights of the Peoples of Russia, recognising the equality of nations and formally permitting secession from Russia. Restive nations at the periphery soon began to break away; Finland, in December 1917, and Estonia and Lithuania, in February 1918, were among the first to declare independence. Bolshevik Russia renounced its sovereignty over the Baltic states "voluntarily and for ever" later in 1918, and, in a series of treaties in 1920, formally recognised the secession of Estonia, Latvia and Lithuania.

In their campaign for independence, the Baltic states had won the support of the Western powers, who wanted to create a buffer zone around communist Russia. Estonia, Latvia and Lithuania, which had a combined population of just six and a half million in the interwar period, occupied a strategically vulnerable position as three tiny nations located between two major European powers, Germany and Russia.

All three newly independent Baltic states had unicameral legislatures elected every three years by universal suffrage. These immature democracies were rapidly confronted by problems common to the new interwar democracies of East-Central Europe. A lack of political experience led to a multiplicity of parties, fractiousness in parliament and cabinet instability. In all three Baltic states the moderate left was popular, but lost ground soon after independence, a victim of its own success after implementing the land reforms that had initially won the rural vote. As support for the left waned, moderate right-wing and centrist agrarian and populist parties gained strength, but were highly fragmented.

Between the first interwar elections in 1919 and the coup d'etat of 1934, **Estonia** had 21 different cabinets. By 1933 a Right-Radical party, the League of Freedom Fighters, had grown in popularity and adopted increasingly violent tactics. Fearing a Right-Radical takeover, in March 1934 Prime Minister Konstantin Pats staged a bloodless takeover supported by senior military figures and the leaders of the main parties. Pats had popular credibility as a former leader of the wartime independence movement who had been the first prime minister of independent Estonia, and he had a considerable power base as leader of the Agrarians. By May 1935 Pats had dissolved political parties and replaced them with a state umbrella political organisation, the Patriotic Front. Notwithstanding the objections of the liberal intelligentsia, and of the workers whose conditions worsened, the Pats regime was remarkably popular, particularly after the economic revival of the mid-1930s.

Latvia's political scene was highly fragmented. Agrarian nominees held the post of prime minister for most of the interwar democratic interlude, while the Social Democrats, although the largest single party, chose not to participate in government. The rapid succession of 18 cabinets from 1918 to 1934 conveyed a sense of permanent crisis in Latvia's nascent democracy. Economic depression in the early 1930s boosted the popularity of a several Right-Radical groups, notably the Thunder-Cross. Just weeks after the 1934 coup in Estonia, the Latvian Prime Minister and Agrarian leader Karlis Ulmanis launched a similar military-backed coup d'etat. Soon all political parties were dissolved. Ulmanis engineered a state-led recovery from depression and this, combined with his use of populist and nationalist rhetoric (reflected in policies including anti-minority educational measures), won him considerable popularity.

Lithuania's interwar political scene was more nationalistic than that of the other two Baltic states. This was due mainly to insecurities over Vilnius, which was to have been Lithuania's capital, but which had been annexed by Poland (as Wilna) in 1920 and occupied ever since. In addition Klaipeda, Lithuania's only port, was claimed by Germany. Inter-ethnic relations within Lithuania reflected these external insecurities. Religion was a second major source of political confrontation. Right-wing parties which shared a similar social and economic agenda were divided between populist and Catholic parties and this underlay the cabinet instability of 1918-24. The popular legitimacy of the democratic system was undermined by the ferocity and demagoguery of parliamentary debate, and by persistent questions over the competence and alleged venality of the government. A new and politically provocative socialist-populist government was in office for less than six months before a Junta of ultra-nationalist military officers, inspired by Pilsudski's takeover in Poland, seized power in a coup in late 1926. As was to be the case in Estonia and Latvia, a hero of the independence movement, Antanas Smetona, became head of state. The junta became the most extreme of the inter-war Baltic regimes, using ultra-nationalist rhetoric to whip up popular support. By 1935 all political parties, except for Smetona's Nationalist League, had been banned.

As the Second World War approached, the smaller states across Central and Eastern Europe became increasingly nervous of German expansionism. Between March 1938 and March 1939, Smetona effectively accepted Lithuania's loss of Wilna to Poland, and ceded Klaipeda to Germany.

All three Baltic republics, having redirected their trade towards the West rather than Russia, were affected by the depression which struck the Western economy from the late 1920s, but they recovered relatively quickly. Of the three, Lithuania was the poorest and industrially the least developed. As the economy grew rapidly, so did the indigenous professional and economic middle classes, key social groups in bolstering national consciousness. Politically, the ethnic minorities' influence was limited, despite the economic power of Germans (and in Lithuania of Jews and Poles).

Although the Soviet Union had formally relinquished its claims on the Baltic States in 1920, it subsequently reassessed its position. As Nazi Germany became increasingly belligerent, the Soviet Union came to regard the Eastern Baltic coastline as strategically crucial for its security. Germany, meanwhile, had used its economic muscle to establish itself as a regional power in the Baltic. The two powers came to a temporary accommodation with the signature of the Nazi-Soviet Pact in August 1939. Combined with a further agreement in September 1939, the Pact assigned the Baltic states to a Soviet "sphere of influence". On 15-18 June 1940 the Red Army invaded. A month later rigged elections were held. The new, pro-Soviet regimes then applied for membership of the Soviet Union and on 3-6 August 1940 the Baltic republics were admitted to the Soviet Union. The international community regarded the annexation as illegal and never formally accepted it.

The Soviet regime quickly implemented draconian policies of Russification and Sovietisation. Most bank accounts were frozen; land was expropriated and cattle and grain were confiscated; commerce and industry were nationalised and industrial plant was transferred to Russia; the education system was transformed with the mass dismissal of teachers and the replacement of textbooks. Mass deportations to Siberia and Central Asia removed members of rival parties, former government officials, entrepreneurs, landowners, the clergy and leading intellectuals. Together the deportees comprised some 4 per cent of the population of Estonia and up to 2 per cent of that of Latvia and Lithuania.

When war broke out between the Soviet Union and Germany in June 1941 the Red Army withdrew and there were nationalist uprisings in all three Baltic states. Some Baltic citizens then welcomed the invading German forces, and the Nazis launched a recruitment drive there. The Nazi occupation was however extremely costly for the Jews of the Baltic, most of whom were concentrated in Lithuania; of Lithuania's pre-war population of some 240,000 Jews, only 40,000 survived the Holocaust.

By 1944 Nazi Germany was facing defeat. Anticipating the return of the advancing Soviet forces, thousands of Baltic nationals fled the region. The exodus depleted the Estonian population by a further 6 per cent, the Latvian by 8 per cent and the Lithuanian by 3 per cent. When the Red Army returned, some nationalists decamped to the forests to join armed anti-Soviet rebels there; resistance was especially strong in Lithuania, where up to 100,000 people may have been involved. Raids and assassinations were conducted by the rebels until about 1952 when organised resistance all but ceased.

Meanwhile the Soviet regime implemented the twin Stalinist economic strategy of agricultural collectivisation and rapid industrialisation. Both had the effect of binding the Baltic states more securely into the Soviet sphere. Collectivisation, in 1948-9, involved yet more deportations, this time of tens of thousands of *kulaks* or prosperous peasants. The Soviet Union's industrial strategy left Moscow controlling 90 per cent of Baltic industries.

The demographic consequences were serious. The new factories were operated mainly by tens of thousands of Russian, Belorussian or Ukrainian settlers, attracted by the Baltic states' relatively high standard of living. These new Slav communities were concentrated in urban areas and rarely bothered to learn the indigenous language. Lithuania, the scene of some of the worst ethnic tension during the interwar period, was the least affected by the changes, with ethnic minorities comprising a constant one fifth of the population. Estonia and Latvia, in contrast, were dramatically affected. Whereas Estonia's population in 1939 had comprised 8 per cent non-Estonians, many of whom were German, by 1989 this figure had climbed to 39 per cent. In Latvia in 1989 some 48 per cent of the population were non-Latvian, up from 23 per cent in 1939.

Stalin's national policy was, in practice if not in its declared intent, one of ruthless Russification. The use of minority languages was curbed, national history was banned or re-written, and symbols of national pride from the cultural to the religious were suppressed; national flags and songs were banned. Cultural policy was somewhat relaxed after Stalin's demise in 1953, and reforms in 1958 gave parents the right to choose the language in which their children should be educated. In 1959, however, Soviet leader Nikita Khrushchev accused the Latvian party of "Latvianising" the local bureaucracy; the party was immediately purged and subsequently became the most pro-Soviet of the three Baltic regimes. Manifestations of Latvian culture were vigorously repressed, and even the folklore groups so beloved of the Soviet regime elsewhere were suppressed in Latvia until the late 1970s. Further Slav immigration was actively encouraged.

At the 22nd CPSU Congress in October 1961 Khrushchev had presented a new national policy, to be realised in two stages: the first, national "rapprochement", as the nations of the Soviet Union learned to co-operate; and the second, national "fusion", as those disparate nations coagulated into a new, supra-national Soviet identity. In practice, however, "fusion" appeared to mean the absorption of "minor" nations into the dominant Russian nation. The evidence of the 1970 census disappointed the Soviet leadership; it demonstrated that "rapprochement", as measured by rates of national inter-marriage, use of Russian by other nations, etc., was progressing extremely slowly. Even within the party, comrades from the Baltic republics fared poorly, being under-represented at all-union level. At the CPSU's upper echelons, the politburo was consistently dominated by Russians and Ukrainians. At republican level, a modus operandi had been reached, whereby the first secretary was usually one of the local national group while the second secretary (in charge of the local nomenklatura) and the KGB chief were usually Russian or Ukrainian.

The growth of opposition to Soviet rule

In fact, with the increasing urbanisation from the 1950s, national consciousness among the Baltic nations appears if anything to have strengthened. From the 1960s underground nationalist groups began to grow, dissatisfied at being ruled by "outsiders", at the Russification programmes, and with the lack of democracy. In 1972 Roman Kalanta, a Lithuanian student, became a symbol of the Baltic struggle for national self-determination when he killed himself by self-immolation in a square in Kaunas in protest at Russian rule. In the ensuing riots, crowds chanted "Freedom!".

tore down Russian street names and torched party and police offices. (Kalanta's sacrifice recalled that of Jan Palach in Prague three years before - *see Czechoslovakia*).

By 1974 several Lithuanian groups had coalesced to form the National Popular Front, which issued a series of demands, including the observation of human rights and the release of political prisoners, the use of Lithuanian as the republic's principal language, and an end to Soviet "colonialism". The Roman Catholic Church was central to this emerging national consciousness; although itself not advocating nationalism, the *Chronicle of the Lithuanian Catholic Church*, which had been published abroad from 1972, included information on human rights abuses. The *Chronicle* was part of a proliferation of *samizdat* in Lithuania in the 1970s not matched anywhere else in the Soviet Union.

Dissent in the early 1980s was stronger in the Baltic republics than anywhere else in the Soviet Union. Estonia, where a Popular Front similar to its (later) Lithuanian counterpart had been established in 1971, was the location of the first major unrest, as students and schoolchildren participated in mass protests against Russification. Further unrest in Tallinn and Tartu was inspired by the revolutionary events in Poland. Economic factors also played a central role; Estonians, being able to watch Finnish TV, were acutely aware that their once-equal neighbours to the north had acquired a level of prosperity far above their own.

The reforms associated with Mikhail Gorbachev as general secretary of the CPSU from March 1985 began only slowly. The initial aims of *glasnost* ("openness") were limited to the improved presentation of government policy. The explosion at the Chernobyl nuclear power station in Soviet Ukraine in April 1986 exposed the limitations of the policy, as the media failed to provide adequate information to Soviet citizens; Lithuanians gleaned most of their news about the blast from Polish television. Gorbachev persuaded the Soviet regime to adopt a more radical policy, to permit greater freedom of speech and the exposure of the party's mistakes as well as its triumphs past and present.

The opposition in the Baltic moved quickly. Although the Baltic republics were not severely affected by the Chernobyl disaster (the main impact was on Belarus), attention was focused on Lithuania's own Chernobyl-type reactor at Ignalina. But the catastrophe at Chernobyl was symptomatic of the Soviet central planners' contempt for the environment. Over four decades of rapid industrial growth implemented with scant regard for the environment had severely damaged the ecology of the Baltic republics, while the Soviet military had polluted and degraded large tracts of the Baltic countryside and coastline.

Latvia's Environmental Protection Club founded in spring 1986, and the Estonian Heritage Society, founded in late 1987, formed the nucleus of the anti-Soviet opposition in the Baltic republics. In October 1986 environmental activists in Latvia began a campaign against a proposed hydro-electric power station at Daugavpils. Within a month, Moscow had dropped the plans, keen to demonstrate its new responsiveness and to avoid further bad publicity on environmental issues. In Estonia, two years of demonstrations culminated in 1987 with the postponement of an environmentally damaging phosphorite mining project. These victories were a strong incentive to further activism.

Meanwhile *samizdat* had been growing in all three states. In July 1986 Helsinki 86 had been founded in Estonia; its journal *Tevija* ("Fatherland") spread information about human rights abuse. Pressure grew to abolish the Soviet police state and permit freedom of expression. In December 1986 Gorbachev made a dramatic gesture in releasing the veteran Russian dissident Andrei Sakharov from administrative exile in Gorky. The release of most other political prisoners in 1987 freed many Baltic anti-communist activists and improved opposition organisation. In August 1987 the dissident Lithuanian Freedom League organised the first mass demonstrations in the Baltic republics, to mark the anniversary of the Nazi-Soviet Pact. Popular participation gathered pace in 1987-8 with a series of mass demonstrations in Estonia, Latvia and Lithuania to mark the anniversaries of other key national dates, including the mass deportations of 1941, and to demand *glasnost* on the Soviet role in these events.

By 1988 the anti-Soviet opposition had begun to take shape. In Latvia in June the Writers' Union convened a congress of cultural organisations which made a series of radical demands typical of the Baltic opposition in 1988. The congress called for republican sovereignty, including economic autonomy, control over immigration, the designation of Latvian as the official language, diplomatic prerogatives and a separate Latvian military. Shortly afterward the National Independence Movement of Latvia, led by Edvards Birkavs, was established. In the same month, the Lithuanian Restructuring Movement or *Sajudis* was formed as a conservative-nationalist umbrella movement under the leadership of historian Vytautas Landsbergis. Then in August 1988 the Estonian National Independence Party was founded, becoming the first self-declared opposition party in the Soviet Union.

In October 1988 the Estonian and Latvian Popular Fronts and *Sajudis* were formally established. They included communists, intellectuals, human rights activists and clergy. The Estonian front was the most radical, calling for a mechanism for republican secession from the Soviet Union. The fronts held national festivals in which huge crowds sang traditional songs and displayed long-banned national flags and symbols. The communist response to the upsurge of national feeling was uneven. At republican level, many communists actually joined the popular fronts. The Latvian and particularly the Estonian communist parties sought to reduce the distance between themselves and the popular fronts; the latter made a significant gesture in this direction by legalising the Estonian national flag. The Lithuanian communist party, on the other hand, remained stubbornly conservative. In September 1988 a demonstration organised by the Lithuanian Freedom League was violently dispersed by police.

Moscow regarded the Lithuanian leadership's response to the nationalist challenge as likely to destroy communist legitimacy in the republic. Moscow now favoured increasing pluralism; the special 19th CPSU conference of June-July 1988 had approved Gorbachev's campaign of democratisation, with the introduction of election of party officials from a choice of candidates and by secret ballot. In relations with the Union's periphery, Moscow wanted a new relationship built on the law, mutual consent and shared interest. Moscow therefore engineered a reshuffle of the Lithuanian party leadership, appointing the reformist Algirdas Brazauskas as the new party First Secretary. His regime quickly declared Lithuanian to be the official state language, but his radicalism had its limits. When Estonia issued its Declaration of Sovereignty in November 1988, allowing it to veto all-Union legislation, Brazauskas, possibly out of loyalty to Gorbachev, ruled out a similar Lithuanian declaration, allowing *Sajudis* to gain a decisive electoral advantage.

Elections to the all-Union legislature, the Congress of People's Deputies, were held in March 1989, and to the republican legislatures in March 1990. In the intervening 12 months there were fundamental changes in the Soviet Union's strategic position which for the first time made independence appear a realistic prospect for the Baltic republics.

In the 1989 all-union elections, the Baltic popular fronts emerged victorious. Events then moved quickly. By late July Latvia and Lithuania had followed Estonia in declaring republican sovereignty. By October Estonia and Latvia had moved on to declare that independence was their long-term goal. In August Poland's first post-war non-communist government was formed, and in November 1989 the changed geo-political environment was dramatically demonstrated with the fall of the Berlin wall and the toppling of Czechoslovakia's hardline communist regime in the Velvet Revolution.

On 6 December 1989, the Lithuania legislature abolished the communists' monopoly on power, and established the first multi-party system in the Soviet Union. A fortnight later the Lithuanian party seceded from the CPSU. Although the move appeared radical, by February 1990 the CPSU had itself renounced its leading role in advance of the republican elections.

The popular fronts and nationalist allies again chalked up convincing victories in the March 1990 polls, and formed non-communist governments. Lithuania almost immediately declared independence, while Estonia and Latvia waited until the early summer before adopting more cautious resolutions on beginning a process of transition to independence. Estonia and Latvia dropped their titular status as Soviet Socialist Republics.

Neither the election results nor the subsequent moves towards independence should have surprised the Soviet leadership, but Gorbachev nevertheless appeared to dither in his response. In April Moscow imposed economic sanctions on Lithuania, but this punitive measure was soon abandoned in favour of a new plan to re-negotiate the relationship between the Soviet Union's centre and periphery. Gorbachev envisaged devolving considerable powers to the republics while retaining a strong centre responsible for the economy, foreign affairs and defence. But by the time Soviet-Lithuanian talks on revising the 1922 Union Treaty got under way in August 1990, conservative forces in Moscow had strengthened their position, and within one week the Soviet delegation had walked out of the talks. Besides, although confederation might have satisfied the Baltic republics in 1989, by late 1990 independence was their explicit goal. When, in December 1990, Gorbachev set a deadline for signature of the new treaty for summer 1991, all three Baltic republics dissociated themselves from the treaty.

The Baltic republics' confidence in setting the agenda in their relations with the centre was increased by the policy conflict in Moscow and the stalemate between reformist and conservative wings of the CPSU. All agreed that further concessions would be regarded by other republics as a sign of weakness and merely increase the centrifugal pressures on the Union. Ultra-conservatives were indignant that the Baltic minnows were apparently dictating the fate of the Soviet Union, whereas reformers feared that a crackdown in the Baltic would undermine their credibility and pave the way for a conservative takeover. Gorbachev vacillated at the centre.

Within the Baltic republics were extremist organisations with links to the hardliners in Moscow, and dominated by members of the slav communities. Among them was Lithuania's Interfront. These "red-brown" groups combined pro-soviet communist rhetoric with Russian ultra-nationalism. They regarded themselves as vanguard for a hardline resurgence that would re-establish the Soviet Union as a strong, centralised power. In January 1991 the threat of a hardline backlash was demonstrated in a rather mysterious sequence of events in the Baltic. Three crucial developments took place almost simultaneously. Firstly Estonia, Latvia and Lithuania announced unpopular price rises just after the Orthodox Christmas celebrations, prompting violent demonstrations mainly by ethnic Slavs. Secondly Interfront and its counterparts in Estonia and Latvia established "National Salvation Committees" declaring themselves the sole legitimate authorities and denouncing the nationalists as "counter-revolutionaries". And thirdly Soviet special forces arrived ostensibly to detain draft-dodgers. Within days they had seized key government and media buildings in Riga and Vilnius. On 13 January OMON (Soviet special Interior Ministry) forces killed 14 people and injured hundreds among the peaceful crowds gathered to protect the television station in Vilnius. One week later six civilians were killed when OMON troops seized the Ministry of the Interior building in Riga.

The hardline crackdown was brought to an end by the combined forces of reform in Moscow. Boris Yeltsin, the Chair of the Russian legislature, issued a joint statement with the three Baltic presidents denouncing "armed acts damaging each other's state sovereignty". Then Gorbachev, after two weeks of prevarication, finally said publicly that the National Salvation Committees had acted unconstitutionally.

The January 1991 crackdown critically undermined the residual legitimacy of the Soviet Union in the Baltic republics. Referendums held in February and March 1991 registered overwhelming support for independence. Even among the ethnic Slav minorities there was some support for secession, due to fears of the growing economic and political crisis in the rest of the Soviet Union. In the March 1991 All-Union referendum on the preservation of the Soviet Union, turnout was so low in the Baltic Republics that the results in these republics were declared invalid.

By the summer of 1991 the Russian Federation, and specifically Yeltsin (the Russian President from June), had become a significant ally of the Baltic republics in their bid for independence. Russia's own bid for republican sovereignty, which it declared in June 1991, drove the centre into further disarray. In July 1991 Yeltsin signed a treaty recognising Lithuanian sovereignty. Meanwhile, the 12 Soviet republics still involved in negotiations on the new Union Treaty had reached agreement on a radical devolution of powers from the centre to the republics. A signing date had been set for 20 August.

On the eve of the scheduled signing of this Union Treaty, hardliners in Moscow launched an attempted coup. The putschists were undone by their own incompetence; for example, although Gorbachev was detained in his dacha by the Black Sea, Yeltsin, in Moscow, was not; he and the Russian parliament became the focus of resistance to the coup, which was quickly defeated.

Most Union republics, including Estonia and Latvia on 20-21 August, declared full independence. The CPSU was suspended. On 6 September the Soviet Union's interim executive organ, the State Council, recognised the independence of the Baltic states. International recognition followed, and in September 1991 Estonia, Latvia and Lithuania were admitted to the UN. In December 1991 the Soviet Union was formally dissolved and Russia assumed its assets and liabilities.

The state-building process

The newly independent Baltic states had several advantages over other former Soviet republics which facilitated their reintegration into Europe. Since their annexation in 1940, they had never been recognised *de jure* as part of the Soviet Union by the international community. Their proximity to wealthy northern European neighbours in Scandinavia and Germany improved prospects for trade and economic co-operation, and their small size encouraged the international community to believe that financial and other help could achieve visible medium-term results. Besides, the Baltic states had been among the most economically developed parts of the Soviet Union. Apart from these practical considerations was that of image. The Baltic nations' courage in asserting their aspirations for self-determination in the face of the growing Soviet threat had reminded the West of that model of peaceful patriotic protest, Czechoslovakia in 1968. The Baltic states thus represented the acceptable face of nationalism, a creed yet to be tainted by the rise of belligerent extremists in Yugoslavia and Russia. Baltic nationalism, moreover, was closely associated with economic and political liberalism, and the three states had a history of democracy, although the deeply flawed nature of this interwar democratic interlude was poorly understood in the West.

The Baltic states nevertheless faced some fundamental problems, including the presence of large Slavic minorities with little apparent respect for the new states, the lack an effective defence and the continued presence of large contingents of former Soviet troops, outmoded and environmentally damaging heavy industries, and rapidly escalating crime rates.

The Baltic states quickly embarked on the process of consolidating their status as independent, democratic countries. All three had adopted new democratic constitutions by mid-1993, under which the balance of executive responsibilities was spread between the legislature and the cabinet, reflecting suspicion of strong executive presidencies. Controversially, citizenship legislation in Estonia and Latvia withheld the franchise from the ethnic Slav communities. The legislation demonstrated that many Baltic nationalists favoured the re-establishment of Baltic nation-states, despite the presence since the Soviet era of large ethnic minorities. The exception was Lithuania, which with its proportionately smaller non-indigenous community confidently enfranchised most residents. The Lithuanian regime worked hard in other ways to soothe relations with Moscow, and its reward was an early withdrawal of Russian troops in August 1993. Latvia and particularly Estonia in contrast established an ill-tempered relationship with a Russian regime which, keen to establish its nationalist credentials, frequently excoriated them for "apartheid" towards their Russian minorities. Although there was some substance to the rhetoric, the actual direction of Russian policy from 1991 was practically unaltered, and the last remaining Russian combat troops pulled out of Estonia and Latvia in August 1994.

Following independence the Baltic states also acted to lessen their economic dependence on Russia. All three states had introduced new currencies by mid-1993. As the Russian economy staggered under the burden of hyper-inflation, trade was rapidly reoriented to the West. Nevertheless the Baltic states suffered severe recession. Economic reform was implemented unevenly; Estonia, under Mart Laar's government in 1992-4, was the most radical exponent of free market reforms, and had virtually completed privatisation by the end of 1995, whereas Lithuania's regime was rather conservative, particularly after the return to power of ex-communists.

Domestically, perhaps the most severe social problem was the booming crime rate. The threat of organised crime to the nascent Baltic democracies was vividly illustrated by the murder in 1993 of Lithuanian journalist Vitas Lingys. His killer, Boris Dekanidze, was executed only after an attempt to free him by criminal allies who threatened to blow up the Ignalina nuclear power station. Teething troubles with the Baltic states' new security forces, many of which had their roots in eccentric or extremist or otherwise maverick irregular units formed during the latter years of the Soviet Union, compounded this problem.

Domestic politics in the independent Baltic states

Independent **Estonia**'s first prime minister, Edgar Savisaar of the Popular Front, was forced to resign in January 1992 after two years in office, having alienated former allies by demanding emergency powers to deal with the economic situation. Tiit Vahi, a technocrat (who later founded the Coalition Party), took office as interim Prime Minister, an office he was to hold three time by the end of 1995. In the September 1992 elections the Pro-Patria bloc, a successor to the Popular Front, emerged as the largest single group. Pro-Patria formed a coalition under the 32-year old Christian Democrat Mart Laar. Early in October the Pro-Patria nominee Lennart Meri was elected as Estonian president by the legislature, replacing as head of state the chair of the Soviet-era parliament, Arnold Ruutel. Almost immediately, the Laar government announced the first round of privatisation, setting the tone for a radical regime which came to be regarded by many Western economists as a model practitioner of the transition from the command economy to the free market. As in Poland in 1989-90, these radical reforms were less popular with the considerable part of the population that judged itself the loser from the process. The fall of the Laar regime was eventually precipitated by divisions within the coalition, due mainly to Laar's abrasive style. His rump Pro-Patria was heavily defeated in early legislative elections in March 1995. The main beneficiary was the centre-left KMU bloc, dominated by ex-communists, which went on to become the senior partner in a coalition government formed in spring 1995. Tiit Vahi, returning as prime minister, promised to maintain fiscal discipline but balanced this with pledges of state support for agriculture. The coalition quickly unravelled when the minor partner, Savisaar's Centrist party, was engulfed in scandal; the inclusion of the pro-market Reform Party in a new coalition under Vahi from autumn 1995 heralded a renewed emphasis on radical economic policy.

In **Latvia** the Popular Front government of Ivars Godmanis in 1990-3 passed several key reforms: on the Latvian language, extending its official use in the education system; introducing the first privatisations; and on Latvian citizenship, under which ethnic Slavs were required to apply for naturalisation. Following the 1993 elections, Latvia's Way, a successor to the Latvian Popular Front, became the major partner in coalition with the right-wing LNNK and took up the same policy threads from its predecessor, distinguished by new promises on state support for agriculture. Latvia's worst post-independence crisis took place in summer 1994, when the parliament passed legislation establishing strict quotas on naturalisation which would have prevented most non-Latvians from acquiring citizenship. The legislation met with international censure and angered Russia. President Meri persuaded parliament to drop the quota system. Latvia's Way performed poorly in elections in autumn 1995, which resulted in a fragmented legislature dominated by populist parties of the left and right. Eventually, in late 1995, the Latvian parliament approved a new eight-party centrist coalition cabinet including the centre-left In Charge, Latvia's Way, the LNNK and the conservative agrarian LZS; Andris Skele, an independent, became prime minister.

Lithuania's first elections after independence produced a dramatic reverse for the *Sajudis* movement, which was swept from power by the ex-communist Lithuanian Democratic Labour Party, heralding a resurgence of the left across Eastern Europe. The *Sajudis* leader and parliamentary chair (head of state) Vytautas Landsbergis bore the principal responsibility for this defeat. Although charismatic and courageous, Landsbergis was also abrasive and confrontational. Many Lithuanian voters viewed his virulent anti-communism with distaste and regarded his plans for a strong presidency as evidence of overweening personal ambitions. On the other hand, many voters regarded the ex-communists as technically the most competent team and, in contrast to

Lithuania's highly politicised anti-communist parties, the least hidebound by ideology. The LDDP's Algirdas Brazauskas, victorious in Lithuania's first direct presidential elections in February 1993, pledged to continue economic reform but to relax socially punishing austerity measures. The centre-left regime established relatively friendly relations with its historically antagonistic neighbours Russia and Poland, while the emergence of Lithuania as a mainly secular, social democratic country seemed to be confirmed by the rather lukewarm reception to the Papal visit of autumn 1993; new estimates put the number of practising Catholics at just 30 per cent of the population.

ECONOMY

Economic reforms got under way in all three Baltic states in 1991. The pace of change in 1992-5 was fastest in Estonia and arguably slowest in Latvia. The priority was extrication from the economic ties to the former Soviet Union. Accordingly, they successfully engineered a realignment of trade, finding new markets notably in Finland, Germany and Sweden. By mid-1993 all three Baltic states had introduced their own currencies, the first being the Estonian kroon which was pegged to the deutschemark in June 1992; interim Latvian and Lithuanian currencies, respectively the lats and the litas, had been introduced by mid-1993 and pegged to the same currency by mid-1994. A major problem was overcoming dependence on Russia for energy supplies, and Russia's 1992 decision to charge world prices for its energy was a significant blow to the Baltic economies, causing rapidly expanding debt levels and fuelling inflation. (Estonia was somewhat assisted by its own natural deposits of oil shale.) The outdated, environmentally damaging Soviet-era heavy industries that predominated particularly in Latvia presented a further significant challenge. Some Baltic economists advocated that they should be left to wither away, allowing their Slav workforce to return to Russia, Belarus and Ukraine; the Baltic economies should instead concentrate on modern light manufacturing industries and modernised agriculture.

Western countries appeared keen to modernise the Baltic economies and help bind them into Western markets. International assistance, although praised by some Baltic leaders (notably Estonia's Vahi in 1992, who described IMF financial assistance as a new Marshall plan for Eastern Europe), was not always invested in long-term projects, and in Lithuania in particular much IMF cash was squandered on paying off debts, notably for Russian fuel. Estonia was particularly successful in attracting foreign investment, mainly from Germany and Scandinavia. In June 1995 the European Union signed association agreements with Estonia, Latvia and Lithuania, and by December 1995 all three had formally applied for full EC (EU) membership, taking a place in the queue behind the "fast track" Central European states - the Czech Republic, Hungary, Poland and Slovenia.

All three Baltic states practised relatively tight fiscal and monetary regimes which by 1994-5 had succeeded in reducing rampant inflation, caused mainly by price liberalisation. Although the recession in the Baltic states was not as severe as the downturn experienced by other former Soviet republics, notably Russia, there was nevertheless a precipitate decline in production in all three countries. For example, overall industrial production in Lithuania in 1993 fell by 47.1 per cent over the previous year. Official figures exaggerated the extent of the economic crisis because considerable economic activity was "black" and therefore unrecorded. Unemployment remained relatively low, reflecting a lack of fundamental restructuring. Again Estonia was a pioneer, bankruptcy legislation leading to the first insolvency in October 1992.

While there was an end to the queues and shortages so typical of the Soviet era, living standards dropped, with those on fixed incomes suffering particular hardship. Figures from Lithuania in 1993 showed that two thirds of family budgets went on food.

Although the reforming governments of 1992-4 lost popularity to the left, new governments appointed in Estonia and Latvia appeared likely to continue the pro-market direction of economic policy.

Privatisation and property restitution

Estonia. Property restitution legislation was implemented slowly from 1991. Some privatisations began from June 1991, and the first round of mass privatisation was announced in October 1992. Housing was privatised under legislation passed in spring 1993. The privatisation process as a whole was almost complete by the end of 1995.

Latvia. Privatisation legislation was passed in February 1991 and sales began in autumn 1991 using a voucher system. Enterprises earmarked for sale came from a variety of sectors. Progress was relatively slow, with only 30 per cent of state enterprises privatised by the end of 1994, mainly because Latvia had inherited large-scale enterprises which were particularly difficult to break up and sell.

Lithuania. Despite controversy in Lithuania over the slow pace of sales under the ex-communist LDDP regime, some 90 per cent of Lithuania's state-owned enterprises had been privatised by the end of 1994. Unfortunately the sales raised little revenue for investment as for the most part shares were exchanged with vouchers distributed freely. In September 1995 a privatisation agency was established, charged with completing the ownership transformation process.

POST-COMMUNIST JUSTICE ISSUES

The post-communist **Estonian** regime was relatively slow in taking action against the former communist elite. In 1993 President Meri vetoed legislation designed to bar former personnel of the Soviet armed forces or KGB, and former communist party members, from participation in the privatisation of housing. Only in February 1995 were substantial measures adopted in the shape of legislation requiring former agents of the KGB and of the occupying Nazi forces to register with the police or be named publicly; thousands of Estonians were thought to be involved. There were no major trials of ex-communist leaders other than that of Soviet-era Prime Minister Indrek Toome, who was cleared of bribery charges in March 1995.

In contrast, the newly independent **Latvian** parliament acted quickly to exclude the ex-communist elite from power. A parliamentary resolution of May 1992 banned former KGB officers from working in the state defence, interior or security apparatus. By July 1992 the legislature had agreed that its deputies' mandates could be revoked if their activities demonstrably hindered the development of democracy. Such sanctions were initially limited to ethnic Russian deputies of the Equal Rights faction, including former Latvian Communist Party First Secretary Alfred Rubiks, for their "unlawful" backing in 1991 of the coup plotters in Moscow, but in April 1994 Latvian Foreign Minister Georgs Andrejevs was suspended from membership of parliament, having been exposed as a former KGB collaborator. By June a contrite Andrejevs had withdrawn from politics. In December 1994 the Supreme Court convicted deputy Aivars Kreituss of past KGB collaboration, despite doubts over the reliability of the KGB archive. In July 1995 Rubiks was sentenced to eight years in prison for involvement in attempts in August 1991 to overthrow the Latvian government, and in

December 1995 Alfons Noviks, 87, the head of Soviet intelligence in Latvia from
1940-53, was sentenced to life imprisonment on genocide charges for his part in the
mass deportation of tens of thousands of Latvians and the persecution of many others
in 1941-9. Noviks's defence was that he had then been subject to Soviet law, under
which the deportations were permissible, rather than to the pre-war Latvian constitution
under which he had been prosecuted.

Lithuanian politics was tainted by a series of scandals linking prominent nationalist
politicians with the former Soviet KGB. In March 1992, the former secretary-general
of *Sajudis*, Virgilijus Cepaitis, was convicted by the Supreme Court of having
"deliberately co-operated with the KGB". In September 1992 the same verdict was
pronounced on Kazimiera Prunskiene, the prime minister of 1990-1. Prunskiene
protested that she had merely given KGB agents an account of her foreign visits.

The *Sajudis* government strongly favoured a political purge of the civil service to rid
public life of committed communists. Critics accused *Sajudis* of positioning itself the
replace the communist party as Lithuania's dominant political force. In April 1992 the
government gave in to its critics, abandoning its political purge, although continuing
"efficiency" reforms of the bureaucracy. The return to power of the ex-communist
LDDP that autumn stalled the administration of a postcommunist justice process.
Restlessness in nationalist circles over the failure to remove ex-communists from
positions of authority was one factor in a mutiny among maverick military units in
Kaunas in September 1993. However in January 1994 two former leading communists
were arrested in Minsk and deported to Lithuania in connection with the January 1991
killing of 13 people at the Vilnius television station; as of late 1995 their trial had yet to
take place.

ETHNIC AND NATIONAL RELATIONS

For Baltic nationalists, one of the most unwelcome legacies of the Soviet era was the
presence in Estonia and Latvia of large communities of non-indigenous groups, 48 per
cent and 39 per cent of their respective populations, as a result of decades of
immigration officially encouraged by the Soviet regime. Most were ethnic Russians or
Poles concentrated in urban areas and had failed to assimilate with the "host" nation;
even their knowledge of Baltic languages was very poor. Some Baltic nationalists
refused to accept the validity of Soviet law under which the migrations had taken place
and argued that the ethnic minorities were illegal immigrants. Mass deportation was
politically unacceptable to all but a few hardline nationalists, but the minorities were
deliberately excluded from the political process, with legislation limiting citizenship to
the former citizens of the interwar republics and their direct descendants. This
legislation disenfranchised most ethnic Slavs in Estonia and Latvia, and in
consequence their first post-Soviet parliaments virtually excluded ethnic minorities.
The Latvian legislature elected in June 1993 included a handful of deputies of the pro-
Soviet and mainly Russian Equal Rights group, but they were soon suspended for their
alleged role in the "anti-Latvian" activities of 1991, while Estonia's legislature
contained not one single ethnic Russian deputy until the admission of social democrat
Sergey Zonov in March 1994.

Further legislation in Estonia and Latvia eventually clarified the citizenship issue. In
June 1993 the Estonian legislature passed a draft Law on Aliens defining non-citizens
as "foreigners" and requiring them to apply for temporary residence permits.
Opposition from President Meri and criticism by the Council of Europe and the CSCE
led to amendments allowing the provision of permanent residency and guaranteeing

ethnic minorities' social protection rights; separate assurances were provided on the rate of naturalisation of ethnic Slav residents. In June 1994 the Latvian legislature approved a draft citizenship law imposing from 2000 annual quotas on the naturalisation of residents, limiting naturalisation to 0.1 per cent of the total citizenry annually. The draft law excluded from citizenship former Soviet military personnel and supporters of the extreme left and right and imposed other strict criteria, including proficiency in the Latvian language. Again, international criticism persuaded the government to intervene and the quota system was dropped in an amended version of the law passed in July 1994. The citizenship legislation was the principal reason for delays to Latvia's admission as a full member of the Council of Europe.

Estonia has made some policy efforts designed to reassure its ethnic minorities. In October 1993 the Estonian legislature passed a law granting ethnic minorities cultural autonomy, allowing the establishment of cultural, religious and educational institutions. In 1995 Estonian elections were held early, so that people naturalised since the last polls in 1992 could vote. The mainly ethnic-Russian Our Home is Estonia (MKOE) duly won six seats in the Estonian parliament.

In Lithuania, where ethnic minorities had remained at roughly one fifth of the overall population since the interwar period, legislation in 1992 extended citizenship to virtually all residents regardless of their ethnic origins. However, in January 1995 the parliament passed legislation designating Lithuanian as the republic's state language, despite protests by ethnic Polish and Russian leaders.

FOREIGN AFFAIRS

Following Soviet recognition of the Baltic states' independence on 6 September 1991, Estonia, Latvia and Lithuania were rapidly re-integrated into the diplomatic community. On 10 September they acceded to the CSCE and on 17 September to the UN. Their preference for integration into Western economic and political structures was obvious from the outset and their commitment to the pro-market economy quickly led to assistance from the IMF, World Bank and EBRD. EC (EU) membership was the long-term goal. On 1 January 1995 a free trade agreement between the Baltic states and the EC took effect, the Estonian portion being fully implemented immediately, while four- and six-year transition periods applied to the Latvian and Lithuanian agreements respectively, allowing them to continue to use protectionism to favour their agricultural sectors. By June 1995 the Baltic states had become associate members of the EC and in October Latvia formally applied for full EC membership, Estonia and Lithuania following suit in December 1995.

The Baltic regimes also expressed their desire to join Western security organisations. Estonia, Latvia and Lithuania joined NATO's Partnership for Peace (PfP) initiative soon after its launch in January 1994, and were granted "associate partner" status in the Western European Union (WEU) in June 1994.

Diplomatic co-operation between the Baltic states had got under way in 1989 with the creation of the Baltic Council. Common political institutions were the Baltic Assembly, in which delegates from the Baltic states' legislatures debated and liaised, and the Baltic Council of Ministers established in June 1994. A Baltic free trade agreement abolishing tariffs on most non-agricultural goods was implemented from April 1994. Defence co-operation included a Baltic Battalion comprising nationals from all three Baltic states and using English as a common language; Britain announced in early 1994 that it was to provide technical assistance. Baltic leaders clearly regarded the force, which was intended to be used mainly for international peacekeeping duties, as a toe in NATO's door.

In bilateral relations, the Baltic states' vast eastern neighbour Russia was obviously of fundamental importance, not least because tens of thousands of Red Army troop were stationed in the Baltic states when the Soviet Union collapsed in August 1991.

President Yeltsin's Russian republican regime, in its quest for sovereignty, had played a key role in the dissolution of the Soviet Union. Initially Russia was disposed favourably towards the Baltic states, regarding their case for independence as based on sound legal principles, but the rapid rise of Russian nationalism quickly put pressure on the Russian regime to adopt a more assertive stance. Although the Baltic states were still beyond the unofficial "sphere of influence" that Russia began increasingly to assert over other former Soviet republics, it became increasingly clear that Russia would not countenance Estonian, Latvian or Lithuanian membership of NATO. While Lithuania successfully sought an accommodation with Russia by introducing liberal citizenship laws, settling border disputes, and (under the LDDP regime) showing sensitivity on the NATO issue, Estonia and Latvia became a favourite target for nationalists in both the Russian government and opposition. The citizenship legislation in Estonia, which had always been perceived as the most anti-Russian republic in the former Soviet Union, and that in Latvia, was regarded as an impudent provocation. In a bid to remind the Baltic states of its regional pre-eminence, Russia made a show of postponing troop withdrawals and charged world prices for energy supplies, which burdened the Baltic states with major debt problems. By 1993 Russia was explicitly claiming the right to intervene to protect the interests of the ethnic Russian minorities in the Baltic states. In June 1993 Yeltsin warned that Russia was prepared to take "all measures necessary" to defend ethnic Russians in Estonia and in August 1994 he denounced Latvia for "militant nationalism" and for raising "national intolerance...to the level of official policy". There was nevertheless a gap between the sabre-rattling rhetoric of the Russian regime and the more pragmatic reality of its policy, which was a virtually continuous withdrawal of troops from 1991. Having withdrawn from Lithuania in 1993, Russian combat troops had left Estonia and Latvia by late August 1994. Russia's overwhelming regional military superiority was nevertheless a fact of political life. The Russian enclave of Kaliningrad, on the Baltic coast south of Lithuania, alone contained a Russian arsenal capable of crushing the fledgling Baltic defence forces. This political reality was reflected in Russia's unilateral demarcation in summer 1994 of its frontier with Estonia, sweeping aside Estonian claims to the 2,000 sq. km. of territory which comprised the Pechory district (in Estonian "Petseri"), land which had been incorporated into the Russian republic in the Soviet era. In November 1995 Estonia reluctantly agreed to accept the existing border with Russia as the *de facto* frontier between the two countries.

The regionally important bilateral relationship between historic antagonists Lithuania and Poland was improved in April 1994 when Brazauskas and Polish President Lech Walesa signed a historic Polish-Lithuanian Treaty of Friendship and Co-operation in Vilnius. Brazauskas hailed the treaty as "an important step...towards uniting Europe". Although it did not explicitly condemn Poland's 1920 occupation of Vilnius, it did condemn the past use of force to resolve disputes between the two republics. The treaty included mutual guarantees on national minority rights, soothing Polish sensitivity over the alleged mistreatment of Lithuania's ethnic Polish minority.

CONSTITUTIONAL ISSUES

In a June 1992 referendum, **Estonian** voters endorsed a new constitution, establishing a parliamentary republic with a strong presidency. The constitution took effect on 3 July 1992. Despite arguments between President Meri and Prime Minister Laar, Estonia has been relatively free of constitutional dispute between the various organs of power. Controversial issues have included the status of the Russian minority.

On 21 August 1991 the **Latvian** parliament re-adopted the 1922 constitution. In July 1993 the parliament renewed this constitution and the 1925 law on the Council of Ministers. Latvia's basic document balances executive responsibilities between the legislature, the cabinet, and the presidency, the latter being the weakest, without for example the power of veto. Latvia has also been troubled by the issue of citizenship and voting rights for its ethnic minorities.

In October 1992 **Lithuanian** voters approved a new constitution balancing presidential and parliamentary powers, having rejected *Sajudis*'s proposals for a strong executive presidency in an earlier poll.

PRINCIPAL PERSONALITIES

Lennart **Meri** (b. 1929). Estonian president since 1992. In the Soviet era Meri was a filmmaker and novelist. He became politically active as an environmental campaigner in 1986 and joined the Estonian Popular Front. From April 1990 until February 1992 he served as Minister of Foreign Affairs. He was nominated by Pro-Patria for the presidency but when, once in office, he clashed with Pro-Patria leader Mart Laar, it was Meri's pragmatic and liberal approach which proved more popular.

Mart **Laar** (b. 1960). Reformist Estonian Prime Minister in 1992-4 and leader of Pro-Patria. Laar was a teacher and historian before entering politics in 1988 as co-founder of the Estonian Heritage Society. In 1989 he co-founded the Estonian Christian Democratic Union. He was elected to parliament in 1990. The Christian Democrats having co-founded the Pro-Patria bloc, Laar became its leader. Prime minister at the age of 32, he achieved a series of major reforms, but his abrasive style alienated former allies and he was forced to resign in September 1994 after scandal hit the government.

Tiit **Vahi** (b. 1947). Estonian Prime Minister of three cabinets in 1992-5. Vahi studied mechanical engineering, and worked as a local transport manager for nearly two decades. In 1989 he was a surprise appointment as Transport Minister but, assisted by his relative anonymity, he developed his image as a competent bureaucrat, leading to his first, eight-month term as interim prime minister in 1992, during which time he introduced a new currency. Vahi then co-founded the moderate reformist Coalition Party and became its leader in March 1993. In alliance with the leftist Rural Union, the Coalition Party took nearly one third of the votes in the June 1995 elections and Vahi returned as prime minister (and was reappointed after the coalition was re-jigged later in 1995).

Guntis **Ulmanis** (b. 1939). The Latvian President from July 1993. Ulmanis, a grandnephew of Latvia's last President Karlis Ulmanis, was an economist by profession. He joined the Latvian Agrarian Union after the introduction of the multi-party system. Once in office he successfully avoided partisan politics and concentrated on state-building and democratisation and continuing pro-market reforms.

Vytautas **Landsbergis** (b. 1932). Nationalist and Lithuanian head of state in 1990-2, when the country achieved independence; leader of *Sajudis* and of its successor the

Homeland Union. Landsbergis, a historian, was in 1990 a popular symbol of the country's resistance to Soviet rule. By 1992, however, he was distrusted for his personal ambition and virulent anti-communism - a contributory factor in the electoral defeat of *Sajudis* and an obstacle to the creation of opposition alliances after 1992.

Algirdas **Brazauskas** (b. 1932). Long-term Lithuanian communist official popularly elected as Lithuania's first post-communist President. Brazauskas served from 1965 as a minister in the Lithuanian republican government, where he established the reformist reputation which facilitated his 1988 appointment as party First Secretary. He then established his nationalist credentials, backing Lithuanian sovereignty and encouraging the Lithuanian party to declare independence from the CPSU. He remodelled the party as the social democratic LDDP, positioning it for the dramatic return to power which it achieved in 1992. Brazauskas became interim head of state before being elected as Lithuania's first postcommunist president in 1993. In accordance with the constitution, Brazauskas then resigned from the LDDP. He pledged to continue economic reform but to relax socially punishing austerity measures. In office he engineered exceptionally good relations with Russia and achieved a degree of stability and social peace unusual for an ex-Soviet republic.

Adolfas **Slezivicius** (b. 1948). Leader of the ex-communist LDDP from April 1991 and Lithuanian Prime Minister from 10 March 1992. Slezivicius was an agricultural engineer before being plucked from obscurity to become a minister in Brazauskas's republican administration. His lack of any tainting association with the injustices of the communist era, his technocratic credentials, and his good working relationship with Brazauskas explain his meteoric rise to the leadership of the LDDP by April 1991 and to the premiership of the country by March 1993.

POLITICAL PARTIES

The left played a relatively marginal role in the interwar democracies of the Baltic states. The economic depression of the late 1920s and early 1930s had if anything driven all three countries toward the authoritarian right. By 1934 the communist parties had been banned by the nationalist dictatorships. Under the Soviet regime each republic was ruled exclusively by its own communist party, dominated to a greater or lesser extent by the Communist Party of the Soviet Union (CPSU).

Moderate elements in the Baltic communist parties sought an accommodation with the nationalist popular fronts which emerged in the late 1980s. Many communist party members joined the fronts. The Lithuanian communists even declared independence from the CPSU in December 1989. A multi-party system was formally introduced in the Soviet Union in early 1990. Conservative, pro-Soviet elements within all three parties nevertheless remained loyal to Moscow, and were outraged by the implications of the electoral defeats at the hands of the popular fronts in 1990. In Latvia and Estonia hardline communists played a key role in the turmoil of 1991 and in the wake of these events several pro-Soviet communist groups were banned. The reformed communist parties in all three states, on the other hand, were tolerated by the newly independent regimes. Leftist parties more or less directly descended from the Soviet-era communist parties made a significant return to power in 1992 in Lithuania, and in 1995 in Latvia and Estonia. Despite these electoral successes, there were widespread concerns over the power of the ex-communist elite, which still penetrated a significant part of the economy and bureaucracy.

The party situation in the Baltic states since the creation of the popular fronts in the late 1980s has been very fluid. The fronts fragmented in 1991-2, and their successor parties went on to establish various alliances of a more or less temporary nature. Parties have been punished at the polls for their role in government. Partly as a consequence of this parties appear to have a transient quality, and apparently owe more to the personalities of their leaders than to party organisation and ideology - weaknesses which had also been a feature of the ill-fated Baltic democracies during the interwar period.

Estonian parties

The principal successor to the **Estonian Communist Party** was Arnold Ruutel's **Safe Home**, a temporary leftist electoral alliance which finished as the runner-up in the 1992 polls. Ruutel had earned nationalist approval in the late 1980s, and in 1990-92 and had served as chairman of the legislature and *de facto* Estonian head of state. He was one of the few former senior communists to retain a position of prominence in Estonian politics (although many former minor communist officials were spread throughout politics). Ruutel was elected as leader of the **Rural Union** (MU) on its foundation in September 1994.

The **KMU** was a centrist electoral alliance comprising five groups, notably the MU and the **Coalition Party**, which had been led by Tiit Vahi since its foundation in early 1993. The KMU was the clear winner of the 1995 elections, and formed a government under Vahi which was likely to continue the reformist policies of its Pro-Patria predecessor.

The **Estonian Popular Front** was founded in October 1988 as an umbrella nationalist opposition movement. The Front's Edgar Savisaar became Estonian Prime Minister in 1990. By 1992 the Front had begun to fragment, but the rump Popular Front contested the 1992 elections, coming third. Savisaar subsequently founded the centre-left **Centre** party (K), which joined the governing coalition as the junior partner to the KMU in March 1995. By October Savisaar had been engulfed in a phone-tapping scandal which drove his party out of government and forced him to retire from politics.

Pro-Patria (*Isamaa* or "Fatherland front"), another successor to the Popular Front, contested the 1992 elections as a bloc of five pro-market nationalist parties, becoming the largest single group. Lennart Meri was its victorious candidate for the presidency. Pro-Patria leader Mart Laar became Prime Minister; his government was noted as one of the most radical pro-market regimes in post-communist East-Central Europe. Divisions over Laar's leadership style exacerbated political differences within Pro-Patria, which began to fragment in mid-1994. The rump Pro-Patria disastrously contested the 1995 elections in alliance with the **Estonian National Independence Party** (ERSP, which on its foundation in August 1988 had become the Soviet Union's first self-declared opposition party, and had gone on to finish fourth in the 1992 elections).

In June 1994 Pro-Patria's right-wing Republican faction broken away to merge in September with the Conservative Party to become the **Estonian Republican Conservative Party** under Karin Jaani. As the principal component of the **Rightist** bloc (W), the Republican-Conservatives flopped in the 1995 elections, barely clearing the 5 per cent threshold for representation. (Two hard-right nationalist parties, **Estonian Citizens** and the **Independent Royalists**, which had been moderately successful in 1992, failed to win any seats in 1995.)

The **Estonian Reform Party** (R) was a pro-market party founded in November 1994 and led by the governor of the Estonian National Bank Siim Kallas. The party finished as runner-up in the 1995 elections and joined the governing coalition later in the year. The **Moderates** (M) were a bloc of centre-left agrarian parties which came third in 1992 but which only narrowly scraped in to parliament in 1995.

Ethnic Slavs were represented by the **Our Home Is Estonia** (MKOE) bloc, which narrowly secured seats in the 1995 elections.

Latvian parties

The **Latvian Communist Party** (LKP) was officially banned after the August 1991 coup attempt in Moscow, but a rump hardline party under Latvia's communist-era leader Alfred Rubiks continued to use the LKP name. Three other pro-communist organisations were banned in October 1993, accused of seditious activity. In July 1995 Rubiks was sentenced to eight years in prison for anti-Latvian activities. Other successor parties to the Soviet-era Latvian communists were the orthodox communist **Unity Party**, which took 7.2 per cent of the vote in 1995, and the **Latvian Socialist Party** (LSP), which also won a handful of seats in 1995. **In Charge (*Saimnieks*)** was a centre left group including many ex-communists founded in April 1994 and chaired by the former *Komsomol* (Young Communist) leader Ziedonis Cevers. *Saimnieks* was a key partner in the broad coalition which took office in December 1995, taking four portfolios, including those of Deputy Prime Minister, Finance and Interior.

The **Latvian Popular Front** (LTF) was formally established in October 1988 as a broad nationalist umbrella movement. Having led Latvia to independence, by 1993 the Front had fragmented, and although a rump LTF contested the 1993 elections, it failed to win any seats.

Latvia's Way (LC), a centre-right party, was the principal successor to the LTF, attracting several of its former leading lights, and emerged as the clear winner of the 1993 elections. It was the major coalition partner in government between 1993 and 1995. In the 1995 elections voters punished the LC for the social costs of the economic reforms it had introduced.

The **Latvian Agrarian Union** (LZS) was a conservative successor party to the Popular Front which won over 10 per cent in 1993 and entered a coalition with the LC in 1993-1994, before leaving in protest at the lack of state support for agriculture. Its vote was almost halved in 1995.

The **Latvian National Independence Movement** (LNNK) was founded in June 1988 as a rallying point for conservative nationalists and finished as runner-up in the 1993 elections. In June 1994 the movement formally became a party, the **Latvian National and Conservative Party** (also LNNK). In the 1995 elections the LNNK vote was halved, while a right-wing breakaway from the LNNK, the **Zigerists' Party/People's Movement for Latvia** (or *Latvijai*) led by Joahims Zigerists, who had been expelled from the LNNK in 1993 for extremism, finished as one of the poll's three winners.

For the Fatherland and Freedom (TUB) a right-wing populist bloc, just cleared the threshold for representation in 1993, but had doubled its share of the vote by 1995, when it contested the election as the **Union for the Fatherland and Freedom--TUBS**. Finishing just behind the three front-runners, it took four key portfolios, including justice and education, in the broad coalition announced in December 1995.

Ravnopravie ("**Equal Rights**") was the party of ethnic Russians. Although it secured a handful of seats in the 1993 elections, its deputies were subsequently suspended for their alleged anti-Latvian activities during the August 1991 coup. The party was banned before the 1995 polls.

Lithuanian parties

The **Lithuanian Communist Party** had played a key role in the early stages of the campaign for independence, and had declared its own independence from the CPSU in December 1989. Although this earned some of its leaders, notably Algirdas Brazauskas, considerable popularity, the party performed poorly in the elections in 1990-91 and after the August 1991 coup the party was banned and its assets seized by the state. In December 1990 a reformist successor party, the **Lithuanian Democratic Labour Party** (LDDP) was founded and in April 1991 Adolfas Slezivicius became its leader. The LDDP stressed its competence and pragmatism and insisted that it was committed to a market economy and Lithuanian integration into Western economic, political and security institutions. It balanced this with stress on the need for continued social support and a commitment to establishing good relations with Russia. By 1992 the LDDP had achieved a remarkable return to power, defeating *Sajudis* in legislative elections and forming a government under Slezivicius. Brazauskas became interim head of state before winning direct presidential elections in February 1993, promising to slow the pace of economic reform. During its term, the LDDP was tainted by allegations of corruption and of profiting from illegal privatisation. The **Lithuanian Peasants' Party** (LVP) was founded in 1995 and was closely allied to the LDDP.

The **Lithuanian Restructuring Movement** (*Sajudis* or "The Movement") was founded in June 1988 as a popular front designed to attract an array of anti-Soviet political forces. Whilst *Sajudis* comprised mainly intellectuals, and included some communists defying their own party leadership, the movement quickly attracted mass support. *Sajudis* defeated the Lithuanian communist party in the All-Union elections of 1989 and in the republican polls of 1990. Its leader, Vytautas Landsbergis, became head of state, and piloted the republic to independence. Although advocating economic reform and beginning property restitution and privatisation in 1991, the *Sajudis* regime favoured étatist social and economic policies such as price controls and state support for industry and agriculture. The populism of the *Sajudis* leadership tended to give the party a shrillness that jarred with the electorate; its alarmist accusations against the former communist LDDP blunted its attack; and it failed to adopt its own positive programme of government. For these reasons *Sajudis* flopped in the 1992 elections. In May 1993 Landsbergis formed *Sajudis*'s principal successor, **Homeland Union-Conservatives of Lithuania** (TS-LK). Although close to the **Lithuanian Christian Democratic Party** (LKDP), personal differences between the two parties' leaderships prevented a merger.

ELECTIONS

There were eight legislative elections in the Baltic states in 1990-5, and for the sake of brevity full results have been omitted in favour of a short summary of the election results.

Estonian legislative elections

The Estonian Popular Front won 27 of the 36 seats allocated to Estonia in the 1989 All-Union elections to the Congress of People's Deputies. In republican elections in 1990, the Front won a convincing majority in the Estonian legislature.

Independent Estonia held its first legislative elections on 20 September 1992. Pro-Patria won 29 of the 101 seats in the new parliament, the *Riigikogu*; Safe Home took 17 seats; the Moderates 12; the Estonian National Independence Party (ERSP) 10; Estonian Citizens and the Independent Royalists eight each; and others two.

In the legislative elections of 5 March 1995, Pro-Patria (in alliance with the ERSP) won only eight seats. The KMU was the clear winner with 32.23 per cent of the vote and 41 seats. The Reform party took second place (16.19 per cent, 19 seats) and the Centre party came third (14.17 per cent, 16 seats). Three other parties, the Moderates, the MKOE, and the Rightists, scored between 5 and 6 per cent of the vote, sharing the remaining 17 seats.

Latvian legislative elections

The Latvian Popular Front won 26 of the 34 seats allocated to Latvia in the 1989 All-Union elections to the Congress of People's Deputies. In republican elections in 1990, the Front won over two thirds of the 201 seats.

Latvia's Way won the elections of 5-6 June 1993, taking 32.4 per cent of the vote and 36 of the 100 seats in the new legislature, the *Saeima*. The LNNK won 13.4 per cent of the vote and 15 seats, Harmony for Latvia 12.0 per cent and 13 seats, and the LZS 10.6 per cent and 12 seats. With between 5 and 6 per cent of the vote, and taking between five and seven seats each, were four further parties including Equal Rights and TUB.

Three parties emerged from the elections of 30 September-1 October 1995 virtually neck-and-neck. They were In Charge with 15.3 per cent of the vote and 18 seats; LC with 14.7 per cent and 17 seats; and the Zigerists Party/People's Movement for Latvia with 15.1 per cent and 16. The LNNK, TUB and LZS all won eight seats.

Lithuanian legislative elections

Sajudis won 36 of the 42 seats allocated to Lithuania in the 1989 All-Union elections to the Congress of People's Deputies. In republican elections in 1990, *Sajudis* won 81 of the 141 seats in the Lithuanian legislature.

In the elections of 25 October and 15 November 1992 to the new legislature, the *Seimas*, the LDDP won 73 of the 141 seats, and *Sajudis* 30. In that part of the ballot based on proportional representation, the LDDP had defeated *Sajudis* by a two-to-one margin, winning 42.6 per cent of the vote. The Lithuanian Christian Democratic Party (LKDP) won 18 seats and the Social Democratic Party (LSDP) eight; ethnic Polish representatives, smaller parties and independents took the remaining 12 seats.

Presidential elections in Estonia, Latvia and Lithuania

Direct **Estonian** presidential elections on 20 September 1992 were inconclusive as no single candidate gained the overall majority constitutionally required for victory; communist-era head of state Arnold Ruutel finished first with 42.2 per cent of the vote and Pro-Patria nominee Lennart Meri was runner-up with 29.8 per cent. Under Estonian electoral rules responsibility for the election of the president thenceforth passed permanently to the legislature, and on 5 October Meri was duly elected as Estonia's first post-communist president by 59 votes to 31.

Guntis Ulmanis of the LZS was elected **Latvian** president in a second round of voting by the legislature on 7 July 1993, after Gunars Meierovics of LC failed to secure a majority in the first round.

In **Lithuanian** direct presidential elections on 14 February 1993 Algirdas Brazauskas of the LDDP polled 60.1 per cent of the vote and his sole rival Stasys Lozoraitis, an independent "unity" candidate endorsed by the main opposition parties, won 38.3 per cent.

CHRONOLOGY

1721. Estonia comes under Russian rule.

1795. Latvia and Lithuania come under Russian rule.

October 1917. The Bolsheviks seize power in Moscow.

2 November 1917. The Declaration on the Rights of the Peoples of Russia recognises the equality of nations and permits secession from Russia.

16 and 24 February 1918. Declarations of independence by Lithuania and Estonia. Over subsequent months Bolshevik Russia renounces sovereignty "voluntarily and for ever" over the Baltic states. Despite this there are clashes between pro-independence fighters and Bolshevik-backed left-wing forces.

11 November 1918. End of the First World War.

18 November 1918. Latvia declares independence.

1919-20. Legislative elections in Estonia, Latvia and Lithuania.

1920. In a series of treaties, Bolshevik Russia formally accepts the secession of the Baltic states. Polish forces seize Wilna (Vilnius). They occupy the city throughout the interwar period; relations remain antagonistic.

December 1922 Foundation of the Soviet Union (the Union of Soviet Socialist Republics--USSR).

1 December 1924. Estonian communists launch an attempted insurrection covertly backed by elements in the Communist Party of the Soviet Union (CPSU).

May 1926. In Lithuanian elections, Catholic parties, having been the dominant force in parliament since independence, lose their overall majority and a Socialist-Populist coalition subsequently takes office.

16-17 December 1926. Coup d'état in Lithuania by ultra-nationalist military officers; a hero of the independence movement, Antanas Smetona, becomes President. Martial law is announced and strictly implemented; four leading communists are executed; in spring 1927 the junta dissolves the legislature and in May 1928 a presidential constitution is decreed.

October 1933; In a referendum Estonian voters endorse right-radical proposals for a strong presidency.

12 March 1934. Estonian coup d'état. Agrarian leader Konstantin Pats stages a bloodless takeover supported by senior military figures and the leaders of the main parties. The coup is an attempt to pre-empt a putsch by right-radicals. Parties are dissolved and an umbrella Patriotic Front created in May 1935, and on 24 April 1938 Pats becomes President under a new constitution.

15-16 May 1934. Latvian Agrarian leader Karlis Ulmanis launches a military-backed coup d'état, announcing martial law and suspending the right-radical and communist parties. Like Pats, Ulmanis claims that the seizure is a pre-emptive strike to head off a leftist or rightist putsch. Political parties are dissolved. In April 1936 Ulmanis assumes the Latvian presidency.

Autumn 1935. All Lithuanian political parties, except for Smetona's Nationalist League, are banned and press censorship is tightened.

24 February 1938. Estonian legislative elections are won by government supporters.

17 March 1938. Smetona capitulates before a Polish ultimatum, agreeing to reopen the border and establish diplomatic relations without prior settlement of the Wilna question; five days later he also concedes Klaipeda to Germany.

23 August 1939. The Nazi-Soviet Pact is signed by Molotov and Ribbentrop; with a further agreement in September 1939, the deal assigns the Baltic States to a Soviet "sphere of influence".

15-18 June 1940. Soviet annexation of the Baltic States.

14-15 July 1940. In rigged Baltic elections, the communists are victorious.

3-6 August 1940. The Baltic states are incorporated into the Soviet Union at the request of their now Soviet-dominated legislatures; they become three of the Union's 15 constituent republics.

14-15 June 1941. On a single night the Soviet authorities, targeting the intelligentsia, deport 60,000 Estonians, 34,000 Latvians and 38,000 Lithuanians to Siberia and Central Asia; in total the Soviets deport 4 per cent of Estonians and 2 per cent of Latvians and Lithuanians.

22 June 1941. War between Germany and the Soviet Union. German forces rapidly take the Baltic States.

1944. Reoccupation by the Red Army. Vilnius is reincorporated into Lithuania.

1948-9. Collectivisation of agriculture; deportation of tens of thousands of *kulaks* to Siberia and Central Asia, depleting the Baltic population by a further 3 per cent in March 1949 alone.

1958. The Soviet Education Act gives parents the right to choose the language in which their children are educated.

1959-61. Khrushchev orders a crackdown on the Latvian CP leadership, whom he accuses of "Latvianisation". Thereafter the Latvian party becomes the most pro-Soviet in the Baltic.

1971. Establishment of the Estonian National Front.

1972. Roman Kalanta, a student, martyrs himself for Lithuanian nationalism, dying by self-immolation in a square in Kaunas; his protest causes riots during which Russian street names are torn down, party and police offices are torched, and the crowds chant "Freedom!" Also in 1972, publication of the *Chronicle of the Lithuanian Catholic Church* begins, heralding a wave of *samizdat* publishing greater than anywhere else in the Soviet Union.

1974. Several Lithuanian groups coalesce to form the National Popular Front, with demands ranging from the release of political prisoners to a cessation of Soviet "colonialism".

October 1980. Estonian students and schoolchildren engage in mass protests against Russification. Further unrest in Tallinn and Tartu is inspired by events in Poland.

1983. The Estonian party cracks down on nationalists, arresting some 40 known dissidents.

March 1985. Mikhail Gorbachev becomes CPSU general secretary.

April 1986. Lithuanian public opinion is galvanised on environmental issues, after Polish broadcasts reveal the extent of the Chernobyl disaster. Emerging movements in all three states campaign to protect and restore national monuments and sites of historic significance or natural beauty damaged by Soviet military or industrial activity; Latvia's Environmental Protection Club is founded in spring 1986 and the Estonian Heritage Society in December 1987. Protests persuade the authorities to suspend environmentally controversial projects in Latvia and Estonia in 1986-7.

July 1986. Helsinki 86 is founded in Estonia; its *samizdat* journal *Tevija* ("Fatherland") spreads information about human rights abuses in Estonia.

23 August 1987. The first mass demonstrations in the Baltic republics, on the anniversary of the Nazi-Soviet Pact, spark off rallies across the Baltic republics to mark anniversaries of other key events in Baltic history, including the 1918 independence declarations and the deportations of 1941 and 1949. Demonstrators demand full *glasnost* on the Soviet role in these events.

3 June 1988. Foundation of the Lithuanian Restructuring Movement (*Sajudis* or "The Movement").

June 1988. The Latvian Writers' Union convenes a congress of cultural organisations, which demands Latvian republican sovereignty and a Latvian seat in the United Nations.

June-July 1988. The special 19th CPSU conference launches democratising reforms of the Soviet party.

20 August 1988. Foundation of the Estonian National Independence Party, the first self-declared opposition party in the Soviet Union.

28 September 1988. A demonstration organised by the Lithuanian Freedom League is violently dispersed by police; Gorbachev, piqued by the Lithuanian communists' conservatism, reshuffles its leadership, appointing the reformist Algirdas Brazauskas as the new party first secretary.

2-8 October 1988. Formal establishment of the Estonian and Latvian Popular Fronts. The Estonian Front is the most radical, demanding a mechanism for republican secession from the Soviet Union.

March 1989. In elections to the Soviet legislature, the all-Union Congress of People's Deputies, the popular fronts score major victories.

18 May 1989. The Lithuanian legislature declares sovereignty. The Latvian legislature follows suit on 28 July.

23 August 1989. In a demonstration of Baltic unity, two million people participate in creating a 400-mile human chain; the event marks the anniversary of the Nazi-Soviet Pact and is organised by the three popular fronts.

27 November 1989. The USSR Supreme Soviet adopts a law ceding the Baltic republics considerable economic autonomy; central ministries subsequently block implementation of the law.

6 December 1989. The Lithuanian legislature abolishes the communists' monopoly on power, and establishes the first multi-party system in the Soviet Union. Latvia follows suit on 11 January 1990.

20 December 1989. The Lithuanian communists declare independence from the CPSU; a rump communist party remains loyal to Moscow.

February 1990. The CPSU renounces its leading role.

24 February 1990. *Sajudis* wins 88 of the Lithuanian legislature's 141 seats in republican elections. Landsbergis becomes President and Mrs Kazimiera Prunskiene Prime Minister.

11 March 1990. The Lithuanian legislature declares independence: the Supreme Soviet of the USSR rules the declaration invalid. An unofficial Congress of Estonia convenes, having been elected in late February in a poll effectively limited to ethnic Estonians.

18 March 1990. Republican elections in Estonia and Latvia are won by the Popular Fronts. Edgar Savisaar's new government in Estonia declares that the republic is in a process of transition to independence.

3-4 May 1990. Anatolijs Gorbunovs becomes Latvian President and Ivars Godmanis Prime Minister. The legislature declares the annulment of the Soviet annexation of 1940, instead asserting the *de jure* continued existence of the independent Republic of Latvia and the sovereignty of Latvian law; Latvia is renamed the Republic of Latvia, dropping its "SSR" prefix. (On this latter point, Estonia follows suit on 8 May.)

12 June 1990. The Russian Republic's Supreme Soviet declares sovereignty on its territory, a crucial step in weakening the institutions of Soviet rule.

November 1990. Publication of the draft Union Treaty designed to replace that of 1922 with a new document devolving considerable powers to the republics while retaining a strong centre responsible for the economy, foreign affairs and defence. The Baltic States declare in December 1990 that they will not sign the Treaty, and boycott further negotiations, which continue until summer 1991.

7 January 1991. The Prunskiene cabinet in Lithuania orders major price rises prompting immediate protest demonstrations mainly by ethnic Russians and Poles. Similar events occur in the other Baltic states; but in Lithuania the legislature rescinds the price rises on the day of their introduction and the Prunskiene cabinet immediately resigns. Also on 7 January 1991, in all three Baltic republics, Soviet elite troops are deployed and pro-Soviet National Salvation Committees are established with the declared aim of averting economic collapse.

13 January 1991. Thirteen Lithuanian civilians are killed and 500 injured by Soviet troops at the Vilnius television station. Boris Yeltsin, the Chair of the Russian legislature, visits Tallinn for talks with the Baltic presidents; the four issue a joint statement denouncing "armed acts damaging each other's state sovereignty".

20 January 1991. Soviet troops kill six civilians in occupying the Ministry of the Interior in Riga.

23 January 1991. Gorbachev says that the National Salvation Committees have acted unconstitutionally; the crisis draws to a close.

9 February 1991. In a referendum, 90 per cent of Lithuanian voters opt for independence. In their own referendums on 3 March Estonian and Latvian voters also back independence, by 74 and 78 per cent respectively.

28 February 1991. The Lithuanian legislature passes privatisation legislation.

July 1991. Yeltsin signs a treaty recognising Lithuanian sovereignty.

19 August 1991. Hardline communists in Moscow launch an attempted coup on the eve of the scheduled signing of the renegotiated Union Treaty. Yeltsin and the Russian parliament lead opposition to the coup. The coup plotters are arrested and the CPSU is suspended.

20 August 1991. Estonia declares full independence.

21 August 1991. Latvia declares independence and re-adopts the 1922 constitution.

6 September 1991. The State Council, the Soviet Union's interim governing body, recognises the independence of the Baltic states.

17 September 1991. The Baltic states are admitted to the UN.

19 October 1991. Latvia launches an experimental privatisation programme.

11 December 1991. Latvian citizenship legislation requires most ethnic Slavs to apply for naturalisation.

11 January 1992. Estonian austerity measures include food rationing.

23 January 1992. Estonian premier Edgar Savisaar resigns and is replaced by independent Tiit Vahi.

25-6 January 1992. The Baltic Assembly holds its inaugural meeting.

31 March 1992. The Latvian legislature passes measures extending the official use of Latvian in higher education institutions.

14 June 1992. In a referendum 90 per cent of Lithuanian voters support an immediate withdrawal of Russian troops.

28 June 1992. In a referendum 91 per cent of Estonian voters endorse a new constitution, which takes effect on 3 July and establishes a parliamentary system with a strong presidency.

14 July 1992. The Lithuanian legislature dismisses Landsbergis's abrasive premier, Vagnorius, who claims to be the victim of entrenched left-wing interests. He is replaced by Aleksandras Abisala on 21 July.

8 September 1992. Russia agrees to withdraw troops stationed in Lithuania by 30 August 1993.

20 September 1992. In elections to the Estonian legislature, the pro-market Pro-Patria bloc emerges as the largest single group with one third of the seats; Pro-Patria forms a coalition under its 32-year old leader Mart Laar. Most non-Estonians are not permitted to vote.

5 October 1992. Nationalist Lennart Meri is elected as Estonian President by the legislature, no single candidate having won an overall majority in the popular vote on 20 September. Later in October Estonia declares its first bankruptcy and announces its first round of privatisation.

25 October 1992. Lithuanian voters approve a new constitution balancing presidential and parliamentary powers.

25 October and 15 November 1992. In Lithuanian elections, the divided *Sajudis* suffers a surprise reverse, as the ex-communist LDDP wins 73 of the 141 seats; pro-Landsbergis parties win 52; and the SDP plus the Centre Movement 10.

25 November 1992. LDDP leader Brazauskas is elected as chair of the Lithuanian parliament and head of state.

14 February 1993. In Lithuania's first direct presidential elections, Brazauskas wins 60 per cent of the vote. Adolfas Slezivicius is Prime Minister from 10 March.

5-6 June 1993. In Latvian legislative elections, the centre-right Latvia's Way bloc becomes the largest single party and forms a coalition with the LNNK. The elections are marred by the disenfranchisement of 34 per cent of Latvian residents, under 1991 citizenship legislation.

21 June 1993. The Estonian Law on Aliens is widely criticised as anti-Russian; international pressure forces the legislature to moderate the law.

6-8 July 1993. On consecutive days, the newly elected Latvian legislature (i) renews the 1922 constitution and the 1925 law on the Council of Ministers; (ii) elects Guntis Ulmanis of the Latvian Peasants' Union as President in a second-round vote; and (iii) confirms as Prime Minister Valdis Birkavs of Latvia's Way. Birkavs subsequently pledges state support for agriculture balanced by a rapid privatisation programme.

31 August 1993. Russian troops officially withdraw from Lithuanian soil, although a few units remain until December to supervise technical matters. Military transits across Lithuanian territory to Kaliningrad continue.

13 September 1993. The Baltic States' prime ministers sign a mutual free trade agreement abolishing tariffs on most non-agricultural goods from April 1994.

26 October 1993. The Estonian legislature passes a law permitting ethnic minorities autonomy, including the establishment of cultural, religious and educational institutions.

26 April 1994. Brazauskas and Polish President Lech Walesa sign a historic Polish-Lithuanian Treaty of Friendship and Co-operation in Vilnius.

13 June 1994. Establishment of the Baltic Council of Ministers.

21 June 1994. The Latvian legislature approves a new citizenship law, including tight quotas on the naturalisation of non-Latvians. Even the government opposes the quota system which is dropped in an amended version of the law passed on 22 July. Yeltsin nevertheless denounces Latvia on 4 August for "militant nationalism".

26 July 1994. Meri promises to grant the estimated 11,000 Russian ex-servicemen in Estonia "civil and political freedoms...[and] social, political and cultural rights".

11 August 1994. Russia commences the unilateral demarcation of its border with Estonia.

29-30 August 1994. On consecutive days, Russian troops officially pull out of Estonia and Latvia respectively; 600 Russian military personnel remain at the Skrunda radar station until May 1995.

15 September 1994. A new Latvian cabinet is formed under Maris Gailis, the former Minister of State Reform, after the withdrawal of the agrarians has brought down the previous coalition. Birkavs is retained as Minister of Foreign Affairs.

26 September-27 October 1994. Estonia's weakened Laar cabinet falls amid scandal: Laar is replaced by technocrat Andres Tarand.

28 September 1994. In Europe's worst postwar transport disaster, some 900 people are killed when a car ferry, the *Estonia*, sinks in the Baltic.

14-27 November 1994. The Lithuanian authorities are forced to shut down the nuclear reactors at Ignalina, after organised criminals threaten to bomb them in a bid to save gangster Boris Dekanidze, who has been convicted of the murder of journalist Lingys. Dekanidze is executed in July 1995.

1 January 1995. EC (EU) free trade agreements take effect, and are implemented in Estonia immediately, while four and six-year transition periods apply to Latvia and Lithuania.

31 January 1995. Legislation designates Lithuanian as the republic's state language despite protests by ethnic Polish and Russian leaders.

5 March 1995. In legislative elections, Estonia's ruling Pro-Patria is heavily defeated. The KMU bloc, dominated by ex-communists, is the main winner.

17 April 1995. A new Estonian cabinet takes office, comprising mainly the KMU and again led by Tiit Vahi.

12 June 1995. The EC (EU) signs association agreements with Estonia, Latvia and Lithuania, the first time that former Soviet republics have been considered for membership.

27 July 1995. Alfred Rubiks, Latvia's communist-era leader, is sentenced to eight years in prison for involvement in attempts in August 1991 to overthrow the Latvian government.

27 September 1995. The last remaining Russian military specialists leave Estonia, following their role in supervising the dismantling of nuclear reactors at the former submarine base at Paldiski.

30 September - 1 October 1995. In Latvian legislative elections, nine parties share the 100 parliamentary seats. Three leading groups win around 15 per cent: the centre-left *Saimnieks*, the right-wing populist Zigerists' Party/People's Movement for Latvia, and Latvia's Way.

13 October 1995. Latvia applies for membership of the EC (EU).

3 November 1995. A centre-right Estonian coalition takes office, once again under Vahi and with KMU participation but with the additional participation of the Reform party (R).

15 November 1995. Estonia agrees to accept the existing border with Russia as the *de facto* frontier between the two countries.

4 and 8 December 1995. Estonia and Lithuania respectively apply for EC (EU) membership.

21 December 1995. The Latvian parliament approves a new eight-party centre-right coalition after three months of wrangling. The coalition includes In Charge and Latvia's Way and is led by the 37-year old businessman and former Agriculture Minister Andris Skele, an independent.

THE CHANGING SHAPE OF EUROPEAN ORGANISATIONS

The shape of international organisations in post-1945 Europe reflected the Cold War division of the continent. Indeed, at the global level the United Nations itself functioned for over 40 years in the context of a world with two opposing superpowers, and the detente of the late 1980s accordingly provoked a profound readjustment of assumptions about its necessarily very different role in a post-Cold War period. At the European level, a fundamental rearrangement was made inevitable by the revolutionary changes in central and eastern Europe in 1989. The process continued thereafter amid upheavals as far-reaching in their implications as the dissolution of the Soviet Union in 1991 and the wars of the Yugoslav succession in 1991-95.

In central and eastern Europe, five main trends stood out.

Firstly, the institutions which had bound the states of central and eastern Europe into the Soviet sphere (the Warsaw Pact defence treaty organisation, Comecon, and ultimately the Soviet Union itself) had lost their power of cohesion, and in the case of the Warsaw Pact their raison d'être; all were wound up in 1991.

Secondly, in the defence and security sphere, NATO's principal role, as a Western defence organisation against the perceived Soviet threat, came under a reappraisal in which conflicting agendas could be discerned. At one pole was the assumption that Russia's size, interests and historical connections would ensure it at least a powerful continuing sphere of influence in eastern Europe. There was thus a case for preserving NATO's ability to counter any future Russian threat - and a concomitant argument for adding reliable allies but not "diluting" its membership by including countries seen as falling within such a Russian "sphere". At the other pole was the aspiration to extend NATO as a "partnership for peace", to provide an umbrella organisation for pan-European and North Atlantic security. It was a new departure in the 1990s to endow NATO with the capability both for peacekeeping operations within Europe (such as the Rapid Reaction Force deployed in Bosnia-Hercegovina in 1995, and the use of the NATO-commanded I-For to replace UN troops in the implementation of the Dayton accords), and for "out of area" military involvement.

There already existed, of course, the pan-European intergovernmental Conference for Security and Co-operation in Europe (CSCE), first set up in 1972 and redesignated an Organisation (OSCE) in December 1994 to underline its intending permanent status. The OSCE, unlike NATO, was not under Western control; it was thus less amenable as an instrument of Western policy, and correspondingly less likely to have Western manpower and military resources placed at its disposal. Nevertheless, the overlap between the OSCE's peacekeeping and security responsibilities, and any new NATO peacekeeping vocation, left considerable room for ambiguity about the appropriate organisational framework for organising such missions, if NATO's area of activity was not to be confined to an exclusive group of member states.

Thirdly, in the context of building free market systems, there was the issue of economic integration for what were increasingly being defined in World Bank and

IMF parlance as the "economies in transition" of the central and east European countries (CEECs). Significant trends included membership of organisations which could access funds for reconstruction and development (including the World Bank and IMF, which Hungary had joined in 1982 and Poland, an original founder member, had rejoined in 1986 after a 36-year absence), participation in the new European Bank for Reconstruction and Development (EBRD), and co-operation agreements with the European Free Trade Area (EFTA). The most crucial issue, however, was seen to be that of relations with the European Communities (EC), which on 1 November 1993 became officially the European Union (EU). Prospective membership of the EC was seen by former communist states in the post-1989 period as the fullest expression of the goal of "joining Europe".

A fourth trend was that countries newly constituted or reconstituted as pluralistic democracies sought the stamp of approval of membership of the Council of Europe. This was in essence a "club" of European democracies, dating from 1949, whose main objectives were to co-ordinate legislation and promote co-operation particularly in its social, cultural, scientific and legal dimensions. Membership depended on a state undertaking to respect certain common standards notably with regard to human rights legislation.

Fifthly, new groups emerged to help build co-operation among various states of the region identifying a commonality of interest in particular economic spheres. Notable among these (see below) were the Visegrad Group which spawned the Central European Free Trade Area (CEFTA), the broader Central European Initiative (CEI), and the Black Sea Economic Co-operation project (BSEC).

East Germany's position was unique among the former communist bloc countries. In the run-up to German reunification East Germany left the Warsaw Pact in September 1990 and, simultaneously with its reunification with West Germany by merger into the Federal Republic on 2-3 October 1990, it became part of NATO (albeit with provisions that NATO troops should not be stationed on the territory of the former East Germany), the Western European Union, the Council of Europe, the EC (EU), and other bodies of which West Germany was already a member.

Warsaw Pact

The Warsaw Pact, formally known as the Warsaw Treaty Organisation, came into being in May 1955, the month in which West Germany joined NATO. The Warsaw Treaty of Friendship, Co-operation and Mutual Assistance was signed by the Soviet Union, Poland, East Germany, Czechoslovakia, Hungary, Romania, Bulgaria, and Albania (which withdrew in 1968, having never really participated and having been estranged from the Soviet camp since 1961).

The Pact provided the framework within which the member countries participated in military planning and contributed their resources and facilities, although the Soviet Union really determined strategy and the deployment of forces and weapons throughout the Cold War. It was the decision by Hungarian reformists in 1956 to leave the Warsaw Pact which precipitated the Soviet invasion. In August 1968 the Soviet leadership was at pains to emphasise that the next major instance of the use of force in Europe, to crush the Prague Spring reform experiment, was a Warsaw Pact intervention rather than a purely Soviet one, with Polish, East German, Hungarian and Bulgarian troops taking part. Three months later, Brezhnev enunciated the doctrine of "limited sovereignty", with its assertion that the socialist states had an "internationalist obligation" to intervene in the event of a threat to socialism.

The importance of the Warsaw Pact in terms of enforcing conformity within central and east European member countries declined dramatically in 1989 when it became apparent, as stated by Gorbachev at the organisation's Bucharest summit in July, that it would no longer act according to the interventionist Brezhnev doctrine. Only the Romanian leader Ceausescu urged the Pact to use force to bring Poland to heel.

Meanwhile the momentum of arms control and disarmament negotiations was accelerating at the US-Soviet level, with the START 1 talks on strategic arms reductions moving towards their eventual July 1991 agreement in the wake of the breakthrough 1987 treaty on intermediate nuclear forces (INF). Following the demise of communist regimes in the majority of Pact member countries, the dissolution of the Pact itself became a formality after the CSCE summit in Paris in November 1990. At this meeting the participants signed the Treaty on Conventional Armed Forces in Europe (CFE), providing for major reductions in such forces between the Atlantic and the Urals; five days earlier the Pact and NATO had declared solemnly that they no longer regarded each other as enemies. The Warsaw Pact countries agreed on 25 February 1991 to disband their military alliance, and the organisation was formally wound up at a meeting in Prague on 1 July 1991.

The former Soviet bloc states, except for Poland, had by this time already negotiated the withdrawal of Soviet troops from their soil.

There had been no Soviet troops stationed in Bulgaria since the withdrawal of the Red Army in December 1947, and none in Romania since July 1958. On 7 December 1988 Gorbachev had announced unilateral troop withdrawals, involving 50,000 troops and 5,000 tanks then based in Czechoslovakia, East Germany and Hungary. The complete withdrawal of Soviet forces from Czechoslovakia, where troops had remained after 1968 and numbered some 73,000, was agreed on 26-27 February 1990 and completed by July 1991. The withdrawal from Hungary, negotiated in March 1990, was completed by June 1991. In Poland, which had not had a Cold War "front line" with the West, there had nevertheless been some 50,000 Soviet troops, principally in order to ensure the security of the lengthy military supply lines from the Soviet Union to the frontier between East and West Germany. Disagreement about the speed of their departure held up an agreement until October 1991, shortly after the collapse of the hardline coup attempt in Moscow in August. Combat troops left Poland by October 1992, and a contingent of 6,000 support troops, deemed necessary until the end of the Russian military presence in Germany, finally withdrew in September 1994. As regards the Soviet military presence in East Germany, its progressive winding down over four years was negotiated as part of the September 1990 "two-plus-four" Treaty on the Final Settlement with Germany, and arrangements for the withdrawal and troop resettlement process to be heavily subsidised by Germany were included in the German-Soviet "good neighbourliness" treaty signed at the same time. By 1994 the withdrawal had been completed, and the four-power military presence in Berlin ended in August-September of that year, with the withdrawal of the last Russian troops followed by that of the remaining contingents of British, French and US forces.

The Baltic states had never been separate members of the Warsaw Pact, but they had to negotiate the withdrawal of tens of thousands of Russian troops after they became independent and the Soviet Union collapsed. Despite bellicose Russian statements about being prepared to intervene to protect Russian minorities in Estonia and Latvia, and considerable diplomatic friction over the withdrawal of troops, their departure in fact proceeded in a virtually continuous process from 1991 onwards. All combat troops had left Lithuania by 1993 and Estonia and Latvia by August 1994.

Comecon

Comecon, formally known as the Council for Mutual Economic Assistance (CMEA), was formed in January 1949, with the purpose of binding the central and east European states more closely within the Soviet sphere, in the wake of Stalin's 1947 repudiation of the US-sponsored Marshall Plan for European reconstruction. Its members were the Soviet Union, Poland, East Germany, Czechoslovakia, Hungary, Romania and Bulgaria, but not Albania; they were later joined by Cuba, Mongolia and Vietnam, while in April 1955 Yugoslavia became an associate member. In theory Comecon provided a structure for ensuring that the economies of participating countries could pursue the roles most appropriate to them in the context of overall planning at the international level. In practice, Comecon planning from the outset meant imposing the Stalinist "Soviet model" where resources and efforts were directed to building up heavy industry and collectivising agricultural production. Subsequent destalinisation allowed for a greater or lesser degree of divergence from this model, including the Hungarian New Economic Mechanism under Kadar's regime from 1968.

The notion that Comecon should co-ordinate economic planning was undermined further by Gorbachev's application of the policy of *perestroika* from the mid-1980s. It was a dead letter once the governments formed in central and eastern Europe after the political upheavals of 1989 had espoused the goal of discarding central planning and instead building market economies. Any prospect of Comecon surviving as a trading bloc was ended by the introduction of hard currency trade among Comecon countries from January 1991, and the resulting collapse of the traditional markets for central and east European materials and goods in the Soviet Union. All the central and east European countries were thereafter obliged to look westwards for new markets, and their priority was accordingly to seek to negotiate preferential terms for such access, since their economies would otherwise be unable to compete.

The winding up of Comecon was postponed "for technical reasons" at the Budapest meeting on 25 February 1991 at which the decision was taken to disband the Warsaw Pact [*see above*]. However, Comecon was dissolved formally at a subsequent meeting in Budapest on 28 June 1991.

Cominform, the Communist Information Bureau established by the communist parties of Bulgaria, Czechoslovakia, France, Hungary, Italy, Poland, Romania, the Soviet Union and Yugoslavia in October 1947, was dissolved in April 1956 when it was deemed to have "exhausted its function". The Yugoslav party had been expelled on 28 June 1948.

As Czechoslovakia progressively eliminated its remaining links with communist organisations after 1989, Vaclav Havel demanded in October 1990 the closure of the headquarters of the communist-dominated **World Federation of Trade Unions** and other international communist "front" bodies in Prague. As President of Czechoslovakia, Havel was the most prominent of the region's statesmen in 1990-91 in articulating the desire for a "return to Europe".

North Atlantic Treaty Organisation (NATO)

A NATO summit meeting in London in July 1990 confirmed the conclusion that progress on disarmament and the collapse of communism in Europe meant the end of the Cold War. The first major organisational change affecting NATO in this context was its incorporation of the former East Germany. In the "two-plus-four" negotiations on German unification which began in May 1990 Gorbachev initially fought hard for the idea that a unified Germany should be outside NATO. In the end, in conceding a unified Germany's right to choose its own alliances, he settled for a good strategic bargain. Under treaties regulating German unification, Soviet troops were allowed to remain in (eastern) Germany until 1994. Germany for its part (i) confirmed its final acceptance of its borders (notably the Oder-Neisse border with Poland); (ii) confirmed its renunciation of nuclear, biological and chemical weapons, and (iii) undertook to reduce its own troop levels over three to four years. It was also agreed that NATO forces should not be stationed on the territory of the former East Germany.

By May 1991 NATO defence ministers, actively engaged in military retrenchment and a re-evaluation of the organisation's role, were calling for "a network of interlocking relationships" with former Warsaw Pact countries. They nevertheless regarded as premature the overtures coming from Czechoslovakia, Hungary and Poland for integration into NATO membership. They pursued instead the idea of creating an intermediate forum to discuss security co-operation between NATO and former Warsaw Pact countries. The resulting North Atlantic Co-operation Council (NACC) held its inaugural meeting in Brussels on 16 December 1991, attended by foreign ministers from the 16 NATO countries, Czechoslovakia, Hungary and Poland, Bulgaria and Romania, the Soviet Union, Estonia, Latvia and Lithuania. Albania joined the NACC in June 1992, as did the former Soviet republics during the course of that year, and the Czech Republic and Slovakia, having completed their separation, in 1993.

NATO's first full summit since the collapse of the Soviet Union, held in Brussels on 10-11 January 1994, focused on threats to peace in Europe and was heavily preoccupied with the war in former Yugoslavia. The summit's warning on the possible use of air strikes had hardened by 9 February into an ultimatum to the Bosnian Serbs, backed up at the end of that month by NATO's first offensive action in its 44-year history. (*For this and subsequent NATO actions see Yugoslavia chapter and especially Bosnia-Hercegovina sub-chapter.*)

The 1994 NATO summit was also the forum at which US President Bill Clinton launched his Partnerships for Peace initiative. This was designed as a way of extending bilateral military co-operation between former communist states and NATO, beyond the co-ordination and joint training envisaged under NACC, but still some way short of NATO membership. Countries joining the programme would be entitled to send representatives to meetings at NATO headquarters, and would conduct joint military planning and training with NATO, while committing themselves to share information about their armed forces, including their military budgets, and to ensure that they were democratically controlled.

Most of the central and east European countries signed Partnerships for Peace agreements within two months. Slovenia (the first former Yugoslav participant) did so on 30 March, and by February 1995 the only non-members in Europe were neutral Switzerland and Ireland, and the remaining four former Yugoslav states -- one of which, Macedonia, signed up on 15 November 1995.

The biggest success for the initiative was Russia's decision to join it, on 22 June 1994, with the accompaniment of a special "extensive and far-reaching individual partnership programme, corresponding to its size, importance, capabilities and willingness to contribute to the pursuit of share objectives". This resolved a disagreement centring on Russia's desire to consult with NATO as an equal and to have a voice on its future evolution, as against NATO's refusal to countenance a Russian veto over its actions. NATO foreign and defence ministers in May and June 1995 reiterated the intention that the alliance should expand its membership eastwards, but with the intended reassurance to Russia (which opposed such expansion) that this would be "part of an evolutionary process". The presidents of the Baltic states, meeting in Tallinn on 7 September 1995, stressed their desire to join NATO as soon as possible, against strong Russian opposition which went as far as warnings of intervention. Albania was also particularly keen on membership, however unenthusiastic the reaction in Brussels. More significant were the repeated Polish expressions of the desire to join, pressed by the Oleksy government soon after it took office in March 1995, and reiterated by the newly elected President Kwasniewski at the end of the year.

Conference on / Organisation for Security and Co-operation in Europe (CSCE / OSCE)

There was a strong Russian preference for developing the role of the CSCE / OSCE, rather than expanding NATO, as the principal organisation for managing Europe-wide responses on security issues. This approach found some support from Vaclav Havel, who, in 1991 (as president of Czechoslovakia), favoured the use of CSCE conflict prevention mechanisms to seek a solution to the crisis and civil war in Yugoslavia.

The permanent Conference on Security and Co-operation in Europe (CSCE) had been set up on 1 August 1975 under the Helsinki Final Act, signed by 35 countries including Bulgaria, Czechoslovakia, East Germany, Hungary, Poland, Romania, and Yugoslavia. Albania joined in June 1991. Membership numbers swelled with the admission of the Baltic states and the separate former Soviet republics after the break-up of the Soviet Union, as well as Croatia and Slovenia in January 1992, the total thus reaching 52 (not including Yugoslavia which was suspended in July 1992). The creation of a Prague-based secretariat reinforced the CSCE's claim to permanence, which was further emphasised by the change of name to OSCE, decided at its Budapest summit in December 1994.

Hitherto mainly a forum for managing east-west confrontation, the CSCE became increasingly involved in human rights issues and aspired to a role in conflict prevention, especially in areas of particular inter-communal tension. It appointed a high commissioner for national minorities, Max van der Stoel, whose work focused particularly on issues involving Hungarian minorities in Slovakia and Romania, Russian minorities in the Baltic states, and the Albanian minority in Macedonia (*see those country chapters*). CSCE missions, however, apart from those in Macedonia and the Baltic states, were used principally in the former Soviet republics of Moldova, trans-Caucasus and central Asia.

European Communities (EC) / European Union (EU)

Eastern Germany, by dint of its merger into the Federal Republic in October 1990, was simultaneously incorporated within the EC (EU). Other central and east European countries, having emerged by their political upheavals from the "Soviet bloc", also saw

EU membership as central to the principal foreign policy objective of "joining Europe". On 16 December 1991, Czechoslovakia, Hungary and Poland signed association agreements with the EC (EU) after negotiations in progress since February 1991. These "Europe Agreements" provided for free trade within 10 years and possibly eventual EU membership.

By the end of 1995 "Europe Agreements" linked the EU in associations with all the countries covered in this book except Albania, the Baltic States and the former Yugoslav states. Albania was at a less advanced stage along this path, having established a trade and co-operation agreement, and been accepted as eligible for aid under EU-administered reconstruction programmes. All three Baltic states had also taken both these steps, and in addition had signed Europe Agreements, in June 1995, but these had not yet entered into force (apart from interim agreements on free trade). With the former Yugoslav states, except the FRY, the EC (EU) had reintroduced in February 1992 the trade benefits originally accorded in its Yugoslavia co-operation agreement of 1980 but suspended as a sanction in November 1991. However with Slovenia, whose relatively highly developed economy made it a leading candidate for fast-track integration, the EU had gone considerably further, signing trade and co-operation and reconstruction aid agreements in 1993 and initialling a Europe Agreement in June 1995.

As regards actual EU membership status, intending applicants were compelled to recognise that any timetable for this would be set not by their eagerness, but by the priorities of the EU's member states and of its executive arm, the European Commission. Those generally considered to be at the front of the queue were the Czech Republic, Hungary, Poland and Slovenia; those which had formally applied as of the end of 1995 were Hungary, Poland, Romania and all three Baltic states.

	Trade and co-operation agreement		Europe Agreement		membership application
	signed	in force	signed	in force	made
Poland	19 Sep 89	01 Dec 89	16 Dec 91	01 Feb 94	08 Apr 94
Hungary	26 Sep 88	01 Dec 88	16 Dec 91	01 Feb 94	01 Apr 94
Czechoslovakia	08 May 90	01 Nov 90			
Czech Rep			04 Oct 93	01 Feb 95	
Slovakia			04 Oct 93	01 Feb 95	
Romania	22 Oct 90	01 May 91	01 Feb 93	01 Feb 95	22 Jun 95
Bulgaria	08 May 90	01 Nov 90	08 Mar 93	01 Feb 95	
Albania	11 May 92	01 Dec 92			
Slovenia	05 Apr 93	01 Sep 93			
Estonia	11 May 92	01 Mar 93	12 Jun 95		04 Dec 95
Latvia	11 May 92	01 Feb 93	12 Jun 95		13 Oct 95
Lithuania	11 May 92	01 Feb 93	12 Jun 95		08 Dec 95

Enlargement was identified by the EU as a "historic mission", and a "pre-accession" strategy was incorporated in the shaping of the Europe Agreements. However, as the EU's internal debate developed about the relative emphasis on "widening versus deepening", and its member states became increasingly preoccupied with promoting or resisting various aspects of "deeper" integration under the 1992 Maastricht treaty on European Union, it became apparent that the eastward enlargement would not be on the agenda for proper negotiation before 1997. In that year, following conclusion of the

EU's scheduled 18-month intergovernmental conference, the Commission would begin preparing "opinions" on applications received. Candidates for membership might accordingly look forward to the prospect of accession in or around the year 2000.

The Group of Seven major industrialised countries agreed at their Paris summit in July 1989 to set up a programme, administered by the EC Commission, to channel assistance from the wider Group of 24 industrialised countries to assist in the reorientation of the economies of Hungary and Poland. This was extended on 4 July 1990 to Bulgaria, Czechoslovakia, Yugoslavia and East Germany (until unification), on 30 January 1991 to Romania, and on 1 January 1992 to Albania and the Baltic states.

Subsumed within this programme was the EC's own "operation phare" (the acronym initially intended to refer, in French, to aid for economic restructuring in Poland and Hungary), which came into effect on 18 December 1989.

European Bank for Reconstruction and Development (EBRD)

The EBRD was set up following a November 1989 initiative by French President François Mitterrand to assist with the identification of viable development projects and the channeling of funding for reconstruction. The EBRD founding charter was signed in May 1990 and the Bank came into being in April 1991. Bulgaria, Czechoslovakia, Hungary, Poland, Romania, and Yugoslavia were founder members, along with the Soviet Union, 31 other countries including all the OECD members, the EC and the EC's European Investment Bank (EIB). By 1995 the Baltic states, all the former Soviet republics, and all the former Yugoslav states except Bosnia-Hercegovina had also joined.

Organisation for Economic Co-operation and Development (OECD)

The OECD developed from the Organisation for European Economic Co-operation, set up in 1948 to administer reconstruction efforts funded by the US Marshall Plan. OECD membership consequently did not include any of the Comecon countries, although Yugoslavia participated in certain aspects of its work. By 1991, however, Czechoslovakia, Hungary and Poland were participating in a co-operation programme with the OECD resulting in the publication of the first OECD reports on Hungary in July 1991, on Czechoslovakia in January 1992 and on Poland in February 1992. As of the end of 1995 the OECD was intending to consider the membership of the Czech Republic, Slovakia, Hungary and Poland, which had applied in early 1994, once it had finished processing South Korea's membership.

European Free Trade Association (EFTA)

The interest which the former Comecon countries showed in concluding agreements with EFTA was twofold. Their desire to develop new markets attracted them towards free trade agreements under which their vulnerable economies were not pressed to offer entirely reciprocal access, but allowed to maintain some essential protective barriers for transitional periods. Secondly there was the notion of using EFTA as a possible "antechamber" or bridge to membership of the EC (EU), especially once EFTA countries and the EU had concluded their joint agreement on the European Economic Area (EEA), which came into being in January 1994 and established the world's largest common market of some 380 million people. The applications for EC (EU) membership by EFTA members Austria, Sweden and Finland (all of which subsequently joined the EU in January 1995) encouraged the perception of EFTA as an "antechamber", although by 1994 the interest in this idea had waned, and Slovenia was the only country actually to raise (in late 1994) the issue of applying for EFTA membership.

Czechoslovakia, Hungary and Poland in June 1990, Bulgaria, Romania, Estonia, Latvia and Lithuania in December 1991, and Albania, the Baltic states and Slovenia during 1992, signed declarations on co-operation with EFTA with provisions to lead on to free trade agreements. Free trade agreements came into effect with the Czech Republic and Slovakia in April 1993, and in the same year with Romania on 1 May, Bulgaria on 1 July, Hungary on 1 October and Poland on 15 November 1993; free trade agreements with the three Baltic states came into effect on 1 January 1996.

Council of Europe

Hungary was the first of the former communist states to join the Council of Europe, in November 1990, followed by Czechoslovakia in February 1991 and Poland in November 1991. Albania, Bulgaria, Romania and Yugoslavia had all applied for membership by this time and have been given "special guest status"; Yugoslavia's status has been withdrawn since mid-1991, however, because of the civil war.

Bulgaria became a member in May 1992 and Estonia and Lithuania joined in May 1993, although the former came close to being suspended until its President Meri refused to sign its controversial nationality law. Also in May 1993 Slovenia became the first former Yugoslav state to gain membership. The Czech Republic and Slovakia completed the process of becoming separate members in June 1993, and Romania became a member in October 1993, despite concerns over the treatment of its Hungarian minority, after the Council's parliamentary Assembly had adopted the so-called Halonen Order requiring that new members should be monitored to ensure that commitments were honoured. Latvia's admission, delayed by concern over the treatment of its Russian minority, was finally approved in February 1995, as was the accession of Albania and Moldova in July 1995 despite worries over their observance of human rights. The admission of Ukraine and Macedonia in November 1995 brought total membership to 38. A Russian application to join, made in 1992, was still pending and was placed in suspension in 1995 in view of its internal war in Chechenya.

The first ever summit meeting of heads of state and government of Council of Europe member countries was held in Vienna on 8-9 October 1993. Grandiosely described as "the new Congress of Vienna", it issued a declaration reaffirming commitment to its fundamental principles. It also set in train the reform of the structure of the European Court of Human Rights (completed the following year when the new single-tier Court replaced the previous dual arrangement of a Court and a Commission), and endorsed work on a Convention on the Protection of National Minorities, which was ready for approval in November 1994.

Groupings within central and eastern Europe

Poland, Hungary and Czechoslovakia identified a common interest from 1990 in pressing for the opening up of the non-communist European organisational structure to accommodate their new democracies and prospective market economies. After a meeting in Bratislava in April 1990 to discuss their "return to Europe", they met again in February 1991 at Visegrad near Budapest, and became known as the "Visegrad Triangle"; after the separation of the Czech Republic and Slovakia, this became the **"Visegrad Group"**. Havel in particular encouraged their liaisons. A co-operation treaty signed in Krakow on 5-6 October 1991 declared their commitment to a united Europe and affirmed that their security interests were best served by integration within NATO. The cohesion of what was principally an informal lobbying group declined thereafter with the perception that certain of the group, in particular the Czech Republic and Hungary, might more quickly win acceptance by NATO and the EU without the others. However, the realisation that no expansion of either of these bodies was imminent, and fear of the growth of Russian nationalism, led to a revival of interest in links within the group. Having signed a **Central European Free Trade Area** (CEFTA) agreement in December 1992, the four countries agreed in August 1995 to develop this over the next two years into a common market in most industrial goods. On 11 September 1995 they agreed to admit Slovenia to CEFTA (Slovenia signed the treaty on 26 November and became the fifth member with effect from January 1996), and designated the Baltic states, Bulgaria and Romania as potential future members.

A broader **Central European Initiative** (CEI) developed out of what began as the "Pentagonale" group, a meeting on 31 July - 1 August 1990, on an Italian initiative, between leaders from Austria, Czechoslovakia, Hungary, Italy and Yugoslavia, to discuss economic and cultural co-operation. Poland joined the group in July 1991 and on 28 January 1992 it adopted the CEI name, widening its scope to include all the former Yugoslav states except the FRY. In October 1995 the CEI foreign ministers, meeting in Warsaw, agreed to extend the grouping further in early 1996 to encompass Albania, Bulgaria, Romania, Ukraine and Belarus.

Countries around the Black Sea (at that time comprising Bulgaria, Romania, the Soviet Union and Turkey, with Greece and Yugoslavia as observers) met in July 1991 to begin negotiations on an economic co-operation agreement. From this grew the **Black Sea Economic Co-operation** project (BSEC), founded in February 1992. BSEC held its inaugural conference that June and a second summit in Bucharest in June 1995. At Bucharest it identified the aims of co-operating on a range of economic areas including trade, transport, power generation and distribution, telecommunications and banking, as well as on tackling pollution, cross-border crime and pollution. It also considered plans to set up a Black Sea Trade and Development Bank in Salonika. Membership had by this time reached 11 (Turkey, Greece, Albania, Bulgaria, Romania, Moldova, Ukraine, Russia and the three republics of trans-Caucasus).

The Baltic states revived in May 1990 an original 1930s "Baltic entente" association between them, with the new title of the **Baltic Council.** They also took part in the wider **Council of Baltic Sea States** founded in March 1992, which included in addition Finland, Russia, Poland, Germany, Denmark, Norway and Sweden.

Other groupings and initiatives included the Alpen-Adria grouping established in 1978 for regional co-operation on tourism, energy, environment, transport, sport and culture, and involving five Austrian provinces, Hungary's western regions, the northern regions of Italy, Bavaria, Croatia and Slovenia; an agreement between Balkan governments at a conference in Athens in March 1990 to strengthen regional economic and technological co-operation; and an attempt in May 1990 to establish a working community between regions bordering on the river Danube, an idea subsequently shattered by the wars in Yugoslavia and the imposition of sanctions against the FRY.

BIBLIOGRAPHICAL NOTE

To keep up with the rapid, fundamental and continuing changes in central and eastern Europe, the student will need to keep a close watch on the academic journals on the region and on international politics. Research is appearing all the time on history so recent that it is still very much in the current affairs category.

For anyone seeking to monitor current events, a valuable resource is provided by the Open Media Research Institute (OMRI) in Prague with the fortnightly publication of *Transition*. The research and analysis done by OMRI is based on constant culling of information from press and broadcast sources, a digest of which is published daily by OMRI by email or on the Internet (at http://www.omri.cz/Index.html). In an earlier period this function was carried out by Radio Free Europe and Radio Liberty, whose research institute in Munich published the weekly *RFE/RL Research Reports* until 1994.

A number of books capture some of the excitement of the "year of revolutions" in 1989, written for the most part by journalists who witnessed some of the dramatic events of that year. Examples include *Tearing Down The Curtain; the people's revolution in Eastern Europe* by an Observer newspaper team, edited by Nigel Hawkes (Hodder and Stoughton, 1990), *Lighting the Night* by the US journalist William Echikson (Sidgwick and Jackson, 1990), and, rather more considered, *The Patriots' Revolution* by Mark Frankland (Sinclair-Stevenson 1990). The pre-1989 opposition movements of Central Europe are depicted in *The Uses of Adversity* by Timothy Garton-Ash (Granta Books, 1990).

For the pre-communist background, a classic work is *East Central Europe Between the Two World Wars* by Joseph Rothschild (University of Washington Press, 1994) and another point of reference is *Eastern Europe between the Wars 1918-41* by Hugh Seton-Watson. On the subsequent years there is *Eastern Europe since 1945* by Geoffrey Swain and Nigel Swain (Macmillan, 1993), and other works including *The Socialist Regimes of Eastern Europe; their establishment and consolidation* by Jerzy Tomaszewski (Routledge, London, 1989); *Eastern Europe 1968-84* by Olga Narkiewicz (Routledge, 1986) and the series *Marxist Regimes*, ed. Bogdan Szajkowski (Pinter Publishers, various dates). An up-to-date analysis of the structure and functioning of politics within the region is *Politics in Eastern Europe* by George Schöpflin. The major work on economic developments and problems is Michael Kaser's multi-volume *The Economic History of Eastern Europe* which takes 1919 as its starting date.

Background on the Soviet Union is outside the scope of this note, but a good start would be *A History of the Soviet Union* by Geoffrey Hosking (Fontana, London, revised edition 1992).

Finally, *The Death of Yugoslavia* by Laura Silber and Allan Little (Penguin Books / BBC Books, London, revised edition 1996) is a penetrating account of that conflict and its origins.

GLOSSARY OF TERMS AND ACRONYMS

ALP *see* PPS

banovina: area of Croatian autonomy within Yugoslavia

BBB: Bulgarian Business Bloc

BBWR: Non-Party Bloc in Support of Reforms (Poland), a deliberate echo of the inter-war pro-Pilsudski Non-Partisan Bloc for Co-operation with Government (also BBWR)

BCP *see* BKP

BfD: League of Free Democrats (East Germany)

BKP: Bulgarian Communist Party, 1948-90 (previously BKP 1919-24, Bulgarian Workers' Party 1924-48)

BRD *see* FRG

BSP: Bulgarian Socialist Party

Bundesrat: upper house of federal German parliament

Bundestag: (main) lower house of federal German parliament

BZNS: Bulgarian Agrarian National Union

CDR: Democratic Convention of Romania

CDU: Christian Democratic Union (Germany)

CEFTA: Central European Free Trade Area

CEI: Central European Initiative grouping

Chetniks: Serb nationalist movement simultaneously involved in anti-German resistance and in civil war with Partisans, 1941-44; Serb irregular militia force in Bosnia, 1992-94

Comecon: Soviet bloc economic planning arm, the Commission for Mutual Economic Assistance, formed in 1949 and disbanded in 1991

Cominform: Soviet-dominated Communist Information Bureau linking communist parties, 1947-56

CPCz *see* KSC

CPSU: Communist Party of the Soviet Union

CSCE: Conference on Security and Co-operation in Europe, renamed OSCE in December 1994

CSSD: Czech Social Democratic Party

DA: Democratic Awakening (East Germany)

DDR *see* GDR

Depos: Serbian Democratic Movement

DKP: German Communist Party, pre-1933

DPS: Movement for Rights and Freedoms (Bulgaria)

DSU: German Social Union

DUS: Democratic Union of Slovakia

EAD: Human Rights Union (Albania)

EBRD: European Bank for Reconstruction and Development

EC (EU): European Communities, since November 1993 the European Union

EFTA: European Free Trade Association

FDP: Free Democrat Party (Germany)

FIDESz: League of Young Democrats (Hungary)

FKgP: Independent Smallholders' Party (Hungary)

FRG: Federal Republic of Germany (formerly West Germany), German acronym BRD

FRY: Federal Republic of Yugoslavia (comprising Serbia and Montenegro)

FSN: National Salvation Front, 1989-93 (Romania)

FSND: Democratic National Salvation Front, 1992-3 (Romania)

FYROM: Former Yugoslav Republic of Macedonia (official name at UN)

GDR: German Democratic Republic (East Germany), German acronym DDR

glasnost: "openness", the slogan from 1985 denoting greater political freedoms under Gorbachev, leading to reappraisals of past actions and politics

HDF *see* MDF

HDZ: Croatian Democratic Community

HND: Croatian Independent Democrats

HNS: Croatian People's Party

HSD: Movement for Self Administered Democracy, 1990-92 (Czechoslovakia)

HSP *see* MSzP

HSWP *see* MSMP

HVO: Croatian Defence Council, the Bosnian Croat forces

HZDS: Movement for a Democratic Slovakia

I-For: NATO-commanded Implementation Force to implement the 1995 Dayton accords on former Yugoslavia

JNA: federal Yugoslav People's Army

KCS: Communist Party of Czechoslovakia, 1921-92

KDH: Christian Democratic Movement (Czechoslovakia, Slovakia)

KDNP: Christian Democratic People's Party (Hungary)

KDU-CSL: Christian Democratic Union - Czechoslovak People's Party (Czech Republic)

KGB: State security police of the Soviet Union, 1954-91

KLD: Liberal Democratic Congress, 1988-94 (Poland)

KMU: coalition based on Rural Union (MU) in Estonia

KPD: Communist Party of Germany revived in 1945

KPN: Confederation for an Independent Poland

Krajina: borderlands; areas within Croatia heavily populated by Serbs

KSCM: Communist Party of Bohemia and Moravia (Czechoslovakia)

kulaks: Russian word for prosperous peasants who market produce and employ labour

Länder: plural of *Land*, the states of the Federal Republic of Germany

LCY *see* SKJ

LDDP: Lithuanian Democratic Labour Party

LDS: Liberal Democratic Party of Slovenia, latterly Liberal Democracy of Slovenia

LNNK: Latvian National Independence Movement

LSU: Liberal Social Union (Czech Republic)

lustration: term used particularly in Czechoslovakia for the process of bringing to light those who collaborated with the communist-era secret police

LZS: Latvian Agrarian Union

Marshall Plan: The US-funded aid programme for postwar reconstruction in Europe, launched in June 1947

MDF: Hungarian Democratic Forum

MIEP: Hungarian Justice and Life Party

MRF *see* DPS

MSMP: Hungarian Socialist Workers' Party, 1956-89

MSzP: Hungarian Socialist Party

NATO: North Atlantic Treaty Organisation

NDH: The 1941-45 *Ustasha* Nazi client regime in Croatia

NEM: New Economic Mechanism, a Hungarian attempt from 1968 to integrate features of market economy with central planning, emulated feebly in Bulgaria in the 1980s

NLP: National Liberal Party (Romania)

nomenklatura: the privileged elites created by communist party appointments systems (literally "list of names and offices" in Russian)

normalisation: sinister euphemism for purges and repression to eliminate reform communist movements, as used after the 1968 "Prague Spring"

ODA: Civic Democratic Alliance (Czech Republic)

ODS: Civic Democratic Party (Czech Republic)

OH: Civic Movement (Czech Republic)

OMON forces: Soviet special interior ministry troops

OP: Civic Forum, 1989-91 (Czechoslovakia: Czech Lands)

Orszaggyules: the Hungarian parliament

OSCE: Organisation for Security and Co-operation in Europe, formerly CSCE

Partisans: Yugoslav wartime communist-dominated resistance led by Tito

PC: Centre Alliance (Poland)

PCR: Romanian Communist Party (in 1948-65 Romanian Workers' Party)

PD-FSN: Democratic Party-National Salvation Front (Romania)

PDAR: Agrarian Democratic Party of Romania

PdP: Covenant for Poland

PDP: Party of Democratic Prosperity (of Albanians in Macedonia)

PDS: Democratic Party of Albania

PDSR: Social Democracy Party of Romania

perestroika: "restructuring"; slogan from 1986 for Gorbachev's pragmatic economic reforms and decentralisation

PL: Peasant Alliance (Poland)

PLA (Albania) *see* PPS

PNT-CD: National Peasant Party - Christian Democratic (Romania)

Podkrepa ("support"): the independent Bulgarian Confederation of Labour

PPS: Party of Labour of Albania, 1948-91 (1941-68 Albanian Communist Party)

PRM: Greater Romania Party or *Romania Mare*

PRS: Republican Party of Albania

PS: People's Union (Bulgaria)

PSDS: Albanian Social Democratic Party

PSL: Polish Peasant Party

PSM: Socialist Party of Labour (Romania)

PSS: Socialist Party of Albania

PUNR: Romanian National Unity Party

PUWP *see* PZPR

PZPR: Polish United Workers' Party, 1948-90

RCP *see* PCR

Republika Srpska: The Serbian Republic declared by Bosnian Serbs in 1992

Riigikogu: the Estonian parliament

RKL: Conservative Liberal Movement (Poland)

RSK: Republic of Serbian *Krajina* (within Croatia)

Saeima: the Latvian parliament

sahovnica: Croatian chequerboard symbol formerly used by *Ustasha* regime

Saimnieks: "In Charge", Latvian party of former communists

Sajudis: "The Movement", popular anti-communist pro-independence front in Lithuania

samizdat: literally, self-publishing; clandestine opposition literature

SDA: Party of Democratic Action (Bosnia; Muslim)

SDL: Party of the Democratic Left, (Slovakia)

SdPR: Social Democracy of the Polish Republic

SDS: Serbian Democratic Party (Croatian Serb and Bosnian Serb sister groups)

SDS: Union of Democratic Forces (Bulgaria)

SDSM: Social Democratic Alliance of Macedonia

Securitate: Romanian comunist-era secret police

SED: Socialist Unity Party, 1946-90 (East Germany)

Seimas: the Lithuanian parliament

Sejm: until 1989, the Polish parliament; since 1989, the (main) lower house of the Polish parliament

SFRY: Socialist Federal Republic of Yugoslavia, 1963-92

Sigurimi: the Albanian communist-era secret police

SKD: Christian Democratic Party (Slovenia)

SKDH: Slovak Christian Democatic Movement

SKJ: League of Communists of Yugoslavia, 1952-91 (formerly Communist Party of Yugoslavia)

SLD: Democratic Left Alliance (Poland)

SMS: Association for Moravia and Silesia (Czech Republic)

SNS: Slovak National Party

Sobranie: the Macedonian parliament

Solidarity: Poland's mass anti-communist movement (*Solidarnosc* in Polish), founded in 1980 and originally based on trade union organisation

SPD: Social Democratic Party of Germany

SPO: Serbian Renewal Movement

Sporazum: The 1939 agreement on Croat autonomy within Yugoslavia

SPR-RSC: Association for the Republic - Republican Party of Czechoslovakia

SPS: Socialist Party of Serbia

SRS: Serbian Radical Party

SSR: any one of the Soviet Socialist Republics making up the Union

Stasi: East German communist-era secret police

StB: The Czechoslovak communist-era state security police, *Statni Bezpecnost*

SzDSz: Alliance of Free Democrats (Hungary)

TUB: For the Fatherland and Freedom party (Latvia)

UD: Democratic Union (Poland)

UDF (Bulgaria) *see* SDS

UDMR: Hungarian Democratic Union of Romania

Unprofor: the UN Protection Force in former Yugoslavia

UP: Labour Union, formerly Labour Solidarity (Poland)

USSR: Union of Soviet Socialist Republics -- the Soviet Union

Ustasa: right-wing Croats responsible for the wartime Croat regime 1941-45

UW: Freedom Union (Poland), merger of UD and KLD

Visegrad group: Hungary, Poland and Czechoslovakia

VMRO: Internal Macedonian Revolutionary Organisation

VMRO-DMPNE: VMRO-Democratic Party for Macedonian National Unity

Volkskammer: East German parliament

VPN: Public against Violence, 1989-91 (Czechoslovakia: Slovak Republic)

VRS: Patriotic Republican Party (Czech Republic)

ZChN: Christian National Union (Poland)

ZL: United List for Social Democracy (Slovenia)

ZRS: Association of Workers of Slovakia

ZSK: Slovene League of Communists

ZSL: United Peasants' Party, 1947-90 (Poland)

INDEX OF PERSONAL NAMES